ENCYCLOPEDIA OF
NATIVE TRIBES OF
NORTH AMERICA

SECOND EDITION

ENCYCLOPEDIA OF
NATIVE TRIBES OF
NORTH AMERICA
SECOND EDITION

MICHAEL G. JOHNSON
COLOR PLATES BY RICHARD HOOK

FIREFLY BOOKS

A FIREFLY BOOK

Published by Firefly Books Ltd. 2014

First printing

Publisher Cataloging-in-Publication Data (U.S.)

A CIP record for this title is available from the Library of
Congress

**Library and Archives Canada Cataloguing in
Publication**

A CIP record for this title is available from Library and
Archives Canada

Published in the United States by
Firefly Books (U.S.) Inc.
P.O. Box 1338, Ellicott Station
Buffalo, New York 14205

Published in Canada by
Firefly Books Ltd.
50 Staples Avenue, Unit 1
Richmond Hill, Ontario L4B 0A7

Design: Greene Media
Front Cover: Niska mask from British Columbia. *Gary
Fiegehen/AllCanadaPhotos.com/Corbis 42-24119764.*
Back Cover: Navajo man in ceremonial dress as Nayenezgani,
a Navajo deity, photo by Edward S. Curtis, Library of
Congress, Prints & Photographs Division, LC-USZC4-8929;

Printed in China

Author's note
This book is dedicated to my wife, Nancy, and daughters
Sarah and Pauline. Thanks are extended to Samuel and Julia
Cahoon of New Jersey, who made it possible for the author
to visit some of the tribal locations — past and present —
noted in the text. Mr. Timothy O'Sullivan of Stourbridge,
U.K., who read the text and added comments for its
improvement; to Hilary Hook and to Ian West for their
generous assistance during the preparation of the text and
illustrations; to Frank Oppel for making early prints available;
to Mark Franklin for the excellent maps; and to Richard
Green and Simon Clay for many of the artifacts and the
artifact photography.

   Wherever possible, provenance of the photographs is
identified. All the photographs in this book are taken by the
authors or from the authors' collections unless specifically
credited otherwise except for the following: pages 57
(bottom right) University Museum of Archaeology,
Cambridge; 194 (top) Werner Foreman Archive (Phoebe
Apperson Hearst Museum of Anthropology); 317 Bill Yenne.
Thanks to the Royal Albert Memorial Museum and Art
Gallery, Exeter, U.K. for the following photographs of
material in its collections: pages 52 (top left), 57 (TL, TR and
BL), 261 (both), 278 (4), 280 (TR and BL), 287 (TL), 299 (B).

*Page 2: Top to bottom, left to right — Pistol holster (Plains Ojibwa); eagle feather
bonnet (Plains); boy's waistcoat (Sioux); pipes and tobacco bag (Sioux); U-shaped
pouch (Malecite); Kachina doll (Pueblo); steel blade trade head tomahawk; storage bag
(Sioux); female doll (Seminole); moccasins (Gros Ventre); gauntlets (Blackfoot); basket
(Apache); necklace (California); beaded cap (Iroquois). Photo Courtesy of Ian West*

CONTENTS

FOREWORD

By Dr. James A. Clifton Ph.D., Adjunct Professor, U.S. Marine Corps Command and Staff College

I thought that the first edition of this beautiful book was a near-flawless example of the book publishing art. So I am delighted to see this somewhat enlarged new edition, the original gem much improved by the addition of new facets and a polishing of the whole. Author Michael Johnson, illustrator Richard Hook and the publisher's copy editors and book designers have obviously collaborated to superb effect in this upgrading.

In the original, Hook's panoptic multitribal color plates were stunning, but so full of visual information about crafts and costumes as to overwhelm the viewer. These multitribal plates were also separated from the pertinent text entries. In the new edition, the composite plates have been broken up, each separate figure enlarged and relocated adjacent to the appropriate text description, with substantial reinforcing effect. That decision was obviously an editor's or book designer's decision, unnamed talents who deserve credit for contributing to the usefulness of this book. Author and publisher also have added a great many additional photographic plates, historic and contemporary. Altogether, this is the most lavishly illustrated reference book about North American Indians available in print.

Michael Johnson has corrected the few glitches in his original exposition, updated numerous entries following recently published scholarly works, and included a useful, illustrated glossary. Adding to his original scholarship, Johnson has produced a sound, accurate and concise course of instruction about the native tribes of North America.

This new edition is an updated, enlarged (sufficient to lose the "Concise" in the first edition's title) model of excellence in the art of reference volume publishing. With Michael Johnson and Richard Hook, they have produced a beginning student's book, a collector's book, a young person's book, a librarian's book, an artist's book, a general reader's book, a costume designer's book and even a scholar's book. It is a banquet for the eyes, a pleasure to hold and handle, and a resource for the mind.

Johnson, one of the world's most respected savants of North American Indian arts, crafts and material culture, worked in close partnership with famed illustrator, Richard Hook, whose color plates are meticulous in detail and dazzling in artistic quality. Of Johnson (an engineer by profession) it may be said that he is an amateur, meaning his lifelong pursuit of knowledge about Indians has been his avocation and that he lacks academic credentials to tack on to his name. But it must also fairly be said that he shares his status with Darwin and Gibbon. Of Hook it may be accurately said that in preparing his illustrations he had to work from archival or museum materials, visual and textual, rather than from living models, unlike his 19th-century predecessors such as George Winter, George Catlin or Rudolph Frederich Kurz. But it must also be fairly said that Hook is easily the superior in artistic talent and mastery of technique to any of his precursors.

Johnson's introductory essay, covering prehistoric and historic Indian populations, languages and cultural distributions, and his 10 chapters describing the many tribes in North America's culture areas put me in mind of Frederick Webb Hodge's 1907 classic, *Handbook of American Indians North of Mexico*, which had the entire staff of the Smithsonian Institution's Bureau of American Ethnology, and other scholars, as contributors. This book is that sound, useful and handy a reference work. The author's coverage of the tribes in each culture area is comprehensive, not abbreviated, and his summaries of each tribe's affiliations and history are solid and perceptive.

I am particularly impressed by the amount of attention Michael Johnson has given to the distinguishing details of the ethnology of North America. These details include a classification of Indian languages, together with a summary of culture areas; and lists of the tribes and languages (with translations of ethnonyms) preceding each of the 10 culture area chapters, from the Northeastern Woodlands to the Arctic. His brief chapter, "The Indian Today," is honest and perceptive, and is sufficient to remind readers that "the Indian" certainly did not disappear with the passenger pigeon.

For some decades a swelling popular and academic interest in North America's native peoples has caused a flood of hastily prepared "Dictionaries" or "Encyclopedias" of things Indian. The shelves of our libraries now groan with the weight of such poor stuff, typically as shaky in scholarship as they are inferior in accuracy in editing, art, print quality, paper and binding. *The Encyclopedia of Native Tribes of North America* does not belong in this opportunistic genre. It stands in marvelous contrast, in a class, and of a quality, by itself.

James A. Clifton, Ph.D.

INTRODUCTION

In 1993 the first edition of this book was published; it was very different to this version in presentation and content. To begin with, economic exigencies meant the book was produced in black and white and the excellent color illustrations, so meticulously prepared by the late Richard Hook, were reproduced in a short central section, divorced from their captions. Succeeding new editions have allowed the publisher to separate these paintings, integrate them with the text, and — where possible — increase their size. Before his recent death, Richard touched-up and added to most of them to ensure that this separation was effected well and a selection of new paintings was been included.

Second, the photographs — again produced in black and white and in sections in the first book — were integrated with the text and much additional material was added. Where possible this was in color, although the age of many of the original photographs precludes this. The photographs show a broader range of time than in earlier editions, with many more images: the story of the Native Americans, so long considered effectively to have ended following their displacement by settlers, is in fact a continuing reality: census figures show that numbers of enrolled Indians are increasing, although these increases may not be purely for natural reasons. The discovery of mineral resources, the erection of casinos and the benefits of tourism have all contributed to increasing wealth for some Native American populations; this increase in wealth has seen an increase of per capita enrollment leading to the questionable rise in populations.

The third form of illustration, the maps, has altered most in this edition — a few minor errors have been corrected but a significant number of new maps have been added, including a section that looks specifically at the Subarctic and Arctic in more detail, providing a graphic display of the First Nations of Canada and the native peoples of Alaska (see pages 288–293).

So, the presentation and design of the book have changed considerably; additionally, the body text has been corrected and updated: a few typographical errors have been corrected but there has been significant updating of the text particularly in the light of recent Census figures, and close work with the Canadian authorities — for example the new section on the Métis (see pages 99–103). The reference section at the end of the book has also seen a number of changes including the expansion of the glossary, illustrated with more specially commissioned artifact photography by Simon Clay.

To accommodate all these changes, there has been a reorganzation of the final sections of the book and an increase in size by sixteen extra pages.

THE NORTH AMERICAN BACKGROUND

In October 1492 Christopher Columbus "discovered" the Americas. The term "discovered" implies that North America was uninhabited; in fact, the whole of the Americas from Alaska to the southernmost tip of South America was populated by a people whose ancestors came from Asia via land, sea and ice bridges near or at the Bering Strait or the Aleutian Islands chain, possibly as long as 30,000 years ago.

These ancient Paleo-Indians somehow filtered down through an ice-free corridor in North America into Central and South America, and in the course of time occupied the whole continent, including the West Indies. Some of the ancestors of the Indians of North America arrived much later, the Inuit (Eskimo) and Athabascan people probably less than 8,000 years ago; the Inuit have tribes in Asia to this day.

Since Columbus thought he had found the fabled Indies, the native people he encountered in the islands off Florida became known as "Indians." A few years later, mariner-explorers "discovered" other natives in Newfoundland with painted red faces — hence the birth of the misnomer "Red Indians." In truth, of course, they are neither. While recognizing that the term is irritating to many, the author has chosen to use "Indians" throughout this text rather than the now popular title "Native Americans," which can also be confusing and may seem to ignore Canadian Indians.

Archaeological and ethnographical speculations reveal that native North Americans have an antiquity and a hunter-gatherer culture of unparalleled historical depth and complexity, which may explain the extraordinary relationship they have maintained with the land and their sense of absolute and eternal belonging with it. These hunters developed beliefs and behavior patterns that enabled them to exist in an unpredictable physical world where every animate and inanimate object had enormous spirit power that had to be respected and ritually placated. Later, a Meso-American maize culture developed and spread north into much of what is now the United States.

Europeans were fascinated by the New World natives, and the earliest representations of Indians in European art quickly established a series of visual symbols derived from both North and South American descriptions with which to portray the Native American. Indians, shown in suitably dramatic or warlike attitudes and set in scenes of wildly inaccurate geographical and anatomical composition, became visually accepted.

The consequent series of simplistic stereotypes spread far beyond the merely visual; extended by "travelers' tales" and adventure fiction, they were exploited by the late 19th-century "Wild West shows," and subsequently by their 20th-century equivalent, the Western film. Until the most recent times, gross misinformation — or, at best, honest confusion — were widespread, both within America and overseas.

Symbols of material culture such as canoes, totem poles, tipis and feather headdresses are shown as characteristics of a commonly shared way of life, rather than of different cultures separated by thousands of miles. The Indian environment is often portrayed as a vast wilderness of mountain and plain, although a considerable proportion of historic North American natives were river, valley, bay and coastal people. The popular media often suggest that the Indian is nearly extinct, although there are probably more North American Indians or people of Indian descent alive today than in 1492. The Indian is presented purely as a hunter, although in fact a large number of Indians were gatherers of wild foods, or pursued a farming tradition based on the production of maize (Indian corn). We are told that the Indian never scalped before the white man arrived, although in fact the taking of scalps was known in many parts of North America. We are told that the Indian man never had facial hair: again untrue — people of Asiatic origin have less body hair than Europeans, but they do have it. These misconceptions may seem individually trivial; but they are legion, and they contribute to a cumulative myth that may obscure important truths.

The Indian has been portrayed historically as vain, cruel to captives, a brave fighter, but with no taste for pitched battle, and susceptible to alcohol, with resultant brawls, family disruption and inertia. Alternatively, the Indian has more recently been eulogized as enjoying perfect harmony with Mother Earth or nature, as having a perfectly democratic and egalitarian social organization, as being eminently spiritual, and considerate of friend, stranger, young and old. In the past few years the Indian has been portrayed as a model conservationist, taking only what he needed from the natural world — notwithstanding the part played by Indians in the promotion of the fur trade. All these images — partial, unbalanced, or at best taken out of context — are highly misleading, and should be taken with a decent amount of skepticism.

It is obvious that the North American Indian could not for long have successfully resisted the European invasion. Small in number, and scattered over a huge area several times larger than Europe, they had no realistic chance of stemming the tide of white settlement. Intertribal animosities precluded concerted efforts to contain a European invasion until it was much too late. Further, vast regions were very thinly populated: parts of Kentucky, for instance, subarctic Canada and the Plains before the development of the horse-bison culture, were hunting territories with few settlements. Warfare was also endemic in some areas; tribal oral traditions confirm that enmities were often established long before the arrival of whites, and recent archaeological reports from grave sites suggest that intertribal warfare could reach staggering proportions.

The complicated geographical diffusion of tribes with a common ancestral language base suggests continual movement, invasion, migration and conquest long before the white man set foot on the continent. We know of substantial cultures that came and went long before European contact, such as the Adena and Hopewell cultures, which were partly based on Meso-American gardening. The Europeans did not, therefore, disturb a "Garden of Eden," but rather a continent of tribal groups and cultures that were fully dynamic — and that were able in some instances to adapt to the new technology brought from Europe in their constant struggle with the harsh realities of an unremitting climate and variable resources, particularly in the northeast and far north. The Indians of the High Plains, Boreal Forest and Subarctic were

able to modify their native cultures into fairly successful hybrid forms based on the merging of native talents with imported European technology.

While some Indians were able to come to an accommodation with the Europeans, some clearly were not. The coastal peoples of the Atlantic, Gulf of Mexico and California were among the first to suffer conquest, subjection and the effects of European-introduced diseases. Many tribes in these regions disappeared long before the United States became an independent nation. The reduction in population during these early times was the direct result of the influence of the old European colonial powers: Britain, France and Spain. During the United States period, central government policies toward Indians were rarely consistent. Often they were instead crude and condescending, with resultant tragedies. But no U.S. administration in Washington has ever approved a policy aimed at the deliberate extermination of Indians, despite the charges leveled by some of today's dealers in politicized rhetoric. The actions of frontier mobs, land-hungry settlers, overzealous local military commanders, gold prospectors, land dealers, et al., cannot always be blamed on a distant government. Californian Indians, particularly, suffered massacres perpetrated by local settlers.

The purpose of this book is not to add to the already existing mass of fable and subjective comment on Native American history, but to give the average interested reader or student some cogent facts about each of the recognized tribes native to North America, north of the Rio Grande River. These include brief historical sketches, intertribal linguistic family relationships, an indication of traditional cultural horizons, locations, and populations both in olden and modern times. The location of the tribes indicated in the text utilizes modern American and Canadian names for states, provinces, counties, rivers, mountains, towns and villages, and for plotting locations the use of a modern road atlas would be a useful tool. Of course, these are not the boundaries recognized by the Indians themselves; their traditional world view and nomenclature were very different.

Tribal names are for the most part not the old names the Indians knew themselves. Many names translate simply as the "real men" or "original people." The common, popular, modern names used are derived from various sources. Some are from native terms, either for themselves or those applied by neighbors or enemies, or corruptions of these terms. Some tribal names are anglicized forms of translated native names; others are from French or Spanish sources. We use the tribal names most commonly encountered in history and literature, although it should be noted that some modern Indian groups have successfully reintroduced their own names into usage.

We should also recognize that the anthropological and ethnographical reports from which most of our understanding of Native American culture derives have been the work of Euro-American scholars and historians, and that there is considerable resentment over this situation by some modern Native Americans, who suggest that they alone should be the interpreters of their ancient cultures. This again raises the question of the old stereotypes of race and ethnic identity: can modern Native Americans be the only legitimate repository of cultural knowledge, on the basis of racial association?

However, many Indians past and present have written in the language of mass and scholarly communication, e.g., J.N.B. Hewitt (Tuscarora), William Jones (Sac and Fox), J.J. Matthews (Osage) and D. McNickle (Flathead). Many people of Native American heritage are active today in the fields of Indian history and Indian art; and the former Director of the National Museum of the American Indian, W. Richard West Jr., is a member of the Cheyenne-Arapaho tribes of Oklahoma. A visit by the writer to the excellently run native museum — the Woodland Cultural Centre, Brantford, Ontario — revealed no significant difference in the presentation of material culture and native history from that found elsewhere in American or European institutions; and the curatorial staff have resisted the temptation to insert politicized comment into descriptions of native culture of past times. After all, there are not too many different ways to present a feather headdress or beaded pouch in a glass case. We should also remember that a considerable proportion of Native American decorative material culture was made for white consumption and is distinctively hybrid, in common with the cultures from which it came — which is hardly surprising, following centuries of interaction.

NATIVE AMERICAN POPULATIONS

The accurate number of Native American Indians living north of the Rio Grande River in the United States and Canada is unknown both for aboriginal times and for today. A conservative estimate suggested by the ethnographer James Mooney was about 1,250,000 for the late 16th century. This figure has been raised in recent re-examinations, in spite of the paucity of data, to as high as 6,000,000, but that is likely an excessive number. A more rational number is in the 2,000,000 to 3,000,000 range. The highest concentrations were undoubtedly in the coastal regions: the Atlantic slope in the east, the Gulf of Mexico region in the south and California in the west. Ironically, these areas suffered the greatest reduction in population from contact and conflicts with, as well as the effects of diseases introduced by, the Europeans.

During the 20th century, the Indian population figures vary considerably, due mainly to different criteria applied by the various enumerators regarding just who is or is not an American Indian. Since the earliest colonial times there has been a continuous and often increasing mixing of Indian and Euro-American peoples that has resulted in the majority of Indians — at least those outside of the American southwest — being of mixed race. A second problem is that the American Bureau of Indian Affairs, the official bureaucracy controlling some of the remaining Indian lands and federal services to Indians, has few or no special relations with substantial numbers of Indians in Maine, New York, Virginia, North Carolina and other states. Consequently, the figures published by the Bureau of Indian Affairs over the years are usually lower than the figures reported by the U.S. Census, since the former count only Indian people who are enrolled at Indian agencies.

The degree of Indian ancestry required at Indian agencies was often determined by individual Indian councils themselves. The degree of Indian ancestry required for enrollment was usually a minimum of one-quarter Indian descent but in some tribes now even lower. The U.S. Census enumerators, on the other hand, attempted to include all people whom they considered racially Indian, and who were regarded as such in their communities of residence; many eastern Indians not on the bureau rolls were therefore counted in the Census. Until the 1970 U.S. Census, enumerators were the arbiters of who was Indian, whereas that responsibility is now placed on the individual interviewee.

In 1950, the Bureau of Indian Affairs (BIA) reported 396,000 enrolled Indians at its various Indian agencies and reservations across the United States, of whom 245,000 were residents on the reservations and the rest in adjacent towns and cities, with a growing number moving permanently to larger metropolitan and urban centers. The Census reported 237,000 in 1900; 366,710 in 1940; 532,591 in 1960; 827,108 in 1970; and 1,418,195 in 1980; and 2,553,566 in 2010. These U.S. Census figures include Indians inside and outside the federal agency system and a growing number of racially mixed groups in the eastern states who have never been officially recognized as Indians, but who have, to a lesser or greater degree, a claim to such ancestry. Included also are federally terminated groups and people who now feel socially acceptable as Indians in a more tolerant society, and who might feel that financial benefits could be obtained by stressing sometimes justifiable claims to tribal ancestry. Today the number is large enough to make possible a wide range of estimates of the U.S. Indian population: in general terms about 2,500,000, of whom 30 percent still live on reservations, and about the same number who are full-blooded Native Americans. The largest U.S. groups are Navajo, Chippewa, Sioux, Iroquois, Cherokee and Lumbee. The U.S. Bureau of Indian Affairs reported 833,000 "enrolled" Indians in 1985 and 1,816,000 in 2001.

The BIA increases probably include for the lowering of the blood quantum for tribal membership, particularly Oklahoma and the controversial inclusion of Afro-American descendants amongst the so-called former "Five Civilized Tribes," called Freedmen (their antecedants were slaves). At least 21,500 Indians from Mexico, South America, and Canada were also included in the 2000 Census. The 2010 Census also includes any self-identified as Native American not enrolled by the BIA and likely have lower or questionable degrees of native ancestry.

In Canada the Indians were forced to make a succession of treaties with the Crown during the 19th and early 20th centuries, which established approximately 600 Indian bands (reserves) across the country. These are the Indians reported by the Indian Affairs Branch of the Canadian Department of Citizenship and Immigration. The total population of Treaty Indians was reported as 136,407 in 1949, 179,126 in 1959, 244,113 in 1969 and approximately 400,000 in 1990, of which 280,000 were on reserves. By 2005 this total figure increased to 748,371. However, a large body of Canadian people of Indian descent were not enumerated because their ancestors chose to be excluded from the Treaty Band system. Native Indian women married to non-Indians or non-band members and their heirs also lost their status as Indians. These Métis and non-status Indians, now recognized as Canadian native people, probably add another 100,000 to the Indian population. The Métis were initially a mixed French and Indian people living around the Red River area in present day Manitoba, who subsequently fanned out into Alberta and Saskatchewan in the 19th century. Their vocal political campaigns for social and economic rights in recent times have encouraged other mixed and non-status groups to affiliate with them, extending the term Métis far beyond its original limited application. The largest Canadian groups are Cree, Northern Ojibwa, Iroquois, Blackfoot, and the extended Métis.

Adding the returns for both the United States and Canada, the total number of "Indians" with a substantial degree of Indian ancestry was in excess of 1,850,000 by 1987, and in excess of three million by 2010 — probably as high as in aboriginal times. The 19th-century proposition that the Indian would vanish as an identifiable racial and social entity was in error, and Americans are now aware of another vocal racial minority in their midst. However, the increase in population cannot hide the great tragedies inflicted historically on the Indian by Euro-Americans.

CLASSIFICATION OF INDIAN LANGUAGES

In 1891 John Wesley Powell of the Bureau of American Ethnology, Washington, D.C., published the first overall classification of the American Indian languages north of Mexico. Tribes with similar languages may be presumed to have common origins; and the greater the divergence in speech, the longer the period of separation from a common ancestral stock. Some tribes were so weakly organized or so widely scattered geographically that only linguistically can they be called "tribes" in the popular sense. North America had many differing languages, and by the time specialists were making records in the 19th century, some dialects were already verging on extinction.

Native American languages consist of a number of distinct families that differ fundamentally from each other in vocabulary and in phonetic and grammatical form. Some of the families, including Algonkian and Athabascan, consist of a large number of distinct languages; others seem to be limited to a small number of languages or dialects or even to a single language. John Wesley Powell's classification of languages north of Mexico recognized no fewer than 55 of these families. (Note that the names used are derived from one of the major languages or "tribes" within each family.)

The distribution of these language families is uneven; 37 of them are either entirely or mostly found in territory draining into the Pacific. Only seven linguistic stocks were located on the Atlantic coastline. In the Mississippi valley, Gulf states and adjacent coast 10 language families were located. The most widely distributed are:

1 *Eskimoan (Inuit)*, in Greenland, northern Canada, into Alaska and Siberia. Note, while today we use Inuit rather than Eskimo in reference to the people, Eskimoan is still used to describe the language of the Inuit and Aleut. The Inuit of western and southern Alaska are now called Tupik.

2 *Algonkian or Algonquian*, several languages on the Atlantic coast, Quebec, Nova Scotia, Canada west to the Rocky Mountains, with groups on the Plains, and the central and southern groups near and south of the Great Lakes. The Inuit of western and southern Alaska are now called Yupik.

3 *Iroquoian*, in three area groups:
(1) The region of lakes Erie, Ontario and the St. Lawrence River.
(2) Eastern Virginia and North Carolina.
(3) The southern Appalachian country (Cherokee).

4 *Muskogian or Muskogee*, including the Natchez, which occupied the Gulf region from the Mississippi delta to Florida and Georgia, and northward to Kentucky.

5 *Siouan*, in three groups:
(1) In the eastern states of North Carolina and Virginia.
(2) A small southern contingent (Biloxi).
(3) The main group on the Plains, and a colony of the Plains group in Wisconsin near Green Bay (Winnebago).

6 *Caddoan*, spoken on the southern Plains, from Nebraska to Texas and Louisiana, and a group in North Dakota.

7 *Uto-Aztecan (Shoshonean)*, on the American Plateau, in the Great Basin, in Texas and Arizona.

8 *Athabascan or Athapascan*, in three groups:
(1) In the north of Canada from Alaska to Hudson Bay.
(2) On the Pacific coast.
(3) In the Southwest and in northern Mexico.

9 *Salishan*, in British Columbia and northwestern United States in two sections:
(1) On the Pacific coast.
(2) The Interior Salish of the Plateau.

10 *Sahaptian (Shahaptian)*, on the Middle Columbia River in Oregon, Idaho.

The other 45 families are shown in alphabetical order in Table 1, on page 11.

This complex classification of native languages is very probably the first approximation to the historic truth. There are many far-reaching resemblances in vocabulary and structure among linguistic families classified by Powell as generically distinct. Scientific comparative work on these diverse languages is still in its infancy; but the reductions shown in Table 2 on pages 11–12 have been made, and the phyla 2a–2g may be regarded as either probable or possible, but unverified (particularly 2e).

The linguistic classifications shown in Table 2 do not correspond at all closely to the racial or subracial lines that have been drawn for North America, nor to the cultural areas into which the tribes have been grouped by ethnographers. In simple analogy, a language family would approximate the English-German (Germanic) or French-Spanish (Latin) groups of European languages, but the larger groups or stocks would parallel only the designation "Indo-European." Gaelic-Irish-Manx-Welsh-Cornish-Breton = Celtic; or English-German-Scandinavian = Nordic. So Micmac-Ojibwa-Cree-Blackfoot-Cheyenne = Algonkian.

However, it must be said that attempts to find common ancestral people through language presenting the divergence in language as a measure in time from a parent group, by the construction of these linguistic family trees are by no means universally accepted and some authorities are reluctant to agree upon these groupings.

However, there has been little opposition to the grouping of Inuit and Aleut, or the formation of "Nadene" from Athabascan, Tlingit, Haida, and Eyak, however the connection of Algonkian with Ritwan has not always been agreed. There are no serious doubts in the validity in principal of the formation of "Shapwailuta," only in the relationship of the Molala and Cayuse has doubt recently been voiced. Serious doubts have been raised with regard to the Hokan and Penutian super families when extended beyond California. The proposed Coahuiltecan family linking a number of extinct languages in the lower Rio Grande

river area is also in doubt—these languages may have been "Isolates." Conservative studies maintain independence for Kutenai, Beothuk, Iroquoian, Caddoan, Siouan, Muskogian, Yuchi, Timukuan, Tunican, Tonkawa, Keres, and Yuki to phyla status and separate Algonkian from Mosan, Hokan from Siouan or Coahuiltecan, which have been a feature of some 20th century revisions to Powell's original 1891 classifications.

The number of Indian languages now spoken is less than a hundred and many of these are known only to a few older people in each tribe, and will be gone entirely during the first half of the 21st century. The only flourishing languages today and the ones likely to survive long into the century include Inuit, Cree, Ojibwa (in Canada), Blackfoot, Mohawk, Micmac, Cherokee, Miccosukee (Florida), Choctaw (Mississippi), Navajo and Apache. The following classification is one of a number which have been proposed.

Table 1
Families marked ★ are now extinct languages

Family	Location
Atakapa ★	Gulf coast, Louisiana and Texas.
Beothuk ★	Newfoundland.
Chimakuan ★	Washington.
Chimariko★	Northwestern California.
Chinook	Lower Columbia River.
Chitimacha ★	Southern Louisiana.
Chumash ★	Southwestern California.
Coahuiltecan ★	Lower Rio Grande.
Coos or Kus ★	Oregon coast.
Costanoan ★	Western California.
Esselen ★	Southwestern California.
Haida	Queen Charlotte Islands.
Kalapuya ★	Northwestern Oregon.
Karankawa ★	Texas coast.
Karok	Northwestern California.
Keres	Rio Grande in New Mexico.
Kiowa	Southern Plains, Kansas, Oklahoma.
Kootenay or Kutenai	British Columbia, Idaho and Montana.
Lutuami	Consisting of the Klamath and Modoc in southern Oregon.
Maidu	Eastern Sacramento Valley, California.
Miwok	Central California.
Piman or Sonoran	Southern Arizona and Mexico.
Pomo	Western California.
Salinan ★	Southwestern California.
Shasta-Achumawi	Northern California and southern Oregon.
Takelma ★	Southwest Oregon.
Tanoan	New Mexico on or near Rio Grande.
Tumuqua or Timucua ★	Florida.
Tlingit	Southern Alaska.
Tonkawa ★	Texas.
Tsimshian	Western British Columbia.
Tunica ★	Mississippi River in Louisiana and Mississippi.
Waiilatpuan ★	Consisting of Molala and Cayuse, northern Oregon.
Wakashan	Consisting of Nootka and Kwakiutl along the coast of British Columbia.
Washo(e)	Western Nevada and eastern California.
Wintun	North-central California.
Wiyot ★	Northwestern California.
Yakonan ★	Oregon coast.
Yana ★	Northern California.
Yokuts	South-central California.
Yuchi	Savannah River, Georgia.
Yuki ★	Western California.
Yuman	Colorado River in California and Arizona.
Yurok	Northwestern California.
Zuni	New Mexico.

To these later were added:

Siuslaw ★	Oregon coast.
Eyak ★	Alaska.

Table 2
Table 2a: Algonkian-Wakashan
```
Wiyot ).......Ritwan  )
Yurok )            )
.............Algonkian  ).. Algonkian-Ritwan )
...............Beothuk  )                 )
Kootenay...................Kootenay )   ALGONKIAN-
                           )       WAKASHAN
Kwakiutl ) Wakashan)       )
Nootka   )        )        )
         )        )        )
Chimakuan        )...................Mosan )
...............Salishan)
```

Table 2b: Nadene
```
Haida.............................Haida )
Tlingit    )                        ) NADENE
Athabascan)...........Continental Nadene )
Eyak       )
```

Table 2c: Yuki and Keres
```
Yuki.................Yuki
Keres..............Keres
```

Table 2d: Penutian

Miwok-Costano)
Yokuts) Californian Penutian)
Maidu))
Wintun))
)
Takelma.........................))
Kalapuya.........................) Oregon Penutian)
)) PENUTIAN
Coos))
Siuslaw) Oregon Coast)
Yakonan) Penutian)
)
Chinook..)
Tsimshian..)
)
Sahaptin (or Shahaptian))
Waiilatpuan........................)............Plateau Penutian)
Lutuami...........................)

Table 2f: Hokan-Coahuiltecan

Karok.........................)
Chimariko)...)
Shasta-Achumawi)...)..Northern Section)
Yana..........................))
Pomo........................))
)
Washo..)
Esselen)........................Esselen-Yuman)
Yuman))...Hokan)
Salinan)))
Seri)............................Salinan-Seri))
Chumash))) HOKAN-
)) COAHUILTECAN
Chontal (Mexico)....................................)) (unverified)
Tonkawa.................Tonkawa))
Coahuilteco)))
Cotoname) Coahuilteco)............Coahuiltecan)
Comecrudo))
Karankawa)

Table 2e

Iroquoian)...................Iroquois-Caddoan)
Caddoan)
....Siouan)
Tunican-Atakapa)......................Tunican) Distant
Chitmacha) connections
) suggested
Yuchi............................)) but remain
Natchez) Muskogian) Natchez–) unverified
Muskogian)) Muskogee
Timucua)

Table 2g: Aztec-Tanoan

Piman)
Shoshonean) Uto-Aztecan)
Sonoran-Nahuatl (Mexico)))
)
Kiowa................................) Kiowa-Tanoan) AZTEC-TANOAN
Tanoan..............................))
)
Zuni...Zuni)

Below: "Distribution of goods to the Assiniboines," Sarony, Major & Knapp's litho of a John Mix Stanley original of July 8, 1853. The Assiniboines were "arranged to receive their presents. They were seated around in the form of three sides of a square, the open side being opposite to the places occupied by the expedition party, the chief, and the higher order of the Indians. At each of the four corners was posted a brave or a chief. These men never receive a gift, considering it a degradation to accept anything but what their own prowess or superior qualities of manhood acquire for them ... Two old men of the tribe were assigned the duty of making the distribution, and the presents were placed in the center of the area. During the whole distribution the Indians sat in perfect silence." Original print via Frank Oppel.

TRIBES AND CULTURES

DISTRIBUTION OF CULTURES

Archaeological research has been conducted widely in North America, but the territory is so vast, the tribes so numerous and their movements so many that it has been difficult to associate ancient pre- or protohistoric sites with later historic tribes. There have been attempts: the Fort Ancient site of the Hopewell prehistoric culture north of modern Cincinnati, the largest and one of the best-preserved earth-walled sites, c. 100 B.C.–A.D. 500, has been tenuously linked to the historic Shawnee; the Dismal River site in present day Nebraska has been alternatively suggested as Apachean or more probably Puebloan; Hohokam and Mogollon of Arizona have been linked with the modern Piman, and Anasazi with the Pueblo of New Mexico and northeastern Arizona.

Despite general agreement on the dates when these prehistoric cultural horizons flowered, and on the dating of their extensive remains, close correlation with historic tribes is limited (except for the Pueblos, whose ancestors seem to have been the Mesa Verde and Chaco Canyon peoples). Generally the links are unsubstantiated. Ethnologists have therefore independently divided North America into so-called cultural areas, in which the various tribes during the historic period developed generally similar skills and subsistence levels derived from a generally similar environment. These areas thus tend to coincide with ecological zones, but also to blend together with the cultures of adjacent areas rather than eliminating them. The boundaries between these cultural areas are entirely arbitrary, but they are usually designated as follows:

Northeastern Woodlands: The north Atlantic coast, Great Lakes and adjacent southern Canada.

Southeastern Woodlands: The south Atlantic coast, the Gulf, to the Mississippi and beyond.

Plains and Prairie: Mississippi Valley to the Rocky Mountains.

Plateau: The mountainous area of the northwest United States and southern British Columbia, Canada.

Great Basin: Most of the present states of Utah and Nevada.

California: Largely, but not entirely, the present state of California.

Southwest: The present states of New Mexico and Arizona, plus adjacent parts of Mexico and Texas.

Northwest Coast: Coastal Alaska, British Columbia, Washington and Oregon.

Subarctic: The northern interior of Canada and Alaska.

Arctic: The northern edge of the continent between Alaska and Greenland.

Below: Rocky Boy showing off beaded jacket, belt, and leggings. For more details about this Plains Ojibwa leader, see page 108.

GREENLAND

Arctic

Subarctic

Northwest Coast

Subarctic

C A N A D A

Plateau

Great Basin

Plains & Prairie

Northeastern Woodlands

California

U. S. A.

Southwest

Southeastern Woodlands

MEXICO

THE BAHAMAS

CUBA

DOM. REP.

HAITI

JAMAICA

BELIZE

GUATEMALA   HONDURAS

THE TRIBES

The tribal entries are not arranged alphabetically; they are grouped firstly in cultural and geographical areas according to the previously mentioned sequence, and within those areas in groups related by language. The sketch maps provided in each section, while intended only as general guides to historical and present day distribution, will assist the reader by reference from the text entries.

The names of linguistic families are presented as sideheads in **_bold italic_** type — separately, if comprising more than one tribe, and beginning the first line of the tribal entry if not. The names of tribes are presented in **bold** type beginning the first line of each entry; subsidiary groups or bands are discussed in the body of the entry where appropriate, the names of the most significant being presented in _italic_ type. The dictates of logic or historical peculiarity modify these general practices in occasional specific cases.

Major linguistic families cross the necessarily arbitrary borders of some of the cultural and geographical areas. Their general characteristics are each summarized in only one area section; cross-references are given in the lists of contents at the beginning of each chapter where appropriate.

Maps and Tribal Names

The maps show the locations of the so-called tribes in their areas during important historic periods, usually of conflict with Europeans, colonization, cultural change and forced relocation. The eastern tribes for the period c. 1600 to 1750 AD, and the western tribes for the 19th century. Other maps showing the location of present day reservations (U.S.) and reserves (Canada) also include some non-federally recognized groups in the eastern U.S. whose Indian origins are in doubt.

To attempt to give tribal self-designations to even a minority of Native American "tribes" would appear to be a near impossible task. So many groups in the Appalachian Mountains, in the Gulf of Mexico region, and Florida, disappeared so early in the colonization of North America that their languages are, in many cases, unknown or known only from a few words recorded by explorers or missionaries. Even to give reasonably accurate terms for well known tribes presents huge difficulties. The Cheyenne for instance, now also use an anglicised name Tsistsistas—while variants include Tse-tis-tas, Sa-sie-e-tas, and Dzi'tsi'stäs—apparently all derived from tsétsEhéstAhese, their self-designation. However, one would need to know the phonemes of each tribe to get near a reasonable pronunciation. The Crow tribe or Apsaroke in practical orthography is Apsaalooke. Both have numerous slightly varying translations: sparrowhawk people, crow, anything that flies, etc. Previous errors also cloud these issues. Recent re-examination of the term "Sioux" suggest it never meant "snake," although many people now avoid its use for that very reason.

The writer's own view is to continue the use of the common English/Franco/Native derived forms despite the perjorative and eccentric connotations of many tribal names. The recently published _Handbook of North American Indians_ by the Smithsonian Institution, Washington, D.C., have by-and –large continued to use traditional nomenclature for tribal names.

Readers should recognize that both the early and recent tribal populations given in the tribal entries are also a matter of debate, even controversy. Recent populations for the now self-regulating Indian enrollment in the U.S. are at best approximate since tribal membership in some instances has been reduced from a usual quarter to an eighth and even a sixty-fourth. The writer's own view would be to favour conservative figures.

Left: Group of Crow warriors in Montana, 1887, including Pretty Eagle (front left) and Plenty Coups (front, third left). Montana Historical Society, courtesy Ian West.

NORTHEASTERN WOODLANDS

Language family and tribe	Meaning/origin of tribal name, where known	Language family and tribe	Meaning/origin of tribal name, where known
Algonkian (except where noted):		North Carolina Algonkians	
		Shawnee	"southerners"
Micmac	"allies"	Miami	"people of the Peninsula"
Malecite	"broken talkers"	Illini	"people"
Passamaquoddy	"those who pursue the pollock"	Potawatomi	"people of the place of fire?"
Abenaki	"easterners"	Mascouten	"prairie people"
Western Abenaki	"easterners"	Kickapoo	"he stands about"
Pennacook	"downhill"	Sauk	"people of the yellow earth"
Massachusett	"at the range of hills'"	Fox	"red earth people"
Nipmuc	"fresh water fishing place"	Menomini	"wild rice men"
Pocomtuc	–	Winnebago (Siouan)	"people of the filthy water"
Wampanoag	"eastern people"	Ojibwa	"to roast until puckered up"
Narragansett	"people of the small point"	Ottawa	"to trade"
Niantic	"at a point of land on a river"	Mississauga	"river with several outlets"
		Algonkin	"place of spearing fish (or eels)"
Mohegan	"wolf" (or place name)	Nipissing	"at the lake"
Pequot	"destroyers?"		
		Iroquoian:	
Lower Connecticut River Tribes		Huron	"rough" or "ruffian"
Paugussett	"where the narrows open out"	Petun (Tobacco Nation)	French name
		Neutral	English name
Wappinger	"easterners" (possibly)	Wenro	"floating oil"
Mahican	"wolf" (or place name)	Erie	"raccoon nation"
Montauk	place name	Susquehannock	English name
Stockbridge	English name	Iroquois (Five Nations)	"real adders"
Brotherton	English name	Mohawk	"man eaters"
Delaware	English name	Oneida	"people of the stone"
Nanticoke	"tidewater people"	Onondaga	"people on the hill"
Conoy	–	Cayuga	town name
Powhatan	"falls in a current of water"	Seneca	"people of the mountain"
		Mingo	Delaware term
		Tuscarora	"hemp gatherers"
		Nottoway	"adders"

The so-called Woodland cultural area was dominant in the northeastern ecological zone, which comprised a central plain between the ocean and the Allegheny-Appalachian mountain ranges, the rich-soiled river bottoms of the Ohio and Mississippi valleys, the Great Lakes and the coastal Maritimes. This is a huge land of forests, both deciduous and evergreen, which includes from north to south, birch, elm, dogwood, oak, hickory, southern pine, mountain ash and, in the southeastern area, mangrove swamp.

The area as a whole is characterized by divergent cultural traditions that developed distinctive processes of skills, art and religion. However, the importance of slash-and-burn agriculture, an influence from Meso-America, was universal except on the northeastern margins.

The first influences from Central America occurred perhaps around 2000 B.C. — crude pottery and polished stone objects have been attributed to this period. Later, more sophisticated cultures flourished, such as the Adena of Ohio and Kentucky, 800 B.C.–A.D. 200. This is noted for the flexed position of the dead in, at first, natural mounds and, later, in human-constructed burial mounds surrounded by earth walls and precincts — the famous Serpent Mound in Ohio is perhaps the most spectacular. This culture produced domesticated plants, squashes, pumpkins and cord-marked pottery. The

Hopewell culture after 100 B.C. saw the culmination of burial ceremonialism and death ritual cults. This culture also produced pottery, stone carvings, realistic art forms of birds, animals and human forms in clay, copper, mica and shell.

The last cultural complex was "Mississippian," which reentered the old Hopewell area at Cahokia and Fort Ancient from c. A.D. 700 until the time of the European invasion. This late "Temple Mound" period is characterized by intensive agriculture of a Meso-American type, relatively superior pottery, palisaded and fortified villages and flat-topped pyramid mounds (Cahokia). During the 15th century a religious cult, known as the Southern Cult, and associated ritual objects were grafted on to the existing temple platform traditions.

Although this culture scarcely survived to the time of European contact, the earliest white adventurers saw it. De Soto's expedition of 1540 encountered the Mississippian culture as it survived among the Creek, Cherokee and Natchez of the southeast, with their class system, distinctive appearance using ear circles and gorget decorations, and the ritual colors of red and white for war and peace. The northern offshoot of this culture was the Woodland pattern, which, although divided into various local phases, was the genesis of late Woodland culture.

The Iroquoian Huron were the northern limit of extensive agriculture, albeit crude, and their Feast of the Dead witnessed by French Jesuit missionaries relates to Mississippian traits. The Iroquois epitomized Woodland culture, with their belief in a Creator and *orenda*, the life force, which embodied the health and creativity of all nature, opposed by the spirits of evil and destruction. The Algonkians, too, had a world view characterized by an overwhelming fear of sorcery, and a pantheon of destructive spirits such as the Windigowan, cannibal ice giants, the complete natural world being inhabited by spirit forms. Their supreme spirit was Manito or Midemanido, and they had a great culture hero Nanabush. Both Iroquois and Algonkian religions were modified over the years by European influences into a curative ambience.

Wood and bark were important materials for the forest Indian, used to fashion canoes of birch or elm bark, and for the construction of toboggans, bows, arrows, clubs, baskets, containers, spoons, bowls, pestles, mortars, cradleboards, drums, lacrosse rackets and Ball Game sticks. Wigwams were bark or reed mats sewn to a frame of saplings, tied with spruce roots.

Above: Iroquois warrior, c. 1776. He holds a ball-headed maple war club (these often being carved and incised); and wears a silver gorget traded from his white allies, a sash with interspaced beads, buckskin leggings and moccasins decorated with porcupine quillwork.

The Indian peoples of eastern North America experienced a long period of white contact and a gradual Europeanization of their material culture. The destruction of many eastern coastal tribes by diseases and the subsequent adoption of their remnants and of white captives by interior tribes led to a mixed gene pool and introduced a hybrid quality to surviving material culture and costume decoration. Before the end of the 17th century cloth, beads, silver, trade tomahawks, guns, thread, wool and metal trade goods were known to Indians as far west as the Mississippi River.

Indian dress in the northeast was modified by these European influences, but we can speculate that in pre-contact times hide tunics were worn by men, slit skirts by women, with a wide use of wampum shell for beads and decoration. However, European cloth and trade goods were adopted so quickly, that by the 18th century Indians in close association with whites used broadcloth and calico for clothes. The Woodland tribes were expert workers of porcupine quills, fibers, moosehair, paint and later beadwork, to decorate symbolically all manner of articles with representations of celestial and mythical phenomena. In the 19th century, heavy floralist beadwork became popular for dance costumes, as did cut-and-fold ribbonwork, which still remains popular.

Intertribal warfare seems to have been endemic, and bitter wars during the colonial period seem to have been the continuance of conflicts of ancient times. The treatment of prisoners was reported with horror by those who witnessed their torture. There is no doubt that the mutually competitive European colonies exploited and encouraged the Indians in these activities. Conversely, several Indian divines preached against war and the evils brought by whites, and urged the accommodation of the new conditions both materially and psychologically. Such nativistic movements still exist.

Despite centuries of contact and depletion, the Woodland people have survived in many areas. A few mixed-descent people still claim coastal Algonkian ancestry, the Iroquois still occupy fractions of their old territory and the Ojibwa are still numerous in the northern fringes of the Great Lakes states and adjacent parts of Canada. The southern Woodland tribes mostly found their way to Oklahoma, and have participated fully in the pan-Indian cultural revival of recent times. They have lost a major part of the old traditional culture through mass movement away from family ties on the reserves and into the cities, but such is the force of conservatism among some that, for instance, a few Kickapoo retained a semblance of old forest life modified to a Mexican environ-ment, and the Mesquakies purchased their own lands to be free of government influences. Both groups retained a distinctively Woodland culture until quite recent times.

ALGONKIAN or ALGONQUIAN

Algonkian was one of the most important language families of North America, being spoken aboriginally from the Canadian Maritimes to North Carolina, and inland to the Great Plains. The family seems to be divided into three component parts: the divergent Plains branch, including Blackfeet, Cheyenne and Arapaho; a Central branch composed of the Cree, Montagnais, Nascapi group, the Ojibwa, Ottawa, Potawatomi group, and the Fox, Menomini, Shawnee, Illinois, Miami group; and finally an Eastern branch. The Eastern branch is not fully classified, since several tribes became extinct before linguistic records could be made, but the following divisions may be reasonably accurate: Micmac, Malecite-

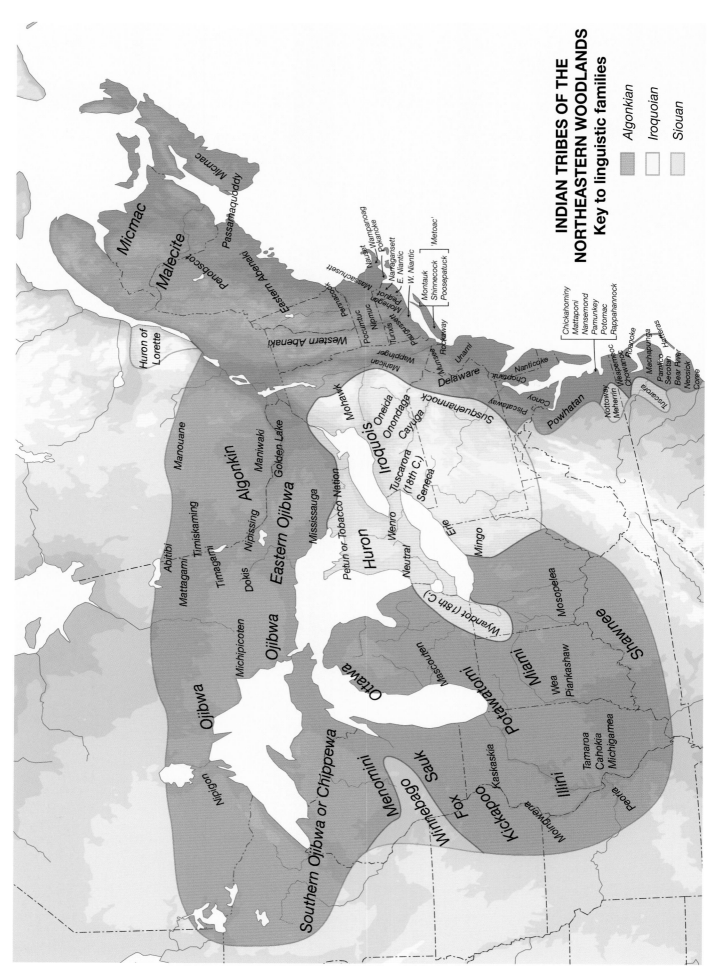

INDIAN TRIBES OF THE NORTHEASTERN WOODLANDS
Key to linguistic families

Algonkian

Iroquoian

Siouan

Micmac

Micmac

Malecite

Passamaquoddy

Penobscot

Eastern Abenaki

Huron of Lorette

Western Abenaki

Pennacook

Pocumtuc

Nipmuc

Massachuset

Nauset

Wampanoag

Pokanoke

Narragansett

E. Niantic

W. Niantic

Mohegan

Pequot

Tunxis

Paugusett

Wappinger

Montauk

Shinnecock

Poosepatuck

'Metoac'

Rockaway

Mahican

Munsee

Unami

Delaware

Chickahominy
Mattaponi
Nansemond
Pamunkey
Potomac
Rappahannock

Nanticoke

Choptank

Piscataway

Conoy

Powhatan

Weapemeoc

Machapunga

Hatteras

Chowanoc

Pamlico

Secotan

Bear River

Neosiok

Coree

Nottoway

Meherrin

Tuscarora

Mohawk

Oneida

Onondaga

Cayuga

Iroquois

Susquehannock

Tuscarora (18th C.)

Seneca

Erie

Mingo

Wenro

Neutral

Huron

Petun or Tobacco Nation

Algonkin

Manouane

Maniwaki

Golden Lake

Timiskaming

Timagami

Nipissing

Dokis

Abitibi

Mattagami

Eastern Ojibwa

Mississauga

Wyandot (18th C.)

Ojibwa

Michipicoten

Ojibwa

Nipigon

Southern Ojibwa or Chippewa

Menomini

Winnebago

Ottawa

Sauk

Fox

Mascouten

Kickapoo

Kaskaskia

Moingwena

Peoria

Illini

Tamaroa
Cahokia
Michigamea

Potawatomi

Wea
Piankashaw

Miami

Mosopelea

Shawnee

Passamaquoddy, Abenaki (two dialects), Nipmuck-Pocumtuck, Massachusett, Narragansett, Mohegan-Pequot, Montauk, Unquachog (Long Island), Quiripi (Connecticut), Mahican, Delaware (two dialects), Nanticoke, Powhatan and Carolina. Of all these eastern dialects only Micmac is still spoken. The name of the whole group derives from the Algonkin (Algonquin) proper, a branch of the Northern Ojibwa in Quebec.

MICMAC (MI'KMAQ) An important Algonkian people of Maritime Canada occupying Nova Scotia, Cape Breton Island, Prince Edward Island and in fairly recent times parts of southern Newfoundland. They were among the first native people encountered by Europeans on the North American continent, when John Cabot took three natives back to England in 1497. Afterwards, they were visited constantly by explorers and fishing vessels from France and England, and became intermediaries in a trade between the French on the St. Lawrence River and tribes further south. Consequently, they became allies of the French, aiding them in colonial conflicts with the English — even after Acadia (roughly modern Nova Scotia) had been ceded to Great Britain. Since 1779 they have been peaceful, scattered occupants of their former domain, never deported, like many tribes, to the south. But a long association with whites, particularly the French, has seen a gradual loss of traditional culture and traditions, and the inevitable mixing of the races. Over the years they have been noted for the fine decoration of their birch bark souvenirs with porcupine quill-work and the production of wood-splint basketry, which has been sold to generations of white curio hunters.

Above: Nova Scotia Micmac woman, c. 1840. The ancient, probably native, double-curve motif is a series of laterally repeated designs probably symbolic (perhaps of canoes). It was used on clothing, pouches, bark containers and canoes by most Northeastern Algonkian peoples, and occurs as far west as the Blackfoot range.

Right: Micmac woman, c. 1830. Early 19th-century Micmac clothing used European materials but retained the beauty of traditional design. Women wore curious peaked hoods with old double-curved designs in beadwork; skirts had rich parallel-lined silk ribbon appliqué. Moccasins were now made with large vamps over the instep, covered with bead- or ribbon work.

Their numbers have usually been reported as about 5,000 in early times. Their present numbers of more than 27,000 includes a large admixture of people of European descent, with close to 20,000 found scattered on about 30 reservations and communities (more than 13,000 are found in Nova Scotia). U.S. numbers of Micmac were reported as 6,722 in the 2000 Census. Native language is still spoken by several hundred people, but Catholicism has replaced most native beliefs for many generations.

In ancient times there seem to have been eight subdivisions. They hunted caribou, moose, otter and beaver, and also fished and collected shellfish. Their dwellings were usually conical bark wigwams, and transportation was by distinctively shaped bark canoes. Hide native dress seems to have been replaced quickly by dark cloth obtained from European traders, which they often decorated with beads and ribbons. They were sometimes also known as Tarrantine; today they prefer to be known as Mi'kmaq (pronounced Mig-maw).

Above: Micmac Indians in front of a makeshift wigwam, Nova Scotia, c. 1900. They are making splint-ash baskets by plaiting strips of wood, a type made throughout the Northeast by Algonkians and Iroquois. Sometimes the splints were stamped with potato designs or dyed. Some baskets were reinforced on the edge with sweetgrass.

Below: Micmac canoes. Birch bark canoes, distributed over the whole Subarctic and Northeastern Woodlands as far south as northern Minnesota, Wisconsin, Michigan, New Hampshire and Maine, were efficient for forest travel, being light enough to be propelled by a single-bladed paddle and carried overland by portage between waterways. Major tribal distinctions in prow and stern shape and sheer of gunwales can be identified; the Micmac canoe had this curved prow and stern, and some were large enough to carry a sail for ocean use. The curved stem pieces, thwarts, headboards, ribs, floor sheathing and gunwales were usually of white cedar, heated into shape; the bark was usually sewn with black spruce roots.

TRIBES OF THE NORTHEASTERN WOODLANDS, c. 1585–1780
Linguistic and cultural boundaries are necessarily approximate; this sketch map is intended only as a general guide to distribution. Modern state boundaries are shown as broken lines, for orientation only.

1 *Micmac porcupine quillwork on birch bark, probably a place-mat. Quills filling gaps between zones indicates late 19th century work, c. 1880.*

2 *Molly Muise, Bear River Micmac, Nova Scotia, wearing a decorated hood, c. 1860.*

3 *Malecite moccasins, c. 1860. Constructed of moosehide with stiffened instep, velvet vamps, and ankle collars, with straight heel seams and gathered to V-shaped vamps. The collars and vamps (insteps) are decorated with beaded clusters and bifurcated vines in the style of the Wabanaki group of Northeastern Algonquians of Maine and New Brunswick (Maliseet, Penobscot and Abenaki peoples). Made primarily for the 19th century souvenir markets.*

4 *Dr. Jeremiah Lonecloud and Annie Gloade. Micmac, Nova Scotia, 1926. Annie is wearing a traditional peaked cap with beadwork, a silver brooch and a ribbon decorated skirt.*

5 *Moccasins, probably Micmac, c. 1850, buckskin, red cloth, ribbon edging and beadwork in the double-curve motifs.*

6 *Sash, Maliseet, c. 1860. The sash is in the shape of a priest's sole or amice and constructed of cloth, silk, and decorated with beadwork. The beadwork style suggests the work of one of the Maritime Indian groups of New Brunswick or Maine collectively known as Wabanaki or Abenaki, and dating from the mid-19th century.*

Left: Penobscot or Malecite woman, c. 1850, wearing a peaked cloth hood with the rounded bottom edge characteristic of the Malecite and Penobscot of New Brunswick and Maine. Hoods were no doubt aboriginal, but these late 18th- and 19th-century Northeastern examples are made from dark trade cloth or velvet, decorated in fine floralistic double-curve and zigzag beaded designs. By this date they were worn only for galas or church festivals.

Right: Penobscot Clown Dancer, 19th century. The only Eastern Abenaki group to remain in Maine were one of the few pockets of eastern seaboard peoples who retained elements of traditional culture late enough to be recorded by ethnographers. The Clown or Trading Dance was a popular gaming ceremony performed at night; the clown wears a deer mask, mooseskin coat and buckskin moccasins with large U-shaped instep vamps.

MALECITE or MALISEET

This is a small group of Algonkian people located along the St. John River in what is now New Brunswick, Canada. They are closely, if not originally, the same people as the Passamaquoddy of Maine, and are related more distantly to the Micmac, Penobscot and Abenaki, the four sometimes known as *Wabanaki*. They were also known as "Etchemin," a term also applied to include their relatives. First recorded by the explorer Champlain, they were thereafter under French influence until the British conquest of Canada. Subsequently they lost most of their lands except for a few acres on the St. John and Tobique rivers, where a number of descendants remain, with a European admixture from 400 years of white contact. Their native culture was overwhelmed generations ago, the tribe being largely converted to Roman Catholicism. They were noted during the 19th century for excellent beadwork, which survives in several museum collections. Their population was rarely given as more than a few hundred. Close to 5,000 descendants are still found at their reserves in New Brunswick and a few in Quebec. Other Malecite may be found in Maine, near Presque Isle and Houlton, Aroostook County, with some Micmac. The Houlton Malecite numbered 550 members in 1990. Total U.S. Malecite population was given as 1,288 in 2000.

PASSAMAQUODDY

Closely related to the Malecite, the Passamaquoddy remained in Maine after the British conquest of Canada in 1759, and have retained a separate identity. They were located on Passamaquoddy Bay, Maine, and along the St. Croix River. Their culture and history is generally the same as other Maritime Algonkian groups. About 3,241 descendants, according to the 2000 Census, are still reported connected with three state reservations near Princeton and Eastport,

Maine. A few have retained their language and a little craftwork, but native traditions, religion and ceremony largely fell into disuse generations ago. In early times they were hunters of moose and caribou, but clams, lobsters, porpoise and salmon were also eaten. In recent times they adopted European cultivated garden produce, including potatoes. Along with their close relatives, they once formed a loose confederacy called *Wabanaki*, modeled on the Iroquois form.

ABENAKI

The Abenaki were Algonkians of central Maine in the valleys of the Androscoggin, Kennebec, Saco and Penobscot rivers in several subdivisions, of which the *Pigwacket* (*Pequawket*), *Norridgewock* and *Penobscot* are the largest. The latter is often given separate status. The explorer Champlain passed through their territory in 1604, and thenceforth they were under French influence and were hostile to the English colonists. They suffered as a result, the Norridge-wock and Pequawket divisions being almost wiped out. Much reduced in numbers, they withdrew in the late 17th century to French Canada, where they settled ultimately at Bécancour and St. Francis. During the various conflicts between the colonial powers the St. Francis Abenaki retaliated against New England settlements. They often adopted white captives, such as the Gill family, whose descendants became chiefs and leaders.

In early times their dwellings were bark houses, conical, square or rounded. They hunted deer, moose, muskrat, otter and bear, and also ate salmon and eels. Like the other northeastern Algonkians they had a strong belief in supernatural beings, with dances to engage their power, but their adoption of Catholicism led to an abandonment of native religion after their settlement in French Canada. They excelled in the manufacture of bark canoes and containers, the latter often finely decorated with incised curving designs.

Above: Penobscot Indians, Maine, c. 1900. They are selling ash-splint baskets. The lady wears a beaded cape and the man a cloth shirt with beaded front and cuffs.

Below: Indian men (probably Abenakis from the St. Francis Reserve, Quebec) c. 1900, with large splint baskets that they made and sold throughout the New England states during the summer months of the 19th century.

Above: Mr. Louis Watso and family, St. Francis Abenaki from Odanak, Quebec, at their basket shop in Blodgett's Landing, N.H. The Abenakis were a people of northern New England but forced to leave for French Canada by English colonists in the 17th and 18th century from where they retaliated until the general peace of 1763. In 1759 the colonial American Militia "Rogers Rangers" made their famous raid on the Abenaki village of St. Francis in Quebec, an episode popularized by the book and film Northwest Passage *of 1939.*

EASTERN WOODLANDS TRIBES, 20th CENTURY

Key to abbreviations:

Ab	=	Abenaki
Al	=	Algonkin
"Cree"	=	Locally called Cree
Da	=	Dakota (Eastern Sioux)
Del	=	Delaware
Iro	=	Iroquois, Six Nations: Mohawk, Oneida, Onondaga, Cayuga, Seneca, Tuscarora
M	=	Mohegan
Mal	=	Malecite
Me	=	Métis
Mic	=	Micmac
Mon	=	Montagnais
Na	=	(in east) Narragansett; (in west) Nakota (Middle Sioux), i.e., Yankton & Yanktonai
Ni	=	Nipmuc(k)
Ot	=	Ottawa
Oj	=	Ojibwa (Chippewa)
P	=	Paugussett
Pas	=	Passamaquoddy
Pe	=	Pequot
Pen	=	Penobscot
Pow	=	Powhatan groups, incl. Pamunkey, Upper & Lower Chickahominy, Mattaponi, Rappahannock
Pot	=	Potawatomi
Sc	=	Scaticook
TdB	=	Tête de Boule (Attikamek)
Wa	=	Wampanoag
Win	=	Winnebago
Wy	=	Wyandot

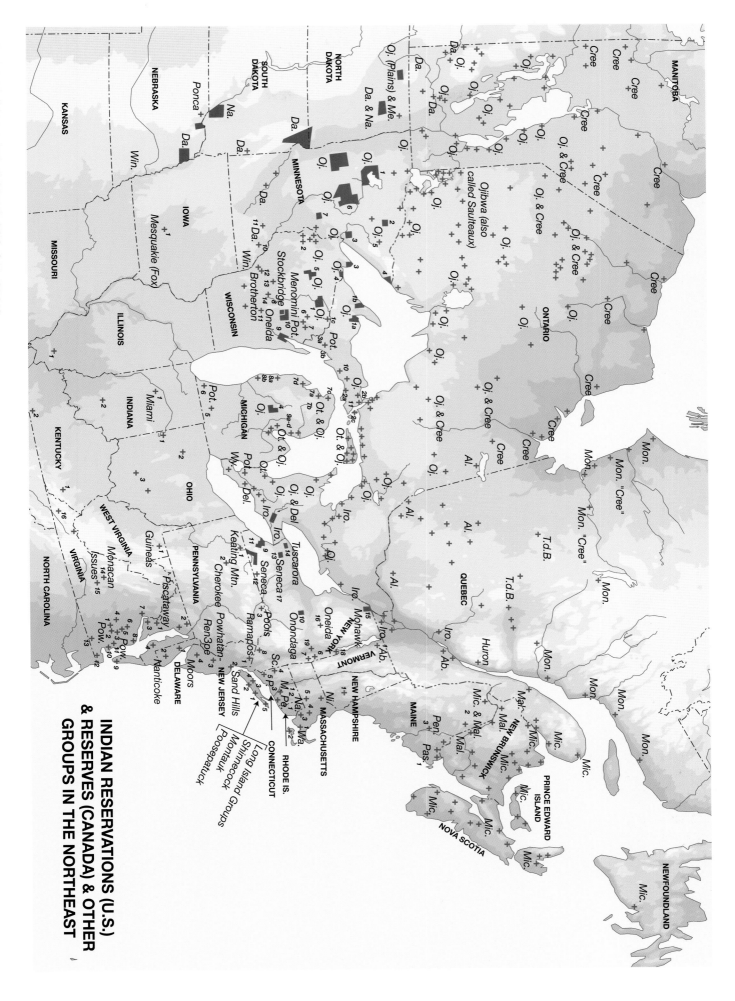

INDIAN RESERVATIONS (U.S.) & RESERVES (CANADA) & OTHER GROUPS IN THE NORTHEAST

Above and Left: The Indian birch bark canoe was made throughout the Subarctic and much of the Eastern Woodlands. Canoes allowed efficient forest travel via the vast network of lakes and rivers. Constructed of birch (and other bark) over a frame of ribs, floor sheathing, thwarts and gunwales of cedar. There were many variations of tribal shapes and this one is an Abenaki canoe. It was made by Aaron York (seen in photo at left), an Abenaki descendant, the first of his people in nearly a century to make the light, strong and versatile canoes so important for travel for his ancestors. European traders quickly recognized their value for long-range travel on the vast inland river and lake systems of Canada. Voyageurs developed their own extra-large versions for the transportation of men and furs. Tribal variations can be recognized by the canoes' profile. Photographs courtesy Aaron York.

Below: Chapel of the Delawares serving the Delaware Indian enclave and descendants on the Six Nations Reserve, Ontario. Photograph courtesy Dave Sager.

Hide dress was replaced largely by blankets and clothes obtained in the fur trade.

These old Maine Abenakis have merged with their relatives, the Western Abenaki, at St. Francis, although the old dialect once spoken at Bécancour was thought to be true Abenaki (called Wawenock). However, the Penobscot remained in Maine after making peace with the English in 1759, and retained a number of settlements along the Penobscot River, the principal one at Old Town, where descendants still remain, with additions from the Passamaquoddy over the years. About 2,194 people in Maine (according to the 2000 Census) now claim Penobscot ancestry, including mixed Euro-American and other Indian. Their language was retained by three speakers in 1970, although some band members spoke Passamaquoddy. The other Abenakis from Maine, sometimes referred to as *Eastern Abenaki*, are now part of the multitribal Abenaki of Quebec, returned as numbering 1,849 at Odanak (St. Francis) and 223 at Bécancour in 2005. Only a portion are actually living permanently on the reserves.

WESTERN ABENAKI The designation Western Abenaki is now given to the Algonkians who spoke one dialect and once inhabited the upper Connecticut River valley in New Hampshire, Massachusetts and Vermont. They were sometimes referred to in history as *Sokoki*, including perhaps the Pennacook on the Merrimack River and the *Missisquoi* on Lake Champlain to the north. Their history is much the same as that of their eastern Abenaki relatives: They gradually abandoned New England for French Canada after King Philip's War (1675-76) and ultimately settled at the St. Francis Mission and Bécancour in Quebec, where other Abenakis and New England remnants joined them, and where multi-ethnic descendants remain. There are few reliable estimates for their early population, perhaps 1,500 excluding Pennacook; the St. Francis Indians were given as numbering 342 in 1783, 370 in 1904, with about 200 descendants still living on the reservation in 1973, and several hundreds living elsewhere. Recently, a mixed-blood group of about 2,300, living around Swanton, Vermont, are also claimants of Abenaki ancestry. During the 19th century many were employed making splint-ash baskets which were sold to whites, and which remain in museums. An Abenaki colony once selling these wares lived near Lake George, New York.

PENNACOOK or **PAWTUCKET** The Pennacook were an Algonkian people of the Merrimac River, New Hampshire, and parts of adjacent Maine and Massachusetts, perhaps exceeding 2,000 people. Their history is similar to both the Western Abenaki to the north (with whom they are now usually classified), and the Eastern Abenaki of Maine. They were defeated by Waldron in 1676 at the close of King Philip's War, and their remnants withdrew to Canada, uniting with the Abenakis at St. Francis, Quebec. A few people claiming Pennacook ancestry have been reported near Manchester in their old territory until quite recently.

MASSACHUSET A group of villages near Boston, Massachusetts, between Salem and Brockton along the coast, and as far inland as the Concord River were home to the Massachuset. They probably spoke the same dialect of Algonkian as the Pawtucket and were probably visited by several voyagers during the 16th century. Before contact with the English settlement at Plymouth in 1621, they perhaps numbered 3,000, but were reduced rapidly by epidemics of smallpox and other pestilence. They were soon influenced by Puritans who settled their country and who gathered their remnants into small villages of "Praying Indians" (those at Punkapog the only ones to survive in any number). These remnants intermarried with African-Americans during the 18th century. A few people of mixed descent (about 60) survived into the 20th century, near Canton and Mansfield in Norfolk County, Massachusetts, but none were reported in the 2000 Census.

NIPMUC or **NIPMUCK** This is a term to cover native villages in central Massachusetts who perhaps spoke an Algonkian dialect connected with the Pocumtuck who lived west of the Connecticut River. They were greatly weakened by the diseases brought by the European settlers, and their remnants settled in villages controlled by whites. Some probably took part in King Philip's War (1675–76), after which only a few survived. A number of descendants still preserve their name, and a few acres of land near Grafton, known as the Hassanimisco Reservation, are privately owned. A few more people near Dudley and Webster may also have their ancestry. The resurgence of Indian identity in recent times has reactivated the group, who are involved in sponsoring pan-Indian events. About 660 people still claim Nipmuc ancestry.

POCOMTUC or **POCUMTUCK** These people lived in Algonkian villages of central-west Massachusetts from Agawam in the south to Deerfield in the north. They may have been connected to the Nipmuc or Wappinger, but all are artificial groupings. Their main settlement was Fort Hill, Franklin County, which was destroyed by the Mohawk in 1666. They joined the hostilities in King Philip's War (1675–76). At its close their remnants fled west to the Hudson and ultimately to the Abenaki at St. Francis, and disappeared as a separate people.

WAMPANOAG or **POKANOKET** A convenient grouping of Algonkian people and villages of southern Massachusetts, including those on the coast below Marshfield, Cape Cod, Martha's Vineyard Island, Nantucket Island and part of Narragansett Bay, Rhode Island, is known as the Wampanoag. The *Nauset* of Barnstable County and *Sakonnet* of Rhode Island have been presented separately in the past, but they probably never formed any unified tribal group. We know that their subsistence consisted of deer, bear, squirrel, fish, seafood, gathering and horticulture. Their houses were of varied shape, covered with slabs of bark or woven mats. They were known to Europeans at least as far back as 1602, and played an important part in helping the Pilgrim Fathers to establish their settlements after 1620, due mainly to the efforts of their chief Massasoit. However, his son Metacom, sometimes known as King Philip, led a general Indian uprising against the colonists in 1675-76, but was defeated so badly that these Indians were never a force again.

Their remnants, about 400 by some estimates, settled in various locations, mostly in Bristol and Barnstable counties, Massachusetts, and a number of descendants were still found near Fall River, Herring Pond, Yarmouth, Assawompsett Pond, Mashpee and Gay Head (Martha's Vineyard Island) in the 19th century. The latter two groups still exist, with a total population of about 3,300. Although they are racially mixed, the force of modern pan-Indianism has strongly reinforced their Indian identity and their participation in Indian events.

NARRAGANSETT The Algonkian people who once occupied the whole of the present state of Rhode Island west of Narragansett Bay are known by that name. They seem to have been closely related to the *Niantic*, with whom they ultimately merged. The smaller Coweset, Pawtuxet and Block Island Indians were all more or less the same people. Probably contacted by the explorer Verrazano in 1524, they were known to the Dutch and English from the early 1600s. They had a large population of several thousand that escaped the first pestilence and smallpox of 1617, but many died in 1633. They became friends of the English in 1636, after Roger Williams laid the foundations of the state of Rhode Island by settling among them. They remained on good terms with whites until King Philip's War (1675–76), when they joined the hostiles, and lost 1,000 men, women and children at the Great Swamp Fight near Kingston. Some fled the country, and others joined the Niantic, these together becoming known as Narragansett.

Since that time they have continued to live in the same area, although many left and joined the Brotherton Indians in New York or the Mohegan in Connecticut during the 18th century. Their descendants, numbering about 2,620, according to the 2000 Census, are still found in the southern part of Rhode Island around Charlestown and Kingston, although greatly mixed with other races, and having lost all traces of their original Indian culture and language. They have, however, absorbed pan-Indian influences, hold an annual powwow and have revived festivals and church meetings, which gives their descendants a persistent identity.

NIANTIC A small group of Algonkian people divided into the Eastern branch in Rhode Island, and Western branch near New London, Connecticut. They were separate from their neighbors perhaps only because of their independent sachems (chiefs), who maintained a nominal pro-English position during King Philip's War (1675–76) under their chief Ninigret. The Narragansett merged with them, and their descendants are no doubt the multi-ethnic group near Charlestown, Rhode Island. The last of the Western Niantic intermarried with Mohegan-Pequot survivors in Connecticut.

MOHEGAN The Mohegan were an Algonkian people who occupied the Thames River valley and its branches in Connecticut, and are often confused with the Mohican (Mahican) in popular writings. They were closely related and perhaps once the same people as the Pequot. They separated from the Pequot after the destruction of that tribe by white colonists, aided by coastal Indians and Mohegans led by Uncas in 1637. They have continued to live in Connecticut, although over the years some joined the Brotherton in New York and the Scaticook. In 1721 they still held 4,000 acres along the Thames River, reduced to 2,300 acres by 1850, by which time many had left their traditional enclave near Uncasville, and in 1861 unoccupied lands reverted to the state. Some descendants still live near Uncasville, Connecticut. Nearby is the Mohegan Church and the Fort Shantok Point burial grounds. The Tantaquidgeons, Gladys and Harold (the 10th generation descendants of the historical Uncas or one of his captain's), still ran a small museum at the rear of their house in 1988, which contained Mohegan material culture. Census 2000 identified 2,428 Mohegan descendents, or about 1,500 (BIA) enrolled 2001. The tribe, now federally recognized, operates a highly successful casino.

The southern New England Algonkians had a subsistence pattern that combined maize horticulture with hunting, and heavy involvement in trade with Long Island Indians for wampum shell money, also used by white settlers, which drew them into the European money exchange at an early date.

PEQUOT The Pequot were an Algonkian tribe, perhaps once one with the Mohegan, together numbering more than 4,000. They occupied eastern Connecticut, particularly around the Mystic River area. Their subsistence foods came from hunting, collecting, maize harvesting, waterfowl and shellfish. The settlement patterns involved villages of several houses built of bark-covered saplings, sometimes large enough for a number of families. Such dwellings were used by all southern New England Algonkians. The Pequot seem to have been at war with their neighbors at the time of first European settlement, which they strongly resisted under their sachem (chief), Sassacus. They were defeated by a combined body of English, Mohegan and Narragansett in 1637, with their principal settlement completely destroyed. Many were sold into slavery in the West Indies, and others fled west. A few who remained obtained two land grants from the English in New London, Mushantuxet, in 1667, and Lantern Hill, 1683, near Ledyard, Connecticut, and both still exist as small state reservations. About 777 people of mixed descent are still connected with these lands. A few families live permanently on the reservations and constitute

Above: Mohegan, c. 1880. Northeastern Algonkians including the Mohegan and Narragansett all but lost native dress by the 19th century. Male dress for special occasions sometimes included a beaded cloth cape as a symbol of rank. The upright feathered headdress with beaded band may be descended from an earlier form, or copied from the popular western war bonnet.

1

1 In May 1879, three Wampanoag women—Zerviah Gould Mitchell (1807–1898) and her two unmarried daughters, Melinda, aka Teweelwma (1836–1919), which means "Bride of the Forest" and Charlotte, aka Wootonekanuske (1848–1930), moved from North Abington, Massachusetts to a fifteen-acre plot of ancestral land at Betty's Neck in Lakeville, Massachusetts.

2 Site of the Uncas Fort at Shantok Point, Connecticut. Uncas was a pro-English Mohegan chief during the Pequot War of 1637.

3 Ms. Gladys Tantaquidgeon, (1899–2005) is given much credit for the Mohegans receiving federal recognition. For years she collected a large number of documents, including tribal correspondence, and birth, death and marriage records, many of which she stored under her bed. That information helped document the continuity of the now claimed 1,700-member tribe, which managed to survive even after its reservation was disbanded. In 1931 she founded the Tantaquidgeon Indian Museum in Uncasville, along with her brother Harold, the tribe's former chief. Tribal officials said it was one of the oldest museums in the country owned and operated by Indians. Here (below left), she is seen as a young woman c. 1915 and at age one hundred.

Right: Wood-splint baskets, Northeastern Woodlands. Baskets made from shaved down ash or oak (sometimes other woods) and simply woven were originally made as utilitarian work baskets for gathering and storing food, or for household or market use. Many large older baskets have elaborately carved handles. More recently, smaller decorative baskets were made for sale to museums, collectors, and tourists. However, it is possible Indian people adopted the plaited wood-splint technique from European settlers during the 18th century—accordingly their baskets may be confused with immigrant basketry, particularly of the Shakers, Pennsylvania-Germans and Swedish peoples. Northeastern Indians, Iroquois, Mohegans and Scaticooks sometimes added painted, swabbed, or stencil designs.

2

FORT SHANTOK
MOHEGAN INDIAN FORT SITE
FROM 1645 TO 1659 IT WAS THE SCENE OF
MANY CONFLICTS BETWEEN THE MOHEGANS AND
THEIR ADVERSARIES THE NARRAGANSETTS
NEHANTICS, POCOMTUC NORWOOTUC AND THE
TUNXIS INDIANS TO THE NORTH WAS THE SP-
RING WHERE DRINKING WATER WAS OBTAINED
IN 1650 JONATHAN BREWSTER ESTABLISHED A
TRADING POST ON THE OPPOSITE SIDE OF THE
RIVER FOR TRADE WITH THE INDIANS

3

Above: Indian girls wearing contemporary pan-Indian dance dress at the powwow organized by the casino-rich Mashantucket Pequots at Ledyard, Connecticut in September 1995.

Opposite, Above: Map showing the main locations associated with the Pequot War 1637 and King Philip's War 1675–1676.

Opposite, Below: Map showing the original homelands of the Mohican (Mahican) and Munsee Delaware in the 17th century, and also locations of subsequent groups with their ancestry.

one of the few surviving Indian groups of southern New England. A casino operation has brought immense wealth to the Mushantuxet band (Mashantucket) recently, along with federal recognition.

LOWER CONNECTICUT RIVER TRIBES This describes a number of small tribes in present-day Connecticut, who were in contact with English settlers from 1639 onward. The noted groups were the *Tunxis*, near Hartford, *Podunk*, near Windsor, *Wangunk*, near Wethersfield, and *Quinnipiac*, near New Haven, centering along the Connecticut River and sometimes collectively called *Mattabesec* by some writers. They have been incorrectly added to the so-called Wappinger group by several historians, but may have shared with the lower Housatonic River groups a separate Algonkian dialect now called Quiripi. They perhaps numbered collectively 2,200 in the early 17th century, but diminished rapidly and sold their lands to English settlers until only a few families remained by the 18th century, and a mere handful of descendants of mixed race by the 19th century.

PAUGUSSETT or **LOWER HOUSATONIC RIVER TRIBES** This is a group of four small tribes formerly living on the Housatonic River, Connecticut, when first in contact with English settlers during the early 17th century. They include the *Paugussett* proper, around present day Derby, *Pequannock*, near Trumbull, *Potatuck*, near Woodbury, and *Weantinock* or *Wawyachtonok*, above Danbury in Litchfield County. This last tribe is sometimes given as a Mahican group. They diminished in numbers due to epidemics brought by whites, and were pressured into land sales. A small mission village, Schaghticoke or Scaticook, developed from an earlier settlement, was established by Mahwee, a Pequot, early in the 18th century, which became a refuge for a mixed tribal group, mostly Paugussett. About 250 or so descendants still identify as Scaticook, mainly from four families. The leading family is surnamed Harris. A few other Paugussett descendants are also reported from Golden Hill, Bridgeport, and near Colchester, Connecticut.

WAPPINGER and **LOWER HUDSON RIVER TRIBES** In the restricted sense, the Wappinger lived on the east bank of the Hudson River, near present-day Poughkeepsie, New York, but the term is sometimes extended to include groups below them as far south as the Manhattan Island Indians. Their closest linguistic relatives were the Munsee-Delaware and Mahican, with whom they are sometimes classed, but the formation of the Wappinger Confederacy proposed by some writers (which includes the Housatonic and Connecticut River groups), now seems wholly without foundation. The lower Hudson tribes perhaps numbered 3,000 before being wasted by wars with Dutch settlers. The transfer of power in the area to the English brought them under pressure for land, and the last withdrew from Westchester County, New York, in 1756. Some joined the Stockbridge in Massachusetts and the Nanticoke and Delaware in Broome County, New York, and ultimately disappeared as a separate group. Early reports called the northern groups Highland Indians (Hudson Highlands).

MAHICAN or **MOHICAN** Apparently the Mahican's name derives from "Muhheakunnuk" or "Moh-he-ka-ne-ok," a location in the tide-water of the Hudson River, New York which reached far up-state to within a few miles of Albany. They were made famous by James Fenimore Cooper's book *The Last of the Mohicans*. The Dutch called them Mahikan or Mahican, the English, Mohican or River Indians.

The original homeland of the Mohicans extended from the southern end of Lake Champlain south to Dutchess County New York and from Schoharie Creek in the west to central Vermont to the east, with their population concentrated along valleys and rivers with villages consisting of about 250 people living in bark-covered lodges and longhouses. They belonged to a cultural tradition known as "Woodland" similar to their close neighbors the Mohawk to the west (a tribe of the Iroquois Confederacy) and branches of the Delaware Indians (the Esopus and Munsee) to the south. They produced maize or Indian corn, beans, various squashes, fished for herring and shad, as well as collecting nuts and berries. Their ceremonials celebrated the exploitation of their main foods culminating with the Green Corn Festival in late August. By November the people scattered into small bands to survive by hunting during the winter before returning to the main villages each spring. Bear, deer, moose and birds were the main food sources during the difficult winter months.

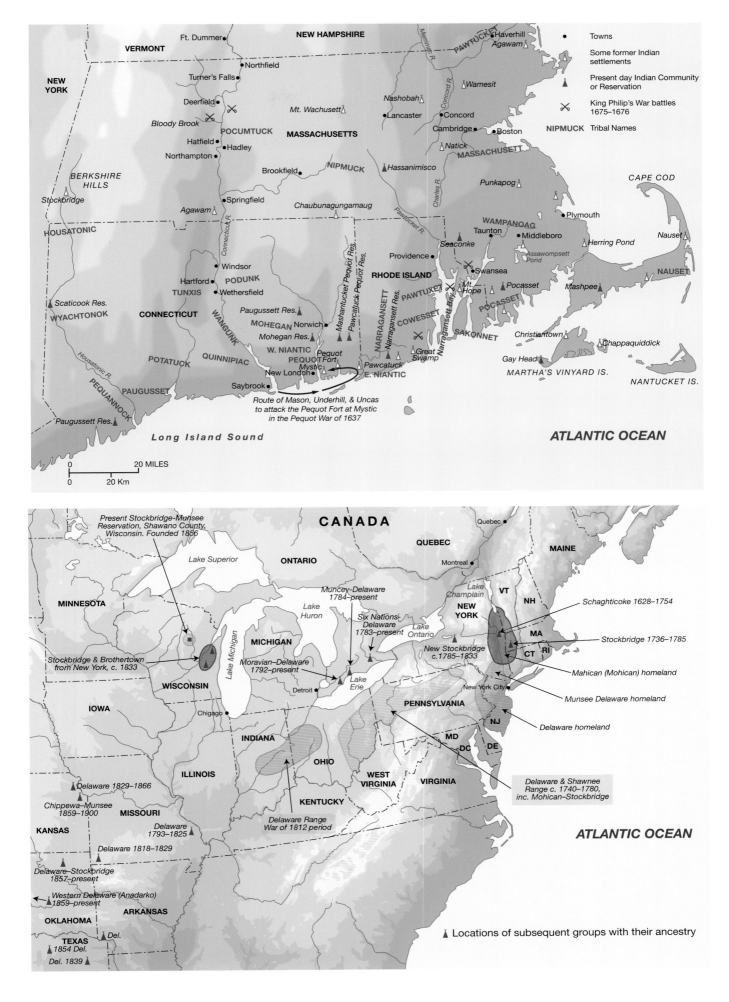

Top map legend:

- Towns
- Some former Indian settlements
- Present day Indian Community or Reservation
- King Philip's War battles 1675–1676
- NIPMUCK Tribal Names

VERMONT
NEW HAMPSHIRE
NEW YORK
Ft. Dummer
Northfield
Turner's Falls
Deerfield
Bloody Brook
POCUMTUCK
Hatfield
Hadley
Northampton
MASSACHUSETTS
Mt. Wachusett
Nashobah
Lancaster
Wamesit
Concord
Cambridge
Boston
Natick
MASSACHUSETT
Charles R.
BERKSHIRE HILLS
Stockbridge
HOUSATONIC
Agawam
Springfield
NIPMUCK
Brookfield
Chaubunagungamaug
Hassanimisco
Punkapog
CAPE COD
Plymouth
WAMPANOAG
Taunton
Middleboro
Herring Pond
Nauset
Seaconke
Assawompsett Pond
Scaticook Res.
WYACHTONOK
Windsor
Hartford
PODUNK
TUNXIS
Wethersfield
CONNECTICUT
WANGUNK
Connecticut R.
Paugussett Res.
MOHEGAN Norwich
Mohegan Res.
Providence
RHODE ISLAND
Swansea
Mt. Hope
Pocasset
Mashpee
NAUSET
Pawcatuck
NARRAGANSETT
Narragansett Res.
PAWTUXET
COWESSET
POCASSET
Christiantown
Chappaquiddick
Housatonic R.
Scaticook
POTATUCK
QUINNIPIAC
W. NIANTIC
PEQUOT Pequot Fort Mystic
New London
Saybrook
E. NIANTIC
Pawcatuck
Great Swamp
SAKONNET
Gay Head
MARTHA'S VINYARD IS.
NANTUCKET IS.
PEQUANNOCK
PAUGUSSET
Paugussett Res.
Long Island Sound
ATLANTIC OCEAN

Route of Mason, Underhill, & Uncas to attack the Pequot Fort at Mystic in the Pequot War of 1637

0   20 MILES
0   20 Km

Bottom map:

CANADA
Present Stockbridge-Munsee Reservation, Shawano County, Wisconsin. Founded 1856
QUEBEC
Quebec
Montreal
MAINE
Lake Superior
ONTARIO
MINNESOTA
Muncey-Delaware 1784–present
Lake Huron
Six Nations-Delaware 1783–present
Lake Champlain
VT
NH
NEW YORK
Schaghticoke 1628–1754
MICHIGAN
Lake Ontario
New Stockbridge c.1785–1833
MA
Stockbridge 1736–1785
RI
CT
Stockbridge & Brothertown from New York, c. 1833
Moravian-Delaware 1792–present
Lake Erie
Mahican (Mohican) homeland
WISCONSIN
Detroit
Munsee Delaware homeland
IOWA
Lake Michigan
Chigago
New York City
PENNSYLVANIA
Delaware homeland
NJ
INDIANA
MD
DC
DE
ILLINOIS
OHIO
WEST VIRGINIA
VIRGINIA
Delaware 1829–1866
KENTUCKY
Delaware & Shawnee Range c. 1740–1780, inc. Mohican–Stockbridge
Chippewa–Munsee 1859–1900
MISSOURI
Delaware 1793–1825
ATLANTIC OCEAN
KANSAS
Delaware Range War of 1812 period
Delaware 1818–1829
Delaware–Stockbridge 1857–present
Western Delaware (Anadarko) 1859–present
OKLAHOMA
ARKANSAS
TEXAS
1854 Del.
Del.
Del. 1839

Locations of subsequent groups with their ancestry

Left: The Mohegan church on the Mohegan Reservation at Montville, Connecticut, near the Thames River. The church was remodeled and enlarged in 1831. A Mohegan festival is held each year in the grounds.

Below: William Penn's Treaty with the Indians in November 1683, *painted oil on canvas 1771–72 by Benjamin West. Penn's first treaty was signed with the Delaware at Shackamaxon, Pennsylvania, in 1682; one of 11 treaties for land cessions between July 1682 and October 1685. Benjamin West's painting was done about a hundred years later. In 1737 Penn's sons and the Philadelphia Quakers subsequently swindled the Delawares out of much of their lands forcing them to move farther west.* Pennsylvania Academy of the Fine Arts, Philadelphia, USA/The Bridgeman Art Library

Opposite: Map showing the homeland of the Mahican.

Mohican social organization consisted of three matrilocal clans—Bear, Wolf, and Turtle—with marriage strictly exogamous (outside one's own clan). Their system of leadership was somewhat intermediate between the grand Chiefs of the Atlantic coastal tribes and the clan based institutionalized sachems (chiefs) of the Iroquois model. Their total population at the time of contact with the early Dutch settlers was likely to have been between 3,000–4,000, but by the end of the 17th century it was perhaps no more than 900.

With the arrival of Henry Hudson and Dutch traders in 1609 and the establishment of Forts Nassau (1614) and Orange (1624) the Mohicans were drawn into the white mans' fur trade which brought them into conflict with the Mohawk, at first holding their own but gradually worn down by a succession of wars beginning in 1628 when the Mohawks gained access to Ft. Orange forcing the Mohicans to look east and north for new hunting grounds. The core of their domain at this period were three villages in present Rensselaer County, New York but by the mid 17th century their diminishing population was augmented by the inclusion of their close relatives the Wyachtonok from around New Milford in Connecticut, the Housatonok from near Stockbridge, Massachusetts, and the Wapping from near Poughkeepsie, essentially forming a confederacy called the "River Indians" by the British who had succeeded the Dutch as masters of the fur trade. Another Mohican village, established after 1628 at the junction of the Hudson and Hoosic rivers, called Scaghticoke later incorporated refugees from New England fleeing the effects of the "King Philip" War of 1676. They were later to move to Odanak in French Canada and lost separate existence.

The sale of Mohican lands began as early as 1630. By 1664 the British became the colonial power of the region with Mohican warriors now largely relegated to act as scouts during the various wars between France and Great Britain in the backwoods of eastern North America. During the 1730s numbers of Mohicans began to gravitate to the Protestant mission at Stockbridge, Massachusetts under the chiefs Konkapot and Quanakaunt (later the Quinney family) and became known as the Stockbridge Indians, a name with which they have ever since been associated. After 1752 some joined the German Moravian missions in Pennsylvania, Ohio, and Indiana, others including the remaining Stockbridges settled among the Iroquoian Oneidas at New Stockbridge in Madison and Oneida counties, New York. The Stockbridges and Oneidas having served the Americans during the American Revolution ultimately looked for new lands in the west and moved to Wisconsin in the 1830s, and finally in 1856 to a reservation obtained from the Menomini Indians in Shawano County which now provided a new home for the Stockbridge people.

After more than 200 years of white colonial corruption, empty promises of both British and later America authorities, and the huge effects of European introduced diseases, the Stockbridge finally had a home. By the mid 19th century they had become largely Christian and rural American in culture. In their new home the Quinney and Metoxen families became foremost in the reformation of community unity and resisting further pressure for yet another removal to Minnesota. Since the establishment of the reservation in 1856 tribal concerns have centered around their churches, leadership, and the role of women. Their matrilineage and language have largely disappeared, and substantial land-loss occurred after the

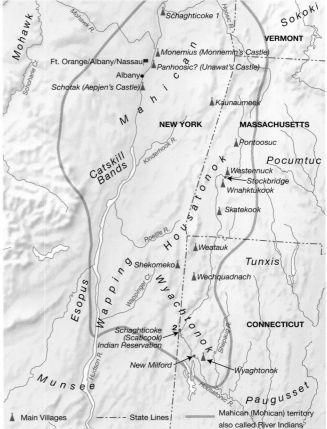

General Allotment Act of 1887. In 1895 the tribe numbered 503, of which 300 lived on the reservation. The tribe agreed to the Indian Reorganization Act of 1934 which began a period of economic improvement, community government, and an elected tribal council. In 1966, of 750 people on the tribal "rolls," 380 lived on the reservation, and in 2000, 1,531 were enrolled "Stockbridge-Munsee" and reported as requiring at least a quarter Indian descent to qualify. At various times during the 18th and 19th centuries they have been joined by small groups of Munsee Delawares, and Brothertown Indians from New Jersey, although the latter became American citizens during the 19th century which subsequently ended their relationship with the U.S. government. Their name, Stockbridge-Munsee, now recognizes the combined tribes.

So, despite their legendary past and Fenimore Cooper's saga which almost obliterated them from the American consciousness, the Mohican descendants are alive and well in northern Wisconsin. Their amazing ethnic persistence celebrated each summer with the "Stockbridge-Munsee Band of Mohican Powwow" a pan-Indian celebration copied from neighboring tribes with songs and dancing and the honouring of men who have served in the U.S. armed forces, now provides a focal point for an annual tribal reunion.

There's no doubt the Mohican (Mahican) and Delaware lacked the organizational genius of the neighboring Iroquois tribes to absorb remnant groups into their matrilineal clans to maintain population and diplomacy in their discourses with Europeans. They were unable to play the role of middlemen in the fur trade and became the geographical buffer which allowed the Iroquois time to form the powerful political position they achieved until the American Revolution fractured them.

A few Mohicans are said to have remained in the Hudson Valley where a number of rural groups have claimed their ancestry.

The term Mahican or Mohican is often confused with another but separate tribe of Connecticut, the Mohegan. Both can claim to have been the inspiration for James Fenimore Cooper's "The Last of the Mohicans," but as both peoples still survive his title was in error.

MONTAUK This general term covers the Algonkians of Long Island, New York, except those at the extreme western end of the island who more properly belong with the Delaware. The same group of tribes are occasionally termed "Metoac." They were famous in history for the production of wampum shell money, which they traded to mainland tribes until the production was taken over by white settlers. They seem to have survived King Philip's War (1675–76) relatively undisturbed, and land grants by the English were given as early as 1666. However, they were subjected to attacks from the Narragansetts, and decreased in numbers due to diseases. After 1775 some joined the Brotherton Indians in New York under Samson Occom, a Mohegan preacher who had formed a new Indian town.

Those that were left on Long Island were the *Shinnecock*, who still retain a reservation near Southampton, with a current population of about 1,200; the *Poosepatuck*, whose descendants still have a few acres at the mouth of the Mastic River; the Montauk proper, a few people near Montauk Point and East Hampton at the eastern end of Long Island; the *Matinecock* on the north shore in Nassau County; and the *Setauket*, a few descendants of whom were once found in Suffolk County but are now no longer reported. Their original population may have been more than 2,000. In 1900 only 150 Shinnecock and 30 Poosepatuck were reported, much mixed with African-American blood, the Shinnecocks having lost many men in an accident at sea in 1876. The present 1,933 or so descendants of the combined bands hold a pan-Indian powwow each summer.

STOCKBRIDGE This is the name given to a group of missionized Mahican (q.v.), Wappinger, Housatonic and others originally settled at Schaghticoke, New York (not to be confused with the group of the same name in Connecticut), who subsequently gathered at the town and mission of Stockbridge, Massachusetts, in 1736. They rendered loyal service to the British in the French and Indian War, and to the Americans in the War of Independence. Between 1756 and 1785 they joined other groups, at first in Broome and Tioga counties, New York; and later joined the Oneida along with the Brotherton refugees. The Oneida, Stockbridge and Brotherton all moved to Wisconsin in 1833, the Stockbridge being given a separate reservation southwest of the Menomini near present Bowler, Wisconsin. In 1966, 380 "Stockbridge-Munsee" were still living on the reservation, with an equal number living away. The 2000 Census reports 1,531 total. They had lost most of their native traditions before or shortly after their move to Wisconsin, and are now highly acculturated and mostly of mixed white and Indian descent. Recently they have organized an armed "Mohican Band of Stockbridge-Munsee Powwow."

BROTHERTON or **BROTHERTOWN** Brotherton is the name of two separate groups of remnant New England

Left: Austin E. Quinney (Ikutauam or "Both Sides of the River"), (1791–1865). Stockbridge leader of the migration from New York to present day Calumet County, Wisconsin in 1834 and the move to Shawano County (1854–1856), their present reservation. In this painting Quinney wears native style leggings, holds wampum and has an iron pipe-tomahawk in his belt. Painting by Amos C. Hamlin Jr., c. 1849. Wisconsin Historical Society.

Below Left: Indian lady dressed in cloth tunic, skirt and shoulder pouch, all decorated with beadwork watching the parade of veterans at the Mohican Band of Stockbridge-Munsee Powwow, near Bowler, Wisconsin, August 2009. M.G. Johnson photograph.

Right: Delaware wigwam, a reconstructed elm bark lodge and dugout canoe at historic Fort Delaware, a reconstructed traders' fort near Narrowsburg, New York, on the Delaware River, July 1998.

Algonkians. The first were a combination of Mahican, Wappinger, Pequot, Mohegan, Narragansett and Montauk who moved to lands given to them by the Oneida in Madison and Oneida counties, New York, under a native minister, Samson Occom (1723–92). They numbered 250 in 1791. The second group were 40 or so Raritan-Delawares from a reservation in New Jersey called Brotherton in Burlington County, who joined the first group in New York in 1802. The combined group moved to Wisconsin in 1833 under the name Brotherton, and about 600 descendants are still reported near Fond du Lac, Wisconsin.

DELAWARE or **LENI-LENAPE** The most important collection of Algonkian groups of the mid-Atlantic coast, once occupying the lower Hudson River valley, the western part of Long Island and the whole of the present state of New Jersey south to Delaware Bay are the Delaware. Their dialectic separation from adjacent people is not clear — perhaps even the Wappinger of the Hudson River and the Matinecock of Long Island should really be included in the group. They included the *Esopus* on the west bank of the Hudson; the *Rockaway* and *Canarsee* of Long Island; the *Minisinks* (later called Munsee) on the Delaware River north of the Delaware Water Gap; the *Unami*, a dialect spoken on both sides of the Delaware River in New Jersey and Pennsylvania; the *Raritans* on the Raritan River; a number of minor subtribes occupying Manhattan Island north to present Westchester County, New York; and a number of small tribes and villages on the lower Delaware, below present Philadelphia, who also spoke a variation of Unami and are for our purposes considered as one. In later years they were usually classified in three groups: Munsee, Unami and Unalachtigo, but only the former two were true divisions.

The Delaware were probably first seen by Europeans in 1524, when Verrazano sheltered in New York harbor, but their history of contact with Europeans began with Hudson's visit in 1609. By the 1630s, the Dutch had introduced the fur trade, and the Delaware fought to secure their villages and hunting territories against the encroaching Dutch and northern Indians. The English, who succeeded the Dutch, induced the River Indians, including the Iroquois, Mahican and Delaware into an alliance known as the Covenant Chain. Throughout the 17th century they were swept by smallpox, measles, influenza and plagues, which halved their population. By the 1740s they were being crowded out by whites and began to move west to the Susquehanna and Allegheny rivers, fighting at times against English settlers, at times for them against the French. They finally made peace at Easton, New Jersey, in 1758, when a reservation was established for some remaining New Jersey bands at Brotherton. By now the Delawares were strung out in settlements from New Jersey to the Ohio country. The western bands were actively engaged in frontier warfare until the Treaty of Greenville (1795) after which some moved west to the White River, Indiana, and later to Cape Girardeau, Missouri. A number of other groups in Pennsylvania and Ohio had been converted by German Moravians and moved to the Thames River, Ontario; still others had joined some Mahican and Nanticoke and sought Iroquois protection, moving with them to Ontario after the Revolution. The Brothertons joined the Stockbridges in New York in 1802, and ultimately moved to Wisconsin with the Oneida in 1833.

During their migration westward, the Delaware maintained a way of life transitional between that of the whites and the less-acculturated Indians of the interior. Bark longhouses had given way to log cabins; European farming with cattle, horses and swine had replaced native slash-and-burn farming; bowls, dishes, pestles and mortars, fiber bags, tumplines, baskets and mats had been replaced by trade goods. During the 19th century, often in concert with the Shawnee, they moved farther west. By the 1820s they were in southern Missouri, and by the 1830s in Kansas, where some settled and became citizens in Ottawa and Franklin counties. The last major move was in 1867–68 to Oklahoma, where the largest group settled in Cherokee Nation.

Their earlier population may have been 12,000. Today they have a total of about 8,304 descendants, all of mixed white or Mahican antecedents. As of 2005, approximately 589 are on the Six Nations Reservation, Ontario, originally from New York; 1,877 on the Moravian Reserve near Bothwell, Ontario; and 523 Munsee near Munceytown, Ontario, who originally came from Ohio. Several hundred are mixed with the Stockbridge and Brotherton in Wisconsin, and there are a few citizen Delaware in Kansas. But the largest group are the Registered Delaware of Washington, Nowata, Craig and Delaware counties in Oklahoma, numbering (along with a few Stockbridge and Munsee) more than 1,500. A thousand or so descendants of Delaware who moved to Oklahoma from Texas with the Caddo and Wichita now live near Anadarko, Oklahoma. There are only a handful of Munsee or Unami speakers today. The Oklahoma Delaware sponsor a pan-Indian powwow each summer. A small number never left New Jersey and a few, near Eatontown, claim their ancestry. The number of Delaware in the U.S. in 2010 was 6,855 according to the census.

The Delawares, occupying a central homeland among the Atlantic coast Algonkians, held the priority of political rank; many other tribes claimed to have diverged from them and

Manito or Creator, whose spiritual agents were present in all living things — trees, flowers, grass, rocks and rivers. Ceremonies were in response to or to control the weather, hunting, harvest, or for the elimination of sickness and catastrophe. The "Big House" Ceremony was still held among the Oklahoma Delawares until the 1920s. A wooden building (originally bark) was constructed with 12 faces carved on the interior posts to watch the ceremonials and to carry prayers to the Creator. Their creation myth (shared with other eastern tribes) held that they sprang from a hole in the earth, and that the world was carried on a giant turtle's back. During the 19th century, a certain Constantine Rafinesque claimed to have found (but probably invented) c. 1830 a series of 183 mnemonic glyphs, which were subsequently reproduced by D.G. Brinton. They claimed the glyphs were a record of ancient Delaware history and myths called the *Walam Olum* or "red score." The originals have not survived, and many historians believe these records and sources are questionable.

No tribe was pushed so far from its homelands. A few bands during the 19th century became "mountain men," and many claimed they were better military auxiliaries than the Pawnee or Cheyenne. They also mixed their blood lines with several tribes in the west, notably the Flathead and Nez Perce.

Above: Portrait of John Caldwell, dressed in Indian costume for an internation council meeting at Wakatomica, Ohio, on January 17, 1780. At the council with the Delaware and other tribes, a Cherokee from Chota (Tennessee) produced a wampum belt he had received from the Americans urging their support (in the Revolutionary War), which was refused. This belt is likely the one shown in this portrait. Caldwell became Sir John Caldwell, Irish Peer, 5th Baronet of Castle Caldwell, County Fermanagh, Ireland. He served in the 8th of King's Regiment of Foot in the American War of Independence. Caldwell's portrait shows him holding a purple wampum war belt over which an axe or tomahawk is woven in white beads. His moccasins are typical eastern Great Lakes type with fringes of deer hair and tin cones. The leggings are red cloth and garters with beads woven in. He has a pouch of black color buckskin decorated with quillwork and beadwork. Across his shoulder hangs a knife sheath decorated with quills and beads. He has several silver gorgets and brooches. He holds an English trade tomahawk. Artist unknown, painted c. 1785. Photograph courtesy National Museums, Liverpool, UK.

Left: Wampum Belt of the Grand Alliance, De Peyster Collection, National Museums Liverpool. The imitation glass wampum designs shows human figures holding hands—meaning alliance, friendship, or peace. Belt collected by Arent De Peyser, a British commandant at Michilimackinac from 1774 to 1779 and later Detroit. Courtesy National Museums, Liverpool.

accorded them the respectful title of "grandfather." The Nanticoke, Conoy, Shawnee and Mahican all claimed a connection with them. Their real name, Leni-Lenape, is equivalent to "real men"; but their common English name is derived from Lord de la Warr, an early governor of the colony at Jamestown, Virginia, although he never set foot among the people who have ever since carried his name.

Although the recording of Delaware culture and religion took place long after Christian and other influences may have blurred many cogent facets, they seem to have believed in a great

NANTICOKE The Nanticoke were an Algonkian people of the present states of Delaware and Maryland, on both sides of Chesapeake Bay and on the north bank of the Potomac River. Although they are frequently delimited to those on the Nanticoke River, a number of other groups can be added as more or less the same people, including the *Nanticoke* (proper); the *Wicocomoco*, on the river of the same name in Maryland; *Choptank*, on the Choptank River; *Pocomoke*, on the Pocomokee River; *Wicomiss* or *Ozinies*, on the Chester River; and *Patuxent*, on the Patuxent River, Calvert County. The *Conoy* are usually given separate status, but a number of minor groups on the Northampton Peninsula, Virginia, could also be added, collectively referred to as *Accomac*.

European contact dates from the 1580s, increasing after the establishment of Jamestown in 1607. Thereafter a series of disputes with the Maryland colonists led to continual outbreaks of violence. Despite the establishment of reservations near the end of the 17th century, many were forced to leave under Iroquois protection for the Chenango River at Otsiningo — present day Binghamton, New York — along with the Conoy and other remnants. The last of these immigrant Nanticoke were counted among the Iroquois at Six Nations, Ontario, or Buffalo Creek, New York, and lost separate identity. Those who remained in parts of their old country intermarried with African-Americans at an early date. Although a mixed-blood people who identify themselves as "Nanticoke" (about 860 in 2001) have remained along Indian River, Millsboro, Sussex County, Delaware, the last native speaker died about 1856. Yet another triracial group near Cheswold, Kent County, Delaware, called "Moors," may also have some Nanticoke ancestry. Both the Moors and Nanticoke number several hundred people. A number of baskets and other utility items were collected from them in the early 20th century and appear to have been native in style. Nanticoke descendants now hold a pan-Indian powwow each year near Millsboro.

CONOY or **PISCATAWAY** An Algonkian tribe related to the Nanticoke (with whom they are often classed) who lived on the western shore of Chesapeake Bay and along the Potomac River were the Conoy. They were in conflict with the Maryland colonists after 1634, and were also harassed by the Susquehannocks from the north. Although reservations were established, they were forced to leave for the north with remnant Nanticoke under Iroquois protection, first to Pennsylvania, then to Chenango, Broome County, New York and Owego, when they were last reported as separate in 1793. Some nevertheless seem to have remained in Maryland, presumably intermixing with whites and African-Americans, since a body of triracial groups survive around Baltimore and in Charles, Prince George's and Dorchester counties under names such as Piscataway, Wesort and Portobacco; but their connection with the old Conoy is uncertain.

POWHATAN The Powhatan are a large and important collection of Algonkian groups located in the Tidewater portion of Virginia, from the Potomac River to the north, through the drainages of the Rappahannock, Pamunkey, Chickahominy and James rivers, and as far south as the Great Dismal Swamp. From 1607 they were in contact — and ultimately in conflict — with the English colonists at Jamestown. Under Powhatan, their paramount chief at that time, the whole group was named the Powhatan confederacy. They cultivated corn, which was stored on raised platforms after harvesting, and hunted, fished and gathered wild plant foods. They wore some buckskin garments (frequently fringed), painted and decorated with shells. Their principal subtribes were the *Potomac*, below the river that bears their name; *Rappahannock*, on the north bank of the Rappahannock River; *Wicocomoco*, in present Northumberland County; *Chickahominy*, on the upper Mattaponi River, and *Mattaponi*, on the lower; *Pamunkey* on the Pamunkey River; *Werowocomoco*, in Gloucester County; and *Nansemond*, below the James River.

Wars with the colonists in 1622 and 1644 broke them, after which they were restricted to English land grants, exposed to continual harassment by Iroquois and Conestogas, and violated for crimes often committed by these northern Indians. By the end of the 17th century they mainly worked as hunters, scouts and servants for the English, with considerable intermarriage with whites, following the famous Pocahontas-Rolfe marriage, and later with African-American slaves. Except on two land grants, formal tribal organization faded; their population of 10,000 at the time of European contact had diminished to a few hundred by the close of the 17th century.

While several hundred people have survived to the present, only the Pamunkey and Mattaponi can claim unbroken links with their 17th century ancestors, due to their two reservations. These are the Pamunkey Reservation, King William County, which has some 350 enrolled members (in

2001), and the Mattaponi Reservation, with about 500 (also in 2001). The remaining groups whose ancestry is less certain — but who claim Indian and tribal descent — are the Upper Chickahominy, Charles City County, Roxbury; and Lower Chickahominy, James City County, Boulevard, with a non-federally recognized combined population of about 1,000 in 2001; Caroline, Essex, King and Queen counties, Rappahannock; the Potomac, near Fredericksburg; Wicocomoco, Northumberland County; Werowocomoco, Gloucester County; Nansemond in Norfolk County; plus a few Accomac in Northampton County (old Nanticoke area). All together these remaining groups reported at about an additional 500 in 2001. Although they are without ancient tribal traditions, they take part in various pan-Indian politics and activities designed to strengthen their Indian identity. Splinter groups have established in New Jersey and Pennsylvania.

NORTH CAROLINA ALGONKIANS

These tribes are famous for their connection with the Raleigh colonists who established a settlement in 1585–87 on Roanoke Island at the mouth of Albemarle Sound in present North Carolina. The artist John White, who accompanied the settlers, made a group of watercolor pictures of their villages, dwellings, fishing techniques and some individual studies that survive in the British Museum, giving us excellent visual evidence of their culture. They show curved-roof wigwams, dugout log canoes, fishing nets, costumes, body paint and ceremonial dances. The fate of the Roanoke colonists, other than those who returned to England, remains unknown. The 17th century saw the exploration and settlement of the area by the Virginia colonists and a decline in native population, but reformed tribes fought on the side of the English in the Tuscarora Wars. During the 18th and 19th centuries they seem to have merged with African-American populations, and only a few of mixed-blood survived.

The following were probably the most important tribal groups: the *Weapemeoc*, on the north side of Albermarle Sound included the *Poteskeit* and *Paspatank*, and these groups maintained themselves until the Tuscarora War of 1712–13; the *Moratok (Moratuc)*, a settlement 160 miles (250 km) into Albemarle Sound at the head of the

Left: Carolina Algonkian warrior, c. 1585. Watercolor sketches made by John White, one of Raleigh's colonists, near the settlement at Roanoke Island in 1585–87 are preserved in the British Museum. He reported that warriors from around present-day Albemarle Sound, North Carolina, decorated their bodies with paint and pearls (probably shells or Roanoke wampum). This warrior, derived from White's drawings, has a skin apron, and a bow probably of maple or hazel.

Roanoke River; the *Secotan*, on Pamlico Sound, who were superseded in that location by the *Pamlico* and *Bear River* Indians who also existed down to the time of the Tuscarora War; the *Neusiok*, on the Neuse River; *Pomeiooc*, a village in an area occupied later by a group called *Machapunga* at Mattsmuskeet Lake, where a reservation with a mixed tribal population survived during the 18th century; *Croatoan*, a village on Cape Hatteras with whom the Raleigh colonists may have taken refuge, were probably the Hatteras Indians who later joined the Machapunga at Mattamuskeet Lake. The *Chowanoc* or *Chawanoke* on the Chowan River, who were probably the largest tribe of the area, submitted to the British in 1675 and were later confined to a reservation on Bennetts Creek. They perhaps ultimately merged with the Tuscarora. During the 20th century a few mixed descendants were reported on Roanoke Island, near Mattamuskeet Lake and near Hertford, but these now seem to have disappeared. The *Lumbee* of Robeson County, North Carolina, claim the ancestry of the coastal tribes and Raleigh colonists, but this is unsupported by historical evidence. Despite their numbers their origins remain unclear.

SHAWNEE This is an Algonkian people whose original home was probably the Cumberland River in Tennessee, but scarcely has any tribe divided so often or moved so much. As far as they can be associated with one area, the Muskingum and Scioto river valleys in the Ohio country were their home during the 18th century, when they were a major frontier tribe actively engaged in warfare against the encroaching white settlers. However, they had also settled in various parts of Pennsylvania during the early part of that century, attracted by the English trade. One band, who have been termed *Saluda* or "Savannas" settled for a time in the southeast, driving the Westo (probably Yuchi) from the middle Savannah region, but subsequently rejoined a main body of the tribe in Pennsylvania. However, a part of these Shawnee did not return home and were incorporated among the Creek.

The tribe had five component parts, perhaps originally separate tribes — *Chillicothe* (Calaka), *Kispokotha* (Kispoko), *Piqua* or *Pickaway* (Pekowi), *Sawekela* or *Hathawekela* (Thawikila) and *Makostrake* (Mekoce) — but their functions

Above: Indian, possibly a Shawnee warrior, scalping a British soldier — an 18th century painting by an unknown artist. The Indian wears black leggings, moccasins with ankle flaps, silver arm bands, tomahawk, breechclout, face paint, feather headdress, and powder horn and strap.

Below from left to right: The famous "Shawnee Prophet," brother of Tecumseh, Tenskwatawa (The Open Door) was a medicine man who announced himself as the bearer of a revelation from the "Master of Life" to return to native practices. However, his influence was destroyed by General Harrison's victory over the Indians at Tippecanoe in November 1811, where he had over a thousand converts. He died in Kansas in November 1837. From a lithograph by J.T. Bowen, Philadelphia, 1836–1844, in McKenney and Hall's History of the Indian Tribes of North America.

Shawnee warrior drawn in Illinois County, c. 1796.

Black Hoof, (c. 1740–1831), Shawnee chief.

Opposite: Paccane, a Miami warrior sketched by Elizabeth Simcoe, wife of the lieutenant-governor of Upper Canada, c. 1790.

seem to have been largely political and ritual. Their subsistence combined hunting with agriculture, but was strongly oriented toward the fur trade since the early 18th century. Their supreme being Creator was female.

They were consistently opposed to white settlement beyond the Appalachian Mountains, switching their alliances between France and Britain to this end. They joined the Pontiac uprising against the British (1763), and fought against the Virginians in Lord Dunmore's War (1774) and later the Americans in the Revolution. They took up arms against the Americans again under the leadership of Tecumseh and Tenskwatawa (The Prophet) at Tippecanoe and in the War of 1812. However, by this time constant warfare had exhausted and split them. Contact with whites over a long period had resulted in a hybrid culture similar to those of other Midwestern tribes. By the late 18th century, a large body of Shawnee and others had begun to settle in Spanish territory, now Missouri, but the main body of the tribe was still in Indiana and Ohio on the White, Auglaize and Miami rivers.

By the 1830s, most of the Indiana bands, with some Missouri bands (later known as Black Bob's band), had rejoined on a reservation on the Kansas River in northeastern Kansas; but others, wishing to be free of white influence, decamped for Arkansas, Texas and beyond, later being known as "Absentee" Shawnee, as they were separate from the main body of the tribe living in Kansas. In 1832, a mixed band of Seneca-Iroquois and Shawnee coming direct from Ohio moved to northeastern Indian Territory, now Ottawa County, Oklahoma. In 1870, following the Civil War, the main body of the tribe moved from Kansas to Cherokee Nation, Indian Territory, while the Absentee Shawnee and Black Bob's band obtained lands between the North Canadian and Canadian rivers in Indian Territory, along with the Potawatomi.

The Ottawa County Shawnee separated from the Seneca in 1867; their descendants are known as the Eastern Shawnee, which numbered about 1,022 in 2000. The Cherokee-Shawnee or Loyal-Shawnee of Craig County, Oklahoma, number about 600; and the Absentee Shawnee number about 1,701 in Pottawatomie and Cleveland counties. One community at Little Axe were a relatively conservative group until recently, maintaining traditional Shawnee rituals including the War Dance and Bread Dances. The Piqua, Ohio, sect of the Shawnee is a small group, numbering only 63 in the 2000 Census. The Loyal and Eastern bands are largely of mixed descent and have been highly acculturated for generations. The census of 1970 counted 2,208 — an underestimation, considering the 2000 total of 5,773. Most Shawnee belong to federally recognized tribes, such as the Eastern Shawnee and Absentee bands. Others, such as the Piqua Sect, are petitioning for federal status, which affords certain rights and privileges afforded previously only through treaties.

MIAMI The Miami are an Algonkian people related to the Illini, centered in present Indiana along the Wabash and Eel River drainages during the 18th century, when they were reduced to three small tribes, including *Wea*, *Piankashaw* and *Miami* proper. They probably came originally from the Fox River area of Wisconsin. Like other tribes of the area they lived in oval lodges covered with cattail mats, bark or hides, in small villages along river banks, with a mixed farming and hunting economy. Their religion recognized the Master of Life, similar to the Illini. Other ritual activity included the vision quest and

the Midewiwin. Their Ohio country became an area of fluctuating colonial intrigue between the French and British in the 18th century, and home to multitribal partly acculturated Indian groups seeking refuge from conflicts farther east. Knowing that the loss of their lands would follow American control, they fought with the British in the Revolution, and continued resistance against American forces under Harmar in 1790, and St. Clair in 1791, until defeated by Anthony Wayne at Fallen Timbers in 1794.

After the Treaty of Greenville of 1795 they remained at peace with the Americans, but declined rapidly in numbers. Between 1832 and 1840 they moved to reservations in Kansas, where the Wea and Piankashaw united with the remnant Illini under the name *Peoria*. The Peoria and Miami removed in 1867 to Indian Territory, now Oklahoma, where two highly acculturated mixed descent groups remain in Ottawa County, numbering about 1,090 in 1970, and 2,677 in 2001. A few escaped removal and maintained themselves in Indiana near Peru, where some 600 mixed descent people were reported in 2001.

ILLINI or **ILLINOIS** This is a group of Algonkian-speaking tribes, more or less closely connected, who lived principally along the Mississippi and Illinois rivers; the *Michigamea*, at Big Lake between the St. Francis and Mississippi rivers, Arkansas; *Cahokia*, near Cahokia, Illinois; *Kaskaskia*, originally near present Utica; *Moingwena*, at the mouth of the De Moines River, Iowa; *Peoria*, originally on the Mississippi near the junction with the Iowa; and *Tamaroa*, near the junction of the Missouri and Illinois rivers with the Mississippi. Their language was closest to the Miami. As the population of these groups dwindled they often reformed in new locations. They were an agricultural people dependent upon

Above: Ojibwa (Chippewa) or Potawatomi baby, Wisconsin, c. 1905, showing the protective wooden hoop characteristic of Woodland cradle boards; and the decorative cloth securing bands, unlike the laced bag used on cradles by the Northern Ojibwa and Cree of Canada. Photograph: W. H. Wessa.

Below: Potawatomi or Kickapoo couple, Kansas, c. 1890. This Indian couple is probably Prairie Band Potawatomi or Kickapoo who were in part resettled in northeastern Kansas. The lady wears a cloth skirt with fine ribbon appliqué and silver brooches. The man wears moccasins beaded in the style popular with the resettled Woodland tribes in Kansas and Oklahoma in the 19th century. Photograph: E. L. Hoppe.

maize. They also gathered wild foods and hunted game, including buffalo.

Their first contacts with the French were with the expedition of Marquette and Joliet in about 1675; they soon came under French influence, and their decline followed quickly. Visited by smallpox, harassed by Iroquois war parties, demoralized by liquor and poverty, and apparently completely missionized, they dwindled from a population of 10,000 to about 400 in 1778. They had gradually moved west of the Mississippi by 1832 when, reduced to a single remnant, they moved to Kansas and united with the Wea and Piankashaw. The final movement was to northeastern Oklahoma under a combined name, "Peoria." There a highly acculturated multi-ethnic group has remained, numbering 439 in 1956, down locally to 400 by 1990, but with 2,600 enrolled in 2001. They recognized an overall being, the "Master of Life," who was the ultimate source of power and visions. Descriptions of ritual practice centered on warfare, shamanism and the calumet dance.

POTAWATOMI An Algonkian-speaking tribe who probably split from the Ojibwa and Ottawa were the Potawatomi. The ancient home of the tribe was evidently the lower peninsula of Michigan, but in about 1680 they were driven to the Door Peninsula near Green Bay in present-day Wisconsin, on the west side of Lake Michigan. During the 18th century they spread south to the present Milwaukee area and the St. Joseph River. By 1790 they had scattered at various times from the Mississippi across the northern tributaries of the Illinois River through southern Michigan to the Detroit area. Their villages were usually established on the edge of the forest adjacent to prairies and lakes. They grew squash, beans and maize, collected plant foods and hunted deer, elk and buffalo. The Potawatomi shared the common Algonkian dual division of clan and social organization, and their beliefs about the spirit world included the curative Midewiwin, the Grand Medicine Lodge Society similar to the Ojibwa and Menomini.

Historically, the Potawatomi first aligned themselves with the French against the English, and with the latter against the Americans, until a general peace in about 1815, after which they changed rapidly. Forced out of their homelands, they mainly withdrew across the Mississippi. In 1841 most of the "Potawatomi of the Woods" from southern Michigan and northern Indiana, already partly acculturated, moved to Kansas, although a few bands remained behind (Potawatomi of Huron and Pokagon). The Illinois-Wisconsin Potawatomi moved to a reservation in Iowa and thence to one in Kansas, thus combining the Woods and Prairie bands. The most acculturated tribal members moved to a new reservation in Indian Territory, now Oklahoma, in 1867. A number of other groups, probably multitribal and multi-ethnic and small in number, have survived in various locations.

Their early population was about 9,000, before a decline due to diseases, warfare and absorption into other groups. Their present distribution in 2001 — by no means all Potawatomi and many no longer living within these communities — is as follows: "Prairie band" near Mayetta, Kansas, about 4,870 in 2001, plus a number with the Kickapoo near Horton; the "Citizen Potawatomi" of Cleveland and Pottawatomie Counties, Oklahoma, locally 3,557; several communities in upper and lower Michigan, 4,100; and two settlements in Forest County, Wisconsin,

Above: Wabaunsee Potawatomi chief (1760–1845). Charles Bird King (1785–1862) was the official painter of Indian delegates to Washington D.C. from many tribes in formal negotiations with the War Department during the 1820s and 1830s. He and George Cooke also copied the slightly earlier works of James Otto Lewis painted in the mid-west. These paintings were transferred from the War Department to the Smithsonian Institution where they were destroyed by fire in 1865. However, despite the loss, many of King's paintings had been copied by King himself and Henry Inman for the three-volume epic by T.L. McKenney & J.Hall History of the Indian Tribes of North America (1836–1844).

Right: Bandolier, no bag, probably Potawatomi, c. 1890. Cloth basic construction with woven beaded panel and strap in similar designs, woven tabs and tassels. Two narrow bands between panel and strap partially beaded in floral designs, letters and commas. British Museum Travelling Exhibition, Worcester City Museum, UK.

Far Right: Bandolier, without a bag, probably Wisconsin Potawatomi, c. 1890. Cloth backing for woven beaded front panel and strap with a woven beaded band between. Bandolier has tabs and wool tassels. The basic Thunderbird and Lightning designs and other figures preserve traditional lore. M.G. Johnson Collection.

1,186. In Canada there are substantial numbers with Ojibwa and Ottawa at Walpole Island, Sarnia, Kettle Point and other locations in Ontario. By 1970, fewer than 1,000 people still spoke their language.

The most conservative groups were the Forest County, Wisconsin, and Prairie Band, Kansas, divisions of the tribe. The former were reportedly living in appalling poverty as late as 1951, although they — like numerous modern tribes — have prospered with gaming and casinos. This group retained the Medicine Dance society, War Dance and the Dream or Drum Dance, a variant of the Plains Grass Dance, which spread through the woodlands promoting friendship. The ceremony centers on a large decorated drum symbolizing friendship — even with whites — which is treated with great reverence. Both groups have the Peyote cult, which spread north during the early reservation period — a part-Christian and part-Indian religion involving the consumption of peyote buttons, a mild narcotic, during night-long rituals, sometimes held in a tipi to aid the sick. Some Kansas Potawatomi are members of the Kenekuk Church founded by a Kickapoo divine in the 19th century. They have sponsored large pan-Indian powwows in recent times on their reservation near Mayetta, and participate in similar events each year on the nearby Kickapoo Reservation — the two tribes are now much intermarried. In past years the Potawatomi excelled in ribbonwork and beadwork, their dress costumes being stylistically similar to the Sac, Fox, Kickapoo and other central Algonkians. The total U.S. Potawatomi numbers were given as 18,329 in 2010.

MASCOUTEN The Mascouten were a tribe of Algonkian-speaking people who probably once dwelt on both sides of the Mississippi, near the present Wisconsin-Illinois border. They were very closely related to the Kickapoo, but were in constant warfare with their neighbors, and were first mentioned by French missionaries as inhabiting southern Michigan, where they had been driven by the Ojibwa and Ottawa. In 1712 they united with the Kickapoo and Fox, after being almost exterminated by the French, and later by the Potawatomi.

The remnant emigrated westward, and they are last mentioned separately in 1779 living with the Piankashaw and Kickapoo on the Wabash River in Indiana. Their name apparently means "Little Prairie People," a title now borne by the Potawatomi Indians in Kansas with whom they have sometimes been confused, although the Potawatomi probably have no Mascouten ancestry.

KICKAPOO An Algonkian-speaking tribe closely related to the Sauk and Fox are the Kickapoo. The movements of the Kickapoo were so frequent that they cannot be associated with any specific area, but it is probable that when first known to whites in 1660-1700, their home was in southern Wisconsin, probably around the Milwaukee area. They seem to have been in northern Illinois, Indiana, Ohio and around the Detroit area during the early 18th century, and later in central Illinois and

Missouri, extending into country formerly occupied by sections of the Illini.

Some Kickapoo worked their way east to the Wabash River, Indiana, becoming known as the Vermillion River Band, while those in Illinois became known as the Prairie Band. Their general culture was similar to that of the Sauk and Fox. Hostile to the French, they were later friendly with the British during the Revolution and the War of 1812; and a few joined Black Hawk in 1832. Both bands were in Missouri by the early 19th century and moved then to northeastern Kansas (1832-34). But some, wishing to remain free from white restrictions, were already moving to Texas. These ultimately decamped to Mexico where a settlement was established near Nacimiento, Coahuila; a basic forest Algonkian culture was reestablished with modifications dictated by their new environment. In 1873 a number (100 or so) from Kansas moved to Indian Territory to a reservation based along the North Canadian River in present Lincoln and Pottawatomi counties, Oklahoma, while about 250 remained on their Kansas reservation near Horton. These three communities still survive, although economic activities take many far outside their boundaries.

In 2001 the Oklahoma Kickapoo numbered about 2,500, the Kansas group 1,606 (the combined total was 1,249 in 1970, 3,000 in 1990). The Mexican band numbered 400 in 1970, but is likely greater now as well. Those in Oklahoma and Mexico have long been noted for their conservatism; and the Kansas group are notable for their adherence to the Kenekuk Church — a nativistic movement, part-Christian, based on the reservation and is still active, although its members are mostly Potawatomis, with whom the Kickapoo are much mixed. They also have a buffalo herd and a bingo hall, and organize a fine annual powwow on the reservation. The Mexican and Oklahoma bands now have a small land base at Eagle Pass, Texas, for transient workers.

SAUK or **SAC** An Algonkian people very closely related to the Fox or Mesquakie, formerly living in the vicinity of Green Bay, Wisconsin, toward the end of the 17th century were the Sauk. Their traditional subsistence was identical with that of the Fox, combining hunting with growing maize, beans and squash. Their social organization consisted of about 12 patrilineal clans whose functions were to arrange the various sacred packs ceremonies. Disputes with French traders led to the initial confederation of the Sauks and the Foxes and their migration south from Wisconsin to present Iowa and parts of northern Illinois.

Their treaties with the U.S. Government in the early 19th century, which ceded their lands in Illinois and Wisconsin, were not agreed to by all their bands. This led to the Black Hawk War of 1832, when they attempted to reestablish control of an old village site near Rock Island, but, hopelessly outnumbered, Black Hawk was finally driven back into Iowa. In 1837, the combined tribes ceded their Iowa lands and were assigned to a reservation in Kansas, but factional disputes resulted in a band of Fox settling at Tama, Iowa, where they

KEOKUK
CHIEF OF THE SACS & FOXES

Opposite: Kansas Potawatomi woman, c. 1870. Silver brooches decorate clothing made entirely of cloth, which had replaced leather among the Woodland peoples by the mid-19th century. She wears the wraparound skirt, an old pattern, but now decorated with the cut-and-fold ribbonwork that had wide distribution from the Canadian Maritimes to the eastern Plains; it developed into its most colorful forms among southern Woodland peoples, some now removed to reservations in Kansas and Indian Territory. The art was also adopted by Missouri valley tribes such as the Omaha, Osage and Kaw, whose women produced superb examples of silk ribbonwork on ceremonial clothes. Both real silver traded from whites, and later "German silver" made by their own smiths, were used for ornamentation.

Above: Keokuk (1767–1848) identified as chief of the Sauk and Fox and his son, Musewont.

Above Right: An illustration from The Indian Tribes of North America, *(Thomas L. McKenney and James Hall): Appanoose, a Sauk warrior painted by George Cooke in 1837.*

Right: Sauk man from Indian Territory (now Oklahoma) photographed in Washington D.C. c. 1868. Reputed to be the grandson of Black Hawk who fought the Americans in 1832.

Below: Sauk elm bark house, c. 1880. Shorter, but of similar construction to Iroquois longhouses, Sauk and Fox bark lodges formed villages of up to 90 houses in the mid-18th century. A few were still being built in the 1880s after removal to Indian Territory.

1 Mesquakie (Fox) youth c. 1890. In this studio photograph, the boy wears a roach, beaded apron, belt, cloth leggings, knee garters and front-flap moccasins. Photograph: Hudson's Gallery.

2 Sauk or Fox warrior of c. 1867 wearing a head roach, widely used by eastern and midwestern tribes and usually constructed of porcupine and deer hair, with a braided woolen turban, silver earrings and bear claw necklace.

3 Black Hawk (1767–1838), leader of the Sauk and Fox Indians in the War of 1832, the last conflict between Indians and whites in Illinois. From a print published by F. W. Greenough, Philadelphia.

remain and now number about 1,260. The remaining Sauk with a few Fox removed from Kansas to Oklahoma (then Indian Territory) and were assigned lands between the Cimarron River and the north fork of the Canadian River, except for one small group who retained land near the Kansas/Nebraska border. The Sauks' interaction with the U.S. Government in the first half of the 19th century led to a division between the so called "British" band and a faction friendly to the government, led by Keokuk and his followers.

The present descendants of the Oklahoma Sac and Fox live around allotted lands near Stroud and Cushing, Oklahoma, reported as 996 in 1950, when the small group near White Cloud, Kansas, numbered 129. Those numbers by 2001 were are 3,025 and 433, respectively. The Oklahoma bands have an annual powwow of the pan-Indian type near the tribal administration complex south of Stroud, Oklahoma, each summer, which incorporates what little remains of traditional Indian culture and reinforces their tribal unity. The Oklahoma Sauk are officially called the "Sac and Fox tribe of the Missouri," and requires only one-eighth Sac descent for enrollment given as approximately 3,800 today with 2,500 living within Oklahoma.

4 *Mesquakie (Fox) children, c. 1890. The boy holds a pipe.*
Photograph: Hudson's Gallery.

5 *Kaipolequa or White-nosed Fox, Sauk chief of his band that amounted to about half his nation. He signed a treaty with the government in Washington D.C. in 1824. From a lithograph by J.T. Bowen, Philadelphia, 1836–1844, in McKenney and Hall's* History of the Indian Tribes of North America.

6 *John Young Bear and wife, Mesquakie, c. 1925. John wears a large porcupine head roach and bear claw necklace. He was a noted carver.*

FOX or **MESQUAKIE** Early reports located the Mesquakie along the Fox River in Wisconsin, living in rectangular bark lodges large enough to accommodate several families, with shelves several feet off the ground on both sides for sleeping and storage of food. They had extensive gardens where squash, beans and corn were grown, usually tended by women. After the harvest was completed the grain and dried squash were cached and the men went on the winter hunts, sometimes making excursions into buffalo country. They also hunted deer and other game to subsidize their horticulture. In recent times the Mesquakie lived usually in wigwams or wickiups of mat-covered bent poles. Their self-given name "Red Earth People," which distinguished them from their kinsfolk, the Sauk, or "Yellow Earth People."

They seem to have been known to French missionaries after about 1640, but were later hostile to the French, who, in 1746, drove them from their homes to the Wisconsin River, where they remained until withdrawing to Iowa at the beginning of the 19th century. They united with the Sauk after the Black Hawk War of 1832 in Iowa, and in 1842 removed to Kansas. But a number, mostly Mesquakie, established themselves near Tama, Iowa, and have remained there, their settlement for years a stronghold of traditional Indian beliefs and religious practices. The 2001 population of the Iowa Fox is about 1,260, although a number live in industrial communities away from the reservation. They have been noted in the past for the production of fine beadwork, ribbonwork and metalwork, and are still producers of fine ceremonial and dance costumes. A number also accompanied their kinsfolk the Sauk to Kansas and Oklahoma and are officially the "Sac and Fox" tribe because of their combined dealings with the U.S. Government during the 19th century. Their language is still spoken by a number of the tribe at Tama, Iowa. Confusingly, the Tama Mesquakie are officially called the "Sac and Fox of the Mississippi in Iowa."

Above: Fox (Mesquakie) warrior, c. 1830. Based on the paintings of Karl Bodmer and George Catlin, this warrior from the period of the so-called Black Hawk War wears a roach with an eagle feather, a bear claw necklace and a blanket. A quirt hangs from his wrist and he holds a metal trade tomahawk.

MENOMINI or **MENOMINEE** This is an Algonkian tribe located on or near the Menominee River, Wisconsin, who were a typical forest people with a subsistence economy based on hunting, fishing and gathering, although one of their main industries was the harvest of wild rice. Their beliefs included

Above: Hoowanneka or Little Chief, a Winnebago chief who allied with the British during the War of 1812. He visited Washington in 1824 and signed the treaty at Prairie du Chien in 1825. From a lithograph in McKenney and Hall's History of the Indian Tribes of North America.

1

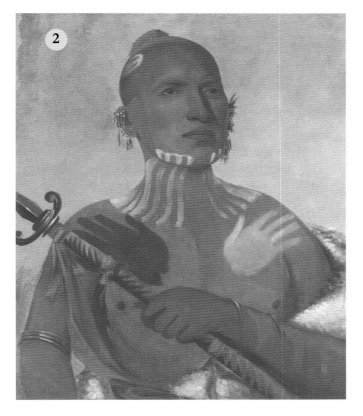

1 Sauk and Fox warrior of the mid-18th century with head shaved except for a small braid to secure the roach (of porcupine and deer hair, or turkey beards). In early times this was much smaller than the still widely used dancer's roach. The spines of the roach feathers are covered with quill-wrapped sticks or rawhide. He wears sashes of natural fiber interspaced with trade beads or wampum, a trade silver gorget and nose and earrings. Shaven-headed warriors were known as far west as the Pawnee and Eastern Sioux.

2 Sturgeon's Head, a Fox warrior, painted by George Catlin in 1832 at Jefferson Barracks near St. Louis at the close of the Black Hawk War of 1832 in the Rock River country of northern Illinois and Wisconsin. He was held with Black Hawk and White Cloud as prisoners of war. He holds a spear and wears metal earrings. Note his painted hand symbols. He claimed to have killed four white men during the late war. Smithsonian American Art Museum.

3 Menominee boy, Wisconsin, c. 1915, wearing a beaded bandolier bag. Photograph Sam Barrett. Wisconsin Historical Society.

4 Chief Souliguy, Menominee Indian, c. 1850, with an early type of bandolier bag.

5 Menominee Indians, Wisconsin, c. 1895. Descendants and family of old Chief Oshkosh who helped found their reservation in 1854. L–R standing: Adell Neff, Peter LaMotte, Perotte, Joe Gauthier, Acquinnie, Oshkosh (son of old Chief Oshkosh), John Gauthier, Louise Amour. L–R seated: Thomas Hogg, Mrs Neopit Oshkosh and son Tom, Neopit Oshkosh, Mose Corn. L–R on floor: Mary Warrington, Mrs Peter LaMotte, Agnes Corn. Photographer unknown.

1 and 3 Two Winnebago families, Wisconsin, c. 1910 (top) and c. 1890 (above).

2 Winnebago women and children, c. 1890. The women are wearing skirts with ribbonwork decoration.

4 Two Winnebago women (today the Wisconsin Winnebago prefer the name Ho Chunk) c. 1900. Each wears a bandolier across her shoulder. Theses bandoliers appear to be pocketless, simply solid beaded in floral designs.

5 Winnebago man, Wisconsin, c. 1900. His apron has typical Prairie-style floralistic beaded designs, however the headdress and the tobacco bag are Plains Indian items.

6 The South Wind, Wisconsin Winnebago, 1899. He wears a floral beaded bandolier bag.

7 Winnebago rush mat domed wigwam.

recognition of spirits above the earth, usually considered benevolent, and those of the underworld, such as the underwater panthers, who were dangerous. They shared most of their major ceremonies with the Chippewa, such as the Midewiwin and Dream Dance, and acknowledged the trickster culture hero called (by the Ojibwa) Nanabozho.

They were probably first known to the French (Jean Nicolet) in 1634 or (Nicolas Perrot) in 1667. A fort was later built at La Baye on the site of present Green Bay, Wisconsin, which became a French settlement. The Menomini were usually firm friends of the French, with whom they intermarried. They quickly adapted to the fur trade, but in the 19th century the Americans encroached rapidly on their territory. In 1854 they were restricted to a reservation in present Menominee County, Wisconsin, where their descendants remain.

Their history since the establishment of the reservation has witnessed factional disputes between the various religious organizations — Christian (Catholic), native traditionalists, and Peyotists — and social divisions opened between several different economic and ethnic groups. In time the traditionalists came to live principally around one community on the reservation at Zoar, these being partly intermarried Potawatomi. This group kept alive the Dream Dance religion, said to be a variant of the Grass Dance of the Plains, along with other old customs. In 1961, the reservation was terminated by the government on the grounds that they were largely acculturated. However, their tribal lumber mill operation became uneconomical, exacerbating various social problems, and a campaign for restoration of reservation status was successful in 1973. They numbered about 3,500 when first known to whites; in 1970, 4,307 were reported, all but a handful being of mixed blood. In 1992 they had 7,000 members, half on their reservation, 8,074 by 2001, and 7,494 in 2010. During the 19th century they excelled in beadwork and ribbonwork. They still hold an annual fair and pageant, and operate a fairly successful casino.

WINNEBAGO (HO CHUNK) The Winnebago were a Siouan enclave largely surrounded by Algonkians, with whom they shared their major cultural traits. They lived between the Rock and Black rivers, including the Wisconsin River drainage, in southern Wisconsin. Their closest linguistic relatives were the Chiwere-speaking group, Iowa, Oto and Missouri. The Winnebago had a rich and complex cosmology, a layered universe, Earth Maker (perhaps before Christian influence, the Sun), Midewiwin, and the sacred war bundles, the focus of important ritual and the property of clans. They were noted by the French (Jean Nicolet) as early as 1634, and permanent contacts came after 1665 with the fur trade, and the establishment of Prairie du Chien, which drew the Winnebago away from their earlier homes at Lake Winnebago and Green Bay to their location on the Wisconsin River.

They usually aided the French during the colonial wars, and took part in the conflicts with Americans until the treaties of 1829 to 1837. Many had removed to southern Minnesota by 1855, and in 1874 moved again, to a reservation in Nebraska purchased from the Omaha, where their descendants remain. However, not all the Winnebagos left Wisconsin, and others returned from Nebraska to form several small communities around Tomah and Black River Falls, Wisconsin. These two divisions remain. The combined population was given as 2,832 in 1970, and 6,000 in 1990. That number has now grown to

Above: Louise Amor, Menomini, Wisconsin, c. 1915. She is wearing a skirt and blanket decorated with fine bands of cut and fold ribbonwork characteristic of the southern Woodland tribes such as the Menomini, Winnebago and Potawatomi, and later the Missouri River valley tribes during the 19th century and early 20th century. Photograph: Samuel M. Barrett.

about 6,145 in Wisconsin alone, and about 4,033 in Nebraska. Although most native traditions have fallen into disuse, both hold pan-Indian powwows. The Wisconsin Winnebago have for years found employment in the tourist center of Wisconsin Dells, and more recently have opened successful casinos. Both groups still have a sizable Peyote membership. The present Wisconsin Winnebago now prefer their own name Ho Chunk.

OJIBWA or **CHIPPEWA (ANISHINABE)** One of the largest tribes of North America, and the principal one of the Algonkian linguistic family, is the Ojibwa. Their original home was Sault Ste Marie, Ontario, and they were first mentioned by Jean Nicolet in 1640, along with other local groups no doubt related to them. They became deeply involved in the fur trade from about 1670, and in the course of the 18th century spread both east (Mississauga, q.v.) and northwest (Saulteaux, q.v.), even to the northern edge of the Plains (Bungi, q.v.), with a

range exceeded only by the Cree, and a descendant population today exceeded only by the Navajo. The Chippewa or Southern Ojibwa are those who spread into the Upper Michigan Peninsula, Wisconsin, Minnesota and the Lake of the Woods area of southwestern Ontario during the early years of the fur trade in the late 17th century in small, widely scattered, autonomous bands. These were not a tribe in a political sense; only in terms of language and some aspects of a commonly shared culture were they one people. Some bands of the Mississaugas and Southern Ojibwa seem to have forged an alliance with the Potawatomi and Ottawa, once designated the "Three Fires," who joined Pontiac's rebellion (1763). But their main energy was directed against the Dakota of central Minnesota, from whom they acquired rich areas of wild rice production.

Top: Winnebago Indians, c. 1900. Photograph probably taken near Black River Falls, Wisconsin. The men wear buckskin leggings and cloth shirts; one man holds bow and arrows, another an eagle feather fan, another a wooden war club. Several wear woven beaded sashes, arm and knee bands. The man second from left wears a cloth apron with abstract floral beadwork typical of the Winnebago, Potawatomi and Fox.

Above: Dolls were made by many tribes. These are from the Wisconsin Winnebago, and are dressed in late 19th-century clothes — the male in aprons, the female in a wraparound skirt, all decorated with cut-and-fold ribbonwork.

The land of the Chippewa was a vast network of interlocking waterways, rivers and lakes with small portages, which allowed relatively swift forest travel in their light birch bark canoes, refined to the most efficient design. Their technology reflected their forest environment, producing bowls, ladles, bows, arrows, snowshoes, lacrosse rackets, musical instruments, cradleboards and fishing lures. Birch bark covered their wigwams of various shapes, and was fashioned into containers for carrying, storing and cooking. Buckskin clothing was replaced by cloth obtained from the traders, and its decoration for festive occasions featured the beads, ribbons and silver they developed to replace quillwork and painting. During the 19th century they developed two distinctive styles of beadwork: one derived from earlier decorative forms using large areas of woven beadwork in geometrical forms, the other, floralistic, and sewn on black or blue broadcloth. The genesis of this style was owed perhaps to the French Canadians, with whom they mixed freely, or other immigrant Europeans. They also continued the use of porcupine quillwork, but this tended to be increasingly restricted to items for the souvenir markets. Their involvement in the fur trade gradually changed native technology: log cabins replaced wigwams, and guns, knives, kettles and steel traps replaced earlier indigenous equivalents.

Social organization was simple, based on family, bands and totemic clans named after animals or birds, usually exogamous and patrilineal. Their religious beliefs centered on the cosmic force that inhabits trees, rocks, sky, earth and all living things. Presiding over all was a paramount spirit, Manito, perhaps personalized as a result of European influences. The Midewiwin

Six beaded Woodland Ojibwa (Chippewa) bandolier bags, c. 1880–1900. These bags were sometimes known as "friendship bags" as they were often given away at tribal and intertribal gatherings. The Sioux would often trade horses for them. The origins of such bags were probably the colonial soldiers' bullet pouches of the 18th century. They were adopted by the eastern Indians and decorated with quill-work or later beaded designs. They were used at one time to carry ammunition and food but later simply as an item of ceremonial dress worn by both men and women, usually diagonally across the chest, as an ethnic symbol. Many bandolier bags were made in the late 19th century by the Southern Ojibwa (also called Chippewa) at first in woven beadwork, later in appliqué sewn beadwork usually onto red or black cloth or velvet with borders around the lower panels. Some very late bandoliers even lacked the opening or bags completely. The bags with geometrically woven designs sometimes contained the X motif — probably stylized thunderbirds — and hence had religious overtones. (**1**) Typical Ojibwa bandolier constructed of wool cloth, military braid edging, yarn tassels, and beads. The floral beading is typical of Ojibwa work of the period 1880–1910. The beaded border to the lower area is sometimes called "otter-tail" design. Some of the beadwork uses "cut" beads. The small design elements suggest possibly a Canadian Ojibwa attribution. Bag length 40cm (16in); width 26cm (10in); strap 122cm (48in); width 13cm (5in). (**2**) Dating to c. 1875–1885, probably from Wisconsin, this bag is made of cloth, velvet, military braid, beadwork. Large beaded shoulder bags descend from early but smaller buckskin shoulder bags (often black dyed buckskin) with porcupine quillwork decoration. Later black cloth or black velvet replaced buckskin, and beadwork replaced quillwork. Wearing bandolier bags amongst the Ojibwa became an ethnic symbol at social and religious gatherings and often carried religious symbolism. Woven beaded bags were popular until about 1885, afterwards, appliqué beaded floral designs predominated. 26cm wide x 112 cm long. (**3**) This exquisite example of 19th century Woodlands bead-work has a floral design in an outstanding blend of colors and with great skill at color combination. The lower part of the bag has a white bead edging that is reminiscent of lace. The back of the shoulder strap is navy and white cotton cloth. The lower portion of the bag is backed by black velvet. The tassels are made of cut glass beads and yarn. This bandolier is in excellent condition and is by far one of the most beautiful examples we have seen. No restoration. 12¾ in wide by 43 in long.

1 *Ojibwa Snowshoe Dance painted by George Catlin, c. 1835.*

2 *Shingwaukonse or Shingwaskonce (Little Pine) 1773–1854. Important Ojibwa chief from the north (Canadian) side of the Great Lakes. Fought for the British in the War of 1812, but was later involved in repairing relations with the Americans, and native-white interactions in the Great Lakes area. His son George Shingwauk (1839–1920) successfully managed the affairs and promoted religious harmony amongst the Anglican and Catholic Ojibwa of the Garden River Band, many of whom had been forcably moved by white settlers from Sault Ste. Marie. After a drawing by Martin Somerville, Monreal, c. 1840.*

3 *Juahkisgaw, an Ojibwa woman and child painted by George Caitlin, c. 1834. She wears a trade cloth strap-dress. The cradleboard is the Woodland type with protective headbow.*

4 *The Round Earth (Wa-wi-eku-mig), Ojibwa 1908. He wears two bandolier bags. Photograph DeLancy Gill, Washington D.C.*

5 *Ojibwa (Chippewa) men, c. 1910–1920. Perhaps a singing group at a Powwow. The men wear floral beaded shirts and the man on the right wears floral beaded leggings as well. These items and moccasins appear to be Ojibwa made, however the feather headdresses and leggings of the center men are adopted Plains regalia.*

6 *Mary Strong Chicog and baby, Ojibwa. Nett Lake, Minnesota 1946.* Photographer Monroe Killy, Minnesota Historical Society.

7 *Buckskin moccasins with center seam, "tee" shaped heel seam, velvet vamp, and cuffs. The vamp and cuffs are decorated with floral beadwork.*

8 *Ojibwa (Chippewa) Indian moccasins. Probably c. 1910, Wisconsin-Minnesota area. Buckskin moccasins with black velveteen vamps and cuffs decorated with floral beadwork in spot-stitch technique. Cuffs or collars edged with silk ribbon.*

9 *Ojibwa Man's Cloth Shirt, c. 1920. A handmade man's cloth shirt with panels of floral beadwork on velveteen at shoulder, chest and cuffs. Probably worn by a male dancer during native celebrations. The beadwork may have been taken from an earlier shirt. Probably from Wisconsin or Minnesota.*

10 *Ojibwa mens' leggings of black velveteen and cloth with floral beadwork, c. 1910. Lac du Flambeau, Wisconsin and Leech Lake, Minnesota.*

11 *Knife case, Ojibwa (Chippewa), c. 1895. Worn as ceremonial regalia constructed with velvet cloth, silk edge and beadwork. The beadwork is typical late 19th century thread sewn floralistic-style of the Ojibwa (Chippewa) of Minnesota, Wisconsin, and adjacent Canada. When used with a knife an inside rawhide or bark sheath would be used inside.*

Above Left: Ceremonial hooded cape of the mid-19th century. Hoods of fur, skin and later of cloth were known throughout the North, Subarctic and Northeast areas, particularly among Algonkian-speaking groups. They gave protection against the weather and some had magico-religious significance. Those with ears like this have been recorded in an area from the Penobscot of Maine west to the Plains Cree. The decoration on the front is similar to that found on examples of East Cree manufacture around James Bay.

Above: Standing Buffalo, Winnebago, c.1860s, probably taken in Sioux City, Iowa, by Gurnsey and Illingworth. He wears a head roach set back on his head, metal earrings, and holds an eagle feather fan. He also wears hide leggings, moccasins, aprons and armbands, wristlets and knee garters with fur drops, which probably confirms his status as a warrior.

Left: Indian doll, c. 1850, from the Great Lakes area, probably Ottawa or Ojibwa. This European trade doll has been dressed by the Indians as a warrior figure with facial tattoos, braided hair, feathers, cloth skirt, breechclout, moccasins and leggings and decorated with ribbonwork and beadwork.

Far Left: Richard Hook's representation of what the doll above would have looked like had he been a real person.

Opposite: Ojibwa wigwam.

or Grand Medicine Lodge was a graded curative society with membership by payment, a feature of which was the shooting of the sacred shell into the candidate's body and subsequent restoration by the Mide priest. In later years they obtained the Dream Dance or Drum religion, an early offshoot of the Plains Grass Dance to which they added religious features.

They began to lose their lands by a succession of treaties after the War of 1812, although they were never transported to areas outside their original domain (except for a small group of Swan Creek and Black River Chippewa, who sold their lands in Michigan in 1836 and moved to join the Munsee in Franklin County, Kansas). They were gradually restricted to reservations in the northern parts of the Great Lakes states where, as the fur trade diminished due to the depletion of game, many gained employment in the logging industry. But these reservations were far from urban centers and the associated opportunities to move to a 20th-century wage-earning economy. Consequently, the reservations often suffered from neglect, social problems, poor housing, poor health and low income. The loss of more reservation land as a result of the Allotment Act in the 1880s also undermined their landbase.

However, in recent times more have moved to urban centers, with perhaps 50,000 or more people of Chippewa descent now living in major cities. Native organizations have now taken over more of the administration and control of their affairs, initiating new social programs. The population of the Ojibwa (Chippewa) in the United States was given in 1970 as 41,946, with 50,431 in Canada (including Saulteaux and Mississauga). This figure would be greater, however, if non-treaty Indians were added in Canada. In 1993, almost 80,000 were reported in the United States alone, and 105,907 in the 2000 Census and an even greater number were reported in Canada — 115,859 in the 2010 Census — with the greatest concentration in Ontario. This population is largely of mixed descent, both from their early contacts and affiliation with French trappers and more recent intermarriage with non-Indians.

The Chippewa reservations in the United States are as follows: *Michigan* — Isabella, Beaver Island, Hog Island, Ontonagon, L'Anse, Bay Mills, and Sault Ste. Marie, plus a number of non-reservation communities; *Wisconsin* — Mole Lake, Lac Courte Oreilles, Bad River, Lac du Flambeau, Lac Vieux Desert, Red Cliff and St. Croix lands; *Minnesota* — Grand Portage, Deer Creek, Leech Lake, Mille Lacs, Vermillion Lake, Nett Lake, Fond du Lac, Red Lake and White Earth. Chippewa reservations in Ontario, Canada, include Pikangikum, Islington, Shoal Lake, The Dalles, Wabauskang, Lac Seul, English River, Eagle Lake, Wabigoon, Rat Portage, Whitefish Bay, Northwest Angle, Big Island, Sabaskong Bay, Big Grassy, Manitou Rapids, Rainy Lake, Sturgeon Falls, Nequagon Lake and Seine River.

A number of reservations hold summer powwows in which they present pan-Indian dances, and wild rice is still collected in a few places. The spoken language and Mide religion survive only among older people or on remote Canadian reserves. Nevertheless, the Ojibwa/Chippewa are still one of the most important Native American peoples. Their own name, Anishineabe, is increasingly preferred by many Ojibwa people.

OTTAWA (ODAWA) A body of Algonkians probably closely related to the Ojibwa, living around Manitoulin Island, Ontario, and the adjacent northern shore of Georgian Bay are the Ottawa. Known to the French in the early 17th century, they later moved west and south ahead of Iroquois expansion. Their name seems to signify "trade." Their culture was much the same as that of the eastern Ojibwa and Hurons, with hunting, fishing and horticulture, until their economy changed due to their involvement in the fur trade. During the late 17th century and in the 18th century they were reported in various locations — Green Bay, Chequamegon Bay, Keweenaw Bay — but gradually Michigan and Manitoulin Island became their main habitat. They ceded most of their Michigan territory during the 1820s and 1830s, and three bands from Ohio were granted a reservation in Franklin County, Kansas, in 1831, from where most moved to Ottawa County, Oklahoma in 1867. Here a highly acculturated group of descendants remain on their old allotted reservation, although many have now left the area.

Of those who remained in their homelands their descendants now occupy a number of reserves on Manitoulin Island and Cockburn Island, Ontario, the largest at Wikwemikong. Much mixed with Ojibwa, they are now usually known as "Odawa," reported as 1,632 in 1970, and more than 7,000 today. The Ottawa in the United States were given as 3,533 in 1970, of which the Ottawa County group in Oklahoma numbered about 500 (2,290 in 2001); the remainder live in Mason and Oceana counties, also in the areas of Traverse City, Burt Lake, Cross Village, Mikado, Oscoda and other locations in Michigan. The total U.S. population of Ottawa according to the 2000 Census was 6,432 rising to

Above: Eastern Ojibwa canoe. This high-ended shape is also found among the Algonkin; they perhaps belong to the same generic form, although some hybrids with the Abenaki construction are reported. This construction and silhouette probably inspired the much larger fur trade canoe used by many tribes, Métis and whites across the interior of Canada in the 18th and 19th centuries.

Right: Ojibwa/Chippewa canoe. This graceful, rounded, "long nose" shape was characteristic of the western Ojibwa (Chippewa) of Wisconsin, Minnesota and western Ontario. Bark seams were sealed with spruce resin gum.

7,975 in 2010. The Ottawa language is still spoken at Wikwemikong, and a large pan-Indian powwow is held there each summer. In years past, the Ottawa were known for their colorful quilled bark baskets and boxes, which were sold to generations of curio collectors and are often found in museum collections.

MISSISSAUGA or SOUTHEASTERN OJIBWA
Part of the Ojibwa who remained close to their traditional home-lands around Sault Ste. Marie, Ontario, and spread eastward perhaps as early as the mid-17th century to trade with the French and Indian groups along the St. Lawrence were the Mississauga. They filled the gap left after the destruction of the Huron, although resisted by the Iroquois. Some made peace with the Iroquois in 1701, forming a loose alliance (those usually termed Mississauga) on the Ontario peninsula along the east coast of Georgian Bay, and

Above Left: Chippewa (Ojibwa) brave, c.1860s. He wears a turban with an eagle feather, treaty medal, trade blanket and holds a pipe and stem. Photograph: J.E.Whitney, St. Paul, Minnesota

Above: Ojibwa (Chippewa), c. 1870. Unusual braided hair at the front, with turkey feathers (widely used by all Eastern tribes) fixed upright.

Left: Ojibwa, c. 1880. The Ojibwa (Chippewa) used two forms of the same basic cradle type, both based on a cedar board roughly 2 feet by 10 inches (60 x 25 cm), with a hickory hoop or bow fixed and braced at the top to protect the child in case the cradle fell. Among the southern Chippewa (U.S.), a short foot brace was attached, and the baby was wrapped to the board with two pieces of cloth. Among the more northern (Canadian) bands and the Cree this was replaced by a U-shaped wooden inner frame, the child being held in a laced bag formed by a rectangular piece of cloth thonged to the sides of the U-frame. In the late 19th century both the wrappers and the bag, usually of dark cloth, were decorated with floralistic beadwork.

Opposite, Above Left: Little Shell Ojibwa (Chippewa), c. 1880. The photograph was probably taken during a visit to Washington, D.C. He wears a treaty or "Peace medal" and a neckband of cloth with floral beadwork.

around the southern end of Lake Huron. Despite active missionaries, traditional religion remained strong. But as the 18th century advanced, a generalized Great Lakes Indian culture emerged with a blending of customs, dress and materials that reflected their interaction with Europeans and other tribal groups in the promotion of the fur trade. During the 19th century, many bands in southern Ontario adopted farming, log cabins and wooden cottages alongside their traditional pursuits — collecting wild rice and maple sap, hunting deer and planting corn — in a number of southern locations. They excelled in decorative arts, both porcupine quillwork (which they developed eventually for the souvenir markets) and beadwork.

Above Right: Kanapima, Ottawa, born 1813 near Mackinaw, Michigan. He and his brother went to a Catholic seminary in Cincinnati, and later to Rome in 1832. On the death of his brother he returned to the United States, became a chief, and resumed the lifestyle of his people. From a lithograph by J.T. Bowen, Philadelphia, 1836–1844, in McKenney and Hall's History of the Indian Tribes of North America

Right: Ojibwa (Chippewa) men on Red Lake Reservation, northern Minnesota, c.1900. Several wear heavily beaded bandolier pouches; the floralistic patterns are thought to have developed through a combination of European folk art with native curvilinear decorative traditions. Courtesy St. Michael Mission, Fort Totten, North Dakota

By the end of the 19th century the easternmost groups were highly acculturated, and today many have left their small reservations (of about 50) to live in urban centers. Excluding any within the United States, the following are the major Canadian groups: Walpole Island, Sarnia, Kettle and Stony Point, Rice Lake, Mud Lake, Scugog, Georgina Island, Rama, Christian Island, Cape Croker, Saugeen, Moose Deer Point, Parry Island, Shawanaga, Magnetawan, Henvey Inlet, Point Grondin, French River, Dokis, Nipissing, Whitefish River, Mattagami, Matachewan, Wahnapitae, Spanish River, Serpent River, a number of reserve bands on Manitoulin Island mixed with Ottawa (Odawa), Pic-Mobert, Goulais Bay, Garden River, Chapleau, Thessalon, Mississagi River and others.Many Canadian bands refer to themselves today as "First Nations."

ALGONKIN or **ALGONQUIN** Algonkin includes a group of bands of the Ojibwa type, who lived on both sides of the Ottawa along the Quebec and Ontario border, Canada. A number of bands were reported by the French, who had contacted them before 1570, but the principal 19th-century groups were the *Weskarini*, or Algonquin proper on the Gatineau River and other northern tributaries of the Ottawa; the *Abitibi*, around the lake bearing their name; and the *Temiskaming*, near Lake Temiskaming.

Their history is one of firm friendship with the French. Champlain visited an Algonquin village on Morrison's Island in 1613 and established trade relations with them. They represented the northernmost penetration of a marginally agricultural economy in eastern North America, but were largely a hunting people who adapted quickly to the activities of the fur trade, which lasted until recent times. They carried on intermittent warfare with the Iroquois, but in the early 18th century were converted by Catholic missions and in part joined the Mohawk and Onondaga at Oka.

Their present descendants, with a mingling of French Canadian ancestry, number more than 10,000, including those at Barrier Lake, Grand Lake Victoria, Lake Simon, River Desert (Manawaki), Argonaut, Hunters Point, Long Point, Kipawa, Timiskaming and Wolf Point, all in Quebec; plus the band at Golden Lake, Ontario, locally called Algonquin, but who spoke the Ojibwa language. They were once famous for their canoe building.

NIPISSING This is a branch of the Ojibwa from the Lake Nipissing area, induced by the French to join the Algonquins at the Oka Mission in 1742. They were involved in the French fur trade, and probably participated in attacks on the English settlers in New York. Since that time they have been a part of the Algonquins; but the present bands at Lake Nipissing and Dokis, Ontario, may also be their descendants, and together numbered about 3,000 in 2005.

IROQUOIAN

One of the most important linguistic families of the Eastern Woodlands was the Iroquoian, consisting of a northern branch originally occupying the St. Lawrence valley from Montreal to Ile d'Orleans, plus the Huron, Petun and Neutral of present southern Ontario; the Five Nations of New York State, and the Susquehannock of Pennsylvania; a southern branch in Virginia and North Carolina, comprising the Nottoway, Meherrin and Tuscarora; and finally a divergent southern branch, the Cherokee. The Laurentian groups noted by the earliest 16th century explorers (Jacques Cartier) seem to have disappeared by the 17th century or had perhaps reinforced the others. The Iroquoians were once proposed as distantly related to the Caddoans of the southern Plains, which fitted their assumed southern origins; but both propositions were subsequently discredited, since they seem to have been a northern people as far back as 1000 B.C.

HURON (WENDAT) The Huron were an Iroquoian people who lived north and west of Lake Simcoe between Nottawassaga and Matchedash bays. They were first contacted during the early 17th century by the French, who established missions among them. The Jesuit missions were able to record much of their culture at that time, and reported a sizable population of 30,000 in more than 30 villages, some defended by fortifications, but the largest number were open and defenseless. They were slash-and-burn agriculturalists and gathered fruits, but were only occasional hunters and fishers. They seem to have been locked in a continuous war with the Seneca, which in 1648-49 became an invasion by the Five

Above: Eastern Ojibwa (Chippewa) woman photographed at Muncey Town, Thames River, Ontario, in 1907. Three small groups of Chippewa, Muncey-Delaware and Oneida-Iroquois have reserves south of London, Ontario. Although probably Chippewa, this lady wears a characteristically Iroquoian cloth dress, cape, skirt and pouch. The same pouch also figures in a contemporaneous photograph of the Oneida Chief John Danford.

Opposite, Top: Mary Kelley, a Wyandot woman in Oklahoma, c. 1912. The Wyandots descend from the Hurons of Ontario.

Opposite, Top Inset: Detail of moosehair embroidery and porcupine quillwork on a black-dyed buckskin pouch. Huron or Iroquois, late 18th century/early 19th century.

Opposite, Below: Three pairs of Huron moccasins and (bottom right) Huron of Lorette moccasins of black dyed buckskin with moosehair embroidery decoration, c. 1820.

Huron Moccasins

The true moccasin forms with soft soles (made without left or right feet) were made and decorated in a wide variety of ways, but there seem to be two main subtypes. One is a southern tradition of a front-seam moccasin; the other a northern tradition with a vamp or apron at the instep. There are many variations of these subtypes, as well as hybrids of both forms. Some have pointed to a European origin for the vamp, as numerous tribes during the 19th century imported it to replace the center-front seam construction. But clearly this form was always present in the far north, reaching back to Siberia. Probably its adoption in the eastern parts of North America was due to the influence of the fur trade and links with the St. Lawrence River and the far north trading companies in the commerce of the 18th and 19th centuries. Most of the Huron moccasins that survive in museums are attributed to the Huron village of Lorette in Quebec. These are sometimes beautifully decorated with moose hair and caribou hair embroidery. The transitional Huron moccasin, c. 1840–1860, had a deep, long, or narrow vamp with the cuffs or flaps turned down. The earliest forms usually had the flaps upright to the leg, and occasionally both an upright flap and a cuff. Some of the early moccasins of the eastern Great Lakes area were characteristically dyed black. Huron moccasins, together with moccasins of the Têtes de Boule (French for "round heads," a branch of the Cree), were sold in large numbers by the Hudson's Bay Company, and this may have been a factor in the spread of the numerous construction variations and decoration techniques across Canada.

Nations in pursuit of expansion and control of the fur trade. Huronia was abandoned, and a large number of Hurons were adopted by the Iroquois or fled west, although a few found refuge at Lorette near Quebec City. The Lorette Hurons have modified their culture with strong French Canadian influences over the years, and have constantly intermarried with these Canadians.

Huron (and some Petun) who moved west seem to have gone first to Mackinac and then to Green Bay, but ultimately to the Detroit area and the Sandusky River region of northern Ohio by the early 18th century. Here they were known to the British as Wyandot, and were often involved in the colonial conflicts of the area. For those in the Detroit area, a reservation was established in the Anderdon township, Essex County, Ontario, in 1790, but later ceded to the Crown, although a few people of mixed descent survived in the area until the 20th century.

By 1817, the Wyandots in Ohio retained only two small reservations, and these were later sold. During the 1840s, they removed first to Kansas, and after 1853 to northeastern Indian Territory, now Oklahoma. Throughout their later history they were much mixed with Euro-Americans, often factionalized between Christians and pagans. A number became "citizens" while in Kansas and never removed to Oklahoma, these numbering about 300.

By 1961, about 900 Wyandot descendants were recorded at the old Quapaw Agency in Ottawa County, Oklahoma, although only a portion lived on their old lands and just two elderly native speakers were left. A few remained in Wyandot County, Kansas, while 1,041 were reported from Lorette, Quebec, in 1969. The latter group, which now numbers about 3,000, were for many years noted for the production of fine craftwork sold to generations of white curio collectors.

PETUN or **TIONONTATI** The Petun were an Iroquoian people living close to the Hurons, near Nottawasaga Bay in present Ontario, Canada. In 1616 they were visited by Samuel de Champlain, and subsequently came under the influence of Jesuits, who reported two major subgroups, the Wolves and the Deer. Their culture and beliefs seem to have been identical to those of their Huron relatives. They were also known as *Tobacco Nation*, as they cultivated and traded tobacco. In 1649 they were attacked and dispersed by the Iroquois and, although they lost separate identity, a number united with the Hurons and apparently formed an element among the later Wyandots.

NEUTRAL An Iroquois people who lived between the Grand and Niagara rivers in southern Ontario — five days' walk south of the Huron villages, according to early forest travelers. They were so named because they were neutral in the hostilities between the Huron and Five Nations Iroquois. As early as 1626,

they were visited by Friar La Roche Dallion, who reported a large population. In 1650-51 they were largely destroyed by the Iroquois, fled west, or were absorbed by the Seneca and others, and disappeared from history.

WENRO Part of the Neutral people but on the Niagara River were the Wenro. Archaeological sites are attributed to them on the New York side of the international boundary. During the Iroquois expansion in the late 1640s they seem to have united with the Huron and lost separate identity.

ERIE The Erie were sometimes called *Nation of the Cat*, and were an Iroquoian tribe who lived on the southern shore of Lake Erie near present Erie City. A number of archaeological sites in the area south of Buffalo, New York, have also been given Erie status. Apparently they should properly be the *Nation of the Raccoon*, referring to the distinctive robes worn by these people. They became known to Europeans in the 1640s, by which time they were already enmeshed in the complex events of the fur trade, which resulted in Iroquois expansion and their defeat after 1653. The *Black Minqua* or *Honniasont*, reported later on the upper branches of the Ohio River in western Pennsylvania and Ohio, may have contained Erie descendants, but these, too, seem ultimately to have been reinforced and absorbed by other Iroquoian groups.

SUSQUEHANNOCK or **CONESTOGA** This is an Iroquois people of the northern branch of the family known to French Jesuits and later Dutch and Swedish colonists. They lived in the valley of the Susquehanna River in present Pennsylvania. Constantly harried by the Iroquois during the early 17th century, they also suffered heavily from epidemics. In an effort to contain Iroquois attacks, they allied themselves with the Maryland colonists, but by the time of general peacemaking at Albany in 1677, they had been greatly dispersed among the Iroquois and Delaware. They continued to decline in numbers, the last of them being murdered by the Paxton Boys in 1765 — an atrocity denounced by Benjamin Franklin.

IROQUOIS or **FIVE NATIONS (HAUDENOSAUNEE)** This is a confederacy of five, later six, Iroquoian tribes living in the central northern area of present upper New York State who, according to legend, were induced to form a league uniting formerly warring nations to preserve the integrity of each, but to bind them to a common council with fixed delegates from each tribe. The date of the foundation of the league was probably about A.D. 1570, possibly in response to European contact. The traditionally reported founders of the league were Dekanawida and the historical Hiawatha. In a sense they were a democracy where lineage, clan and tribe were represented in policy-making. The league comprised the

Mohawk, Oneida, Onondaga, Cayuga and Seneca, living in this order east to west across present central New York State.

They became frequent and bitter enemies of the French, but were friendly to Dutch and English traders working out of Albany. During the 17th century they launched a series of devastating attacks on related tribes who were under French influence, which established their supremacy in the beaver fur trade for a century or more. They were important allies of the British during the French and Indian War (1754–63), but the American Revolution (1775–83) broke them. The Mohawks, Cayugas and some Senecas fought with the British, the Oneida with the Americans. The Americans had laid waste to much of Iroquoia by the end of the war. The Mohawk and Cayuga withdrew mainly to Canada, the Onondaga and Seneca remained in New York, and the Oneida in time moved to Wisconsin.

Culturally the Iroquois seem to have been descendants of the prehistoric Mississippian culture, a complex derived from Meso-american agricultural practices. They raised fields of corn (maize), beans and squash, flanking their semipermanent villages, which supplemented hunting and gathering. The entire process of planting, cultivating, harvesting and preparation of food was in the hands of women, their leaders called "Matrons." The ceremonial spirits of Maize, Beans and Squash were called the "Three Sisters." Their religion was dualistic, with the object of pleasing the spirits both friendly and unfriendly. They seem to have had a Creator, at least in later ceremonial practices, and a belief in *orenda*, the natural power of creativity in all things. As the fur trade and ultimately farming became the principal lifestyle of Iroquois communities, a curative image predominated in later Iroquois religious life, with important medicine societies such as the False Faces, a mask-wearing society devoted to group well-being and healing processes.

At the end of the 18th century, a time of despair for many Iroquois communities, a Seneca divine named Handsome Lake revitalized Iroquois religious life by introducing a strict moral code to a modified ceremonial life, partly influenced by Quakers. This "Longhouse" religion still survives in 12 Iroquois communities, preserving the remnants of Iroquois culture, language, ritual and drama for a small percentage of their descendants. The term "Longhouse" derives from their ancient bark dwelling, which housed several families and they now prefer the name Haudenosaunee "People of the Longhouse." From the time of the American Revolution they have gradually modified to a Euro-American culture and have for many generations lived similarly to rural whites, or more recently as wage-earners, a large number living in towns and cities away from their reservations and communities. Their population by 1980 exceeded 50,000 descendants, and by 2010, 90,000 of which 48,000 were in the U.S. This total includes a large number of persons of mixed European and other tribal ancestry added over four centuries of expansion, conflict and acculturation.

MOHAWK This is the easternmost tribe of the Iroquois League, who once lived mainly in the valley of the Mohawk River in present east-central New York State. After the formation of the League of Five Nations they were the "keepers of the eastern door" of the confederacy. With the encouragement of the Dutch traders at Albany they became perhaps one of the most aggressive peoples of the area, and were, no doubt, responsible for the depletion of some of the

Opposite: Huron of Lorette chief c. 1840. The remnant Huron group that settled near Quebec City gradually adopted French cultural traits, but retained a number of indigenous crafts. Moosehair embroidery and quillwork, used to decorate souvenir trade items, also appeared on the cuffs, shoulders and collars of mens' dress clothes. He wears a French Canadian–made assumption sash, probably derived from and replacing the native-made finger-woven sash of fiber or traded woolen yarn.

Above: Conical-shaped birch bark wigwam photographed on the Golden Lake Reserve, Ontario, c. 1880. Houses were covered with birch bark or elm in the boreal forest regions or with rush mats farther south in New England and south of the Great Lakes. Conical, domed, rectangular and gabled shapes were common. The Golden Lake people are usually called Algonkin proper but they spoke a dialect of Ojibwa.

Below: Joseph Brant (1743–1807). Painted by Charles Willson Peale in 1797. Mohawk chief called Thayendanega fought for the English in the American Revolution. Original in Second Bank of the United States Portrait Gallery, Independence National Historical Park, Philadelphia, Pennsylvania.

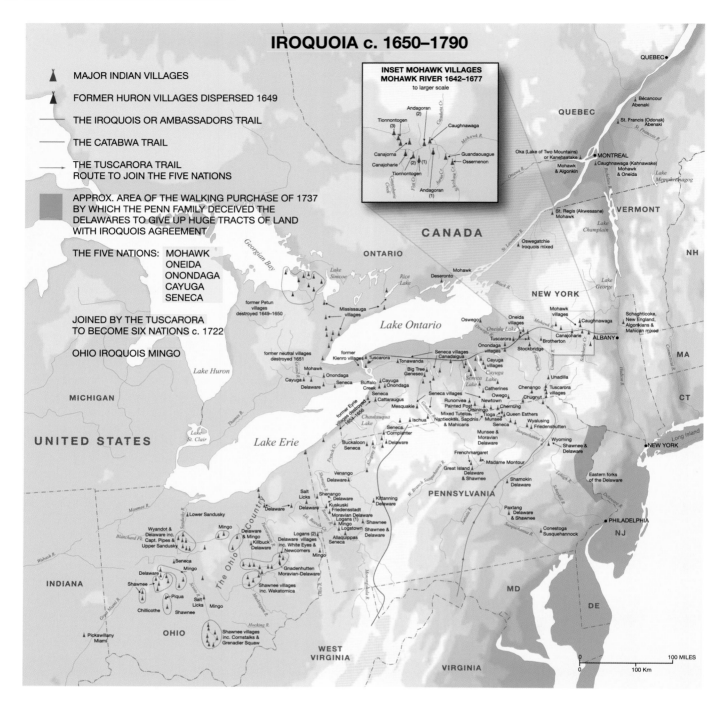

IROQUOIA c. 1650–1790

INSET MOHAWK VILLAGES
MOHAWK RIVER 1642–1677
to larger scale

▲ MAJOR INDIAN VILLAGES

▲ FORMER HURON VILLAGES DISPERSED 1649

— THE IROQUOIS OR AMBASSADORS TRAIL

— THE CATABWA TRAIL

→ THE TUSCARORA TRAIL
ROUTE TO JOIN THE FIVE NATIONS

■ APPROX. AREA OF THE WALKING PURCHASE OF 1737
BY WHICH THE PENN FAMILY DECEIVED THE
DELAWARES TO GIVE UP HUGE TRACTS OF LAND
WITH IROQUOIS AGREEMENT

THE FIVE NATIONS: MOHAWK
ONEIDA
ONONDAGA
CAYUGA
SENECA

JOINED BY THE TUSCARORA
TO BECOME SIX NATIONS c. 1722

OHIO IROQUOIS MINGO

Above: Iroquoia, c. 1650–1790, showing major Indian villages. Note the red Tuscarora Trail, showing the movement of the people northward after the Tuscarora War to join the Five Nations.

Opposite, Top: Significant military campaigns with Indian involvement, 1649–1783.

Opposite, Below Left: "The Death of Wolfe" by Benjamin West, 1770. This depicts the death of the British General James Wolfe at the Battle of Quebec in 1759. The painting (one of five known) is a jingoistic British political montage. There were few, if any, Iroquois warriors at the battle, but one is shown to represent their aid to the British during the French and Indian War in North America 1763–1760. The American colonial militia are also represented by the figure wearing a green coat and Indian attire, probably Sir William Johnson, British Superintendent of Indian Affairs) who led significant victories against the French at Lake George in 1755 and Fort Niagara in 1759, although he was not present at Quebec. Alternatively, the figure may represent Major Robert Rogers and his Rangers who led the assault on the Abenaki village of St. Francis in 1759, whose warriors had been assisting the French with attacks on New England settlements throughout the war. It is also possible that the image represents a combination of the two colonials. Benjamin West, the colonial American painter was born in 1738, emigrated to Europe to pursue a successful career

as an artist. In a number of his works ("William Penn's Treaty with the Indians" and "The Death of Wolfe") West used several Native American Indian specimens in his paintings. Objects such as headdresses, moccasins, bags, and women's skirts clearly show he had access to authentic material likely provided through family connections that remained in America. Between 1989 and 1990 West's descendants gave 17 specimens to the British Museum, of which eight are depicted in West's paintings and are contemporary with his time in London during the third quarter of the 18th century. However, West's portrayal of Indians have been criticized as they pose in classical Western models setting a pattern for later visual distortions of the mythic Indian past.

Opposite, Below Right: Iroquois whimsy, c. 1905. A six-lobed, beaded pin cushion of a type made in the late 19th century and early 20th century for the souvenir trade at Niagara Falls, Montreal and other locations. Often attributed to the Mohawk of Caughnawaga. Using large glass beads such objects are often called "flights of fancy" or Whimsies.

SIGNIFICANT MILITARY CAMPAIGNS WITH INDIAN INVOLVEMENT 1649–1783

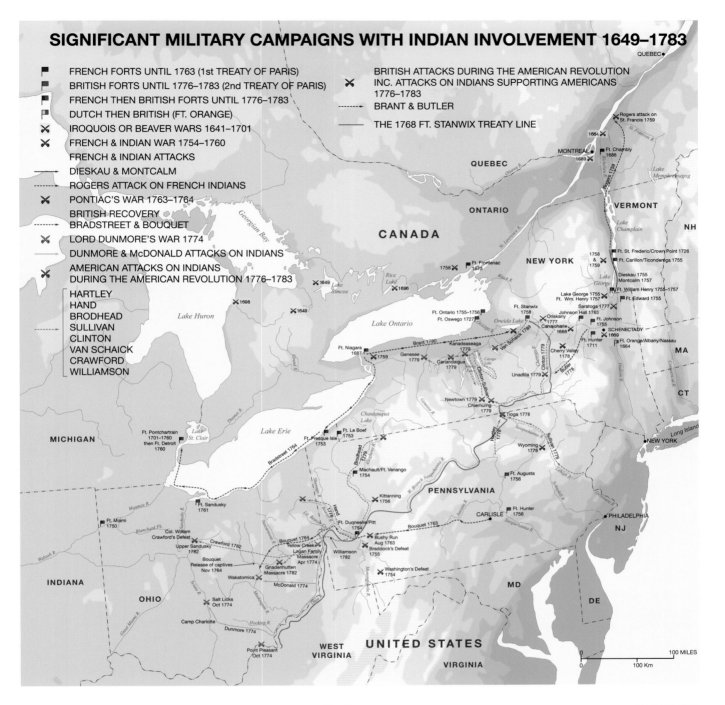

Legend:

- 🚩 FRENCH FORTS UNTIL 1763 (1st TREATY OF PARIS)
- 🚩 BRITISH FORTS UNTIL 1776–1783 (2nd TREATY OF PARIS)
- 🚩 FRENCH THEN BRITISH FORTS UNTIL 1776–1783
- 🚩 DUTCH THEN BRITISH (FT. ORANGE)
- ✕ IROQUOIS OR BEAVER WARS 1641–1701
- ✕ FRENCH & INDIAN WAR 1754–1760
- FRENCH & INDIAN ATTACKS
- ⟶ DIESKAU & MONTCALM
- ROGERS ATTACK ON FRENCH INDIANS
- ✕ PONTIAC'S WAR 1763–1764
- BRITISH RECOVERY BRADSTREET & BOUQUET
- ✕ LORD DUNMORE'S WAR 1774
- DUNMORE & McDONALD ATTACKS ON INDIANS
- ✕ AMERICAN ATTACKS ON INDIANS DURING THE AMERICAN REVOLUTION 1776–1783
  - HARTLEY
  - HAND
  - BRODHEAD
  - SULLIVAN
  - CLINTON
  - VAN SCHAICK
  - CRAWFORD
  - WILLIAMSON
- ✕ BRITISH ATTACKS DURING THE AMERICAN REVOLUTION INC. ATTACKS ON INDIANS SUPPORTING AMERICANS 1776–1783
- BRANT & BUTLER
- THE 1768 FT. STANWIX TREATY LINE

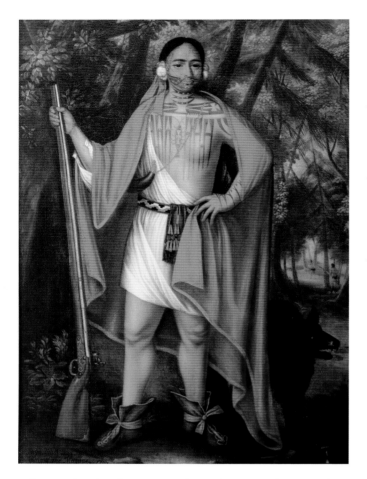

Left: Sagayengwarahton or "Old Smoke" also known as Brant, died before 1753. He was a Mohawk war chief of the Bear Clan as confirmed by the totemic animal recorded at the bottom right of his portrait painted by Verelst in London in 1710 when he was a member of a deputation of "American Kings." His grandson was likely the Brant who married Margaret, a Seneca widow already with two children, Mary (Molly) and Joseph, who took his stepfather's English surname to become the famous Joseph Brant. Note the facial and body tattoos.

Right: Joseph Brant or Thayendanegea was born in 1742 or 1743, his Indian name refers to two wagers (sticks, as in bets) bound together. His parents were Canajoharie Mohawks, but his father was killed in the Ohio country and his mother remarried an Indian known to the whites as Brant. Thayendanegea's career as a warrior began at the age of 13 when he joined the Mohawks at the Battle of Lake George in 1755. He and his half-sister Molly, became protégés of Sir William Johnson who sent him to Dr Wheelock's school in Connecticut, whilst Molly became Johnson's third wife. He was also present at the Battle at Fort Niagara in 1759 and took part in the Pontiac War of 1763. In November 1775 Brant accompanied Guy Johnson to London, for the first of two visits, and King George III conferred upon him the rank of Captain. He devoted his energies to the British cause during the Revolution during which he was raised by Gov. Carleton to the rank of Colonel. He may have been present at Cherry Valley in 1778 and was associated by the Americans with atrocities on the frontier. After the British defeat he moved to Canada where he was instrumental in obtaining the Grand River tract (Six Nations Reserve). He lived the remainder of his life as an English squire at Burlington, Ontario, and was criticized for conveyancing land on the Six Nations Reserve to whites. He supervised a new edition of the Prayer Book and Psalms in the Mohawk language and was reported to have translated a version of the Gospel of St Mark. He died in 1807 and is buried in the grounds of the Mohawk Chapel close to the city that bears his name — Brantford.

tribes on their borders. During the 17th century they were firm friends of the Dutch and British. The French explorer–soldier Samuel de Champlain had attacked their settlements and henceforth they were enemies of the French until, between 1667 and 1720, during breaks in the conflicts between France and Britain, more than a third of the Mohawks withdrew to French Canada under Jesuit missionary influence.

The Mohawks remaining in New York continued to support the British during the French and Indian War, and gave great assistance during the Revolutionary War under Joseph Brant (Thayendanegea), an Anglicized Mohawk leader. At the end of the war the Mohawks in the British cause took refuge in Canada with a large party of Loyalists, and obtained a tract of land on the Grand River, along with groups of other Iroquois, until all six Iroquois tribes were represented (the Tuscarora having joined as a sixth nation). In 1784, another group established a settlement near Kingston, Ontario, known as the Tyendinaga Band. A few subsequently left for the west as fur trappers and finally settled in Alberta; a few others went to Gibson and Watha near Georgian Bay, Ontario.

The history of the French Mohawks developed separately. During the late 17th century they went first to La Prairie, where they were joined by some Onondagas and Algonkians. They formed settlements at Oka (Lake of Two Mountains); later Caughnawaga (Kahawake) and St. Regis (Akwesasne) were founded. They usually assisted the French in colonial conflicts. All these groups have survived as reservation bands, and the Mohawk population consists

Below: Iroquois longhouse, c. 1650. Used by all northern Iroquoian peoples including the Six Nations and Huron, this community dwelling ranged from 30 to 200 feet (9 to 60 m) in length and 15 to 25 feet (5 to 8 m) in width. The frame of forked upright posts and horizontal beams had flexible horizontal tie poles and triangular or rounded roof supports. The sheathing of elm, hemlock, basswood or cedar bark formed overlapping shingles, secured by outer poles tied through to the interior poles. The longhouse had two doors and several smoke holes, but no windows. Inside was a central hallway between curtained-off family booths. Logs replaced bark due to 18th-century white contacts. The 12 remaining longhouses on various reservations synonymous with the survival of Iroquois traditions, and used for meetings and ceremonials — have two stoves, a central bench for ritualists and side seats for various clans, although externally they are conventionally boarded rural buildings.

of the following groups: Oka, on the north side of the St. Lawrence, Quebec — 1907 population 507; 777 in 1970; and 2,017 in 2005; Caughnawaga, on the south side of the St. Lawrence — 3,198 reported in 1949; 4,515 in 1970; and 9,392 in 2005; St. Regis, on the U.S. border partly in Quebec, Ontario and New York, 1,800 reported in 1945 on the American side (9,020 in 2005), 1,100 in Quebec, and 600 in Ontario in 1949. In 1970, 2,963 were on the Canadian side, with closer to 7,000 in 2005. At Tyendinaga at Bay of Quinte, Ontario, 2,111 were reported in 1970, and 7,533 in 2005, and Six Nations Reserve on the Grand River, Ontario, 3,974 were reported in 1970 as Mohawk by descent. A few are at Gibson and Watha on Parry Sound, Georgian Bay, Ontario; and a few (Michel's band) in Alberta, descendants of fur traders, numbered 125 of mixed descent in 1949.

The figures of all Canadian and U.S. Mohawk give a present population in excess of 48,000, although largely of mixed ancestry. They are noted for having accepted the various forms of Christianity, although a Longhouse is now thriving on the St. Regis-Akwesasne Reservation among a largely Catholic population. Their men have also been noted in recent times for working as steel erectors on high-rise structures and bridges

Below: Northeastern Woodlands: Iroquois ceremonialists, c. 1840. Two male societies performed at several of the annual festivals in the agricultural calendar. The Corn Husk Faces heralded the Maize, Bean and Squash deities — the life-supporting "three sisters." Wooden masks are worn by members of the False Face Society that represent earth-bound supernatural forest beings, who provided they are given offerings in return, give curing powers to the doctors who wear them.

Above: Iroquois False Face Mask from Six Nations Reservation, Ontario, c. 1950. It is in crooked face style, a form derived from the mythological facially disfigured "rim of the world" figure after a struggle with the Creator. This form of mask was used in the curing rites during the Midwinter Festival. Below is a turtle shell rattle used when doctoring the sick.

throughout the United States and Canada. Recently several families from Akwesasne have established another community at Ganienkeh near the northern end of Lake Champlain, also near their old homes in the Mohawk valley near Fonda.

ONEIDA "People of the stone" is the name given to these people in allusion to the Oneida stone; a granite boulder near their former village. They are a tribe of Iroquoian stock forming one of the Six Nations of the Iroquois League. They lived around Oneida Lake and in the region southward to the Susquehanna River. They were not loyal to the league's policy of friendliness toward the British, and were inclined toward the French, being practically the only tribe to fight for the Americans in the Revolutionary War. They were attacked by Joseph Brant's Mohawks during that war, and were forced to take refuge in the American settlements until the war ended. Factionalism and a reduction in their land base in New York State persuaded a large body of Oneida to remove to new homes in Wisconsin, where the Menomini relinquished land for their use in 1838. Another group purchased 5,200 acres near London, Ontario in the 1840s, independently from the Oneidas already at Six Nations. A few remained in New York State at a small settlement near their old homes or on the Onondaga Reservation.

Left: Beaded box, Mohawk, c. 1915. Souvenir beadwork on purses, boxes, picture frames, etc, were made by the Mohawks of Caughnawaga for sale in nearby Montreal and other tourist locations. This decorative beaded style was popular in the late 19th and early 20th centuries. There is a similar example in the National Museum of the American Indian, New York 21/2980.

Right: Iroquois, c. 1880. Woman pounding corn with pestle and log mortar, her child hanging safely nearby. The cradle was a board about 2 feet (60 cm) long, with a projecting bow similar to those described for the Ojibwa (Chippewa) but lacking their distinctive recurve. The bow and top edge of the board were often carved, and near the bottom was a foot support. The baby was bound to the board with red or blue cloth decorated with beads or moose hair, and a blanket or netting could be drawn over the bow to protect the face. A burden strap secured the cradle behind the mother's shoulders.

Below: Iroquois, c. 1812. European trade tomahawks, guns, cloth and silver had already been used among Northeastern Woodlands peoples for more than a century. Use of the bow was by now rare in many areas, restricted to some hunting or circumstances when firearms were in short supply. Woodland bows, often of hickory or hazel with braided sinew strings, could exceed 6 feet (1.8 m) in length. Arrows were sometimes of elder, quivers of bark or rush. The buckskin cap is decorated with   traded feathers, cut feather clusters and ermine skins.

Below Right: Iroquois couple pounding corn with pestle and mortar, probably photographed on the Six Nations Reservation, Ontario, c.1890. The split log house is typical of the adaption to white rural life. The basket appears to be of the native splint ash type. Cambridge University Museum of Archaeology & Anthropology.

In 1926, some 3,238 Oneidas remained in the United States, 2,976 on or near their Green Bay Reservation, Wisconsin. By 1972, that number had grown to more than 6,000, although only about a third lived on tribal lands. By 2001, the number of Wisconsin Oneida had increased to 14,745. There were 262 in New York State in 1926, and 1,893 in 2001. In 1972, the Oneida of the Thames near London, Ontario, included 1,964 members, of whom 1,200 were residing on the reserve lands (5,127 in 2005); and 802 Oneidas by lineage were reported from Six Nations Reserve, Brantford, Ontario, in 1973 (1,734 in 2005). A few hundred were mixed together with several Iroquois groups in New York, chiefly at the Onondaga Reservation or near the Oneida settlement. The majority of Oneida became Christians before leaving New York, although a Longhouse minority survives at the Thames Band Reserve near London, Ontario. The small Oneida Reservation in New York now boasts the Turning Stone Casino and a museum.

ONONDAGA The Onondaga were an important tribe of the Iroquois Confederation, formerly living on the mountain, lake and creek bearing their name in present Onondaga County, New York State, extending northward to Lake Ontario and southward perhaps to the head waters of the Susquehanna River. In the Iroquois Councils they are known as "they are the bearers." Their principal village, also the capital of the Confederation, was called Onondaga, later Onondaga Castle. It was situated from before 1654 to 1681 on Indian Hill in the present town of Pompey, and in 1677 contained 140 cabins (500 population). It was removed to Butternut Creek, where the fort was burned in 1696. In 1720 it was again moved to Onondaga Creek, and their present reservation in New York State is but a few miles away.

The Onondaga of the Grand River or Six Nations Reserve, Ontario, Canada had nine clans: Wolf, Turtle, Bear, Deer, Eel, Beaver, Ball, Plover (Snipe) and Pigeonhawk. The Wolf, Bear, Plover, Ball and Pigeonhawk clans each have only one federal chieftainship; the Beaver, Turtle and Eel clans have two federal chieftainships, while the Deer clan has three. The marked difference in the quota of chieftainships may be due to the adoption of other clans and chieftainships, which have long been extinct. In the Iroquois ceremonial and social assemblies that still exist, the Onondaga tribe itself constitutes a tribal phratry, while

the Mohawk and the Seneca together form a second, and the Oneida and Cayuga (originally) and later the Tuscarora formed the third tribal phratry. The functions of the Onondaga phratry are in many respects similar to those of a judge holding court with a jury.

In the middle of the 17th century their population was 1,700, but during the 18th century the tribe divided; part stayed loyal to the League's historical friendship with the British while others, under the direct influence of the French Catholic missions on the St. Lawrence River, Canada, migrated there to form small Iroquois colonies. By 1751 about 800 Onondaga were said to be living in Canada. On the outbreak of the American Revolution nearly all the New York Onondaga, together with the majority of the other Iroquois tribes, joined the British, and at the close of the war the British granted them a tract of land on the Grand River, Ontario, where a portion of them still live, mixed with other Iroquois groups. The rest are still in New York State, the greatest number being on the Onondaga Reservation and the others with the Seneca and Tuscarora on several reservations.

In 1906, those in New York were numbered at 553; and in 1920, 510 were enumerated on the Onondaga Reservation alone. On the Six Nations Reserve, Ontario, about 400 of a total Iroquois population of 5,400 were reported as Onondaga in 1955. In 1956, 894 Iroquois were returned from the Onondaga Reservation, and 1,034 in 2001, the greater proportion of these of Onondaga descent, although most tribal members have some white ancestors and an admixture from other Iroquoian tribes, including Cayuga. In 1973, 560 Onondaga were reported among the Six Nations at Grand River, a

Above: Iroquois, c. 1900. Gustoweh or "whirling feather" headdress traditional to Iroquois men, and still favored for ceremonial wear. It was often constructed of hide or cloth over an ash splint framework with a central eagle feather attached in a tube. Occasionally a cluster of smaller split heron, hawk, turkey or owl feathers was also attached. The band was of silver, other metal or embossed beaded cloth.

Below: Onondaga Longhouse, Six Nations Indian Reservation near Brantford, Ontario, seen in August 1990. This Longhouse is one of four on the reservation, where some modern Iroquois people preserve their religion and ritual dramas. Note the kitchen and cookhouse to the right. Part of the latter's construction is more than 150 years old. The old longhouse was recently been replaced by a new building.

Above: Indian Chief of Six Nations (Iroquois) c. 1860s, photographer unknown. The man wears beaded cap with feathers and horsehair. He also wears a beaded baldric over a buckskin jacket. According to the late Dr. James H. Howard, the headdress was a type worn and remembered by the Oklahoma Seneca-Cayuga Iroquois descendants.

Opposite, Above: Red Jacket or Sagoyewatha ("Keeps them awake"), chief and orator of the Senecas, signed treaties with the Americans at Canandaigua in 1794 and at Big Tree in 1797. He visited President Washington and received his medal in 1792. He opposed Christian missionaries at Buffalo Creek. He died in 1830 at about 74 years of age.

Opposite, Below: Ottawa man c. 1860 wearing a cloth turban. Most Ottawa (Odawa) remain scattered through Michigan and adjacent Canada, although a small group were removed to Oklahoma, then Indian Territory.

number that grew to 1,193 in 2005. The Onondaga in New York and Ontario continue to practice the Longhouse ceremonials, including the Midwinter and Harvest rites. The New York Onondaga Reservation remains the theoretical center of traditional Iroquois political and legislative life.

CAYUGA A tribe of the Iroquoian family and of the Iroquois Confederation, formerly occupying the shores of Cayuga Lake in present New York State were the Cayuga. Their local council was composed of four clan phratries, and according to tradition, this form became the pattern of that of the confederation of the Five (later Six) Nations, in which the Cayuga had 10 delegates. In 1660, they were estimated to number 1,500, and in 1778 about 1,100. At the beginning of the American Revolution, a large part of the tribe removed to Canada and never returned, while the rest were scattered among other tribes of the Iroquois League. After the Revolution they sold their lands in New York; some joined the Seneca of Sandusky in Ohio, and some the Oneida who later moved to Wisconsin. The mixed Seneca-Cayuga ultimately found their way to Oklahoma.

The Cayuga of the present time are much mixed with the other Iroquois people, as well as having an admixture of white blood; the largest element of them in New York State are on the Cattaraugus Reservation, where some of their descendants have mixed with the Seneca. The largest number, however, live on the Six Nations Reserve on the Grand River, Ontario, where 1,450 were reported in 1955 among the general Iroquois population; the same group were reported to number 2,525 in 1973 and 6,147 in 2005. On the Grand River today two Cayuga Longhouse congregations number about 300 each, and continue the traditional ceremonials organized by the Seneca revivalist Handsome Lake at the close of the 18th century. Another Longhouse group survives amongst the Seneca-Cayuga of Oklahoma — a group of many Iroquoian elements. This group, which contains both Seneca and Cayuga, had 3,674 enrolled in 2001. They have recently repurchased a small tract of land in their original homeland at the head of Cayuga Lake, New York.

SENECA The Seneca are a tribe of Iroquoian lineage and of the Iroquois Confederation. They called themselves "people of the mountain," and were once the most populous tribe of the Iroquois Confederation, with a range in western New York State between the Genesse River and Seneca Lake. They became the most important tribe of the confederation, and on the defeat of the Erie and Neutral tribes they occupied the country near Lake Erie and south along the Allegheny Mountains. Consistently friendly toward the British, the Seneca fought for them in the French and Indian War and later in the Revolution, although some remained neutral. General John Sullivan destroyed Seneca villages and crops in 1779, and many fled to British protection. The last time the Seneca took up the hatchet was in 1812, during the American invasion of British Canada.

Instead of receding before the Europeans as their rapidly increasing population pressed upon their remaining lands in New York, they tenaciously maintained their ground, and when forced to make territorial concessions to the whites they managed to preserve a few tracts for their own use, which they continue to occupy. The present Seneca descendants are on three reservations in western New York at Allegany and Cattaraugus (the Seneca Republic), plus Tonawanda near Akron. The small Cornplanter tract in Pennsylvania was flooded by the Kinzua Dam in the 1960s. In 1890 these groups numbered about 3,000; in 1906, 2,742; in 1956, 3,528; in 1970, 4,644; and just over 8,000 according to the 2000 Census. There are also many Senecas among the descendants of the mixed Seneca-Cayuga of Oklahoma. In addition, 345 Seneca were reported from Six Nations, Ontario, in 1973, and 786 in 2005. Each Seneca reservation has a Longhouse congregation, and the Allegany Senecas run the Seneca-Iroquois National Museum at Salamanca, New York.

MINGO In the 18th century, detached branches of various Iroquois groups occupied parts of northern Ohio. These were usually known as Mingo — the name appears as early as 1750 — and they were constantly reinforced by kinsmen from New York. They were known collectively as "Seneca" by the early 19th century, when they had ceded most of their lands to the United States and settled on two reservations in Ohio: one at Lewistown on the Great Miami River (mixed with Shawnees), and the other on the Sandusky River near

Fremont. By this time a number of Cayugas had also joined them, bringing total numbers to perhaps 500. They were subsequently forced to cede these reservations in 1831–32 for new lands in Kansas and, now called "Seneca of Sandusky," they were ultimately united with more relatives from New York on the Neosho Reservation. In 1869, after the Civil War, they and other eastern relocated groups of the area were reassigned lands in the southern portion of the Neosho Reservation within Indian Territory, present Ottawa County, Oklahoma. During the past century they have been known as the Seneca-Cayuga. Although their ancestry is mixed with a dozen other tribes and with whites, close to 4,000 people are still members of the group (though only 11 fluent native speakers remained in 1962). A Longhouse with an annual Green Corn Dance is held each August near Turkey Ford, Oklahoma. However, most members of the group no longer live permanently in the area.

TUSCARORA The Tuscarora were an Iroquoian tribe originally of present North Carolina who divided from their northern kinsfolk perhaps 600 years ago. They lived along the Pamlico, Neuse and Trent rivers in northeastern North Carolina in the Piedmont and coastal plain. Their final defeat by white settlers in 1711–1713, following years of persecution and usurpation of their lands in the Carolinas, resulted in their move north to join the Iroquois League of New York State as a sixth nation. They were formally adopted in 1722. Nevertheless, there was a Tuscarora Indian band in Bertie County, North Carolina, later during the 18th century, and the last of them did not move north until 1803. During the American Revolution part of them moved to British Canada, where their descendants are among the Iroquois of the Six Nations Reserve on the Grand River near Brantford. Others remained in New York State on a reservation near Niagara Falls that bears their name. In the War of 1812 some Tuscaroras performed meritorious service for the Americans and protected the life of General Peter B. Porter. As a result, Tuscarora women from their reservation were permitted to sell their craftwork on the Porter family property next to Niagara Falls for many years. The tribe has been one of the most acculturated of the

New York Iroquois groups. The lack of the diagnostic northern Iroquoian mask-making complex and the revised Longhouse religion that are associated with other Iroquois groups reflects the abandonment of native culture in favor of Christianity (Baptist) and rural farming. However, apparently not all of Tuscarora blood moved north; a number, perhaps mixed with Pamlico, Mattamuskeet and Machapunga, may have added a strain to the modern Person County Indians and Lumbees of North Carolina. In their North Carolina days, they perhaps numbered 5,000. In 1890, 400 Tuscaroras were on their New York Reservation, about 700 in 1970 and 664 were identified specifically as Tuscarora in the 2000 Census. Those at Grand River numbered 789 in 1973, and 1,926 in 2005.

NOTTOWAY A small tribe of Iroquoian lineage who lived around the middle course of the Nottoway River in the southern area of Virginia in present Southampton County were the Nottoway. A second tribe on the Meherrin River below them, the *Meherrin*, also of Iroquoian stock, were closely related. They are part of the same branch of the family as the Tuscarora. They seem to have acquired elements of Euro-American culture before the close of the 17th century, and the Nottoways finally settled on lands near Sebreel and Courtland, perhaps largely merging with African-Americans. In 1825 they numbered 47, but only nine were reported in 1859. Bill Lamb, who died in 1960, claimed to be three-quarters Nottoway and the last of his people.

Two other small ethnic groups may have completed this section of the Iroquoian family: the *Coree* and *Neusiok* or Neuse River Indians, who lived southeast of the main Tuscarora area, but almost nothing is known of them. Some Meherrins apparently left Virginia and crossed to North Carolina and reportedly had a reservation between 1705 and 1729, of which parts were still being sold by an Indian named Sallie M. Lewis (1838–1904) in the 19th century. A few people around the towns of Ahoskie and Winton in North Carolina still claim their descent. The last we hear of the Coree is a remnant who joined the Indians at Mattamuskeet Lake in Hyde County, North Carolina, after the Tuscarora Wars; a few descendants of these "Machapunga" survived until the 20th century.

SOUTHEASTERN WOODLANDS

Language family and tribe	Meaning/origin of tribal name, where known	Language family and tribe	Meaning/origin of tribal name, where known
Muskogean (except where noted):			
		Atakapa	"man eaters"
Apalachee	"people on the other side"		
Chatot	–	**Caddoan**★:	
Hitchiti	"to look upstream"	Adia	–
Alabama	"to camp" or "weed gatherer"	Natchitoches	"paw paw"
Koasati	"white cane"	Hasinai	"our own folk"
Tuskegee	"warrior"	Kadohadacho	"real chiefs"
Biloxi (Siouan)	"first people"		
Pascagoula	"bread people"	**Iroquoian**★★:	–
Ofo (Siouan)	"dog people"	Cherokee	"people of a different speech"
Pensacola	"hair people"		
Mobile	"to paddle"	**Siouan**★★★:	–
Napochi	"those who see"	Manahoac	"they are very merry"
Chakchiuma	"red crawfish people"	Monacan	"digging stick"
Houma	"red crawfish"	Tutelo	–
Acolapissa	"those who listen and see"	Saponi	"shallow water"
Bayogoula	"bayou people"	Nahyssan	–
Taensa (Natchez)	–	Occaneechi	–
Natchez (Natchez)	"warriors of the high bluff"	Cheraw	–
Chickasaw	"to leave"	Moneton	"big water people"
Choctaw	"red" or "flat"	Keyauwee	–
Muskogee	"swampy ground"	Sissipahaw	–
Seminole	"separate","runaway", "wild"	Eno–Shakori	"mean"
Yamasee	"gentle"	Cape Fear Indians	–
Cusabo	"Coosawhatchie River people"	Waccamaw	–
Calusa (affiliation unknown)	"fierce people"	Pedee	"something good"
Timucua (affiliation unknown)	"earth"	Wateree and others	—
		Catawba	"separated or strong people"
Yuchi	"those far away", "yonder"		
Tunica	"those who are the people"		
Chitimacha	"those who have pots"		

★ see p. 155
★★ see p. 56
★★★ see p. 124

The agricultural basis that provided the northern woodland peoples with their subsistence economy provided an even stronger basis for the Indians of the southeastern area of the United States, within the present states of Alabama, Georgia, Mississippi, South Carolina, Tennessee and neighboring states to the north. The Mesoamerican influences on the prehistoric cultural horizons of the Ohio valley, such as Adena and Hopewell, called "Mound Builder" cultures, left a strong legacy with the later Mississippians, whose descendants became known to the Europeans. While the Mississippian culture left

PREHISTORIC CULTURAL SITES AND HISTORIC NATIVE TRIBES OF THE SOUTHEAST, c. 1540–1850

This map shows the principal prehistoric archaeological sites of the southeast and Ohio-Mississippi valleys. Note also the route of explorer Hernando de Soto. He died on May 21, 1542, and his expedition returned to Mexico City. Only 300 of the original 700 men survived.

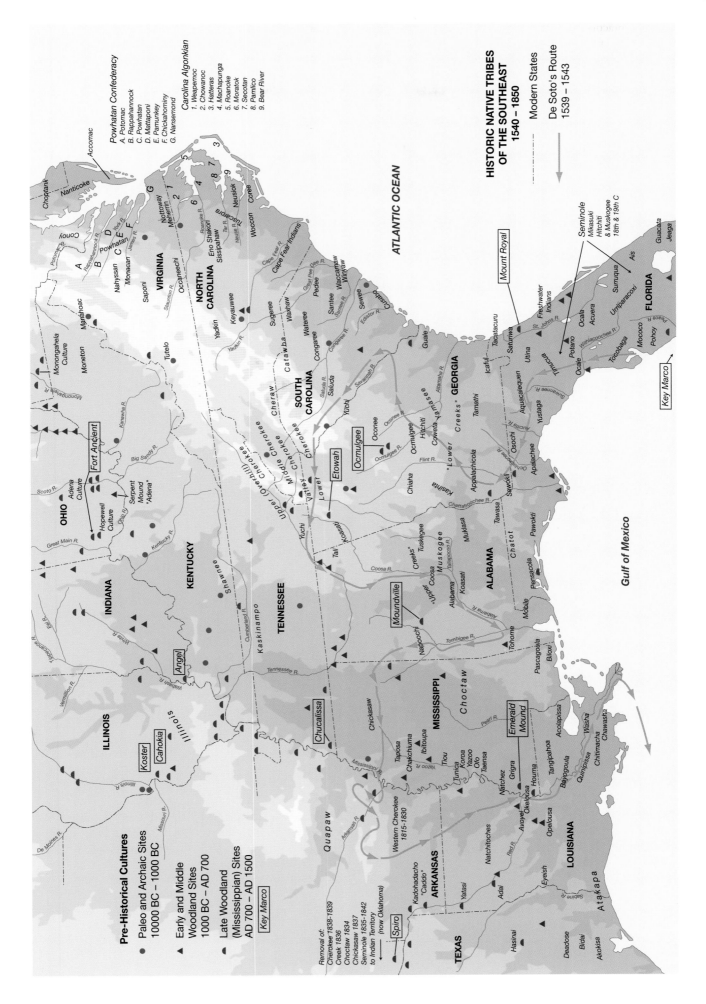

HISTORIC NATIVE TRIBES
OF THE SOUTHEAST
1540 – 1850

Modern States

De Soto's Route
1539 – 1543

Pre-Historical Cultures

● Paleo and Archaic Sites
10000 BC – 1000 BC

▲ Early and Middle
Woodland Sites
1000 BC – AD 700

◗ Late Woodland
(Mississippian) Sites
AD 700 – AD 1500

Key Marco

Removal of:
Cherokee 1838-1839
Creek 1836
Choctaw 1834
Chickasaw 1835-1842
Seminole 1835-1842
to Indian Territory
(now Oklahoma)

Powhatan Confederacy
A. Potomac
B. Rappahannock
C. Powhatan
D. Mattaponi
E. Pamunkey
F. Chickahominy
G. Nansemond

Carolina Algonkian
1. Weapemoc
2. Chowanoc
3. Hatteras
4. Machapunga
5. Roanoke
6. Moratok
7. Secotan
8. Pamlico
9. Bear River

agricultural practices, ritual and religious traits, social and class systems of honored men and common people, Caribbean-type material such as feather mantles, litters, wooden stools, platform beds, cane weaving, fish poisoning and blowguns linking the Gulf tribes to the Arawak and Carib of the West Indies have been proposed, but are doubted by many historians.

The largest linguistic family of the Southeastern area were the Muskogian people or smaller groups who may have been in lesser degrees distantly related to them, except for the Iroquoian and Siouan representatives and a few independents. The land occupied by these tribes was almost unbroken forest that once stretched from the Atlantic to the Mississippi, providing a varied supply of nuts, berries, roots, fish and game to add to the agriculture of the interior tribes. Villages were clusters of reed- or bark-covered dwellings, usually ranged along the rivers and creeks, with open central plazas or squares where the chiefs and nobles lived close to the council and ritual houses.

The most important religious festival projected to modern times has been the Green Corn celebration, or Busk, as it is called by conservative Creeks in Oklahoma. This is a maize festival, and part of a complex that extended from the Seminole of Florida to the Iroquois in the north. The celebration was an occasion of amnesty, forgiveness and absolution from crime. It lasted four to eight days and was performed in the town square, the "square grounds" of the present Oklahoma Creeks. The ceremonial involved taking emetic drinks to produce vomiting. This ceremonially cleansed the body, around the lighting of the new fire constructed of logs pointed at cardinal points — a world renewal complex of doubtless Mississippian origins. The persistent and symbolic use of the colors red for war and white for peace, plus regard for the Sun, sanctification, priesthood, animal spirits, theory of disease and certain medical practices, also echo back to Mississippian origins; but there were few animal medicine societies such as we see in Iroquoian culture.

The Southeastern tribes had regular trails running through the present Gulf states, allowing travel over long distances for war and trade. Canoes, usually the dugout type, facilitated some water travel. War parties were highly organized, made solemn and binding by pipe, calumet and war bundle ceremonials.

The French and Spanish explorers of the 16th and early 17th centuries saw these southern cultures in their pristine condition. However, by the 18th century, many of the coastal tribes had been ruined by diseases and wars with the Europeans, who had also turned tribe against tribe in colonial conflicts. For a time the larger interior tribes maintained themselves effectively enough by wholesale adoption of European material culture and frontier life, reflected in log cabin dwellings, clothing, domesticated farm animals and the adoption of Christianity. The Cherokee even had their own newspaper and kept African slaves. This did not save them from removal to Indian Territory, now Oklahoma,

Above: Choctaw Ball Game player, c. 1830. Catlin recorded the face paint, broad decorated belt and horsetail ornaments in c.1830. Known in both Northeastern and Southeastern Woodlands, this team game — often played violently as a substitute for war — was named "lacrosse" by the French, from the racket's resemblance to a bishop's crozier. In recent times the Iroquois used one racket, the Choctaw and Cherokee two.

where a substantial number of Cherokee, Creek, Choctaw, Chickasaw and Seminole survive, much mixed with white and African-American ancestry, although a group of Cherokee remained in North Carolina, Choctaw in Mississippi, Seminole in Florida and a few Creeks in Alabama.

Early French Contacts and Trade with Southeastern Indians

The French first established a post at Biloxi in 1699 making contact with the Pascagoulas, Biloxis, Moctobis and Capinas. These Indians formalized friendly relationships with calumet ceremonies and striking the post rituals with their clubs, boasting of their deeds in war. Iberville the command-ant distributed knives, glass beads, vermilion, guns, etc, to the Indians. Following the expedition of Marquette and Jolliet through Illinois country and along the Mississippi, La Salle led a party of 31 Indians and 33 Frenchmen to the mouth of the Mississippi, contacting the Quapaw, Taensa, and Natchez villages en route, in 1682. His commercial drive into the Lower Mississippi Valley ended with his assassination in 1687, so French activity in the Lower Mississippi Valley remained minimal. Henri de Tonti continued their interests and trade in the central Mississippi Valley from posts on the Illinois and Arkansas rivers. Through these contacts the Indians in the Lower Mississippi Valley had been drawn into France's mercantile economy. This was despite challenges from English traders originating from the Carolinas pursuing deerskins and Indian slaves, and Spanish expeditions from Texas. Voyagers, missionaries, and traders could now approach Louisiana from Canada or direct from France.

Many small Indian groups turned to Iberville's fledgeling colony for assistance and arms against the Creek, Chickasaw and Natchez who in turn were trading with the British and supplying hundreds of Indians for slaves. Many more died of diseases brought from Europe to which the natives lacked immunity. Iberville found evidence of the effects of epidemics among the Mobilian and Tohomé villages on the Mobile and Pascagoula rivers in 1700–1701. In 1702 Bienville (Iberville's brother) and Tonti attempted to make peace with the Chickasaw and Choctaw but these diplomatic overtures were short-lived due to continuing inter-colonial hostility between Britain and France. The Alabamas who lived at the confluence of the Coosa and Tallapoosa rivers also continued to harass the French colony and their Mobilian allies.

Several different tribes lived near the Mississippi below the junction with the Red River, including the Bayogoula and Chitimacha who suffered most during these early years of

French colonization and who absorbed refugees from other villages. The Taensa after being driven from their homes on Lake St. Joseph turned against the Bayogoula and Chitimacha in 1706. The latter killed the missionary Saint-Cosme and in response the French destroyed the Chitimacha village on Bayou Lafourche and took many as slaves.

In 1716 Fort Rosalie was constructed among the Natchez Indians and they became exposed to epidemics and violence after a French party had refused to parlay and smoke the calumet, a sign of hostility. French traders extended their influence and had built trade stations amongst the Kadohadacho and Hasinai Indians by 1721. However, French-Natchez relations were in crisis by 1722, their population halved by disease and they struck at French settlements. The deaths of two Natchez chiefs—Stung Serpent in 1725 and his brother the Great Sun in 1728—strengthened the anti-French fervour. They erected warpoles, drank war medicine, and in 1729 killed over 300 whites and 300 negroes and captured some slaves. During the winter of 1730–1731 the French campaign against the Natchez resulted in many Natchez being shipped to the Caribbean as slaves, their subsequent near extinction and the inevitable loss of their unique culture.

MUSKOGEAN This family constituted one of the largest of the continent and the one dominant in the Southeastern area. They seem to fall into several dialectic divisions and a large number of so-called tribes. The extent of these tribes is the subject of considerable debate, since their movements were so numerous between initial contact with the Spanish in the 16th century and the more extensive contacts with the French and British in the 18th century. The dialectic groups were perhaps: (a) the Apalachee and their associates in northern Florida; (b) Hitchiti, mostly in central Georgia, later becoming Lower Creeks; (c) Alabama in Alabama State, later becoming Upper Creeks; (d) Choctaw and Chickasaw in Mississippi; (e) Tuskegee, Upper Creeks; (f) Yamasee-Cusabo; (g) Muskogee of Alabama and Georgia; then more diversely, (g) the Natchez of Mississippi and (i) Calusa of Florida.

The Muskogean linguistic family has in turn been distantly linked to the Timucua, Yuchi and Tunican families, and more improbably to the Iroquois and Caddoans. The true Muskogeans had crystalized into the Creek, Seminole, Choctaw and Chickasaw by the early 19th century, when they removed to Indian Territory, now Oklahoma.

APALACHEE The Apalachee were once a large and powerful Muskogean tribe of northern Florida, numbering 7,000 people, who lived between the Aucilla and Ochlocknee rivers, around St. Marks. The Spanish gathered them into collective and defenseless mission towns, which were gradually destroyed by the Creeks and Yuchi (under British influence) from South Carolina, with a final invasion in 1702–1704. The remnant seems to have moved to Mobile Bay and then to Louisiana or Oklahoma, where a few remained in the 19th century, and a number of descendants are still reported in Rapides Parish, LA.

CHATOT This group was first contacted by the Spanish in 1539, west of the Apalachee on the lower reaches of the Apalachicola and Chipola rivers of northern Florida. They suffered the same fate as the Apalachee, and moved to Louisiana in the 18th century, where a few remained later on

the Sabine River, but nothing more is known of them. They perhaps numbered 1,000 in Spanish colonial days. Although geographically closest to the Apalachee, their linguistic relatives may have been the Yamasee and their associates.

HITCHITI This is a substantial group of Muskogean-speaking tribes that form a dialectic division of the family, divided originally into several tribes occupying the area near the Chattahoochee and Flint rivers in Georgia, also at various times the Apalachicola River in northern Florida. During the 18th century, they became associated with — and part of — the Lower Creeks, and ultimately shared their fortunes and fate. The original tribes were the Hitchiti proper, *Apalachicola*, *Sawokli*, *Okmulgee*, *Oconee*, *Tamali (Tamathli)*, *Chiaha*, *Mikasuki* and probably the *Osochi*. After forming the "Lower Creeks" during the 18th century, some Oconee and Tamathli, joined later by Mikasuki, moved to Florida, and have become one of the two Seminole groups still associated with southern Florida. After the removal of the Creeks to Oklahoma, a few Hitchiti, Apalachicola and Chiaha remained separate, but are now counted as part of Creek Nation.

ALABAMA The Alabama were a Muskogean tribe on the Alabama River, close to its junction with the Coosa and Tallapoosa rivers in Alabama. They formed with the Koasati a separate dialectic division of the family, and came to be regarded as part of the Upper Creeks, although some retained their separate identity. They probably absorbed two smaller tribes who may have been closely related, the *Tawasa*, once on the Chattahoochee River, and the *Pawokti* of the Choctawhatchee River. After 1763, they began a movement westward, which ultimately led in 1854 to the establishment of a reservation in Polk County, Texas, where they combined with the Koasati. Some moved with the general Creek emigration to Indian Territory, where descendants retain their identity near Weleetka, Okfuskee County. In 1700 they numbered perhaps 2,000; in 1944, 152 were returned as separate in Oklahoma, and 415 Alabama-Koasati were reported from Polk County, Texas, but largely of Alabama descent. The Texas Alabama-Coushatta (Koasati) numbered 800 in 1990, and 882 in 2000.

KOASATI or **COUSHATTA** This is a Muskogean tribe closely related to the Alabama, whose later history is associated with the area at the junction of the Coosa and Tallapoosa rivers, Alabama. The *Muklasa*, another group of that area (Montgomery County), may have been an associated tribe. During the 18th century they became politically part of the Upper Creeks, and ultimately removed as part of the Creeks to Oklahoma in the 19th century. Their descendants are found in Okfuskee and Hughes counties. However, before this move, a number had already settled on the Red, Sabine, Neches and Trinity rivers in Louisiana and Texas. A number later joined with the Polk County Alabama in Texas, and others settled in the Kinder-Elton area in Allen, Jefferson-Davis, Washington and St. Landry parishes, Louisiana. The Oklahoma Koasati numbered about 150 in 1950; the Alabama-Koasati of Texas, about 500 in 1970; and the Louisiana Koasati about 500 of mixed descent. Census 2000 reported 974. There is good reason to believe that the *Kaskinampo*, an ancient tribe reported by the explorers De Soto, and (later) Marquette and Joliet on the Tennessee River in northern Alabama were

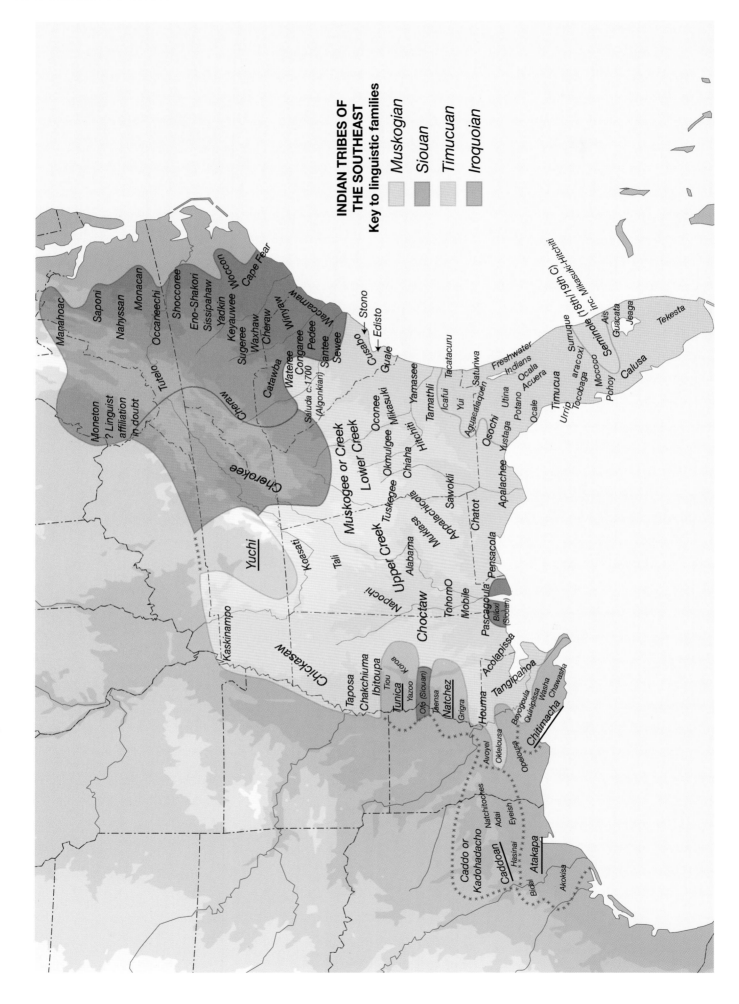

INDIAN TRIBES OF
THE SOUTHEAST
Key to linguistic families

Muskogian

Siouan

Timucuan

Iroquoian

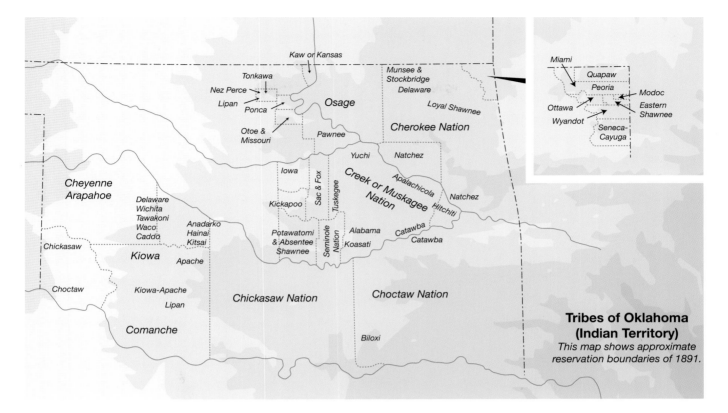

Tribes of Oklahoma (Indian Territory)
This map shows approximate reservation boundaries of 1891.

connected with the Koasati, and probably ultimately united with them or the Chickasaw.

TUSKEGEE Another Muskogean people, probably related to the Alabama group, are the Tuskegee. They were known at various times in several locations, mostly in Alabama, including the Tennessee River in the northern part of the state, on the Chattahoochee near Columbus, and near Fort Toulouse (Alabama Fort) on the junction of the Coosa and Tallapoosa rivers, when they established themselves as an Upper Creek faction. With removal to Oklahoma they finally settled around Beggs, where their descendants are counted as Creeks.

BILOXI A small Siouan enclave among the Muskogeans, located on the lower Pascagoula River and near Biloxi, Mississippi, the Biloxi were noted by the French explorers

Iberville and Bienville in 1699, but they may have come from the north not long before. The *Moctobi* and *Capinans* were possibly subgroups. Under French influence they moved to the Pearl River area until 1763, transferring later to the Red River country of Louisiana, and Angelina County, Texas. A few ultimately joined the Choctaw in Oklahoma and Louisiana. A number of their descendants are merged with the Louisiana Choctaw at Jena, LaSalle Parish, Lecompte, Rapides Parish and among the mixed Tunica-Avoyel-Ofo-Choctaw remnants in Avoyelles Parish — perhaps 100 or so of mixed descent. They never numbered more than a few hundred.

PASCAGOULA This is a tribe closely associated with the Biloxi, but perhaps of Muskogean connection, on the Pascagoula River in Jackson, George and Perry Counties, Mississippi. Visited by Iberville in 1699, they later moved to Louisiana with the Biloxi and merged with local Choctaw in the 19th century.

OFO The Ofo were a small tribe of probably Siouan extraction who are believed to have descended the Mississippi River by 1673 from somewhere in southwestern Ohio, where they were known at one time to the French as *Mosopelea*. By 1686 some of them were with the Taensa, and as late as 1784 had a separate village above Point Coupée, Louisiana. A remnant is supposed to be merged into a mixed group of Indian descendants near Marksville, Louisiana.

PENSACOLA A small Muskogean tribe, the Pensacola were apparently of the Choctaw dialectic division, who occupied Pensacola Bay in northwest Florida when first known to the Spanish in the 16th century. However, by the time the Spanish post at Pensacola was established in 1698, they had moved inland and presumably westward. Their remnants merged with other groups, perhaps the Choctaw. They probably never numbered more than a few hundred.

TRIBES OF THE SOUTHEASTERN WOODLANDS, c. 1600-1730

Linguistic and cultural boundaries are necessarily approximate; this sketch map is intended only as a general guide to distribution. Modern state boundaries are shown as broken lines, for orientation only. Note that the Caddoan family are included by some in the Plains cultural area, and that the linguistic affiliation of the Timucuan tribes is in doubt. Underlined names indicate small linguistic groups distinct from the larger groupings indicated by the shading key.

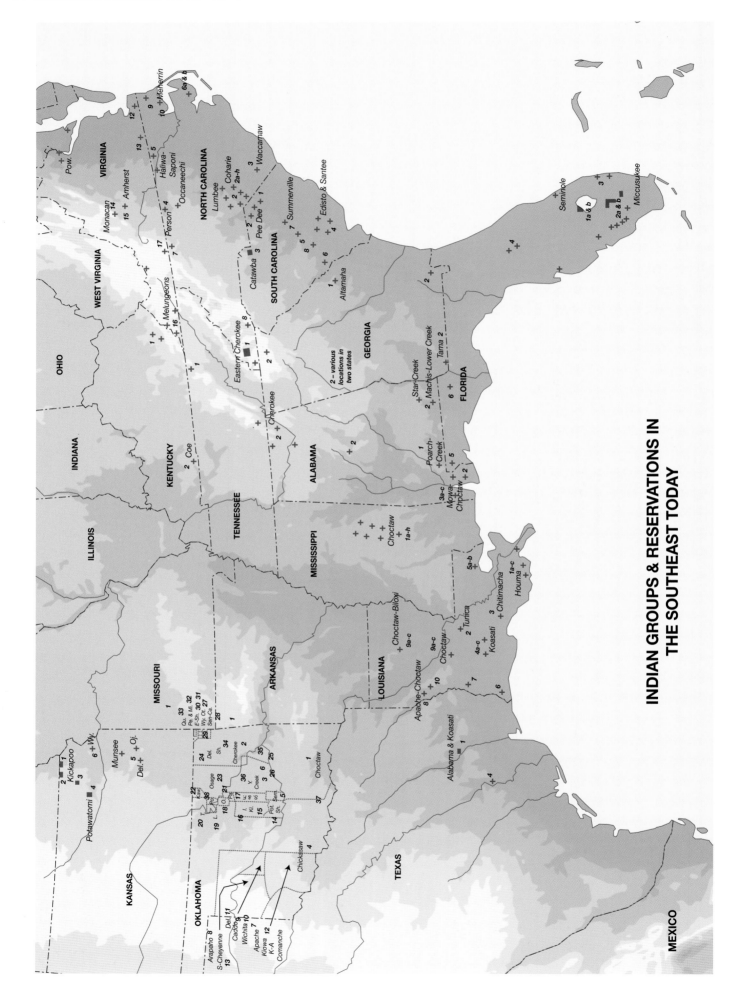

INDIAN GROUPS & RESERVATIONS IN THE SOUTHEAST TODAY

MOBILE This was the largest of a group of Muskogean tribes who occupied an area around Mobile Bay, Alabama, when first known to the Spanish, who inflicted heavy losses in a battle with these people in 1540. Later, they were farther north in Wilcox County, returning closer to Mobile post (the present city of Mobile) during the French occupation. They must have numbered several thousand in the 16th century, but perhaps only 1,000 by the mid-18th century. Their ultimate fate is unknown, but they perhaps merged with the Choctaw. The *Tohome* on the west bank of the Tombigbee River, Washington County, Alabama, and the *Naniaba* were probably subdivisions or closely related. They gave their name to "Mobilian," a trade jargon used in the Gulf region.

NAPOCHI A tribe reported living somewhere around the junction of the Tombigbee and Black Warrior rivers in Hale County, Alabama, by early Spanish expeditions was known as the Napochi. They may have become the Acolapissa, Quinipissa and Napissa of the 17th and 18th centuries, living in Mississippi and Louisiana.

CHAKCHIUMA These were a Muskogean people of the Choctaw group, known to Spanish explorers (1540-41) and, later, to French settlers in Louisiana. They seem to have lived around Leflore County in Mississippi at the junction of the Yazoo and Yalobusha rivers. During the 18th century they were at war with the Choctaw and Chickasaw, with whom their remnants probably united (or they may possibly have joined the group known as Houma). Two other groups of the same area were the *Taposa*, mentioned by Iberville (1699), living close to the Chakchiuma, and the *Ibitoupa* on the Yazoo

River in present Holmes County, Mississippi. These probably merged with the Choctaw.

HOUMA Houma were a Muskogean tribe possibly descended from the Chakchiuma. When first known to the French in the 17th century, they lived on the east side of the Mississippi River in Wilkinson County, Mississippi. Later, they established themselves near New Orleans, where they remained throughout most of the 18th century, near Ascension parish. During the 19th century, they seem to have moved into the more inaccessible areas of Terrebonne and Lafourche parishes, where as many as 6,000 of their descendants, virtually all French-speaking Creoles, are still reported around the Grand Caillou, Dulac and Golden Meadow areas. Claude Medford (1972 personal correspondence) reported one woman who knew some of their words and phrases. He also suggested that the Biloxi, Atakapa and Chitimacha combined with the Houma to form these descendants. In earlier times they may also have absorbed the Acolapissa tribes and the *Okelousa*, a tribe reported in the 18th century as having lived in Pointe Coupée Parish on the west side of the Mississippi in Louisiana, which may have been descended from an ancient people of De Soto's time. These are not the Opelousa of Atakapan connection. The 2010 Census reported 10,837 Houma.

ACOLAPISSA A Muskogean tribe reported by Bienville in 1699, located on the Pearl River, Louisiana, was the Acolapissa, but they may have descended from the Napochi of the 16th century. In 1702 they moved to Lake Pontchartrain. Another people, the *Tangipahoa*, on the river of that name in Louisiana, were probably an associate tribe. During the 18th century they seem to have moved to the Mississippi above New Orleans and merged with the Bayogoula and Houma. Near the beginning of the 20th century, a small Indian group was reported near Bayou Lacombe, St. Tammany Parish, Louisiana, which may have been of Acolapissa and/or Choctaw ancestry, but nothing has been heard of them recently.

BAYOGOULA These were a people of Bayou Goula, Iberville Parish, Louisiana, visited by Iberville in 1699. They seem to have been connected with the *Mugulasha* and *Quinipissa*, perhaps with the *Acolapissa*, as divisions of a single tribe numbering perhaps 1,500 in 1650. During the 18th century they seem to have merged with the Houma.

TAENSA The Taensa were a Muskogean tribe, related to the Natchez, who lived near present St. Joseph in Tensas County, Louisiana, and who were reported by La Salle in 1682. They moved several times during the 18th century, ultimately merging with the Chitimacha. Another group known as Little Taensa or *Avoyel*, apparently closely related, were mentioned by Iberville in 1699 in the neighborhood of Marksville, Avoyelles Parish, Louisiana. A small mixed-blood Indian remnant combined with Tunica, Ofo, Biloxi and Choctaw still survived in the area in 1980.

NATCHEZ This was the largest of a group of three tribes, including the Taensa and Avoyel, who spoke a divergent language of the Muskogean family, living close to the present site of the city of Natchez, Mississippi. After a bloody war with the French in 1729–30, they were defeated, and their remnants ultimately settled among the Upper Creeks and Cherokee. A

SOUTHEASTERN TRIBES, 20th CENTURY

Compare Oklahoma section with p. 73 sketch map of Indian Territory. This map includes communities today claiming Indian descent.

Key to abbreviations:

Del	=	Delaware
E.Sh	=	Eastern Shawnee
I	=	Iowa
K-A	=	Kiowa-Apache
Kaw	=	Kaw or Kansas
Ki	=	Kickapoo
L	=	Lipan
O	=	Otoe & Missouri
Ot	=	Ottawa
Pa	=	Pawnee
Pe&Mi	=	Peoria & Miami
Po	=	Ponca
Pot	=	Potawatomi
Qu	=	Quapaw
Sem	=	Seminole
Sen-Ca	=	Seneca-Cayuga
S&F	=	Sac & Fox
Sh	=	Shawnee
T	=	Tonkawa
Wy	=	Wyandot
Y	=	Yuchi

Left: Chickasaw Nation Council House, Tishomingo, Oklahoma. The large Southeastern "Five Civilized Tribes" were forced to move to Indian Territory—now Oklahoma—in the 1830s–1840s. They re-established themselves reflecting the institutions of the U.S. and customs of European-Americans of the South. A large number of the Creek, Cherokee, Choctaw, Chickasaw and some Seminole were of mixed descent by this period.

Below: Choctaw Nation Council Building, Tuskahoma, Oklahoma.

Right: Yoholo-Micco an Upper Creek chief wearing a "V" shaped flap on the pouch of a shoulder bag, as painted by Charles Bird King in Washington D.C. in 1826. The lithograph derived from King's painting was used in McKenney and Hall's Volume 2 of The Indian Tribes of North America, 1836–44 *and subsequent editions.*

Below Right: Menewa, a mixed blood "second chief" of the Lower Creeks wearing a beaded pouch with a "V" shaped flap when painted by Charles Bird King in Washington D.C. in 1826 from which this lithograph was made for McKenney and Hall's three-volume epic The Indian Tribes of North America. *He was wounded fighting the Americans and Cherokees at Horseshoe Bend in 1814, and despite later aiding the Americans against the Seminoles, he was forced to move beyond the Mississippi.*

number accompanied the Cherokee and Creek to Oklahoma, where a few descendants survive near Braggs and Concharty, Muskogee County. A few other descendants are said to be among the multi-ethnic so-called Summerville Indians of South Carolina. They were generally similar in culture to the Muskogeans. They developed a sun worship with a perpetual fire in a temple, and a caste system of suns, nobles, honored men and commoners or "stinkards." They perhaps numbered 3,500 before 1700, and were reported at about 386 in 2000 (with 87 identifying solely Natchez descent).

CHICKASAW An important Muskogean tribe of northern Mississippi and adjacent Tennessee and Arkansas, and at one time along the Tennessee River in northern Alabama were the Chickasaw. They were first mentioned by De Soto in 1541. In the 18th century they were first in contact — then in conflict — with French explorers and settlers during the colonial wars between France and Britain, when they remained consistent allies of the British. They fiercely repelled all invasions of their territory by other Indians and whites, or at least up to the time of the American Revolution.

In the early 19th century, the Chickasaw gradually ceded their lands to American settlers, and between 1836 and 1847, moved to Indian Territory, forming one of the so-called "Five Civilized Tribes," setting up a quasi self-governing nation with a capital at Tishomingo until the Civil War. During this period they seem to have completely modified to Euro-American rural culture, native culture, dress, with ancient institutions falling into disuse. Their descendants live in several southern Oklahoma counties, particularly Pontotoc, Johnston and Love, and adjacent towns and cities. They are today largely of mixed Indian, white and African-American descent, numbering 4,204 in 1910; 5,616 in 1970; 9,080 in 1990 and 20,887 in 2000, according to the Census. Most are now either Methodist or Baptist, and about 500 still speak the Chickasaw language. Their closest relatives are the Choctaw. The 2010 Census returned 19,685.

CHOCTAW The largest Muskogean tribe, living in present south-central Mississippi when noted by Hernando De Soto in 1540, were the Choctaw. More than a century passed before they were again contacted by whites, the French explorer Pierre Le Moyne d'Iberville. Like the Creeks, they grew corn as a staple crop, as well as beans, pumpkins, melons and sunflowers. They had more than 100 villages. Following French settlement in Louisiana in 1699, they formed a close association with the colony in their struggles with the Chickasaw and the British. During the American Revolution their warriors served on the side of the Americans, and in the War of 1812 they fought with Andrew Jackson against the Creeks. In 1805 they began a series of treaties with the United States. Finally, in 1830 at the Treaty of Dancing Rabbit Creek, they ceded most of their remaining lands in Mississippi for new lands in Indian Territory, now Oklahoma.

Before removal west they had partly modified to a Euro-American culture, adopting garden vegetables, poultry, hogs, cattle, horses and European clothing. By 1838 some 18,000 Choctaws were in Indian Territory, forming one of the so-called "Five Civilized Tribes," having a separate form of government based at Tuskahoma until adopted into the state of Oklahoma. The acculturation process begun in Mississippi continued during the 19th century, so that little native culture remained.

However, not all Choctaws moved to Oklahoma. A substantial number maintained themselves in several communities in Mississippi at Pearl River, Tucker and Bogue Chitto, Neshoba County; Red Water and Standing Pine, Leake County, Conehatta, Newton County; and Bogue Homo in Jones County. A few are also found near Jena and other places in Louisiana. The present Oklahoma Choctaw are found principally in McCurtain, Pittsburg, Le Flore, Pushmataha and Choctaw Counties, and in many towns and cities of southeastern Oklahoma; they were reported to number 19,000 in 1944. The Mississippi Choctaw were reported as numbering about 3,000 in 1950. A combined census of 23,562 in 1970 included Oklahoma, Mississippi and Louisiana Choctaw. The combined Census 2000 number was reported at 87,349, and 88,913 in 2010. The Oklahoma Choctaw are largely of mixed descent, with some white and African-American ancestry. Today there are three federally recognized Choctaw tribal entities, including the Choctaw Nation of Oklahoma (at least 50,000), the Jena Band of Choctaw in Louisiana (84) and the Mississippi Band of Choctaw (7,626). Other, smaller groups are seeking federal recognition. The Mowa Band numbers 1,572, and the Clifton Choctaw are reported at 76 members. As with the Chickasaw, the majority of the Choctaw are Baptist or Methodist, although some sing their hymns in the Choctaw language (there are very few fluent speakers, however). The economic base of the the Choctaw includes gaming facilities, some factories and (in Mississippi) lumber. There is a tribal museum, a monthly newspaper (*Bishinik*) and an official website.

MUSKOGEE or **CREEK** One of the largest and most important groups of the Muskogean family, comprising a loose confederacy of tribes closely related by language in Georgia and Alabama are the Muskogee. This group, called "Creeks" by the British, is in allusion to their villages being located close to rivers and creeks. They were generally divided into two branches. The "Upper Creeks" of Alabama were centered along the Alabama, Coosa and Tallapoosa rivers. They comprised the *Coosa* and *Tulsa* in Tallapoosa County; *Abihka* in Talladega County; *Atasi*, Macon County; *Pakana* and *Tukabahchee*, Elmore County; *Hilibi*, Tallapoosa County; *Holiwahali* (who probably included the *Kolomi*, *Fus-Hatchee*, and *Kanhatki*) in Elmore and Montgomery counties; and the *Okchai* and *Wakokai* in Coosa County. The "Lower Creeks" resided chiefly east of the Chattahoochee River in Georgia. There they comprised the *Kasihta*, close to the present site of Columbus, Georgia; *Coweta* on the Ocmulgee River, later moved near Columbus; and *Eufaula* in Clay County, Georgia, and Talladega County, Alabama (some also emigrated to Florida and became Seminoles). During the 18th century, both

Left: Choctaw warrior, c. 1735. Two French artists recorded lower Mississippi valley tribes in the early 18th century: Antoine du Pratz, the Natchez and Chitimacha, 1718–34; and A. de Batz, the Choctaw, Natchez, Tunica and others, 1732–35. This Choctaw, with warrior face paint, holds Chickasaw scalps on a pole.

the Upper and Lower groups were reinforced by other local Muskogean groups — the Alabama and Koasati affiliated with the Upper Creeks, while the Hitchiti groups joined the Lower Creeks, and non-Muskogean Yuchi and Shawnee also joined the confederacy at various times.

The Creeks and Muskogeans generally were heirs of Mississippian horticulture, involving the planting of maize, beans, cane, millet, tobacco and sunflowers. They gathered nuts and wild fruits, hunted deer and bison in the west, and stored nut oil and bear fat. Their settlements were formed of a main town with small villages surrounding them. The towns contained a "square," where public and religious gatherings were held. Most tribes were divided into matrilineal totemic clans. Houses were of logs and poles with mud or thatched roofs, sometimes palisaded villages. Later, log cabins of the white frontier-type were adopted. Also, there was considerable Euro-American material culture adopted from the early 18th century onward. The Green Corn festival, or *busk*, was a major religious rite, a form of which still survives among a number of conservative Oklahoma Creek communities. Each town or small tribe elected a chief or *micco*. Certain towns were consecrated to peace and were designated "white towns." Others, set apart for war ceremonials, were designated as "red towns." From a method of time-keeping with sticks to record the days a war party might be on the trail, the term "Red Stick Creeks" was sometimes used by whites.

Their history of contact with whites begins with De Soto's expedition in 1540, and further Spanish contacts were made in 1559 and 1567. Later, they became at first enemies but eventually allies of the British colonies of South Carolina and Georgia, and aided the British against the Apalachee (1703–1708) and Spanish Florida. After the Revolution, constant hostilities with Americans climaxed in the Creek War of 1813–14, with the defeat and submission of Weatherford, their principal leader, followed by the cession of a greater part of their lands to the United States. In 1832, they finally agreed to move to new lands in the west — Indian Territory, now Oklahoma. In 1836, the majority of Creeks made the journey, by land and river, in appalling conditions and at great cost in lives.

With remarkable fortitude, they adjusted to their new rich soil lands along the Arkansas River, and organized a quasi-government at Okmulgee, with a legislature composed of two houses — the House of Kings and the House of Warriors. The mixed-bloods, descended from early European traders, claimed the largest tracts of good farmlands, while the poorer full bloods sought the rural back country. The Civil War disrupted the Creek, now one of the so-called "Five Civilized Tribes." As slave-holders, they were mostly drawn in on the Southern side, and subsequently lost many possessions as whites pillaged their country. After the Dawes Act in the 1880s allowed tribal lands to be allotted with spare domain opened to white settlement, a substantial proportion of their lands passed to whites.

Left: Louisiana Choctaw woman with large burden basket on a chest tumpline, c. 1880. Almost all eastern basketry used simple plaiting technique and available materials. The Choctaw and Creek made fine river cane baskets of this "cow nose" shape. The Chitimacha made colorful baskets of narrow cane splints, the Cherokee and Catawba used mainly oak splints and the Northeastern tribes, ash.

The present descendants of the Creeks and their associates are in McIntosh, Hughes, Okmulgee, Creek and Muskogee counties, Oklahoma, formerly Creek Nation; also in the cities of Tulsa and Sapulpa and throughout Oklahoma and the United States. Their population prior to their removal from Georgia and Alabama was about 22,500; in 1857 they were reported to number 14,888. Later figures have been confused by the division into full bloods, Creeks by "blood," African-American freedmen and intermarried whites. In 1930, 8,760 were returned from Oklahoma; in 1950, 9,752; and in 1970, 17,004 including Alabama and Koasati. In 1990 the Creeks were reported to number more than 28,000, of which 16,000 were in Oklahoma and 1,800 were Poarch-Creeks near Atmore, Alabama. The combined number reported in the 2000 Census was 40,223, of which 36,654 were reported simply as "Creek." The descendants of those who remained in the east live near Atmore, southern Alabama, and were reported as numbering 2,228 in 2001. The census in 2010 returned 44,085 "Creek."

SEMINOLE The later Muskogean tribe of Florida consisted initially of immigrant Lower Creeks from the Chattahoochee and Flint rivers, Georgia — mostly Oconee and Mikasuki of the Hitchiti group, who occupied the area of northern Florida following the destruction of the Apalachee people. They seem to have been known as Seminole from about 1775. More Creeks and African slaves fled into Spanish territory from hostilities in the Alabama and Georgia areas as the newly independent United states pressured the Creeks for land. These later immigrants, mostly true Creeks (Muskogee speakers) from the Upper Creek villages, tripled the Seminole population following the "Red Stick War" of 1813–14.

The Americans invaded Florida in 1817–18, and destroyed African-American and Seminole towns in present Jefferson County. By 1819, Florida passed to the United States by treaty, and in 1823, the Seminoles agreed to move south to a tract of land in the center of Florida. In 1832 a number of chiefs agreed to move west to Indian Territory (now Oklahoma), and subsequently the majority were induced to follow or were captured and sent west. But a number continued with stubborn irregular warfare, although continually driven south (the Second Seminole War, 1836–1842). Their leader, Osceola, seized while under a flag of truce, was taken to Fort Moultrie, Charleston,

South Carolina, where he died in 1838. Although the majority of Seminoles had left Florida a few hundred were allowed to remain in the southern swamps, where a number still remain.

Those who were forced to move to Indian Territory formed one of the so-called "Five Civilized Tribes" in present Seminole County, Oklahoma, and their subsequent history is much the same as that of the neighboring Creeks. Two "square grounds" are still used for old Green Corn festivals and ball games. Most Seminoles are Baptist or Presbyterian, and are fully integrated into the economic life of the wider society of Seminole County. The Seminole numbered about 8,000 in 1980, and 12,431 according to the 2000 Census and 14,358 in 2010. In 2001 the Oklahoma Seminole were reported as numbering 13,642 and those whose ancestors had remained in Florida were returned as 2,817 Seminole and 550 Miccosukee, having officially separated in 1962. The Miccosukee (Mikasuki) descend from the old Hitchiti speaking branch of the tribe while the Seminoles are Muskogee speakers and descend from Upper Creeks.

The Florida Seminole remained largely independent from white influence until the early 20th century. They still occupy the Brighton, Immokalee and Big Cypress federal and state

Above: William McIntosh, a mixed-blood Creek (son of a Scottish trader and a Creek woman), became a leader of the pro-American faction of his people at the time of the British-American conflict of 1812. Some of his followers aided the Americans against the Creeks at Atasi in 1813 and Horseshoe Bend in 1814. His agreement to the sale of Creek lands to the Americans in 1823 led to his murder in 1825 for "selling the graves of their ancestors." The painting was done in 1820, although some doubt exists about the artist's name. Photograph courtesy of the Alabama Department of Archives, Montgomery, Alabama

Left: Three cloth bandolier bags, Seminole, Creek or Cherokee, c. 1830. All are decorated with beadwork, although the interpretations of the designs are unknown. Symbolic figures in abstract form are known to have been incorporated in similar bead embroidery from this period. From the permanent collection of the Montclair Art Museum, Montclair, New Jersey

Below Left: Seminole group, Florida, c. 1855. A few of the Seminole people escaped removal to Indian Territory by surviving in the dense southern Florida swamplands. Before the 20th century development of their distinctive patchwork quilting they had adopted European-type clothes, fashioned in unique styles, with horizontal bands of contrasting colored cloth stitched to coats and skirts.

Below: The Seminole Chief Billy Bowlegs, from a daguerrotype, c. 1885. A leader during the Third Seminole War (1856-58), he wears a silver headband with traded ostrich feathers, and bandoliers of braided wool and beadwork. Cambridge University Museum of Archaeology & Anthropology.

Opposite, Top: Seminole Chickee. This design probably evolved after the Seminoles' forced retreat into the Florida swamplands. They can still be seen in use. Frame and rafters were poles cut from small trees, effectively roofed with overlapping palmetto fronds. Living quarters were raised internal platforms, and kitchens were separate. Similar dwellings were probably once common throughout the Gulf Coast territories of extinct peoples such as the Calusa.

Opposite, Below Left: Warrior chief of the Second Seminole War, 1835–42, by which date Seminole costume was a unique blend of native and European materials. The belt, garters and perhaps the sash echo aboriginal prototypes seen on figures engraved on shell objects from Spiro Mound, Oklahoma, though by this date were made of trade wool and beads. The buckskin moccasins are a form of the classic Eastern one-piece center seam type. The bandolier and pouch (usually with a triangular flap) are probably syncretistic in origin, derived from both aboriginal and European models. The native breechcloth and leggings were made in both buckskin and cloth at this date. The cut of the cloth smock-coat is thought to be of European inspiration, though early reports suggest that buckskin prototypes existed in the Southeast. Crescentic gorgets of silver or other metals were traded or made from coins. The uniform insignia of the 18th- and early 19th-century European military officer, the gorget was widely popular among the Eastern peoples.

reservations, plus land along the Tamiami Trail and in recent times additional lands (small reservations) have been added at Dania, Coconut Creek, Ft. Pierce, and Tampa. The Florida Seminoles still perform the sacred Green Corn Dance; and have also developed colorful quilted costumes which have become popular with tourists. Africans who fought with Seminoles against the Americans in the early 19th century called "Maroons" are still found in the Bahamas, Coatunla, Texas, and Oklahoma.

YAMASEE The most important Muskogean tribe of eastern Georgia, the Yamasee were likely dialectically connected with the coastal tribes; they were always located inland on the Ocmulgee River above its junction with the Oconee. They are probably the "Altamaha" mentioned in 1540 and were in contact with Spanish missions in Florida in the 17th century, when some moved to St. Augustine. They appeared in South Carolina in 1715 when a war broke out between them and the English colonists, which sadly largely destroyed them. A few Yamasee ultimately joined with Seminoles and Creeks; a mixed-blood group has survived in Burke County, Georgia, until recent times, although their connection with the old Yamasee is still unverified. This group is sometimes reported as "Altamaha-Cherokee" and numbers 100 or so.

CUSABO A Muskogean people of the coast of South Carolina between Charleston and Savannah, Georgia, and along the Ashley, Edisto and Coosawhatchie rivers were the Cusabo. The

Guale on the Georgia coast, the lower Savannah River and St. Catherine's Island, in contact with the Huguenot colony at Port Royal from 1562, seem also to be connected with them. The Spanish from St. Augustine, Florida, made several attempts to missionize the Cusabo until the arrival of English settlers in 1670. A number of Cusabo assisted Barnwell in his expeditions against the Tuscarora in 1711–12, and against the St. Augustine mission in 1720. They seem ultimately to have joined the Catawba, Creek or Florida Indians, although a large multi-ethnic group known as the "*Summerville Indians*," who live in and around Dorchester County, South Carolina, may contain a portion of their ancestry, particularly from the Edisto River group. Spanish missionary influence on the Guale towns alternated with periods of warfare, thereby reducing them to submission until their virtual extinction in the 18th century.

CALUSA An Indian people of southern Florida, including all the groups south of Tampa Bay to the Florida Keys and in the interior around Lake Okeechobee were known as the Calusa. They were visited by the Spanish as early as 1513, but missionary attempts do not seem to have been successful and were finally abandoned in 1569. Thereafter no permanent settlement was ever made by the Spanish in that area. They were nomadic hunters and fishers, moving from place to place with nature's cycle. Despite their isolation, they once numbered close to 3,000, but are now extinct. A few remained until the Seminole came into Florida and some, no doubt, incorporated with them or finally crossed to Cuba. They are presumed to have been of Muskogean connection, perhaps closest to the Choctaw, or alternatively, to the Timucua. The following tribes were probably also connected with them: *Ais, Guacata, Jeaga* and *Tekesta*.

TIMUCUA or UTINA This is a collective term for the Indians of northern Florida, possibly of the Muskogean family or a divergent branch, probably a separate family. They lived in large houses grouped in permanent towns with extensive cornfields surrounding their villages. They probably numbered 13,000 when De Soto passed through their country in 1539, followed by French settlers who were supplanted in turn by Spanish in 1565. They were gradually conquered by the latter, and missionized by Franciscans. They rebelled in 1656 and suffered from pestilences that raged in the missions at various times. The remaining Timucua were concentrated into missions near St. Augustine, Florida, but continued to be harassed by northern Indians and the English. The last of them were in Volusia County, Florida, in 1736, probably ultimately becoming incorporated into the Seminole. The following tribes were perhaps associated with them: *Acuera, Fresh Water Indians, Icafiu, Mococo, Ocale, Pohoy, Potano, Saturiwa, Surruque, Tacatacuru, Tocobaga* and *Yustaga*.

YUCHI The Yuchi were an important Southeastern tribe of Georgia, who apparently lived in a number of locations, including present-day Tennessee, but they usually are associated with Georgia and South Carolina, particularly the Savannah River country and even northern Florida. At various times they lived with the Creeks on the Ocmulgee, Chattahoochee and Tallapoosa rivers during the 18th century. Their language is classified as a separate linguistic family or a very divergent Muskogean branch. In general culture they were similar to the Creeks. The Yuchi moved to Indian Territory in two main groups: one identified with the Lower Creeks (McIntosh party), which arrived at Fort Gibson in 1829; and a larger party with the Upper Creeks from Alabama in 1836. During the Civil War, they divided in sentiment between Union and Confederacy, basically echoing the old Lower and Upper Creek alliances. There were four Yuchi settlements in Indian Territory, near Depew, Kelleyville, Bristow and Mounds. In recent times, they have been concentrated around Sapulpa and Mounds, and were reported to number 1,216 in 1949, although often counted among the general Creek population, which probably accounts for the reduction to 302 reported by the 2000 Census. The Yuchi still have two squaregrounds where they hold annual Green Corn

Right: Timucua man, c. 1562. From paintings by Jacques Le Moyne of the Timucua peoples in the fortified towns of northern Florida, 1562–64. LeMoyne was cartographer and artist to the French Huguenot colony on the St. John River. The Timuca men had distinctive hairstyles, wore feather crowns and ear plugs, were heavily tattooed and seem to have used metal ornaments.

dances in summer, one near Bixby, the other near Kelleyville. The *Westo* and *Stono* may have been Yuchis in conflict with the Carolina settlers in 1664 and 1669–71, although a more recent theory suggests they may have been Erie refugees from western Pennsylvania.

TUNICA The Tunican linguistic family consisted of a small group of tribes that occupied the valley of the Mississippi, close to where the present states of Louisiana, Arkansas and Mississippi adjoin. They were composed of the *Koroa* on the lower Yazoo, but were often reported in other locations; *Yazoo*, also on that river; *Tiou* on the upper Yazoo (united with the Natchez after having been driven from their homes); *Grigra* on St. Catherine's Creek, Mississippi (also adopted by the Natchez); and the *Tunica proper*, a few miles north of the junction of the Yazoo River with the Mississippi.

They were probably visited by early Spanish and French explorers, and missionary priests were in

Above Left: Seminole woman sewing a colorful skirt, c.1950. The arrival of the hand-cranked sewing machine in the camps of the Florida Seminoles during the 1890s transformed their costumes using bands of horizontally sewn multi-colored cloth or "patchwork." The craft continues, and skirts and jackets are sold to tourists along the Tamiami Trail in southern Florida.

Above: Miccosukee Seminole woman working at her sewing machine making dolls with patchwork decoration. Postcard photograph c. 1980.

contact with them from 1699. They were usually firm friends of the French, and suffered at the hands of the Natchez as a consequence. After 1731, they gradually decreased in numbers, some remaining in their old haunts, others combining with other tribes, until some time between 1784 and 1803, when their combined remnants moved to an area near Marksville in Louisiana, near the Red River. Here, a small tribally and racially mixed group has survived until recent times. The whole group probably numbered about 2,500 before suffering the effects of European diseases, and by the early 18th century perhaps only a few hundred were left. The census of 1910 gave 48 "Tunica," and by 1970, about 200 Indian people of mixed descent are reported from Avoyelles Parish, Louisiana, including a few occupants of the old Marksville Reservation. They are, however, of Ofo, Avoyel, Biloxi and Choctaw, as well as Tunican ancestry. The extension of the language family to include the tribes other than the Tunica proper is largely circumstantial, although some authorities have suggested a connection with the Chitimacha and, perhaps, with the Atakapan tribes on the gulf coast of Louisiana.

Above Left: Seminole woman, c. 1930. Some still wear this hairstyle, combed over a cardboard frame extending from one side of the head. After about the age of 12, strings of multicolored glass beads are worn around the neck, with strings added for virtue or as gifts. After middle life they are sometimes removed, strand by strand, the last going to the grave with its wearer.

Left: Seminole dugout canoe. In the absence of tree bark of suitable quality, Florida and Gulf Coast peoples used simple hollowed tree trunk canoes with rounded or pointed ends. Until recently the Seminole made slender boats from single cypress logs, with stern platforms for poling through the swamps.

CHITIMACHA This is a group of three tribes forming a linguistic family who lived on the shores of Grande Lake, plus parts of the coast and delta regions of the Mississippi River in Louisiana. These include the *Chitimacha proper* of Grande Lake, *Chawasha* on Bayou La Fourche, and *Washa* in Assumption Parish. They went to war with the French in 1706 after the killing of St. Cosme, a missionary to the Natchez, in response to treachery against them. The war lasted 12 years, after which the eastern groups, Washa and Chawasha, settled near Plaquemine and gradually diminished. The Chitimacha at Grande Lake, however, retained a small reservation near Charenton, Louisiana, where a mixed-blood remnant has continued to live.

The population of the whole group may have exceeded 3,000 in 1650. The census of 1910 reported 69, and 51 in 1930. The Bureau of Indian Affairs reported 89 living on the Chitimacha Reservation, St. Marys Parish, in 1950. During the early 1990s a total count, including all descendents, found 720 enrolled members. The Census 2000 report is 1,001. They are a federally recognized tribe. There is a museum and a cultural complex, but the language of the Chitimacha is no longer spoken. They are famous for their basketry, and a few women have continued the craft until recent times. In pre-French times, and in common with others along the lower Mississippi, their houses were of palmetto leaves over a framework of poles. They hunted deer with bow and arrow or blowguns with cane darts, collected vegetable foods and planted maize and sweet potatoes. Linguists have linked them with the Tunica and Atakapa families into the Tunican stock, but this is largely speculative.

ATAKAPA A group of tribes who occupied the Gulf coast of Louisiana and eastern Texas from Vermillion Bay to Galveston Bay, are known as the Atakapa. They include the *Akokisa* on the Trinity River, Texas; the *Atakapa* proper on the Neches, Sabine and Calcasieu rivers; an *Eastern Atakapan* group on the Mermenton River; and Vermillion Bayou *Opelousa* near present Opelouses, Louisiana. Later the *Bidai*, *Deadose* and *Patiri* — small groups on the middle course of the Trinity River, Texas — were added.

They were first noticed by Spanish and French explorers, including Bernard de la Harpe, who carried some of them off to New Orleans in 1721. In 1779, the Eastern Atakapas helped Spanish expeditions against the British. However, they had sold most of their lands to the French Creoles by the early 19th century, and ultimately disappeared. The Atakapa in the Calcasieu Parish area near Lake Charles, Louisiana, held together longer, and the ethnologists Gatschet (1885) and Swanton (1907–1908) visited the few remaining members of the tribe and recorded their language. A few Atakapa descendents were reported in the early 20th century under derogatory terms — Creoles and "Sabines" — and today a group called Atakapa-Ishak of the area claim their ancestry. Of the Texas branches, nothing is known after about 1805. They are perhaps distantly related to the Tunica and Chitimacha.

ADAI Adai were a Caddoan tribe formerly located near present Robeline, Natchitoches Parish, Louisiana. Iberville found them in 1699. Missions were established among them, but destroyed by the French in 1719. By 1805 they were at Lake Macdon near the Red River, and in about 1830, the last of them joined other southern Caddoans and merged into a composite group "Caddo," losing separate identity. Another small tribe, the *Eyeish*, probably connected to them linguistically, lived on Ayish Creek, a tributary of the Sabine in northeastern

Above: A postcard showing a Seminole dugout canoe.

Below: Florida Seminole man's dress mid-19th century before the development of patchwork decoration. He wears an ostrich feather in his turban and a beaded baldric. He is not the famous "Billy Bowlegs," the Seminole hero of the Third Seminole War 1856–1857.

Texas. They were visited by the Spanish in 1542, but by the early 19th century they were extinct or had joined other related groups. The Adai, Eyeish, Natchitoches, Hasinai and Kadohadacho constituted the southern branch of the Caddoan family.

NATCHITOCHES A small confederacy of Caddoan tribes in northwestern Louisiana, principally along the Red River from the present city of Natchitoches to Shreveport were known as the Natchitoches. The *Yatasi* were the largest subtribe of the group. In 1700 Bienville reported 400–450 members. Later they descended the Red River closer to French settlements, and probably united with French Creoles or joined their relatives the Hasinai in Texas. They are no longer a separate group.

HASINAI This is a Caddoan confederacy of small tribes of northeastern Texas, including the *Anadarko* and *Hainai*, living on the upper Neches, Trinity and Angelino rivers in Nacogdoches, Rusk and Cherokee Counties. Encountered by the Spanish in the 16th century, and by survivors of the la Salle expedition in 1687, they were missionized by the Spanish after 1690. They later moved west to the San Antonio area, to a reservation on the Brazos River in 1855. By 1859, their remnants were united with the Kadohadacho as a composite group called "Caddo" in southern Oklahoma, where their descendants remain. They perhaps numbered 3,000 in 1700, but are now not reported separately from Caddo.

KADOHADACHO or **CADDO** This is the largest of the southern Caddoan confederacies who lived in northeastern Texas and adjacent Arkansas and Oklahoma, particularly around the Great Bend of the Red River near present Texarkana. They were probably known to the Spanish and French before the establishment of La Harpe's trading post in about 1719, which cemented permanent white contact with them. They provided a bulwark against the northern Indians, and suffered as a consequence, withdrawing to the vicinity north of Shreveport, Louisiana. In 1835 the Caddo ceded their lands to the United States and moved to Texas, joining the Hasinai, Cherokee or Chickasaw. Those with the Hasinai on the Brazos River moved in 1859 to Indian Territory, where their descendants still live in the vicinity of Binger, Caddo County, now Oklahoma. They perhaps numbered 2,400 in 1700. In 1872, the composite "Caddo" including Natchitoches and Hasinai numbered 392; in 1944, 1,165 Caddo were reported, and 1,207 in 1970, although now mostly of mixed descent through intermarriage with Euro-Americans and Wichitas. In 1992, the group numbered 3,371, and in 2000, 2,675. Of that number, 72 were given as the Caddo Indian Tribe of Oklahoma and 301 Caddo Adais Indians, Louisiana.

They were originally a sedentary people, cultivating their fields and raising corn, beans and pumpkins like other tribes of the Southeastern Woodlands. They did take to horses, however, and raised livestock. Although now rural Americans, they still hold tribal dances near Binger and join the inter-tribal American Indian Exposition held annually at Anadarko, Oklahoma.

CHEROKEE This is a large, important and well-known tribe who once occupied the southern Appalachian Mountains, the Great Smoky Mountains and valleys of the upper Kanawha, Savannah, Hiwassee, Tuckasegee, Coosa and Tennessee rivers in present eastern Tennessee, western North Carolina and northern Georgia and Alabama, comprising an area of 40,000 square miles (104,000 sq km). Echota, a settlement on the south bank of the Little Tennessee River, seems to have been

Above: Seminole man, c. 1880. Turbans were popular with Seminoles and men of other Southeastern tribes during the 19th century; figurines recovered through archaeology may show their use in aboriginal times. The form shown was made by folding and wrapping a commercial woolen shawl; they were sometimes decorated with silver and plumes.

Right: Caddoan grass house. Early French and Spanish reports indicate long use of this type by ancestors of the Wichita and Caddo of Arkansas, Oklahoma, Texas and Louisiana, in semi-permanent villages of up to 80 houses. A circle of heavy cedar beams supported a secondary circle of lighter poles leaning in against them, then drawn and tied together at the apex. Horizontal ribs secured the construction, with long grass thatch tied to the ribs in overlapping layers. Communal lodges may have been as tall as 25 feet (8 m), family lodges smaller. They have not been in use since about 1900, but there are a few reconstructions at "Indian City," Anadarko, Oklahoma.

Opposite: Cherokee lands of the 18th and 19th centuries.

Below: Seminole men and women in front of Chickees wearing dress decorated with patchwork, c. 1933. Postcard photo.

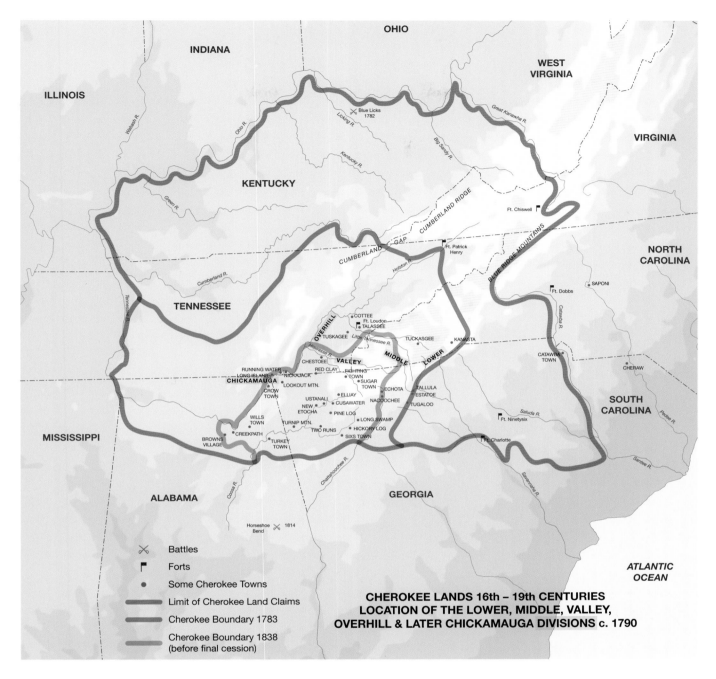

CHEROKEE LANDS 16th – 19th CENTURIES
LOCATION OF THE LOWER, MIDDLE, VALLEY,
OVERHILL & LATER CHICKAMAUGA DIVISIONS c. 1790

considered the capital of the nation. They were first known to Europeans following De Soto's expedition in 1540, and later held a great mountain area between the English settlements on the Atlantic coast and the French and Spanish garrisons along the Ohio and Mississippi. However, unlike their distant relatives, the Iroquois, they lacked the political cohesion to assert a balance of power, and were often factionalized and divided among themselves. There seem to have been a number of minor dialects spoken within the group, but their distant linguistic connection with the Iroquoian family has been firmly established, although their separation from the parent stock may have taken place more than 2,000 years ago.

The Cherokee had more than 60 villages, which were connected to the outside world by seven main groups of trails. By these trails the Cherokees could visit the Iroquois, Chickasaw, Catawba and the Gulf tribes. Early Cherokee dwellings were built of poles covered inside and out with interwoven twigs or mixed clay and grass, and some structures housed several families. However, by the 18th century, Cherokees had largely adopted the

log cabin styles of white frontier settlers, along with other European material and social influences. At the center of each village was a circular council house where religious, political and social gatherings took place. They were a farming people, growing maize, beans, squash, pumpkins and tobacco, mostly controlled by the women. They also were gatherers, hunters and skillful fishers. They used bows and arrows and reed blowguns before the introduction of firearms. Pottery and basketry were expertly made, as were elaborately carved pipes, some of which have been preserved in museum collections. Europeans introduced horses, pigs and other farm animals, and the Cherokee became accomplished at husbandry.

The religious and political activities of the people were organized by the White Peace Organization, the rituals of war by the Red War Organization. Each had a complex round of ceremonials, including six great festivals held in the council house. These included Planting Corn, First Green Corn and Ripe Green Corn; Feasts of the New Moon and of Reconciliation; the New Fire Rite; and Bounding Bush Feast. The Red War Organization

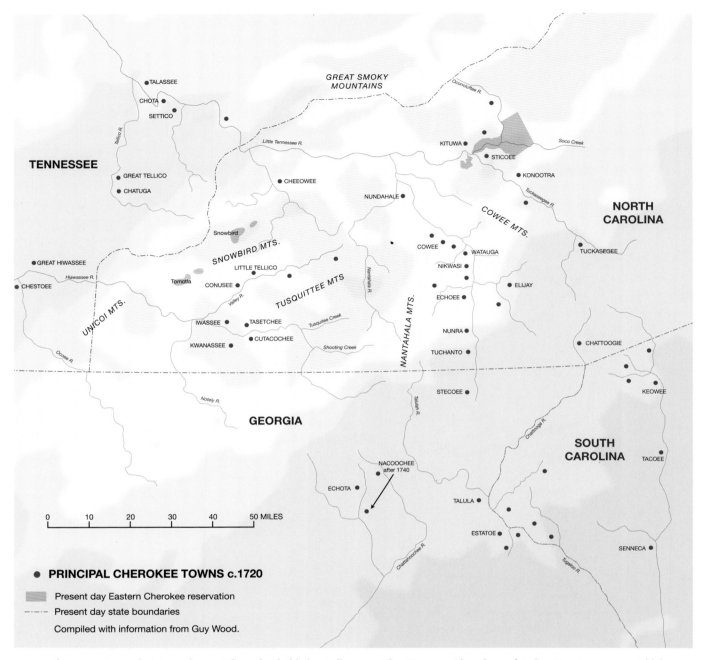

PRINCIPAL CHEROKEE TOWNS c.1720

Present day Eastern Cherokee reservation

Present day state boundaries

Compiled with information from Guy Wood.

arranged war parties and victory dances. They also held the Ball Game indigenous to eastern North America, a rough team game still played by Eastern Cherokees.

The Cherokee were mostly on the side of the French in the French and Indian War and on the side of the British in the Revolutionary War. They became the object of hatred for land-hungry settlers, and peace was not restored until 1794. From this time until their removal to Indian Territory they suffered a period of increasing political pressure and cessions of lands, which resulted in groups moving to Arkansas and Texas. Finally, following the Treaty of New Echota in 1835, a large portion of the tribe, including most of the mixed-bloods under John Ross, were forcibly removed to Indian Territory during 1838–39. This journey, which involved intense suffering and the loss of a quarter of their numbers has been known ever since as "The Trail of Tears." A number of Cherokee escaped removal, and in 1889 a reservation was formally established around a number of conservative communities near the Great Smoky Mountains, North Carolina. This is known as the Qualla Reservation of the Eastern Cherokees.

The Western Cherokee of Indian Territory, now Oklahoma, contained the highest percentage of the most acculturated members of the tribe, operating schools, newspapers and churches, as well as owning African-American slaves. They also included a number of conservatives who had moved west ahead of the main body in 1838. The Western Cherokees had a quasi-national government and were known as one of the "Five Civilized Tribes" of Oklahoma. As supporters of the Confederacy during the Civil War, they suffered war casualties, and retribution under the 1866 Treaty, but they have maintained a substantial population within their old area in northeastern Oklahoma. In 1920, 36,432 Cherokees were reported in Oklahoma, and in 1930, 45,238. In 1970 they were returned as 66,150, which included the Eastern band, separately returned as 1,963 in 1930. The present Oklahoma Cherokee (about 285,476 in 2010 Census) are largely of mixed descent and live predominantly in Cherokee, Adair and Delaware counties, particularly around Tahlequah, their 19th-century capital. However, members of the tribe live throughout the state and widely across the country, and have (mostly) become one of the best integrated Indian people

CHEROKEE IN THE WEST AND THE TRAIL OF TEARS

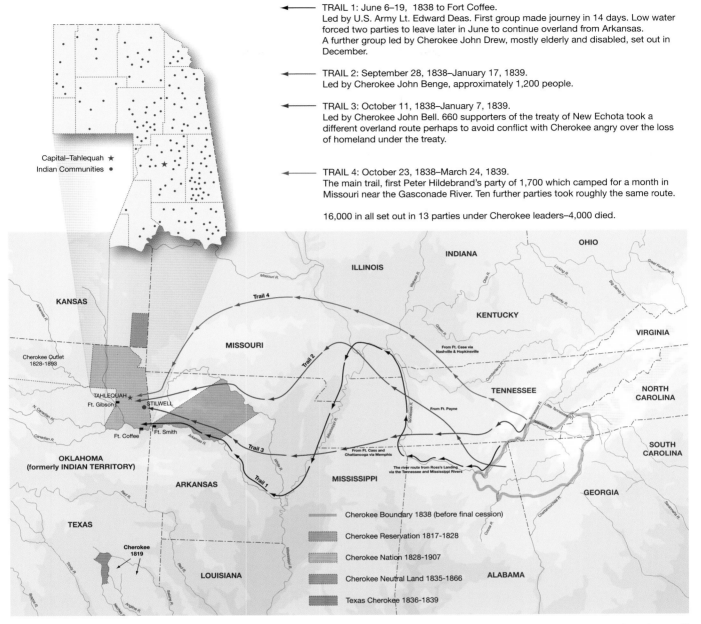

TRAIL 1: June 6–19, 1838 to Fort Coffee.
Led by U.S. Army Lt. Edward Deas. First group made journey in 14 days. Low water forced two parties to leave later in June to continue overland from Arkansas. A further group led by Cherokee John Drew, mostly elderly and disabled, set out in December.

TRAIL 2: September 28, 1838–January 17, 1839.
Led by Cherokee John Benge, approximately 1,200 people.

TRAIL 3: October 11, 1838–January 7, 1839.
Led by Cherokee John Bell. 660 supporters of the treaty of New Echota took a different overland route perhaps to avoid conflict with Cherokee angry over the loss of homeland under the treaty.

TRAIL 4: October 23, 1838–March 24, 1839.
The main trail, first Peter Hildebrand's party of 1,700 which camped for a month in Missouri near the Gasconade River. Ten further parties took roughly the same route.

16,000 in all set out in 13 parties under Cherokee leaders–4,000 died.

Capital–Tahlequah ★
Indian Communities •

Cherokee Boundary 1838 (before final cession)
Cherokee Reservation 1817-1828
Cherokee Nation 1828-1907
Cherokee Neutral Land 1835-1866
Texas Cherokee 1836-1839

in American society. The use of Sequoyah's alphabet in their schools during the 19th century was a major reason why the Cherokee rapidly became a literate people.

The Eastern Cherokee were a more conservative portion of the tribe until recent times. The present population is 8,166 (according to the 2000 Census), with a number of relatively full-blood communities. They have retained the Ball Game (played by each man with two sticks to catch the ball, the object being to get the ball through a goal); old games, dances and basketry are seen at their annual Cherokee Indian Fair; and they operate a reconstructed Oconaluftee Indian Village and museum. However, a now more dominant mixed-blood element in the main Cherokee village has exploited the local tourist trade with the provision of "fake" Indian attractions in recent years. Both Eastern and Western Cherokee also operate outdoor dramas, called *Unto These Hills*, in an attempt to show their own version of Cherokee history. Besides the two main bodies of the tribe, substantial numbers of rural people — in Tennessee particularly — also claim their ancestry. In 1990, the Cherokee were reported to number 122,000, and many more claimed their blood. That number

increased to 281,069 in the 2000 Census. A relatively small number, about 13,000 still speak their language in Oklahoma, one of the few thriving Indian tongues outside the Southwest.

The primary economic activities of the Cherokee living on reservations include oil and gas sales, gaming, ranching, logging and arts and crafts.

EASTERN SIOUANS

A number of ancient tribes in the central eastern states of the United States are now included in an eastern branch of the Siouan linguistic family, largely on circumstantial evidence based on old historical associations. The linguistic position of the Catawba is well known as a divergent Siouan branch; they plus Sara, Sugeree, Waxhaw, Wateree and Woccon are now sometimes considered sufficiently divergent from Siouan to be regarded as a sub-family Catawban. However, a vocabulary collected from Tutelo descendants among the Grand River Iroquois in the 19th century, thought to be of Siouan extraction and much closer to the Plains languages, suggests an extensive distribution of old tribes of the Piedmont region of Virginia and the Carolinas who

may have been Siouan in speech. The Tutelo and their Saponi kinsfolk incorporated a number of remnant splinter groups before seeking refuge among the Iroquois. The formation and limits of the grouping are by no means fully accepted, however. The total population of the whole group (exclusive of Catawba) was perhaps no more than 6,000 in the 17th century. The ethnologist James Mooney suggested that the later Robeson County Indians (now called *Lumbee*) of North Carolina were probably of mixed Eastern Siouan ancestry. This large and probably multi-ethnic people have not, as yet, been recognized by the U.S. Government as "Indians," and were reported to number over 66,000 in 2010.

MANAHOAC This was a small tribe, possibly of Siouan extraction, who lived about the upper Rappahannock River in northern Virginia, numbering perhaps 1,000. They apparently joined the combined Saponi, Occaneechi and Tutelo, but nothing else seems to be known of them after 1728.

MONACAN A group of small tribes who held the upper valley of the James River in Virginia are known as Monacan.

Above, Left and Right: Cherokee men, probably the mixed bloods Moses Price and Richard Justice, painted by William Hodges in London in 1790–91, when they accompanied William Augustus Bowles during an "unofficial" delegation of Creeks and Cherokee to England in an attempt to re-establish commercial and military activity between the British and the Southern tribes, following the Revolution. Courtesy of the Royal College of Surgeons, London, U.K.

Below Left: Buckskin moccasins, Cherokee or Creek, c. 1830. Typical Southeastern style beadwork. Courtesy John Painter.

Below Right: Cherokee Nation Capitol Building, Tahlequah, Oklahoma.

First contacted by colonists in 1607, they were still noted separately as late as 1702. A few people of Amherst County, Virginia, still claim their ancestry. They may have been of Siouan stock.

TUTELO Tutelo is a name given to several combined tribes of Virginia, but specifically to those people around Salem, Virginia. Their remnants, along with others, were settled at Fort Christanna on the Meherrin River in 1714, and ultimately journeyed north to be formally adopted by the

Cayuga in New York in 1753. Later their descendants moved to the Six Nations Reserve in Ontario, where the last full blood Tutelo died in 1871, and the last speaker, John Key, in 1898 — though not before their language was recorded.

SAPONI A tribe originally from near Lychburgh, Virginia, thought to be of the Siouan family due to their association with the Tutelo, was known as the Saponi. It is thought that some merged with the Tutelo at Fort Christanna before they finally united with the Iroquoian Cayuga in New York State in 1753. However, two considerable groups of mixed-descent people survive not far from their old territory across in North Carolina in Person, Warren and Halifax Counties. Called *Haliwa*, these people claim Saponi ancestry. It is also possible that they have left an element among the modern Lumbee. A splinter group of Haliwa live near Lancaster, Pennsylvania. The 2000 Census reported 3,452 Haliwa-Saponi.

NAHYSSAN This was a small tribe found by John Lederer in 1670 on the Staunton River, Virginia. Their history was probably essentially similar to that of the Saponi and Tutelo.

OCCANEECHI A small tribe who lived near Clarksville in Mecklenburg County, southern Virginia, was the Occaneechi. They seem ultimately to have joined the Saponi and Tutelo in the 18th century, and nothing further is known of them. They are thought to have been of Siouan stock by their association with the Tutelo. A number of people in North Carolina still claim descent.

CHERAW or **SARA** This is a tribe originally located close to Chattooga Ridge, in the northwestern corner of what is now South Carolina, when first contacted by Spanish explorers. In 1670 John Lederer reported that they were on the Yadkin River, North Carolina, and later moved near the southern boundary of Virginia. The last of them seem to have joined the Catawba, and a number may possibly have merged with the Indians of the Lumber River. They are thought to have been of Siouan connection, and numbered 510 in 1715. The *Yadkin* reported on the river of the same name in 1674 may have been the same or a closely related people.

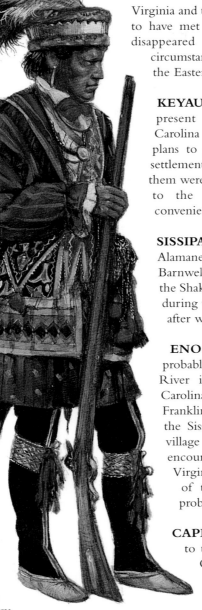

Above: Cherokee chief c. 1825. The ceremonial dress of Southeastern leaders at the time of removal to Indian Territory mixed European materials with native styles. Moccasins remained the eastern center-seam type. Cloth or occasionally buckskin leggings with front seams may have been native derived. This European style coat has an open front and large collar, and the cloth turban features a silver band and imported feathers. Some Cherokee, Creek and Seminole triangular flap bandolier pouches survive, decorated in unique curving symmetrical beadwork designs of an almost African quality. One example has gold-plated beads.

MONETON An ancient tribe west of the Blue Ridge in Virginia and the Kanawha River, West Virginia. They seem to have met Europeans first in 1671, but subsequently disappeared or merged with other tribes. On circumstantial evidence, they have been grouped with the Eastern Siouan tribes.

KEYAUWEE A tribe found by Lawson in 1701 near present High Point, Guildford County, North Carolina are known as Keyauwee. Despite reported plans to join the Saponi and Tutelo closer to the settlements near Albemarle Sound, the last reports of them were in 1761, when their town was located close to the boundary of the two Carolinas. For convenience they are classified as Eastern Siouans.

SISSIPAHAW This group lived on the Haw River, Alamanee County, in North Carolina. Lawson and Barnwell noted them, and later connected them with the Shakori. They apparently united with other tribes during the Yamasee War of 1715 against the English, after which nothing is known of them.

ENO-SHAKORI The Eno-Shakori were probably two separate tribes: the Eno on the Eno River in Orange and Durham counties, North Carolina, and the Shakori in Vance, Warren and Franklin counties, who may have been identical to the Sissipahaw. They apparently combined in one village called *Adhusheer* in about 1700. Although encouraged to join other groups closer to the Virginia settlements for protection, the last report of them was in South Carolina, when they probably united with the Catawba.

CAPE FEAR INDIANS This is the name given to the Indians on the Cape Fear River, North Carolina, who were probably known to early voyagers and were friendly to early European settlements in the area. In 1711–12, their warriors accompanied Barnwell against the Tuscarora, and later aided the whites against the Yamasee in 1715. They probably numbered several hundred in 1600, and about 200 in 1715. A few of the modern so-called *Summerville Indians* of South Carolina claim their ancestry.

WACCAMAW These were a small group of Indians, probably of the Siouan family, who lived on the Pee Dee River, South Carolina, near the border with North Carolina, about 100 miles (160 km) northeast of Charleston. The *Woccon* may have been a division of the same people. It is possible that a number of their descendants are included in the Lumbee of Robeson County, North Carolina, and about 1,536 people of mixed descent near Wilmington, North Carolina (in Columbus and Bladen counties), perpetuate the name "Waccamaw." The *Winyaw* were very probably connected with them in ancient times.

Top: Sequoya or George Gist, a Cherokee with mixed German descent. He invented the syllabary that bears his name and was submitted to the Cherokee leaders for their approval in 1821. Its adoption led to thousands being able to read and write within a few years. He was born about 1760 and died in Mexico in 1843 searching for lost members of his tribe. From a lithograph by J.T. Bowen, Philadelphia, 1836–44, in McKenney and Hall's History of the Indian Tribes of North America.

Above: John Ridge, Cherokee son of Major Ridge, a distinguished mixed blood Cherokee chief. The family name apparently derives from the Cherokee "one who follows the ridge." He acted as his father's secretary after his education in Tennessee and Connecticut and was a contributor to the Cherokee Phoenix and Advocate. After the Cherokee removed to Indian Territory in 1838–1839, the major, his son, and Elias Boudinart — all leaders of the Treaty Party — were killed by adherents of the National Party, John Ross's party, for their acquiescence to the removal and its consequences, on

June 22, 1839. From a lithograph by J.T. Bowen, Philadelphia, 1836–44, in McKenney and Hall's History of the Indian Tribes of North America.

Top: William Augustus Bowles, American Loyalist at the time of the American Revolution, married into the Lower Creeks and visited Great Britain twice in the 1790s. Painted by Thomas Hardy while in London, wearing wampum and other dress accessories of the Creek Indians of the period.

Above: Eastern Cherokee man and woman preparing and making cane baskets, Qualla Reservation, North Carolina, c. 1950. Cherokee baskets are still made from white oak, river cane and recently honeysuckle and various dyeing and decorating materials. Cane is split into splints, then peeled and trimmed, and finally plaited into a variety of basket shapes using wickerwork, checkerwork and twilling techniques. Post card of Oconaluftee Indian village, Cherokee Historical Association.

Right: Cherokee log cabin, c. 1840. Eighteenth-century association with Carolina settlers led to the gradual replacement of houses built of vertically set interwoven poles, covered inside and out with clay mixed with grass, by the log cabins typical of white frontier settlers. A few Eastern Cherokee in North Carolina still used stone-chimneyed log houses until recent times.

PEDEE A small tribe of supposed Siouan connections who lived on South Carolina's Great Pee Dee River, the Pedee were most probably closely related to the Cape Fear and Waccamaw. The name Pedee is used by Lumbees living in Marlboro and other counties of South Carolina, but has no connection with the old Pedee.

WATEREE Probably the most powerful tribe of central South Carolina as far back as the time of the Spanish settlements at St. Helena. They lived on the Wateree River, below present Camden. Although they aided Barnwell against the Tuscarora, their involvement in the Yamasee War of 1715 caused their ultimate decline. But they remained as a separate tribe until 1744, when they sold their remaining lands to a white trader and disappeared from history. Other small tribes who survived up to the Yamasee War period, and who are assumed to be connected in the Eastern Siouan linguistic group in South Carolina, were the *Santee*, of the Santee River; *Sewee*, near Moncks Corner, Berkeley County; *Congaree*, on the Congaree River near Columbia; *Sugeree*, in York County; and *Waxhaw*, in Lancaster County. They all suffered because of the Yamasee War, some being sold into slavery; others emigrated to Florida or united with the Catawba, to whom most may have been related. A group of mixed-blood people called *Summerville Indians* — descended from Winyaw, Edisto and others — survives in Dorchester County and probably contains their ancestry.

CATAWBA or **KATAPU** The largest of the Siouan tribes of the east, and the only one of the whole group to survive into the 20th century under their old name. Their language seems to have formed a divergent Siouan branch, now called Catawban, which possibly extended to include other tribes, such as the *Santee*, *Congaree*, *Sewee* and *Sugeree* — small tribes whose remnants seem to have merged with the Catawba during the 18th century. They were probably contacted by the Spanish in 1566–67; and in 1701 John Lawson found them on the Catawba River near the present state boundary between North and South Carolina. At constant war with the Iroquois and Shawnee, they were usually friendly with the English of South Carolina, aiding them against the Tuscarora in 1711-13, and later against the French and northern Indians.

Smallpox reduced them in 1738 and 1759, and they were less important thereafter, although they served as scouts for the Americans in the Revolution. They continued to decline in numbers but obtained a reservation in York County near Rock Hill, South Carolina, a portion of which they still occupy. During the 19th century, a few Catawba journeyed west: some settled near Scullyville, Oklahoma, some in Arkansas and a few with the Mormons in Colorado (about 60 reported recently).

The York County Catawba numbered 490 in 1780; 450 in 1822; 120 in 1881; 166 in 1930; and 300 in 1970. By 1990 the Indian population on reservation had fallen to 124, but 2,480 had enrolled in 2000. By then the tribe had received nonprofit corporation status and was a federally recognized entity. The tribe also filed legal claims for restitution of its original 144,000-acre (58,000 ha) reservation, granted during the colonial era. They were awarded $50 million in 1993. The present Catawba are of mixed blood. The last full-blood, Robert Lee Harris, died in 1954, and the last fluent speaker of their language, Chief Sam Blue, in 1959. In 1690 the Catawba probably numbered 4,000. They were skillful in making pottery and baskets.

LUMBEE The collective name given to a large body of people claiming Indian descent centering in Robeson County, North Carolina and adjoining counties and extending across into South Carolina. They were once known by the derogatory term "Croatan." Subgroups include the so-called Coharies (Sampson Co. N.C.), Smilings, Sinkers, Brookses, Martins, Cherokees (Hoke Co.) all in North Carolina; Blues (Marion, Dillon, and Marlboro Cos. S.C.) and Shakories (Horry Co. S.C.). Although recognized as a separate people by the state of North Carolina in 1885, the federal government has continued to refuse their recognition as an Indian people and thus any entitlement to federal (BIA) services as Indians. Having no surviving Indian language or place-names in their locations, some doubts exist that such a large number of Indian descendants could have emerged from the depleted tribes of the region of colonial times. However, that some Indian families survived to the mid-18th century has been demonstrated by the historian Wesley White and the studies of John Swanton and James Mooney of the Smithsonian Institution who have suggested that they may be descended from the remnants of the Siouan tribes of the region, Cheraw, Keyauwee, and Waccamaw, however the Eastern Cherokees of N.C. refuse to regard them as Indians. They were consistently reported to number 30,000 during the 20th century; the census of 2000 gave 55,000, and of 2010, 66,000.

SUMMERVILLE The collective name given to a number of groups claiming Indian ancestry in South Carolina centering in Colleton, Dorchester, Berkeley, Richland, Sumter, Orangeburg and other counties. They formerly went by several derogatory local names such as Brass Ankles, Buckheads, Turks, Red Bones, Goins and Red Legs; but now known as Edisto River, Crane Pond (Holly Hill), Creeltown, Four Holes, Varnertown and Beaver Creek communities.

Their Indian ancestry is likely to have come from the remnant Siouan tribes of the 18th century frontier, Pedee, Wateree, Cape Fear, Santee and Winyaw; also perhaps Yuchi and Natchez. They are usually referred to as "tri-racial," being of mixed European, Afro-American and Indian origin. Some have obtained state recognition as Indian but not federal. During the 20th century they were collectively reported to number about 5,000 people.

PLAINS AND PRAIRIE

Language family and tribe	Meaning/origin of tribal name, where known
Algonkian★ (except where noted):	
Plains Cree	–
Plains Ojibwa	–
Sarsi (Athabascan)	"not good"
Blackfoot or Blackfeet	English, "black moccasins"
Gros Ventre or Atsina	"gut people"
Assiniboine or Stoney (Siouan)	"one who cooks with hot stones"
Cheyenne	"red talkers"
Arapaho	"trader"
Siouan (except where noted):	
Sioux or Dakota	"little adders" (Ojibwa) "allies" (Dakota)
Mdewakanton Sioux	"spirit lake dwellers"
Wahpekute Sioux	"leaf shooters"
Wahpeton Sioux	"village in the leaves"
Sisseton Sioux	"swamp villagers"
Yankton Sioux	"dwellers at the end"
Yanktonai Sioux	"little dwellers at the end"
Teton Sioux	"dwellers on the prairie"
Crow	"bird people"
Mandan	Dakota name
Hidatsa or Minitaree	"willows"
Arikara or Ree (Caddoan)	"horns" or "elk"

Language family and tribe	Meaning/origin of tribal name, where known
Omaha	"those going against the wind" or "current"
Ponca	"sacred head"
Iowa	"sleepy ones"
Oto or Otoe	"lechers"
Missouri	"people with dugout canoes"
Kansas	"wind people"
Osage	"one who carries a message"
Quapaw	"downstream people"
Caddoan:	
Pawnee	"a horn"
Wichita	"big arbor"
Tawakoni	"neck of land in the water"
Waco	English name
Kichai	"going in wet sand" or "red shield"
Shuman (affiliation unknown)	–
Kiowa	"principal people"
Uto–Aztecan★★:	
Comanche	Spanish term
Padouca	–

★ see p. 17
★★ see p. 202

Of all North American Indians, the former native inhabitants of the Prairies and Plains are the most popularly and widely known. Their area ranged from the Mississippi valley in the east to the Rocky Mountains of the west, and all the way from the Saskatchewan River in the north to the Rio Grande in the south. The western High Plains are very arid, and are marked off by their short grass vegetation. The east, with a higher level of precipitation, is the Prairie, characterized by its dark soil and tall grass. The whole area was once home to teeming game, bison, pronghorn antelopes, wolves, coyotes, deer and bears. The main river systems run west to east to link to the Missouri and the Mississippi, along which forested patches were found.

The cultural traits that came to characterize the High Plains peoples were dependence on the bison (buffalo), limited use of roots and berries, limited fishing, absence of agriculture in the High Plains, use of the tipi, skillful use of bison and deer skins, rawhide, geometric art and the travois. Social characteristics included camp circle organization, division into bands and men's societies. Religious traits included the Sun Dance, sweat lodge and vision quest observances, and scalp dances. However, this culture was relatively late, and was dependent upon the introduction of the horse and, to a lesser extent, changes in tribal locations farther east pressing tribes into the eastern plains, along with the introduction of the gun, fur trade and trade goods, which caused continuous change from the 17th century onward. The tribes that are firmly associated with this way of life were the Blackfoot, Gros Ventre (or Atsina), Assiniboine, Crow, Sioux, Cheyenne and Arapaho, all of whom entered the plains from the east; the Kiowa, who came from the north; and the Comanche, who split from the Shoshone.

The Prairie culture is much older, and is characterized by semi-sedentary village tribes along the Missouri, Republican and Platte rivers, whose subsistence was based on maize agriculture, supplemented with seasonal hunting. Such tribes included the Pawnee, Arikara, Hidatsa, Mandan, Omaha, Ponca, Oto, Missouri and Osage. They had been influenced by the highly developed Mississippian culture, which in turn developed from prehistoric Mexican impulses. Several

C. S. Co. 2 — BEARDY'S WARRIORS.

Above Left: Plains Indian man wearing a porcupine hair and deer hair head roach, c. 1900. These headdresses are associated with the Plains "Grass" or "Omaha" dance ritual which spread to many tribes during the second-half of the 19th century. It continues to be the popular headgear for many male dancers' today at "Powwows" across the U.S. and Canada.

Above: Beardy's Warriors, Parkland Cree people, c. 1890, who settled on the reserve that still bears his name, Beardy's, in Saskatchewan.

Left: Plains Cree Warrior painted by Paul Kane, c. 1846. He wears a "straight-up" eagle feather headdress, quilled shirt, and leggings. The horse has a quilled crupper.

elements contributed to the ultimate mix in Plains culture from this source: earth lodge dwellings, steatite sculptures for pipes, ceremonial and religious organizations, small effigy altar platforms, perhaps the medicine bundle complex and the calumet or peace-pipe complex. A third influence came from the Rocky Mountain tribes — the Shoshone, Salish and Shahaptian groups — whose mythology concentrated around the Trickster and culture hero Coyote, and seems to have been integrated into Plains Indian folklore. Marginal groups were the Caddoan tribes in the southeastern regions, partly modified eastern groups such as the Cree and Ojibwa in the north, and Apachean groups in the southwest. For 300 years these three cultures intermingled increasingly.

The old Prairie tribes belonged to two language families: the Siouan, a word derived from the Sioux (Dakota), and the Caddoan. The Winnebago, a woodland people, were a remnant of the Siouans left in the east as they gradually moved west, then north and south to occupy the river bottoms and raise beans, squash, tobacco and corn. The Caddoans spread out from America's agricultural heartland; the Arikara followed the Siouan Mandan north; the Pawnee occupied the central Republican, Platte and Missouri areas; while the southern Caddoans were found in Kansas, Texas, Oklahoma and Arkansas — the Wichita erected their grass-thatched lodges as far north as the Great Bend of the Arkansas. The three Blackfoot tribes were the vanguard of Algonkian movement in the north. The most important movement, however, was the appearance in the northern plains area of the Sioux from the prairies and woods of Minnesota. The Western Sioux turned into nomadic Plains Indians, plundered the Missouri village tribes, and dislocated ethnic groups who were on their way west, such as the Arapaho, Gros Ventre and Cheyenne. The latter were a semi-sedentary group in the Prairie region until this period.

The major impetus in forming the Plains culture was given when horses were introduced from the Spanish colonies in the southwest. The horse was soon integrated into the existing culture patterns; it supplanted the dog travois, added the horse cult complex and allowed these now-mounted peoples to spread over the western plains. Two routes for the spread of horses have been suggested from the minimal documentation. One traces them from the Spanish and Pueblos in the Santa Fé area to the Utes of the Basin by 1640, then to the Shoshone, then to the Plateau and the Crow, and finally to the Blackfoot by about 1730. The alternative route combines horses from two sources, Santa Fé and San Antonio, thence to the Kiowa and Comanche, and then north to the Sioux. From both probable routes horses were traded for corn and robes at the Mandan villages, and from them to the Assiniboine, Cree and Plains Ojibwa, in exchange for European trade goods.

The religious patterns of the equestrian Plains tribes were partly a reformulation of the religion of the Prairie people adapted to the nomadic way of life in amalgamation of older features of different groups. The Prairie tribes reflected a half-sedentary way of life combining seasonal cultivation of the soil with seasonal hunting of buffalo. The corresponding religious patterns were a mixture of hunting beliefs and rituals connected with the agrarian calendar and social functions, notably the Calumet ritual, peace and war pipes, and ceremonies for the promotion of the growth of corn. The Pawnee developed a high god concept, star and cosmological mythology, medicine bundles and even human sacrifices to the Morning Star. The

Below: Participants in the Sun Dance on the Pine Ridge (Oglala Sioux) Reservation, South Dakota, c.1964. Outlawed by the U.S. Government during the early reservation days, Sun Dances are now held, sometimes in attenuated forms, on several reservations.

world view of the Plains and Prairie tribes conceived the everyday world of the Indian as a mysterious part of the great cosmic structure. Over this world the sky elevates its dome, the seat of the great powers, a Supreme Being, star gods, supernatural beings held by great supernatural power known to the Sioux as Wakan. Two great ceremonials stand out above all others: the Sun Dance, and the Okeepa of the Missouri River village tribes, such as the Mandan.

The Sun Dance

The Sun Dance was the most important of all Plains Indian ceremonies, although missing among the Pawnee, Kiowa, Apache and Comanche (who held one dance in 1874). The term Sun Dance is a misnomer, although male dancers gaze toward the rising morning sun or center pole during the public phase of the ceremony. The purpose of the ceremony is very diverse. Basically, however, it is a re-creation ceremony or world renewal rite. The Plains Cree in the north considered it a thank-offering for the reawakening of all nature after the silence of winter. They call it the "Thirsting Dance" because the participants did not drink during its performance. Formerly it was held mostly in June, the springtime of the northern plains. However, recent modified nativistic and part-Christian versions of the rite are usually celebrated in July and August.

Of all Plains tribes, the Cheyenne had the most concisely and consciously preserved meaning of the Sun Dance. They called the Sun Dance shelter New Life Lodge or Lodge of New Birth, where the ceremony re-creates, re-forms and re-animates the earth, vegetation, animal life, etc., while offering thanks to a Supreme Being. There is no doubt that the Sun Dance has attracted ritual and cultural traits that have little to do with its original meaning, such as the Crow tribe's vow for revenge, and overemphasized elements, such as the self-torture of the Western Sioux rite.

The basic pattern of the Sun Dance is highly uniform, and was usually initiated during the winter months by a man or woman who had made a vow to do so in thanks, or who had a visionary command to do so. In the pre-reservation days, scattered bands would gather, often approaching the rendezvous in a ceremonial manner, making four stops en route. Secret preliminaries began in a tipi between the pledger and shamans (priests), usually old men with esoteric knowledge of the ritual. These preliminaries were to purify the participants, and to learn the sacred songs and ritual paint designs. At the same time, a distinguished warrior or group of warriors killed a buffalo bull with one shot. Similarly, scouts located a suitable forked tree which would be "killed" by a virtuous woman or captive and cut down. Both would be transported to the Sun Dance site. In the meantime, a larger number of men would erect a circle of 10 to 20 posts, up to 20 yards (20 m) in diameter, with an entrance to the east. The center pole would be erected with a bundle of brush near the top (the Thunderbird nest); the head or skin of the killed buffalo bull, and other objects, such as a Sun Dance doll (Blackfoot) or offering of cloth, might be affixed. Rafters would join the posts to the center pole.

The second public phase of the ceremonials would begin with the formal procession of barefoot, kilt-clad, white-painted dancers into the lodge, taking their places on both sides of the altar. Gazing constantly at the center pole or the sun they would raise and lower their heels, bending their knees, blowing their eagle-humerus whistles at every beat of the drum. They continued dancing for several days and nights, hoping in this way to obtain a vision, or at least arouse the pity of a supernatural being.

In both the preliminary and public phases of the rite, lesser ceremonies would interwork. These included male and female initiation into societies, the curing of the sick, exhibitions of supernatural power, the recounting of warrior deeds and the distribution of wealth. Finally, among several tribes, those participants who had vowed to do so would have themselves pierced through the pectoral muscles with skewers, by means of which they would be tethered to the center pole. They would dance back and forth attempting to tear themselves free, gaining supernatural aid through their ecstasy of pain. The public ceremony usually lasted four days.

The history of the Sun Dance remains obscure. Superficially it resembles the Okeepa ceremony of the Mandan of North Dakota, suggesting a Siouan origin for the rite. Others believe that the impressive resemblances between the Sun Dance and the Spirit Dance of the Plateau may indicate a common origin — a belief reinforced by the easy adoption of the ceremony,

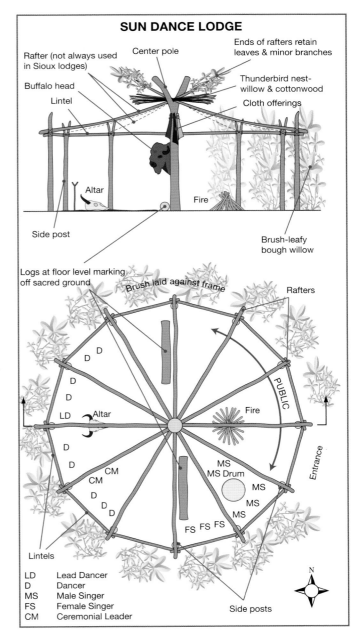

SUN DANCE LODGE

Rafter (not always used in Sioux lodges)
Center pole
Ends of rafters retain leaves & minor branches
Buffalo head
Lintel
Thunderbird nest-willow & cottonwood
Cloth offerings
Altar
Fire
Side post
Brush-leafy bough willow

Logs at floor level marking off sacred ground
Brush laid against frame
Rafters
PUBLIC
Fire
Entrance
D
D
D
D
LD
Altar
D
D
CM
CM
D
D
D
MS
MS Drum
MS
MS
MS
FS FS FS
Lintels
Side posts
N

LD — Lead Dancer
D — Dancer
MS — Male Singer
FS — Female Singer
CM — Ceremonial Leader

Above: Plains Cree Woman, c. 1880, wearing a buckskin dress with floral and geometrical beadwork, and leggings and moccasins in geometric designs. The Cree moved to the margins of the Plains during the fur trade era and their culture and dress reflected the Woodland and European influences from the east and true Plains culture to their south. The dress is a specimen in the Glenbow Museum, Calgary, Canada. Oil painting by Richard Hook.

Above: The Plains Cree Chief Poundmaker, photographed c. 1880 by G. Moodie, Maple Creek, Saskatchewan. Poundmaker was an important Cree leader — an adopted son of the Blackfoot Chief Crowfoot — and a guide for the Marquis of Lorne, Governor General of Canada, during a visit to the West. He was imprisoned for his part in the Northwest Rebellion (1885) and died in 1886. He gave his name to a band and a reserve of his people, who still live in Saskatchewan.

albeit Christianized, by 20th-century Plateau-Basin groups such as the Shoshone, Bannock and Ute as a nativistic revitalization movement. Still others look to a recent origin of the Sun Dance, with rapid diffusion from a possible Cheyenne or Arapaho genesis. The following tribes share significant resemblances: (1) Arapaho, Northern and Southern Cheyenne; (2) Blackfoot and Sarsi; (3) Ponca and Western Sioux; (4) Assiniboine, Plains Cree, Plains Ojibwa; (5) Santee Sioux; (6) Shoshone, Ute, Kiowa and Kutenai.

The Sun Dance was probably related to the Okeepa ceremony vividly described by the artist explorer George Catlin in the 1830s. It centered on "Lone Man," who restored the earth after a great flood by use of the "Big Canoe" or ark of wooden planks symbolically representing a protective wall. The ritual was a cosmic new year ceremony to ensure abundance of bison and a new beginning, involving collective — as opposed to individual — vision quests, and spiritual instruction and initiation for youths. Both rituals communicated an idea of a unified religious universe.

Besides the great collective festivals, warriors and individuals sought the help of animal spirits through visions induced by fasting and dreaming. High Plains warriors developed a range of age-graded military societies, each having its chiefs. Other

organizations, mystical in character, were dream societies, deriving power from dreamed animals, buffalo or elk, which provided sexual power. In a time of despair following the loss of much of their culture in the 19th century, there appeared several nativistic movements, such as the Ghost Dance of the 1880s–90s and the Peyote cult — a mixture of Mexican Indian, Christian and Plains Indian symbolism. Recently pan-Indianism has taken on some features of tribal rejuvenation; the old Prairie Grass Dance has provided its ritual features.

Among the characteristic features of material culture, the hide tipi probably originated in the far north, and some buckskin apparel and large combat shields perhaps came from the Plateau, linked to the Plains via trade routes. Plains warriors developed militaristic and religious art with geometric painting and pictographs. Male society costume contained animal and bird elements associated with game tracking and battlefield scavengers. The Plains peoples were superb quillworkers and later beadworkers, and decorated male and female dress with geometric designs, perhaps influenced heavily in the late 19th century by imported Middle Eastern rugs. Elements of material culture that may have come from the eastern forests were rawhide box trunks, but now shaped as rawhide envelopes; and certain forms of pictographic art that seem related to the art of the forest people, particularly memory aids etched on bark. The 19th century saw the influx of European trade goods — cloth, beads, metals and guns — together with the spread of material culture from the Cree, Ojibwa and Métis from Canada, which added to the cultural mix of the whole region.

PLAINS CREE (NAHIAWUK) This is the general term given to cover the Cree bands living partly or wholly on the prairies and parklands of Saskatchewan and Alberta from the mid-18th century onward. On cultural grounds they have been considered distinct from their Woodland Cree cousins, because of their adoption of Assiniboine traits, which are essentially "Plains" in format. Most notably, these include ceremonials and the development of a dependence on the buffalo (bison), in common with the Blackfeet, Assiniboine and Gros Ventre, whom the Plains Cree displaced from the Saskatchewan River. In the late 18th century they were reinforced by bands of Swampy Cree who partially modified to the Plains culture, but were to remain largely marginal. The marginal bands between the Swampy and Plains Cree were sometimes referred to as "Bush Cree." However, we consider here the true Plains Cree and the "Bush Cree" together and independent from the Swampy and Woods Cree — in fact a distinct tribe. The Plains Cree bands were:

(1) *Calling River* of the Assiniboine and Qu'Appelle valleys, mostly now under the File Hills and Crooked Lake Agencies. The Calling River Cree or Qu'Appelle Cree were a marginal division of the "Bush Cree" and have mixed considerably with the Plains Ojibwa.

(2) *Cree-Assiniboine* is an extension of the Calling River band in association with the Assiniboine and are probably a mixture of the two tribes, located near the Wood and Moose mountains (Saskatchewan), now mostly under the File Hills-Qu'Appelle Agency (Piapot's band) and Crooked Lake Agency (White Bear). Mr. N.J. McLeod, Superintendent of the File Hills-

Qu'Appelle Agency, in a well-documented description of the Cree and Saulteaux of his agency (personal correspondence, December 16th, 1955), claims: "Piapot's Band are of the Plains Cree tribe of Indians, and are somewhat different from other in that they are descendants of Indians who lived by hunting the buffalo, whereas some of the Cree tribes lived in and along the fringes of the bush areas and are known as Willow or Bush Crees." He thus asserts that the Calling River people were "Bush" or marginal, in sharp contrast to Piapot's band.

(3) *Touchwood Hills* lived between Long Lake and Touchwood Hills, now largely on the Poormans, Day Star and Gordons reserves.

(4) *Rabbitskins* roamed the Assiniboine River, between the Calling River and Touchwood Hills bands, with whom they are now mixed under the File Hills-Qu'Appelle and Touchwood Agencies. The Rabbitskins were a "Bush" group, tethered to the trading posts during the 19th century, at which time they were closely associated with groups of Bungi or Plains Ojibwa.

(5) *House People* lived near the junction of the North and South Saskatchewan rivers, mostly above the north branch. The House People were partly "Bush Cree" and partly true Plains Cree, and are now principally on the Mistawasis and Sandy Lake (Ahtahkakoops) reserves under the Shellbrook Agency.

Above: Plains Cree man, c. 1780. The Cree had penetrated the northeastern plains of present Saskatchewan and Manitoba by the late 18th century. Surviving evidence of male dress suggests that these marginal Plains people retained partly fitted hide tunics and quilled and painted decoration reminiscent of Subarctic Algonkian prototypes. The placement of diminished discs and strips appears intermediate between Subarctic garments, and the loose-fitting hide shirts with larger strips characteristic of early 19th-century northern Plains warriors.

Below: Plains Cree Indians photographed in Saskatchewan, c. 1890.

(6) *Parklands People* were a "Bush" or Willow Cree group on the South Saskatchewan, near its junction with the north branch. They are now under the Duck Lake Agency at Beardy's and Fort-a-la-Corné reserves. These were a late extension of the Swampy Cree under fur trader influence.

(7) *River People* lived on and below the north branch of the Saskatchewan River and the Battle River. These are true Plains people, and were one of the largest Plains Cree groups. Their descendants are mostly on the Poundmaker, Sweet Grass, Red Pheasant and Little Pine reserves of the Battleford Agency. These people were closely related to the Alberta or Beaver Hills Cree.

(8) *Beaver Hills People* were the largest Plains Cree grouping, and are the most important division of the Prairie Cree. These Plains Cree inhabited the Saskatchewan beyond Onion Lake, Neutral Hills, and Beaver Hills to the headwaters of that river. They are now mostly on the following reserves: Onion Lake (Saskatchewan), Saddle Lake, Alexander, Ermineskin, Samson, Montana, Sunchild and John O'Chiese, under the Saddle Lake, Edmonton, Hobbema and Stoney-Sarcee agencies. On many reservations they have mixed with their old allies, the Assiniboine (Stoney), particularly at Wabamun, Stoney-Plains and Morley, and with the Blackfeet and Sarsi — their former enemies — near Calgary.

(9) *Rocky Boy and United States Cree* came about after the development of the United States fur trade on the Missouri during the early 1800s. Plains Cree, Swampy Cree and Métis wandered in small groups through Montana and North Dakota. After the second Métis rebellion in Saskatchewan in 1885, some hundreds of Plains Cree removed to Montana to escape the Canadian authorities for their part in the Riel uprising. A reservation called Rocky Boy, near Havre (Montana), was established for landless Plains Cree and Plains Ojibwa in 1916, but many more remained as landless refugees on several Montana reservations.

The total number of Plains Cree in the early 19th century may have been 15,000, before smallpox took its toll. Cree conquest of the western forest seems to have been complete by the late 18th century, when Alexander Henry met them on Lake Winnepeg in 1775; and by Daniel Harmon's day, about 1820, they were linked to the Assiniboine and venturing out on the Prairies. Finally, by 1876, most of the Plains Cree had submitted to Canadian authority, although they participated in the uprising against the Government in 1885 alongside the Métis.

Plains Cree culture included procuring buffalo for meat and hides. The acquisition of the horse, probably as early as 1750, facilitated bison hunting

Above: Plains Cree woman, c. 1790. A dress of this type collected in the Upper Missouri region by Lewis and Clark in 1804–1805 is no doubt of Cree origin. It is constructed with one seam on the side and along the top. The painted decoration is clearly related to early Subarctic garments where red and black bands predominate. The beaded discs perhaps derive from central Subarctic sun symbols, as present on fitted coats with multicolored designs attributed to late-18th/early-19th century Cree, Ojibwa and Métis.

and regulated tribal movements. Their material culture also resembled High Plains forms in the use of the skin (later canvas) tipi, buckskin clothes for male and female, some tattooing, and decorated ceremonial costume with fine quillwork and beadwork in geometrical and later floralistic designs. Warrior and rank societies existed for men, such as Buffalo Dancers, Kit Fox and Prairie Chicken societies. The concept of a single all-powerful creator and supernatural power in all phenomena was endemic. They had the Sun Dance (some reservations still hold them) or Thirsting Dance, the vision quest, smoking tipi rite, medicine bundles and other Plains ceremonial complexes. The present Canadian population of Plains Cree descendants exceeds 61,000, with approximately 7,000 additional Plains Cree and Plains Ojibwa in Montana.

PLAINS OJIBWA or **BUNGI** In parallel with the Plains Cree, groups of woodland Ojibwa first established themselves on the edges of the Plains (the Parklands) by about 1790, and later some bands became true High Plains Indians. They left their homelands in Minnesota and Ontario and finally occupied an area of southwestern Manitoba, northern North Dakota and southeastern Saskatchewan. The great expansion of the Ojibwa began in the 18th century after they secured firearms from the French and English. Those who lived on the northern edges of the Prairies are often called Saulteaux (pronounced "sotoe"), but those who successfully adapted their culture to life on the Plains are Plains Ojibwa or Bungi, although no sharp division actually existed. They now employed the hide tipi, the horse and the Red River cart obtained from the Red River Métis. They also exploited the bison and pronghorn antelope, which replaced deer, moose and beaver as the chief sources of sustenance in their new environment. Clothing styles were also modified, including shirts and leggings for men, and single-piece dresses for women. Both geometrical and, later, floralistic decoration for their ceremonial clothes were common. They also adopted the Sun Dance, although the Midewiwin (Great Medicine Society) survived among a few bands; and they had a warrior-police society, "Okitsita," similar to other Plains tribes. During the later 19th century they adopted the Grass Dance, a variant of the Omaha Dance, the Drum Religion and later the Peyote cult.

Today many Plains Ojibwa reserves hold secular powwows, sharing features with other northern Plains Indian groups. In most areas they are heavily mixed with Métis, with perhaps most of their current 59,000 population being of mixed descent. Their present descendants are at Turtle Mountain, North Dakota; Rocky Boy Reservation, Montana (merged with Cree); Gamblers, Keeseekoowenin, Long Plain, Peguis, Rolling River, Roseau River, Sandy Bay, Swan Lake and Waywayseecappo, all in Manitoba; and Cote, Fishing Lake,

Kahkewistahaw, Keeseekoose, Kinistino, Muscowequan, Muscowpetung, Nut Lake, Ochapowace, Pasqua, Sakimay, Shesheep, Saulteaux and White Bear in Saskatchewan. A number are descendants of marginal Plains bands, and some are also of Cree origin.

MÉTIS A term with a number of meanings for people of mixed European and Native ancestry. The name is derived from the Latin term mixticius. In North America the French term Métis is employed, or "Mestizo" in Latin America. In its strictest meaning it was once applied to people of French and Indian genealogy who formed settlements at the Red River of the North's junction with the Asiniboine River in present day Manitoba. However, in its wider sense, the term Métis has been increasingly applied and adopted by people of mixed European and Native descent, especially in northern and western Canada, whose forebears may have had no connection with the Red River Métis. However for various reasons they were excluded from registration as Indians in the treaties between the Native people and the British Crown, and denied enrollment in the U.S. where they have been regarded as Canadian nationals.

The origins of the Métis were the natural outcome of the North American fur trade where Europeans (particularly French and British) took native wives. The foundations for the settlement of the Great Lakes by French Canadian fur traders followed the explorations of the second half of the 17th century and by mid 18th century there were perhaps 50 major mixed blood communities in the region ranging from Detroit, Kaskaskia, and Michilimackinac. Subsequently this region passed from French control to the British, then Americans which together with the diminishing fur returns, resulted in the mixed bloods rejoining their native communities, or absorbed into the growing white communities, or found their way to the Red River area where many were employed by the newly formed North West Company (NWC) towards the end of the 18th century. These Métis were now in direct competition with the older Hudson's Bay Company (HBC) founded in 1670, whose traders worked west and south from Hudson and James bays through a vast region claimed by the British as Rupert's Land. Many of the mixed bloods of HBC were of Cree origin, those of the NWC, whose French ancestors came originally fro Lower Canada, were of Ojibwa and Ottawa extraction and largely Roman Catholic.

In 1811 in order to gain pre-eminence in the fur trade, the HBC (claimants to much of western Canada) gave jurisdiction of an area of present day southwest Manitoba and adjacent areas of Saskatchewan and Minnesota to Thomas Selkirk, 5th Earl of Selkirk, an area known as Assiniboia. He recruited Scottish and Swiss colonists. In 1816 a confrontation took place at Seven Oaks between the two fur trade companies and their respective personnel and mixed bloods that was only resolved when the two companies merged in 1821 due to the diminishing quantity of fur.

Below: Great Lakes mixed blood communities of the 18th–early 19th century.

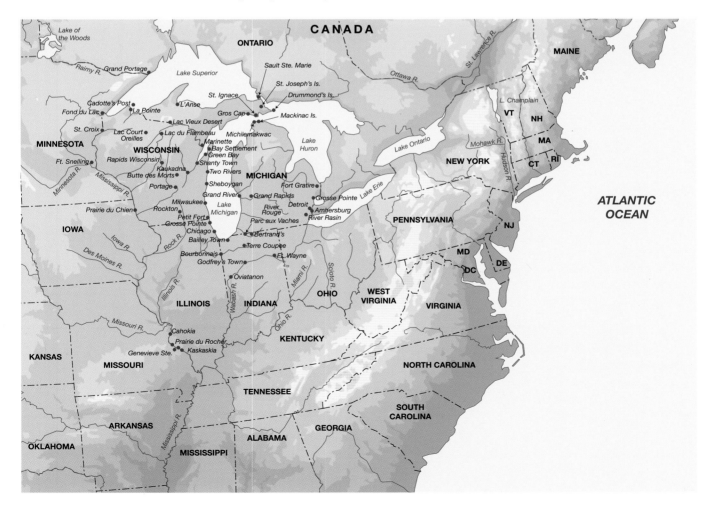

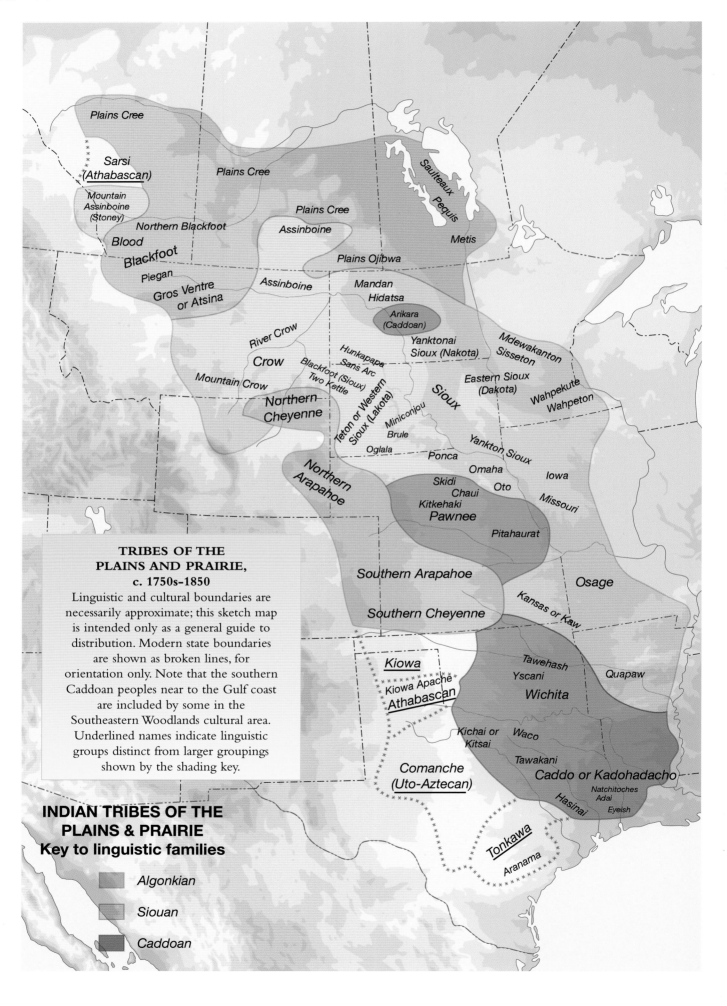

Plains Cree

Sarsi
(Athabascan)

Mountain
Assinboine
(Stoney)

Plains Cree

Northern Blackfoot

Blood

Blackfoot

Piegan

Gros Ventre
or Atsina

River Crow

Plains Cree

Assinboine

Plains Ojibwa

Assinboine

Saulteaux

Pequis

Metis

Mandan

Hidatsa

Arikara
(Caddoan)

Yanktonai
Sioux (Nakota)

Mdewakanton
Sisseton

Crow

Mountain Crow

Hunkapapa
Sans Arc

Blackfoot (Sioux)
Two Kettle

Northern
Cheyenne

Teton or Western
Sioux (Lakota)

Miniconjou

Brule

Oglala

Eastern Sioux
(Dakota)

Sioux

Wahpekute

Wahpeton

Yankton Sioux

Ponca

Omaha

Iowa

Northern
Arapahoe

Skidi
Chaui
Kitkehaki

Pawnee

Pitahaurat

Oto

Missouri

**TRIBES OF THE
PLAINS AND PRAIRIE,
c. 1750s–1850**

Linguistic and cultural boundaries are
necessarily approximate; this sketch map
is intended only as a general guide to
distribution. Modern state boundaries
are shown as broken lines, for
orientation only. Note that the southern
Caddoan peoples near to the Gulf coast
are included by some in the
Southeastern Woodlands cultural area.
Underlined names indicate linguistic
groups distinct from larger groupings
shown by the shading key.

Southern Arapahoe

Southern Cheyenne

Osage

Kansas or Kaw

Kiowa

Kiowa Apache
Athabascan

Comanche
(Uto-Aztecan)

Tawehash

Yscani

Wichita

Quapaw

Kichai or
Kitsai

Waco

Tawakani

Caddo or Kadohadacho

Natchitoches
Adai
Eyeish

Hasinai

Tonkawa

Aranama

**INDIAN TRIBES OF THE
PLAINS & PRAIRIE
Key to linguistic families**

Algonkian

Siouan

Caddoan

Above: Plains Ojibwa family (probably Manitoba) c. 1880. The woman is holding a cradle board of a Woodland form, which has a double-curved head bow guard. The tipi (canvas), a Plains habitation, indicates the intermediate position the Plains Ojibwa held between Woodland and Plains cultures.

Right: Plains Cree woman painted at Fort Union in 1833 by Karl Bodmer. She has blue-black facial tattoos and her ears adorned with dentilium shells. She wears a hide dress, probably constructed with two large elk skins, tails up and folded back to make a yoke.

Below: Beaded "Vest" or waistcoat, Saulteaux or Cree c. 1890. Vest with solid beaded front on canvas with a cloth back. The floral beaded designs reflect Ojibwa origins from the Great Lakes area. The term "Saulteaux" identifies people of Ojibwa origin who moved west into present day Manitoba and Saskatchewan during the fur trade period. The dark veins link the floral elements in a stiff or more angular layout than woodland Ojibwa work and gives the workmanship a Cree or Plains borderland feel. There is a label inside which states, "vest of Big Moose Saulteaux." Laura Peers (Un. of Oxford, UK) claimed this name appears in the Hudson's Bay Company records of the period.

Redundant employees and fur traders from both companies had produced two separate populations. The English and Scottish traders and their part-native descendants and Indian wives, mostly Protestant from the area of Rupert's Land and the French speaking Métis who were mostly Catholic and anti-British. There was also in this latter group a small English and Scottish presence from the period 1812–1821 when the NWC was under Anglophone management.

By the early years of the 19th century the Métis had established trade alliances with the Plains Ojibwa, Plains Cree, Assiniboine, and Blackfoot of the northern Plains, and more than holding their own in inter-tribal warfare. In 1851 they defeated a war party of Sioux at Grand Coteau. They defended their territorial and political rights during the "Red River Rebellion" of 1869–1870 when confronted with

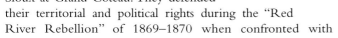

Manitoba's entry into the Canadian Confederation. The Métis center of influence as a result moved on west to the Saskatchewan River around Batoche and beyond to Fort Edmonton. A second Métis confrontation, the "Northwest Rebellion" of 1885 around Batoche and Duck Lake took place, where they were defeated by superior Canadian forces which ended their provisional government and resulted in the execution of their political leader Louis Riel in November 1885. Some Métis took refuge in the United States, along with some Cree allies.

They became increasingly isolated from mainstream politics until the early 20th century when demands for a land base resulted in the foundation of several Métis communities in Alberta. However, by then a complex set of problems had emerged which had led to the general loss of Indian status by the descendants of the unions of Indian women and non-Indian men which had resulted in their enfranchisement as recognized Canadian "Treaty" Indians. Many such "non-treaty Indians" now gravitated towards the Métis to find their political and cultural aspirations. It was not until 1989 that the Métis (now including formerly non-status Indians) were fully recognized by the Canadian government as an Aboriginal people, equal to the First Nations (Treaty Indians) and Inuit (Eskimo). Perhaps the number of Métis in this wider sense is about 300,000 of which perhaps one third descend from the old Red

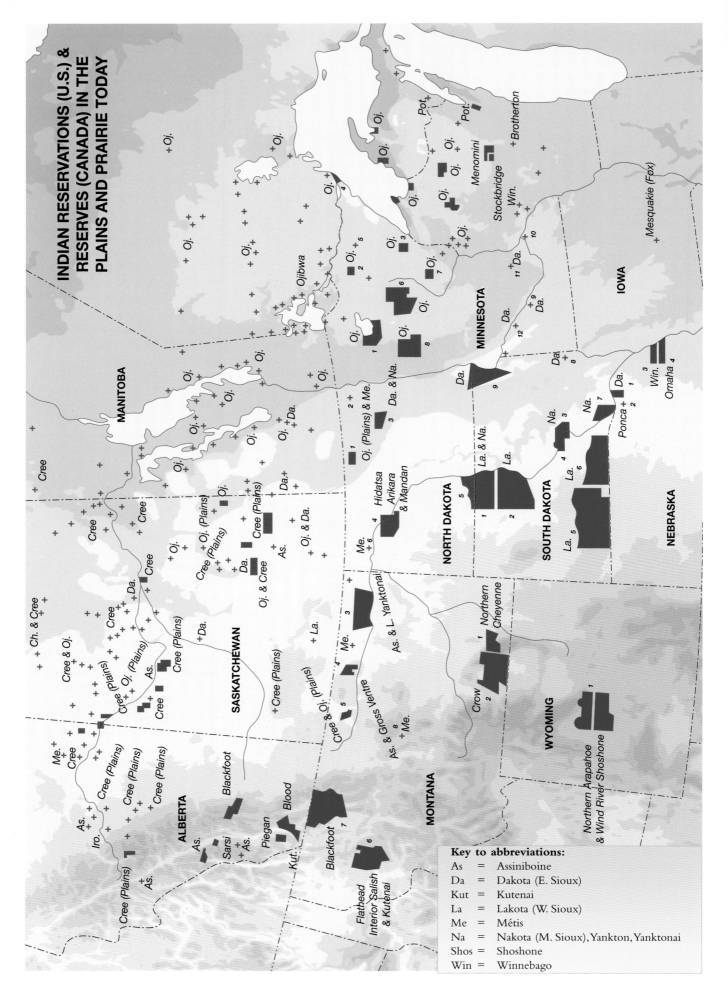

INDIAN RESERVATIONS (U.S.) & RESERVES (CANADA) IN THE PLAINS AND PRAIRIE TODAY

Key to abbreviations:

As	=	Assiniboine
Da	=	Dakota (E. Sioux)
Kut	=	Kutenai
La	=	Lakota (W. Sioux)
Me	=	Métis
Na	=	Nakota (M. Sioux), Yankton, Yanktonai
Shos	=	Shoshone
Win	=	Winnebago

A series of photographs showing the deconstruction of a tipi. While they are not all of the same structure, the sequence does show the process well.
*(**1**) "Wolf Tipi," Sarsi, Alberta, c. 1900. Such painted lodges were medicine bundles and similar designs appear among the three Blackfoot tribes (Blood, Blackfoot proper and Piegan) and the Sarsi. The designs were "transferred" to new canvas tipi covers as the old ones wore out. There are still painted lodges amongst the Blackfoot and Sarsi.*
*(**2**) Sarsi Indians removing a canvas tipi cover from the pole frame. The painted designs are typical of the Blackfoot tribes and the Sarsi of southern Alberta.*
*(**3**) Sarsi Indians removing tipi poles, Alberta, c. 1900. The Sarsi or Sarcee were a small Athabascan tribe who joined the Blackfoot group and became totally integrated into the culture of the dominant people.*

Above: Skin coat, mittens, moccasins and a so-called octopus bag. Coats of this type of European form were the final development from much older painted Subarctic tunics and are usually attributed to the Red River Métis. All the items are decorated with delicate stylized floral patterns in quillwork, a merging of native and European influence. The sash is of braided yarn a type also popular among Red River Métis. The items probably date from the 1840s.

River people. In North Dakota and Montana groups of Métis arrived following the Red River and Northwest rebellions and some settled with the Plains Ojibwa at the Turtle Mountain Agency, Pembina, and Walhalla and ultimately enrolled as Indians by the BIA (Bureau of Indian Affairs). At one time these Métis spoke an old French-native patios called Mitchif, and adopted a number of Indian cultural traits, including buffalo hunting, and produced a range of beautifully decorated items of clothing which recalled their Indian heritage using porcupine quills, beadwork, ribbonwork, and silkwork. Refined by the influence of Catholic teaching establishments they became the extraordinary confluence of native and European artistic cultures which ultimately spawned its own dynamics across the vast Canadian north and American

west. The term Métis has rarely been used in the U.S. outside North Dakota and Montana, but all the Great Lakes and Prairie tribes of the Missouri Valley have substantial amounts of old French ancestry.

SARSI or **SARCEE (TSUU TINA)** A small Athabascan-speaking tribe who once lived along the upper waters of the Saskatchewan River in present Alberta, were known as Sarsi. They were probably at one time part of the Beaver Indians, but joined the Blackfoot for protection against their enemies, the Crees and Assiniboines, perhaps some time in the late 18th century. Their customs thereafter were greatly modified by their long residence among the Blackfoot. They seem always to have been a small tribe, perhaps numbering 750 people before smallpox decimated them in 1836, and scarlet fever in 1856.

In 1877, along with other southern Alberta Indians, they ceded their lands for a small reserve near Calgary where a small group, much mixed with other Indian groups, has continued to live. In 1881 they numbered 396; in 1924, only 160; in 1949, 201; in 1970, 467; and in 2005, 1,544. Their language is now used by only a few older people, and they have lost their Sacred Peace Pipe and Beaver bundles. They do, however, sponsor an annual powwow and run a cultural center on the reserve. Their close proximity to Calgary has resulted in almost complete acculturation. The Sarsi today prefer their own name for themselves; Tsuu Tina.

BLACKFOOT or BLACKFEET
(SIKSIKAH) The historic Blackfoot, an Algonkian people, were a loose confederacy of three closely related tribes: the Blackfoot or *North Blackfoot* (Siksika), the *Blood* (Kainah), and *Piegan* — also spelled Peigan in Canada — (Pikuni), with a close alliance with the Atsina and Sarsi. They once held an immense territory, stretching from the North Saskatchewan River, Canada, to the headwater of the Missouri River in Montana, including the foothills of the Rocky Mountains.

They seem to have moved from the east and were the vanguard of Algonkian relocation in the west. David Thompson, an explorer for the Hudson's Bay Company, made the first extensive record of Blackfoot culture when he wintered with them in 1787–88. He found that horses, guns and metal objects of European manufacture had preceded him by at least 50 years. They seem to have been in conflict with the Snake Indians, usually assumed as Shoshone, whom they ultimately appear to have expelled from the area. Despite the ravages of smallpox, particularly among the Piegans, the pre-reservation Blackfoot became the most powerful tribe of the northern Plains.

They were a typical Plains tribe, as exemplified by a dependence on the buffalo for food, tipis, bedding, shields, clothing and

containers; by the development of bands from common ties of kinship; and by functional age-graded men's societies and warrior societies, including formalized religious organizations. The band functioned as a group, with a dependence upon the generosity of the able and wealthy few among the young and old. Religion included the wide use of "bundles" containing symbols (usually remnants of birds, animals and objects) of the power of dreamed or vision experience. These personalized sources of power were opened at times, with accompanying rituals for group benefit, for health, hunting and prestige. Each of the three tribes held an annual Sun Dance, the Plains world renewal complex enacted in a specially constructed "Medicine Lodge," which, in spite of Government pressures, has been held periodically until recent times. As late as 1958 the Bloods still held the Medicine Pipe Dance by the Horn Society, the strongest native religious group extant. Their principal deities were the Sun and a supernatural being, Napi, or "Old Man." Their dead were deposited in trees, sometimes in tipis erected for the purpose on hills.

During the 19th century they diminished in number, from some 15,000 to about 6,750 in 1862. Many died of starvation with the final disappearance of the buffalo. After 1877 the Canadian Blackfoot settled in three reserves: the North Blackfoot, near Gleichen; the North Piegan, near Brocket; and the Blood at Cardston. The South Piegan were finally restricted to a reservation on the eastern side of the Glacier National Park, Montana, with the administrative agency at Browning. These Blackfoot had established relations with the U.S. fur companies on the Missouri and had suffered the worst in smallpox outbreaks. The years after 1884, following the collapse of their hunting economy, were largely dominated by trying to adjust to white rural life, farming, stock-raising, and more recently to an industrial wage economy. The Montana (American) division are officially called Blackfeet.

In contrast to pre-reservation days, Blackfoot culture has become no longer monolithic. They are socially divided by religion, by social achievement and by blood.

1 Blackfoot man, c. 1890. Pierced skin decoration was recorded in the east among the Ojibwa and Eastern Sioux, and in the west among the Blackfoot, Flathead and Plateau tribes. Members of the Brave Dog Society of the Blackfoot wore shirts of this type when in dress, representing the grizzly bear. Blackfoot moccasins were originally of side-seam construction or, later, separate sole forms, but usually soft-soled. This youth also wears a loop bead necklace, porcupine head roach and topknot hairstyle, and carries a saber, probably as society insignia but also as a useful weapon.

2 Blackfoot woman, c. 1895. Blackfoot dresses were originally made of two large elk skins, joined at the shoulders with a fold-over, although a small separate yoke became more common. Later, a deeper yoke, shaped and curved around an imaginary deer tail relating to the original shape of the hides, was sewn or laced to the two hides forming the skirt. In 1885–1905, square-cut dresses of red or dark blue stroud cloth became popular. Later still, separate cloth yokes or capes reinforced with sacking, over cloth or sateen dresses, were in vogue. Blackfoot women usually covered the upper part of dresses and capes with horizontal bands of wide lazy stitch beadwork in seed or pony beads fringed with tubular "basket" beads and traded thimbles. Triangular cloth patches on the front of the skirt, possibly a uterine or bison symbol, were a Blackfoot feature. The feathered headdress signifies an officer of a women's society.

*3 Blood dog travois, c. 1870. The dog travois of the thinly populated High Plains in pre-horse nomad times seems to have been a uniquely Native American device, and was the only alternative to back-carrying for lodges and other burdens.
It was carried forward into the 19th century horse culture as the "big dog travois."
Spanish 16th-century explorers met villages of pedestrian hunters in the south with dog travois — perhaps Athabascan/Apachean groups; northerly explorers reported the Snakes, at least partly of Shoshonean origin, using them while retreating west on foot before the Blackfoot; and among the latter the dog travois was occasionally used until reservation days.*

4 Two tobacco bags, Plains Cree or Blackfoot, c. 1890. Buckskin bags with beaded panel both sides. Squared top, dissimilar to most tobacco bags of the Canadian Parklands. Simple, symmetrical angular floral designs suggest Plains origin. Red stain to fringing on one bag. 800cm long.

5 Man's trade cloth leggings, Blackfoot, c. 1890. Rectangular pieces of folded cloth with bias cut edges and beaded strips. Courtesy Dave Sager.

6 Blackfoot parfleche, c. 1870. Parfleches were folded envelopes of rawhide — untanned buffalo or other skin — which can be molded when fresh and wet, and dries hard, waterproof but semi-flexible. Usually folded from a single sheet, with flaps secured by thongs through burned holes, they were used for carrying dried food and clothing; the Blackfoot made additional holes allowing attachment to a saddle or travois frame. They were painted, usually only on the end flaps, with bold designs in pigments mixed with buffalo hoof glue. Characteristically smaller than most, Blackfoot parfleches tended to curved designs and triangles in solid colors.

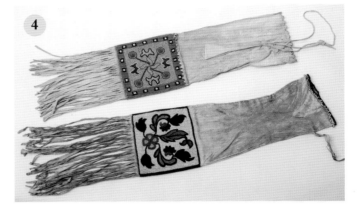

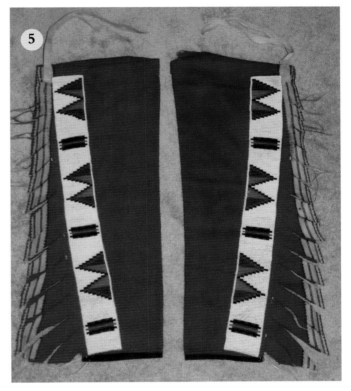

7 The Blackfoot travois were usually considered the property of women. The shafts of lodge pole pine were crossed and tied above the horse's neck and also tied to the saddle. The flared, dragging poles were secured as a frame by two notched main cross struts; secondary struts and willow tipi backrests formed the load platform.

1 *Four Blackfoot men, c. 1900. Three wear skin shirts, and three wear skin leggings, all trimmed with ermine skins. The ermine was recognized as a fierce fighting animal which would imbue warriors' clothes in pre-reservation warfare. The man on the right holds a metal pipe tomahawk with a beaded triangular tab and an eagle wing feather fan.*

2 *Wolf-Plume, Curly-Bear, and Bird Rattler, Blackfoot, 1916.*

3 *Blackfoot, c. 1910. Ceremonial split-horn bonnet, constructed on a headpiece of felt or skin covered with weasel (ermine) pelts, as was a cloth trailer usually added behind, with a beaded browband and shaped and polished buffalo horns.*

4 *Blackfoot, c. 1900. Sacred "Natoas" (Sun's Turnip) headdress of the holy woman in the Blackfoot Sun Dance ritual, honoring the myths concerning Grandfather Sun, Morningstar, his wife Tailfeather Woman, her son Scarface, Spider and the Forbidden Turnip. The lack of women with knowledge of the ritual led to its decline among the Blackfoot.*

5 *Blackfoot, c. 1890. Chief wearing older-style upright ceremonial bonnet of eagle feathers on a skin or felt base, the browband was usually quilled, beaded or, as here, studded with brass. There was usually lavish ermine trimming. This ancient style was widely seen on the northern Plains among Upper Missouri tribes, Plains Cree and Blackfoot, among whom both men and women could be entitled to them. Characteristic of the Blackfoot is the red-dyed rooster plume at the front. This style was largely replaced by the flared crown bonnet by the early 20th century.*

7 *Blackfoot Brave Dog Society members, c. 1910.* Harry Pollard Collection, Provincial Museum & Archives of Alberta, Edmonton

8 *Two Guns White Calf, a Blackfoot, photographed c. 1910 with a youth, probably by Walter McClintock. He wears a fine buckskin shirt and leggings beaded in typical Blackfoot designs of the period.*

9 *Bird Rattler (1859–1939), photographed in 1927. After an adventurous youth, this Blackfoot man eventually became a successful Montana farmer, a tribal judge and keeper of the Piegan sacred Circle Dance Medicine Pipe Bundle until his death.* Photograph: Glacier Studio, Browning, Montana; courtesy Ian West

6 Bird Rattler, Blackfoot, 1916. He wears a traditional "straight-up" eagle feather headdress, a loop necklace, and a buckskin shirt with beaded strips. The Blackfoot are three tribes; Piegan, Blood, and North Blackfoot, split between Montana (U.S.), and Alberta (Canada). Americans call the tribe "Blackfeet," in Canada "Blackfoot," and by themselves "Siksika."

Top: Rocky Boy (see also page 13) or Stone Child, chief of the Landless Plains Ojibwa of Montana and successor of Little Shell in 1901. In 1916 the Rocky Boy Rservation was established, a home for Ojibwa from various reservations and for Little Bear's Crees from Canada.

Above: Blackfoot women, photographed c. 1910, probably by McClintock. Left, buckskin dress with elk-tooth and beadwork decoration. Right, trade cloth dress with basket bead and thimble decoration.

Top: Four Souls, Plains Cree, Rocky Boy Reservation, Montana, c. 1930. He was the son of Little Bear and grandson of Big Bear, who had joined the Métis in the Northwest Rebellion in Canada in 1885.

Above: Joe Iron Pipe, of the South Piegan division of the Blackfoot nation, with his wife and son, c. 1910. The woman wears a cloth dress with beaded belt. He wears typical Blackfoot full dress, with the traditional "straight up" bonnet, and holds a beaded guncase. Provincial Museum & Archives of Alberta

Top, Left and Right: *Blackfoot chief Thundercloud (left) and Mountain Chief are colored prints of photographs from the F.A. Rinehart Studio, Omaha, Nebraska. Rinehart's Studio photographed many Indians who participated in the 1898 Trans-Mississippi Exposition held in Omaha. Another local studio, Heyn, also produced some superb studies of Indian subjects around the same time.*

Above Left: *Pretty Young Man (Blackfoot name Ma-Ko-Yo-Mah-Kan ?) photographed c.1910 with a tipi painted with Elk designs. See commentary in Tipi*

entry of Glossary for discussion of motifs. Harry Pollard Collection, Provincial Museum & Archives of Alberta

Above Right: *This superb portrait of Eagle Child illustrates the facial characteristics of the Blackfoot. He wears the flaring eagle-feather bonnet, with white discs and horsehair trim at each feather tip, beaded browband and ermine drops, which replaced in popularity the "straight up" style during the late 19th century.* Glacier Studio, courtesy Ian West

Above: North Blackfoot headmen (from left to right) Calf Child, Wolf Chief, and Red Leggings photographed by Arnold Lupson, Glenbow Museum, Calgary c. 1920. Note that Calf Child holds the tobacco bag also shown here below). The pipe bag is made of buckskin with appliqué beadwork in typical stepped and block geometrical designs c. 1890.

Right: Calf Child holding the tobacco bag. Painting by Richard Hook

However, in the recent past a renewed awareness of "Indian culture" has led to an increased participation even by the mixed-bloods in pan-Indian powwows, which are often performed several times a year. The South Piegans promote the annual North American Indian Days at Browning, and similar events are held by the Bloods, North Piegans and North Blackfoot, but the sacred bundles have mostly fallen into disuse. They still have colorfully painted canvas tipis that are erected at major social gatherings, including the Calgary Stampede. The Blackfoot historically made beautiful costumes — elaborately decorated men's warrior costumes of shirts and leggings with eagle feather headdresses, and full-length buckskin women's dresses, adorned with beadwork. This ceremonial dress, modified over the years, is still worn at modern powwows, together with an ever-changing array of dancers' costumes having little reference to older Indian dress. The Blackfoot population in 1970 was 18,000, of whom 9,900 were Montana Blackfeet, largely of mixed antecedents. The total Blackfoot population now stands at 39,000 — more than double the 1970 number — of whom 23,500 are enrolled

on the Blackfeet Reservation Montana. The contrasting Canadian population is interesting as well. In 1970 the Bloods numbered 4,262. They now number 9,842. The North Piegan were numbered at 1,413 and North Blackfoot 2,355 in 1970, for a combined total of the two at 3,768. That combined total of the two bands is now 9,428. All three bands live in Alberta.

GROS VENTRE or **ATSINA (HAANININ)** An Algonkian tribe of the northern Plains, considered once part of the Arapaho (but for much of the 19th century allies of the more powerful Blackfoot) are the Gros Ventre. Their French name derives apparently from the movement of the hands over the abdomen to indicate hunger, used by Indians of differing speech to communicate in Plains Indian sign language. This sign also signifies abdominal tattooing, and thus confuses these people

Above: Man's buckskin shirt, Blackfoot, c. 1900. Man's tailored and fringed ceremonial shirt with beaded arm and shoulder strips, and disk. Courtesy Dave Sager.

Above Right: Man's buckskin long shirt, probably Northeastern Plains (Canadian Parklands) c. 1820. Large quilled disk and narrow sleeve strips with integrated disks. Refined neck flap, no horse hair decoration suggests possible Cree origin. National Museums of Scotland.

Right: Porcupine quillwork details of strips and disk on a Blackfoot man's buckskin shirt made c. 1830–1840. The design on the large disk is probably a conventionalized thunderbird and may actually be the work of their friends the Assiniboine. Pitt Rivers Museum, Oxford, UK.

Below Right: Detail of a large rectangular porcupine quilled panel, plus bulrush and (possibly) maidenhair fern decoration on the back of a Blackfoot shirt together with quilled strips and hair lock dangles wrapped with pericardium and quills. Below the large quilled panel are warrior painted figures. Detail from a Blackfoot shirt collected by Edward Hopkins who accompanied Sir George Simpson to western Canada 1841–1842. Pitt Rivers Museum, Oxford, UK.

with the Hidatsa (Gros Ventre of the Missouri), who are a completely separate Siouan tribe. Their culture and history parallel those of the Blackfoot, their powerful neighbors to the west. Their home for most of the 19th century was between the South Saskatchewan River in Canada and the Missouri River in Montana, particularly around the Milk River. They share the Fort Belknap Reservation, Montana, with some Assiniboine. Their recent population history is 1,045 in 1954; 1,519 in 1970; 2,900 in 1992 and 5,426 in 2001. For many years a considerable amount of craftwork was carried on by the women of the reservation.

Above: Blackfoot Indians. Old Horn Society parade with Holy Women (Virgins) to call people to the Sun Dance, c. 1910. Ceremonial staffs include (left to right) the Otter Staff, Swan Staff, White Spear Staff, Kit Fox Staff, Buffalo Spear, Yellow Spear. Each staff was renewed each year. Photograph: Harry Pollard; Provincial Museum and Archives of Alberta

Right: Blackfoot painted canvas otter lodge at Browning, Montana, c. 1950.

Below: Inside a Blackfoot Medicine tipi, c.1910. Center foreground — medicine pipe altar. Directly behind is the medicine pipe bundle. H. Pollard Collection

Above Left: Blackfoot war tipi (back view) with painted pictograph battle scenes, c. 1895. Photograph: Walter McClintock

Above: Golden eagle feather headdress, Blood, c. 1957. Headdress given to Sir Douglas Bader, the legless World War II fighter pilot hero, in 1957, during his adoption as honorary chief of the Blood Band of the Blackfoot Indians of Alberta. This sloping black form of the popular Plains Indian "War bonnet" was adopted by the Blackfoot from the Crow and Sioux about 1880. Photograph: Michael Johnson

Left: Stoney (Assiniboine) Indians from Morley, Alberta, photographed at Banff Indian Days, c. 1950. Second right is George Maclean (Walking Buffalo), who toured the world for the Moral Rearmament Movement. Photograph: Nicolas Morant

Pan-Indian powwows include social dances such as the Grass Dance, Tea and Owl Dances, danced by couples and derived from white two-steps, and the Fool or Clown Dance, also associated with the Gros Ventre, Assiniboine and Blackfoot of Montana and Alberta.

ASSINIBOINE and **STONEY** The Assiniboine were formerly a large Siouan tribe whose language confirms a close link with the Yanktonai Sioux, from whom they probably separated not long before the appearance of white traders in their vicinity. They occupied an area between Lake Superior and James Bay, adjoining territory then dominated by the Crees and their association with the Hudson's Bay traders.

Early reports distinguish between Assiniboine of the meadows and woods during the 18th century. They appear to have been in a slow migration westward during the 18th century, when they seem to have formed a northern division from Moose Mountain, along the South Saskatchewan and Qu'Appelle rivers, and a southern division that ranged south to the Missouri River and west to the Cypress Hills. During the 19th century they suffered a drastic reduction in population due to the ravages

Above Right: Assiniboine warrior, c. 1833. Inspired by a Bodmer painting of a visitor to Fort Union on the Missouri in June 1833, he wears a loose-fitting hide shirt and a robe, and holds a rawhide combat shield with protective designs and "medicine." The bowlance, reported from a number of tribes, was probably dually-functional.

Right: Moccasins Assiniboine, c. 1900. A pair of solidly beaded moccasins in light blue, turquoise blue, dark blue, red (inside white), and green beads in geometrical designs. These moccasins were reported to have been collected on the Umatilla Reservation, Oregon, however the construction and beadwork designs suggest they may be from Montana and perhaps Assiniboine.

Below: Stoney Indian tipis, Alberta, c. 1910.

of smallpox, which persuaded a number of the Saskatchewan Assiniboine to move to the foothills of the Rocky Mountains. This group became known as "Stoney," apparently an allusion to their method of cooking with hot stones. Their culture was much the same as that of the Blackfoot during the 19th century but, like the Crees, they have a long association with white traders.

Those who remained in Canada were located on several reserves. The Mosquito, Grizzly Bear's Head and Lean Man's bands settled near Battleford, Saskatchewan; Pheasant Rump's and Ocean Man's bands settled near Moose Mountain (later moved to the White Bear Reserve); Carry-the-Kettle settled at Fort Qu'Appelle; Joseph's and Paul's bands near Edmonton and Chiniquay, Wesley and Bearspaw near Morley — the largest group. The Canadian Assiniboine-Stoney numbered 1,371 in 1904, and 13,510 in 2005, but this figure also included the Canadian Sioux. Those who settled on two reservations in Montana — Fort Peck and Fort Belknap — totaled 1,234 in 1904, a huge reduction from an aboriginal population of perhaps 10,000. In 1970, Mosquito-Grizzly Bear's Head numbered 387, a few were at White

Above: Stoney Indian tipis, near Banff, Alberta, c. 1910.

Left: Assiniboine, c. 1898. The many forms of war bonnet, collections of military symbolism with animal skins, feathers, shells and mirrors added — were once considered sacred. Exact ritual meanings faded with the end of the old warrior days. The bonnet was adopted simply as an ethnic symbol, or by men who had recently been in U.S. military service. The flamboyant eagle bonnets worn for parades by older men among the Assiniboine ("Stonies") at Morley, Alberta, were once famous.

Bear, and Carry-the-Kettle numbered 734 — all in Saskatchewan. The Mosquito-Grizzly Bear's Head and Lean Man now number 1,180, and Carry-the-Kettle reports 2,237 in 2005. In 1970 Alexis recorded 490 (1,516 in 2005), Paul's 575, and Chiniquay, Wesley and Bearspaw (Stoney) 1,610 (4,352 combined in 2005). All are in Alberta. The U.S. Assiniboine (5,274 in 2000) were divided almost equally between Fort Peck, where they are mixed with Yanktonai, and Fort Belknap, where they are mixed with Gros Ventre. The Assiniboine and Stoney often now prefer the name Nakoda derived from their Siouan background.

As a rural, and now an urban minority ethnic people, their 20th-century condition is much the same as that of other western Indian groups. The Morley Stoney participated for years in the "Banff Indian Days" celebration, a colorful show of tipis and Indian costume. The Assiniboine are one of those upper Missouri River tribes who were immortalized by the artists Catlin and Bodmer, who recorded Plains Indian life in its near-pristine grandeur during the 1830s.

In 1990 there were reported 8,120 Assiniboine in the United States, a number that grew to more than 11,000 by Census 2000.

CHEYENNE (TSISTSISTAS) An important Algonkian tribe of the high Plains whose earliest known home was Minnesota between the Mississippi and Minnesota rivers. They seem to have been in contact with La Salle's Fort on the Illinois

Above left: Little Wolf or more correctly Little Coyote, Northern Cheyenne chief, born c. 1820 died in 1904. He and Dull Knife led the dramatic escape of some Northern Cheyenne from Oklahoma, after their confinement, back to their homeland in Montana in 1878. The party of about 300 split after reaching Nebraska. Dull Knife's band surrendered at Ft. Robinson, whilst Little Wolf's band made their way back to Montana. He later became an army scout under Gen. Nelson A. Miles. The man in this photograph is identified as Little Wolf in the Smithsonian Archives, photographed by William Dinwiddie in Washington D.C. in 1895. Smithsonian Institution National Anthropological Archives, Bureau of American Ethnology Collection.

Left: Moccasins, Southern Cheyenne, c. 1900. Partly beaded moccasins in white, light and dark blue, rose (red), with white opaque center, and yellow beads. Cheyenne beaded moccasins dated from the 19th century to the present time almost always have a lane of beads across the instep just below the opening, and a lane (row) over the heel seam. Southern Cheyenne moccasins from Oklahoma usually have a welt of buckskin reinforcement between the moccasin upper and the hard sole on their moccasins, a trait introduced by white traders. These moccasins are typical Plains area buckskin construction with hard (rawhide) soles. The beadwork colors used — red, yellow, blue, and white — are the sacred colors of the Cheyenne Beadworkers Guild.

Below: Cheyenne buckskin tobacco bag, c. 1860, with beadwork formed into long narrow triangles by horizontal stripes.

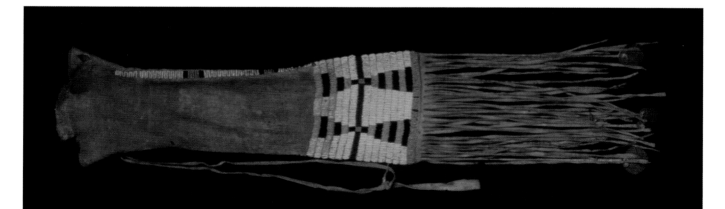

Above: "Jacob Two-Young-Man," a Stoney indian, c. 1950, wearing eagle feather headdress, beaded shirt and gauntlets, probably at Banff Indian Days. Photograph: Nicholas Morant

Left: Another Rinehart photograph of 1898, Assiniboine Chief Wets It.

Right: Cheyenne Woman with Cradle, c. 1870. She wears a beaded buckskin dress, and a German silver concho belt. Plains Indians became expert metalworkers using the inexpensive substitute for real silver. The cradle is a lattice-type with the pointed back boards visible. The cradle is now in the Buffalo Bill Museum, Cody, Wyoming but formerly belonged to the artist Frederic Remington and hung in his studio. Acrylic painting by Richard Hook.

Below: Blackfoot man, c.1910. He appears to be holding a "medicine pipe" during ceremonial preliminaries. He wears a Hudson's Bay trade blanket. The photographer was probably Walter McClintock.

River in 1680. At this time they lived in fixed villages, practised agriculture, and made pottery, but lost these arts after being driven out onto the Plains to become nomadic bison hunters. They became one of the focal points of the Plains culture, characterized by tipi dwelling, development of age-graded male societies, geometrical art, and the development of ceremonial world renewal complex, the Sun Dance. They were constantly pressed further into the Plains by the Sioux, who later became their firm allies.

After moving west from their original Woodland homeland the Cheyenne were ultimately joined by a related tribe, the Sutaio or Suhtai, an event according to tradition, taking place at Bear Butte in the Black Hills of South Dakota. This event was recounted in the legends of the culture heros Sweet Medicine and Erect Horns. They shared with other High Plains tribes cultural features such as military societies (the Cheyenne had the famous Dog Soldiers), band divisions of which they may have had ten, and the Sun Dance. However, they differed in having a central council of 44 chiefs. Their principal sacred tribal objects were and still are the Medicine Arrows and the Sacred Buffalo Hat. The tribe as a whole came together only in the summer when enough food was available for everyone. At least one great ceremonial was then held, the Sun Dance, Animal Dance (Massaum), or the Renewal of the Medicine Arrows. The Animal Dance was performed to perpetuate the supply of meat, particularly buffalo, and contained the symbolic killing of animals by clowns or Contararies who performed their rituals backwards.

After establishing themselves on the upper branches of the Platte River in Wyoming and Colorado they were in constant warfare with the Crow, Shoshone, and Pawnee. Later in consequence of the building of Bent's Fort on the upper Arkansas River in Colorado in 1832, a large part of the tribe moved south to the Arkansas while the rest remained on the North Platte, Powder, and Yellowstone rivers. Thus came into being the geographical division of the tribe into the Northern and Southern Cheyenne. Their population before the cholera epidemic of 1849 was about 3,000 to 4,000.

By the early 1840s the Cheyenne encountered American emigration and in 1851 at the Fort Laramie Treaty the Americans recognized the two divisions of the tribe. Between 1854 and 1879 the Cheyenne fought more than 50 military actions against

Above: Cheyenne woman, c. 1880. A buckskin dress of classic southern Plains three-hide type: front and back forming the skirt, with the yoke a large, folded rectangle sewn to the skirt tube in a straight seam. Two bands of beadwork are sewn halfway between head aperture and seam, and one band along the shoulder fold. Along the bottom are zigzag motifs, and corner extensions simulating the legs of the original animal shape. Sioux women also wore a three-hide dress, although the yoke hide was less deep, and was sometimes separate and covered with seed beadwork. All Plains women substituted cloth for hide in the early reservation years.

Left: Cheyenne Sun Dancer, c. 1890. This most important Plains festival is described in the introduction to the Plains and Prairie section of the text. Details of this world renewal rite varied between tribes. Cheyenne dancers were painted symbolically: the lower body white, the upper body black (clouds) with white dots (hail), the blue central rectangle representing the morning star and the blue facial circle, the sun. Wreaths of willow were usually worn around head, limbs and body.

American soldiers and consequently lost more fighting men in comparison with their numbers than any other Plains Indian people. In 1864 Colonel J.M. Chivington led a troop of militia against a camp of more than 500 Cheyenne and Arapaho, killing many women and children. In 1866 Cheyenne warriors were among the Sioux who annihilated Fetterman's troop near Fort Phil Kearney in Wyoming, but in 1868 Roman Nose was killed at Beecher Island, and Black Kettle's Southern Cheyenne village was destroyed by Lt.Col. George A. Custer on the Washita River, Oklahoma. The Dog Soldiers were defeated at Summit Springs in Colorado in 1869, but they took part in Custer's defeat at the Little Big Horn on June 25, 1876, after the U.S. government's failure to protect hunting grounds from gold prospectors and railroad surveyors, as specified in the 1868 Fort Laramie Treaty. Despite the tribes' success in the battle of the Little Big Horn that June, Mackenzie secured their surrender, and in 1877 a portion of the Northern Cheyenne was brought to Oklahoma to be colonized with the Southern Cheyenne who had agreed to move to a reservation located in western Indian Territory by the terms of the Medicine Lodge Treaty of 1867.

Reservation conditions were harsh and became intolerable, causing Little Wolf and

Above: The Cheyenne often completely covered the bag of their lattice cradles with lazy stitch beadwork in their characteristic stepped, elongated triangles enclosing rectangles, and figures of birds, dragonflies and horses. The colors used were symbolically important, representing life-giving powers.

Far Right: Arapaho man c. 1880. Wholesale use of white trade goods had considerably modified central Plains dress by the third quarter of the 19th century. This man wears a set of horizontally strung "hairpipes" and a nickel-silver cross. His pipe has a red catlinite bowl; his pipe bag and moccasins show geometrical patterns also favored by the Sioux and the Cheyenne (although details differed), executed in seed beads in sinew-sewn ridged lanes— "lazy stitch." Central plains moccasins by now had hard soles sewn to separate uppers, a style thought to be white-influenced.

Right: Cheyenne warrior, c. 1870. The Dog-Men (to whites, "Dog Soldiers") were the largest of several age-graded military societies, numbering perhaps half the Cheyenne males of 15 and older and including the chief, seven assistants, and four warriors selected for bravery to protect the society from enemy raids. These four, as illustrated, wore special skin or cloth scarves decorated with eagle feathers over their heads or one shoulder and trailing to the ground; the supreme demonstration of bravery was to stake this to the earth with a red peg, symbolizing willingness to fight to the death on that spot. Their headdress was of erect magpie, owl, hawk or crow feathers surmounted by eagle tail feathers. Ceremonial regalia included eagle bone whistles, dew claw rattles and skunk skin belts, and they held a bow and arrow during ritual dances.

Dull Knife to make an heroic return to the north country. Despite internment at Fort Robinson, Nebraska, and a second break for liberty, about 60 had rejoined those who remained in the north, and in 1884 were assigned to a reservation on the Tongue River, Montana, where their descendants remain. In this comparatively rugged, isolated country Cheyenne descendants have struggled with problems of poverty and readjustment to rural and recently urban American culture.

In 1954 the Northern Cheyenne numbered some 2,120 but there has been an increase in the numbers of those of mixed Cheyenne and white blood in recent years (8,036 in Montana in 2001). However, the traditional beliefs surrounding the Sacred Buffalo Hat and the Sun Dance still persist. The Southern Cheyenne are found in various counties in Oklahoma, specific-ally Custer, Roger Mills, Canadian, King-fisher, Blaine, and Dewey. Parts of the allotted Cheyenne and Arapaho Reservation opened to white settlement in 1892.

In 1950 there were 2,110 Southern Cheyenne, 11,459 in 2001 (including some Arapaho). They too have retained traditional symbols of ethnic unity such as the Sacred Medicine Arrows, although they are nominally Christian.

Peyotism has a strong following in the south. Both groups sponsor pan-Indian powwows at various times when other tribes attend.

In 2011, 11,688 were given as Cheyenne alone, presumably counting both Northern and Southern together.

ARAPAHO (HINANAEINA) The Arapaho are an Algonkian-speaking tribe of the Plains, being originally one people with the Atsina. The origins of the tribe are not known, but tradition has it that they came from the headwaters of the Mississippi River, or even Canada. They formed the most aberrant group of the whole Algonkian family, which points to a long separation from their parent group. The Arapaho were often noted for their religious and contemplative disposition, less warlike than the Cheyenne. They were a nomadic equestrian people, hunting bison, developing military and age-graded organizations, and observed the annual Sun Dance. After crossing the Missouri River they pressed on to the headwaters of the Platte River, to the edge of the Rockies in present eastern Wyoming by 1820. By 1835 a portion of the tribe had moved south to the upper Arkansas River in eastern Colorado, thus

Opposite, Above Right: Arapaho Chief Black Man wearing a Ghost Dance shirt, another Rinehart photograph of 1898.

Opposite, Above Left: Southern Cheyenne Chief Killer, a colored print of 1899 from a painting by E.A. Burbank, Chicago.

Opposite, Below: A group of Cheyenne men, c. 1909.

Left: Arapaho man wearing an eagle feather "war bonnet" and holding a tobacco bag and fan. Photograph: Charles Carpenter, Saint Louis Exposition, 1904

Above: Pitatapiu, Assiniboine, painted at Fort Union by Karl Bodmer in 1833. He holds a rawhide bison hide shield and a long bow-lance. Behind him stands another Assiniboine warrior who wears a skin shirt with a large porcupine-quilled chest disk and bison hide robe. He carries an English-made flintlock sold by the American Fur Co.

Below: Southern Cheyenne woman's moccasins, Oklahoma, c. 1930.

Right: Arapaho, c. 1875. Although the Arapaho used cradles similar to the Sioux and Cheyenne, a number of unusual specimens have survived that are attributed to them. A branch of willow, chokecherry or sumac was held in an inverted U-shape by transverse sticks. The cover was a plain piece of buckskin or canvas, folded lengthwise and stitched together along one short side. The quilled ornaments usually consisted of a large disc at the top and wrapped ladder-like rawhide bands down the front opening. Pendants were either plain or quill-wrapped buckskin strips with small bells or deer claws attached.

Below: Arapaho, c. 1870. The Arapaho, Cheyenne and Western Sioux of the central Plains resembled one another in dress, ornamentation and use of trade goods. The latter included blanket cloth, bone hairpipes, silver, German silver and beads. These partly replaced hide robes, shell beads and native forms of decoration — notably porcupine quillwork, by the mid-century. The development of seed beadwork after the 1850s is characterized by hourglass, triangle, diamond and stripe designs, perhaps derived from earlier quilled or painted parfleche and rawhide designs. The warrior holds a rawhide shield and a typical Plains lance. A quirt hangs from his wrist, and a blanket with beaded strip ornamentation lies across his lap. His horse is painted and decorated with eagle feathers, its bridle with German silver.

Right: Two views of the interior of an Arapaho or Cheyenne tipi.

forming the Northern and Southern branches of the tribe. At this time they were in constant alliance with the Cheyenne, but were often at war with the Shoshone, Ute and Pawnee, and also raided with the Kiowa and Comanche, with whom they had friendly relations.

The history of the Southern Arapaho is similar to that of the Southern Cheyenne. They entered into treaties with the United States in 1861 and at Medicine Lodge River in southern Kansas in 1867, which assigned them to lands in western Indian Territory, now Oklahoma, where descendants remain. The Northern Arapaho were assigned to the Wind River Reservation, Wyoming, after making peace with the Wind River Shoshone with whom they share the reservation. Wind River is well watered, with rich natural resources, and supports Indian-owned cattle. But the Arapaho have had serious social and economic problems over the years. The Southern Arapaho are found mostly in rural Blaine and Washita counties, Oklahoma, much mixed with the Cheyenne. In pre-reservation days the Arapaho probably numbered 3,000. In 1923 the Southern Arapaho numbered 833 and the Northern branch 921; in 1950, the Southern branch 1,189; and in 1960, the Northern Arapaho 2,279. In 1970 the combined population was given as 2,993, and in 1990 about 6,000. The Northern Arapaho numbered 7,131 in 2001. Although a separate number was not given from the Cheyenne, the Southern Arapaho likely number close to 7,000 as well (6,350 in 2000). They were strong adherents of the Ghost Dance movement of 1890.

Right: Sioux, c. 1900. The symbol of the Native American: the eagle feather crown or war bonnet. Feather crowns are probably ancient in the Americas, associated with chieftainship, war and ritual. The flared crown bonnet probably evolved among the Upper Missouri tribes, and was recorded in this form by George Catlin as early as the 1830s. It was particularly associated with the Sioux, Cheyenne and Arapaho, but during early reservation days was adopted by many tribes as an ethnic symbol. The feathers were laced to a hide skullcap (or, later, a traded felt hat with the brim removed).

Below: Sioux, c. 1885. The cradle was a rectangular bag of hide, backed with rawhide or canvas, with a piece of parfleche inserted under the top and extending to form a square or rectangular back tab beaded with symbolic protective designs. The sides of the bag were often fully beaded in geometrical designs, including box shapes with extending prongs. The Sioux occasionally mounted cradles on frames similar to those of more southerly tribes.

Below Right: Sioux amulets. The Plains peoples customarily enclosed the umbilical cord of a newborn infant in a decorative bag in the shape of a turtle or lizard, which was hung on the cradle as a protective charm.

Opposite: The Sioux domain, 1800–1850, highlighting the location of the seven divisions (in yellow) and seven sub-groups (red) of the Teton.

SIOUAN

Siouan is an important language family of American Indians whose ancestors probably originated in the Mississippi Valley where some of the most highly developed North American civilizations existed. Tribal traditions seem to indicate movement from this general area along the Mississippi, ultimately to dominate the central Plains. However, a divergent branch, the Catawba and their associates, are found in the Carolinas. Late 19th century texts collected on the Iroquois Grand River Reserve in Ontario from adopted Tutelo descendants strongly suggest a close relationship to the western division of the family. Subsequently, a number of absorbed or extinct tribes of the Tutelos' ancient home — Virginia, — have been added to the family on purely circumstantial evidence.

The Western Siouans — the Dakota-Assiniboine group — comprises the Dakota, Nakota, and Lakota (including the seven Sioux tribes speaking three dialects, although the separation of the Nakota from Dakota is now in question), and the Assiniboine, now regarded as the Assiniboine and Stoney (Nakoda); the Dhegiha, comprising the Omaha, Ponca, Kansa, Osage and Quapaw; the Chiwere, comprising Iowa and Oto-Missouria, the Winnebago, Mandan, and finally the Hidatsa-Crow.

SIOUX or DAKOTA

These are collective terms used by the united States and Canadian governments to designate the largest section of the Siouan linguistic family—seven tribes, all very closely related. When first mentioned by early white explorers in the mid-17century, all seven tribes lived within what is now the southern half of the state of Minnesota. Several of the Sioux tribes have traditionally resided at Mille Lacs, Minnesota, which seems to have been a home for several bands when Hennepin and DuLuth visited them 300 years ago. Culturally they seem to have been a Woodland and Prairie people, living in bark lodges and practicing slash-and-burn horticulture, fishing, and hunting.

French maps only separated Sioux of the East and Sioux of the West as late as the 1700s with their western advance barred by a score of Arikara villages strung along the Missouri in present day South Dakota until that tribe were weakened by smallpox and measles during the early 18th century. The Western Sioux diaspora from Minnestoa has recently been placed much earlier at least as far west as the lower Sheyenne River by some authorities. Pressure during the 18th century from the Ojibwa, who were

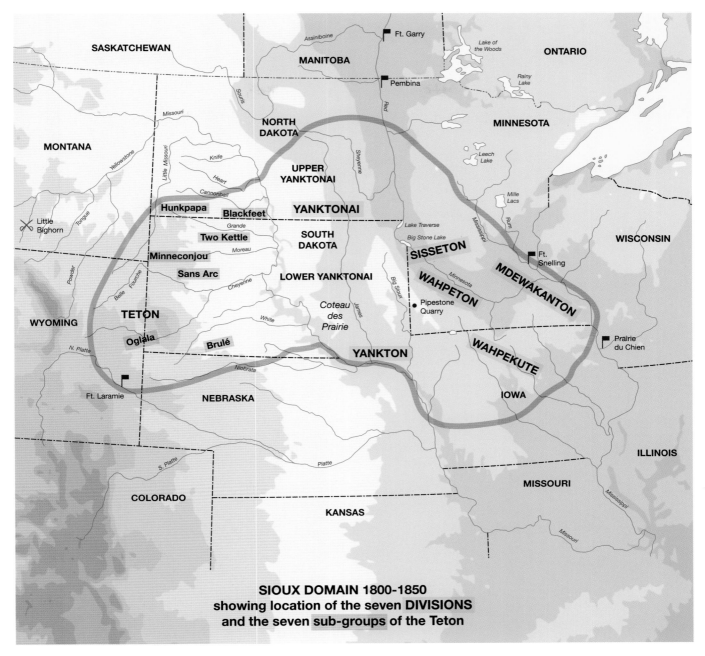

SIOUX DOMAIN 1800-1850
showing location of the seven DIVISIONS
and the seven sub-groups of the Teton

supplied with firearms by the French, probably hastened their western movement with two main groups finally crossing the Missouri River and developing a strong horse culture dependent upon the bison, tipi dwelling, and a truly nomadic way of life. In time they became known for their stubborn resistance to white encroachment.

Their name, Sioux, seems to be of Ojibwa-French extraction, meaning "adders" or snakes, a translation now regarded as inaccurate. Their own name, Dakota, means "allies," and they were once known as the Seven Council Fires before their westward dispersal. Dakota is the name of the whole nation in the eastern dialect, Nakota in the middle dialect, and Lakota in the western dialect. Although the separation of Nakota from Dakota has recently been challenged.

The seven tribes were:
1 Mdewakanton or Mdewakantonwan, sometimes Bdewakanton—meaning "Spirit Lake village," referring to Mille Lacs in Minnesota.
2 Wahpekute—"Leaf shooters."

3 Wahpeton or Wahpetonwan—"Village in the leaves."
4 Sisseton or Sisitonwan—"Swamp villagers."
These four tribes formed the Dakota or Santee (Isanti) section.

5 Yankton or Ihanktonwan—"Dwellers at the end village."
6 Yanktonai or Ihanktonwanna—"Little dwellers at the end."
These two tribes formed the Nakota or middle section.

7 Teton or Titonwan—"Dwellers on the Prairie."

This single tribe were the Lakota or western branch of the nation. In 1990 there were reported 75,000 descendants of all branches of the Sioux in the United States, perhaps 20 percent full blood. By the time of the 2000 Census, that number had swelled to 108,272, with an even smaller percentage of full-blood ancestry.

MDEWAKANTON SIOUX These people are a Sioux tribe of the Eastern or Santee division of the nation who formerly lived at Mille Lacs at the head of the Rum River, Minnesota,

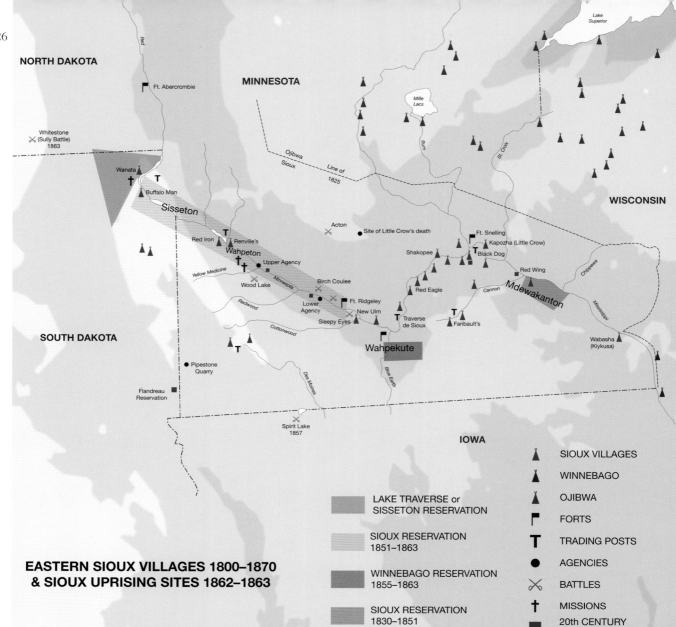

EASTERN SIOUX VILLAGES 1800–1870
& SIOUX UPRISING SITES 1862–1863

LAKE TRAVERSE or
SISSETON RESERVATION

SIOUX RESERVATION
1851–1863

WINNEBAGO RESERVATION
1855–1863

SIOUX RESERVATION
1830–1851
(mixed bloods)

SIOUX VILLAGES

WINNEBAGO

OJIBWA

FORTS

TRADING POSTS

AGENCIES

BATTLES

MISSIONS

20th CENTURY
RESERVATIONS

Right: Eastern Sioux brave, c. 1860s, probably photographed in Minnesota by J. E. Whitney. Note gunstock-shaped wooden club, and pipe with twisted stem and catlinite bowl, typical of western Woodland groups.

Left: Map showing Eastern Sioux villages 1800–1870 and Sioux uprising sites 1862–1863.

Below Left: Santee (Eastern Sioux) graves. Painting by Seth Eastman, c. 1850. Collections of the Minnesota Historical Society

but are later associated with the region of the west bank of the Mississippi River from Winona to Red Wing in southeast Minnesota. The economy of the Santee rested on hunting, fishing, gathering (wild rice) and a horticulture complex of respectable antiquity. They lived in bark gable-roofed houses, and also wigwams. Bison hunts were organized by appointed hunt chiefs, and band chiefs were usually hereditary, with an appointed *akicita* (police) from the warrior societies. Dress was modified during the 18th and early 19th centuries by the adoption of cloth, sashes and coats from traders, but they retained shirts, leggings and soft-soled moccasins. Santee women wore the two-piece Central Algonkian style dress, consisting of a wraparound skirt and loose blouse. The Santee were expert at ribbonwork and beadwork, including floralistic, zoomorphic and geometrical designs applied to ceremonial dress. Their chief ceremonies were the Medicine Dance, which resembled the Algonkian Midewiwin, and the Thunder Dance. Some bands also adopted the Sun Dance.

In 1851 they sold their lands to the government and moved to the upper Minnesota River area. They were the principal participants in the 1862 uprising against the whites in Minnesota, which resulted in their capture and dispersion. Some fled to Canada under their chief, Little Crow, while those who survived the ordeal were placed principally on the Santee Reservation, Knox County, Nebraska (mixed with Wahpekute); Upper Sioux Reservation near Granite Falls, Lower Sioux Reservation near Morton, Prairie Island near Red Wing, Prior Lake near Shakopee (all in Minnesota), and the Flandreau settlement on the Big Sioux River, South Dakota, all mixed with other Santee. Before 1851, there were seven bands of Mdewakanton, including the Kiyuksa (a name used by bands of other Sioux tribes) and Kapoza. The Santee of the Niobrara Reservation, Nebraska, numbered 1,075 in 1904 and 1,400 in 1955, but many had left the area. A few are in Canada at Sioux Valley (Oak River) and Birdtail near Birtle, Manitoba, but are not reported separately.

WAHPEKUTE SIOUX These are a branch of the Santee or Dakota division of the Sioux group on the Cannon and Blue Earth Rivers in southern Minnesota, particularly around the old Faribault's Trading Post. Lewis and Clark found them on the Minnesota River below the Redwood River junction. After the sale of their lands in 1851, some joined the Mdewakanton, with whom they are sometimes referred to as the "Lower Council Sioux," in distinction from the Sisseton-Wahpeton, the "Upper Council Sioux." Following their participation in the affair at Spirit Lake, Iowa in 1857, and the Minnesota outbreak of 1862, the Wahpekute fled mostly to Canada, and to the Missouri. Those on the Missouri combined with the Mdewakanton on the Santee Reserve on the Niobrara River, Knox County, Nebraska, where a portion of their descendants, about 400 strong, remained in 1955. They were reported as numbering 2,663 in 2001.

In Canada, where some descendants of Chief Inkpaduta's band remain, they are found at Sioux Valley Reservation (Oak River) near Griswold, Manitoba, mixed with the three other Santee tribes, numbering 899 in 1970. A few others were incorporated among other Santee at Oak Lake near Pipestone, Manitoba, and Sioux Wahpeton Reservation (Round Plain) near Prince Albert in Saskatchewan.

A handful no doubt merged with the few Mdewakanton in the small remaining Minnesota communities, and a few more are said to have accompanied the Yanktonai to Fort Peck, Montana.

Most of the Eastern Sioux groups have over the years assumed the rural culture of the European immigrant farmer, but at a lower economic level. The Wahpekute Sioux today do not exist as a separate tribal group, having mixed with other communities as a direct result of the 1862-63 campaign, during which General Henry H. Sibley and his troops scattered the Santees, many fleeing to Canada.

WAHPETON SIOUX The traditional home of the Wahpetons was near Little Rapids, some 45 miles (70 km) from the mouth of the Minnesota River's junction with the Mississippi. But after 1851 they removed to Lac-Qui-Parle and Big Stone Lake in the western part of Minnesota. They are sometimes grouped with the Sisseton into the "Upper Council Sioux." They were involved in the outbreak of hostilities between the Eastern Sioux and whites in 1862, as a result of which they were scattered over a wide area. Most were ultimately gathered on the Sisseton or Lake Traverse Reservation in South Dakota, where, in 1909, the combined Sisseton-Wahpeton numbered 1,936. A few Wahpeton were

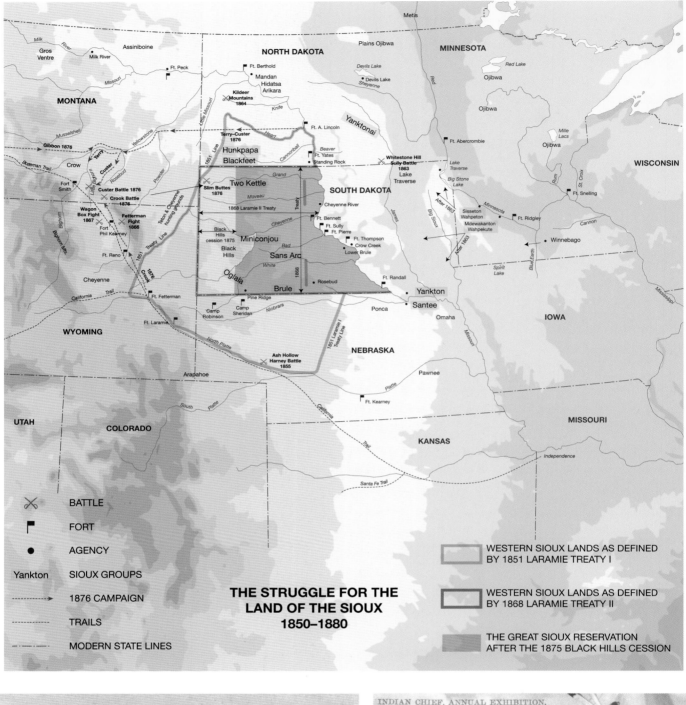

THE STRUGGLE FOR THE LAND OF THE SIOUX 1850–1880

BATTLE
FORT
AGENCY
Yankton SIOUX GROUPS
1876 CAMPAIGN
TRAILS
MODERN STATE LINES

WESTERN SIOUX LANDS AS DEFINED BY 1851 LARAMIE TREATY I

WESTERN SIOUX LANDS AS DEFINED BY 1868 LARAMIE TREATY II

THE GREAT SIOUX RESERVATION AFTER THE 1875 BLACK HILLS CESSION

INDIAN CHIEF, ANNUAL EXHIBITION, BRANDON MAN.

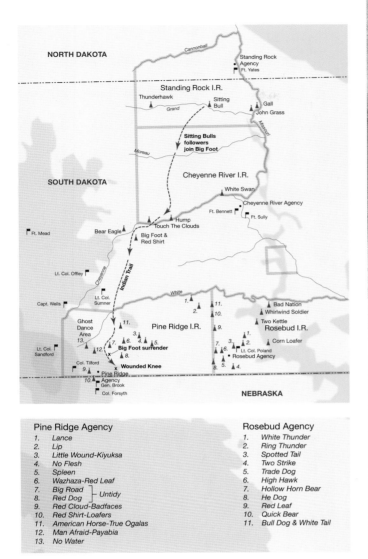

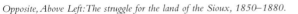

Opposite, Above Left: The struggle for the land of the Sioux, 1850–1880.

Opposite, Below Left and Below Right Mounted Indian at Brandon, Manitoba, c. 1900. Probably Santee Sioux with their reserve at close-by Sioux Valley. Note the scalp hanging below the bridle and the tied eagle feathers in the horse's tail, usually a warrior symbol. He wears trade cloth leggings in Plains style but the decorated saddle or bag just visible, appears to be Woodland beaded style, or possibly Métis. Amost 100 years before the Brandon photograph the artist Peter Rindischacher in 1829 had painted a Sioux warrior on horseback with feathers tied in the horse's tail, apparently a Sioux trait. The warrior holds a feathered lance and wears buckskin leggings with quillwork decoration.

Above: Map of the Ghost Dance War, 1890, showing the Indian trail to Wounded Knee and Indian bands (numbered).

Above Right: Joseph Tawapaha Waskena "Good Coup Stick" Santee Sioux (Dakota) of Griswold, Manitoba with his wives. He is holding an Ojibwa-Cree style tobacco bag. After moving to Canada after 1862 the Santee adopted regalia of these northern peoples. Photograph courtesy Louis Garcia.

Center Right: Early 20th century Indian men wearing eagle feather headdresses. The man on the right wears a beaded shirt and holds a pipe. The other man holds a beaded fire bag and wears beaded gauntlets. They are thought to have been Canadian Santee Sioux (Dakota), in Manitoba. Photograph credits Alvina Alberts and Louis Garcia, Ft. Totten, N. Dakota.

Below Right: Mr and Mrs Claude Irish and daughter Dora Irish, Santee Sioux (Dakota), Ft. Totten, aka Spirit Lake Reservation, North Dakota, early 20th century. The lady wears vertically strung "hairpipes" (commercially turned from animal bones) and the man wears horizontally strung hair pipes. Originally of silver or shell made for eastern trade to decorate the hair. Bone hairpipes became popular after about 1872. Indians today continue to use hairpipes for dance regalia.

Above: Wahpeton Sioux dancers, c. 1900, at Fort Totten Reservation, North Dakota.

Above Right: Eastern Sioux warrior, Wa-kan-o-zhan-zhan (Medicine Bottle), who was executed in November 1865 for his part in the 1862 Minnesota outbreak. Photographed by J.E. Whitney in June 1864 at Fort Snelling, Minnesota.

included with Sisseton and Yanktonai at Devil's Lake (Fort Totten) Agency, North Dakota, where the three together numbered 1,013 in 1904. In 1956, the enrolled population at Sisseton was 3,672, and at Devil's Lake (Fort Totten) 1,500. In 2001 the Sisseton Sioux numbered 10,759, and those on the Flandreau, 716. A number also fled to Canada, their descendants in Manitoba at the Birdtail Reserve near Birtle numbering 187 in 1970 (686 in 2005), and those at Long Plain Sioux Reserve near Portage La Prairie, 224 the same year. These are mostly Wahpeton descendants, as are a few mixed with other Santee at Oak River, Oak Lake, Manitoba, and Standing Buffalo and Round Plain, Saskatchewan. The Eastern Sioux in Minnesota and Yankton have traditionally been the only persons who possessed the rights and permissions to work the pipestone quarries of southern Minnesota, where ceremonial pipes were made, and more recently, novelty souvenirs.

SISSETON SIOUX This is the largest of the four Eastern Sioux or Dakota tribes, who claim an origin around the headwaters of the Rum River, Minnesota, in the area of Mille

Lacs when first met by whites in the 17th century. Later, they seem to have been located near the junction of the Minnesota and Blue Earth Rivers in Minnesota, and at Traverse des Sioux. By the 1840s, some had moved to the Lake Traverse and the James River country. The majority were located on the Sisseton Reservation in South Dakota and combined with the Wahpeton. A few joined other Santee at Oak River (Sioux Valley), Manitoba, and larger numbers of their descendants are at Standing Buffalo Reserve near Fort Qu'Appelle and Moose Woods or White Cap Reserve near Dundurn, both in Saskatchewan. In 1956, the Sisseton-Wahpeton at Lake Traverse (Sisseton Reservation) numbered 3,672 (10,759 in 2001); in 1970 Standing Buffalo numbered 514 (1,078 in 2005), and Moose Woods 148. Before their dispersal following the war of 1862, there were about six bands, including those of Sleepy Eyes, Red Iron and Gray Thunder, all prominent chiefs. The band called "Dryers on the Shoulder" lived near Lake Traverse and were great buffalo hunters; they apparently formed the principal group of the Standing Buffalo Reserve in Canada.

YANKTON SIOUX The Yankton Sioux are one of the seven divisions of the Sioux, and one of the two that form the Nakota or, geographically, the Middle Sioux. They were probably in the vicinity of Mille Lacs with their relatives during the 17th century. In 1708 they were on the east bank of the Missouri River near the site of Sioux City, Iowa. They were not noted separately again until Lewis and Clark found them in the region of the James, Big Sioux and Des Moines rivers in southeastern South Dakota, neighboring Iowa and Minnesota. In 1842 they were noted on the Vermillon River in South Dakota. They seem to have been well known to traders along the Missouri, and through the efforts of Chief Palaneapape they were restrained from joining the Santee in the Minnesota outbreak of 1862.

In 1858, they ceded all their lands to the United States, except for a reservation on the north bank of the Missouri near Wagner, South Dakota, where their descendants have lived since. They were generally indistinguishable from their close relatives the Yanktonai. Lewis and Clark estimated their numbers at 4,300 with the Yanktonai. In 1867 there were 2,530 Yankton alone; in 1909 they were reported as numbering 1,739; in 1945, 1,927; in 1956, 2,391; and in 2001, 7,570. A few incorporated with other Sioux on various reservations and are no longer reported separately, and many have intermarried with non-Indians over the years. Perhaps fewer than half of the present inhabitants of reservations in eastern South Dakota are full-blood members of their respective tribes. The Yankton are said to have had eight bands, the Cankute or "Shooters-at-the-Tree" being the most noted.

YANKTONAI SIOUX The more dominant of the two Nakota branches of the Sioux nation, speaking the same dialect as the Yankton, were the Yanktonai. Their homeland included the drainages of the James and Big Sioux rivers and the Coteau du Missouri. The economy of these Middle Sioux, like the Missouri River groups they had displaced, rested on a base of hunting, fishing, gathering and river bottom horticulture. Great tribal bison hunts took place twice a year, taking them far west of the Missouri. They used the skin tipi, and skin-covered

wikiups resembling those of bark found among the Santee. They also made or used abandoned earth lodges, and employed the "bull boat," a round hide river craft probably adopted from the Mandan, Hidatsa and Arikara. The Sun Dance was their most important religious ceremony. The Yanktonai divided into two divisions: the Upper Yanktonai in six bands of which the Kiyuksa ("Breakers of the Rule") and Pabaksa ("Cutheads") were the most prominent, and the Lower Yanktonai or Hunkpatina. In the 17th century the Assiniboine are said to have divided from the Yanktonai and moved to Canada. They still refer to themselves as *Nakoda*, but are now considered as a separate people.

The Yanktonai took part in the War of 1812 on the side of Great Britain. They took no part in the Minnesota War of 1862, and made treaties of peace with the United States in 1865, being divided between reservations on the Missouri. The Upper Yanktonai descendants are on the Standing Rock Reservation on the North–South Dakota border, and on the Devil's Lake — now known as Spirit Lake — (Fort Totten) Reservation, North Dakota (mostly Pabaksa). The Lower Yanktonai are found on Crow Creek Reservation, Fort Thompson, South Dakota, and on the Fort Peck Reservation, Wolf Point, Montana. In 1956 the combined Sisseton-Wahpeton-Upper Yanktonai of Fort Totten numbered 1,500; the combined Teton and Upper Yanktonai of Standing Rock 4,324; the Lower Yanktonai and Teton of Crow Creek 1,132; and the Lower Yanktonai (locally called Yankton) and Assiniboine of Fort Peck were reported to number 3,881. In 2001, the combined Yanktonai, Yankton and Teton on the

Below: Wahpeton and Yanktonai Sioux dancers, c. 1900, probably 4th of July powwow, Ft. Totten Reservation (Devil's Lake now called Spirit Lake), North Dakota.

Crow Creek Reservation, South Dakota, numbered 3,507. The North Dakota Standing Rock Reservation, with Yanktonai and Teton, numbered 7,380.

TETON SIOUX This was the largest and most powerful of all the original seven branches of the Dakota or Sioux Indians. In fact, they outnumbered the other six tribes together. They became the Western Sioux, or in their own dialect, Lakota, following their migration onto the High Plains in the late 18th and early 19th centuries. They were divided into seven bands: Hunkpapa, Minneconjou, Sihasapa (or Blackfoot — no connection with the Algonkian Blackfoot), Oohenonpa (Two Kettle), Sicangu (or Brulé), Itazipco (Sansarcs) and Oglala. Leaving their original home in Minnesota, they were around Lake Traverse by 1700 and on the Missouri by 1750. By about 1820 they claimed the whole of western South Dakota

centering on the Black Hills. They transformed completely to a bison-hunting economy, supplemented by deer and antelope, lived in conical skin tipis and secured vast herds of horses.

The Western Sioux had an elaborate system of warrior societies, including the *akicita* or soldiers, Kit Foxes, Crow Owners (referring to a special type of dance bustle), Strong Hearts (famous for their unique ermine skin horned headdresses worn in battle). These societies often fought as a unit. Another type of organization, completely mystical in character, were the dream societies such as Buffalo and Elk Dreamers. Although details of organization differed from band to band, the council and chiefs emerged as the principal governing body. The supreme counselors among the Oglala were "Shirt-Wearers." Their dress consisted of skin shirts and leggings for men, decorated with porcupine quills or later, beads. Women wore skin dresses, often heavily beaded, with much decoration in

Below: Delegation of Brulé Sioux (Lakota) to Washington, D.C., June 1870. Left to right: Fast Bear (Mato Ohanco), a senior warrior of the Wazhazha band; Spotted Tail (Sinte Gleska), head chief of the Brulé subtribe; Swift Bear (Mato Luza), chief of the Corn Owner's band; Yellow Hair, another senior warrior of the Wazhazha. Right rear is Capt. D.C. Poole, to whose Carlisle Indian School in Pennsylvania children were often forcibly sent for insensitive indoctrination in white ways.

Opposite, Above Left: A man's skin shirt, probably antelope, with war exploit painting and plaited quilled strips, dating prior to 1850 (and perhaps much earlier). Plaited quillwork edged with blue, red, and white pound beads suggests a possible Crow origin. The warrior figures, horses, and weapons belong to the early style of the Siouan tribes of the Northern Plains and upper Missouri River. Later on a more realistic painting style emerged with European influences. National Museum of the American Indian, New York.

Opposite, Above Right: Conquering Bear, Oglala (Western Sioux) 1898, wearing eagle feather headdress. Photograph F.A. Rinehart, Omaha.

Opposite, Below: Spotted Tail (Sinte Gleska) and wife. A Brulé Teton Sioux (Western Sioux) born about 1823 and killed near the Rosebud Agency in August 1881, Spotted Tail rose to the position of chief after proving his prowess in battle, and won his wife in a dual with a subchief. He was present at the Grattan fight in 1854 and the retribution by Harvey at Ash Hollow in western Nebraska. He signed the Laramie Treaty of 1868 as Chief of the Lower Brulés and was henceforth acknowledged as an important agency chief. The facts relating to his death are in dispute as he was leading a hostile party against Crow Dog at the time. The quilled and beaded shirt he is depicted wearing is now in the National Museum of the American Indian, New York and Washington (NMAI), and was collected at Fort Laramie in 1855. It is heavily fringed with hair-locks. Oil painting by Richard Hook

Above: Little Wound of the Oglala subtribe of the Western or Teton-Sioux (who today prefer the term Lakota), photographed by Heyn of Omaha, probably during the 1898 Trans-Mississippi Exposition at Omaha. He wears typical ceremonial clothing of his nation, with the then-popular "war bonnet" with eagle feather trailer.

Above Right: Sioux Shield, 1899, by E.A. Burbank.

Below: Sioux Indians gambling, c. 1909, probably at a "Wild West" touring show. Several men wear beaded vests and blanket strips, hairpipes and feather bonnets. Photograph: W.H. Martin

Opposite 1 Sioux Chief Red Cloud, 1899, by E.A. Burbank. This Oglala chief was born in 1822 and led the Sioux against the U.S. Army on the Bozeman Trail in the 1860s. He destroyed Fetterman's detachment but lost many warriors at the Wagon Box Fight in 1867. He agreed the 1868 Laramie Treaty and lived to a ripe old age, dying at Pine Ridge in 1909.

2 Sioux High Bear, 1898, from a photograph by Rinehart.

3 Sioux Iron Crow, 1899, by E.A. Burbank.

4 Sioux Annie Red Shirt, 1898, from a photograph by Rinehart.

CHIEF RED-CLOUD.
SIOUX.

1

HIGH BEAR
SIOUX—

HIGH BEAR
—SIOUX—

2

IRON-CROW.
SIOUX.

3

ANNIE RED SHIRT
—SIOUX—

4

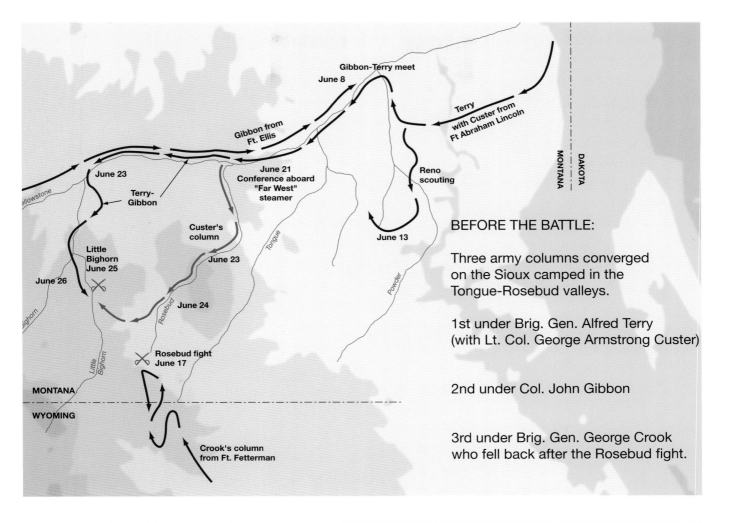

Gibbon-Terry meet
June 8

Terry
with Custer from
Ft Abraham Lincoln

Gibbon from
Ft. Ellis

MONTANA
DAKOTA

June 23
Terry-
Gibbon

June 21
Conference aboard
"Far West"
steamer

Reno
scouting

Custer's
column

June 13

Little
Bighorn
June 25

June 23

June 26

June 24

Rosebud fight
June 17

MONTANA

WYOMING

Crook's column
from Ft. Fetterman

BEFORE THE BATTLE:

Three army columns converged on the Sioux camped in the Tongue-Rosebud valleys.

1st under Brig. Gen. Alfred Terry (with Lt. Col. George Armstrong Custer)

2nd under Col. John Gibbon

3rd under Brig. Gen. George Crook who fell back after the Rosebud fight.

Right and Below Right: One of the most controversial military engagements in American history, the Battle of the Little Bighorn in southeastern Montana was fought on June 25, 1876. Custer split his command, attacked a large encampment of Sioux and Cheyenne, and was annihilated. Major Reno, who failed to reach Custer during the battle, is often blamed for the defeat. Although Sitting Bull was present or nearby, the following chiefs and bands also took part: Hunkapapas under Gall and Black Moon; Oglalas under Crazy Horse; Minneconjous under Fast Bull; Sans Arcs under Fast Bear; Blackfeet under Scabby Head; Cheyennes under Two Moon and Ice Bear; Santees, Yanktons, and Yanktonais under Inkpaduta. Many details of the battle are still unknown, including the exact route of Custer to his "last stand." The battle actually took place in the land of the Crows and on the present-day Crow Reservation.

1 Sioux Kicking Bear, 1899, by E.A. Burbank. Kicking Bear (1846–1904), was an Oglala Lakota who fought in several battles during the War for the Black Hills, including the Battle of Little Bighorn. He joined Buffalo Bill Cody's Wild West Show in 1891.

2 Sioux Chief Little Wound, 1899, by E.A. Burbank.

3 Sioux Chief Spotted Elk, friend of Red Cloud, 1899, by E.A. Burbank. This not the Spotted Elk, also called Big Foot by Americans, who was murdered with many of his people at Wounded Knee during the Ghost Dance troubles of 1890.

4 Sioux Chief Hollow Bear, 1898, from a photograph by Rinehart. Hollow Horn Bear — Sioux name Matihehlogego (1850–1913) — was a Brulé Sioux leader during the Indian Wars. He became a celebrity and featured on a 14-cent postage stamp issued in 1922 and on a five-dollar bill. He was appointed the head of Indian police at the South Dakota Rosebud Agency.

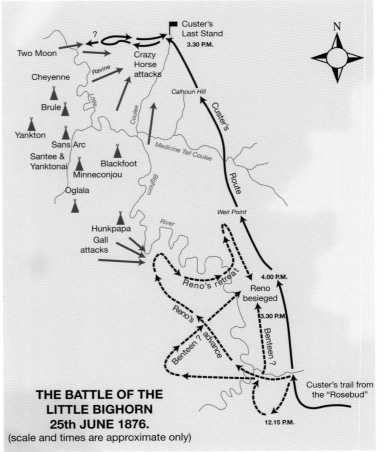

THE BATTLE OF THE LITTLE BIGHORN 25th JUNE 1876.
(scale and times are approximate only)

Above left: Jack Red Cloud, Teton Sioux, Oglala band. Son of the celebrated Chief Red Cloud. Descendants of the family are still living on the Sioux reservations in South Dakota. Photographer, Charles Carpenter, Saint Louis Exposition, 1904.

Above center: Red Shirt or Bear Stop, a Minneconjou Teton Sioux, had been a warrior at the time of the Custer battle of June 1876 and was with Sitting Bull at the Yellowstone River when later he counciled with Colonel Nelson A. Miles. While Sitting Bull headed on north to Grandmother's country (Canada), Red Shirt returned to the Standing Rock Agency. Later a "Red Shirt" toured with "Wild West" shows and was photographed here at Earls Court, London, c.1910, when he was reported as Oglala.

Above right: "Buffalo Bill" Cody with Red Cloud (left) and American Horse c. 1890s. Red Cloud was the famous Oglala (Western Sioux) leader who led Indian resistance along the Bozeman Trail in Wyoming at the Fetterman and Wagon Box fights 1866–1867.

Right: Beaded vest (waistcoat), probably Crow or Flathead (Plateau area) c. 1930. Floral style beadwork probably came to the Crow and Plateau tribes via contact with Crees and Canadian Métis during the 19th century. This vest has a fully beaded front with "cut beads" used to form floral shapes on a white-beaded ground. The vest is constructed with heavy cloth and silk back. The beadwork has a false collar effect, sometimes noted on other similar vests. The floral beadwork style on this vest seems to have developed after about 1900 and was popular among the Crow, also the Shoshone and other western tribes.

Below right: Moccasins, Western Sioux, c. 1890. Rawhide soles, probably buffalo hide uppers with sinew-sewn lazy stitch (lane stitch) beadwork. Typical Western Sioux style beadwork, possibly Oglala or Brule (Pine Ridge or Rosebud reservations). Note the buffalo head design on the instep and possible Ghost Dance figures around the outside.

Opposite, above: Teton (Western) Sioux woman and child, c.1885, probably at Rosebud or Pine Ridge Reservation, South Dakota. Both wear Plains Indian metalwork on belts, decorated moccasins and dresses made from trade cloth. The vertically strung bone "hairpipes" were also obtained from white traders and are still popular today with Indian women at powwows.

Opposite, below: Western Sioux Grass Dancer, c. 1890. The Grass or Omaha Dance was adopted by the Sioux from Missouri valley tribes in the 1860s–70s, presumably to replace redundant rituals of their own warrior societies. They added their own (usually social) rites to the performances. The symbolism of the traditional dress was retained: the roach, braids of sweetgrass in the belt, two upright feathers and a back bustle — a collection of feathers from birds that scavenged the battlefield; these elements were often worn over dyed sets of trade underclothes.

defeat of Custer's command in June 1876 on the Little Bighorn River, Montana (see map on page 137), and the ultimate surrender of Crazy Horse in 1877, and Sitting Bull in 1881. The Great Sioux Reservation was divided into smaller reservations — Pine Ridge, Rosebud, Lower Brulé, Cheyenne River and Standing Rock — followed by further losses of land during the allotment and subsequent sale of unoccupied areas.

Thus began years of squalid reservation life, restrictions on religious ceremonies, poor housing, the boarding school system that took children away from their families and lack of employment opportunity in areas far from economic activity.

Today there is a wide racial and cultural range on the Sioux reservations and, despite some recent improvements, they are beset by social problems. The distribution of the modern Western or Lakota Sioux is as follows: the Hunkpapa are mostly at Standing Rock Reservation, with a few at Wood Mountain Reserve, Saskatchewan; the Minneconjou are at Cheyenne River Reservation; the Sansarc, Sihasapa and Two Kettle are also at Cheyenne River; the Upper Brulé are at Rosebud Reservation; the Lower Brulé at the Lower Brulé Reservation; and the Oglala at Pine Ridge Reservation — although there has been some mixing. It was at Pine Ridge that the Wounded Knee massacre of Indian people took place in 1890 during the Ghost Dance movement. This has become a tragic symbol of Indian subjection by whites, and was the last significant "military" engagement between whites and Indians.

Despite poor surroundings the Sioux have a tremendous *ésprit de corps* and some still possess a hauteur and openness of character; much of the belated understanding and reverence for "Indian culture" found today stems from the activities of modern Sioux people. During the 1860s the Grass Dance (so called because of sweetgrass braids worn by the participants) or Omaha Dance (because it came from the Omahas) was adopted by the warrior societies, whose own rites were falling into disuse. The lively songs and male dances, called "war dances" by whites, became a main social activity at Indian gatherings on the reservations, and quickly spread to most northern Plains tribes. The Assiniboine, Blackfoot and Gros Ventre each added their own rites, usually of a social nature, to the performance. For years only men participated, but in recent times women and children take part as well. The Omaha Dance became the basis for the modern powwow complex in the central and northern Plains (where it is still called Grass Dance), an outward manifestation of pan-Indianism, which parallels and even merges with a similar movement that spread from Oklahoma. Today, as in the past, powwows are held on all reservations.

In 1904, the Lakota were distributed as follows: Cheyenne River, 2,477; Lower Brulé, 470; Pine Ridge, 6,690; and Rosebud, 4,977 — when added to the Middle and Eastern branches they totalled 26,175, including Assiniboine, within the United States. In 1956 there were 4,983 enrolled at Cheyenne

6

characteristic geometric designs. The Sun Dance was the great focal point of summer camps. They also had Yuwipi, a night cult, probably Woodland in origin, and the "shaking tipi rite." Burial was invariably of the scaffold type; "winter counts" were pictographic calendar histories on buffalo robes. Warfare and hunting were important male activities, the elaborate warrior societies each having their own customs.

As a result of the California Gold Rush of 1849, and the discovery of gold in Colorado and Montana in the 1860s, white men in greater numbers began crossing Western Sioux lands and killing buffalo. The Sioux became resentful, attacking wagon trains and prospectors, and outfighting soldiers. Finally, at the treaty of Fort Laramie in 1868, Chief Red Cloud demanded that white men should be kept out of their country — that the Great Sioux Reservation, the whole of present South Dakota west of the Missouri — be reserved exclusively for Sioux use. For a few years the treaty held, until in 1874 gold was discovered in the Black Hills, traditionally a sacred area. This, together with the U.S. government's complete inability to keep white prospectors, immigrants and hunters out of the area, led to a series of bitter conflicts that climaxed in the

7

Left: Teton Sioux, c. 1872. Painted eagle feathers fixed upright in the hair, along with an arrow, indicate warrior status. His braids are wrapped with fur, and he wears dentalium and abalone shell earrings. He also wears a "peace medal," as given by various agents and usually bearing likenesses of presidents' heads.

Right: Western or Teton Sioux woman, c. 1900. Lakota woman wearing a blue trade cloth dress, heavily decorated with dentalium shells — slender, cone-shaped shells open at each end, brought to the central Plains by white traders from c. 1860. Tubular ornaments in conch shell (later in silver and brass) for hair decoration (hence "hairpipes") were used by Eastern tribes, and by the 19th century shell pipes were being drilled by white manufacturers in New Jersey for the Western Indian trade. After 1880 these were made from polished cattle bone. Women usually strung them vertically, men horizontally, into breastplates.

Below: Western or Teton Sioux man, c. 1895. Lakota ceremonial dress gradually lost its religious symbolism as warrior societies fell into disuse and ceremonials tended toward a merely social character. War bonnets and war shirts were worn by some older men, irrespective of the spiritual, obligatory or status requirements of pre-reservation days. However, the reservation Sioux developed distinctive beadwork in increasingly complex geometrical designs, including matching strips for buckskin shirts and leggings. Leggings of buckskin or cloth were sometimes made with outstanding flaps, a style originally brought to the New World by the Spanish.

River; 705 at Lower Brulé; 9,875 at Pine Ridge; and 8,189 at Rosebud. In 1970 there were 47,825 Sioux (Western, Middle and Eastern) in the United States and 5,155 in Canada (the only Teton representatives in Canada are 70 people at Wood Mountain). Today, more 131,048 Sioux are reported in the United States (2010 Census), with an additional 13,000 in Canada. A large number of Sioux people live in Denver.

CROW An important Siouan people of the northwestern Plains who split from the Hidatsa, perhaps beginning 350 years ago. Both oral tradition and linguistic evidence confirm this origin. At least two separate divisions took place giving rise to the Mountain Crow and River Crow. The Hidatsa had once been three distinct groups, the once nomadic Awaxawi, an old agricultural sedentary group the Awatixa, and the Hidatsa proper—the last of the three to settle on the Missouri River from the east learning the arts of cultivating corn from the Mandans. It is likely the Mountain Crow, separated from the Awatixa and later the River Crow from the Hidatsa. The map produced under the direction of William Clark in 1805 located the Paunch Indians (Mountain

Crow) and Raven Indians (River Crow) separately. The last Crow separation from the Hidatsa was under way by the middle of the 18th century although an association remained until an outbreak of smallpox in 1782 no doubt hastened the split. Trading ties were almost completely severed by the further outbreak in 1837 which destroyed the Mandans and partly destroyed the Hidatsa and Arikara. These peoples (particularly the Mandans) had been long residents in the valley of the Missouri in sedentary, agriculturally based villages of earth lodges in what is now North Dakota. The Verendrye brothers exploring west of these villages in 1738–1739 reported another Hidatsa-type people who were probably to be the later Mountain Crow but still earth lodge dwellers. By the time of Lewis and Clark's epic journey 1802–1804 the River Crow were located along the middle course of the Yellowstone River and the Mountain Crow in the mountainous regions of the upper course in one of the richest territories of the Great Plains for natural resources. The ideally positioned Mandan and Hidatsa had become a center of an aboriginal trading system that drew a succession of white traders following in the footsteps of the Verendryes. The relative abundance of material culture and population stability (until the ravages of smallpox) led to elaborate social and religious structures, clan system, annual religious ceremonialism, and a rich and varied artistic background that remained with the Crow long after it was

Right: Crow man, c. 1880. Crow men were among the most impressively dressed of all Plains people. The earliest known surviving warrior shirts have porcupine quill strips on the arms and over the shoulders, in techniques known as quill-wrapped horsehair and diagonal weave. In the late 19th century, linked by trade to other, notably Plateau peoples, the Crow developed geometrical beaded designs in characteristic flat mosaic surfaces of greens, blues, yellows and pinks. Men's shirts were heavily fringed with ermine tails, and trade cloth leggings often had contrasting colored "boxes" at the front with beaded lanes. Northern Plains tribes also favored the loop bead necklace.

Far Right: Crow, c. 1880. Noted for their impressive hairstyles, the Crow probably took some forms from their friends the Nez Perce, perhaps including this: an upstanding forelock or pompadour and long back hair stuck together with rows of small spots of pitch. To slim braids at the temples were attached ornaments — coiled brass wire, dentalium shells. hairpipes and trade beads.

Below: Crow, c. 1870. Ceremonial warrior headdress of antelope hide, red stroud cloth, pronghorn antelope horns, hawk, magpie and prairie chicken feathers, beads, bells, ribbon and paint. Sacred war regalia was often decorated with the feathers of birds that scavenged on battlefields.

extinguished among the Missouri River peoples. Their clan system was unique among High Plains nomads reflecting their Hidatsa origin.

Through the Hidatsa connection the Crow were able to obtain surplus agricultural products and ultimately white men's trade goods in exchange for horses, skins, robes, and dried meat. In turn the Crows traded with the Nez Perce to the west and Shoshone to the south from whom they obtained huge numbers of horses. This interchange of trade goods witnessed a sharing of tribal art styles which continued through the Plateau tribes to the peoples of the Columbia River. This secondary trading route ultimately became a primary source of intertribal art and dress diffusion in which a clan group known as the "Kicked in the Bellies" band shared ceremonial dress, parfleches, horsegear, and cradles with their Plateau friends. Their ceremonial organizations however continued to reflect their Hidatsa connections such as their Tobacco Society.

Prior to the Lewis and Clark Expedition of 1804–1806, few white men had seen the Absarokee or Crow Indians, although the Verendrye brothers had visited them in 1743 and called them

"Beaux Hommes." After Lewis and Clark came various fur traders, and trading posts, such as Forts Liza and Cass, forged permanent white contacts with the Crow. The artist Catlin portrayed them as one of the most colorful native tribes on the northern Plains in the 1830s. By 1864, the Bozeman Trail led right through Crow country, and this was followed by the building of military forts — Reno, Phil Kearny and C.F. Smith — to protect the immigrants (despite their abandonment during the Sioux wars). On the whole, relations with whites — though often strained — remained largely peaceful. They signed treaties with the United States in 1825, and recognized their boundaries as defined by the Fort Laramie Treaty of 1851. This was followed by a second Laramie Treaty in 1868, which established the Crow Reservation, although this was subsequently reduced in area. The present Crow Reservation is south of Billings, Montana, in Bighorn County. The administrative center is Crow Agency.

Except for the cultivation of tobacco, the Crow abandoned agriculture after their separation from the Hidatsa and became a true, nomadic Plains people, heavily dependent on the horse for bison-hunting, though they also gathered roots and berries for food. They also developed their own styles of ceremonial costumes, with dyed porcupine quillwork and, later, beadwork decoration of unique composition. The Crows have fared better than most Indians in their adaption to American culture, although they are still distinctively Indian, and hold the colorful "Crow Indian Fair" each August. They originally numbered perhaps 8,000 before smallpox reduced them. In 1944 there

Left: Shavings, a Crow chief photographed in Montana in 1880. He wears a typically resplendent Crow shirt, panel leggings and moccasins with animal tails hanging from the heels — probably signifying warrior status. Montana Historical Society, courtesy Ian West

Below: Burial scaffold, probably Crow, Montana c. 1900.

Right: Pretty Eagle, a member of the Crow delegation to Washington, D.C., 1880, photographed by C.M. Bell. His hairstyle and shirt decoration are typical of his people. Pitt Rivers Museum, Oxford

Far Right: Crow woman wearing traditional cloth dress of two contrasting colors, with imitation elk teeth, while participating in the parade at the 1987 Crow Fair, Montana. Photograph: Jonathan Smith

were 2,467; in 1954, 3,416; in 1970, 3,779; 1991, 8,491, and 13,394, including mixed-bloods in 2000 Census.

MANDAN The largest and most important of the three Upper Missouri River horticultural tribes is the Mandan, who lived in dome-shaped earth-covered lodges stockaded into villages. They planted maize, beans and pumpkins, but also hunted bison. They no doubt once resided somewhere near the Mississippi valley and the heartland of gardening North America. The Winnebago were perhaps their closest relatives, but their speech shows a long separation from their parent Siouan family, and they entered their historic region several generations before the Hidatsa. Prior to the 1782 smallpox epidemic they outnumbered the three Hidatsa villages, with perhaps 3,800 people. Their first recorded contact with whites was in 1738, when Verendrye visited them, at which time they had nine villages near the Heart River. These had been reduced to only two at the time of Lewis and Clark in 1804: Metutehanke and Ruptari, below the mouth of the Knife River on the west bank of the Missouri River. During the 1830s, the artists Bodmer and Catlin captured in paint some of the most outstanding scenes of native America ever recorded, including chiefs, villages, and important religious ceremonies such as the Okeepa.

In 1837, the Mandan were destroyed by smallpox, with only 137 people being said to survive. These joined the Hidatsa and settled on the Fort Berthold Reservation in North Dakota, where a few descendants perpetuate their name. In 1906, they numbered 264, and in 1937, 345, but they are now largely merged with the Hidatsa. Together with the Arikara they form the "Three Affiliated Tribes of the Fort Berthold Reservation." Among the ceremonies observed by the three tribes, the Okeepa warrants special attention because of its complexity and great antiquity. It is a four-day spectacle involving self-torture, the drama of "Lone Man," who saved the tribe from disaster, and other origin myths. The Mandan villages were an important trade center for nomadic tribes and the northern tribes. From them material culture diffused over a wide area. Reconstructions of Mandan villages can be seen at Knife River, near Stanton, and Fort Abraham Lincoln State Park, Mandan, North Dakota.

There are two Mandan origin myths, one depicts the Mandan as an indigenous people in their historic location where two culture heros, Lone Man and First Creator (Coyote) created the flat prairies east of the Missouri River and the rugged hunting terrain west of the Missouri, respectively. The alternative myth suggests they had emerged from beneath the earth on the right bank of the Mississippi bringing corn with them. From somewhere around the pipestone quarries in Minnesota they split and reformed on the Missouri until they reached the Heart River. Sometime later the three Hidatsa tribes also moved from the east and advanced to the Missouri where they established their villages near the mouth of the Knife River. Village sites were selected by Corn bundle owners and laid out by impersonators of Lone Man and Speckled Eagle representing the People Above. The center of the village plaza contained a cedar post representing the body of Lone Man surrounded by the ark, a barrel-shaped wall of planks symbolizing the protection against a mythological flood. The plaza was the site for the Okeepa ceremony.

At the time of European contact the Mandan and Hidatsa were living in relative prosperity in the fortified villages along the Missouri River which were important centers of trade between the nomadic hunters to the west and southwest, particularly with the Crow who in turn obtained goods from the Shoshone Rendezous in southwestern Wyoming. The nomads brought dried bison meat and robes for corn and other horticultural products. Dentalium shells from the Pacific Ocean

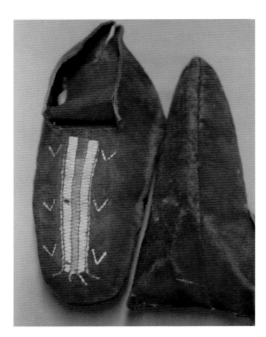

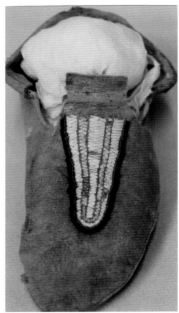

Above Left: Moccasins pre 1822, possibly Sioux or Hidatsa with quillwork representing either the corn plants or Water/Underground Monster. An early side seam construction moccasin form. Courtesy Dave Sager.

Above Center: Moccasin with quillwork and pony beads pre 1830, probably Sioux. Courtesy Dave Sager.

Above Right: Hardsoled (rawhide) Crow moccasins, c. 1880 with typical Crow style beadwork of the latter half of the 19th century. Courtesy Dave Sager

Right: Crow, c. 1880. One of the elements of material culture linking the Crow to the Plateau peoples was their cradle construction, which resembled those of the Flathead and Nez Perce except that they replaced the bag with a series of wide straps laced together down the front. Crow cradles were beaded in large geometrical shapes often outlined with white beaded lines.

Below: Crow dancers, c.1885.

Far Right: Two Leggings, Crow Indian, c.1910. The Crows were always considered as one of the most impressively attired of all the Plains Indians. Two Leggings wears a buckskin shirt decorated with ermine skins and beadwork. He stands before a canvas tipi — usually left unpainted by the Crows.

Above: White Man Runs Him — Crow Indian army scout with Custer in 1876, seen here in c. 1909. Photograph: Wanamaker

Right: Chief Plenty Coups, Crow Indian, Montana, c.1910, a celebrated leader and spokesman for his people. He wears a typical Crow shirt and an eagle feather headdress with ermine skin drops, often known as a "war bonnet." A headdress belonging to Chief Plenty Coups is on display at the National Cemetery, Arlington, Virginia, near Washington D.C., close to the Tomb of the Unknown Soldier.

Opposite, Below Left: Crow Chief Curley, his wife and Chief Long Tail, c. 1907. Curley was a noted Army scout of the Custer campaign of 1876.

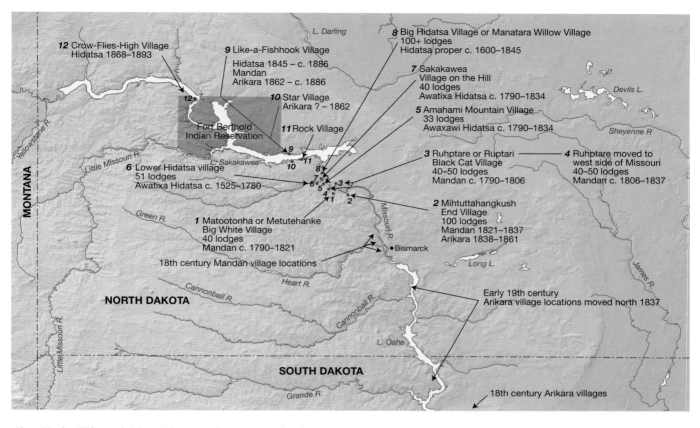

12 Crow-Flies-High Village
Hidatsa 1868–1893

9 Like-a-Fishhook Village
Hidatsa 1845 – c. 1886
Mandan
Arikara 1862 – c. 1886

10 Star Village
Arikara ? – 1862

Fort Berthold
Indian Reservation

11 Rock Village

8 Big Hidatsa Village or Manatara Willow Village
100+ lodges
Hidatsa proper c. 1600–1845

7 Sakakawea
Village on the Hill
40 lodges
Awatixa Hidatsa c. 1790–1834

5 Amahami Mountain Village
33 lodges
Awaxawi Hidatsa c. 1790–1834

6 Lower Hidatsa village
51 lodges
Awatixa Hidatsa c. 1525–1780

3 Ruhptare or Ruptari
Black Cat Village
40–50 lodges
Mandan c. 1790–1806

4 Ruhptare moved to
west side of Missouri
40–50 lodges
Mandan c. 1806–1837

2 Mihtuttahangkush
End Village
100 lodges
Mandan 1821–1837
Arikara 1838–1861

1 Matootonha or Metutehanke
Big White Village
40 lodges
Mandan c. 1790–1821

18th century Mandan village locations

Early 19th century
Arikara village locations moved north 1837

18th century Arikara villages

MONTANA

NORTH DAKOTA

SOUTH DAKOTA

Yellowstone R.
Little Missouri R.
Green R.
Little Missouri R.
L. Sakakawea
Missouri R.
Bismarck
Heart R.
Cannonball R.
Cannonball R.
L. Oahe
Grande R.
L. Darling
Devils L.
Sheyenne R.
Long L.
James R.

Above: Mandan, Hidatsa and Arikara 19th century village sites in North Dakota. At the time of Lewis and Clarke (1804–1805) the Arikara lived in semisedentary earth lodges just below the state line in South Dakota, while the Hidatsa occupied three villages at the junction of the Knife River and Missouri River, with the three Mandan below them. After the smallpox of 1837, an epidemic that virtually exterminated the Mandan, the Hidatsa experienced a period of wandering. However, in 1845 they began to construct a new village on the north bank of the Missouri named "Like-a-Fishhook" where they were soon joined by the remnant of the Mandan. The Arikara moved upstream to occupy the abandoned site of the Mandan village near Ft. Clark

(Mihtuttahangkush) and lived there from about 1838 until 1861 when the timber shortage and continual harassing raids by the Dakota forced them upstream again. In 1862 they began construction of two villages on the right hand side of the river, but after another Dakota attack they abandoned these sites and joined the Hidatsa and Mandan at Like-a-Fishhook where the three tribes occupied one large village from 1862 to the mid 1880s, thereafter accepting allotments.

Below Right: Chief Long Tail's wife wearing a typical Crow dress decorated with elk teeth, c. 1907.

found their way to the Mandans via this trade route. Other trade routes came via the Kiowa bringing Spanish and Ute goods and they also exchanged goods with the Cree and Assiniboine to their northeast.

HIDATSA or **MINITAREE** This was a Siouan tribe on the upper Missouri River in North Dakota who, according to tradition, came from somewhere to the northeast, but met and allied themselves to the Mandan and shared with them the agricultural pursuits for which they have become famous. They were in reality a group of three closely related village tribes — *Hidatsa, Awatixa,* and *Awaxawi* — who were visited by the explorer-trader Thompson in 1797 on the west side of the Missouri, near the mouth of the Knife River in present Oliver County, North Dakota. their population was then estimated at about 1,330. Before this time, but after their arrival on the Missouri, the people later called Crow split from the Hidatsa after a dispute. The Hidatsa movement to the Missouri has

been put as early as c. 1550. Despite low rainfall, the Hidatsa, Mandan and Arikara were successful as horticultural, earth lodge-dwelling peoples, and became known to a succession of traders and explorers during the 18th century, their villages being a focal point of trade between the nomadic Plains people and the Indians to the north, who were in closer contact with the fur trade. They were visited by Lewis and Clark in 1804, and by the artists Catlin and Bodmer in the early 1830s.

In 1837 a terrible smallpox epidemic reduced them to a few hundred survivors, consolidated in one village, which was moved in 1845 to Fort Berthold, where they have resided since. In 1907 they numbered 468; in 1970, 1,705, including a number who are part Mandan. They were also once known as "Gros Ventre of the Missouri," but have no connection with the Atsina, also known as Gros Ventre. In 2000, 1,571 Hidatsa were reported.

ARIKARA or **REE** The third of the upper Missouri River horticultural tribes, the Arikara, are a Caddoan people and a relatively late offshoot of the Skidi Pawnee. In the 1780s French traders reported them below the Cheyenne River in present South Dakota. In 1804, Lewis and Clark found them between the Grand and Cannonball Rivers, close to the

Above: Mandan warrior, c. 1833. From a Bodmer painting, winter 1833-34. The warrior, Flying Eagle, has a bear claw necklace and eagle wing fan indicating high rank. Wolves' tails attached to his heels indicate warrior status. His robe is decorated with a quilled band with rosettes, his leggings with "pony" beadwork, and his moccasins with both beads and quills.

Left: Mandan Buffalo Bull Dancer, c. 1833, after Bodmer. A member of the Buffalo Bull Society, who imitated the motions and sounds of the animal when dancing, he wears a bison's head mask, carries a shield, and holds a lance, perhaps of a ceremonial type similar to bow-lances and society staffs of other tribes.

Right: Mandan White Buffalo Cow Dancer, c. 1833. The women's White Buffalo Cow Society of the Mandans was seen dancing at Fort Clark by Karl Bodmer at Christmas 1833. These aged women wore face paint, and on their heads a broad piece of the skin of the white buffalo cow with a tuft of feathers.

present boundary between North and South Dakota, and already weakened in numbers due to smallpox. They were also often on unfriendly terms with the Mandan, Hidatsa, and surrounding Sioux. For a time they apparently rejoined the Skidi on the Loup River, Nebraska, but subsequently returned north, and by 1851 were on the Heart River. In 1862 they finally joined the Hidatsa and Mandan on the Fort Berthold Reservation, North Dakota, where their descendants have remained. Despite their early hostility to Americans, some Arikara served as scouts for the U.S. Army during the Indian Wars. Over the years their lands were allotted, and the Missouri bottom lands were lost during the Garrison Dam development in the 1950s.

In 1804 the Arikara numbered 2,600. The census of 1930 gave 420. In 1945 the reported figure was 780, and in 1970, 928. The "Three Affiliated Tribes of the Fort Berthold Reservation" (Mandan Hidatsa and Arikara) now run a museum that exhibits buckskin clothing and historical items. There are usually at least four powwows held each year on the reservation: The White Shield, Mandaree, Little Shell and Twin Buttes powwows, which are combinations of the northern Plains and pan-Lakota intertribal forms. In 1990, the three tribes numbered 6,000, with approximately half living in the Fort Berthold Reservation. The total 2001 population of the three affiliated tribes (Mandan, Hidatsa and Arikara) enrolled at Fort Berthold was 10,789 of which only 1,583 were Arikara alone.

OMAHA The Omaha are a Siouan tribe of the Dhegiha dialectic group who are thought to have moved west from the

Above Right: Pehriska-Ruhpa (Two Ravens) Hidatsa, painted at Fort Clark in 1834 by Karl Bodmer. Apparently the elaborately fringed shirt with bright yellow quillwork had been obtained from the Crows. He also wears a grizzle bear claw necklace and painted buffalo robe and holds a magnificent quilled pipe.

Right: Meraparpa or Lance-Mandan, probably photographed during a Mandan and Arikara delegation to Washington, D.C. in 1874. His buckskin shirt is decorated with quillwork strips; his hair is wrapped in fur, and the three upright, decorated eagle feathers perhaps signify warrior status.

Left and Below Left: Hidatsa bullboat. Made from two buffalo hides stretched over a willow bough frame, these were light enough to be carried on the back, but large enough to hold several people or a considerable load. They were used by the Missouri River tribes, Mandan, Hidatsa and Arikara, and occasionally by neighboring Sioux.

Mississippi valley, perhaps even from the Ohio valley. Unverified connections have been made to link these Siouans with the ancient people who built the great earthworks of southern Ohio. The Dhegiha, according to tradition, moved along the Missouri River, except for the Quapaw who crossed the Mississippi into present Arkansas. The Omaha continued along the Missouri for about 800 miles (1,300km) above its confluence with the Mississippi, where the explorers Lewis and Clark found them in 1804, in what is now northeastern Nebraska between the Platte and the Niobrara rivers. In common with other tribes of the region, the Omaha lived in earth-covered lodges in permanent villages but also used the conical skin tipi during hunting trips in pursuit of buffalo. In 1820 the Omahas had a p e r m a n e n t village in present Dakota County, Nebraska. They planted maize, beans, pumpkins and watermelons and were also employed in obtaining furs for white traders. They were visited in 1833 and 1847, respectively, by the artists Bodmer and Kurz who made important records of their material culture.

In 1854, they ceded their lands to the United States in return for a reservation in Thurston County, Nebraska, a portion of which was ceded to the Winnebago in 1865. They were reported to number 2,800 in 1780, but were reduced by wars with the Sioux and by smallpox in 1802 to a few hundred. In 1906 they numbered 1,228, and in 1954 about 1,700, of whom fully half were no longer on the reservation, a large proportion of which was occupied by non-Indians. In 1993 the Omahas were reported to number 6,000, a number that was actually 5,427 in 2001. Omaha descendants hold an annual powwow near Macy, Nebraska, each summer on the Omaha Reservation, which serves as a unifying tribal event. Many of the customs, beliefs and ceremonies of the tribe were recorded in the 19th century with the help of Francis La Flesche, a prominent mixed-blood member of the tribe.

PONCA The Ponca are a branch of the Omaha Indians who separated from their parent tribe at the mouth of

Above: Arikara Bear Dancer, c. 1900. The Bear Society was one of nine making up the prestigious Medicine Fraternity. Annual medicine bundle ceremonies began with the first thunder of early spring and continued through the summer in public, secret and conjuring performances. The ceremonies coincided with various stages in the growth of maize and squash crops.

Right: Omaha chief, c. 1870, wearing otter fur turban, the tail decorated with ribbonwork, the other side with ermine and a single horn. He wears a grizzly bear claw necklace.

Above: Omaha man, c. 1868. His costume is characteristic of the Missouri valley tribes. The otter fur turban, with the tail folded and protruding at the side, is decorated with ribbonwork and beaded at the front with the hand motif common among the Omaha, Osage and Pawnee. Grizzly bear claw necklaces were characteristic of the southern Woodlands and Prairies, although never numerous because of the difficulty of obtaining them (particularly from the now-extinct Plains grizzly). Highly valued, the claws were considered to be imbued with the strength and valor of the bear. The hunter might offer a speech of apology after killing one. The necklace sometimes had an otter skin pendant down the back. He wears buckskin leggings, (probably untailored) with bottom tabs and frontal beadwork in realistic animal designs, also noted among the Pawnee. The Omaha, in common with the Winnebago, also made moccasins with the ankle flap extending around the front over the instep.

the White River, South Dakota, and finally associated themselves with the region around the junction of the Niobrara River with the Missouri in present Knox County, Nebraska. Ponca villages were usually located on a river or creek terrace, where gardens could be cultivated on nearby bottom lands. They also hunted bison, deer and antelope. Their dwellings were both earth lodges and skin tipis. They were usually at war with the Sioux, from whom they seem to have adopted the Sun Dance. By treaty in 1858 they ceded their lands to the United States for a reservation at the mouth of the Niobrara River. The Poncas were forced to leave that reservation in 1876–77 for Indian Territory, where they were finally given lands on the Salt Fork of the Arkansas River, which became the Ponca Reservation until allotment. A few Ponca under Standing Bear made a dramatic return home to Nebraska and were allowed to stay after nationwide publicity had been given to their plight. The "Northern" Ponca retained lands near Niobrara, but quickly assumed white culture, and finally were federally terminated in 1962, most tribal members having left the old reservation.

The Southern Ponca still live partly on their old reservation lands near White Eagle in Kay and Noble counties, Oklahoma, and have been one of the principal groups contributing to the Oklahoma pan-Indian complex during the 20th century. Their powwows have been developed from the remains of Prairie tribal warrior society rituals, the Hethuska or Inlonska dances. These secularized ritual forms, and some with rather baroque male "feather" costumes, have become popular with many tribal groups, and their modern powwows are a focus of ethnic unity. The Southern or Oklahoma Ponca numbered 784 in 1907; 950 in 1950; about 1,200 in 1970; 2,360 in 1993; and 2,618 in 2001. Only a handful are full-blood, however. The Northern Ponca numbered 263 in 1906, and 397 in 1937, but are now so scattered as to make enumeration difficult, but 2,095 were enrolled in 2001.

IOWA The Iowa were a small Siouan tribe who lived on the Blue Earth River, Minnesota, when first reported by the French explorer Le Sueur in 1701. Later, they were located near the Platte River in Nebraska, Iowa and northern Missouri, where Lewis and Clark met them in 1804. In 1824, they agreed to a move from their home-

Above: Iowa chiefs, c. 1900. Like many Missouri River Valley peoples they were forced to live in Oklahoma (then Indian Territory) in the 19th century.

Below: Iron Man Coming, Otoe, 1895, holding an eagle-feather fan.

Above:David Tohee (Blue Hair), Iowa, 1901. He wears buckskin leggings with woven beaded garters, beaded moccasins, an apron, and holds an eagle-feather fan.

Below: Howard Frost, Omaha, 1898. F.A. Rinehart photograph during the trans-Mississippi International Exposition in Omaha.

Above: Plain Owl, Crow Indian, Montana, c. 1910. He holds an iron pipe-tomahawk and wears a buckskin shirt trimmed with ermine skins.

Below: Robert Headman, Otoe, 1898. The Otoes still live in the vicinity of Red Rock, Oklahoma.

Above: Osage man and wife, 1911. He wears a beaded vest in Prairie-style floralwork, knee garters, and moccasins. His wife's moccasins look Delaware-style.

Below: Otoe lady, Oklahoma 1935. A member of the Old Eagle family (American name Dailey). She wears a typical Oklahoma woman's dress of the period.

land to Great Nemaha Reservation in north-eastern Kansas, along with some of the Sauks and Foxes, where they settled in 1836. During the allotment of the Nemaha Reservation, a number of Iowa moved to seek homes in Indian Territory. In response to a plea to government officials, they were assigned a reservation in present Payne and Lincoln Counties, Oklahoma, to the west of the Sauk and Fox of Oklahoma. The Iowa spoke a dialect of the Chiwere branch of the Siouan family, being closely related to the Oto and Missouri, and more distantly to the Winnebago. Culturally they were close to the Sauk and Fox, but by the time of Lewis and Clark they were involved with traders from St. Louis and lived in a single village of 800 individuals, raising corn and maize, but hunting buffalo seasonally.

The Kansas Iowa are still connected with their allotted reservation on the Nebraska-Kansas border north of Hiawatha, Kansas. They numbered 246 in 1907; 540 in 1945; and 2,897 in 2001. The Oklahoma Iowa numbered 78 in 1920 and 114 in 1945, mostly near Perkins in Lincoln and Payne Counties. As of 2001, they numbered 491. Their descendants are much mixed by intermarriage with whites and other tribes.

It has recently been suggested that the Iowa, Oto, and possibly the Winnebago, may have descended from the Oneota prehistoric Upper Mississippian Culture of the Woodland/Prairie borderland of Iowa and adjacent areas.

OTO or **OTOE** The Oto were a Siouan tribe of the Chiwere group, with a tradition of a separation from the Winnebago, and a later separation from the Missouri Indians near the mouth of the Iowa River. They gradually removed west, first to the Des Moines River, then to the Missouri River, then to an area on the south side of the Platte River in present southeastern Nebraska. They were always a small tribal group who maintained themselves among enemy tribes. They were rejoined by the remnants of the Missouri at the time of the establishment of a reservation on the Big Blue River near the present Nebraska-Kansas state border line. They were finally removed to Indian Territory in 1882. The Oto were never prominent in history. They lived in permanent villages of earth lodges similar to the Omaha and Kansas, but when visited by Lewis and Clark in 1804, they were already in poor condition. In Oklahoma their reservation in Noble County was allotted against considerable opposition, but the Oto-Missouri descendants still live partially around their old agency and near Red Rock, Oklahoma. Each July the Otoe-Missouria (current spelling) host a typical Oklahoma pan-Indian powwow near the old agency lands of which representatives of many tribes attend for colorful dances. On tribal lands today they run a successful bingo hall — disparities in gambling laws on Indian lands make this a useful commercial opportunity. In 1993, 1,550 Otoe-Missouria were reported, with that number shrinking somewhat to 1,506 in 2001.

Left: Deer Ham, an Iowa Indian, photographed in Washington, D.C. c.1870, probably by A. Zeno Shindler.

Below: Oto (Otoe) male dancer's breechclout. Heirloom made about 1900 and shows the abstract floralistic beadwork style of the Missouri Valley tribes removed to Oklahoma in the 19th century. Seen at the Otoe-Missouria Powwow, July 1989. Courtesy Doug White Cloud

Bottom: Otoe-Missouria Powwow, Red Rock, Oklahoma, July 1989. A modern "Southern"-style powwow, with singers under shade. Parade led by the head woman dancer. Note her shawl with horse motifs.

Above: Peyote cult accoutrements, c. 1930. The Peyote cult or Native American Church, the most widespread pan-Indian religious movement of this century, combines elements of Mexican, Plains Indian and Christian religions. Of ancient Mexican origin, the ceremonial use of the narcotic peyote seems to have reached the Oklahoma Indians via the Lipan or Mescalero Apache. It developed into two rituals: the Big Moon Way, and the Half Moon Way — describing the shape of sacred altars. Ceremonials take place by night in a canvas tipi; the ceremonial leader, or Roadman, uses a hawk feather fan, gourd rattle, and staff, all appropriately decorated, and the peyote is usually consumed in "button" form — as shown here, with an Arapaho fan and an Osage rattle.

MISSOURI The Missouri were a small Chiwere Siouan tribe, at one time the same people as the Oto, with a tradition of a separation from the Winnebago. Later the Missouri and Oto divided, the former living for a time on the Grand River, a branch of the Missouri in present northern Missouri State, while the Oto moved to the Des Moines River in Iowa. Wasted by wars with the Sauk, Fox, Osage and Kansa as far back as 1748, they reunited several times with the Oto. Finally, about 90 Missouris joined the Oto on the Big Blue River and accompanied them to Oklahoma, where the two tribes became officially the "Otoe-Missouri tribe of Oklahoma," the Missouri having since disappeared as a separate people.

KANSAS, KANSA or **KAW** An important Siouan tribe of the Dhegiha group very closely related to the Osage were the Kansas. Their name signified "Wind People." They lived on the Republican, Kansas and Big Blue rivers in northern Kansas, and in adjacent Nebraska. The explorer Marquette heard of them living there as far back as 1673, apparently succeeding some Caddoan tribes on the prairies of the Kansas River, but their western advance was checked by the Cheyenne. They had semipermanent earth lodge villages, grew crops, hunted bison and were often considered warlike by surrounding tribes. In 1815 the Kansa were said to have 130 earth lodges and a population of 1,500; the agent O'Fallon estimated 1,850 in 1822. But they were reduced drastically in number by smallpox over the next few years. They first agreed with the U.S. authorities to move to a reservation at Council Grove on the Neosho River in 1846, where the Kaw Indian Mission still stands. However, these lands were directly on the Santa Fe Trail and, in a succession of agreements, they finally moved to Indian Territory in 1873. There were only 209 left in 1905.

The Kaw Reservation in Oklahoma is located in Kay County, where approximately one-third of 2,553 descendants still lived in 2001, being mostly of mixed blood. Some old French-Kaw families are still extant, having been well educated over the years, their Indian traditions largely disappearing within the first generation of their move to Indian Territory. In 1993 only five Kaw full-bloods were known.

OSAGE The Osage was the largest and most important Dhegiha Siouan tribe, part of a Siouan movement that divided into the Omaha, Ponca and Kansas, who ascended the Missouri River, the Quapaw going south to the Arkansas. The Osage remained on the Osage River in central-western Missouri state.

The tribe was divided into the Great Osage, centering in Vernon County, and the Little Osage on the west side of the Little Osage River. They were in part an agricultural people, raising small crops of corn and squash near their permanent villages, but they depended upon the bison for much food and clothing. Their hunting territory extended to the west, which brought them into contact — and continuous enmity — with the Kiowa and Comanche of the High Plains. Although tribal life and religion existed until the late 19th century, they had a long association with various Spanish and French traders, with whom there were some quite early intermarriages, resulting in a reputation for haughty Latin manners. The first European notice of them was by Marquette in 1673, and they had already established relations with the French traders before 1719. After 1802 the Osage also traded at the "Three Forks," near present Okay, Oklahoma, at the junction of the Arkansas with the Neosho and Verdigris rivers, having separated from the Missouri bands.

The Osage made several treaties with the United States during the early 19th century, by which they ceded their lands in Missouri and Oklahoma for part of southeast Kansas centering in present Neosho County. After the opening of these lands following the Civil War, they faced intolerable conditions. However, the sale

Right: Osage woman, c. 1900. The Osage and Kaw of the southern Prairies came into proximity with resettled southern Woodland tribes after their removal to Oklahoma, and probably adopted from them the techniques of ribbon appliqué. Besides cut-and-fold geometrical patterns, the Osage are noted for horse and hand motifs, sometimes found on so-called "friendship blankets." The hand was an old, possibly Mississippian symbol of esoteric significance. This young woman also wears "German" (nickel) silver brooches.

of remaining lands allowed the purchase of a reservation in Indian Territory, now Osage County, Oklahoma. Having recovered from the many difficulties suffered in Kansas, they fell heir to oil and mineral deposits during the late 1890s and early 1900s, which brought great wealth to some Osage families. The present Osage population is widely dispersed. About one-third of their membership lives in three towns on the old Osage Reservation at Gray Horse, Hominy and Pawhuska.

By 1980 the language was known fluently to only about 25 old people, and almost all tribal members were of mixed white and other, Indian tribal descent. They are, however, presenters of three annual powwows at each village, in which they promote their Inlonska dances, derived originally from the Kansa and Ponca to the west of them in about 1880. Their male dancers are widely known as "straight" dancers, lacking the baroque feather "fancy" costumes associated with other pan-Indian Oklahoma powwows. The Osage once numbered 6,500 before being reduced partly by smallpox to 1,582 in 1886. In 1950 there were 4,972 enrolled members of the tribe, of whom only about 480 were full Osage. As of 2001 there were 18,415 who claimed Osage descent, but only 7,242 were reported in the 2010 Census. Over the years their association with French settlers and missionaries has resulted in most present day Osages being nominally Roman Catholic. The Osage are noted producers of fine ribbonwork decoration on their dance clothing, and run their own museum at Pawhuska.

QUAPAW or **ARKANSEA** Another member of the Dhegiha Siouan group the name Quapaw apparently signified "Downstream People," and they were the most southern of the group. According to tribal traditions, they continued down the Mississippi into present Arkansas state, while others turned up the Missouri River. Although De Soto's expedition may have met them in 1541, the first recorded contact was by Father Jacques Marquette, who during his memorable journey down the Mississippi in 1673 rested at the Quapaw village on the Arkansas River, not far above its junction with the Mississippi. He describes their dome-shaped bark-covered cabins, their corn kept in baskets, and they made wooden dishes and pottery. They were also visited by La Salle in 1682, and Tonti in 1686. They were an important people of the area, with remarkable pottery, and lived in palisaded villages. However, their early contacts with the French on the Mississippi brought diseases, and intertribal conflicts in promotion of the fur trade, hence most Quapaw left the Mississippi valley for the south side of the Arkansas River.

By 1761 they had merged with ruined tribes, notably the Illini, and remained the nucleus of a diminishing people.

In 1818 the Quapaw ceded all their lands to the United States, except for a strip between Little Rock and Arkansas Post below Gillett, Arkansas. This was ceded in 1835 for lands in southern Kansas and northern Indian Territory, which in turn were ceded except for a section in the northeastern corner of Indian Territory, now Ottawa County, Oklahoma. This became the Quapaw Reservation, but was allotted in 1895. Over the years their population dropped from perhaps 6,000 in the 16th/17th centuries to a meager 305 in 1909, these mostly of mixed French and other Indian ancestry from groups who had merged with the Quapaw. In 1945 they numbered 610, and by 1970 about 750. In 1993 about 1,800 were enrolled, and by 2001 they numbered 2,657. Despite their acculturation, the Quapaw descendants sponsor a large annual powwow of a pan-Indian type near Devil's Promenade, Miami, Oklahoma, including Straight Dances, Stomp Dances and other activities.

CADDOAN

An important language family who probably once lived in the Lower Mississippi valley region, according to tribal traditions, were the Caddoan. Their agricultural background suggests links with Mississippian culture. The family consisted of many small tribes grouped into confederacies. Commencing in the south, these were the Kadohadacho or Caddo, Hasinai, Natchitoches with the Adai and Eyeish, of Louisiana, eastern Texas and Arkansas; the descendants of the first three tribes became the later "Caddo." In Oklahoma and adjacent Texas were the Wichita, Tawakoni, Waco and Kichai (Kitsai), who ultimately became the "Wichita." On the Platte River, Nebraska, were the four Pawnee tribes and, finally, there were the Arikara, who seem to have split from the Pawnee two and a half centuries ago and migrated along the Missouri into what is now North Dakota.

PAWNEE The Pawnee were originally among the largest and most powerful tribes on the Plains. From the late 18th century four bands have been recognized. The Skidi or Skiri, the northernmost on the Loup River in central Nebraska, also

Below: Pawnee Tribal Council, Oklahoma, 1939. For the photograph they wear a mixture of materials of their own and other tribes. The settlement of more than 50 tribes in Indian Territory led to the merging of many styles of dress and art from several different areas.

Top, inset: Pawnee earth lodge, c. 1865. The floor was excavated to about a foot deep; the framework was a skeleton stockade of heavy posts on which rafters were laid upward to central posts supporting the smoke hole and outward to an outer bank of earth. Willow purlins laid horizontally on the rafters supported the earth and sod covering. The entrance was a long covered way built of poles with earth covering. This faced east, and its length varied among the Missouri valley tribes. The west side of the lodge, where corn was stored, was considered sacred. Several related families usually occupied the lodge, which was about 40 feet (130 m) in diameter and 15 feet (50 m) high.

Top: Earth lodge, probably Pawnee. The extended vestibule suggests a Pawnee lodge.

Above Left: Buffalo Bull, aka La-doo-ke-a, a Grand Pawnee warrior, 1832. Painted by George Catlin and described as a warrior of great distinction. He appears with his medicine or totem painted on his chest and face and holds a recurve bow. Probably painted at Ft. Leavenworth, Kansas. Smithsonian American Art Museum.

Above Right: Petalesharo (Generous Chief) Skidi Pawnee Chief (c. 1797–c. 1832) by Charles Bird King, c. 1822. Tradition claims that it was Petalesharo who carried out his father's wish to abolish the practice of sacrificing young captive women at the Spring Solstice ceremony to the Morning Star, He stopped the killing of a Comanche girl, c. 1817, and gained national fame for his action. The last known sacrifice was in 1838.

Above: Pawnee, c. 1880. Otter fur turban decorated with multicolored cut-and-fold ribbonwork; note also silver ball and cone earrings.

Right: Southern Plains woman, Kiowa or Comanche, wearing a typical buckskin dress of that area. She also wears moccasin boots and metal German silver conchas; c. 1896.

Below: Pawnee, c. 1870. The Pawnee shared a similar type of cradle with Prairie Siouan groups such as the Osage, Iowa, Omaha and Ponca. Of the same general form described for the Ojibwa (p. 54), they made the backboard usually of cottonwood (Pawnee) or cedar (Osage), and the protective upper hoop, but lacked the foot board. Pawnee cradle hoops were partly supported by a thong stay from the carved area, while the Osage had thongs holding the hoop below the carved area. Pawnee carvings derive from ancient symbolism connected with the Morning Star, the Sun and other natural phenomena.

called Loups or Wolf Pawnee. Living south of them were the Chawi (Chaui) or Grand Pawnee, the Kitkahahki (Kithehaki) or Republican Pawnee, and the Pitahawirata (Pitahaurent) or Tappage Pawnee. These three bands, sometimes called the South Band, spoke a dialect of Pawnee slightly different from the Skidi who claimed a closer affinity with their Caddoan relatives the Arikara of South Dakota, and later North Dakota. The South Bands lived below the Platte River in Nebraska and into Kansas. As late as 1818 when the U.S. government concluded their first treaties with the Pawnees, each of the four bands were politically independent. In the 17th century the Pawnee lived in small scattered earth lodge villages which gave way later to larger, more compact towns that gave more protection (by the 19th century) from constant harassment by the warlike Sioux. During the 19th century the four bands were forced onto a reservation on the north side of the Platte River and their population of perhaps 12,000 in the late 18th century, had dropped to about 3,000 by 1870 due to disease, the disappearance of the buffalo herds and encroaching white settlers. In 1873 they lost about a hundred people, mostly women and children, massacred by Sioux, and by 1875 they were persuaded to leave their exposed reservation in Nebraska for one in Indian Territory (now Oklahoma) and consequently the entire tribe moved there.

By the time of their move to Oklahoma, the demoralized tribe had radically changed from their earlier semi-sedentary horticultural way of life, similar to their relatives to the south the Wichita, Kitsai, and Caddo. Although hunting was an integral part of their subsistence, they raised corn (maize), pumpkins, squashes, and beans in several varieties which reflected prominently in their religious and ceremonial life. Maize ceremonialism reached its highest development on the Plains among the Pawnee and Arikara. On winter buffalo hunts the Pawnee lived in temporary camps of conical tipis, but their permanent homes were earth lodges, large dome-shaped structures of wood covered with packed sod and earth in sizes which varied in diameter from 26–50 ft (8–15 m) with a height of about 16.5 ft (5 m) at the center. These contained several families of thirty or more people. Each village had its own fields for cultivation and burial ground.

Before the Euro-American influences had radically changed Pawnee culture, each village had its own origin myth. The village founder was created by a star or star group who had also provided the founder with a sacred bundle(a collection of paraphernalia such as rocks, feathers, corn ears, animal skins, etc) which would form an altar around which the bundle's own ritual was performed. The bundle served as a source of power for good fortune and

Above: White Man, a Kiowa, 1898, from a photograph by Rinehart.

assistance for procuring food. In time the bundle and paternal inheritance was passed on to his son, who was thus a descendant of the founder and new village chief. Since all the people of the village were regarded as the founder's descendants, they had a common origin and a common source of power.

Foremost among the star bundles were the Evening and Morning Star (Venus) bundles, the North Star bundle, and Skull bundle. The organization of the priests was parallel to, but separate from, that of the chiefs, since both were patterned on the sacred bundle scheme. However, shamanistic medicine societies ministered to individuals obtaining power from animals, whereas priests were associated with celestial power and concerned with group welfare. The Pawnee also had several men's societies similar to other Plains tribes each with distinctive insignia, dress, and functions. Celestial (star) phenomena were arranged hierarchically, and at the top stood Tirawa or Tirawahat, an amorphous being who had created the universe. The Sun, Moon, and Stars, were subordinate to him but also involved with many aspects of creation. Most ritualistic procedures were annual, but a number were held according to visions: the most important was the human sacrifice to the Morning Star.

Viewing Pawnee ceremonialism as a whole, we find them at the center of North American Indian agricultural and hunting traditions with parallels with Eastern and Southwestern cultures and the human sacrifice ritual links to Mexico. Perhaps these elements were grafted onto a basic Mississippi Basin hunting culture or point to a southern origin for the Caddoans. However, the link with Mexico has recently been disputed by some authorities. The last known child sacrifice was of a Sioux girl in 1838, news of which spread to the eastern cities.

Following which missionary endeavors were undertaken together with the rapid population reduction witnessed the near collapse of their ceremonial life before removal to Oklahoma.

The Pawnees' first contact with Europeans was probably with the Coronado expedition in 1541. A guide in his party is thought to have been a Pawnee. They obtained horses either directly or indirectly from the Spanish settlements, and French traders were established among them by 1750. After the Louisiana Purchase, St. Louis became an American trading center, and subsequent contact with immigrants through their territory brought decimation from cholera and smallpox, which reduced their population from perhaps 10,000 in 1838 to about 1,300 in 1880. In a succession of treaties with the United States, they ceded all their lands except for a reservation in present Nance County, Nebraska. But in 1874–76, all four bands moved to Indian Territory, where an agency and reservation was established below the Arkansas River adjoining the Osage. However, their surplus lands — after the infamous allotments were completed — were opened to white settlement in 1893. Pawnee rural descendants still live in and around Pawnee and Skedee, Pawnee County, Oklahoma. They numbered about 1,260 in 1950; 1,928 in 1970; 2,500 in 1990; and 2,560 in 2001, with a considerable admixture of white and other Indian ancestry.

They still sponsor the Pawnee Homecoming Powwow each summer, to which other tribes are invited, and to which Pawnee men serving with the U.S. Army often return (a military tradition which goes back to the 19th century). This powwow is of the popular pan-Indian type established in Oklahoma during the early 20th century, which has been derived from the blending of the culture of a number of tribes forced to Oklahoma during the second half of the 19th century. The songs and dances are based on old Ponca, Kaw and Osage forms, in turn influenced by warrior society rituals of the Omaha, Sauk and Fox, which are known as Hethuska or Inlonska. Subsequently modified in form, dance and dress, the Oklahoma Powwow has become a highly successful social function that has spread far beyond the tribes who developed it.

WICHITA The largest known historic tribe of the southern Caddoan-speaking group are the Wichita, who lived along the Canadian River in present Oklahoma, and were presumably the people the explorer Coronado found in 1541 in the area called "Quivira." In 1719 the French commandant Bernard de la Harpe found them on the Arkansas River, Oklahoma, one of several related tribes of the area known collectively as "Pani Pique." Government relations began in 1834, when Colonel Dodge from Fort Gibson, Indian Territory, held a council with the Wichita and others on the North Fork of the Red River.

In 1859 they agreed to settle on a reservation south of the Canadian River, where they were joined by most of their relatives, and by the Caddo with their associates from the Brazos Reserve in Texas. They were disrupted by the Civil War and, generally in an impoverished condition, were subsequently allotted lands in severalty by 1901. In early times the Wichita probably numbered 1,600, with their related tribes perhaps more than 3,200. In 1910 there were 318 "Wichita," 385 in 1937; and 485 in 1970. In 2001, there were 2,174 reported. Most Wichitas now live around Gracemont, north of the Washita River in Caddo County, Oklahoma, and are the descendants of true Wichita, Tawakoni, Waco, Kichai and others. The *Tawehash* of early reports were probably at least part of the Wichita. In 1993 only 20 speakers of their language remained.

TAWAKONI The Tawakoni were a tribe of Caddoan speech and of the Wichita group who lived on the Arkansas River in present Muskogee County, Oklahoma, when visited by La Harpe in 1719. They subsequently drifted south into Texas after the close of the French and Indian War in 1763. They were with the Wacos on the Brazos River near present Waco, Texas, in 1779, and were among the tribes on the Brazos in 1859 when persuaded to move, along with the Caddo, to a reservation on the Washita River in Indian Territory. They ultimately affiliated with the Wichita people and are no longer reported separately, but no doubt have descendants among the present day Wichita-Caddo of Oklahoma. They were buffalo hunters and good horsemen, but they also raised crops of corn, and later wheat and vegetables. They also owned livestock before leaving Texas.

WACO These Caddoan people were no doubt part of the tribes visited by La Harpe in 1719, and may have been the *Yscani* of early reports. However, they were in northern Texas by 1779 under this name. Part of the people moved in 1859 from the Brazos River to the Washita River, Indian Territory, where they combined with the Wichita and are no longer reported separately. Their descendants are counted as "Wichita" and are in Caddo County, Oklahoma. Villages of the Wichita tribes were distinguished by dome-shaped houses covered with grass thatch.

KICHAI or KITSAI These were a Caddoan people who were living on the upper Trinity River in Texas in 1701, probably intermediate between the tribes that became collectively either Caddo or Wichita. Some were part of the Indians who moved to the Wichita Agency, Indian Territory, from the Brazos Reservation in Texas in 1859. Their descendants are counted as "Wichita" and live in rural Caddo County, Oklahoma. Recent studies have suggested that the Kitsai are linguistically a bridge between the "Witchita" group and the Pawnee.

SHUMAN or **JUMANO** These were a people who from early Spanish reports were associated with various places in Texas and adjacent states, once thought to have been Caddoan, Apache or Uto-Aztecan. They were reported on the Rio Grande in 1535, and trading in eastern Texas in 1685. They are not clearly reported after 1740. If they were indeed Caddoan, then some no doubt merged with the Wichita. More likely, the last of them joined the Hispanicized groups around El Paso, Texas, and in Mexico, where a descendant was still living at Senecú in 1897.

Above: Kiowa, c. 1875. The Kiowa of the southern Plains, often allied with the Comanche, were known for elegantly painted and fringed hide garments. Some shirts and leggings were painted yellow or blue-green, with twisted fringing, but at this period they had only minimal edge and seam beadwork. Moccasins often had heel and instep fringes and double tongues. Here an otter fur turban with trailer is decorated with ribboned and beaded rosettes. He has an otter skin bowcase and quiver, with strike-a-light and whetstone cases hanging from the latter; and he carries a painted rawhide shield. Although known throughout the Plains, in later years the use of lances seems to have been largely ritualistic, as firearms became more widely available.

KIOWA According to their own tradition the Kiowas' earliest known home was in Montana, and they were in possession of the Black Hills of western South Dakota during the 18th century. They were probably expelled from this region by the Sioux arriving from the east, and began a movement south to the Arkansas and the headwaters of the Cimarron River and northern Texas. By 1790 they had established friendly relations with the Comanche. At some time, perhaps in the late 17th or early 18th centuries, a small Athabascan tribe, the Kiowa-Apache, joined them, and remained as a subtribe until reservation days. The Kiowa developed into a formidable and typical Plains tribe. Their language forms an independent family, but is distantly related to the Tanoan family of Pueblo Indians. Despite ravaging the southern Plains and even northern Mexico with their Comanche allies, they developed a lucrative trade relationship with the Pueblos.

Above: The Kiowa developed the lattice cradle, constructed on a pair of narrow boards with pointed ends extending far above the top of the bag, held in place by crosspieces near its head and foot. The sides of the deep buckskin bag, lined with cloth and reinforced with rawhide, were laced together with deerskin thongs. The bag was beaded with geometrical or — more commonly — abstract floralistic designs probably adopted from neighboring Eastern tribes relocated in Oklahoma. The boards were often decorated with brass studs. The Comanche had similar cradles; use of the boards was also adopted by the Cheyenne and sometimes by the Sioux.

Above: The Kiowa warrior Tape-Day-Ah ("Standing Sweat House"), c.1875. He was reputed to have been a member of every Kiowa war party between 1870 and 1874. Note the southern style of tailored, fringed shirt, decorated fur turban and bowcase and quiver made from mountain lion skin. Photograph: Soule Photos, courtesy Ian West

Below: The Comanche used a rawhide night cradle — simply a rectangle of hide laced tightly around the baby.

They became known to the Americans in the early 19th century and were reported on the prairies of the Arkansas and Red rivers in 1820. A treaty at Fort Atkinson in 1853 attempted to establish peace on the Sante Fe Trail, which ran through Kiowa territory, but with little success. The Kiowa suffered from the cholera epidemic of 1849 and smallpox in 1861. But despite their reduced numbers and agreement to relinquish their tribal lands for a reservation in present southwestern Indian Territory, now Oklahoma (1865 and 1867), they continued to raid Texas. These raids climaxed in the fight at Adobe Wells in 1874, after which the Kiowa Chief Satanta was arrested and later committed suicide. Some Kiowa warriors were even imprisoned and sent for three years to Florida. Much of Kiowa history was contained in a pictographic form known as "calendar histories," recorded by the ethnologist James Mooney.

By the late 1870s the Kiowa and Comanche were finally restricted to their reservation in southwestern

Oklahoma, suffering further tragedies from epidemics and starvation after the disappearance of the buffalo by 1879. Their transition from tribal to reservation life was attended by much misery. Their population before the epidemics of the early 19th century may have been more than 2,000, but was barely 1,000 by the time of their final surrender at Fort Sill in 1875. In 1924 they were reported to number 1,699, in 1970 4,357, nearly 10,000 in 1992 and more than 11,000 by 2000, with a considerable number of mixed tribe and race, including Mexican and other Indian ancestry — particularly Comanche. In the 2010 Census the figure had dropped slightly to 9,253.

The present population live mainly in Caddo County, Oklahoma, with the largest community near Carnegie. After several decades of dormancy a Kiowa warrior society has been revitalized, representing a distinctively Kiowa flavor to Oklahoma pan-Indianism, the "Gourd Dance." It has now been formally organized in four separate factional divisions that promote Kiowa ethnic identity among both rural and urban tribal members. Gourd Dance members are often invited to attend powwows throughout Oklahoma. They sing and dance, holding distinctive rattles and fans. Their language is now thought to be spoken by fewer than 400 people.

COMANCHE The Comanche spoke a Shoshonean language, and perhaps split from the Shoshone after obtaining horses during the late 17th century. They became the most skilled horsemen of the southern Plains and were truly nomadic. They were then associated with the area around the North Platte River. Later moving south, they ranged at the headwaters of the Cimarron, Brazos, Red and Canadian rivers. They harried the Spaniards all the way into Mexico, replenishing their herds of horses by trade or by attacks on settlements. They were at first enemies of — and later friends with — the Kiowa, and together they often closed the Santa Fe Trail. They often adopted white women captured on their raids.

One of their first official dealings with Americans came in 1834 when Colonel Henry Dodge met several Comanche representatives at a Wichita village on the Red River. They remained periodically hostile to Texans and Americans until the famous Medicine Lodge Council of 1867, held in Kansas just north of the Oklahoma state border. This was one of the most memorable and colorful gatherings of southern Plains Indians. As a result of this treaty, and because of military action against the Cheyenne on the Washita in 1868, the Comanche settled on a reservation in southwestern Indian Territory, now Oklahoma. Early reservation life was marked by much suffering and starvation resulting in hostile outbreaks and military reaction. The last of the Comanches to accept reservation life were the Kwahadi band under Quanah Parker, who surrendered in 1875. Parker, son of a white captive, became an influential leader during early reservation life.

The Comanche had several subtribes, the best known being the *Kwahadi* or "Antelope" band, the *Yamparika* or "Yap eaters," the *Nokoni, Tanima, Kutsveka* and *Penateka,* or "Wasps," the most-southern band and vanguard of the Comanche southward migration. The Comanche lacked the

Above: Comanche warrior, c. 1840. The principle defense of the Plains warrior was the rawhide shield, usually made from the bison's thickest breast hide and protected — when not in use — with a soft buckskin case. Shields were painted with symbols and had small "medicine" attachments. This warrior's eagle feather bonnet is taken from a known example collected before 1850, the browband with pony beads and triangular designs recalling Plateau/Basin Shoshone work. The Comanche had previously separated from the Shoshone.

extensive ceremonialism of other Plains tribes, the Sun Dance not being an important aspect of their culture. Their bands were more self-managing. Their buckskin clothing was emphasized by heavy fringing rather than by beadwork or other decoration. Their tipis were built on a four-pole basis like those of their Shoshone relatives, and unlike the three-pole form used by their neighbors. Their population has frequently been overstated. It was perhaps 4,000 in the early 19th century, and 2,538 in 1869; reduced to 1,476 in 1910, it recovered to 4,250 in 1970, including a considerable admixture of Spanish, Mexican-Indian, Anglo and recently other Oklahoma Indian ancestry. The Comanches numbered 8,500 in 1993, 9,580 in 2001 and 12,784 in 2010, but only about 250 elderly members were fluent in their language.

Most modern Comanches live in the rural and urban parts of present Caddo, Kiowa, Comanche and Cotton counties, Oklahoma. The changes brought by acculturation to white American life have resulted in tribal schisms between liberals and conservatives, Christians and Peyotists, and full-bloods and mixed-bloods. The Comanche — together with the Kiowa —were the principal conduit of the Peyote cult to other Oklahoma tribes.

The religion, derived from Mexican Indians by way of Lipan and Mescalero Apaches, and was adopted by the Comanche in the 1880s. It involved the sacramental eating of peyote, a mild narcotic, and compounded elements of native and Christian beliefs. But it developed in Oklahoma into its present two divergent rites. The Comanche have also been keenly involved with the pan-Indian Oklahoma Powwow complex of the 20th century.

PADOUCA Early in the 18th century the Padouca are recorded as a people of western Kansas, usually considered as Comanche. However, several historians have suggested that they may have been Apachean, even the first great tribe to have attempted to form settlements and grow crops in the heart of the High Plains country — although archaeological evidence now suggests that the agriculturalists at least were Puebloan. If they were Apachean, perhaps the Lipans and Kiowa-Apache were all that were left of them by the 19th century. Recently the Comanche theory seems more acceptable to historians. A tribe reported as *Gatakas* seem to have been close allies of the Kiowa, and this was probably an early term for the Kiowa Apache; or alternatively part of a composite "Padouca," who moved south through the Great Plains before the Kiowa-Comanche but who subsequently disappeared from history, or at least under that name.

PLATEAU

Language family and tribe	Meaning/origin of tribal name, where known	Language family and tribe	Meaning/origin of tribal name, where known
Shahaptian:		**Salishan:**	
Nez Perce	French — "*pierced noses*"	Flathead or Salish	"*people*"
Palouse	–	Kalispel	"*camas*" (plant)
Wallawalla	"*little river*"	Coeur d'Alene	French — "*awl heart*"
Umatilla	–	Spokan	"*sun people*"
Yakima	"*runaway*"	Colville	English name
Klickitat	"*beyond*"	Senijextee	"*lake people*"
Tenino	–	Okanagan	place name
		Sanpoil & Nespelem	–
Waiilatpuan:		Sinkiuse	band name
Cayuse	–	Wenatchee	place name
Molala	place name	Chelan	–
		Methow	–
Lutuamian:		Thompson	English name
Klamath	"*people*"	Shuswap	–
Modoc	"*southerners*"	Lillooet	"*wild onion*"
		Kutenai	division name

The Indians living in the present states of Idaho, Washington, eastern Oregon, parts of adjacent states and Canada constitute a culture area known as the Plateau. Generally, the area consists of barren uplands, mountains with patches of forest and lakes. It is cut by two great river systems, the Columbia and its tributary, the Snake.

The culture of the Plateau Indians has often been regarded as partly a transitional culture, its elements drawn from both the Plains and from the Pacific Coast. While the Nez Perce may have had a heavy overlay of Plains culture, for some others it was superficial and very late. Political unity rarely extended beyond village autonomy in the south, and band autonomy in the north, although settlements of ethnically mixed composition, often bilingual were common. Each village had its chief, its fishing place and its territory along a river. Anything resembling tribal organization must have arisen subsequent to the acquisition of the horse, placed for this area around 1710. Tradition from the Cayuse and Umatilla declare they obtained their horses from the south, probably from the Shoshone, not from the Plains. The Shoshone of southern Idaho were the main conduit of horse

trade to the Plateau tribes before horses were common among the Assiniboine and other Plains groups. Chieftainship was received through inheritance or by selection by achievement. The powers of a chief varied greatly from tribe to tribe. In the south central Plateau the chief was leader, counselor and arbitrator in disputes. Among the Canadian Plateau Salishan and Chilcotin chieftainship and war leadership are quite divorced, the latter merely an accomplished warrior selected for the occasion.

Habitations in the Plateau fell into three general types: the earth lodge, the mat lodge and the tipi. The earth lodge, a circular pit covered with a conical roof of radiating rafters and central posts, was the commonest form in the area with its highest development in the north-central region. The mat covered lodge of cattail or tule was also widely distributed often side-by-side with the earth lodge, the most popular form being pitched in cross-section with a rectangular ground plan with rounded ends. The tipi was an intrusive form found among the Kutenai and Flathead as a typical dwelling but adopted as a temporary shelter for Indian celebrations in recent times farther west. Plank houses and extended lodges using a ridge pole with leaning side poles were used for feasts, councils and ceremonials.

Right: Nez Perce woman, c. 1900. Cloth replaced hide late in the 19th century. The dress's square-cut yoke gave a "bat wing" effect, and sleeves terminated above the elbow. The dress was worn over a blouse. The yoke often was decorated with cowrie shells and elk's teeth or carved-bone imitations. The primary source for this example seems to show brass tacks, an unusual addition. The Nez Perce are famed for their large, twined storage bags of cornhusk with designs in native fibers or traded wool (see page 144 for description). The designs probably influenced the rather massive quality of late-Plateau beadwork. Nez Perce moccasins were usually of side-seam construction; floralistic beaded designs appeared quite early during the fur trade era in the Plateau region.

Below Left: Nez Perce, c. 1860. Basketry caps appear among women of the western peoples from California to Washington State. Those worn by the Nez Perce and some other Plateau peoples were made of cornhusk and other dyed fibers, embroidered with colored grass or wool.

Below: Nez Perce, c. 1877. Material culture and dress show similarities borne of friendly trade relations with the Crow of Montana: horse collars, gun cases, bandolier bags, and blanket strips, bore similar beaded designs, such as hourglass shapes, isosceles triangles and crosses, and similarly sophisticated use of colors such as pink and blue, stitched down on hide or cloth in a flat mosaic form. Nez Perce warriors wore both upright and flared bonnets; a style intermediate between the two is illustrated. The Nez Perce were famous for these Appaloosa horses.

Plateau people subsisted on fishing and hunting which included deer, elk and water fowl, and many varieties of plants and edible roots were collected including camas, onions and wild carrots or bitterroot. During the 19th century several Plateau tribes made seasonal visits to the Montana plains to hunt bison, often in combined groups of Flathead, Kalispel, Nez Perce, Cayuse and Umatilla. Contact with Plains Indians began the adoption of Plains-type clothing, horse gear and certain aspects of Plains military and social ceremonialism. However, recent evidence suggests this interaction was by no means one way.

The eastern Plateau tribes such as the Kutenai were partly located east of the Rocky Mountains and were marginal to the Plains culture adopting the coup system, warrior societies, and the Sun Dance. Distinctive art and material culture developed with the interaction and trade between Plateau groups and the Crow of Montana and Shoshone of Idaho and Wyoming, resulting in trade goods from the east being available at The Dalles, in the middle of the Columbia River, then exchanged with goods from the Northwest Coast. The environment of this area being the most receptive to Plains influence.

Canoes of the dugout type were known in all parts of the Plateau except among the Flathead. In the northern part of the Plateau, bark canoes predominated with the curiously shaped sturgeon-nosed canoe associated with the Kutenai and their neighbors.

Religious beliefs and ceremonies largely revolved around the belief in dreams, visions and spirits, usually guardian spirits, ghosts, animals (Grizzly Bear)—some dangerous, some benevolent. Before any ceremony, people had to be cleansed by participation in a sweat lodge (which also had spirit) to achieve purity of mind, body and spirit. Midwinter Spirit Dance ceremonies provided the opportunities for people with spirit power to demonstrate their power from the spirits, by dances, curing and ensuring continuing subsistence and health. Some Christian elements incorporated during the 19th century gave rise to newer religious practices such as the Prophet Dance, the Washat Religion (also known as Smohalla's religion after a Wanapum divine) whose ceremonies are still held in special longhouses. The Bluejay Dance of the Kutenai was similar to the Spirit Dances of the western Plateau.

Trade goods of the white man were reported by Lewis and Clark in 1805 and the beginning of the fur trade in 1811–1812 brought European traders and eastern Indians into the region. Smallpox preceded them, coming east from ships exploring the Pacific Coast and from the Missouri River in the 1780s.

The Plateau peoples excelled in basketry. There were three main basketry techniques: coiling, plaiting and twining and all three were known on the Plateau, the area between the Cascades and Rockies. In the Thompson River and Fraser River areas and also among the Klickitat and Yakima rigid coiled storage basketry was decorated by imbrication, a technique where a separate decorative element is folded and held parallel to the coils. The foundation coils were split cedar root stitching, with decorative material of cherry bark, horsetail root, bear grass and other

Above: Nez Perce men and women, c. 1907. Note the upright eagle feather headdress worn by the man kneeling, and the fine beaded shirt and leggings worn by the young man on the right.

Right: Yakima woman, c. 1885. The older, classic dress of the Plateau and northwestern Plains was constructed of two elk skins forming the front and back, sewn together. To straighten the shoulder line, the tail ends were folded over and stitched down. Plateau women decorated the upper part with bands of large pony beads, strung loosely and sewn to the skin. Her basket hat of native fiber has a deep triangular design in bear grass false embroidery.

Below: Umatilla mat lodge, c. 1860. Before adoption of Plains-type canvas tipis in the late 19th century, Plateau peoples used pole lodges covered with either cattail (bullrush) or tule (reed) mats, usually sewn but sometimes twined. The conical shape was only one of several ground plans, including rectangular, and parallel-sided with one or both ends rounded. The Yakima had a structure with vertical walls and gable roof resembling West Coast house shapes.

the Cayuse, Molala and others close to the Columbia River. The Columbia River Wasco and Wishram are included with their Chinookian relatives in the Northwest Coast section see p. 262.

SHAHAPTIAN or SAHAPTIAN

Shahaptian was a linguistic family of the American Plateau region, occupying the valleys of the Columbia and Snake rivers in Washington, Oregon and Idaho. They have been linked with the Cayuse, Molala, Modoc and Klamath into the larger so-called Shapwailutan stock. The Shahaptians as a whole were noted for their superficial adoption of cultural traits from the Plains Indians during the 19th century.

NEZ PERCE The most important tribe of the Shahaptian family, the Nez Perce occupied lands between the Bitteroot Mountains in the east, to the junction of the Snake and Columbia rivers in the west. They made their homes along the Clearwater and Snake rivers and in the Wallowa valley of what is now Idaho. They had strong trading links with the northern Plains Indians, particularly with the Crow, and made seasonal bison-hunting visits to the Montana plains. In 1805 the explorers Lewis and Clark passed through their territory. The Nez Perce concluded treaties with the United States Government in 1855 and 1863 (which only a portion of the tribe recognized), and agreed to the reservation set aside near Lapwai, Idaho. In a desperate attempt to reach Canada in June-October 1877, some Nez Perce under their famous leader, Chief Joseph, made a masterly 2,000-mile (3,200 km) retreat through Idaho and Montana, but were forced to surrender to Generals Miles and Howard only a few miles from the border. As a result, some of Joseph's band were sent to Indian Territory, but returned later, either to the Lapwai Reservation or Colville Reservation, Washington. They numbered 6,000 in the early 19th century. In 1895, 1,457 were on the reservation at Lapwai; in 1906, 1,534, with 83 on the Colville Reservation. In 1985, they numbered 2,015 — perhaps 400 of these being fullblood — mostly on or near their Idaho reservation. Census 2000 reported 3,983 Nez Perce, with an additional 2,552 of mixed ancestry. They continue to hold root festivals and powwows,

grasses. Plaiting was used for mat-making and cover mats for lodges and were usually made of cattail or tule rushes. Twinned flat bags were particularly common among Nez Perce, Umatilla, and others of the central Plateau and also the Upper Chinook Wishram and Wasco of the Columbia River. Three structural elements are used in plain twining, a pair of wefts passed around the front and back of each warp, and a fourth non-structural element wrapping around each weft appears on the bags' exterior surface as false embroidery of colored cornhusk (corn was introduced to the Plateau about 1820). The weft and warp elements were often of two-ply Indian hemp and the cornhusk colors, brown, green or yellow. These bags were usually for gathering and root storage, but later for personal belongings and square-shaped with more elaborate designs.

Following the explorers Lewis and Clark, missionaries and traders had modified native life in the area by the 1840s, and a number of conflicts occurred between white intruders and the Cayuse, Yakima, Nez Perce and Palouse. Although most of the larger inland Salish and Shahaptian tribes survived the invasion, smaller western groups suffered greatly, particularly

---

TRIBES OF THE
GREAT BASIN AND PLATEAU, c. 1750s–1850

Linguistic and cultural boundaries are necessarily approximate; this sketch map is intended only as a general guide to distribution. Modern state boundaries are shown as broken lines, for orientation only. The numerals in the Shapwailuta linguistic areas indicate (1) Shahaptian, (2) Waiilatpuan, and (3) Lutuami linguistic families. The Kutenai, an independent linguistic group, are so indicated by underlining.

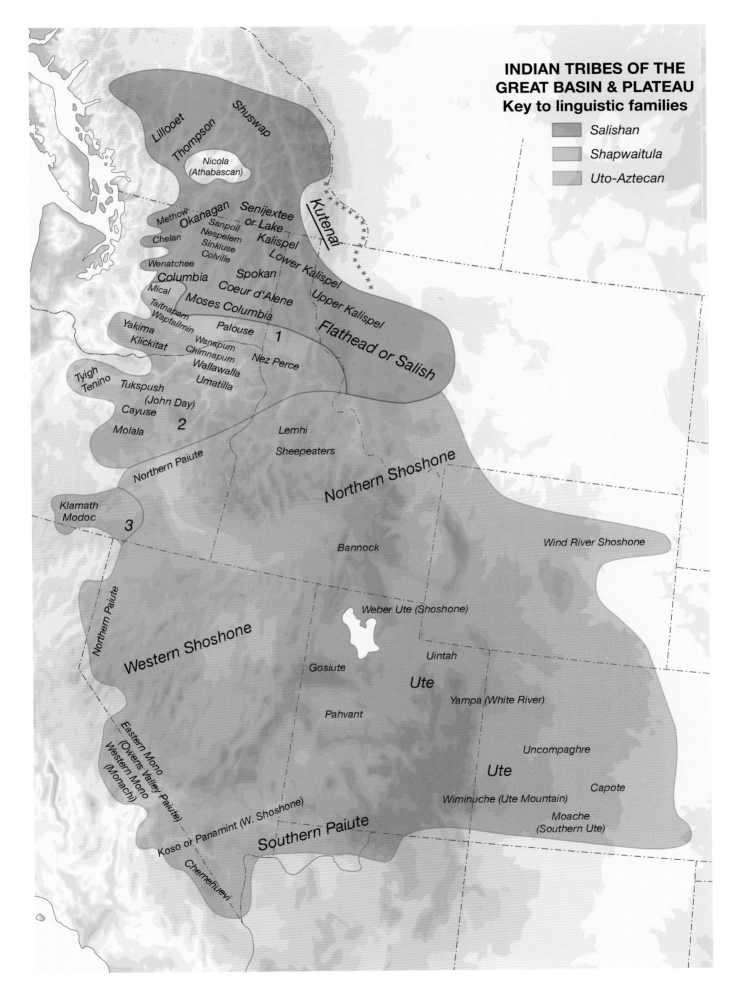

INDIAN TRIBES OF THE GREAT BASIN & PLATEAU
Key to linguistic families

- Salishan
- Shapwaitula
- Uto-Aztecan

Lillooet

Thompson

Shuswap

Nicola (Athabascan)

Methow

Okanagan

Senijextee or Lake

Kutenai

Chelan

Sanpoil
Nespelem
Sinkiuse
Colville

Kalispel

Lower Kalispel

Wenatchee

Columbia

Spokan

Mical

Coeur d'Alene

Upper Kalispel

Taitnapam

Moses Columbia

Waptailmin

Palouse

Yakima

1

Flathead or Salish

Klickitat

Wanapum
Chimnapum

Nez Perce

Wallawalla

Tyigh
Tenino

Umatilla

Tukspush
(John Day)

Cayuse

2

Molala

Lemhi

Sheepeaters

Northern Paiute

Northern Shoshone

Klamath
Modoc

3

Bannock

Wind River Shoshone

Northern Paiute

Weber Ute (Shoshone)

Western Shoshone

Gosiute

Uintah

Ute

Pahvant

Yampa (White River)

Eastern Mono
(Owens Valley Paiute)
Western Mono
(Monachi)

Uncompaghre

Ute

Capote

Wiminuche (Ute Mountain)

Koso or Panamint (W. Shoshone)

Southern Paiute

Moache
(Southern Ute)

Chemehuevi

Above: Nez Perce beaded heavy leather saddle bag or pommel bag, c. 1900.

Left: Edward Sheriff Curtis (1868–1952) is the best-known of the photographers of Native Americans due to his 20-volume series published from 1907 into the 1930s. Each volume included a superb portfolio of photographs printed in a red sepia tone. This full-length portrait of a Nez Perce man was taken around the turn of the 20th century. Library of Congress Print & Photographs Division, LC-USZC4-8865

Below: This image of two Interior (Plateau) Salish women drying meat on a stick frame was published in The North American Indian, *volume 7, p. 60. This was published in 1911 and covered the Yakima, the Klickitat, Salishan tribes of the interior, and the Kutenai.* Library of Congress Print & Photographs Division, LC-USZ62-113093

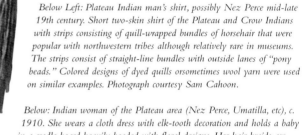

Right: Women from both the Plateau and northern Plains wore the two-tail deer or mountain sheep skin dress, formed using the tail up then folded down a few inches front and back to create straight shoulder seams. The edge of the skins formed an undulating horizontal contour across the front and back of the garment. This contour was echoed on Plateau women's dresses by broad bands of beadwork often using large or pony (pound) beads in contrast to the smaller and solidly beaded yokes of Plains dresses.

Plateau women's dresses often massed heavy waves of wide lazy-stitch bands interrupted at intervals by bold vertical triangular or rectangular blocks. On this example the yoke or cape is separate and could be transferred to a new skin dress if required. The skin dress was reported to have been collected at the Colville Reservation, Washington and the yoke is Nez Perce, both dating from the first half of the 20th century.

Below Left: Plateau Indian man's shirt, possibly Nez Perce mid-late 19th century. Short two-skin shirt of the Plateau and Crow Indians with strips consisting of quill-wrapped bundles of horsehair that were popular with northwestern tribes although relatively rare in museums. The strips consist of straight-line bundles with outside lanes of "pony beads." Colored designs of dyed quills orsometimes wool yarn were used on similar examples. Photograph courtesy Sam Cahoon.

Below: Indian woman of the Plateau area (Nez Perce, Umatilla, etc), c. 1910. She wears a cloth dress with elk-tooth decoration and holds a baby in a cradle-board heavily beaded with floral designs. Her hair braids are wrapped with fur.

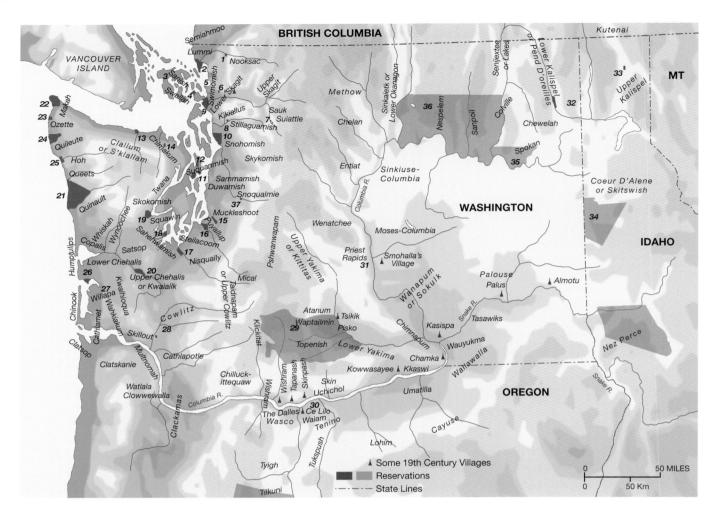

The Indian Tribes of Washington State and Columbia River Valley

Key to reservations and communities of Washington State with tribal origins:

1   NOOKSACK   Nooksack
2   LUMMI   Lummi, Duwamish, Snohomish, Suquamish, Samish, others now "Lummi"
3   SAN JUAN-MITCHELL BAY   Samish, Songhees, others
4   SAMISH   Samish, Skagit
5   LOWER SKAGIT   Skagit
6   UPPER SKAGIT   Skagit
7   SAUK-SUIATTLE   Skagit, Kikiallus
8   STILLAGUAMISH   Stillaguamish
9   SWINOMISH   Swinomish, Snohomish, Samish, Skagit, Kikiallus
10   TULALIP   Snohomish, Suquamish, Samish, Duwamish, Snoqualmie, now "Snohomish"
11   PORT MADISON   Duwamish, Snohomish, Suquamish, now "Suquamish"
12   PORT GAMBLE   Clallam
13   LOWER ELWHA S'KLALLUM   Clallam
14   JAMESTOWN S'KLALLUM   Clallam
15   MUCKLESHOOT   "Muckleshoot" several small original groups
16   PUYALLUP   Puyallup, Nisqually, Steilacoom, others now "Puyallup"
17   NISQUALLY   Nisqually, Puyallup, Steilacoom, others now "Nisqually"
18   SQUAXIN IS.   Nisqually, Puyallup, Steilacoom, others now "Squaxin"
19   SKOKOMISH   Skokmish, Twana, Clallam, Chimakum, now "Skokomish"
20   CHEHALIS   Chehalis (Upper & Lower), Chinook
21   QUINAULT   Quinault, Quaitso (Queets), Humptulips, Satsop, Copalis, Chehalis, Chinook, now "Quinault"
22   MAKAH   Makah, Quileute
23   OZETTE   Ozette
24   QUILEUTE   Quileute
25   HOH   Hoh
26   SHOALWATER BAY   Chehalis (Upper & Lower), Satsop, Chinook
27   CHINOOK   Chinook
28   COWLITZ   Cowlitz
29   YAKAMA (YAKIMA)   Yakima (Upper & Lower), Palouse, Pisko, Wenatchi, Klickitat, Wishram, Columbia River Shahaptians, now "Yakama"
30   CELILO   Fishing sites Waiam, Wasco and Wishram
31   PRIEST RAPIDS   Wanapum
32   KALISPEL   Kalispel
33   BONNERS FERRY (Idaho)   Kutenai
34   COEUR D'ALENE (Idaho)   Coeur d'Alene
35   SPOKAN   Spokan
36   COLVILLE   Colville, Methow, Okanagan, Lakes, Sanpoil, Nespelem, Chelan, Entiat, Moses–Columbia, Wenatchi, Nez Perce, Palouse, now "Colville"
37   SNOQUALMIE   Snoqualmie

which show a continuing Indian tradition. Much of their livelihood now depends on farming, logging, leases and tourism. Although few young people speak the Nez Perce language, the tribal council is attempting to preserve it through publishing a dictionary and other texts.

PALOUSE A group of Shahaptians occupying the Columbia River valley above its junction with the Snake and along the Palouse River valley are the Palouse. They included the *Chimnapum*, *Wauyukma*, and *Wanapum* or *Sokulks*. The confusing term "*Wanapam*" has also been added, but this is probably the same as Wanapum, the people who lived around Priest Rapids on the Columbia. Although included in the Yakima Treaty of 1855, only a few moved to various reservations, most choosing to remain in their homelands. As a result, few Palouse or Wanapum remain today. The Shahaptians were a village people with few political tribal organizations. On the whole, Plateau life involved wintertime occupancy of river villages and summertime camping at fishing and root-digging grounds. The Winter Guardian Spirit Dance was the major religious ceremony of the Plateau tribes. Smohalla, an Indian religious leader of the 19th century, was a Wanapum.

A few descendants still survive at Priest Rapids and other locations along the Columbia River.

WALLAWALLA or **WALULA** These were a group of Shahaptians on the Wallawalla River, on the south side of the Snake, near its junction with the Columbia. Closely related to the Nez Perce, they were met by Lewis and Clark in 1805, and, subsequently, traders and trappers soon filtered into their domain. They moved to the Umatilla Reservation, Oregon, following the Wallawalla Treaty in 1855. Perhaps numbering more than 1,000 in pre-reservation days, they were returned as 397 in 1910 and 623 in 1945. They have now largely merged with the Cayuse and Umatilla and are known as the "Confederated Tribes of the Umatilla Reservation."

UMATILLA The Umatillas lived on the lower Umatilla River, near its junction with the Columbia in present Umatilla County, Oregon. Reported to number 1,500 in 1780, the Umatilla had dwindled to a few hundred by the time of the Wallawalla Treaty of 1855, when they were assigned to the Umatilla Reservation, along with the Wallawalla and Cayuse. They numbered 272 in 1910 and 161 in 1950; but are a large element in the confederated "Umatilla," including the other groups, given as 1,234 in 1956; 1,578 in 1985; and 2,140 in

Above: Umatilla woman, half-length portrait, wearing beaded buckskin dress, shell bead necklaces, shell disk earrings, and woven corn husk and beargrass hat. Published in volume 8, pl. 269 of The North American Indian, *a volume that concentrated on the Nez Perce, Wallawalla, Umatilla, Cayuse and the Chinookan tribes. Library of Congress Print & Photographs Division, LC-USZ62-111291*

Left: Gauntlet-gloves with floral beadwork in the style of the Plateau tribes, from the first half of the 20th century. Probably Yakima. M.G. Johnson Collection.

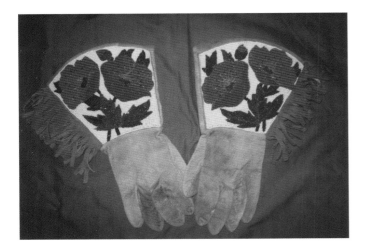

2001. They still hold root feasts, and participate in the powwows at the Pendleton Roundup each September.

YAKIMA (YAKAMA) In its modern and inclusive sense the Yakama Nation comprises the enrolled members of the Yakima Reservation Washington, descendants from five major groups of Shahaptian speaking villages, and a few Interior Salish and Upper Chinook, who once occupied approximately 60 independent villages bounded by the Columbia River on the south and east, the Cascade Mountains on the west, and the upper course of the Yakima River to the north. The five Shahaptian groups were the Lower Yakima (Yakima proper), Upper Yakima or Kittitas including the closely related Pshwanwapam and Mical, Taitnapam or Upper Cowlitz, Klickitat (q.v.) and Wanapum (q.v.).

Above: Alby and Hattie (Hatty) Shawaway, Yakima Indians, c. 1950, wearing beaded costume partly influenced by Plains Indians. Photograph: Santa Fé Railway

Opposite, Above: Salish man, c. 1880. The Hudson's Bay Company was the primary European influence in much of the Canadian interior and western United States until the early 19th century. Among the trade goods they introduced were the English woollen "point" blankets, so named from lines marked on the edge denoting the weight and thus the value in trade for furs. Traders, Métis and Indians made them into winter capote coats. These were popular among northern Plains tribes and marginal Salish (Flathead), whose western Montana location was a crossroads for styles of native dress and ornamentation. The fur cap is embellished with peacock and eagle feathers. Note the loop necklace and pipe bag.

Below and Below Right: Two women's beaded flat bags, probably Yakima (right) and Klickitat, c. 1900. These probably derive from earlier corn husk bags, and were carried by women at celebrations.

In 1855 Governor Stevens, on behalf of the U.S., concluded a treaty with 14 groups by which they ceded their lands for the Yakima Reservation. These appear to correlate with some of the above, plus the Palouse (q.v.) from along the lower Snake River; these were the Yakima, Palouse, Pisquouse or Pisko (Salish), Wenatshapam or Wenatchee (Salish), Klikitat or Klickitat, Kowwassayee, Liaywas, Klinquit, Skinpah or Skin (also known as Rock Creek), Wisham or Wishram (Chinook), Shyils, Ocheehotes or Uchichol (also known as Tapanash or Topinish), Kahmiltpah and Seapcat. All Shahaptian speakers unless noted.

These 14 groups completed the treaty which was not ratified until 1859 and in the interim serious problems arose after settlers began moving into Yakima territory violating the treaty agreements and thus sparking a series of confrontations known as the Yakima War, which ended in 1858. The treaty established the Yakima Reservation under chiefs Kamiakin and his brothers Skloom and Shawaway (Lower Yakimas) and Teias and Owhi (Upper Yakimas). In 1862 the groups on the Yakima Reservation were numbered 667 Yakima, 633 Klikitat, 808 Columbia River Shahaptians, and 471 Wishram. In 1863 most Taitnapam (Upper Cowlitz) moved to the reservation giving a combined total of 3,000 in 1865. A number of Palouse, Wanapum and Taitnapam have never lived on the reservation.

Their traditional round of subsistence activities began in February when the first of the numerous wild plants were gathered. In mid-spring they gathered at their fishing stations along the Columbia and Yakima Rivers and later dispersed to root-digging grounds and then to the higher elevations to hunt deer, elk, mountain sheep and goats. Many foods were stored in woven baskets, a specialized craft of the Plateau people, using cedar, spruce roots, grass and strips of willow, cedar or elder bark. Soft twined cylindrical bags and flat cornhusk bags were also used.

Before the arrival of horses in about 1730, the Yakima lived in semi-underground circular pit houses, roofed over with poles covered with mats and grasses in winter, or mat-covered conical lodges in summer. Later rectangular lodges were built covered with layers of tule mats. When they began to hunt bison on the Plains they adopted the skin tipi of the three-pole foundation. Canvas covered tipis are still used today for special celebrations.

Traditional Yakima beliefs and religious practices fell into two distinctive spheres, the old guardian-spirit complex, which protected and restored spiritual and physical purity by means of sweetloges and Winter Spirit dances controled by shaman. Later cults incorporating some Christian elements such as the Washat or Seven Drum Longhouse religion and the Shaker Church, which combined fundamental Christian and Indian doctor characteristics, have still a following.

The collective name Yakima (now since 1994 Yakama) has for much of the 20th century been used to designate all the confederated groups of their reservation, and require "one fourth or more" Indian descent of one of the original 14 groups or their successors to be enrolled as a member. This collective group numbered 2,933 in 1937; 6,853 in 1984; 8,315 in 1992; 8,624 in 2001; and 8, 643 in 2010, with more than half living on the reservation, and a large number of full blood.

They continue to hold a large number of annual Indian events, powwows, Longhouse celebrations, and memorials. Tribal income is derived from logging, light industry, fruit and vegetables.

Two small bands identified in the late 19th century living on the Yakima Reservation, Atanum and Waptailmin may have been reformed from the afore-mentioned groups.

KLICKITAT This group lived along the Klickitat and White Salmon rivers, Klickitat County, Washington. They were related to the Yakima groups, but also intermarried with the Cowlitz to the west, and possibly numbered 600 in 1780. They were included in the Yakima treaty of 1855 and moved to the Yakima Reservation, where they have merged over the years into the Yakima population. In 1910, 405 were reported separately; in 1970, only 21.

TENINO A group of Shahaptian bands and villages principally along the Deschutes and John Day rivers, mainly on the south side of the Columbia River in Oregon, were known as Tenino. These include the *Tyigh, Tilkuni, Tukspush* (or *John Day Indians*) and *Waiim* (or *Wyam*), to which can be added for convenience the *Tapanash* and *Skinpah* on the north side. Although a few seem to have gone to the Yakima Reservation, the majority, following the Wasco Treaty of 1855,

Below: Flathead singers, c. 1907. With the increasing social function of Plains/Plateau ceremonialism of the early 20th century, specialist "singing" groups (never called "drummers") provided accompanying songs for Owl, Grass, Tea and Rabbit Dances. Western bass drums, more reliable in sound, often replaced native drums. Each "singer" used a single drumstick, and for certain dances performers kneeled around the drum.

moved to the Warm Springs Reservation, Oregon, where a merged Wasco-Tenino-Paiute population remains. In 1945, 544 Tenino were reported, plus a few John Days. In 1985 more than 2,000 "Warm Springs" were enrolled, and 3,831 in 2001. A few Waiams continued to occupy old fishing sites along the Columbia until recent times (Celilo). Root feasts and powwows are still popular on the Warm Springs Reservation.

WAIILATPUAN

This was a small linguistic family, now thought to be close enough to both Shahaptian and Lutuamian to constitute one stock, "Shapwailutan." Only two tribes form the family — the Cayuse and Molala. However, the validity of this grouping has recently been contested.

CAYUSE Cayuse is a tribe of the upper Wallawalla, Umatilla and Grand Ronde rivers in northeastern Oregon, although they originally came from the Deschutes River area. They are particularly famous for their horses. They were involved in the so-called "Whitman mission massacre" of 1847, largely caused by squabbles over land ownership and fears about measles epidemics. Settled on the Umatilla Reservation, they numbered 404 in 1904, and 370 in 1937, but have largely merged into the "Confederated Umatilla," a composite of Umatilla, Wallawalla and Cayuse.

MOLALA This second branch of the Waiilatpuan family lived on the eastern slopes of the Cascades Mountains of central Oregon, and later on the Santiam and Molala rivers on the west side. The last of these people were said to be on the Grand Ronde Reservation, and a few may still be in the Lincoln County area of Oregon. The census of 1910 gave 31, but they are no longer separately reported.

LUTUAMIAN

This was a small linguistic group formed by two tribes of southern Oregon, the Klamath and Modoc. The group is connected with the Shahaptian and Waiilatpuan into the larger Shapwailutan stock.

KLAMATH The Klamath lived in the area of rivers and marshes around upper Klamath Lake, Oregon. They ceded their lands to the United States in 1864 and were provided with a reservation, which they shared with the Modocs and some Paiutes. Over the years they became very mixed with Euro-Americans and lost much of their Indian culture, which led to the termination by the Bureau of Indian Affairs of the reservation's status and of all government programs and assistance. However, the tribe's descendants are pressing for renewed government recognition. In 1958 a total of 2,133 were enrolled, being all the people of Klamath, Modoc and Yahooskin Paiute descent living on and off their former reservation. Census 2000 reported 2,632 Klamath.

MODOC The southern branch of the Lutuamian family, the Modoc lived around lower Klamath Lake, Tule Lake and Clear Lake in northern California. The Modocs are remembered for their stubborn resistance to American troops in the Lava Beds of northern California in 1872 under their leader, Captain Jack. As a

Indian girls of the Flathead Reservation, Montana, 1907, riding ponies with beaded saddles upon which unlimited time has been spent. The girls' ponies are adorned with a variety of Plains and Intermontane finery.

Louis Charlemain ("He Rolls Around"), Flathead man and daughters, c. 1907. He is holding a Civil War bayonet.

Above: Flathead man "Loma," photographed in Montana, c. 1907. He has his hair in braids and wears a shirt decorated with strips of floral beadwork.

Right: Salish (popularly known as Flathead) man, c.1907. Photograph taken on the Flathead Reservation, Montana. He holds a bow and arrows. His belt appears to be decorated with brass tacks.

Left: Double saddle bag, Flathead, Montana, c. 1890. Indian brain tanned buckskin double saddle bag, a woman's item of luggage. A large rectangular piece of hide lined cloth doubled on the long dimension and edges sewn together. A long slit cut in its length serves as the opening of the bag. Long fringes are added at each end of beaded panels. Usually they were thrown over the center of a woman's saddle hanging equal distance on each side, or placed over the cantle of the saddle through the slit. The distance between the pommel and cantle of a woman's saddle determined the proper width of the saddle bag, about 30cm (12in). The long fringes, according to Blackfoot tradition, should fall below the horse's belly when the bag is placed on the horse's back. Collected on the Flathead Reservation, Montana. Length approximately 275cm (9ft).

Right: Mrs. John Bushman ("Ma-Lee"), Flathead woman in buckskin costume, c. 1907.

result a number were sent into exile in Indian Territory, although some returned, few descendants (12 reported in 2000) remain in Oklahoma. The majority of Modocs, however, were incorporated among the Klamath on the Klamath Reservation, and had 478 descendants according to the 2000 Census, some around the town of Chiloquin, Oregon. Few, if any, are full-blood Modoc.

SALISHAN (INTERIOR)

While linguistically connected to their kin of the coast, the Salishan tribes of the mountains, valleys and rivers of the Canadian Cordillera and the American Plateau regions were different in culture. Their house types were the conical mat lodge, sometimes extended to communal lodges, and winter semi-underground dwellings. In common with other Plateau Indians they were well developed in the skills of fishing, making baskets and woven bags, and dressing skins. In later years they obtained a veneer of Plains culture and adopted the tipi of the popular type, particularly the eastern groups such as the Flathead.

FLATHEAD or **SALISH PROPER** The easternmost Salishan tribe living in western Montana in the valleys between the Rocky Mountains and the Bitterroot Range were the Flathead. They apparently obtained their name because, in contrast to tribes farther west, they did not deform the heads of children by compression with a board in the cradle. During the first half of the 19th century the Flatheads were involved in the fur trade, and relations with whites were generally friendly. They were missionized by the Roman Catholics in the 1840s. They signed a treaty with the United States in 1855 and were assigned a reservation around Flathead Lake, Montana, where they were ultimately combined with part of the Spokan, some Lower Kalispel, most of the Upper Kalispel, or Pend d'Oreilles, and some Kutenai.

The true Flathead were usually reported to number around 600. In 1909, they numbered 598. The population of the whole

Left: Spokan man, c. 1846. The Canadian artist Paul Kane traveled west across the interior, reaching Fort Vancouver in December 1846. Near Fort Colville he painted an Indian with combined bowcase and quiver, as well as a second bow, and wearing this pierced buckskin shirt imbued with protective power.

"Confederated Salish-Kutenai" of the Flathead Reservation was given as 3,085 in 1937; 3,630 in 1945; 5,937 in 1980; and 6,950 in 2001, of which only half resided on the reservation. Flathead culture was superficially much like that of the Plains tribes, although they never held the Sun Dance. The Arlee powwow is held in July, and other cultural events are expressions of their continuing cohesion as an Indian people.

KALISPEL This Salish tribe was also known as Pend d'Oreilles, in reference to the large shell earrings some of them wore. They were divided into the Upper Kalispel of western Montana, around Thompson Falls on the Clark Fork of the Pend d'Oreille River, and the Lower Kalispel, extending into present northern Idaho up to Priest Lake, almost to the Canadian border. Like the Flathead, they participated marginally in the horse-bison culture, but Plains traits were superficial. They were dominated by the fur trade and Catholic missionaries from the 1840s. Most of the Upper Kalispel and a few of the Lower Kalispel joined the Flatheads on the Flathead Reservation, numbering 640 and 197, respectively, in 1905. The Lower Kalispel are also found on the Kalispel Reservation at Usk, Washington, established in 1914, and a few on the Colville Reservation. The Kalispel element of the combined confederated "Salish-Kutenai" are no longer reported separately, but the Usk Lower Kalispel numbered 259 in 1985, and 329 in 2001.

COEUR d'ALENE or **SKITSWISH** The country occupied by this Salish tribe was almost wholly within the present state of Idaho on the headwaters of the Spokane River, Coeur d'Alene Lake, below Lake Pend d'Oreille. Missionary work began among them in the 1840s. The Coeur d'Alene Reservation in Benewah County, Idaho, was established in 1873, and for the majority of their descendants has been home since that time. They numbered 494 in 1905; 608 in 1937; 440 in 1970; 800 in 1990; and 1,493 in 2001, of which most were resident on their reservation. They sponsor an annual powwow at Worley.

SPOKAN A Salishan tribe on the Spokane and Little Spokane rivers in eastern Washington, closely related to their eastern neighbors, is the Spokan. They became associated with white traders after the establishment of Spokane House in 1810, and were assigned to several reservations in the late 19th century, but principally live on the Spokane Reservation, Wellpinit,

Left: Flathead (Salish) girls in western Montana, c. 1907. Their horses are in parade attire with decorated martingales, saddles, saddle blankets and headstalls. Behind them is a canvas tipi.

Washington, and with the Flathead in Montana. They were reported as 454 and 135, respectively, in 1910. In 1937 they were reported to total 847; in 1985, 1,961; and 2,306 in 2001. Summer dances, games and exhibits are still held at Wellpinit. In 1990 approximately 1,000 lived on their reservation.

COLVILLE Originally a small Salishan tribe around Kettle Falls on the Columbia River below the Canadian border, the Colville became associated with the Hudson's Bay post at Fort Colville after its establishment in 1825. In 1872 the Colville

Reservation was established on the western and northern sides of the Columbia, adjacent to the original Colville domain, and the Colville have been there since, although they are now incorporated with many other tribes to form the modern "Confederated Tribes of the Colville Reservation." The following tribes formed constituent elements in the present "Confederated Colville": Methow, Okanagon, Lakes, Sanpoil, Nespelem, Chelan, Entiat, Colville, Moses-Columbia, Wenatchee, Nez Perce, and Palouse. True Colville numbered 334 in 1907, and 322 in 1937, but the whole "Confederated

Colville" numbered 3,799 in 1985, 8,842 in 2001, and 10,081 in 2010. Rodeos and powwows are still held regularly in summer at Omak, Washington.

SENIJEXTEE or **LAKES** This Salishan tribe lived on the Columbia River, north of Kettle Falls, and on the Kettle River into Canada to Lower Arrow Lake. Those on the south side of the international border joined the various tribes of the Colville Reservation, being reported as 542 in 1909. Any north of the border seem to have merged with the Okanagan.

OKANAGAN or **SINKAIETK** This interior Salish tribe lived along the Okanagan River, Washington, north across into Canada on the Similkameen River and Lake Okanagan. They were estimated to number 2,500 in around 1790. The Canadian bands were settled on reservations around Lake Okanagan, at Okanagan, Westbank, Penticton, Upper and Lower Similkameen and Osoyoos, numbering more than 1,500 in 1970, and 1,708 in 2005. A few southern Okanagan were enrolled at the Colville agency, numbering 187 in 1906, and are now part of the "Confederated Colville."

SANPOIL & **NESPELEM** These are two closely related Salishan groups on the Sanpoil and Nespelem rivers in north-central Washington state. They made no treaty with the government, although ultimately most appear to have moved to the Colville Reservation. The Sanpoils numbered 202 in 1915 and the Nespelem 45 in 1910, about 150 full-blood in 1959, but they have now largely merged with the "Confederated Colville." The 1970 Census reported 1,674 Sanpoil, Nespelem, Okanagan and Spokan in the United States. That number, according to Census 2000, is 7,833, but again refers to merged tribes.

SINKIUSE or **COLUMBIA** The Sinkiuse were a group of Salishan bands on the east side of the Columbia River, from Fort Okanagan to Priest Rapids, Washington State, where one band called *Moses-Columbia* lived. They were originally estimated to number 1,000. The census of 1910 reported only 52, and the 150 full-blood reported in 1959 largely merged with the "Confederated Colville" on the Colville Reservation. In 1970, 33 Columbia and Wenatchee were reported.

WENATCHEE and **ENTIAT** These were two small Salishan groups on the west side of the Columbia River, on the Wenatchee and Entiat rivers around Leavenworth, Washington State. Not all moved to the reservations, but some to the Colville Reservation. These numbered 52 in 1910, and 268 in 1959, both on and off the reservation. They are now part of the "Confederated Colville."

CHELAN A Salish group on the west side of the Columbia, related to the Wenatchee, were the Chelan. A few remained until reservation days, but appear to have joined the Wenatchee and Columbia on the Colville Reservation.

METHOW A small group on the Methow River in north-central Washington were the Methow. They joined the Columbia or Sinkiuse on the Colville Reservation and lost separate identity.

THOMPSON or **NTLAKYAPMUK** The Thompson were a large tribe of interior Salishan, living on the Fraser River, British Columbia, from Spuzzum in the south to above Lytton, then along the Thompson River to an area above Spencer Bridge, and east along the Nicola valley. First noted by Simon Fraser in 1809, they subsequently came under the influence of the Northwest and Hudson's Bay traders. Although depleted during the 19th century, they continued to occupy village sites that became small reserves. The most important are Spuzzum, Boston Bar (230 in 2005), Boothroyd (259 in 2005), Kanaka

Above: A selection of so-called "imbricated" baskets and trays, c. 1920s–1930s. Made by the northern Plateau peoples of the Thompson and Fraser Rivers region of British Columbia. Coils of cedar, spruce root, or grasses with red and black cherry bark imbrication. Courtesy Ian West.

Below: Nespelem (Nespilim) woman, c.1907. The Nespelem was a small Interior Salish tribe related to the Sanpoil and Okanagan. Their descendants are now part of the many related groups called "Confederated Colville" of the Coville Reservation in Washington State. Photograph: Edward S. Curtis.

Bar (191 in 2005), Lytton (1,781 in 2005), Oregon Jack Creek (57 in 2005) and Upper and Lower Nicola (858 and 959, respectively, in 2005). The total population numbered 2,742 in 1970, and 4,335 in 2005.

SHUSWAP (SECWEPEMC) The Shuswap were an important Salishan tribe north of the Thompson, from the vicinity of Ashcroft north to Williams Lake in the upper valleys of the Fraser River, and along the Thompson River above Kamloops, and also in the valley of the upper Columbia River. Known to the early explorers and later traders and miners, they never moved from their ancient homes, although they were restricted to small reserves, usually near old village sites. Their main groups are at Bonaparte (765 in 2005), Ashcroft (236 in 2005), Kamloops (1,039 in 2005), Adams Lake (716 in 2005), Spallumcheen (738 in 2005), Clinton (127 in 2005), Shuswap (227 in 2005), Canoe Creek (644 in 2005), Williams Lake (505 in 2005), Canim Lake (616 in 2005), Soda Creek (345 in 2005) and High Bar (66 in 2005). Other locations include a total of 2,331. The total population was numbered at 3,862 in 1970.

LILLOOET (STL'ATL'IMX) These were a substantial Salishan people on the Fraser River around the town of Lillooet and Anderson Lake, also along the valley of Harrison Lake, Lillooet Lake and Lillooet River. They show a similar history to their relatives, the Shuswap and Thompson, but lost more members in the smallpox epidemic of 1865. Their principal present reserves are at Douglas, Skookum Chuck, Anderson Lake, Lillooet, Fountain, Seton Lake, Cayoose Creek, Bridge River and Mount Currie. They were reported as numbering 2,494 in 1970, but that number grew to 5,776 in 2005.

KUTENAI or KOOTENAY

The Kutenai are a tribe and independent linguistic family of Indians who either migrated or were forced, probably by the Blackfoot, across the Rocky Mountains into what is now southeastern British Columbia. They seem to have split into the upper and lower divisions.

The Upper Kutenai pushed south into present Montana on the Tobacco Plains and were influenced by the horse-buffalo Plains Indian culture complex. They used horses for transportation and as a source of wealth, and adopted the Sun Dance and material culture and costume associated with the northern Plains Indians.

By comparison, the Lower Kutenai were partly sedentary, of the true Plateau culture, subsisting on fish, roots and game, and are famous for a remarkable canoe (see below). In aboriginal times they perhaps numbered 2,000, but only 500 or so by 1855. Most of the Upper Kutenai, originally from around Jennings and Libby, Montana, under the name Dayton-Elmo band, joined the Flathead and their associates on the Flathead

Above: Thompson River Salish woman. Of particular interest is the beaded and studded headband worn over the burden strap, which supports her basket. Courtesy Ian West.

(Jocko) Agency; the Lower Kutenai, with accessions from the Tobacco Plains band, obtained reserves in British Columbia around Creston, Windermere and Cranbrook, and also near Bonners Ferry, Idaho. In 1907, 573 were recorded in Montana and 549 in British Columbia. The Bonners Ferry group returned 106 in 1945, 115 in 1982 and 121 in 2001.

The Kutenai perhaps constitute a quarter of the present, so-called "Confederated Salish-Kutenai," numbering 3,225 in 1985, but many now live off the reservation. In 1970 the Canadian Kutenai at Columbia Lake, Lower Kootenay, St. Mary's and Tobacco Plains numbered 446. That number was 713 in 2005.

Below left: Thompson pit house, c. 1850. Tribes of the Southern Cordillera of British Columbia and the Plateau area used differing types of semi-subterranean houses, up to 30 feet (9 m) wide and 4 to 6 feet (1.2 to 1.8 m) in depth, entered by a roof ladder. Exclusive to the Okanagan, Thompson, Lillooet, Shuswap and Chilcotin was the pyramidal roof with a circular pit obtained by hip rafters on internal posts, and the use of four or six logs to form the hatchway.

Below right: "Sturgeon nose" canoes were characteristic of the Kutenai and Shuswap.

Left: Kutenai, c. 1885. Several eastern Plateau and northern Basin tribes used a cradle based on a long elliptical board, the broad upper part covered with skin or cloth. The lower part was made into a bag to hold the child. The Kutenai beaded the upper area in geometric or floralistic patterns. Cradles were usually carried on a chest strap.

Right: Kalispel couple, full-length portrait, the man standing, the woman seated, facing front, wearing traditional dress 1861.

Below: Margaret Tenasse, Kootenay (Kutenai) and examples of her beadwork at her home near Windermere, British Columbia, c. 1945.

GREAT BASIN

Language family and tribe	Meaning/origin of tribal name, where known	Language family and tribe	Meaning/origin of tribal name, where known
Uto–Aztecan★:		Ute	Spanish name
Western Shoshone	–	Southern Paiute	Spanish name
Northern Shoshone	–	Eastern Mono	–
Bannock	English name	Western Mono	–
Eastern or Wind River		Northern Paiute	Spanish name
Shoshone	–		★see p. 202

The Indians who lived in the vast area of present Nevada, Utah, western parts of Colorado and Wyoming, southern Idaho and adjacent parts of Oregon and California, shared a similar lifestyle and formed the Great Basin cultural area. The area is bounded by the Snake River in the north almost to the Colorado River in the south. Although the area is not all desert, sparse vegetation, sagebrush and meager grassland characterize the region. In the east, woodland and brush are found in canyons and valleys, and occasional marshy patches dot the area. Animal resources are sparse: squirrels, rabbits and fish were the principal meat, with occasional antelope, deer and bison. Even gophers and grasshoppers were eaten. The Indian also depended upon piñon (pine) nut and acorn harvests, from which mush, flour and cakes could be made, augmented by wild plants, seeds, berries and roots. The Indians of the Great Basin were dominated by their daily food quest in a very largely inhospitable and exceedingly demanding climate that regularly produced both extremes of heat and cold.

The area became known to the Spanish in the late 18th century, and to Americans after the explorations of Jedediah Smith (c. 1824-31) and John Fremont. Settlement by whites was limited, however, as most immigrant parties crossed the Great Basin en route to California. Consequently the Indians did not suffer removal as elsewhere, but gradually modified to the predominant culture, though at the lowest economic level.

Reservations and "colonies" for homeless groups were often established in the late 19th and early 20th centuries. The Indians of the area belong mainly to the old Shoshonean linguistic family, specifically to the Numic division, now designated as the Uto-Aztecan family except for the Washoe, whose distant relatives are the Hokans of California.

Right: Goshute (or Gosiute) couple. Photograph: C. R. Savage, Salt Lake City.

WESTERN SHOSHONE This is a collective name for a group of scattered bands extending from the arid Death Valley of California through the highlands of central Nevada into northwestern Utah, including the upper reaches of the Owyhee and Humboldt rivers. They belonged to the Numic division of the Shoshonean or Uto-Aztecan linguistic family. Usually designated in small subgroups such as the "Pine Nut Eaters," two groups are sometimes given separate status: the *Panamint* on the west side of Death Valley, Inyo County, California, and the *Gosiute* of western Utah. The so-called "Weber Ute" of the Great Salt Lake are also classified as Western Shoshone. Shoshone culture was the Great Basin type, with plant procurement a subsistence mainstay, together with harvesting nuts and seeds and some hunting.

White settlers, miners and ranchers followed the earlier explorations of Jedediah Smith and John Fremont. In 1863, a treaty with the United States provided the establishment of reservations, notably Duck Valley on the Nevada-Idaho border. But not until after 1900 did any substantial numbers of Western Shoshone occupy the "colonies" scattered in their old territory. They slipped unnoticed into the white man's mode of living, but at a low economic level. Their population may have been more than 3,000 before white contact. In 1937, 1,201 were reported, including Gosiute and Panamint. In 1980, 2,923 were reported. The largest groups as of 2001 were at the Duck Valley Reservation, Nevada (1,888); Skull Valley (118) and Goshute (433), both in Utah; Wells (202), Elko (1,594), South Fork, Carlin, Ely (418), Ruby Valley, Winnemucca, Battle Mountain (575), Fallon (1,002), Yomba (205) and Duckwater (337) reservations, all in Nevada (6,772). A few others are scattered in other reservations in Nevada and Utah. The last of the Panamint seem to have merged with the two branches of Mono in Inyo County, California. The Shoshone produced fine coiled basketry. Hand games and Fandangos are still frequently held.

NORTHERN SHOSHONE The Northern Shoshone were bands of Numic-speaking Shoshoneans living in the Snake River Valley, Idaho, and as far north as the Salmon River. They are linguistically very close to the Western Shoshone. Their environment was marginally Plateau, where it merges into the Great Basin. Their subsistence depended on salmon and other fish, collecting wild roots (yampa, bitterroot and camas) and hunting, which included the bison. Subgroups included the "*Salmon-Eaters*" and "*Mountain Sheep-Eaters*," around the Salmon and Lehmi rivers, "*Yamp-Eaters*" of the Camas Prairie, and some bands of mixed Shoshone and Paiute on the Oregon border. Historical evidence suggests they they may have been the "Snakes" who once occupied the northern Plains before the Blackfoot expelled them west of the Rockies. Nevertheless, they developed a veneer of Plains culture, and inthe 19th century they also visited the Montana plains to hunt bison. They participated in the development of trade relations with the Crow, and adopted the Plains-derived Grass Dance and the Sun Dance, to which they added Christian features. Their form of Sun Dance is now shared with the Crow and Wind River Shoshone.

The Shoshone had obtained horses by the late 17th century, which established them as travelers and traders. Whites established trading posts within Bannock and Shoshone territory as early as 1810, and they participated in the annual summer rendezvous with the whites on the Green River,

Wyoming. Independent life ended in the 1860s, when the Lehmi and Fort Hall reservations were founded, although Lehmi was closed in 1907 and the population was transferred to Fort Hall. There are no reliable population figures for pre-white contact Shoshone. An estimate for 1860 gives 3,000 Shoshone and Bannock; in 1937, 3,650 "Northern Shoshone" were reported, in 1983 about 3,900 were enrolled at Fort Hall Reservation, Idaho. In 2001, the Fort Hall Shoshone and Bannock numbered 4,536. The Shoshone and Bannock still hold annual festivals, powwows and rodeos, including their Sun Dance at Fort Hall, despite overwhelming modern influences.

BANNOCK The Bannock were a detached branch of the Northern Paiute on the Snake River, Idaho, who became associated with the Northern Shoshone and, in time, intermixed. In culture they were similar to the Shoshone, and moved with them to the Fort Hall Reservation, Idaho, in 1869. In 1878 an Indian uprising in the area involved some Bannock. In 1910 they numbered 413; in 1937, 342; and in 1945, 337. They are now part of the "Shoshone-Bannock Tribe" of Fort Hall, Idaho.

EASTERN or **WIND RIVER SHOSHONE** The ancestors of the Eastern and Northern Shoshone are probably the "Snakes" or "Gens du Serpent" reported by the earliest white traders. Ranging as far north as the Saskatchewan River,

GREAT BASIN AND PLATEAU TRIBES, 20th CENTURY

This sketch map necessarily duplicates part of the Northwest Coast area.

Key to abbreviations:

C.Sal	=	Coastal Salish
Chil	=	Chilcotin
Cx	=	Comox
He	=	Heiltsuk
Hl	=	Halkomelem
Ka	=	Karok
Kut	=	Kutenai
Kw	=	Kwakiutl
Li	=	Lillooet
N.Pa	=	Northern Paiute
No	=	Nootka
Ok	=	Okanagan
S.Pa	=	Southern Paiute
Se	=	Seechelt
Sh	=	Shuswap
So	=	Songish
Sq	=	Squamish
St	=	Stalo (Cowichan)
Th	=	Thompson
Yu	=	Yurok
N. Shos	=	Northern Shoshone
W. Shos	=	Western Shoshone

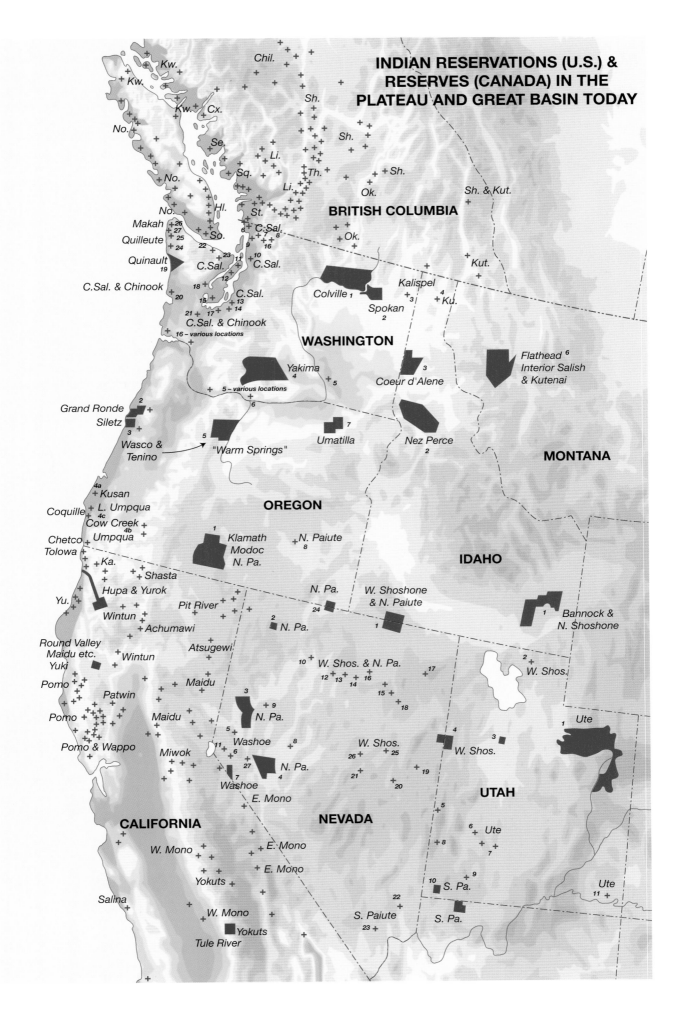

INDIAN RESERVATIONS (U.S.) &
RESERVES (CANADA) IN THE
PLATEAU AND GREAT BASIN TODAY

Kw.
Kw.
Chil.
No.
Kw.
Cx.
Sh.
Se.
Sh.
Li.
No.
Sq.
Th.
Sh.
Li.
Ok.
BRITISH COLUMBIA
Sh. & Kut.
Hl.
St.
Ok.
Makah
26
C.Sal.
27
Kut.
Quilleute
25
So.
6
7
8
24
22
23
11
16
9
Quinault
19
C.Sal.
12
10
C.Sal.
Kalispel
Ku.
18
Colville 1
3
4
C.Sal. & Chinook
13
17
20
21
14
Spokan
C.Sal.
2
C.Sal. & Chinook
16 – various locations
WASHINGTON
Yakima
4
5
3
Coeur d'Alene
Flathead 6
Interior Salish
& Kutenai
5 – various locations
6
Grand Ronde
2
7
Siletz
3
Umatilla
Nez Perce
Wasco &
5
2
Tenino
"Warm Springs"
MONTANA

OREGON
4a
Kusan
L. Umpqua
Coquille
4c
Cow Creek
Chetco
4b
Umpqua
IDAHO
Tolowa
Klamath
1
N. Paiute
Ka.
Modoc
8
Shasta
N. Pa.
Hupa & Yurok
N. Pa.
W. Shoshone
& N. Paiute
1
Bahnock &
N. Shoshone
Yu.
Pit River
24
Wintun
2
Achumawi
N. Pa.
1
Round Valley
Atsugewi
2
W. Shos.
Maidu etc.
Wintun
10
W. Shos. & N. Pa.
Yuki
12 13
16
17
Pomo
Maidu
14
1
Ute
Patwin
3
15
18
Pomo
Maidu
9
4
3
Pomo & Wappo
N. Pa.
26
W. Shos.
25
Miwok
5
8
W. Shos.
6
21
19
11
27
N. Pa.
20
Washoe
4
5
E. Mono
UTAH
CALIFORNIA
NEVADA
6
Ute
W. Mono
E. Mono
8
7
Yokuts
E. Mono
10
9
S. Pa.
Salina
22
Ute
W. Mono
S. Paiute
11
Yokuts
23
S. Pa.
Tule River

Above: Bannock mother and child, 1910, showing typical Basin/Plateau cradleboard. Although the mother is largely obscured, note her dress decorated with cowrie shells, and beaded and brass-studded belt.

Right: Ute, standing, c. 1895. The Northern Ute probably adopted the Plateau style cradle (see p. 178) late in the 19th century, adding an eye shade of willow basketry. There was some concern over possible harmful effects of confining a baby in a cradle for extended periods, but Indians claimed beneficial effects for developing erect posture, apart from ensuring safety during the day. At night a mother would transfer her baby into a soft buckskin bag, or place it in beddings.

Below right: Shoshone, kneeling, c. 1890. Pine board covered with buckskin, the area above the bag is elaborately beaded in geometric or floralistic designs — these probably were quite a late development. The laced bag front had minor variations for gender, allowing for the insertion of a soft pad between the legs of infant girls, or with holes in the central flap tied over the lacing which allowed infant boys to urinate outside the buckskin pouch.

they were subsequently expelled from the north by the Blackfoot and ultimately restricted to the Plateau and Basin — except for the Eastern Shoshone, who have occupied western Wyoming periodically since about A.D. 1500, particularly in the watersheds of the Snake, Wind and Sweetwater rivers. The Comanche split from them in the 18th century. Culturally they were intermediate between Plains, Basin and Plateau, gathering berries and roots, but also skilled buffalo hunters whose women were noted as skilled and rapid butchers. Their material culture resembled that of true Plains people, their tipis, ritual objects, horse equipment and ceremonialism, including the Sun Dance, reflecting their association with the Plains culture.

They remained generally on good terms with whites during the 19th century, through the efforts of Chief Washakie, and the Wind River Reservation was established, which they were forced to share with former enemies, the Northern Arapaho. Religion involved the acquisition of supernatural powers, and tribal welfare derived from the Sun Dance. A modified Sun Dance with some Christian elements is shared with the Northern Shoshone, Ute and Crow and has been an important element in reservation life. Peyote and pan-Indianism including annual powwows are also part of continuing Indian life. The total Shoshone population may have been 10,000 or more in 1700. The recent Wind River Shoshone population reports 1,672 (1950), 2,400 (1981) and 3,400 (2001). In 2010, 8,299 "Shoshone" were recorded.

UTE A Shoshonean (Uto-Aztecan) people of central western Colorado and central-eastern Utah, occupying the drainages and tributaries of the Green and Colorado rivers. They are closely connected to the Southern Paiute in language. Their historic culture reflected both Great Basin and Plains traits; eastern and southern bands foraged for bison, but they also collected berries, roots, nuts and seeds. They were divided into a number of subtribes: *Capote* and *Moache*, in southern Colorado; *Wiminuche*, north of the San Juan River; *Uncompahgre*, in the area of the Gunnison River, Colorado; *White River Ute*, including the *Yampa* on the White, Yampa and Green rivers; *Uintah*, in northeastern Utah; *Pahvant*, around Sevier Lake; *Timpanogots*, around Utah Lake, *Sanpits*, around Manti in San Pete Valley; and *Moanunts* or *Fish Ute*, on the upper course of the Sevier River, Utah.

Left and Right: Buckskin Charlie, aka Buck Sopiah was a Southern Ute chief who became a celebrity after saving women and children during the so-called "Meeker Outbreak" on the White River Reservation, Colorado in 1879. He is shown (left) wearing the Benjamin Harrison 1890 Peace Medal. Buckskin Charlie rode with Geronimo in President Theodore Roosevelt's Inaugural Parade in 1905.

Below Left: Ute couple and child, c. 1900. The cradle is the type used by tribes of the Great Basin and Plateau using a curved skin-covered board and skin bag with an eye shade. Neidhardt Collection.

Left: Ute man, Quin-cha-ke-cha, c. 1900 by B.A. Burbank, Ignacio, Colorado. He wears an eagle-feather headdress with trailer, and a fully beaded vest, and beadwork wrapped hair braids and arm bands.

Below: Chief Ouray (Arrow) and Chipeta in 1880 — the year he tried to negotiate a treaty for the Uncompahgre Ute, who wanted to stay in Colorado. In fact, in 1881 the government forced the Uncompahgre and the White River Ute to reservations in present-day Utah.

Above: Ute camp, photographed in 1913 at Garden of the Gods, during the Shan Kive—Colorado Springs Carnival—in El Paso County, Colorado. Buckskin Charlie, with a mustache, stands near center holding a sheath of white feathers. His wife, To-wee, stands in the front and holds the hands of two girls. She wears a feather bonnet. Chipeta, widow of Chief Ouray, sits in the front row near Buckskin Charlie, between two girls in dresses decorated with elk's teeth.

Left: Shoshone tepees.

Below: A group of Paiutes in Nevada, photographed by T.H. O'Sullivan in 1875.

Left: Ute woman, c. 1885. Late 19th-century costume showed the characteristics of the neighboring Shoshone, Jicarilla and Plains tribes. Eastern Ute bands adopted lazy stitch beadwork superficially resembling Cheyenne and Arapaho work. Note facial and hair paint. The ankle-length dress is made of two skins (probably deer), tails up, with a fully beaded yoke (sometimes separate) forming the upper part. The silver concho belt is a traded Navajo item.

Right: Ute man, c. 1885. Men's shirts had long triangular neck flaps, probably an exaggeration of the original hide shape (or representing knife sheaths worn from the neck by Eastern tribes). Shirts and leggings were usually heavily fringed, with beaded strips in stepped and large triangular elements.

Above: Ute warrior wearing shirt and leggings, typically decorated with broad beadwork strips and many bells. Note the characteristic beaded strips of the leggings around his ankles and the broad bandolier strap over his left shoulder.

In later years they were concentrated in four bands — Uncompahgre, White River, Uintah and Wiminuche. They were known to the Spanish from the 1600s, and they raided the Hopi, Paiute and Plains tribes. However, from 1750 onward Apache, Arapaho and Cheyenne exploited Ute hunting grounds in their eastern mountain valleys.

In 1868 a reservation was established in Colorado for Uncompahgre, Moache, Capote, Wiminuche, Yampa and Uintah Utes. In 1880, following the "Meeker Massacre," two reservations were formed in Utah to become the Uintah and Ouray reservations, and the Uncompahgre and White River Ute moved there in 1880 and 1882. The Wiminuche, Moache and Capote were subsequently located on the Southern Ute Agency along the San Juan River Valley of southern Colorado and adjacent New Mexico — now the Ute Mountain and Southern Ute reservations. The Utes probably numbered 4,500 before the reservation period, but were reduced to 3,391 by 1885. In 1920 there were 449 Uintah, 257 White River,

Above Left: The Pauvan or Pahvant were a Ute group in Utah, 1860s.

Above Right: Southern Paiute man, c. 1872. At this date John W. Powell (later of the Smithsonian Institution), and photographer John K. Hillers recorded Southern Paiute men and women wearing buckskin clothing, which resembled that of the Ute and Shoshone. It has not been confirmed as Paiute make, but the buckskin cap and sandals are more typically Paiute.

Right: Southern Paiute baskets, c. 1880. Woman with twined conical burden basket on chest tumpline, and close-coiled tray used to sift mesquite meal.

421 Uncompahgre (Uintah-Ouray Reservation), and 456 on the Ute Mountain and Southern Ute reservations. In 1980 there were 2,000 Northern Ute, exclusive of 1,000 mixed-bloods and 900 Southern Utes. In 1990 there were 1,044 Southern Ute, 1,264 Mountain Ute and 2,650 Northern Ute (Uintah-Ouray). In 2001 there were 1,375 Southern Ute, 2,012 Ute Mountain Ute and 3,174 Northern Ute (Uintah-Ouray). The Bear Dance and Sun Dance are still prominent festivals.

SOUTHERN PAIUTE The term to cover linguistic related Numic-Shoshonean bands of southern Utah Nevada, including parts of Arizona above the Colorado R and extended to include the *Chemehuevi* of San Bernard County, California, as Southern Paiute. They can be divi for convenience into a number of other subgroups — *Mo Shivwits, Pahranagat, Kaibab*, etc. — but there was no tr organization. They were divided into bands l together for mutual aid and subsiste collaboration. The Southern Paiute were typical Great Basin people; the quest food kept them on the move in searc small game, grasshoppers, gophers, fish, n seeds and wild vegetables. Their shelters v simple brush constructions, but they made basketry. They seem to have been known to the Spa from the 16th century, but felt the impact of Euro-Ameri contact in the 19th century, when they were gradually set on reservations.

Their present descendants have been connected with following reservations in 2001: Moapa River on the Mu River, southern Nevada (295); Shivwits, Kanosh, Kooshar Indian Peaks, Kanarraville, all terminated and restored as "Paiute Indian Tribe of Utah" (799); Kaibab in north Arizona (252); Las Vegas Colony, Nevada (55); Chemehu Reservation, Arizona (708); and Colorado River Reservat Arizona (mixed with others), for a total of approxima 2,109. Only about half live on their reservations, and there longstanding off-reservation communities.

EASTERN MONO or **OWENS VALLEY PAIUTE** This is a branch of the Uto-Aztecan family closely connected linguistically with the Northern Paiute, who occupied the valley of the Owens River parallel with the southern Sierra Nevada Mountains, Inyo County, California. They are sometimes locally called Paiute, and their descendants are at Benton (with the Paiute), Bishop, Big Pine, Independence, Lone Pine (with Panamint) and throughout Inyo County. They number perhaps about 2,000, including the Western Mono (Monache) and Panamint, the three being almost indistinguishable. In 1991 there were 2,266 Owens Valley Paiute with about 950 on reservations.

WESTERN MONO or **MONACHE** These are a group of six small Shoshonean (Numic) Uto-Aztecan speaking tribes related to the Eastern Mono and Northern Paiute. Strictly, they were more Californian in culture than Great Basin, since they lived beyond the Sierra Nevada Mountains on the upper reaches of the San Joaquin (North Fork), Kings and Kaweah rivers, California, where they shared a general culture with the neighboring Yokuts. Their subsistence depended primarily on hunting, fishing and gathering. They probably numbered 4,000 before 1770, reduced to 1,500 by 1910, but both figures combine Western and Eastern Mono. They are now part of the mixed tribal group of the Tule River Reservation and have largely merged with Yokuts at Tule River and in Tulare, Fresno and Madera counties. About 1,100 descendants were still reported separately in 2001 at North Fork (510), Big Sandy (331) and Cold Springs (271).

NORTHERN PAIUTE This is a term that covers Numic-speaking bands of the Uto-Aztecan family and the branch that relates them with the two branches of the Mono of California. They lived in a vast area, from Mono Lake, California, in the south, through the Walker and Humboldt river drainages, Nevada, north, beyond Malheur Lake, Oregon, and west into northeast California. Their habitat was scrub desert and freshwater marshes. They were seminomadic gatherers with some hunting and fishing. Their dwellings varied throughout the region, including dome-shaped structures covered with brush mats. They seem to have obtained horses in the mid-1700s, which initiated a series of changes introduced by whites, and there were hostile encounters during the mid-1800s.

They were ultimately placed on reservations, with total populations given as 3,038 in 1910; 4,420 Northern and Southern Paiute in 1930; 2,590 in 1950; and 5,123 in 1980. In 1992 the Northern Paiute alone numbered 4,750 on their reservations. By 2001, that number was much closer to 7,500. The largest reservation populations are at Pyramid Lake, Walker River and Fort McDermitt in Nevada, but others are at Benton and Bridgewater, Mono County, California; Burns, Warm Springs and Klamath Lake, Oregon (mixed with other tribes); Duck Valley, Nevada (with Shoshone); Summit Lake, Winnemucca, Lovelock, Fallon, Reno-Sparks and Yerington, Nevada; Fort Bidwell, XL Ranch, Cederville, Alturas in Modoc County, California (mixed with Pit River); and Susanville, Lassen County, California (mixed with Maidu). In 2010, 13,728 North and South Paiute were reported together.

Above: Paiute, c. 1880. The cradle has a flat, wedge-shaped foundation of willow rods with an inverted U-shaped top, covered with buckskin or canvas. A basketry awning protects and shelters the child's head.

Above Left: Western Mono bark house, c. 1860. The Monache used conical thatched, oval earth, and conical bark houses, sharing the first two forms with the Yokut, Eastern Mono and Northern Paiute. The third was primarily Monache, as suitable bark was only available at higher elevations on the western slopes of the Sierra Nevada. The bark house was unexcavated, with a center post (or two with a ridge beam) supporting a few large poles covered with cedar bark slabs.

Below Left: Northern Paiute mat lodge, c. 1860. This group, with the Eastern Mono, Washo, Monache and some Yokuts, used three main dwelling types. Those used in winter (and in large versions as mens' assembly or sweat lodges) had a frame of beams on four forked posts (or a ridge beam on two) over a circular floor excavated to about two feet (60 cm). Outer rafters leaning in against the beams gave an oval shape. A thatched grass-and-earth covering left a central smoke hole. A conical type (illustrated) lacked the beams and posts, with outer rafters set inside the excavated depression being brought together, tied to a hoop at the apex, and covered with rush mats, again with a smoke hole. Thirdly, many types of temporary, unexcavated traveling dwellings used cone-, dome-, or gable-shaped bough frames usually covered with brush.

CALIFORNIA

Language family and tribe	Meaning/origin of tribal name, where known	Language family and tribe	Meaning/origin of tribal name, where known
Ritwan:		**Penutian:**	
Yurok	"downstream"	Wintun	"people"
Wiyot	district name	Maidu	"person"
		Miwok	"people"
Hokan:		Costanoan	Spanish — "coast people"
Karok	"upstream"	Yokuts	"person"
Chimariko	"person"		
Shasta	–	**Uto-Aztecan:**	
Achomawi	"river"	Tubatulabal	"pine nut eaters"
Atsugewi	–	Tataviam	–
Yana	"person"	Gabrielino	Spanish — mission name
Pomo	"village"	Luiseño-Juaneño	Spanish — mission names
Esselen	–	Kitanemuk	"house"
Salina	Spanish name	Serrano	Spanish — "mountaineers"
Chumash	–	Cahuilla	Spanish name
Washo	"person"	Cupeño	place name
		Kawaiisu	"people"
Yukian:			
Yuki	"stranger"		
Wappo	Spanish — "brave" or "fine"		

The typical cultural characteristics of the Californian area were those found among the tribes who lived along the two main valley systems, those of the Sacramento River and San Joaquin Valley, including the eastern slopes of the Sierra Nevada north to Mount Shasta, and west to beyond Clear Lake. In terms of linguistic diversity, the area was one of the most complex in North America. The principal families were Maidu, Wintun, Miwok, Costano and Yokuts, now loosely linked to form the Penutian stock; and the Karok, Shasta, Achomawi, Yana, Pomo and others linked into the Hokan superfamily.

Food was mainly gathered, including vegetables, acorns, buckeye nuts, seeds and a variety of grasses. They dug roots and bulbs from the ground and collected kelp and seaweed from the ocean, these often being dried or boiled for soups. They hunted rabbits, quail and gophers, collected grasshoppers and caterpillars, and fished for salmon. Houses were constructed either of coarse grass or bunches of bulrushes in dome shapes, or of redwood plank slabs in conical shapes among the coastal people. Clothing was sparse except for elaborate ceremonial dress using abalone shells, many types of feathers, skirts of vegetable fiber or deerskin and some tattooing. Many tribes were excellent basketmakers, and the Pomos made reed canoes at Clear Lake.

Religion centered on the worship of ancestral ghosts through the Kuksu cult, a society of spirit or ancestral impersonation involving colorful costume and the initiation of youths by ghosts. Old men with special knowledge often acted as directors, including instruction on morals, hero gods and healing. A variant religion among the Patwin was known as the Hesi. These old religions were in part associated with nativistic movements in the second half of the 19th century, incorporating neo-Christian elements. These include the Ghost Dance of 1870, the Earth Lodge Cult and the Bole-Maru "Dream Dance." Ceremonies usually took place in large, circular, semi-underground wooden buildings.

The remaining regions of California reflected other cultural areas. The Mono and Paiute of the mountainous eastern parts of the state belong to the Basin. The tribes in the northwestern section are sometimes classed with the Northwest Coast culture because of their wealth accumulation traits, prestige displays and World Renewal rituals. Wooden house types, dugout canoes, salmon weirs and twined basketry reflect, if only weakly, the northern culture.

For convenience the Californian Athabascans are treated under the Northwest Coast section with their linguistic relatives to the north see pages 264–266.

The Yurok and the Karok had villages along the Lower

Klamath River; the Hupa lived along the Trinity River, a tributary of the Lower Klamath. All three tribes were culturally very similar, intermarried and shared religious beliefs. Principal ceremonies were the White Deerskin Dance and the Jump Dance, publicly performed as World Renewal ceremonies. The White Deerskin Dance was usually held in the fall and aimed to spiritually recreate their universe and pray for plentiful game and fish. The ceremony could last up to sixteen days. Men held skins of albino or light-colored deer on poles aloft and held large obsidian blades. The dance gave the participants the opportunity to display their wealth in public — usually tusk-shaped dentalia shells imported from Vancouver Island and used for currency.

In the Jump Dance, the dancers wore elaborate costumes including woodpecker scalp headdresses, dentalia shell necklaces and deerskin skirts and carried cylinder-shaped dance baskets all made for public display. Staging of these great ceremonial dances was an inherited privilege and sponsors constituted the highest level of society. There has been recent renewal interest and performances of these World Renewal ceremonies throughout the Lower Klamath basin.

Southern California had cultural affinities with the Southwestern culture, with coiled basketry, large polychrome cave paintings by the Chumash, ocean-going dugout and plank canoes, and communal dwellings, usually round. Toloache or Jimsonweed Religion was found in most of the area, with visions obtained from taking the toloache drink. Boys and girls had initiation ceremonials with religious and moral instructions from chiefs.

The reduction of the native population was nowhere greater than in California. In precontact times the population was in excess of 300,000, but by 1910 perhaps no more than 25,000 remained, many of these of mixed white and Indian ancestry. The greatest sufferers were the coastal and central valley tribes — the former as a result of Spanish colonization, the valley tribes because of the influx of gold-seekers after 1848, when villages were broken up and Indian peoples driven from their land (and often killed) in quasi-military clearance operations by whites. Only where substantial reservations were established did the native population survive in sizable groups. Many were left landless, engulfed by white communities, as a result of which most small groups that remained merged into white culture with resultant intermarriage. Government intervention in the late 19th and early 20th centuries saw the foundation of small reservations around the state called "Rancherias," which managed to give a few hundred people a landbase, but more lived scattered among the white population. Descendants survive there, and today California has the largest Indian population of any state, but these are mostly immigrants from other areas of the United States.

RITWAN

This term includes two tribes of northern California, usually considered distinct: the Wiyot and Yurok. These are separate

Left: Yurok Jump Dancer, c. 1896. Frequently performed by visiting Hupas, at Weitchpec in Northwest California, where Northwest Coast cultural traits were influential, this dance was held semi-annually, alternately with the White Deerskin Dance. Headdresses were of redheaded woodpecker feathers, worn with buckskin aprons and dentalium shell currency necklaces. The latter were also carried in cylinder-shaped dance baskets.

families, perhaps divided 2,000 years ago. An even more remote association with the Algonkian family has been speculatively suggested.

YUROK The Yurok was an important and relatively large and linguistically distinct tribe of northern California, living principally along the lower parts of the Klamath River between its junction with the Trinity River and the coast at Requa. They were part of a culture linking them to the Hupa, Karok, Tolowa and Wiyot. Shamans, sometimes women, obtained power directly from spirits. World renewal ceremonies were important, including the White Deerskin Dance. Houses included the redwood plank type and ceremonial plank sweathouses. Facial tattooing, deerskin clothes, basketry, shell money, slaves and wealth display traits that paralleled the Hupa and, more remotely, the northern tribes.

They probably numbered in excess of 3,000 in precontact times, but were disrupted after 1827 when the first Hudson's Bay traders invaded their country. Violent clashes with gold-seeking whites occurred after 1850. However, the Yuroks retained some portions of their old land, and there are still sizable groups at Weitchpec, Johnson's (Hoopa-extension), Requa (Coast Indian Community) and Trinidad.

As of 2001, they still numbered more than 4,700 (959 on reservations in 1968), though largely of mixed white-Indian ancestry. There have been recent attempts to revitalize their language and dances. The Shaker Church has its southern limit among the Yurok.

WIYOT A small family of Indians on the coast of northwest California between the Mad and Eel river estuaries were the Wiyot. They are now thought to be related to the Yurok, with whom they shared much of their culture, but were more orientated to a coastal environment. There was heavy emphasis on salmon fishing and on the hunting of deer, elk and sea mammals. Their ceremonialism was the same as that of the Yurok and Hupa. They suffered a series of atrocities at the hands of whites, which reduced their population from 1,000 in 1850 to 131 in 1968, on two small reservations, Blue Lake and Table Bluff (Loleta) in Humboldt County, California. In 2001, 408 Wiyot were enrolled on those reservations, although most lived in Eureka.

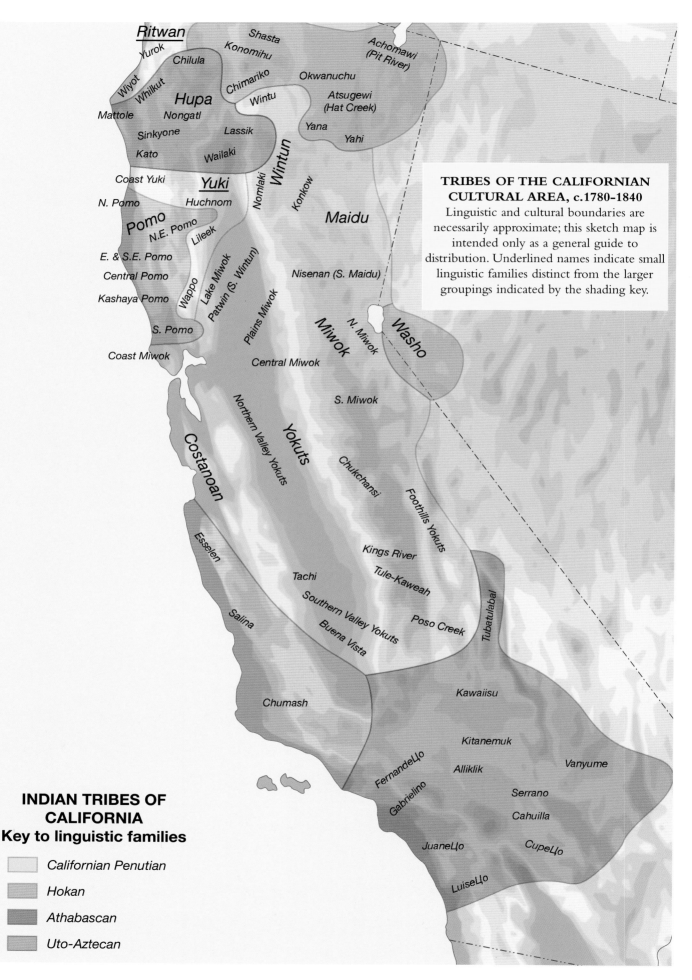

Ritwan

Yurok

Shasta
Konomihu

Achomawi
(Pit River)

Chilula

Wiyot

Whilkut

Chimariko

Okwanuchu

Hupa

Mattole

Nongatl

Wintu

Atsugewi
(Hat Creek)

Sinkyone

Lassik

Yana

Kato

Wailaki

Yahi

Coast Yuki

Yuki

Wintun

N. Pomo

Huchnom

Nomlaki

Konkow

Pomo

N.E. Pomo

Maidu

Lileek

E. & S.E. Pomo

Nisenan (S. Maidu)

Central Pomo

Wappo

Lake Miwok

Patwin (S. Wintun)

Kashaya Pomo

Plains Miwok

S. Pomo

Miwok

N. Miwok

Washo

Coast Miwok

Central Miwok

S. Miwok

Costanoan

Northern Valley Yokuts

Yokuts

Chukchansi

Foothills Yokuts

Esselen

Kings River

Tachi

Tule-Kaweah

Salina

Southern Valley Yokuts

Poso Creek

Tubatulabal

Buena Vista

Chumash

Kawaiisu

Kitanemuk

FernandeƚƚO

Alliklik

Vanyume

Gabrielino

Serrano

Cahuilla

JuaneƚƚO

CupeƚƚO

LuiseƚƚO

**TRIBES OF THE CALIFORNIAN
CULTURAL AREA, c.1780–1840**
Linguistic and cultural boundaries are
necessarily approximate; this sketch map is
intended only as a general guide to
distribution. Underlined names indicate small
linguistic families distinct from the larger
groupings indicated by the shading key.

**INDIAN TRIBES OF
CALIFORNIA**
Key to linguistic families

Californian Penutian

Hokan

Athabascan

Uto-Aztecan

Above Left: A Yurok woman wearing a dentalium shell skirt.

Above: Yurok author, Lucy Thompson — Che-na-wah-Weitch-ah-wah — (1856–1932) known for her 1916 collection of her people's stories, To the American Indian: Reminiscences of a Yurok Woman.

Below: Yurok canoe on Trinity River. Redwoods were the Yuroks' tree of choice for canoes, preferably ones that had been felled naturally. The interior of the tree became the bottom of the canoe, and the outside the top because the interior wood has a much tighter grain and is, therefore, heavier. This Edward S. Curtis image was published in the supplement to volume 13 of The North American Indian. Library of Congress Prints and Photographs Division.

Above Left: Shasta man, c. 1890, Northern California, probably in Siskiyon County. Fort Jones Museum.

Above Right: Shasta Indian woman, c. 1890. The beaded "flat bag" tucked into her belt may be the work of one of the Oregon tribes with whom the Shasta were culturally linked. Fort Jones Museum.

Far Left: A Curtis photograph: "Achomawi basket-maker."

Left: Beaded "flat bag" constructed of heavy sacking and trade cloth and beaded in Plateau style floral beading. From an Oregon Coastal collection, but similar to the one held by the Shasta lady; c. 1900. M. G. Johnson Collection.

Left: Karok, pre-1870. In northwest California, family or village feuds usually resulted in little more than retaliatory activity, and might be settled by payment, with the parties acting out a formalized war dance. Male dress was limited to a buckskin breechclout or apron, with moccasins for long journeys. Warriors might add wooden slat armor. The principal weapon was the yew bow, with sinew backing and string. Syringa wood arrows were carried in shell-decorated fur quivers.

Below: Karok, c. 1895. Scoop-shaped cradle made of wooden rods sewn together, with a top hanging hoop. The infant was bound in with leather thongs, its feet hanging free. The mother wears the traditional basketry cap of northern California.

with world renewal, manifested in annual ceremonials similar to those of the Yurok and Hupa.

Despite being overrun by whites, the Karok have continued to occupy parts of their old territory, though there has been much intermarriage with whites over the years. They were reported to number 994 in 1905, 775 in 1910, 755 in 1930 and 3,781 in 1972, the last figure including many with little Karok ancestry. In 1992 approximately 1,900 Karok were officially enrolled, and in 2001 there were slightly more than 3,300. However, the World Renewal rites and Brush Dances still survive as an outward expression of continuing Karok identity.

CHIMARIKO This was a small tribe and linguistic family that occupied a short stretch of perhaps 20 miles of the Trinity River, from its junction with the South Fork to Big Bar, in northern California. They seem to have been destroyed by white miners in the 1850s and 1870s. In 1849 they may have numbered 250. Only nine survivors were found in 1903. While a few people of mixed descent may survive, essentially they are extinct.

SHASTA The Shasta are a group of tribes of northern California, culturally partly Californian and partly Plateau. The principal tribe of the group was the Shasta proper, who occupied the upper course of the Klamath River, Shasta River and Scott River as far south as Callahan and as far north as Jacksonville, Oregon. There were three small southern groups: the *New River Shasta*, of the New and Salmon rivers; *Konomihu*, also of Salmon River; and the *Okwanuchu*, of the upper tributaries of the Sacramento River, below Mount Shasta — in total most of present Siskiyou County. The Shasta hunted deer and rabbits, fished salmon and collected acorns and wild greens. House types were of low-roofed plank construction with side entrance, gathered into villages of five or six dwellings with a sweat house. They also used and obtained in trade buckskin, obsidian, dentalia, haliotis, nuts and woodpecker scalps. The Gold Rush and Rogue River Indian Wars shattered Shasta life and culture, and their population dropped from 3,000 to 100 or so by the 20th century. A few were incorporated on the Grand Ronde and Siletz reservations in Oregon and Round Valley, California, and a few descendants are still reported from Siskiyou County, including about 50 people at Quartz Valley, Alturas, and Ruffeys rancherias; but the aboriginal culture is now practically non-existent. The Shasta formed a language family sometimes extended to include the Achomawi and Atsugewi.

HOKAN

In 1913 two ethnologists, Dixon and Kroeber, suggested that a number of small Californian families should be considered as one super-family or stock, and suggested the term *Hokan*, derived from the word "two" in some northern California languages, to cover the grouping. The group included the Karok, Chimariko, Shasta, Achomawi, Yana, Pomo, Washo, Esselen, Yuman, Salinan, Seri and Chumash. More recently a link has been suggested with the Lower Rio Grande Coahuiltecans, but the proposal of a link with the Siouan and other families has been abandoned.

KAROK A distinct tribe occupying the middle course of the Klamath River in northern California, starting just north of the Yurok village at Weitchpec and extending northward to the vicinity of Seiad close to the Oregon border is the Karok. Their population, more than 2,700 in the early 19th century, was densest in three clusters: around Camp Creek, at Orleans; Salmon River, at Somes Bar; and Clear Creek, below Happy Creek. Except for a few groups of Hudson's Bay Company traders, the Karok knew little of the white man until 1850–57, when a swarm of miners invaded their lands. The Karok displayed a similar culture to that of the Yurok, subsisting on fish, hunting and the gathering of wild plant foods. Houses were made from split-log planks, canoes from hollowed-out redwood. They dressed in deerskin, heavily decorated with nuts and shells for ceremonial use. Their principal rites were those concerned

ACHOMAWI or **ACHUMAWI** This is one of two tribes who formed the so-called Achomawi or Palaihnihan branch of the Hokan family of languages. They are popularly known as *Pit River* Indians, as they occupied the Pit River basin from Big Bend to Goose Lake in north-central California. They fished for salmon, bass, catfish and trout, caught wildfowl, and collected vegetable foods and insects. They suffered somewhat less than most native Californians from white invasion, and still numbered about 750 in 1963 — perhaps half their aboriginal population. The present Pit River people live in Shasta, Lassen, Modoc and Siskiyon counties, at XL Ranch Indian Reservation near Alturas, Likely, Big Bend, Fall River and Hot Springs. Elements are also found on two reservations in Oregon. In 1990 more than 1,000 Pit River people were reported being the Achomawi and Atsugewi together, a number that doubled by 2001. Like many neighboring tribes they excelled in basketry.

ATSUGEWI This, the second tribe of the Palaihnihan branch of the Hokan linguistic stock lived south of their distant relatives the Achomawi, in two groups. The *Atsuge* lived in the lava-strewn valleys north of Mount Lassen, and the *Apwaruge* in the barren plain to the east around Eagle Lake, Lassen County, California. In common with most northern Californian tribes, fish and acorns were staple foods. Although they were out of the salmon area, they were allowed to take a ration from Pit River by the Achomawi. They recognized countless native spirits, but had few major ceremonials other than puberty rites. Hudson's Bay trappers visited their region in the 1830s, followed in the 1850s by Gold Rush prospectors and settlers, who completely disrupted native life, with murder on both sides leading to virtual annihilation of the tribe. A few Atsugewi survived at Hat Creek, Dixie Valley and Burney, and perhaps 100 or so descendants are still counted but usually as "Pit River."

YANA This was a small linguistic family on the northeastern tributaries of the Sacramento River, between Shasta Lake and Tehama, in three geographical groups plus the *Yahi*, a southern branch. They numbered perhaps 1,500 before a series of bloody massacres by whites (c. 1850–70) reduced their numbers to a mere 100 or so by 1910. Ishi, the last of the Yahi, lived under the protection of the University of California for five years until his death in 1916, during which time he provided a wealth of information on their culture.

POMO Pomo were an important group of seven related tribes speaking differing dialects and forming a family of the Hokan stock centered around Clear Lake and along the coast from Fort Bragg in the north, to beyond Stewarts Point in the south in present Mendocino, Lake and Sonoma counties, California. They were a populous people, numbering more than 14,000 in the 18th century. In the mild climate the Pomos used little clothing; in cool weather mantles, capes, robes and skirts of vegetable fiber or skins were worn. They hunted rabbits, deer, sea mammals and bears with bows and arrows, heavy spears, nets and snares. They had ample supplies of fish.

The Pomos lived in conical huts of redwood bark or planks, and around Clear Lake houses were built of bunches of

Above: The most celebrated Yahi was Ishi — "the last Yahi" or "the last wild Indian in North America." He was captured in 1911 near Oroville, California, and later befriended by University of California anthropologists Alfred Kroeber and Thomas Waterman, who housed him at the University Anthropology Museum in San Francisco until his death in 1916. During those five years, he provided a wealth of information about California's precontact native culture. In the 1990s, Steven Shackley, a research archaeologist at the Hearst Museum of Anthropology, theorized that Ishi was actually Wintun. This is his death mask.

bulrush (tule) or coarse-textured grass. They are also known for their excellent-quality baskets, which survive in abundance in museums. The social core of Pomo life was the family and the small village. Their beliefs were part of a religious complex called the Kuksu, which stressed curing rituals and elaborate forms of dancing and fire-eating to ensure the absence of danger from ghosts.

The Russians established a settlement at Fort Ross in 1811, but the Mexicans made the first serious inroads into Pomo life and culture in the 1820s and 1830s, taking lands and introducing cholera and smallpox. Land loss continued under the Americans, and they ultimately became almost landless in their own country, working on the ranches and farms of white settlers. They did, however, reestablish small settlements in the late

Right: Pomo balsas. Canoe-shaped raft of tied reed (tule) used by fishermen on Clear Lake and its swampy environs, but unsuitable for ocean mammal hunting.

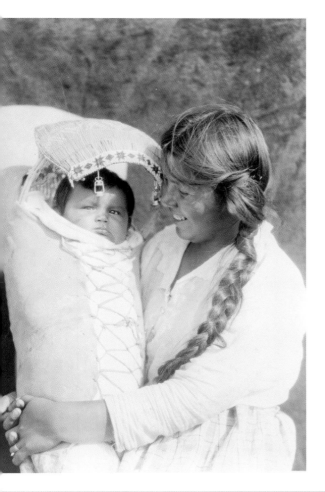

Above Left: Edward S. Curtis image of Achomawi mother and child published in the supplement to volume 13 of The North American Indian. *Library of Congress Prints and Photographs Division.*

Left and Above Right: Two images of the Pomo: gathering seeds on the upper Lake Pomo and cooking acorns in front of a tule hut. These Edward S. Curtis images were published in volume 14 of The North American Indian. *Library of Congress Prints and Photographs Division.*

Below: Otterskin (probably) quiver decorated with abalone shells, strips of white deerskin and woodpecker (probably) feathers. 19th century, Canbridge. N.W. California.

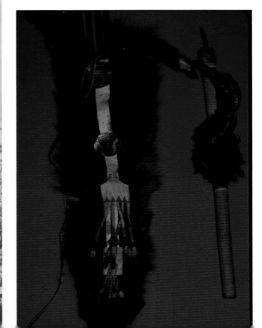

Above: Petroglyphs at the Chumash Painted Cave State Historic Park, high above Santa Barbara, CA. There are numerous drawings in the cave said to depict the Chumash cosmology and other subjects.

Right: Cemetery at Santa Barbara Mission, Santa Barbara, California. Several thousand Chumash, as well as many early settlers and Franciscan padres, are buried in the cemetery.

Below: Depicting a Chumash coastal village with a fishing boat, this mural in the city of Lompoc was the first of the Mural-In-A-Day creations, painted in 1992 by volunteer artists under the direction of master artist Robert Thomas. The Chumash were carpenters in the pre-Spanish-contact era, and their boats, caulked with local tar or pitch, could reach the Channel Islands.

All three images on this page: The Jon B. Lovelace Collection of California Photographs in Carol M. Highsmith's America Project, Library of Congress, Prints and Photographs Division.

Left: Pomo man in Bole-Maru dress, c. 1925. The Kuksu religious system of secret mens' societies performed rituals to restore perpetual harmony with ghosts, ensure fertility and first fruits, and aid curing. Performers impersonated spirits, human and animal ghosts and divinities, wearing elaborate costumes, including large feathered headdresses ("Big Heads"). The Kuksu fell into disuse from the 1870s, but revitalization cults later infiltrated north-central California, and one echoed the remnant of Kuksu, though limited to human ghosts evoked by male or female dreamer priests (Maru). The Bole-Maru cult also included end-of-the-world and ultimately Christian concepts. It still has a few Pomo reservation adherents.

19th century, and a number of small reservations or rancherias have been maintained since.

A revitalization movement, the Bole Maru Cult, still survives, alongside their own branch of the Methodist Church. About 500 live on tribal lands at Manchester, Stewarts Point, Cloverdale, Lytton, Lower Lake, Upper Lake, Sulpher Bank, Hopland, Scotts Valley, Potter Valley, Sherwood, Mark West, Big Valley and other locations, including a few at the larger Round Valley Reservation, where a multitribal group of about 500 have long been established. The recent population was 2,626 in 1970, 4,766 people in 1990 and more than 5,000 identified as Pomo in 2001.

ESSELEN This was a tribe and small linguistic family which, based on only fragmentary evidence, has been placed in the so-called Hokan stock. They occupied the coast of mid-California between the Carmel River and Point Lopez below Monterey. First known to the Spanish in 1602, the native Esselen culture vanished with the destruction of the mission San Carlos Borromeo de Monterey in 1770, when they were absorbed by other missions and ultimately lost separate identity. They may have numbered about 500 in the 18th century, but were almost extinct by 1820, although a few people in Monterey County, California, still claim their ancestory.

SALINA or **SALINAN** A group of tribes formerly occupying the coast of central-south California and the rugged mountainous interior, from the upper Salinas River near the Soledad Mission almost to San Luis Obispo are known as the Salina. There seem to have been two dialects that formed the Salinan language family, now tentatively included in the Hokan stock. They probably numbered more than 3,000 before 1771, when the Spanish began missions among them, but by the early 19th century, rapid acculturation had taken place, and their population was no more than 700 by 1831. This decrease continued after the secularization of the missions in 1834, and only three families were known by the early 20th century, near Jolon, descendants from the old San Antonio Mission. In 1928, 36 people were reported, and a few descendants are still living, but as a distinct group they have gone. The 1970 census, however, gave 360 Salina and Chumash.

CHUMASH The Chumash were a group of linguistically related people, now included in the Hokan stock, of present Santa Barbara County, California, along the coast from San Luis Obispo to Ventura. They numbered perhaps in excess of 15,000 before the Spanish missions were established in 1772. There seem to have been eight subdivisions of this docile and friendly people. The Spanish were determined to make industrious farmers of the Chumash, but subjected them to a life of toil, mistreatment and destruction of native culture. Following the secularization of the missions in 1834, the Chumash merged or intermarried with Mexicans, or were decimated by disease. One small reservation at Santa Ynez was set aside in 1855, and about 50 people of mixed descent were all that were left as a separate Chumash group in 1972, and 159 were reported in 2001. Other descendants likely survive among the Mexican Americans of the area.

WASHO This is a linguistic family and tribe who inhabited the large valleys of the Feather, Yuba and American rivers of east-central California, and the areas north and south of Lake Tahoe, as far as Honey Lake south to Walker River, split equally between present Nevada and California. They have been suggested to belong distantly to the Hokan stock. Culturally they were intermediate between the true Californian and Great Basin cultural types. The many rivers and lakes supplied them with fish; they gathered camas roots, pine nuts and acorns, which were cooked into gruel; they also hunted deer and mountain sheep. House types were conical, of bark slabs leaning against a frame of poles, or temporary dome-shaped brush structures. They were very fine basketmakers of both coiled and twined weaves, and several makers became nationally well known.

Religion and ceremony were usually associated with the spirits of their subsistence and in connection with communal harvesting. Permanent contact with whites began in about 1840, and the alienation of their resources and lands followed. They numbered about 1,500 in 1850; 725 in 1970; 695 in 1980; and about 1,272 in 2001. Their main modern groups are at Woodfords, Alpine County, California, and Dresslerville, Carson and Reno-Sparks in Nevada. About 100 people still speak the Washo language.

YUKI The Yuki were a group of small tribes in the upper Eel River valley in the Coast Range Mountains of northwest California, and also along the coast between Rockport and

Fort Bragg. The Yuki proper lived in the Round Valley area; the *Huchnom* on the south Eel River; and the *Coast Yuki*, perhaps a branch of the Huchnom, in the coastal area described. These tribes, together with the detached southern branch, the Wappo and Lile'ek, form a language family with no known relatives.

Culturally, the Yuki led a hunting and gathering existence of typical California pattern and of a fairly simple type, but they had an elaborate ceremonial life. Their existence as an independent people came to an end in 1856 when white farmer-settlers destroyed the ecology of their valley homes; many starved or were massacred by settlers. The establishment of the Round Valley Reservation in 1858 probably saved the handful of survivors. Some estimates put the number of these three groups combined at more than 8,000. In 1970 there were 350 Yuki, Wailaki, Nomlaki and Pomo on the Round Valley Reservation or in nearby communities, of whom perhaps 30 to 35 people were true Yuki by descent. That number increased to 3,494 by 2001, a total of Round Valley and other local Indian groups, but again, few were true Yuki, and there were only a few native speakers left. The last of the Huchnom, known as Redwood Indians, were also merged with others at Round Valley, where a handful of descendants may still be traced. The Coast Yuki seem to be extinct.

WAPPO The Wappo were related to the Yuki, Huchnom and Coast Yuki, and form the Yukian linguistic family. They lived in the valleys of the Napa and Russian rivers in Napa and adjacent Sonoma counties, California, with a detached branch on the south shore of Clear Lake, sometimes known as the *Lile'ek*. The culture was a simple central Californian type with subsistence use of plant foods, river life and small game. They excelled in basket making in common with their northern neighbors, the Pomo. They were within range of the Spanish settlements and missions, and a number were Hispanicized before American settlers moved in. The census of 1910 reported 73 Wappo; and 12 Wappo were reported from the Alexander Valley Rancheria in 1951. Perhaps 50 descendants remained by 1970.

PENUTIAN

This is a language stock of central California, composed from five families previously considered distinct: Maidu, Wintun, Costanoan, Miwok and Yokuts. The name Penutian is a composite of the stems of the numerical word "two" in Maidu, Wintun and Yokuts and "uti" in Costano and Miwok. The stock also has been extended to the Coos, Yakonan and Siuslaw of Oregon, and even to the Chinook and Tsimshian, but the unity is not considered proved by all authorities.

WINTUN The territory of the Wintun consisted substantially of the west side of the Sacramento River valley from the river to the crest of the coastal mountain range, and they consisted of three distinct dialectic divisions. The *Northern* or *Wintu* division occupied upper sections of the Trinity River and Sacramento River, north of Cottonwood Creek to the edge of Shasta County. They were the largest division of the family. The central division, the Wintun proper or *Nomlaki*, occupied the Sacramento valley from Cottonwood Creek south to Grindstone in Glenn County. They numbered some 2,000 at the time of first contact with whites. Finally, the *Patwin* or Southern Wintun lived from just beyond Colusa to San Pablo Bay in Colusa and Yolo Counties. All these divisions were further subdivided into groups who lived either in the hills, or

Above: Wintu pit house. The peoples of the upper Sacramento River area spent part of the year in substantial circular earth-covered family lodges, about 12 to a village. Larger versions served as mens' assembly and "Big Head" dance houses. They had one or more center posts, a ring of posts, and supported beams and rafters covered with brush, bark and earth. Access was by ladder via the roof smoke hole.

plains or river valleys. They were typically Californian in culture; their bark houses were gathered in villages around semisubterranean earth lodges for ceremonials of the Kuksu type, including the Bole-Maru cultists who performed the "Big Head Dance" (see p. 197) — male and female spirit impersonators who wore impressive feather headdresses.

The Patwin suffered first from their exposure to the Mexicans in the late 18th century and, subsequently, from American contacts from the 1840s onward. The whole family numbered perhaps 15,000 in the mid-18th century. About 1,000 Wintun were reported during the 20th century, but are mixed racially and tribally. The Northern Wintun are mostly in Tehama, Trinity and Shasta counties, including Redding (Clear Creek); the Nomlaki are at Paskenta and Grindstone Creek in Glenn County. A few Patwin are at the Colusa Rancheria in Colusa County and Rumsey in Yolo County, and others among the mixed Round Valley population. In the returns of the 1990 census 2,244 Wintu were identified, and 332 Nomlaki, but no Patwin. In 2001, 157 Nomlaki-Wintu were reported at Grindstone, 75 Patwin and Nomlaki at Colusa (3 Parcels); 136 Patwin and Miwok at Cortina; and 44 Patwin at Rumsey.

MAIDU The Maidu are a linguistic family of north-central California, now usually considered a part of the Penutian stock. They are further dialectically subdivided into three tribes: the *Maidu proper*, who occupied the upper reaches of the Feather River south of Eagle Lake around Susanville, Butte Valley and Quincy; the *Konkow*, who lived on the east side of the Sacramento River around Chico; and the *Nisenan* or Southern Maidu, who occupied the Yuba, Bear and American river valleys around Marysville, Nevada City, Placerville and Auburn. Physiographically they can be divided into groups who formed cultural cleavages into valley, foothills and mountain Maidu. They were participants in the important Kuksu religious cult of the Sacramento Valley, with its wide variety of rituals, impersonations of spirits, distinctive costumes and use of large semisubterranean dance houses. They used bark or brush

Right: Konkow-Maidu earth lodge, c. 1870. Semisubterranean, earth-covered multifamily dwelling or mens' assembly house, usually constructed in spring for winter use. It was circular, 20 to 40 feet (6 to 12 m) in diameter, and excavated to a depth of about 4 feet (1.2 m).

Above: Nisenan, c. 1870. Southern Maidu boy wearing "flicker feather" headdress across the forehead, large abalone shell gorget and bandolier covered with abalone pendants and beads. Abalone objects were considered great wealth among the Maidu tribes.

lean-to house structures and had an elaborate system of shell money exchange between mourners and their friends. They also burned property at funeral rites, including some fine baskets made especially to be consumed in this way, all in honor of the dead. Clothing was scant. They often went naked or wore breechcloths of buckskin or aprons.

The Spanish contact was limited to the Nisenan, but American and Hudson's Bay trappers appeared in the 1820s, and the Gold Rush after 1848 saw the disastrous invasion of their territory by whites. Settlers' livestock upset the ecological balance; Indians killed livestock, and natives were killed in retribution. From a population of 9,000 in 1846, only about 1,100 were reported to survive in 1910 — mostly Maidu in Plumas County, Konkow in Butte County, and Nisenan in Yuba, Placer and El Dorado counties.

Top: Miwok Indian boys, c. 1960, wearing traditional ceremonial dress, including headbands of flicker feathers, in front of a roundhouse in Tuolumne County, California. These boys were part of a cultural group reviving Californian Indian traditions.

Above: Miwok shelter made from strips of wood and bark.

In 1970, 2,546 Maidu and Miwok were returned, largely of mixed descent. A small number have lived on small reservations and rancherias in these counties, at Susanville, Taylorsville (Maidu), Chico, Mooretown, Enterprise, Berry Creek, Strawberry (Konkow), Nevada City, Colfax, Auburn and Shingle Springs (Nisenan). Despite the economic disadvantages affecting most modern Californian native descendants, there is a heartening renewed interest in their own cultural and traditional values, including the continuation of the Maidu Bear Dance each spring at Janesville. In 1990 the Maidu had about 2,500 descendants, and 3,000 in 2001.

MIWOK This is a large group of Indians forming a linguistic family in central California, comprising the main body of the family, the *Eastern Miwok*, in five subdivisions, and two small detached groups, the *Coast Miwok* and *Lake Miwok*. The Coast Miwok were a number of small tribulets in Marin County between Bodega Bay and San Pablo

Bay who came under the influence of the Spanish missions, particularly at San Francisco. They numbered about 2,000 in aboriginal times, but have largely disappeared or were absorbed by Spanish colonists. Only a handful of mixed-blood survived to the 20th century. The Lake Miwok held a couple of small streams flowing into Clear Lake, and perhaps numbered 500 in precontact times; in 1905, 41 were reported, and a few still remain at Middletown mixed with Pomo people.

The main body of the family, the Eastern or Valley Miwok, comprised the Bay Miwok between Walnut and Stockton; the Plains Miwok, from Rio Vista to Sacramento; the Northern Miwok, centering on the Mokelumne River in Calaveras and Amador Counties; the Central Sierra Miwok, between Knights Ferry and Murphy's in Stanislaus and Tuolumne counties; and the Southern Sierra Miwok, on the western edge of the Sierra Nevada and Yosemite National Park. War was usually confined among themselves. Males were captured and killed in the dance house. The Bay and Plains Miwok disappeared through the combined effects of the Spanish missions and epidemic diseases, but the interior Miwok and Yokuts blocked Mexican settlement. Following California's annexation by the United States and the Gold Rush, remnants eked out a meager existence on the edges of Sierran towns.

In the early 20th century, small reservations or rancherias were established, and some of their descendants still live on these. The Miwok population was given as 670 in 1910, and 763 in 1930. Perhaps 1,700 people, some of mixed descent, continue in their old locations today. In 1770 the whole group numbered in excess of 15,000. The few on reservations are found at Shingle Springs, Wilton, Jackson, Sheep Ranch, in El Dorado, Amador, Calaveras, Tuolumne and Mariposa counties; a few are also reported at Cortina in Patwin country. The census of 1990 returned 3,381 Miwok, a number that remains about the same, since several tribes are reported together.

Above: Californian headdress. Royal Albert Memorial Museum and Art Gallery, Exeter, Devon, U.K.

COSTANOAN Costanoan is a linguistic term to designate a group of perhaps eight small tribes in 50 villages living south of San Francisco Bay, along the coast of California south to Big Sur and inland for about 60 miles (100 km). They had a population that probably exceeded 7,000 in 1750. Originally, they lived in domed structures covered with thatched tule or wild grass on a frame of poles. They were first contacted by Spanish explorers in the 17th century, and permanent missions were established in the second half of the 18th century. The changes in lifestyle introduced by the Spanish, together with diseases, reduced their population to 2,000 by 1832, and the Costanoans largely merged with other Indians and Mexicans throughout the 19th century. Perhaps 150 descendants still survive, much mixed with other peoples, but calling themselves "Ohlone." The language is extinct, but early texts and words gathered from survivors show it to be a separate family within the Penutian stock, forming with the Miwok language a subgroup called "Utian."

YOKUTS This was an extensive and large group of 40 or 50 minor tribulets who spoke varying dialects forming a family within the Californian Penutian stock. They were the main people of the San Joaquin valley south to Buena Vista Lake, east to the Sierra Nevada foothills and north to the Stockton area. They are divided geographically and culturally into three groups: the *Northern Valley*, *Southern Valley* and *Foothills Yokuts*. The Northern Valley group occupied the San Joaquin River valley from Fresno to the Sacramento River, but their aboriginal culture was quickly modified by the Spanish, then after 1822 by Mexicans, and they have few survivors. The Southern Valley Yokuts are about 14 groups, of which the Tachi are the most prominent, occupying the southern San Joaquin valley below Fresno in present Kings, Tulare and Kern counties around Tulare Lake. The Foothills Yokuts are about 15 minor groups; starting in the north from Oakhurst are the Northern Hill group in Fresno County (Chukchansi); the Kings River group (Choynimni) in eastern Fresno County; Tule-Kaweah group (Mikchamni and Yawdanchi) in Tulare County; Poso Creek group (Palewyami) in Kern County; and the Buena Vista group in Kings and Kern counties — the last is sometimes included with the Southern Valley section of the family.

For most central Californians, wars were usually minor affairs. Food resources were generous enough for villages of 200 or so people. The Yokuts were not a political group, their relationship being linguistic, but all their related groups made excellent basketry. Shamans who derived their powers from spirit animals had much influence, but the Kuksu Cult did not extend as far south as the core of Yokuts territory. The Ghost Dance of the 1870s had some converts. The Yokuts were encountered by the Spaniards in the late 18th century, but the latter's influence was mainly among the northern villages. The Mexican period, 1822–46, saw punitive expeditions into Yokuts country, and final cultural collapse followed American settlement in the 1850s. Yokuts survived in small isolated pockets throughout their old territory, but epidemics and absorption into white communities saw their population drop from about 18,000 in 1770 to 533 in 1910, the apparent low point. In 1970 there were 791 reported, 2,000 in 1990 and about 3,400 in 2001. The reservation and rancheria groups are at Picayune (Chukchansi) and Table Mountain (Chukchansi) in Fresno County; Santa Rosa (Tachi) in Kings County; and Tule River (Kings River and Tule-Kaweah).

CALIFORNIAN TRIBES, 20th CENTURY

Key to abbreviations of mission groups:

Ser	=	Serrano
Ca	=	Cahuilla
Lu	=	Luiseño
Die	=	Diegueño and Kamia (Ipai-Tipai)

Klamath
Modoc
N. Paiute

1c Tolowa
1b Karok
1a 2a 2c Shasta
7d 2b
7a 7g Yurok
Yurok 7c Hupa
7b 7h
Wiyot 7f
7e

N. Paiute

N. Paiute
2

W. Shoshone & N. Paiute
1

3f 3c
3g 3a
Pit River 3b
3e 3d

4a
Atsugewi
4b

10
W. Shos & N. Pa.
12 13 14 16 17
15
18

Yuki, Maidu &
Wailaki etc.
Round Valley
Reservation
8j 9b Wintun
9a
8a-h 13a 12b 12e 10c
Pomo 13a 12a 10a
8k+l 13b 12d Maidu 10b
Patwin 12c
14a-c 3
8c 18b 11 N. Paiute
Pomo Maidu 19a 5 Washo
15a-j 17b 18a 20c 19b 8
16g 17a 20b 20a 11 26
16a-h 6 W. Shos 25
Pomo & Wappo 28 27 21 19
42 Miwok 26b 7 N. Paiute 20
21a 21b Washo 4
Ione Miwok 26a
22 23b 23c
23a 24a 27 E. Mono

CALIFORNIA 43 24b 25b
25c 33b E. Mono
25a
28

35 29a 33a NEVADA
Ohlone 29b W. Mono
36 29c
30a-d E. Mono
Yokuts 33c

31b W. Shoshone
Salina 31a 33e
37 W. Mono 33f S. Paiute
32a 22
Yokuts 23
32b 33d
Tule River

34

Chemehueui
& Mohave
38 Chumash

13

Ser. 39c
39a Ca. 39b 18
Ser. 40a-l
Ca. Ca. For these
Lu. reservations
see Arizona
Lu. Ca.
Die. 41a-u 12
Die. Yuma 11

INDIAN RESERVATIONS IN
CALIFORNIA & NEVADA TODAY

UTO-AZTECAN

A large and widespread linguistic superfamily of Mexico and the United States, formed by joining the old so-called Nahuatl family (Aztec) of central Mexico with their northern related Sonoran language, and hence to the old Shoshonean family of the western United States, is the Uto-Aztecan. The Aztec and their relatives seem to have formed one complete branch; the *Cora, Huichol, Tubar, Mayo, Yaqui, Eudeve, Opata* and *Tarahumara* another; the *Pima-Papago* (formerly "Piman") with the *Tepehuan*, yet another. The old Shoshonean family comprises the *Hopi, Takic* (a group of tribal languages in southern California), *Tataviam, Tubatulabal* and *Numic* (Paiute, Shoshone, Comanche) of California, the Great Basin and the Plains.

TUBATULABAL This is a name for three small tribes in the upper part of the Kern River valley, California: *Bankalachi, Palagewan* and *Pahkanapil* (Tubatulabal proper). They formed linguistically a separate division of the old Shoshonean family now termed Uto-Aztecan. They were first visited by Father Francisco Garcés in 1776. The American invasion after 1850 completely disrupted native life. A massacre by whites in 1863, and epidemics of measles and influenza, saw their population collapse from about 750 in 1850 to about 50 by 1970, with only six native speakers left. Their present descendants are on the Tule River Indian Reservation or in the Kern Valley area of California, and number several hundred of mixed descent.

TATAVIAM or **ALLIKLIK** Tataviam was a language, or a remnant of a tribal language, spoken by Indians at the San Fernando Mission, formerly living to the north on Santa Clara River, California, beyond Piru. By 1916 the language was extinct and the descendants of the Indians who spoke it had merged with other Indians, Hispanic or Anglo people.

GABRIELIÑO The Gabrieliños spoke a language of the Takic section of the Shoshonean family. They occupied an area now covered by the city of Los Angeles in present southern California and adjacent lands and nearby islands. They are so named from the mission of San Gabriel founded in 1771, although Spanish explorers had contacted these people as early as 1520. They shared many of their arts with the Chumash people of the Santa Barbara coast, and had developed a religion with named gods, such as Chingichngish. They also erected temples and used vision-producing narcotics, which spread to neighboring tribes. They were missionized at San Gabriel and San Fernando (Fernandeño) missions. Diminishing in numbers from 5,000 to a few hundred, they became largely Hispanicized and merged with larger dominant local races. Although a few people still claim their ancestry, they are, for all intents and purposes, extinct. Small Indian groups on the islands of Santa Barbara may have been related; the *Nicoleño* are sometimes given separate status.

LUISEÑO This was a Shoshonean (Uto-Aztecan) tribe of the so-called Takic section of the family, closely related to the Gabrieliño, Cupeño and Cahuilla, who together form a dialectic subsection. They lived between San Juan Creek and San Luis Rey River in the coastal region of southern California, in small sedentary villages dependent on gathering plant foods, fishing and hunting. Houses were conical structures covered with reeds, brush or bark. Their first recorded contact with Europeans occurred in 1796, with the founding of the San Diego Mission, at which time they numbered perhaps 4,000 people. They were later missionized at the San Juan Capistrano (Juaneño) and San Luis Rey missions. In 1834 the missions were secularized. Following revolts against Mexicans and Anglo-Americans, the Indians suffered displacement and merged with others into the so-called "Mission Indians." By 1970 about 600 Luiseño descendants were on the La Jolla, Rincon, Pauma, Pechanga, Pala (with others) and Soboba reservations, with others scattered throughout southern California. Attenuated forms of their old religion mixed with Catholicism and colorful fiestas are still a major activity. There are approximately 3,500 Luiseño descendants.

KITANEMUK A small tribe belonging to the Takic division of the Uto-Aztecan family and closely related to the Serrano, the Kitanemuk lived on Tejon and El Paso Creeks in the western valleys of the Tehachapi Mountains in present Kern County, California. In general culture they seem to have differed little from either Tubatulabal or Yokuts. They appear to have merged with other Indians at San Fernando and San Gabriel missions, but a few survived separately until the 20th century around Fort Tejon and on the Tule River Reservation, with perhaps 100 descendants. Their language is now extinct.

SERRANO A group of Takic speakers who lived east of present-day Los Angeles in the San Bernardino Mountains are known as Serrano. A northern group, the *Vanyume* on the Mohave River, are sometimes given separate status. Like their neighbors they were gatherers, hunters and fishers. Although the valley floors were largely desert, the upper-mountain slopes provided streams and a food supply of nuts, acorns, berries and small game. Family dwellings were usually circular willow structures covered with tule thatching. In addition they had large ceremonial houses where chiefs or religious leaders lived.

The Serrano are noted for the manufacture of fine coiled baskets. Contact with the Spanish first occurred in about 1771, and they were collected into missions in about 1820. During the American period they have been grouped with Cahuilla and Cupeño on the San Manuel, Morongo and possibly Twentynine Palms reservations. They probably numbered 1,500 or more before 1770. More than 550 descendants are among the present day multitribe "Mission Indians" of southern California.

Top: A Curtis photograph of a Cahuilla house in the Californian desert. Library of Congress, Prints & Photographs Division LC-USZ62-111286.

Above: A Curtis photograph of a Cahuilla woman harvesting taken in 1905. Library of Congress, Prints & Photographs Division LC-USZ62-96454.

Opposite: Tubatulabal girl, 2012. Approximately 280 people from the Tule River Reservation and near by Lake Isabella claim Tubatulabal descent. They were expert basket makers.

CAHUILLA The Cahuilla were a substantial Takic-speaking tribe closely related to the Cupeño, Serrano and Kitanemuk, who lived in the mountains, canyons, valleys and deserts north of Salton Sea between the Little San Bernardino and Santa Rosa Mountains of southern California. They lived in rectangular and dome-shaped brush-covered shelters in small villages. Food consisted of small game, acorns, piñon (pine) nuts, beans, seeds and wild fruits, with marginal agriculture providing corn and squash. They had a rich ceremonial life — their rituals reaffirming a relationship to all things, the sacred past, present and nature. The Spanish passed through their country in 1774, and subsequently they were integrated into the mission system. Their population may have been as high as 6,000, but they were reduced to 1,000 by the 1880s. By 1970 they numbered more than 1,600, about half

on several reservations in southern California, including Agua Caliente, Augustine, Cabazon, Cahuilla, Los Coyotes, Morongo, Ramona, Santa Rosa, Soboba and Torres Martinez. There has been considerable intermarriage over the years with the Cupeño, Serrano and Luiseño. By 1990, their population had risen to about 2,300, and to about 3,000 by 2001, although many are of tribal mixtures.

CUPEÑO This was a small Takic-speaking tribe of the Shoshonean family, now called Uto-Aztecan, who lived east of Lake Henshaw and west of the Santa Rosa Mountains, California. They are very closely related to the Cahuilla, but also strongly influenced by Luiseño religious complexes. They probably numbered 500 when first encountered by the Spanish. Subsequently they were missionized and reduced to the social status of near serfs during the Mexican and American periods. They probably number fewer than 150 people today, but a few are still found on the Pala, Los Coyotes and Morongo Indian reservations.

KAWAIISU The Kawaiisu were a small Uto-Aztecan tribe belonging to the Numic dialectic group who once lived on the southern foothills of the Sierra Nevada Mountains, around present Havilah, California. They were strictly a hunting and gathering people, similar in culture to their neighbors the Tubatulabal and Southern Yokuts. Except for puberty rites for boys and girls, ceremonials were few, but they had developed shamanism. They were probably contacted by the Spanish, along with other local tribes, in about 1780. Their culture collapsed following the 1850s, when a rush of trappers and farmers invaded their territory. Their original population was about 500, but there are only some 50 to 100 mixed-blood descendants today. A few may survive in their old territory and on Tule River Reservation, but they appear to have disintegrated as a group. The Kawaiisu are often classified as a Basin people.

TEJON TRIBE A present day, federally recognized Indian tribe in the general vicinity of Bakersfield, California in the area of the 19th century Sebastian Reservation, which was sold during the late 19th century. The present enrolled members number about 600 and claim Kitanemuk, Kawaiisu, Chumash and Yokuts ancestry. They live around Wasco, Bakersfield and Lake Isabella in Kern County.

IONE BAND OF MIWOK A federally recognized band of Miwok in Amador County, near Plymouth, California.

OHLONE TRIBE A non-federally recognized people of probable Costanoan ancestry living in a general area south of San Francisco Bay. There are several groups petitioning for federal recognition. They had been absorbed into the Spanish missions by 1806, but their descendants are now organizing politically.

SOUTHWEST

Language family and tribe	Meaning/origin of tribal name, where known
Non-Pueblo Dwellers:	
Yuman:	
Havasupai	"blue water people"
Walapai	"pine tree folk"
Yavapai	"people of the sun"
Mohave	"three mountains" (possibly)
Maricopa	–
Yuma	Spanish form of native term
Baja California Yumans	–
Cocopa	Spanish form of native term
Diegueño	Spanish mission name
Kamia	–
Uto-Aztecan★:	
Pima	"no"
Papago	"bean people"
Mexican Border Tribes:	
Seri	Spanish form of native term
Uto-Aztecan★:	
Yaqui & Mayo	–
Tarahumara	–
Tepehuan	–
Lower Pima	–
Eastern Sonoran tribes	–
Northern Chihuahua and Coahuila tribes	
	–
Coahuiltecan	Mexican place name
Karankawa	–
Tonkawa	"they all stay together"
Athabascan★★:	
Apache	"enemy"
Lipan Apache	"people"
Kiowa Apache	–
Chiricahua Apache	"great mountain"
Mescalero Apache	Spanish — "mescal people"
Jicarilla Apache	Spanish — "little basket"
Western Apache	
Navajo	area name

Language family and tribe	Meaning/origin of tribal name, where known
Pueblo Dwellers:	
Pueblo	Spanish — "village," "town"
Keres	coined term
Cochiti	self-designation, i.e., "person of"
San Felipe	Spanish name
Santa Ana	Spanish name
Santo Domingo	Spanish name
Zia	"person of"
Acoma	"person of"
Laguna	Spanish name
Tanoan:	
Northern Tiwa	
Taos	"in the village"
Picuris	Spanish form of native term
Southern Tiwa	
Sandia	Spanish — "water melon"
Isleta	Spanish name
Tigua	–
Piro	–
Northern Tewa	
Nambe	"earth"
San Ildefonso	Spanish name
San Juan	Spanish name
Santa Clara	Spanish name
Tesuque	"structure at a narrow place"
Pojoaque	"drink water"
Southern Tewa	
Hano	–
Towa	
Jemez	self-designation
Pecos	self-designation
Zuñi	Spanish form of native term
Uto-Aztecan★:	
Hopi	"peaceful ones"

★ see p. 202
★★ see p. 264

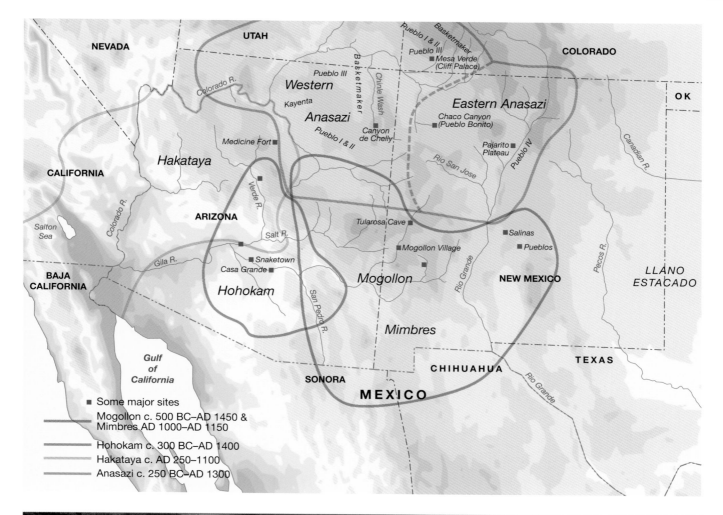

Above: The prehistoric southwest.

Below: The so-called Cliff Palace is a multi-storied masonry archaeological site in southwestern Colorado part of the Mesa Verde complex of the Anasazi Culture. It dates from c. AD 550–AD 1300 from the Developmental and Great Pueblo periods. Abandoned partly due to climate change, the people probably joined or formed some of the later Rio Grande Pueblos. Photograph courtesy Barry Corbett.

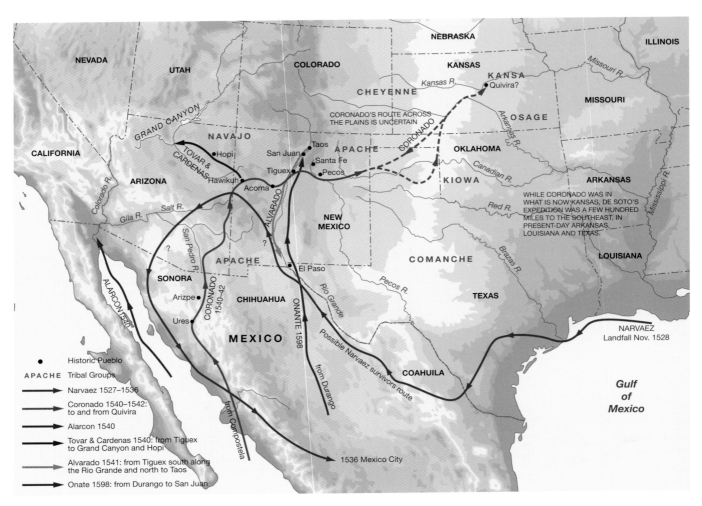

NEBRASKA

ILLINOIS

NEVADA

UTAH

COLORADO

KANSAS

Missouri R.

KANSA

● Quivira?

MISSOURI

CHEYENNE

Kansas R.

CORONADO'S ROUTE ACROSS
THE PLAINS IS UNCERTAIN

OSAGE

Arkansas R.

CALIFORNIA

GRAND CANYON

NAVAJO

● Hopi

Taos

San Juan

Santa Fe

Tiguex

Pecos

APACHE

CORONADO

OKLAHOMA

ARKANSAS

Mississippi R.

TOVAR &
CARDENAS

Hawikuh

Acoma

Colorado R.

ARIZONA

Salt R.

Gila R.

San Pedro R.

?

ALVARADO

NEW
MEXICO

KIOWA

Canadian R.

WHILE CORONADO WAS IN
WHAT IS NOW KANSAS, DE SOTO'S
EXPEDITION WAS A FEW HUNDRED
MILES TO THE SOUTHEAST, IN
PRESENT-DAY ARKANSAS,
LOUISIANA AND TEXAS.

?

APACHE

El Paso

Red R.

COMANCHE

LOUISIANA

ALARCON 1540

SONORA

Arizpe ●

Ures ●

CORONADO 1540-42

CHIHUAHUA

MEXICO

ONATE 1598

Rio Grande

Pecos R.

Brazos R.

TEXAS

NARVAEZ
Landfall Nov. 1528

● Historic Pueblo

APACHE Tribal Groups

Narvaez 1527–1536

Coronado 1540–1542:
to and from Quivira

Alarcon 1540

Tovar & Cardenas 1540: from Tiguex
to Grand Canyon and Hopi

Alvarado 1541: from Tiguex south along
the Rio Grande and north to Taos

Onate 1598: from Durango to San Juan

from Compostela

from Durango

Possible Narvaez survivors route

COAHUILA

1536 Mexico City

Gulf
of
Mexico

*Above: Spanish expeditions
into the American southwest.*

*Left: Montezuma Castle
National Monument in
Arizona has well-preserved
cliff-dwellings built by the
Sinagua, northern cousins of
the Hohokam, around 700
A.D.*

*Right: Havasupai man
standing in front of branch
wickiup photographed by
Henry G. Peabody c. 1901.*
Library of Congress Prints
& Photographs Division
LC–USZ62-112673.

The historic southwestern culture derives basically from two sources: one an ancient agricultural tradition, the other a much later northern hunting tradition, which the Navajo and Apache — relative newcomers to the area — introduced about A.D. 1400. Three major prehistoric cultures contributed to the older cultural traditions of the region; Mogollon and Hohokam, who geographically preceded the Pima and Papago, and Anasazi, which preceded the Pueblo.

The Mogollon culture, c. 500 B.C.–A.D. 1400, acquired agriculture and pottery from Mexico. They were mainly pit-house farmers, and the originators of later developments in the Southwest. This complex originated in Cochise County, Arizona, and spread to neighboring areas. Hohokam culture, c. 300 B.C.– A.D. 1450, developed farther west, centering along the Gila River around present Phoenix, Arizona. It developed irrigation canal systems, fine pottery and stonework. These cultures declined during the early 15th century, and we can assume that the modern Pima and Papago are their descendants.

The Anasazi ("the ancient ones"), is a collective term to cover the development of Puebloan culture from about 250 B.C.–A.D. 1700, and incorporates sites within eastern Arizona, western New Mexico and adjacent Colorado. The earliest phases are termed "Basketmaker," 250 B.C.– A.D. 700, and "Modified Basketmaker," A.D. 400–700. These were followed by three Pueblo periods: the "Development Period"; the "Great Pueblo Period," characterized by large towns with fine masonry apartments, and their abandonment about A. D. 1276 when drought forced the people south to Hopi, Zuni and to the Rio Grande; and finally the "Regressive Pueblo Period," A.D. 1300–1700, which climaxed with Spanish occupation. Their most famous sites are Mesa Verde, Chaco Canyon, Pueblo Bonito and Kayenta.

The Pueblos possessed elaborate, formal ceremonials, based upon a tradition of sacred myths. Most dances are dramatized prayers with participants dressed to impersonate divine spirits, moving in unison exactly rehearsed. Some impersonate Kachinas or animal spirits, who act as intermediaries between man and god. Through such rituals the Pueblo people prayed for rain, crops, sunlight and fertility. All this has survived a Spanish conquest, a revolution, reconquest and vigorous attempts to Christianize them.

Although many Pueblo villages postdate initial Spanish contact, most seem to have been located close to earlier sites after resubmitting to Spain and accepting a veneer of Catholicism. From the Spaniards they adopted domesticated animals, horses, wheat, fruit trees, sheep and cattle. The use of adobe bricks from molds to rebuild larger rooms in the Pueblo structures was also of Hispanic origin. From the early 1700s until the American annexation of the Southwest in 1848, the Pueblos and Spanish (or Mexicans, after the 1820s) stood back-to-back, fighting off the Athabascans, who first appeared in the 15th century. Although warfare between the Navajo and Apache and the Pueblo and Spanish often reached alarming proportions, the former still adopted weaving, pottery, masked dances and even marginal agriculture from the Pueblos. The Athabascans retained their roving, hunting and raiding northern ways, however. Hardy, skilled in combat, incredibly observant and gifted at concealment, they were without equals as warriors.

Of all Native American cultures there is no doubt that those of the Southwest are the best preserved, despite the merging of Anglo-American material culture with their own. They still have a timeless quality, with a strong attachment for the still well-supported old religion and ceremonials, from which whites are often excluded. The Navajo are still struggling with dual culturism, but the Apache, despite very harsh treatment during early reservation days, have become successful stockmen, and retain a strong identity as a separate people. Southwestern Indian culture includes the Piman, Yuman, Pueblo, some northern Mexican tribes and some Texas border tribes, plus the southern Athabascans.

YUMAN

Yuman is a language family named after the Yuma tribe, located near the middle and lower Colorado River in Arizona, California and adjacent Mexico in a distinctly desert habitat. The Yumans had a relatively simple culture, and were first exposed to Europeans in 1540, when the Spanish explorer Alarcón visited Cocopa country. Some groups were agricultural, representing the northwestern frontier on the continent for the native practice of maize farming. They made basketry and pottery. Linguistic studies have suggested a tentative connection to the Esselen of coastal California and hence to the Hokan stock; but their nearest linguistic relatives were the Cochimi, an extinct group of languages of Baja California, Mexico. The Yumans are located at the junction of three cultural areas, California, Southwest and Baja California, Mexico. The Upland or Arizona plateau branch are the Havasupai, Yavapai and Walapai; the River branch are the Mohave, Yuma or Quechan, Maricopa, Halchidhoma and Kavelchadom; the Delta-California branch comprises the Diegueño, Kamia and Cocopa; and, finally, the Baja California branch, the Kiliwa.

The River Yumans lived in low, rectangular, earth-covered houses, while the Maricopa adopted the Piman round houses. They practiced floodwater agriculture, growing corn, beans and cucurbits (pumpkin and squash). The Upland groups ranged over a wide and arid territory, collected a variety of wild plant foods and had considerable dependence on hunting. They lived in dome-shaped grass-covered shelters. Religion and ceremonialism were not elaborate; beliefs were expressed through shamanism, curing by means of spirits and dreams. They were often warlike and aggressive, but usually among themselves. In 2010, 10,262 "Yuman" were counted in the Census.

HAVASUPAI The Havasupai were an Upland Yuman tribe who occupied the plateau area on both sides of the Colorado River, including Cataract Canyon, through which flows the Havasu River, a tributary of the Colorado. During the 19th and 20th centuries they consolidated into one group under pressure for land from whites and Navajo, and were ultimately restricted to a reservation of only 500 acres (200 ha). They were both an agricultural and a hunting and gathering people, living in domed and conical logwood structures covered with thatch or earth. They usually spent their winters on the canyon rim hunting and gathering. Summer was spent in the canyon, farming their tiny gardens. They excelled in basketry. Met by Spanish explorers in the 16th century, they changed little until increased contact with whites as late as the 1930s. In 2001, the Havasupai numbered 674, but not all live on the reservation. Today their income is derived primarily from outside wage work. Their reservation has recently been extended to 160,000 acres (65,000 ha).

WALAPAI or **HUALAPAI** These are a Yuman-speaking tribe of the Upland group, very closely related to the Havasupai and Yavapai. They live in the canyons of the Colorado River in Arizona, particularly on the south side of the river, from the Coconino Plateau almost to the big bend of the Colorado, near present Lake Mead. Their first contact with the Spanish was in 1776. Hostilities between the Walapai and Anglo-Americans in 1866 led to the destruction of their crops and internment on the Colorado River Reservation. They later returned to their old lands and received a reservation there (though representing only a fraction of their old domain), which they continue to occupy. They were originally gatherers and hunters, and more recently stock raisers. The Walapai originally probably never numbered more than 1,000, and today about 1,900, about half of them on their reservation, including two extensions at Big Sandy and Valentine.

YAVAPAI This Yuman tribe occupied north-central Arizona between the Pinal Mountains in the east as far north as present Flagstaff, then west almost to the Colorado River. They have also been termed "Apache-Mohaves" on the incorrect assumption that they are descended from two tribes. While there has been intermarriage with Apaches, they are an independent, separate people. Their habitat was mostly a vast desert with subsistence dependent on plant foods, nuts, acorns, piñon (pine nuts) and berries. They also hunted deer, antelope and rabbits. They led a seminomadic existence and lived in simple brush shelters and caves. They excelled in coiled basketry. The Yavapai were involved in bloody feuds with Anglo prospectors and miners in the 1860s-70s, and some were interned on the San Carlos Apache Reservation. Ultimately, a reservation was established at Fort McDowell, east of present Phoenix, Arizona, and smaller

reservations at Camp Verde, Middle Verde, Clarkdale, and Yavapai, near Prescott. They probably numbered more than 1,500 before 1860. As of 2001, their descendants numbered about 2,171, about half at the Fort McDowell Reservation, the rest divided between the other reservations and adjacent towns.

MOHAVE The northernmost Yuman tribe of the Colorado River group, living where the present states of Nevada, California and Arizona adjoin at the Mohave Valley are the Mojave. Although they were known to the Spanish from the 17th century onward, they were too remote from them to be much affected by their missions.

However, after the 1820s they came increasingly into conflict with Anglo-Americans, including the U.S. military. Their culture was of the simple desert Yuman type, with plant gathering, some fishing and hunting. They were assigned to the Fort Mojave and Colorado River Indian reservations, close to their original homes. Today they number well over 2,000 descendants, perhaps slightly more than half their population in the 17th century. They enjoy increasing prosperity, due to the development of irrigated farmlands and income from land leased to whites.

MARICOPA The Maricopa are a Yuman people of the River group, probably occupying lands along the Colorado River in the distant past, but by the time of the Anglo-American presence in the Southwest, concentrated along the Gila River. The people now called Maricopa appear to be an amalgam of several older Yuman subgroups: the *Halchidhoma*, of the Colorado River; *Kavelchadom*, of the Gila River; and *Kohuana* and *Halyikwamai*, close to the Cocopa south of the international border. Some of the modern Maricopa families claim the descent of these incorporated groups. Their present descendants are with the Pima at Laveen, on the Gila River Reservation and at Lehi, on the Salt River Reservation, Arizona, with a total number of about 1,100 people.

Above: Mohave woman, c. 1880. Women originally wore only skirts of willow bark or, later, of cloth or yarn. Some photographs show a large shawl, however. Hair was worn loose, and complex facial tattoos were common. Elaborate netted beaded collars were characteristic. A simpler necklace is worn here, with a jew's-harp hanging from it.

YUMA or **QUECHAN** The Yuma are one of the principal tribes of the Yuman linguistic family, who lived at the junction of the Gila and Colorado rivers in the extreme southwestern corner of Arizona. They were gatherers of wild foods but also planted maize, pumpkins and beans. Their house types were dome- or rectangular-shaped wooden structures, covered with earth or brush. Clothing was minimal due to the extreme heat — usually aprons front and rear and, in cooler weather, rabbitskin robes. The Spanish explorer Alarcón passed through their territory en route to meet Coronado in 1540. There followed sporadic subjection to Spanish, Mexican and Anglo-American influences. In 1884 the government established the Fort Yuma Indian Reservation, although some lands were

Above: Yellow Feather, a Maricopa woman, supporting a basket on her head and wearing a beaded collar. Photographed by Frank A. Rinehart, 1898.

Below: Maricopa women gatherers, c. 1907. This tribe originally lived in the lower Colorado River region but were driven out by inter-tribal warfare and settled along the Gila River in Southern Arizona. Edward Curtis photograph.

Above: A limited number of basket types are produced in New Mexico: coiled baskets from the Jicarilla and Mescalero Apache and Ute, plaited yucca baskets from Jemez Pueblo and a few open wickerwork bowls from the Rio Grande pueblos. The Indians of Arizona have produced a much greater quantity. The Hopis of the third Mesa produced wicker trays, bowls of rabbit brush or sumac colored with both native and aniline dyes. Second Mesa villages produced woven coiled plaques and baskets of grass sewn with strips of native-dyed yucca. The Papagos made more baskets than any other tribe in the U.S. typically coiled beargrass sewn with yucca, The Pima, Yuman tribes and Paiute all produced baskets. The Western Apache are famous for their fine bowl baskets and burden baskets decorated with long buckskin fringes.

Left: Her-Loo-A-Lah, an Apache woman, posed with willow jugs and woven wash basins.

Below: Naiche hereditary Chief of the Chiricahua Apache, 1898. Photograph by F.A. Rinehart during the Trans-Mississippi International Exposition in Omaha. USS/crossed arrows on cap signifies U.S. Scout status. Second son of Cochise, he raided white settlements with Geronimo, transported to Florida, Alabama and Oklahoma. Later became a U.S. Army scout.

lost during the allotments that followed. Originally numbering perhaps 4,000, they were reduced to 848 by 1937, but numbered about 3,000 by 2001.

BAJA CALIFORNIA YUMANS A number of small groups of Yuman peoples live in Baja California, Mexico. The *Aka'wala* or *Paipai* have descendants around San Miguel, and their language seems to be connected with the Upland groups in Arizona. The *Kiliwa* or *Yukiliwa*, also in northern Baja California, are near Santa Catarina and still have a few speakers. The *Cochimi* and other small and almost extinct tribes of southern Baja California are thought now to be sufficiently divergent in language from Yuman to be considered as a separate family.

COCOPA A Yuman tribe who lived at the delta of the Colorado River where it empties into the Gulf of California, now Baja California Norte, Mexico, but also extending into southwestern Arizona were known as Cocopa. They were a typical River Yuman tribe, but not always on friendly terms with their relatives. They were encountered by the Spanish explorer Alarcón in 1540, and subsequently were slowly modified by Mexican and Anglo-American influences. They probably numbered in excess of 3,000 at one time, but only 1,200 in 1900. Two small reservations have been established near Somerton, Arizona, and had an enrolled population of 500 or so in 1980, and 880 in 2001. A few are still reported from Mexico, around the Hardy River in Baja California and in Sonora, totalling perhaps 300-400.

DIEGUEÑO or **IPAI** These were a people occupying the border country of southern California in present San Diego County, south of the San Luis Rey River — an area of coast, mountain and desert. They form with the neighboring Kamia (Tipai) and Cocopa a branch of the Yuman linguistic family. They lived principally on wild plant foods, supplemented by hunting and fishing. They became part of the so-called "Mission Indians" of southern California, of both Yuman and Takic origin, who were to a large extent under the influence and control of the Spanish missions from 1769 until secularization during the Mexican period. During the American period they have labored on ranches, in mines and in towns, with a land base of 13 small reservations, which they share with the Kamia. The Diegueño and Kamia together numbered about 1,500 in 1980; 2,500 in 1992; and 3,284 in 2001. The two tribes are sometimes now called "Kumeynay."

KAMIA or **TIPAI** These Yuman people — now usually considered with the Diegueño as one tribe, "Tipai-Ipai," lived on both sides of the border between California and Baja California, Mexico, and they were usually considered as part of the "Mission Indians." The reservations with Tipai-Ipai resident descendants are at Barona, Campo, Capitan Grande, Cuyapaipe, Inaja-Cosmit, La Posta, Manzanita, Mesa Grande, Pala (with Takic), San Pasqual, Santa

Ysabel, Sycuan, Viejas and Jamul. They number about 650. Others are in the general San Diego County area; the Mexican Baja California groups seem to have merged with Hispanic or other natives.

PIMA The Pima or Upper Pima and their close relatives, the Papago, speak a distinct language within the Uto-Aztecan linguistic family. They occupied with the Papago an area of the Sonoran Desert, now part of southern Arizona and northern Sonora, Mexico. The Lower Pima, or Pima Bajo (referred to elsewhere), live far to the south and are also related. The extensive range of the Pima and Papago villages was generally south of the Gila River to the Rio Magdalena, Mexico. Before the arrival of the Spanish in the mid-17th century, they were part of a desert food-collecting culture grafted on to the successful farming of domesticated plants, corn, beans and squash. This irrigation agriculture, of central American origin, was developed by the Hohokam people, who were skillful builders of canals, to lead river or arroyo water to their fields. Culturally the Pima and Papago are descendants of the Hohokams, who seem to have disappeared about A.D. 1400. Maintaining a sufficient water supply was the major concern of Piman life, so larger communities were found along the San Pedro and Santa Cruz Rivers, where a subtribe, the *Sobaipuri*, were located.

The Spaniards brought livestock, wheat and improved implements for canal and ditch irrigation. They also converted the Pima-Papago population to nominal Catholicism through the establishment of missions. The Americans came after 1854 and, although they exerted control over their territory, there was little settlement pressure and relations were usually satisfactory. While tribal fortunes reached a low point around 1900, on the whole the Pima have adapted to an Indian-Hispanic-Anglo culture adequately. The Pima descendants live on the Gila River, Salt River and Ak-Chin reservations, and in off-reservation communities in Casa Grande, Chandler, Coolidge and Phoenix. During the American period the Pima were those generally settled closer to the Gila River. In 1945 there were 4,702 on the Gila River Reservation and 1,113 at Salt River Reservation. Today they number 20,479 and 7,371, respectively. In recent years the Pima have preferred to call themselves *O'otam* or O'odham, specifically Akimel O'odham and the Papago Tohono O'odham. The 2010 Census gave 19,921 "Pima" alone.

PAPAGO (TOHONO O'ODHAM) A division of the Upper Pima Indians of the desert region of southern Arizona and northern Sonora, Mexico, are the Papago. The division between Pima and Papago became widely recognized during the American period after 1854, with the transfer of their territory from Mexico to the United States. The Papagos were delimited to the border area with Mexico, while the Pima were adjacent to the Gila River and its tributaries. Food resources were crops of corn, beans and squash, which depended on irrigation, often

Above: Pima earth lodge, c. 1900. Basic construction of the Pima and Papago house was around beams set on four forked posts, forming an 8-foot (2.5 m) square. Willow poles set in the ground around the perimeter were bent inward and lashed to the beams, extending across to form a flattish dome roof, with a thatched exterior. It was then covered with a thick layer of earth. Smoke escaped through the single low doorway, usually facing east.

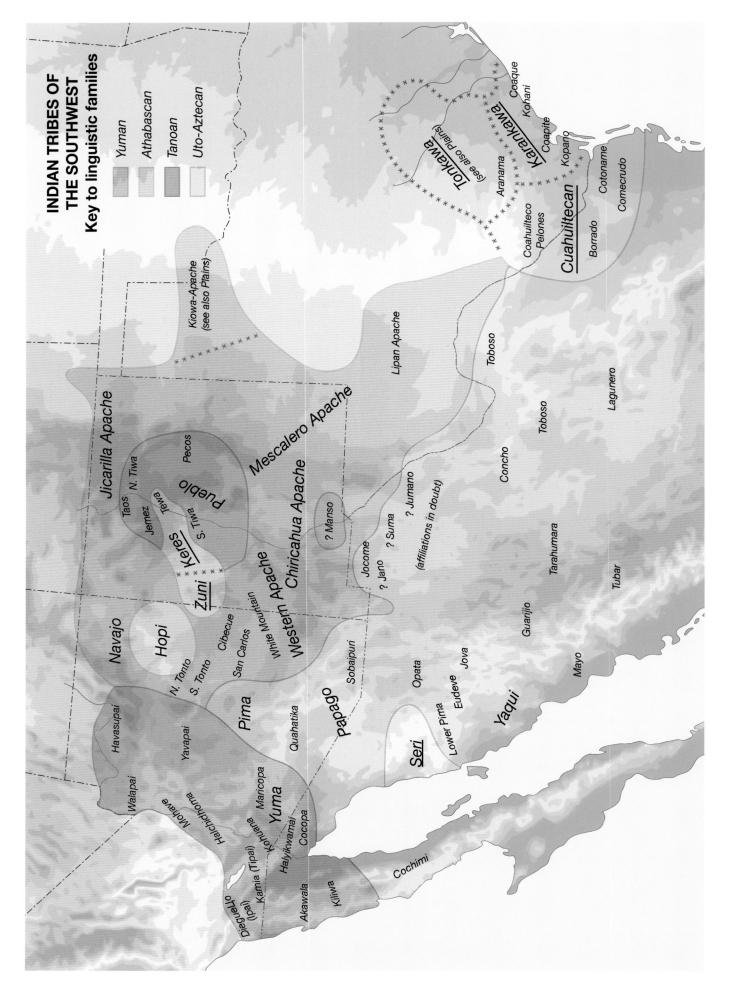

INDIAN TRIBES OF THE SOUTHWEST
Key to linguistic families

Yuman
Athabascan
Tanoan
Uto-Aztecan

Kiowa-Apache
(see also Plains)

Jicarilla Apache

N. Tiwa

Taos
Jemez
Tewa

Pueblo

Pecos

S. Tiwa

Keres

Zuni

Mescalero Apache

Chiricahua Apache

? Manso

Lipan Apache

Toboso

Concho

Toboso

Lagunero

? Suma

? Jumano

(affiliations in doubt)

Jocome

? Jano

Tarahumara

Tubar

Navajo

Hopi

Western Apache

Cibecue

N. Tonto

San Carlos

White Mountain

S. Tonto

Guarijio

Havasupai

Yavapai

Pima

Quahatika

Papago

Sobaipuri

Seri

Opata

Lower Pima

Eudeve

Jova

Guarijio

Mayo

Yaqui

Walapai

Mohave

Halchidhoma

Yuma

Maricopa

Kohuana

Halyikwamai

Cocopa

Diegueño (Ipai)

Kamia (Tipai)

Akawala

Kiliwa

Cochimi

Tonkawa
(see also Plains)

Karankawa

Coaque
Kohani
Coapite
Kopano

Aranama

Coahuilteco
Pelones

Cuahuiltecan

Borrado

Cotoname

Comecrudo

TRIBES OF THE SOUTHWEST
AND MEXICAN BORDER, c. 1600-1860
Linguistic and cultural boundaries are necessarily
approximate; this sketch map is intended only as a
general guide to distribution. Underlined names
indicate small linguistic families distinct from larger
groupings indicated by the shading key.

limited. They also depended on wild foods and hunting. During the Spanish period, 1687-1821, European-derived crops, livestock and improved gardening techniques modified Papago culture. Beginning in 1687 the Papago were Christianized, following the foundation of the San Xavier Mission, which became the center of Papago religious life. Politically, each Papago village was autonomous, usually with two locations — one near an arroyo where flash floods provided water for their fields. Papagos were often raided by the Apaches, but they have usually been on friendly terms with the Americans. They seem to have had a belief in a creator, "Earthmaker," before their acceptance of Christianity.

Their culture has been one of gradual modification to Hispanic and American gardening and cattleowning village communities, subsequently extended to wage-earning permanent settlements off the reservations. Reservations were established at San Xavier, Gila Bend, Ak-Chin and Sells in the late 19th and early 20th centuries. In 2001, the Papago numbered about 26,267, about half on their reservations, the rest at Ajo, Marana, Florence, Tucson, Phoenix and elsewhere. In 2010, 23,313 Tohono O'Odham were reported. They still hold festivals and dances for harvests and rain, using their own musical instruments, and they still excel in coiled basketry. A few hundred Papago live in Sonora, near Caborca.

MEXICAN BORDER TRIBES

Brief reference should be made to the Indians of northern Mexico in the states, east to west, of Tamanlipas, Nuevo Leon, Coahuilla, Chihuahua and Sonora. The whole area was colonized by the Spanish in the 16th and 17th centuries, and the Indians were successfully missionized. By the time of Mexico's independence from Spain, the Indians and Mestizos (mixed-descent population) had formed the lowest stratum of the social system. In the eastern states, tribal independence had collapsed, but in the western states, particularly Sonora, a large Indian population has survived to the present. Over the years, substantial numbers of the Mestizo population have found their way into the United States. Many of the following tribes are part of the general Southwestern culture of the Pima-Papago type, and many are linguistically related to U.S. tribes as members of the Uto-Aztecan language family. The following tribes are worth noting in this regard:

SERI Of Tiburon Islands and adjacent coastal Sonora, Seri are a small tribe with an independent language, perhaps related to the Chontal of Central Mexico and distantly to the Hokan languages of California. About 500 descendants survive.

YAQUI AND MAYO These are two closely related Uto-Aztecan peoples of central coastal Sonora; the Yaqui number 20,000, the Mayo 30,000, the latter in the Rio Mayo region. As of 2001, about 13,231 Yaqui-Mayo are in Arizona in six communities at Tucson, Tempe, Marana, Scottsdale, Eloy and Pascua. They are noted for their masked dancers and deer dancers with deer antler headdresses.

TARAHUMARA These are a largely Hispanicized Uto-Aztecan people of southwestern Chihuahua. They have numerous descendants, mostly Mestizos, but 50,000 are distinctly Indian.

TEPEHUAN These people of the Sierra Madre region of southern Chihuahua are now largely Mestizo. Their language belonged to the Uto-Aztecan family.

LOWER PIMA This is a Piman enclave in Mexico, east of the Yaqui in east-central Sonora. A few survive exclusive of Mestizos.

EASTERN SONORAN TRIBES A number of tribes of this region are now culturally extinct, being largely Mestizo. They are the *Opata, Jova, Eudeve, Guarijio* and *Tubar.* All spoke dialects of the Uto-Aztecan language family.

NORTHERN CHIHUAHUA AND COAHUILA TRIBES The extinct *Concho* and *Toboso* are thought to have been Uto-Aztecan speakers, but the *Jumano, Suma, Manso, Jano* and *Jocome* of the Rio Grande region, whose original territory extended into Texas and New Mexico, may well have been Athabascans. They may have been the bands of Apachean people pushing south who are known to have been in contact and conflict with the early Spanish settlers and missionaries, but there is no proof. We know that all these peoples were in revolt at times during the 17th century, were subsequently assimilated into Hispanic society and are now extinct as separate cultural identities. Possibly the last of them joined the hispanicized Pueblos near El Paso, Ysleta, Senecú and Socorro.

COAHUILTECAN This is a name given by ethnologists to a large number of relatively unknown minor tribes on both sides of the border in southern Texas, north of the Rio Grande to San Antonio, thence to the Gulf coast and as far west as Eagle Pass, then south into Mexico in northern Nuevo Leon, Coahuilla and Tamaulipas. The truth is that we know almost nothing about them except for the mass of minor tribal, group, band or mission names left from the Spanish colonial period. On the evidence of some linguistic data from Spanish mission records, the Coahuiltecan language family was proposed, but it is by no means certain that all the groups of the area were related. Recently the *Comecrudo, Cotoname, Borrado* and *Waikuri* have been given separate status. Speculatively, the Coahuiltecans have been linked to the Karankawan family of the Texas coast, and even more remotely to the Hokan stock, but all is yet unverified.

KARANKAWA A group of small extinct tribes who lived along the Texas coast from present Corpus Christi to Galveston Bay are known as Karankawa. They have been given independent linguistic status on very limited information. Speculative affiliations have been proposed with the Tonkawa and Coahuiltecan but are unverified. From the 16th century onward they were in contact with an assortment of Spanish, French and American castaways, explorers and missionaries. During the American settlement after 1821 the coast tribes subjected the intruders to constant pilfering, and the

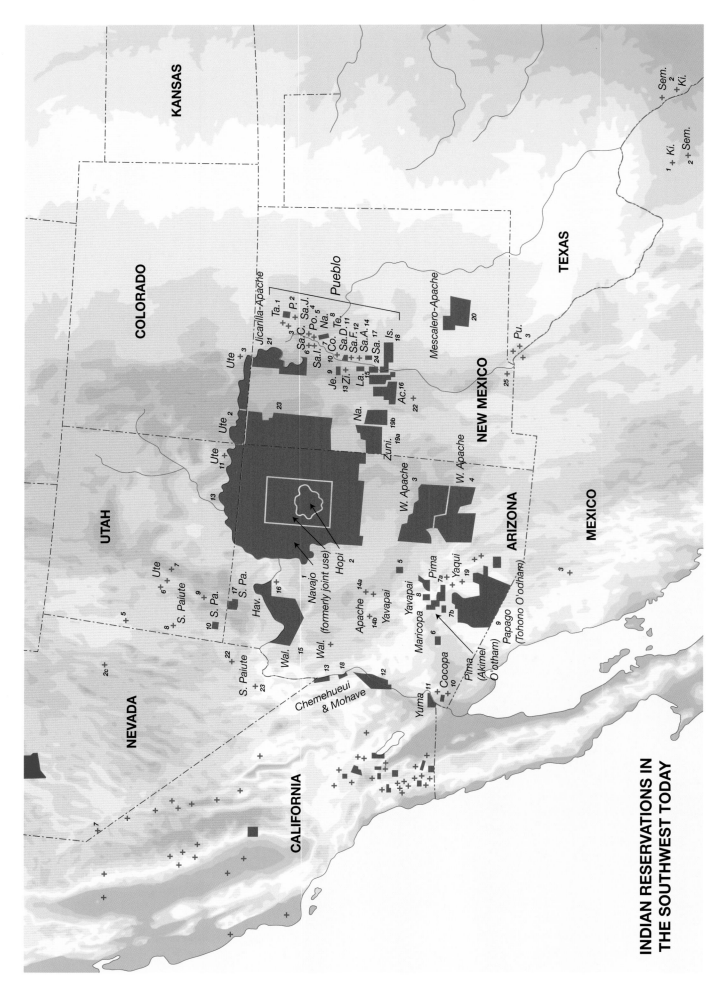

INDIAN RESERVATIONS IN THE SOUTHWEST TODAY

SOUTHWESTERN TRIBES, 20th CENTURY

Key to abbreviations:

Hav	=	Havasupai
Na	=	Navajo
Wal	=	Walapai

Po	=	Pojoaque
Sa	=	Sandia
SaA	=	Santa Ana
SaC	=	Santa Clara
SaD	=	Santo Domingo
SaF	=	San Felipe
Sal	=	San Ildefonso
SaJ	=	San Juan
Ta	=	Taos
Te	=	Tesuque
Zi	=	Zia

Pueblos:

Ac	=	Acoma
Co	=	Cochiti
Is	=	Isleta
Je	=	Jemez
La	=	Laguna
Na	=	Nambe
P	=	Picuris

Karankawas suffered reprisals that finally destroyed them entirely. We hear of a band being exterminated by a group of ranchers in 1858. A few may have crossed into Mexico, but all traces of them are now lost. In later years there seem to have been five tribes. Their reputation as cannibals seems unfounded.

TONKAWA A group of small Indian tribes of central Texas, the Tonawa were contacted by the Spanish as early as 1542 on the Trinity River. At one time, before the arrival of the Apache and Comanche, they seem to have been the most important of the peoples of central Texas. They had a distinct language, forming a separate family, which on circumstantial evidence has been linked to the Karankawa of the Texas coast. By the mid-18th century, much reduced in number, the Tonkawa seem to have been connected with the San Xavier missions on the San Gabriel River, Texas. In 1855, the remaining Tonkawas were moved to a reservation on the Brazos River, Young County, Texas. But the hostility of the Texans enforced their removal to Indian Territory (now Oklahoma) in 1859.

They suffered a massacre in 1862, when Delaware and Shawnee, with others, killed 137 men, women and children in reprisal for old disputes. The surviving Tonkawas lived for a time at Fort Arbuckle in Chickasaw Nation and later took refuge at Fort Griffin, Texas. They returned to Indian Territory in 1884, when a small reservation was established in present Kay County, Oklahoma. Their total population was perhaps over 1,700 at the time of Spanish contact but only 350 when first removed to Indian Territory in 1857. Just 92 members of the tribe survived when brought from Fort Griffin. A few people have continued to identify themselves as Tonkawa

through the 20th century: 53 in 1910; 46 in 1936; 186 in 1993; and 420 by 2001, although they mixed with Lipan Apaches over the years. They are found around Tonkawa, Kay County, Oklahoma. Although it is difficult to delimit Tonkawan tribes in Spanish colonial times, they seem to have been a warlike people who followed the bison herds for long distances, lived in skin tipis and were fine horsemen.

APACHE (INDE) The southwestern division of the Athabascan linguistic family known as Apache is composed of seven tribes: the Chiricahua, Jicarilla, Kiowa Apache, Lipan, Mescalero, Western Apache and Navajo (Navaho). All but the Kiowa Apache language seem to be closely related branches of a single tongue that were perhaps unseparated before about A.D. 1300.

There has been lengthy debate over the route taken by these Athabascans following their separation from their northern relatives of the Mackenzie River drainage of Canada. One theory suggests a migration through the inter-montane region of the American Plateau and Great Basin. A second view suggests a route through the Great Plains, and these Apachean people are credited as the first Great Plains people to be in contact with the earliest Spanish exploration on the Plains in the 16th and 17th centuries. A number of archaeological sites such as Dismal River and others in Nebraska and Kansas have been presented as Apachean, although some historians consider them more probably Puebloan. In the course of the debate a number of tribal names in old Spanish and French records have been given Apache status, including the *Padouca*, alternatively presented as Comanche, a relatively ancient people of the Plains.

The first hypothesis, however, seems to be generally favored, with the entry of these Athabascans into the Southwest about A.D. 1400, with an early spatial separation, either before or very shortly after their arrival in the Southwest — first of the Kiowa Apache and later of the Lipan to the Plains of Oklahoma and Texas. Certainly the Kiowa Apache represent the greatest problem for the favored theory, because of their adoption of Plains cultural traits, their long association with the Kiowa, and a tradition — albeit tenuous — of a link to the southernmost group of the Northern Athabascans, the Sarsi.

A number of Indian groups of northern Mexico, such as Manso, Suma, Jumano and Janos — names from old Spanish mission records —

Apache Mountain Spirit Dancer, c. 1930. Also called Gaan Dancers, they impersonate the sacred spirits who drive away sickness and evil and bring good fortune. Over black buckskin hoods with false eyes of abalone or turquoise, they wear towering wooden headdresses painted with symbols of strength, and challenge the forces of evil by charging at each other in the dark beside a fire. Several Apache groups retain the ceremony, usually combined with the girls' puberty rite. He wears a buckskin kilt, and characteristic Apache boots with rawhide upturns at the toe.

Above: Chief Josh, a San Carlos Apache as photographed by Rinehart in 1898.

Above Right: Ndee Sangochonh, Apache Indian, half-length portrait, facing front by Edward S. Curtis, c. 1906. Library of Congress, Prints & Photographs Division LC-USZ62-106797.

Right: Apache buckskin knee length boots with upturned rawhide soles and Gaan dancers depicted in the beadwork. W. Reid Collection.

Below: Four Apache men on horseback at the edge of a stream, Edward S. Curtis c. 1903. Library of Congress, Prints & Photographs Division LC-USZC4-8805.

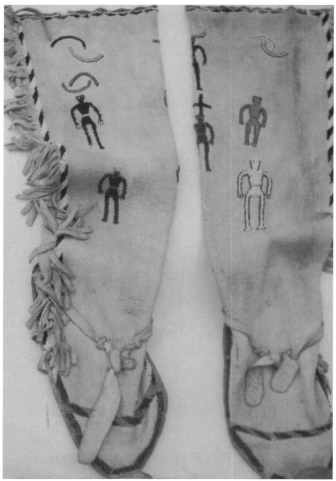

Above Left: Pacer, a Kiowa Apache, was an advocate for friendly relations with whites. His small tribe, part of the Kiowa at the beginning of the reservation period, was the remnant of an older independent Plains people. Others believe the Kiowa Apache separated from the Southwestern Apache. Photograph by William S. Soule in 1872.

Above Right: Apache girl with baby in cradle with sun shade. LC-USZC4-8845.

Below Left: Apache feast march ceremony—an Edward Curtis photo from January 1905. LC-USZ62-48375.

Below Right: Striker, Kiowa Apache, 1872. He has a combined bow case and quiver (probably Mountain Lion) and a beaded pouch slung across his back; he holds a bow.

Above: Apache wickiup, c. 1880. Light poles were set in a rough circle of shallow holes, bent inward, tied together and covered with thatched grass or brush tied on with yucca fiber in regular overlapping courses. The structure, 5–7 feet (1.5–2.1 m) high and 6–10 feet (1.8–3 m) in diameter, was partially covered with earth in winter.

have also been presented as Apachean, but none survived until reservation days, so their connections are unknown. In 2010 the U.S. Census gave 64,869 "Apache."

LIPAN APACHE An Athabascan tribe of the southwestern Apache group, Lipan are usually given separate status. They were in the upper Red River area of northwestern Texas as long ago as 1670. At that time they numbered perhaps 3,000 people and already had the advantage of horses and metal weapons. They seem to have pushed several Caddoan peoples eastward, who were subsequently armed by the French. This halted and reversed their advance. They seem to have played a large part in destroying Spanish settlements and missions in the San Antonio area. However, the entry of the Comanche into Texas led to diminished numbers and domain.

In later years they occupied an area between the Colorado River (of Texas) and the Pecos River. A few crossed into Mexico. Their language was closest to Jicarilla, and they perhaps split from them in about A.D. 1500.

Below: Apache Indians at Gallup, New Mexico, c.1910. Several are dressed to represent the Mountain Spirits or Gaans, wearing masks of black hoods with attached split yucca laths painted with mythological and sacred designs. Photograph: J.R.Willis.

The last of the Lipan were settled in 1905 on the Mescalero Reservation, New Mexico, and there were only two or three old women living in 1981 who knew anything of their ancient language. A few others are said to have been incorporated among the Kiowa Apache and Tonkawa of Oklahoma, but are no longer reported separately. The Lipan, together with the Mescalero and Tonkawa, are thought to have been the original spreaders of the Peyote cult among Indians north of the Mexican border.

KIOWA APACHE These are the most divergent group of the southwestern Apachean people, who have been associated with the Kiowa of the southern Plains since long before white contact, perhaps for 400 years. It has been proposed that they may have moved from the north with their allies, the Kiowa, and not separated from the main southern group. Superficially, they are a Plains people, who formed a distinct band within their adopted tribe. In the 1860s they moved to the Fort Sill Reservation, Oklahoma, along with Kiowa and Comanche, with whom they are much mixed. In 1907 they were reported to number 156. The modern Kiowa Apache live in and near the towns of Anadarko, Fort Cobb and Apache in Oklahoma, and were reported to number about 400 in 1960, including about 40 people who could speak their language. In 1981 they had an enrollment of 833, with only 20 remaining speakers of the language. By 2001 there were 1,854 reported, but the number of speakers is unknown.

CHIRICAHUA APACHE This is a tribe of the southwestern Apachean group who lived on the west side of the Rio Grande in southwestern New Mexico and adjacent Arizona and Mexico. Although they had almost no tribal cohesion they are sometimes divided into four bands: Chiricahua, Mimbreños, Mogollon and Warm Springs. Their closest linguistic relatives are the Mescalero Apache. Although mission records from the Spanish colonial days do not mention the Chiricahua by this name, they found Indians in their region who were consistently hostile, and many of them were clearly Chiricahua Apaches. By 1853 most of the Chiricahua territory had been transferred from Mexico to the United States, but the hostilities continued

Above: Mescalero Apache Crown Dancers. Masked and painted dancers representing mountain spirits (Gaans) appear during girls' puberty ceremonies. Their elaborately painted head boards and bodies enshrine symbolism for well-being connecting the participants with the supernatural world. This photograph was taken at Ruidoso, Mescalero Reservation, New Mexico, c. 1947.

Below: Apache woman doing beadwork, c. 1950. Some Apache bands excelled in beadwork, particularly those closest to the Plains tribes, such as the Jicarilla and Mescalero. The cradleboard with its sun shade and yucca slats has also been adopted by some Navajo women.

between miners, ranchers, settlers and these nomadic Indians. The government made several attempts to settle at least some on reservations through overtures to leaders Mangas Coloradas and Cochise, and when these failed some were interned on the San Carlos Reservation. Thus began a long, dramatic and tragic duel between a few hundred Apaches and the troops, scouts and citizens of the United States and Mexico.

Victorio and most of his followers were killed by Mexican soldiers in 1880, and not until 1886 did Geronimo and his band surrender to General Crook in Sonora, Mexico. The entire Chiricahua people were sent first to Florida and then to Alabama, but in 1894 were transferred to Fort Sill, Oklahoma. In 1913, 187 of the remaining Chiricahuas returned to their homelands and settled on the Mescalero Reservation, New Mexico, while 84 chose to remain in Oklahoma. Over the intervening years the Chiricahua people have all but merged with the Mescalero, but perhaps 500 still claimed their descent in 1970. The

Oklahoma branch have descendants near Apache and Fletcher towns and number about 450, known as the "Fort Sill Apache."

MESCALERO APACHE Mescaleros are a branch of the southwestern Athabascan Apachean peoples who have occupied essentially the same territory of southeastern New Mexico, Texas and the adjacent parts of Chihuahua, Mexico, since the 17th century. Their territory combined high mountain valleys and flats, with cold winters and hot, dry summers. Despite treaties at various times with the Spanish and later Mexican authorities, when Texas and New Mexico were transferred to the United States, the new government recognized no Indian claims to land. A bitter struggle between the Americans and the Mescalero saw many taken prisoner at Bosque Redondo, along with the Navajos. In 1872 a reservation was established on the eastern slopes of the White and Sacramento mountains, New Mexico, and the Mescalero — with additions from the Chiricahua and a few Lipans — have been there since.

Like most southwestern Apaches, they lived by hunting wild game, antelope, rabbit and, occasionally, buffalo. They harvested wild plants, particularly agave (mescal), prickly pear, wild pea,

Left: Jicarilla Apache woman, c. 1895. From the most Plains-like Apache tribe apart from the Kiowa-Apache, she wears a separate yoke cape similar in construction to Sioux, Cheyenne and Southern Ute capes, beaded in the curving parallel lines and solid blocks of lazy stitch beadwork popular among Rocky Mountain tribes. Wide leather belts with silver button decoration were characteristic of Jicarilla women. Small bags of horse mint were sometimes tied to garments, for perfume, and as love charms.

Below: Jicarilla Apache group, 1904. Although the costumes of this tribe were Plains-influenced, there were many purely Jicarilla traits, such as the women's broad, tacked leather belts, woolen hair ties and the style of dress yoke shown at right.

Above: Chiricahua Apache girl, the granddaughter of Cochise, photographed in 1886.

Right: Apache boots, perhaps Mescalero, c. 1900. W. Reid Collection.

Below: A group of San Carlos Apaches in 1898, probably photographed by the F.A. Rinehart studio or Heyn studio during the Trans-Mississippi International Exposition in Omaha. Left to right: James Stevens (interpreter), Forgetting, Josh Jingling, Long and Net the Whites.

Left and above: Back and front views of Western Apache female doll, c. 1900. This shows the two-piece Western Apache woman's dress, poncho, and skirt and the knee length boots with upturned rawhide soles. June Bedford Collection.

Left: Western Apache, c. 1860. Perhaps the hardiest of all Native American warriors, a few hundred Apaches defied other tribes, Mexicans and the U.S. Army until the 1880s. Although popularly shown wearing much Euro-American clothing, they had their own distinctive dress. Buckskin shirts with cut or applied fringing were decorated with yellow ocher and lines of beadwork and silver buttons. Warrior and ceremonial buckskin caps bore eagle, turkey, ibis or owl feathers. Calf-length moccasins with rawhide soles extended at the toe were often painted and beaded in lines. Rawhide shields were invested with great protective and concealing powers by painted black, yellow, green, and white designs of stars, crescent moons, sun, birds, bats and spirit forms, often split into cardinal sections or groups of four elements.

Above: Western Apache woman, ceremonial dress, c. 1930. For the girls' puberty ceremony, Western, Chiricahua and Mescalero Apache women wore the two-piece buckskin dress, a large cape extending to the waist over a separate skirt, which was heavily fringed, painted and decorated with single lanes of beadwork and tin cone "jingles." Yellow-colored moccasin-boots, with hard soles turned up at the toe, were sometimes beaded with mountain spirit motifs. Her necklace is of loomed beadwork.

Right: Western Apache water basket, c. 1900. Young woman carrying water in a *tus,* a twined basket of coarse splints caulked with juniper leaf paste and sealed with pine pitch.

Right: Western Apache woman, c. 1890. For moving camp, or a food-gathering expedition, the horse bears rawhide saddlebags decorated with cutouts and red cloth, a *tus* (water container) and a buckskin-fringed burden basket. The best construction technique for pack baskets was twining: a set of vertical warps with two or more horizontal wefts which were twined around each other.

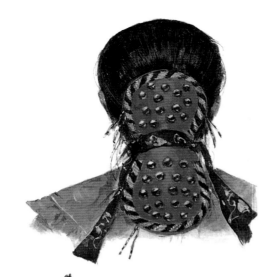

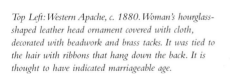

Top Left: Western Apache, c. 1880. Woman's hourglass-shaped leather head ornament covered with cloth, decorated with beadwork and brass tacks. It was tied to the hair with ribbons that hang down the back. It is thought to have indicated marriageable age.

Top Right: Western Apache, c. 1880. He wears a thick patterned headband, buckskin war amulet decorated with shell braided into the hair, and typical Apache face paint.

Above: Western Apache, c. 1880. He wears a ceremonial war-medicine headdress of clipped turkey feathers and two eagle feathers — imparting protection and swiftness in battle. Several Apache war and ceremonial caps were secured by chinstraps.

Right: Western Apache, c. 1890. Some groups used a cradle with a U-shaped or ovoid frame of heavy rods, crossed by wooden slats, with a broad bow over the child's head made of narrower yucca slats. The cover was usually deerskin, often colored yellow. The infant was strapped in with buckskin ties, and cushioned with layers of cloth or crushed cedar bark.

berries and choke-cherries. The Apaches were expert basket makers, and they had buckskin clothing for male and female. Their house types were brush wickiups, but also, among the Mescalero, Lipan and Jicarilla, the tipi of the Plains type. The Apache had no large pantheon of gods, but revered two powerful supernaturals, "Child of the Water" and his mother "White Painted Woman." These culture heroes destroyed monsters with objects and substances that became incorporated into ritual practice. Two important observances are the girls' puberty rite, and masked dancers who impersonate the Mountain Spirits capable of protecting the Apache from hostile forces and disease with their distinctive hoods and headdresses. The Mescalero likely numbered about 2,000 in 1850. In 1888, only 431 remained, 868 in 1945; 1,300 in 1980; 3,000 in 1992; and now there are almost 4,000 reported. The last four figures include the mixed Mescalero-Chiricahua population.

JICARILLA APACHE A tribe of the southwestern Athabascans closest to Lipan in language are the Jicarilla. Their territory was the high country of mesas and basins in the area of northern New Mexico on both sides of the Rio Grande, and the upper valleys of the Red River. Their hunting territory extended into present Colorado. Their location enabled subsistence to include the hunting of bison as well as antelope and small game, and they also gathered wild berries and fruits. Their early use of the horse and relative proximity to Plains Indians allowed the adoption of cultural traits and material culture from the east and north.

Like their kinsfolk they raided the Pueblos extensively, and also incorporated both ritual and material culture from that source. They were the Apaches most influenced by Pueblo gardening practices. They probably encountered the Spanish in the 16th century and thereafter waged constant war on them. They were in turn harassed by the Comanche during the 18th century, and hostilities with the Americans continued until 1855.

In 1874 the Jicarilla Reservation was established near Dulce, New Mexico, and has been their home since. Their major ceremonials were the Bear Dance, a curing rite; and the Relay Race between two sides, enlisting the aid of culture heroes and deities to ensure food supply. The Jicarilla have retained a surprising amount of traditional religion and beliefs, despite modern influences, but do not have the Mountain Spirit rituals of the Western Apache. They numbered 815 in 1900 and have steadily increased since, being reported to number 2,308 in 1980; 3,100 in 1992; and 3,403 in 2001. Stock raising has now given way to wage earning for most Apaches.

WESTERN APACHE

The Western Apache form a group of Athabascan subtribes speaking similar dialects in southeastern Arizona, from the San Pedro River in the south to the Verde River in the north. They comprise the *San Carlos, White Mountain, Cibecue, Southern Tonto* and *Northern Tonto* in that order, south to north. The whole group are sometimes known as *Coyoteros.* They have become one of the legendary Indian peoples due to their prowess as warriors, usually fancifully represented in popular books and on film. They probably reached their present location in about A.D. 1525, and remained isolated until hostilities with the Spanish intensified after 1765, although no settlements were established by the Spanish in Western Apache domains. The Apache adoption of the horse and the material culture of equestrian raiders ensured independence until the Americans obtained control of Arizona in 1853. Anglo-American efforts to destroy the Apaches intensified with the concentration of Western Apaches on the San Carlos Reservation, established in 1872 in eastern Arizona south of the Colorado Plateau (San Carlos, Tonto) and

Left: Navajo hunter, c. 1895. Navajo silverwork, copying Mexican techniques, perhaps dates only from the return from imprisonment at Fort Sumner. At first, Mexican coins were worked with simple metal tools, but by 1930, commercial blowtorches and solder were being used along with files, saws, punches and other tools. This hunter (note fur and skin quiver/bowcase slung over his right shoulder) wears a "squash blossom" necklace, and a sand-cast naja pendant of supposed Islamic inspiration. The shoulder strap of a pouch for tobacco and small items bear plain silver buttons. His belt conchos have embossed centers stamped from large dies, the sparse decoration hammered with chisels. Later, turquoise and more elaborate designs were introduced, spreading to the Zuñi and Hopi, and increasingly designed for sale to whites. But good Navajo work retains its massive quality. Navajo moccasin-boots have rawhide soles and buckskin uppers, varying only in their extent.

Below Left: Navajo conical hogan, c. 1900. This older form than that on p. 186 was built around three forked logs, locked in a tripod. Two logs were added 4 feet (1.2 m) apart on the east side to support a door frame. Poles, brush and sometimes cedar bark were piled around the framework, the whole being covered thickly with earth, leaving a smoke hole at the apex. Doorways sometimes projected like dormers, and were usually closed with a blanket.

Below: Navajo sandpainting, c. 1950. Dry "paintings" using pulverized materials serve as temporary altars during the various "ways" or healing rites, depicting supernatural beings in human or anthropomorphic forms, often in pairs or larger multiples. Yeibichai masked dancer spirit representations are often depicted during night-long curing rites and — unlike fixed sand paintings for commercial sale — are always destroyed before dawn. Another ceremonial, the "Blessing Way," is performed for general well-being and to restore harmony with a universe that the Navajo recognize as an orderly, all-inclusive system of complimentary good and evil spiritual components.

the Fort Apache Reservation to the north (White Mountain, Cibecue).

The Western Apache world view was expressed in a cycle of myths that explained the origin of the world and supernatural powers. Their major ceremonials were connected with curing or protection against illness, usually performed in special structures.

The traditional Apaches have a belief in an impersonal deity, "Life Giver," and culture heroes "Changing Woman" and her son, "Slayer of Monsters."

The puberty ceremony survives, and Gaan or Crown dancers (Mountain Spirit Dances) continue to perform regularly. In 1972 the Western Apache population was 9,622. But the 15,825 reported in 1981; the 21,572 in 1992; and 24,860 in 2001, perhaps an overestimate for the San Carlos and Fort Apache reservations, with a few at Camp Verde, Middle Verde and Clarkdale with the Yavapai. Over the years the Apaches have become fairly successful stockmen and operate tourist facilities, but on the whole, social conditions remain below those enjoyed by white Americans.

NAVAJO or **NAVAHO** A tribe forming one of the seven divisions of the southwestern Athabascan Apachean group is the Navajo. They call themselves Diné, and they likely entered the American Southwest during the 15th century. Linguistically, they are closer to the Western Apache than the latter are to Lipan or Kiowa Apache. Their location was — is — the dry desert regions of the northeastern section of Arizona and the northwestern parts of New Mexico, between the San Juan River in the north to the area of the Puerco and San Jose rivers in the south. The Navajo seem to have been more heavily influenced by Pueblo culture than other Apachean groups, and the adoption of elements of Pueblo population, perhaps before and after the Pueblo revolt against the Spanish in 1680, reinforces a strong Puebloan link. Their pottery and weaving arts are of Pueblo origin.

Above: Navajo, c. 1900. Navajo cradles were backed with two boards with pointed or rounded upper ends, a footrest, and a hoop or canopy of thin, bent wooden splints. All parts were thonged together through holes in the wood. Ornaments and charms were often attached to the bow-shaped canopy. The mother is shown weaving a blanket. The Navajo copied the vertical loom from the Pueblos c. 1700, first weaving cotton, later wool. The earliest Navajo serapes and blankets closely resembled those of the Pueblos. But they gradually developed their own increasingly complex rug designs, associated today with various parts of the Navajo Reservation, e.g., Ganado, Two Grey Hills and Wide Ruins.

Below: Navajo woman weaving a rug, c. 1950. The Navajo learned their weaving techniques from the Pueblo Indians, however they used the wool from sheep introduced to the Southwest by the Spanish. Originally they used their own herds and native dyes for blankets, later they imported wools for rugs styled to American tastes.

Above: Navajo woman and child, c.1960. She holds the characteristic cradle board with sunshade, and wears a blouse decorated with coin silver. The Navajo today are the largest tribe, with an enrolled membership of well over 250,000 — although there are perhaps more Cherokee and Cree descendants who have intermarried with whites over generations, so that many are no longer regarded, enrolled or identified as Indian people.

Right: Navajo yebichai dancer representing the god (holy person) Zahadolzha, with a leather mask and basket cap. His belt has large silver conchas. Edward S. Curtis, 1904.

Below: Female "Yei" figures in a Navajo rug design, c. 1980. These representations of divine beings from Navajo mythology have only appeared in recent times on rugs, and in this form are imitations devoid of the religious content. Many "Yei rugs" are made in the Shiprock area. M.G. Johnson Collection

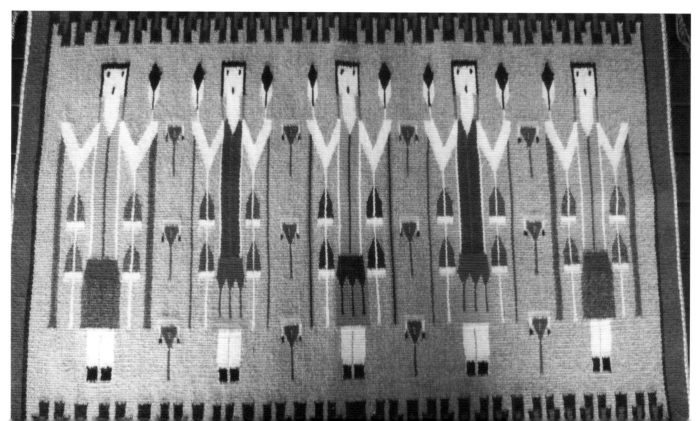

22 ENCYCLOPEDIA OF NATIVE TRIBES OF NORTH AMERICA

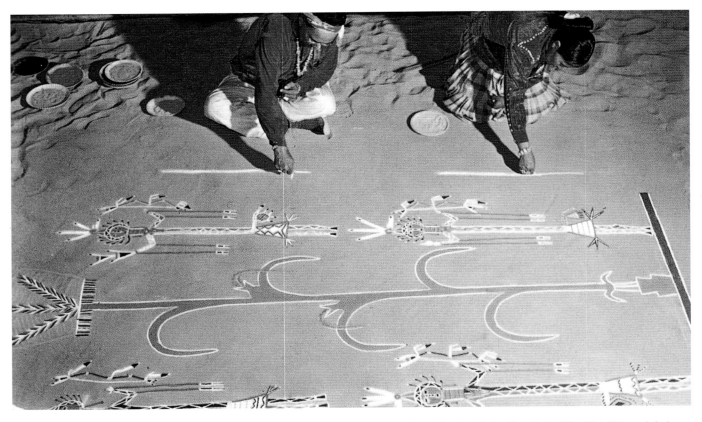

Above: Navajo sandpainting, c.1950. Mythological figures produced by finely ground colored sands on the floor of a Hogan, aided the Navajo in curing ceremonies. These paintings must be destroyed before sundown on the day they are prepared, or they will have no effect on patients.

Below: Corn Dance, Santa Clara Pueblo, New Mexico. Courtesy Ray Whiteway-Roberts.

Opposite, Above Right: Manuelito Segundo was the son of Manuelita and his wife Juanita, 1874.

Opposite, Above Left: Navajo leader Manuelita in 1874. He led his people back to their homeland from Bosque Redondo in 1868 after negotiations in Washington D.C. Note the buckskin guncase, fur bowcase and quiver, probably made from mountain lion, and also his huge blanket.

Opposite, Below: Santa Clara Pueblo Buffalo Dance, 1990. The men wear buffalo headdresses and kilts decorated with the serpent symbol, the unmarried girls wear sun-disc bustles. Courtesy Ray Whiteway-Roberts.

Although the Navajo were involved in wars against the Spanish and were often successful in driving them away, their culture gradually modified under Spanish influence, including the domestication of sheep and horses. This influence also affected food gathering, agriculture, trade, religion and the arts, which resulted in a hybrid Apachean-Puebloan-Hispanic tradition, which survives.

The Navajo origin myth describes ascending from the underworld. The majority of their ceremonials are primarily for curing disease — actual or anticipated. They also are for the ritualistic restoration of universal harmony once it has been disturbed, usually expressed as the "Blessing Way," through group rituals and singing, which give psycho-therapeutic benefit to patients and participants. Other important rituals include the Yeibichei or "Night Chant," and recently the Peyote cult has become popular with many Navajos.

After the United States obtained control of the Southwest the legendary government scout, Kit Carson, was commissioned to round up the Navajo, and in doing so destroyed their sheep, orchards, food and horses. Some 8,000 Navajo were interned at Bosque Redondo in 1863. They returned some five years later, and the Navajo Reservation was established, ultimately covering an area larger than West Virginia. It straddles four states — Arizona, New Mexico, Utah and Colorado. During the 20th century, three additional communities have been added at Ramah, Valencia County; Canyoncito, west of Albuquerque; and Puertocito, northwest of Magdalena, Socorro County, all in New Mexico. In the years between their captivity and today, the Navajo have increased in population from perhaps 10,000 to 166,519 in 1981; 195,938 in 1990; 255,727 in 2001; and 308,013 in 2010. They are the largest enrolled Indian tribe north of the Rio Grande.

Navajo life today centers on attempts to cope with the many economic and political problems that stem from their cultural isolation, and to ensure that exploitation of the mineral resources on their lands by various corporations will benefit "The People." The Navajos are noted for their fine silverwork, woolen blankets and rugs and for their continued distinctive dress, particularly of the women, which is derived from 19th-century full skirts and long blouses of European fashion.

THE PUEBLOS

The name of the so-called Pueblo Indians of the American Southwest, derived from the Spanish for "village," is a collective term for Indians who lived in permanent stone or adobe structures in compact villages along the Rio Grande in New Mexico, the Zuñi of western New Mexico, and the Hopi villages of northern Arizona. The

Top Left: Navajo log hogan, c. 1950. The more recent form, still in use in remote areas, is hexagonal, and of horizontally laid logs. From the eaves upward (5 or 6 feet / 1.5–1.8 m above the ground) the log courses are drawn in progressively to form a dome, which is covered with earth. The interior is excavated to about 2 feet (60 cm), leaving a low "shelf" running around inside the walls, with a central fire pit.

Above Left: Indian silversmiths, probably Navajo, making jewelry, c. 1930.

Below Left: Navajo woman weaving a rug, c. 1930.

Opposite: The Pueblo villages.

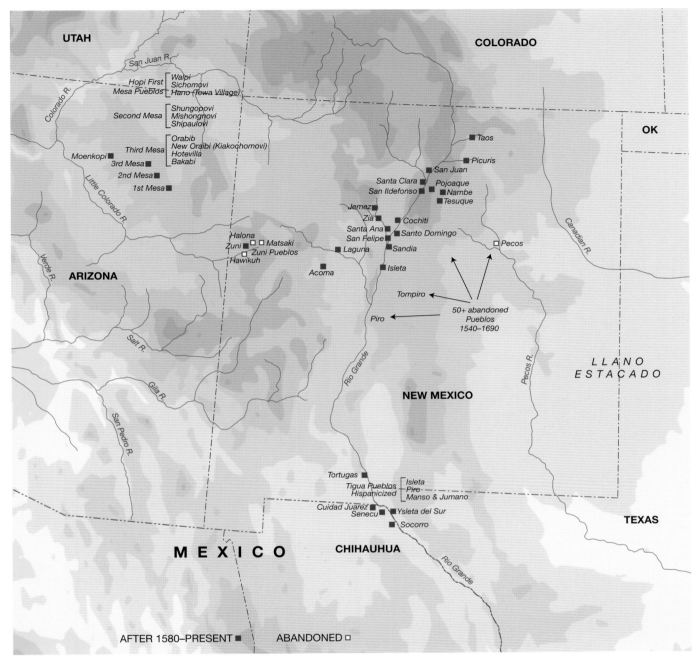

UTAH

COLORADO

OK

San Juan R.

Hopi First
Mesa Pueblos
Walpi
Sichomovi
Hano (Tewa Village)

Colorado R.

Second Mesa
Shungopovi
Mishongnovi
Shipaulovi

Moenkopi ■
Third Mesa
Orabib
New Oraibi (Kiakochomovi)
Hotevilla
Bakabi

3rd Mesa ■

Little Colorado R.

2nd Mesa ■

1st Mesa ■

■ Taos

■ Picuris

San Juan ■

Santa Clara ■
San Ildefonso ■
Pojoaque ■
Nambe ■
Tesuque ■

Jemez ■

Zia ■
Santa Ana ■
San Felipe ■
Cochiti ■
Santo Domingo ■
Sandia ■

Halona □ □ Matsaki
Zuni ■ □ Zuni Pueblos
Hawikuh □

Laguna ■

ARIZONA

Verde R.

Acoma ■

Isleta ■

□ Pecos

Canadian R.

Tompiro ◀

50+ abandoned
Pueblos
1540–1690

Piro ◀

Salt R.

Gila R.

Pecos R.

LLANO
ESTACADO

San Pedro R.

Rio Grande

NEW MEXICO

Tortugas ■

Tigua Pueblos
Hispanicized
Isleta
Pire
Manso & Jumano

Cuidad Juarez ■
Senecu ■
Ysleta del Sur ■

Socorro ■

TEXAS

M E X I C O

CHIHAUHUA

Rio Grande

AFTER 1580–PRESENT ■   ABANDONED □

historic Pueblos seem to be descendants of people who built the great architectural wonders at Chaco Canyon, Mesa Verde, Casa Grande and other places spread over five states, which were perhaps at the height of their cultural development during the 13th century. The Pueblos who survived the Spanish conquest are divided into four linguistic families: Tanoan, Keresan, Zuñi and Hopi — the latter a divergent branch of the old Shoshonean family, now Uto-Aztecan.

Pueblo dwellers were sedentary horticulturists with intensive farming, usually in small fields irrigated from streams or storage reservoirs, the chief crops being corn, pumpkins, melons, beans and squash. They also raised a native cotton, a product that was woven into everyday clothing. In addition to agriculture they hunted deer, and antelope and occasionally bison on the plains. After contact with the Spanish, the Pueblos adopted horses, cattle and sheep. Wheat, grapes, peaches and apples were also grown extensively. They domesticated turkey, which were herded in large flocks, and eagles were kept in captivity for their feathers, prized for ritual use.

The ancient clothing of the Pueblo men consisted of a short tunic of deerhide, and leggings reaching the knees, either of skin or of cotton, breechcloth and moccasins. After the introduction of sheep, woven woolen garments largely replaced skin, including brightly colored blankets of native or imported wool, bayeta or yarn. Womens' dresses were knee length, in the form of a blanket, whose two ends were sewn together over the right shoulder and under the left, belted at the waist. Both men and women often wore their hair fringed at front and sides. They made ornaments of drilled shell, turquoise beads and other stones, and developed a skillful metalworking process derived from the Spanish.

The Zuñi Pueblo seems to have been the first known to the Spanish, in 1539, which inspired the Coronado expedition of 1540. Expecting to find great wealth (the seven cities of gold), and encouraged always by news of what lay beyond, he explored Pueblo country for two years without finding the hoped-for riches. It was not until 1598 that Juan de Oñate set up a permanent colony, near the present town of Española,

Above: Pueblo Indians probably from Cochiti Pueblo, displaying cottonwood drums, c. 1930.

Below: Buffalo Dance of the Rio Grande Pueblo Indians. Note the large cottonwood drums, c. 1930.

New Mexico, and there followed vigorous attempts to missionize; that is, to suppress native religion and enforce labor and tribute, which eventually led to the Pueblo Revolt of 1680. It was not until 1696 that the Spanish regained control of the Pueblo Indians. They were thereafter less harsh in their treatment, and the Pueblos continued in their ancient beliefs while adopting a veneer of Catholicism.

Few Rio Grande Pueblos maintained their exact original sites after the Revolt, perhaps only Acoma and Isleta. Since that time the Pueblos have been notably peaceful toward whites, with a relatively stable culture extracting from the Anglo-American world only that which helps to sustain their own culture in a continuing, preordained, timeless existence.

Their homes were originally without doors, the upper floors being reached by ladders. Corner fireplaces and dome-shaped ovens were derived from the Spanish. Floors were paved with stone slabs or plastered like the walls and roofs. The building material used in the western Pueblos is mostly stone, held together with adobe mortar, the whole covered with adobe plaster. In the east, since the Spanish conquest, unmolded adobe brick has been used. The roof beams are usually cottonwood, pine or spruce, with crosspoles covered with brush and earth. Modern tools and materials have made possible larger rooms with the use of longer timber beams. The Pueblos were excellent basket makers; and their earthenware vessels — ancient and modern — consist of elaborately burnished, incised or painted jars, bowls and platters, each Pueblo often developing its own style.

The Pueblos, in common with many Native Americans, have a conception of Nature and God as one. They revered the sky, earth, sun and the subterranean "Great Ones," recognizing a pantheon of supernatural spirits usually living under the world or in the sky and at the four cardinal points. These forces of nature, both cosmic — sun, moon, earth, wind and fire — and animal spirits, such as water serpents and spiders, or the dead, all exhibit anthropomorphic characteristics. These are friendly or hostile, requiring respect and veneration by secret societies and fraternities such as Kachina or Kiva societies, who dress in impersonation of the supernaturals in ritual dances to bring rain or good health. Such rituals usually take place in specially constructed semisubterranean chambers known as Kivas, or on village plazas. These ceremonies were arranged in calendrical cycles.

The Kachina cult impersonations of supernaturals, mostly cosmic forms, are associated with the Western Pueblos of the Hopi and Zuñi, while animal impersonations are more common among the Rio Grande Pueblos — a reflection of their traditional reliance on hunting as well as farming. These animal-propitiating ceremonies share the stage with Church Saints' days where Catholicism has been more influential. Other societies were the Clowns (Koshares) who, in addition to fun-making, were sacred. Membership in

Above: Throughout the Pueblo region, infants were often carried in a blanket on the mother's back, though several cradle types were also originally used. Variants of the basket cradle were found among the Mohave, Pima, Yuma and Hopi; but the Rio Grande Pueblos and Navajo used a board type, the former frequently carving the top in terraces symbolizing clouds, with a flexible wooden hoop canopy.

these esoteric societies was by initiation at adolescence. The Spanish introduced the official position of "Governor" at each Pueblo as part of their colonial administration, a political appointment sometimes passed on by descent, which continues.

In 1885, the Indians of the 19 Pueblos of New Mexico, including Zuñi, were reported as numbering 7,762, a drop from about 10,000 after the Pueblo Revolt of 1690. By 1946 this number had risen to about 14,500. In 1970 the total population, including Zuñi and Hopi, was reported as 30,971, and by 2001 that number had increased to 62,221.

A number of the Pueblos operate highly successful casinos in New Mexico, but there is still a deep level of poverty among the people.

KERES or KERESAN

This is an independent linguistic family of Pueblo Indians of the Rio Grande, New Mexico, composed of the Pueblos of Cochiti, San Felipe, Santa Ana, Santo Domingo and Zia, constituting the eastern or Queres group, and Acoma and Laguna, who form the western or Kawaiko group. They trace their origins to the underworld, from where they emerged from an opening, and took up residence on the Rio de los Frijoles.

They later abandoned the Rio and moved south, where Coronado visited them in 1540. They took part in the Pueblo Revolt of 1680, and were subsequently missionized, at least superficially, although they have remained a conservative people until the present time. In 1930 they numbered 4,134 in total, and in 1945, 6,036. The Keres people of those Pueblos numbered 24,470 in 2001.

COCHITI PUEBLO This Pueblo village is in Sandoval County, New Mexico, on the west bank of the Rio Grande, and is the northernmost of the Keresan-speaking villages. This small Pueblo witnessed all of the Spanish expeditions into New Mexico and took an active part in the Revolt of 1680. A large number of people no longer live on the reservation, although they return for the feast of San Buenaventura in July, when the Corn Dance is performed. They are noted for creamy-yellow pottery with black designs and also for making cottonwood drums. They numbered 465 in 1956; 799 in 1968; and currently number 1,189, but only about half live in the Cochiti Pueblo itself.

SAN FELIPE PUEBLO This is the central village of the five eastern Keresan Pueblos on the west bank of the Rio Grande, 10 miles (16 km) north of Bernalillo. They hold a special relationship to Cochiti and were perhaps once a single people, but there were villages in this area when Coronado passed

5733. Indian Pueblo Village.

Above: The northernmost Pueblo village in New Mexico, Taos Pueblo, is partly six stories high. It was the closest Pueblo village to the Plains and was once an important trading center.

through in 1540. Although few arts and crafts are now pursued, the secret societies function and ceremonials are still held. In 1956, they numbered 941; in 1970, 1,811; in 1991, 2,619; and 3,131 in 2001. A large number of them live away from the Pueblo.

SANTA ANA PUEBLO This is a small but conservative Keresan-speaking Pueblo on the Jemez River 8 miles (13 km) from its junction with the Rio Grande, plus the village of Ranchitos. In 1956 they numbered 353; in 1977 there were 498; and in 2001 there were 716. Pottery making was revived in 1973.

SANTO DOMINGO PUEBLO The Santo Domingo Pueblo is located on the east bank of the Rio Grande, 7 miles (11 km) south of Cochiti, and is the largest of the eastern Keresan Pueblos. Their ancestors probably occupied the Pajarito Plateau at one time. They have managed to maintain a core of basic Indian religion and beliefs. A cacique selects tribal, civil and religious officers for their dramatic ceremonials held in August. Pottery of varying quality has been made, and large amounts of jewelry. In 1956 they numbered 1,455; 2,511 by 1970; and 4,492 in 2001.

ZIA PUEBLO (SIA) A Keresan-speaking Pueblo on the Jemez River about 30 miles north of Albuquerque, New Mexico is the Zia. Presumably, they are descendants of an older, larger Pueblo, "Old Zia." Although they have been nominally Catholic since 1692, a few societies are extant. They

have gained a livelihood in the recent past from grazing sheep and goats on surrounding lands. They are noted for making fine pottery with white or yellow-buff backgrounds and varied naturalistic designs of deer, birds and leaves. In 1956 the Pueblo had a population of 327; rising to 555 in 1972; 820 in 1992; and 773 in 2001.

ACOMA PUEBLO Acoma is the western-most Keresan Pueblo, and one of the most impressive, situated on a mesa almost 400 feet (120 m) high some 50 miles (80 km) west of Albuquerque, New Mexico — sometimes known as the "Sky City." A number of satellite communities have been established over the years at Acomita, Santa Maria de Acoma and McCarthys. Traditionally, they share a basic culture with other Puebloan groups, particularly the Keresans, in social structure, religious and political systems.

The Acoma Pueblo vies with Hopi for the title of the oldest continuously inhabited village in the United States. Acoma pottery has hard, thin walls, with white to yellow-brown slip and is decorated with geometric motifs and parrotlike birds in overall designs. In 1956 the tribe numbered 1,888, rising to 2,512 in 1966, about 4,000 in 1991 and is now about 6,344.

LAGUNA PUEBLO Laguna is one of two western Keresan-speaking Pueblos and is the largest of all Rio Grande Pueblos. They now occupy six villages at Paguate, Mesita, Encinal, Paraje, Seama and Casa Blanca, plus the Laguna Pueblo 40 miles (65 km) west of Albuquerque, New Mexico. The Pueblo was established in 1699. Their close location to Spanish and Anglo communities during the 19th century resulted in some acculturation, but religious and secular officers (that of "governor" imposed by the Spanish in 1620) still follow the

Keresan pattern, despite internal factionalism. They numbered 3,475 in 1956; about 5,800 in 1975; 7,023 in 1992; and 7,825 in 2001, of whom some 2,500 live away from the reservation in towns and cities throughout New Mexico and the United States. Rich uranium deposits have been found on Laguna lands.

TANOAN

This is a major linguistic grouping of primarily New Mexico Pueblo Indians, apparently distantly related to the Kiowa language to form the Kiowa-Tanoan stock. An even more distant relationship has been suggested with Uto-Aztecan and Zuñi. As a large grouping, the Tanoan is commonly broken down into what is known as the "Eight Northern Pueblos" of New Mexico, plus the Sandia and Isleta Pueblos near Albuquerque, and the Jemez, west of Los Alamos. Lingusitically, the Tanoan family is divided into Tiwa, Tewa and Towa as follows: Northern Tiwa (Taos and Picuris); Southern Tiwa (Sandia, Isleta, Tigua and Piro); Northern Tewa (Nambe, San Ildefonso, San Juan, Santa Clara, Tesuque, Pojoaque); Southern Tewa (Tano, now Hopi-Tewa); and Towa (Jemez and Pecos).

In 1937, the Tiwa numbered 2,122; the Tewa 1,708, excluding Tano; and the Towa 648 (Jemez). The Pecos merged with the Jemez and the Piro, who with refugees from Isleta moved to the El Paso area after the Pueblo Revolt of 1680 and joined with others to form three Hispanicized Pueblos, of which only Tigua is still extant. Some authorities have placed the old Manso of Mesilla valley in southern New Mexico into the Tanoan family, but more probably they were Athabascans and long Hispanicized.

Above Left: Pueblo Indian pottery maker, c.1950. Maria Martinez from the San Ildefonso Pueblo, New Mexico, was one of the most famous of the Pueblo potters of the 20th century.

Below Left: Maria Martinez and husband Julian, famous Indian pottery makers of San Ildefonso Pueblo, New Mexico, 1934. They re-created prehistoric black-on-black Pueblo pots.

Below: Nampeyo, a noted Tewa Hopi potter of the Hano pueblo in northeastern Arizona, decorating pottery.

TAOS PUEBLO Taos is the northernmost Pueblo, located 10 miles (16 km) east of the Rio Grande Gorge and 70 miles (110 km) north of Santa Fé, New Mexico, just north of Taos. Their language is Northern Tiwa, a dialect of Tanoan. Traditionally one of the more prosperous communities, surrounded by fertile agricultural land, this impressive multistory Pueblo is about 600 years old. It is geographically close to the Plains Indians, from whom the tribe adopted elements of material culture — and recently the Peyote religion, which has caused much factionalism. In 1956 they numbered 1,137; 1,463 in 1970; 1,601 in 1991; and 2,443 in 2001. In 1847 there was a revolt against the Americans, which resulted in the destruction of the old mission at the Pueblo.

PICURIS PUEBLO This is a small Tiwa-speaking Pueblo town 20 miles (32 km) south of Taos, New Mexico, numbering 158 in 1956; 172 in 1972; and 324 in 2001. Good micaceous pottery has been traditionally made at Picuris. The Pueblo has been in the same vicinity as the present buildings since at least 1591. They are closely related to Taos.

SANDIA PUEBLO One of the three Southern Tiwa dialects of the Tanoan family is spoken by the people of this Pueblo, located 14 miles (22 km) north of Albuquerque, New Mexico. Although the site is a post-contact village, there are a number of prehistoric sites in the vicinity. The Pueblo was burned by the Spanish after the Pueblo Revolt of 1680.

Religion remains a means of retaining their identity in a location close to Anglo-Hispanic communities. They have retained the Corn, Eagle, Buffalo and other dances, plus their cacique and governor, a position instigated originally by the Spanish. Their population was 74 in 1900; 265 in 1971; and 485 in 2001.

ISLETA PUEBLO The second of the three Southern Tiwa dialects of the Tanoan family is spoken by the inhabitants of this Pueblo, situated on the west bank of the Rio Grande 13 miles (20 km) south of Albuquerque, with an outlying settlement, Chiskal.

The Spanish destruction of religious chambers, masks and paraphernalia led to the Revolt of 1680, which drove out the Spanish settlers for several years. Farming has remained

Above: Tesuque Pueblo Eagle Dancer, c. 1930. The Rio Grande Pueblos have several animal dances involving impersonation and mimicry. The Eagle Dance — dramatizing the relationship between humans and the sky powers — has become a popular exhibition, performed by groups even as far afield as the northern Plains. The dancer wears a headpiece, gourd beak and wing feathers.

important until recent years, and they have produced a commercial style of pottery. In 1956 they numbered 1,759, in 1974 there were 2,710, in 1990 it grew to 3,971, and in 2001 the population was reported as 4,441.

TIGUA PUEBLO This is a hispanicized Pueblo located south of El Paso, Texas, near the Mexican border at Ysleta del Sur, a village founded for refugees fleeing from the Tiwa villages (particularly from Isleta), following the Revolt of 1680. They have about 350 descendants, including another community, Tortugas, in Las Cruces, New Mexico.

PIRO Another Hispanicized group of Tiwa refugees from the upper Rio Grande are the Piro, who established villages just inside Chihuahua, Mexico, at Senecú and Socorro. Both groups have long ceased to exist as separate Indian communities, and probably merged with various other Indian remnants, Manso and Tigua, in the area. The ancient Piro probably numbered 6,000 before being exposed to Apache attacks in the early 17th century.

NAMBE PUEBLO Nambe is a small Pueblo, now largely Hispanicized, 15 miles (24 km) north of Santa Fé, New Mexico. They formerly spoke a Northern Tewa dialect of the Tanoan family. The present village is probably postcontact, but there are ruins of an earlier Pueblo close by. The population was 184 in 1956; 356 in 1972; 487 in 1993; and 643 in 2001. Women from this village once produced a good grade of micaceous cooking ware and wove belts of cotton.

SAN ILDEFONSO PUEBLO This Pueblo is situated on the Rio Grande, 20 miles (32 km) northeast of Santa Fé. They speak a Northern Tewa language of the Tanoan family, and claim descent from people who moved out of the valleys and cliff homes on the Pajarito plateau. This Pueblo was involved in the Revolt of 1680, and was one of the last to accept Catholicism in the 19th century. Since then they have often been factionalized. Maria and Julian Martinez, both famous potters, came

Right: Zuñi Pueblo woman, c. 1970. Womens' dress changed more slowly than men's, and traditional styles are retained for fiesta occasions. They are based on the old-style manta, a fine wool rectangle in black or brown, woven in a diagonal twill, held together at the sides with ornate silver pins, and worn over sateen blouses and lace petticoats. Pueblo women wear white buckskin moccasins with a wide strip wound round the legs up to the knee. The ceremonial bowl is of characteristic Zuñi design.

Left: Zuñi Rain Dancer, c. 1890. The Zuñi have probably the most complex of all Southwest native religions, with six esoteric cults, plus an ancestor cult. This dancer has a half-mask of painted leather with a horsehair beard, pink clay body pigment, a kilt traded from the Hopi and spruce garlands.

from this Pueblo, producing highly hand-burnished black ware, with dull accent areas of sharp geometric design. The Buffalo and Deer dances and the Plains-orientated Comanche Dance are still performed on San Ildefonso's Day. They numbered 138 in 1900; 413 in 1973; and 628 in 2001.

SAN JUAN PUEBLO The largest and northernmost of the six Tewa-speaking Tanoan Pueblos is the San Juan Pueblo. It is located 5 miles (8 km) north of Española on the east bank of the Rio Grande. It was in this vicinity that the Spanish founded their first provincial capital in New Mexico before moving to Santa Fé in 1610.

They suffered considerable persecution by the Spanish civil and ecclesiastical authorities until they arose in revolt in 1680. San Juan pottery is generally hand-burnished red and black ware with some incised and carved types. In 1956 they numbered 934; 1,721 in 1977; to 2,301 in 1991; and 2,723 in 2001.

SANTA CLARA PUEBLO Santa Clara is a Northern Tewa-speaking Pueblo town of the Tanoan family located on the west bank of the Rio Grande in Rio Arriba County, just south of Española. They traditionally lay claim to the cliff dwellings of Puye. The present day Pueblo occupies almost the same site as viewed by the 16th century Spanish.

Santa Clara Indians are often regarded as one of the wealthiest Pueblos, with a resource-rich land base. The Santa Clara Indians make polished black and red pottery with modern variations. Their population was 669 in 1956; 1,204 in 1974; about 2,000 in the mid-1980s; and 2,800 in 2001.

TESUQUE PUEBLO The southern-most of the six extant Rio Grande Tewa Pueblos, just 10 miles (16 km) north of Santa Fé, New Mexico, is the Tesuque pueblo. Despite their close proximity to Spanish and late Anglo-American influences, they have retained many ceremonials which have an ancient quality. Tesuque women formerly made grey-cream pottery. In 1956 they numbered 185; 281 in 1973; 488 in 1993; and 404 in 2001.

POJOAQUE PUEBLO Pojoaque is a small Pueblo, now largely Hispanicized, located 16 miles (26 km) north of Santa Fé, New Mexico. Although archaeological investigations on the Pojoaque Reservation suggest a large population with extensive farming in protohistoric times, by 1712 they numbered only 79. In 1970 there were 46 residents, and there were 327 in 2001. Their former language was a Northern Tewa dialect of the Tanoan family. Religious ceremonials are no longer held. As one of the eight Northern Pueblos, they are located very close to Nambe, San Ildefonso and Santa Clara.

HANO AND POLACCA These are two small Puebloan villages on the easternmost mesa of the Hopi Reservation in northeastern Arizona. They are thought to be descendants of a Rio Grande Tewa people known as *Tano*. They emigrated to the Hopi First Mesa in about A.D. 1700, and have largely intermarried with their hosts over the years. Hano is now known as *Tewa-Village* and still looks like an old Hopi style Pueblo. They are a fully integrated Hopi people, sharing their culture and ceremony. In 1972 there were 218 at Tewa-Village and 782 at Polacca, a more recent settlement.

JEMEZ PUEBLO The people of this Pueblo speak Towa, a dialect of Tanoan. The Pueblo is located on the Jemez River, 30 miles (48 km) northwest of Bernalillo, in an area where several villages were reported by the 16th-century Spanish explorers. They were participants in the Pueblo Revolt of 1680 and suffered the traumas and punitive expeditions that followed. Although native arts have weakened over the years, their political and religious organizations still function under a cacique and his staff, who appoint the officers of societies, the moieties and clans. Like most modern Pueblo cultures, theirs has been a mixture of native, Spanish and Anglo influences. In 1956, they numbered 1,137; 1,939 in 1970; and 3,486 in 2001.

PECOS PUEBLO Pecos was a Pueblo formerly located about 18 miles (29 km) southeast of Santa Fé, New Mexico. In the early 18th century they were subjected to attacks by Comanches and Apaches, and

Left: Hopi Snake Dancer, c. 1900. Rain brings rattlesnakes to the surface. They are thus associated with this rain dance for the benefit of crops. The ceremony is still performed in Hopi villages by the Snake-Antelope societies in alternate years with the Flute societies. Continual brushing of the snakes' backs with an eagle feather wand prevents them from coiling and striking. During the dance, a gatherer or guard controls them in conjunction with the carrier. Note the dyed feather headdress, black and white face and body paint, the kilt embellished with the sign of the serpent, and numerous silver and turquoise necklaces.

Above: Santa Clara Pueblo, Rainbow Dance, c.1960. Santa Clara is the third-largest of the six northern Tewa-speaking Pueblo towns located on the west bank of the Rio Grande between Taos and Santa Fé, New Mexico.

Below: Photo shows a crowd of people seated on the walls and standing at Taos Pueblo, watching native dances, c. 1910.

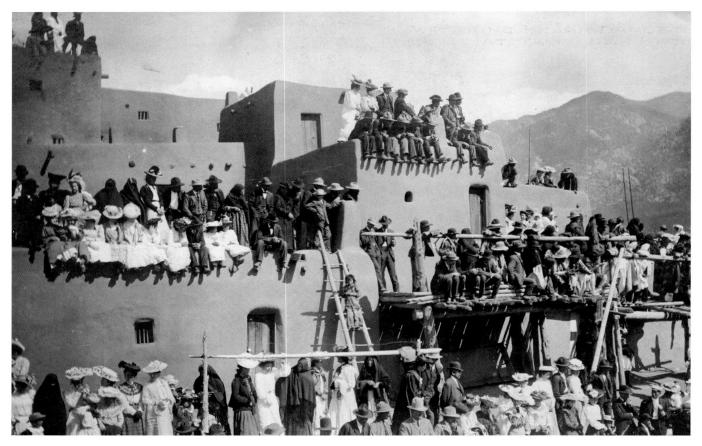

Right: Zuni Kachina doll, c. 1920. This doll represents "Sayatasha" the Rain God of the North with one long horn on the right side of his head symbolizing long life. During the Shalako ceremonies the actual impersonator leads a retinue of four different kachinas to the six kiva shrines at Zuni offering blessings.

Far Right: Zuni women dressed in formal attire carrying polychrome painted ollas, and wearing traditional textile dresses and skin moccasins, c. 1950.

Below: Zuni man in ritual costume and mask impersonating a Kachima spirit.

Above Left: Governor Diego Narango from Santa Clara Pueblo as photographed by Rinehart in 1898.

Above: Another Rinehart image, this of Pueblo woman Ts-I-Do-We-Tsh, who is wearing a Sioux dress.

were weakened further by smallpox epidemics that reduced their population from about 1,000 to 189 in 1792. In 1838 the last of them, just 17 in number, finally moved to Jemez Pueblo. They spoke a Towa dialect of Tanoan.

ZUÑI PUEBLO The Zuñi form a tribe, a Pueblo and a linguistic family whose villages and present reservation are in McKinley County in the western part of New Mexico. Hawikah, one of their towns, was first seen by the Spanish in 1539, and the following year Francisco Vásquez de Coronado captured the town during his expedition to find the "Seven Cities of Cibola," perhaps the seven villages of the Zuñi. The Spanish were only partly successful in their attempts to missionize the Zuñi, and in 1820 further attempts were abandoned, partly due to increasing raids by Navajo and Apache. The heritage of Spanish contact was the adoption of some crops, horses, burros and a system of secular government. Three summer farming villages — Ojo Caliente, Pescado and Nutria — were established around Halona, the remaining central Zuñi Pueblo. Tekapo, a fourth village, was established about 1912.

The population grew from about 1,500 at the beginning of the American period in 1848 to 3,439 in 1956. In 1970 there were 7,306 reported — a number that grew to 9,000 in 1990 and 9,780 by 2001. The Zuñis have been noted for their pottery; chalky-white slip with large brown-black designs, often large rosettes, deer, frogs and dragonflies, but the art has diminished in recent times. The Zuñis produce a great deal of turquoise and silver jewelry. Their social and religious organizations were composed of four interlocking systems of clans, the Kiva-Kachina society, the curing societies and the priesthoods. The Shalako, a splendid portrayal of religious pageantry, is held in late November.

HOPI PUEBLOS The Hopis speak a language of the Shoshonean family, now called Uto-Aztecan, and have lived in the same area of northeastern Arizona for more than 1,600 years. Their present Pueblos are located on three mesas west of Kearns Canyon, the main administrative center for the Hopis. On the First Mesa are the Tewa towns of Hano and Polacca, who joined the Hopi in the 18th century, Shitchumovi (Sichomovi) and Walpi. On the Second Mesa are Shipaulovi, Mishongnovi and Shongopavy (Shungopovi), and on the Third are Bakabi, Hotevilla, Oraibi (which claims to be the oldest inhabited village in the United States), Upper and Lower Moenkopi, and Kyakotsmovi (Kiakochomovi) or New Oraibi. Hopi country is the southern escarpment of Black Mesa, a highland area about 60 miles (100 km) wide, and their present reservation, a square within the Navajo Reservation, is a continuing source of disagreement between the tribes concerning ownership.

The basis of Hopi life — in a harsh, dry environment — has been the cultivation of corn, beans, squash and melons, to which they added European fruits. Spanish activity in the area

Above: Hopi Snake Dancer in costume. c. 1910. Edward S. Curtis photograph.

Above Right: Hong-ee Hopi (Moqui) holding a Black Ogre mask, by B.A. Burbank, c. 1898.

was never extensive, although they were known from 1540 to the invaders, who made various attempts to establish missions. But all churches were destroyed in 1680, and further attempts were abandoned after 1780, the Hopis being left in isolation to follow the indigenous culture lost to so many tribes. Their American experience began in 1848 when the United States obtained the Southwest from Mexico. This initiated a series of factional splits, particularly at Oraibi, between conservative and liberal forces. Hopi social structure contains a number of interlocking social and religious organizations, the latter exhibited in an annual cycle of masked Kachina or unmasked ceremonials in Kivas, or on plazas. The Hopis' pottery is characteristically mottled yellow-orange with asymmetric curvilinear black designs. They are the only major basketmaking Pueblo tribe in recent times, mainly using flat coiled technique, with abstract birds, whirlwinds and Kachina designs. In 1970 7,236 Hopis were reported, and 11,267 in 2001 — a large increase in recent years. The Hopis are renowned for their Snake Dance, held to bring rain for crops — see also pages 237 and 244.

HOPI CEREMONIALS The cycle of Hopi ceremonies begins in winter. The dates of all winter ceremonials are established by the position of the sun as it sets on the western horizon, whilst those of the summer are fixed by the position of the rising sun on the eastern horizon. Many of the rituals during the first half of the ceremonial year are Kiva based (ritual chambers) and in the second half take place on the Pueblo plazas. The important ceremonials are:

Wuwuchema Held in November and re-enacts the Hopis emergence from the Underworld. Spirits of the dead are invited to return and Masau (God of Earth and Death) kindles the new fire. Sometimes called the New Fire Ceremony. Members of the One-Horned and Two-Horned Societies participate.

Soyal Sometimes known as the Prayer-Offering Ceremony. Held in December. A winter solstice ritual to bring the sun back from its northward journey. Time for good wishes and blessings to mark the rebirth of the new year. To prevent ghosts returning, prayer sticks at the end of cords decorated with paint or feathers or cornstalk packets as charms (pahos) are distributed to families.

Pamuya Held in January for one day to announce the time of the summer Snake or Flute ceremonies and making the pahos to be used in them.

Powamu Also called the Bean Dance. Held in February. The first major ceremony of the Kachina season including the Mong or Chief Kachinas. Beans are forced to germinate in hot kivas to predict a successful growing season. Children are initiated and receive presents of dolls from Kachinas.

Palolokon Also called Water Serpent Ceremony. Held in March, (not annually), a theatrical display of plumed and horned serpents sweeping away a miniature cornfield. The placated monsters will ensure the crops and springs upon which villages depend will not fail.

Above: Edward S. Curtis photograph, c. 1907, of 10 Hopi snake priests, standing, facing front, carrying sticks, some with bags. Library of Congress, Prints & Photographs Division LC-USZ62-124229

Kachina Dances Held in April, May and June, usually one day's duration, and out-of-doors after the weather becomes milder. A sponsor determines which Kachina (out of over 250) will be performing. Promotes harmony, ensures health and brings clouds and rain. Social dances during this period include impersonating Navajos, Apaches and Spaniards, as well as Butterfly dances adopted from the Rio Grande Pueblos.

Niman Dance Also called the Home Dance. Held in July. Marks the final ceremony of the Kachina season. When the Kachinas return home to the San Francisco Mountains. The Hemis Kachina with elaborate tablita often impersonated, also the Koyemsi (clowns) entertain. Coincides with the early harvest; captive eagles killed with feathers used for pahos.

Flute Ceremony Also called the Lalent Ceremony. Held biennially in August, by members of the Gray and Blue Societies to bring late summer rain to bring crops to full maturity. Also commemorates the creation of the sun. Flutes used to imitate the sound of locusts and insects associated with summer.

Snake Dance Also called the Chechukta Dance. Held biennially in August (alternating with the Flute Ceremony) by members of the Snake and Antelope Societies. Ceremony based on a legend of a Hopi man initiated into the Snake tribe, marries and becomes ancestor of all reptiles. Dance renowned for the lines of dancers holding snakes with "huggers" who distract the serpents during performance. Snakes returned to the ground where they will act as messengers carrying the Hopis' prayers for rain to the spirits of the Underworld. In even numbered years the Snake Dance takes place at Hotevilla, Shipaulovi, and Shungopovi and in odd years at Walpai and Mishongnovi and the Flute Ceremony vice-versa.

Marau Society Ritual held in September and reported one of the oldest Hopi woman's dances closely duplicating those given by the men. Fertility, curing and weather control being the primary purposes.

Lakon Also called Basket Dance. Society ritual, held in October by women who spend several days making baskets then, on the eighth day, give them away. The ceremony is a prayer for health and weather control and brings an end to the year's sacred dramas.

Oaqol Also called Basket Dance. Society ritual, held in October (or March), once an important eight-day women's dance but now has become a one-day public dance.

Principal Hopi deities — culture heroes and major gods

Sotuquangu: God of the Sky, Creator of the Earth, Supreme Being

Masco: God of Earth, God of Death

Muinwu: Germ God, also known as Alosaka

Huruing Wuuti: Mother of the Universe

Kwanitaqa: One Horned God

Tawa: Sun God or Father Sun

Kokyang Wuuti: Spider Woman

Pookanghoya and Palongaohoya: Twin War Gods

Palolokon: Water Serpent

Muyao: Moon God

Ong Wuuti: Salt Woman

Kachinas These are not gods but are symbolic representations in human form of the spirits of plants, animals, birds, places or ancestors. When a dancer wears a mask and appropriate costume he believes he has received the spirit of the Kachina and the Hopis' prayers given to the Kachina through a priest are carried to the gods. There are five basic types of masks, leather face masks, upper half face masks, circular, spherical sack masks and helmet masks. There is no attempt at realism although some clue to the Kachina's identity is usually present. Kachina representations wearing masks appear only in the first half of the Hopi religious annual cycle, the supernatural beings themselves retiring to the San Francisco Mountains. Wooden painted dolls, small representations of Kachinas are given to instruct children, and non-religious forms are sold to tourists.

Above: Zuni Shalako kachina dolls, c. 1960. Probably Hopi made, these represent the Giant Couriers of the Rain Makers. The actual impersonators are 10 feet tall dancers wearing masks balanced on poles under a blanket.

Below: Hopi Kachina dolls do not have any ceremonial function. They are made to depict the dancers and are given to children so they may recognize specific kachinas.

This kachina doll represents the Mudheads or Clowns (Koyemsyhi) who appear in many Hopi dances and are always cheerful and friendly. Courtesy Leslie Atkins.

Below: Hopi White Ogre Kachina doll representing "Soyoka" or Ogre Woman (a costumed male). Similar kachinas with a black face are Black Ogre or "Natacka." These dolls represent dancers who frighten children who misbehave. Courtesy Leslie Atkins.

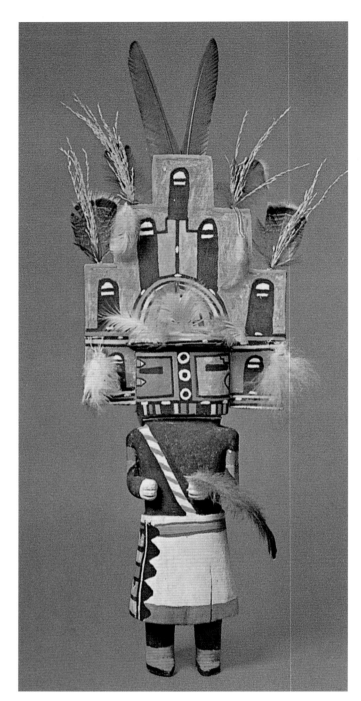

Left: Hopi Kachina doll of Cottonwood, c. 1915. These were used to instruct children about numerous forms of spirits that link humans to the gods, who are believed to live part of the year among the Hopis. This is the Hemis or Hümis Kachina doll (a model of the costumed dancer), with black painted body, kilt, sash and mask with painted sun, clouds and rainbow, and sprouting cornflower representations. Such dancers appear during the Niman ceremony — the celebration of the return of the Kachinas to the World Below in July.

Right: Edward S. Curtis photograph of four young Hopi Indian women grinding grain c. 1906. Library of Congress, Prints & Photographs Division LC-DIG-ppmsca–05085

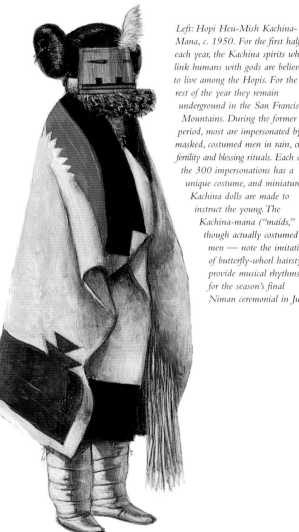

Left: Hopi Heu-Mish Kachina-Mana, c. 1950. For the first half of each year, the Kachina spirits who link humans with gods are believed to live among the Hopis. For the rest of the year they remain underground in the San Francisco Mountains. During the former period, most are impersonated by masked, costumed men in rain, crop, fertility and blessing rituals. Each of the 300 impersonations has a unique costume, and miniature Kachina dolls are made to instruct the young. The Kachina-mana ("maids," though actually costumed men — note the imitation of butterfly-whorl hairstyle) provide musical rhythms for the season's final Niman ceremonial in July.

Left: Hopi Snake Dance, as depicted on a postcard of about 1900. Photography has been banned at the ceremony for many years.

Right: Hopi Butterfly Dancer, c. 1970. The second half of the Hopi religious year sees the unmasked plaza dances of the Snake-Antelope, Flute, Butterfly, Maraw and other societies, on dates set by the solar or lunar calendar. Hopi women Butterfly dancers wear black mantas, woven belts in red, black and green, false hair fringes and carved tablita headdresses with painted butterfly and other designs.

Above: Hopi, c. 1900. Traditional "butterfly" or "squash blossom" hairstyle symbolizing virginity; the hair is wrapped around two curved sticks into large whorls. Married women wore their hair tied with a cloth hanging down at the side of the head and over the shoulders. This postpubescent style is still occasionally seen.

Right: Hopi She-Eu-Mish Kachina, c. 1950. One of the most dramatic Kachinas, this black-painted singer-dancer in the Niman ritual wears a kilt, sash and a masked headdress bearing complex symbolism of sprouting cornflowers, the rainbow and sun and rain clouds. He carries a gourd rattle and a feather.

NORTHWEST COAST

Language family and tribe	Meaning/origin of tribal name, where known
Tlingit	*"people"* or *"human beings"*
Haida	*"people"*
Tsimshian	*"inside of the Skeena River"*
Wakashan:	
Nootka	*"circling about"*
Makah	*"cape people"*
Ozette	—
Kwakiutl	*"beach on the north side of the river"*
Salishan:	
Bella Coola	English name
Comox	*"house"*
Seechelt	place name
Puntlatch	—
Squamish	*"people"*
Nanaimo	*"bunch people"*
Cowichan	*"warm the back"*
Songish	name of local group
Stalo	*"upriver"*
Semiahmoo	—
Nooksack	*"place of bracken roots"*
Lummi	*"facing each other"*
Samish	—
Upper and Lower Skagit	—
Swinomish	place name
Snohomish	place name
Snoqualmie and Skykomish	—
Suquamish	place name
Duwamish	place name
Twana	*"a portage"*
Clallam	*"strong people"*
Muckleshoot	—
Puyallup	place name
Nisqually	place name
Squaxon	—
Cowlitz	*"people of the river"*
Upper Chehalis,	
Lower Chehalis	village name (or *"sand"*)
Queets	—
Quinault	village name
Tillamook	place name
Siletz	—

Language family and tribe	Meaning/origin of tribal name, where known
Chimakum:	
Chimakum	—
Quileute	village name
Hoh	—
Chinookian:	
Chinook	village name
Clatsop	*"dried salmon"*
Cathlamet	village name
Skilloot	
Cathlapotle	*"people of the Lewis River"*
Multnomah	*"those toward the water"*
Watlala	—
Clowwewalla	—
Clackamas	—
Chilluckittequaw	—
Wishram	—
Wasco	*"cup (or small bowl) of horn"*
Coos	—
Yakonan	*"people of bay (or river)"*
Kalapuyan	—
Takelma	*"those dwelling along the river"*
West Coast Athabascans:	
Coquille	*"people who live on the stream"*
Umpqua	*"grass people"*
Tututni	—
Chastacosta	—
Taltushtuntude	—
Dakubetede	—
Chetco	*"close to the mouth of the stream"*
Tolowa	—
Hupa	place name
Chilula and Whilkut	*"people of the Bald Hills"*
Mattole	place name
Nongatl	—
Sinkyone	—
Lassik	chief's name
Wailaki	*"north language"*
Kato	*"lake"*

The Indians of the Northwest Coast occupied a relatively narrow strip between the interior mountains and the Pacific Ocean, being relatively isolated from the rest of the continent. It was — and is — a heavily forested land, mild and wet, covering the area of the Pacific coast from Yakutat Bay, Alaska, to northern California. The mountainous coast is deeply indented by sounds and fiords encompassing many islands. The coastal peoples were set apart by their industries, arts, beliefs and customs from interior tribes. Notwithstanding the uniformity of their culture, closer study discloses many independent tribal characteristics and divergent development.

The peaks of Northwest Coast culture were formed by the Haida-Tsimshian-Tlingit of the far north, and the Kwakiutl of British Columbia, with the Nootka of Vancouver Island, both characterized by a highly developed red cedar wood carving art of totem poles, house fronts, masks and other ceremonial items, distinctive totemic painting and superb basketry. In the southern area, through present Washington and Oregon, this distinctive culture weakened, although the Coast Salish produced some carving and fine basketry, and the Chinook held occasional Potlatch ceremonies like those of the north. The Potlatch was basically a wealth display and distribution festival held by prominent men, which became exaggerated due to the activities of the Hudson's Bay Company, who infiltrated the coastal areas during the early 19th century.

The art of carving and erecting large memorial columns (totem poles) is probably not ancient on the north Pacific coast. Early explorers do not seem to have remarked on them, so we may speculate that it was the acquisition of metal tools from traders that gave the Indians the means of developing techniques to express their wood carving art in its most exaggerated forms. Before these totems had reached their imposing proportions, carving seems to have been used for grave posts, house fronts, masks and stone objects of considerable antiquity. We can also speculate that carved poles were fashionable, with ambitious chiefs announcing their wealth and identity by the comm-emoration of ancestors whose

spirits could be beautifully represented in animal, bird or mythological forms — Eagle, Raven, Owl, Bear, Beaver, Wolf, Frog, Shark, Whale, Halibut and Salmon—on impressive poles (see also Glossary).

Along the coast of Washington and Oregon, the zoomorphic carving and painting of the northern tribes diminished. The Chinooks were great traders of dried salmon, dentalium shells and sometimes slaves from California, in return for goods from the northern tribes. Houses were more crudely made, and for single families. In southern Oregon and northwestern California, head deformation, as practiced in the north on young children, was unknown. Redwood replaced cedar as the primary wood, and deerskin robes and skirts replaced the woven cedar bark robes of the north.

Shamanistic secret societies, such as the Cannibal Dancers of the Kwakiutl, were unknown in the south. The southern tribes made fine basketry or imported it from the Californian tribes further south.

Northwest Coast culture collapsed largely through the conversion of the tribes to Christianity, the influence of the Gold Rush in Alaska and the Yukon, and the invasion of the Oregon and Washington river valleys by settlers during the 19th century. Their population was drastically reduced in some areas, and the whole culture fell into decay, while Canadian governmental pressure forced potlatching to be abandoned among the Kwakiutl, with the confiscation of many ceremonial objects that have only recently been returned.

TLINGIT The Tlingit were a group of Northwest Coast Indians along the south coast of Alaska, between the present northern part of British Columbia and the ocean. Although primarily a fisher folk they were favorably situated to become highly successful traders, acting as middlemen between the interior Alaskan tribes and white traders. They were fine woodcarvers, rank high as basket makers and are renowned for their "Chilkat blankets" of mountain goat wool and cedar bark. The basic political group was the village, divided

Above: Kwakiutl woman (standing). Chief's wife holding a broken "copper," inviting a rival chief to at least match its value or acknowledge his social inferiority. Her tunic-dress of trade cloth is covered with cut-out totemic figures in contrasting colors. The "button blanket" cloak is covered with designs outlined in white shell-like traded buttons. A Haida woman sits below her. She is wrapped in a trade blanket and wears a silver nose ring and a large labret through the lower lip — a symbol of high rank.

Above: Tlingit, c. 1860. Armor of heavy hide and wooden slats is worn with a heavy wooden helmet with totemic crest mounted on a wooden collar with vision and ventilation slits. The knife and club had blades of whalebone, trade iron or copper, and crest images. Early hide clothing probably approximated that of the interior Athabascans. Moccasins resembled the Subarctic form with vamp, front toe seam, or sometimes blunt squared-toe seam. Interclan wars to avenge injury or insult were sometimes settled by mock battles.

Above: Tlingit, c. 1900. Woman wearing shaman's headdress with exaggerated simulated bear claws, probably of mountain goat horn, and a beaded cloth tunic.

Above: Tlingit bark sling cradle, c. 1890. The button cap is Tlingit in style, the moccasins and bark sling probably of neighboring Athabascan origin.

into two phratries, Wolf and Raven totems. They lived in large community houses like most West Coast people, and were dependent on the sea for food. Recent linguistic studies suggest that the Tlingit are related to the Athabascan and Haida, together termed "Na-Dene."

The principal Tlingit subtribes were, north to south (but excluding the so-called "Inland Tlingit," an Athabascan people), as follows: *Yakutat* (Yakutat Bay), *Gonaho* (mouth of Alsek River), *Chilkat* (Lynn Canal), *Huna* (Goss Sound), *Auk* (Stephens Passage), *Taku* (Taku River and Inlet), *Hutsnuwu* or *Killisnoo* (Admiralty Island), *Sitka* (Baranof and Chichagof Islands), *Sumdum* (Port Houghton), *Kuiu* (Kuiu Island), *Kake* (Kupreanof Island), *Stikine* (Stikine River), *Henya* (west coast Prince of Wales Island), *Hehl* (on Behm Canal), *Sanya* (Cape Fox) and Tongass (Portland Canal).

They numbered some 10,000 in 1740; 6,763 in 1880; and 3,895 in 1950. By 1970, their numbers had recovered to about 7,000. By 2001, there were 15,000 reported in Alaska. Their main locations today are Yakutat, Klukwan, Juneau, Mount Edgecumbe, Sitka, Kake, Wrangell, Ketchikan and Klawak.

Above: Tlingit c. 1900. Decorated with carved and painted totemic designs, this hat has a raven crest topped with two woven rings (reflecting clan status or the number of Potlatches given), to which are attached ermine skins.

Left: Tlingit and Haida canoe. The southern Tlingit made canoes of red cedar, but all Tlingit preferred the great Haida canoes, up to 60 feet (18 m) long with masts and sails, which could carry several tons of freight. Such "war canoes," purchased by Tlingit chiefs, bore their carved and painted crests at bow and stern.

HAIDA These people were the original inhabitants of the Queen Charlotte Islands, Canada, and part of Prince of Wales Island in Alaska. They had the most spectacular culture of the Northwest Coast tribes. They lived in large community houses of heavy hand-hewn timber, decorated inside and out with carved and painted figures of massive proportions. Their totem poles were the finest and tallest, and they are equally noted for their carvings in black argillite, a soft stone found in the Queen Charlotte Islands. Spanish explorers were probably the first Europeans to reach the islands in the 18th century, followed by numerous traders and, finally, by the establishment of a Hudson's Bay post at Masset.

Originally the Haida numbered 8,000, but by 1895 had been reduced by smallpox, consumption (tuberculosis) and liquor to only 593 in two remaining villages, Masset and Skidegate, Queen Charlotte Islands, with about the same number (known as *Kaigani*) at Kassan and Hydaburg on Prince of Wales Island, Alaska. In 1960 there were 391 in Alaska (2,000 in 2001), and in 1970 there were 1,367 in Canada, mostly at Masset and Skidegate. That number increased to 2,265 by 2001. The Haida language formed a separate speech family, but a distant connection with the Athabascan and Tlingit has been suggested as a stock called "Na-Dene."

Above: Haida Indians from Queen Charlotte Islands, late 19th century, wearing Chilkat blankets made of cedar bark twine and mountain goat wool. These blankets were called "Chilkats" as they were made by a Tlingit tribe of Southern Alaska who bore the same name. The men wear carved wooden headdress frontlets decorated with abalone shell and ermine fur.

Above Left: Masked Haida shaman, c. 1880, with bird-down decoration in his hair and around his neck. The blanket of commercial wool is worn over a tunic-kilt of native textiles, shredded cedar bark and twisted mountain goat wool, with brilliant blue-green designs, woven like the so-called Chilkat blankets imported from the Tlingit of southern Alaska. The bottom edge is fringed with puffin beaks.

Below: Haida house, c. 1880. Northwest Coast peoples used varying construction forms for houses of thick cedar planks on massive beams and columns with portal-framed gable ends, the roof beams supporting overlapping plank roofs. The Haida often used six roof beams, supported on corner columns and via portals at each gable positioned either side of façade posts carved with the crests of the owner and his wife. The original entrance was at the base of the post. Many families could live in such a house, some of which were up to 50 feet (15 m) long, each with their own apartment on platforms separated by mats or partitions.

Left: Haida chief c. 1888. The ceremonial basketry hat is painted in red, white and black designs showing the crest of the wearer. His Chilkat blanket is woven by women, with cedar bark and goat wool motifs designed by men to represent their clan or lineage crests. Shield-shaped plaques of sheet copper, (brought in by Europeans) were highly prized as wealth symbols — representing the value of wealth distributed at Potlatch ceremonies to validate the social status of the sponsor.

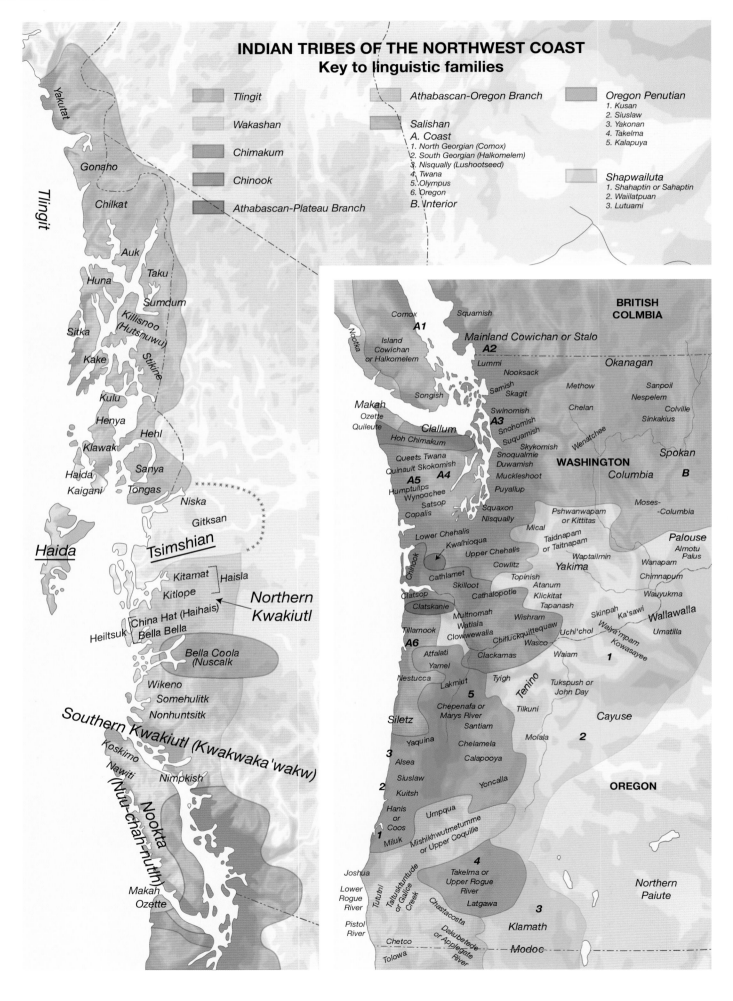

INDIAN TRIBES OF THE NORTHWEST COAST
Key to linguistic families

Tlingit

Wakashan

Chimakum

Chinook

Athabascan-Plateau Branch

Athabascan-Oregon Branch

Salishan
A. Coast
1. North Georgian (Comox)
2. South Georgian (Halkomelem)
3. Nisqually (Lushootseed)
4. Twana
5. Olympus
6. Oregon
B. Interior

Oregon Penutian
1. Kusan
2. Siuslaw
3. Yakonan
4. Takelma
5. Kalapuya

Shapwailuta
1. Shahaptin or Sahaptin
2. Waiilatpuan
3. Lutuami

Tlingit

Yakutat
Gonaho
Chilkat
Auk
Taku
Huna
Sumdum
Sitka
Killisnoo (Hutsnuwu)
Kake
Stikine
Kulu
Henya
Hehl
Klawak
Sanya
Haida
Kaigani
Tongas

Haida

Tsimshian

Niska
Gitksan

Kitamat
Kitlope
Haisla
China Hat (Haihais)
Heiltsuk
Bella Bella

Northern Kwakiutl

Bella Coola (Nuscalk)

Wikeno
Somehulitk
Nonhuntsitk

Southern Kwakiutl (Kwakwaka'wakw)

Koskimo
Nawiti
Nimpkish

Nootka (Nuu-chah-nulth)

Makah
Ozette

BRITISH COLUMBIA

Comox
Squamish
A1
Nootka
Island Cowichan or Halkomelem
Mainland Cowichan or Stalo
A2
Lummi
Okanagan
Makah
Ozette
Songish
Samish
Skagit
Methow
Chelan
Sanpoil
Nespelem
Colville
Sinkakius
Quileute
Clallam
Swinomish
A3
Snohomish
Suquamish
Wenatchee
Spokan
Hoh Chimakum
Skykomish
Snoqualmie
Duwamish
Queets Twana
Muckleshoot
WASHINGTON
Quinault Skokomish
A4
Puyallup
Columbia
B
Humptulips
Wynoochee
Satsop
Copalis
Squaxon
Nisqually
Pshwanwapam or Kittitas
Moses-Columbia
Mical
A5
Lower Chehalis
Kwalhioqua
Taidnapam or Taitnapam
Waptailmin
Palouse
Almotu Palus
Upper Chehalis
Chinook
Cowlitz
Yakima
Wanapam
Cathlamet
Topinish
Atanum
Chimnapum
Skilloot
Clatsop
Cathlapotle
Klickitat
Tapanash
Skinpah
Ka'sawi
Wauyukma
Clatskanie
Multnomah
Watlala
Wishram
Wallawalla
Tillamook
Clowwewalla
Chifluckquittequaw
Wasco
Uchi'chol
Waiya'mpam
Kowasayee
Umatilla
A6
Atfalati
Clackamas
Waiam
Nestucca
Yamel
Uchi'chol
1
Lakmiut
Tyigh
Waiam
Siletz
5
Tenino
Tukspush or John Day
Chepenafa or Marys River
Santiam
Tilkuni
Cayuse
Yaquina
Chelamela
Molala
2
3
Alsea
Calapooya
Siuslaw
Kuitsh
Yoncalla
OREGON
Hanis or Coos
Umpqua
2
Miluk
Mishikhwutmetumme or Upper Coquille
1
Joshua
4
Takelma or Upper Rogue River
Northern Paiute
Lower Rogue River
Latgawa
Pistol River
Chastacosta
Klamath
3
Chetco
Dakubetede or Applegate River
Modoc
Tolowa
Tututni
Taltushtuntude or Galice Creek

TSIMSHIAN This family is a combination of three closely related tribes of northern British Columbia: the *Tsimshian proper*, on the lower Skeena River and Annette Island, Alaska; the *Niska* or *Nishga*, on the Nass River and neighboring coast; and the *Gitksan* or *Kitksan*, on the upper Skeena River. They may be distantly related to the Chinook and hence to the speculative stock, the Penutians. As fishers they took salmon, codfish and halibut, and at the same time hunted seals, sea lions and whales. The interior bands hunted bear and deer and collected berries. Villages consisted of large wooden houses of cedar planks, arranged in a row facing the sea or river. Canoes and boats were placed in front on runways or on the beach. Four phratries — Raven, Wolf, Eagle and Grizzly Bear — were distributed amongst the three tribes. They were part of the strong art and carving tradition of the coastal people, and shared with the Tlingit and Haida the northern center of this remarkable culture.

The coastal Tsimshian were probably visited by Spanish, English and American navigators, and later the Hudson's Bay Company established posts in the early 19th century. Their country was also overrun by miners during the Klondike Gold Rush. The Tsimshians have reserves in their old territory at Metlakatla (Alaska), Port Simpson, Metlakatla, Kitselas (Tsimshian proper), Gitlakdamix, Canyon, Greenville, Kincolith (Niska), Kispaiox, Hazelton, Kitwancool, Kitwanga and Kitsegukla (Kitksan). In 1780, the whole group numbered 5,500. In 1908, there were 1,840 Tsimshian. In 1906, there were 814 Niska, and in 1902 there were 1,120 Kitksan. In 1970, the same groups numbered 2,863, 2,364 and 2,503, respectively in British Columbia. By 2005, those numbers had increased to 6,045 Tsimshian and 5,515 Niska. In 1950, there were 797 at New Metlakatla, Alaska; 1,209 in 1990; and 2,200 in 2001.

WAKASHAN

This is a language family of Indian tribes formed by two separate groups: the Nootka, of the west coast of Vancouver Island, and the Kwakiutl, of the northern coast of the Island and large parts of the adjacent coastal mainland of British Columbia. The Wakashan group has been suggested to be remotely connected to the Salishan and Chimakum into a larger linguistic grouping known as "Mosan."

NOOTKA or **NUTKA (NUU-CHAH-NULTH)** An important native people of the western shore of Vancouver Island, from Cape Cook on the north to beyond Barkley Sound were the Nootka. Although they were known to European maritime explorers from 1592 on, Captain Cook gave the first accounts of these Indians in 1778. The settlement of Victoria and the missionary work of the Roman Catholic

Above: Tsimshian memorial ("totem") poles, c. 1910, at Kitwanga on the Skeena River, British Columbia, home of the Gitksan tribe, an important Northwest Coast people who excelled at wood carving.

Below: Nootka man, c. 1778. A sketch made at Nootka Sound, Vancouver Island, during James Cook's third voyage is the basis for this man, wearing a woven hat depicting a whaling scene and a fur cloak. He has ear pendants and facial painting and carries arrows with barbed bone points in a fur quiver, and a bow of the type used for warfare and hunting land game and sea otter.

Church gradually modified the traditional Nootka culture. The Nootka were both a sea and river people. They fished for halibut and cod, gathered kelp and hunted whales, seals and sea otters as well as gathered berries, fruits and roots. They were an integral part of Northwest Coast culture. While their carving and painting were generally not as elaborate as those of the northern tribes, they excelled in basketry. They are believed to have numbered 6,000 in 1780, slowly reduced to 2,159 by 1907. By 1970, however, they had recovered to 3,409; 4,720 in 1984; and 5,127 in 2005. They have continued to occupy 18 small village reserves on Vancouver Island, the main ones at Kyoquot, Ahousaht, Clayoquot, Hesquiaht, Nootka, Ochiet, Port Alberni (Sheshaht) and Ucluelet.

MAKAH Makah is a branch of the Nootka, located on Cape Flattery, Washington. Spanish, British and American trading vessels contacted the Makahs by the end of the 18th century. Their economy was based upon the sea, and they hunted whales and seals. The Makah were

---

TRIBES OF THE NORTHWEST COAST, c. 1780–1850

The geographical nature of this area dictates that it be illustrated in two vertical halves, northern on the left, southern on the right. Linguistic and cultural boundaries are necessarily approximate; these sketch maps are intended only as a general guides to distribution. Underlined names indicate small linguistic families distinct from larger groupings indicated by the shading key.

Left: Bella Coola Indian wearing a mask dramatizing the supernatural being Echo. The dancer wears a cloth blanket decorated with trade buttons. The Bella Coola—also called Nuxalk—were an isolated Salishan tribe below Dean Channel, British Columbia, where their descendants remain. Photograph by Harlan I. Smith c. 1910.

Below: Nootka woman, c. 1900. This young woman wears her hair in woolen bands with strings of beads tipped with traded thimble "jinglers," signifying puberty. The comb pinned to her cedar bark cloak enables her to touch her head without violating menstrual restrictions.

Opposite, Below: Masked dancer of the Kwakiult Hamatsa Society. These mechanical masks are earthly representatives of a giant cannibal spirit in the form of a raven, a Crooked-Beak of Heaven, and a Crane. They try to lure a young initiate into evil while relatives and tribal members work to reclaim him. These masks have moveable beaks making clacking sounds.

Below: Kwakwaka'wakw Nation (Kwakiutl) Crooked Beak Hamat'sa mask, carved by the Nimpkish artist Godfrey Bruce of Alert Bay.

Above: The Vancouver Island Nootka weavers Annie Williams and Emma George, photographed at the 1904 St. Louis Exposition where they demonstrated their expertise in basketry.

Below: Nootka, c. 1850. Ordinary woven basketry cradles were regarded as temporary and expendable. Others, usually of cedar boards, padded with shredded bark and mountain goat wool, were carved and painted with the crest of the child for whom they were intended, and had permanent and sometimes ceremonial value.

involved with a treaty in 1855, which established their reservation on the tip of Cape Flattery, within their former homeland. They probably numbered 2,000 in 1805, but declined due to smallpox to about 500 in 1850. They numbered 435 in 1905; 919 in 1985; 1,079 in 1992; and 2,389 in 2001. The modern Makah have a museum, and hold native language classes. "Makah Days," annual gatherings for salmon barbecues, canoe races and Indian dances, are held each August.

OZETTE This is probably a subgroup of the Makah, occupying a village at the mouth of the Ozette River, Washington, south of their kin. Sites around the village seem to have been occupied for several hundred years. In 1872, some 200 people lived there, and at a small reservation established at Cape Alava in 1893. However, in the years since then the Ozettes have drifted away to other reservations, and by 1937 only one person remained. Recent archaeological excavations at the old village site have revealed the importance of whaling and other maritime pursuits. Various fine examples of material culture have also been recovered from the site.

KWAKIUTL The Kwakiutl is the second division of the Wakashan family, who occupied the whole coast of British Columbia, except for the Bella Coola, from Douglas Channel to Cape Mudge. They effectively formed a number of village tribulets, which can be arranged dialectically as follows:

Above: Makah man, Neah Bay, Washington State, c. 1910, wearing wolf mask and blanket decorated with buttons in totemic designs. Displayed in the foreground are other carved and painted masks typical of Northwest Coast tribes. The Makahs still inhabit the northwest tip of the Olympic Peninsula, Washington.

Below Right: Kwakiutl winter ceremony dancers, c. 1900. These expressed, in long, dramatic public ceremonial, the characteristics of sinister supernatural beings, to reclaim for humanity tribal members believed to have fallen victim to their influence during winter visitations. Standing is the briefly seen bee or wasp dancer, whose arm slats clack when in motion. Crouching is the Hamatsa bird monster, whose masks had clacking, string-operated lower beaks. Shredded cedar bark fringes covered the shoulders under a full-length bark cape. Dancers became members of the secret societies they had represented in the dramas.

Above: Part of a Kwakiutl village on Gilford Island, between the mainland and Vancouver Island, c. 1885. The cedar plank houses show white influence (jack roofs, windows), but the painted sea monster and carved double-headed serpent (sisiutl) on the gables indicate the house of an important leader. Villages usually faced the water — note the beached canoes.

The most important winter ceremonial of the Kwakwaka-wakw (Southern Kwakiutl) was that of the Hamatsa Society during which a number of articulated masks were worn representing a complex cast of characters including maneating associates of the Great Cannibal Spirit (Baxwbakwalanuksiwe). The most spectacular of these masks represents "Crooked Beak of Heaven," one of the mythical birds of the upper regions. The dramatic ritual which took at least four days to complete was based on legends of the bird-monsters who inhabited the sky-world and were eaters of human flesh, terrifying apparitions as they searched for human bodies to consume. During the course of the ritual initiates became increasingly calm as their spirits were recaptured by their human families. The example on page 253 was carved by Godfrey Bruce Nimpkish (a branch of the Southern Kwakiutl at Alert Bay and Hope Island) Vancouver Island.

They were known to English and American coastal marine explorers during the late 18th century, but it was the establishment of the Hudson's Bay posts in the mid-19th century that profoundly modified Kwakiutl culture, particularly among the northern groups. In 1780, the northern branches numbered 2,700 and the southern tribes 4,500. But by 1906, they numbered only 852 and 1,257, respectively. In 1970, the Haisla and Heiltsuk numbered 848 (Kitamaat) and 1,245 (Bella Bella, Oweekano etc.), respectively; and the Southern Kwakiutl 2,715 (Alert Bay, Fort Rupert etc.). They are particularly noted for their superb woodcarving and painting art, for totem poles, house gable fronts and columns, mortuary posts and masks. They also participated in the wealth display and distribution complex known as the Potlatch ceremony, which was accompanied by feasting, hospitality, and the bestowal of gifts in honor of important headmen, but which also led to family

starting in the north, the *Haisla* division were the Kitamaat on Douglas Channel and the Kitlope on Gardner Canal; the *Heiltsuk* division were the Bella Bella on Dean Channel and Milbanke Sound, China Hat or Haihais on Mussel Inlet, Somehulitk and Nohuntsitk on Wikeno Lake, and Wikeno or Oweekano on Rivers Inlet; the Southern Kwakiutl (or Kwakwaka-wakw) were the *Kwakiutl* proper of Smith Inlet, Kingcome Inlet, Gilford and Turnour Islands, Knight Inlet on the mainland, Hope Island (Nawiti), Alert Bay (Nimpkish), Klaskino Inlet (Koskimo), Quatsino and Fort Rupert (Kwawkewltk) on Vancouver Island.

feuding. In recent years Alert Bay has seen a revival of Kwakiutl art and culture. The Campbell River and Cape Mudge bands presently considered Kwakiutl may have been at least in part Comox.

In 2005 there were a reported 3,957 Northern and 4,493 Southern Kwakiutl living throughout British Columbia.

SALISHAN (COAST)

The coastal division of the Salishan family occupied the coastal area of British Columbia, from the Strait of Georgia south through the Puget Sound area of Washington State, along the coast as far south as the Siletz River, Oregon, except around the mouth of the Columbia River (occupied by the Chinook). There was one detached northern branch, the Bella Coola of Burke Channel, British Columbia. The Coast Salish practiced the wealth and gift distribution ceremony known as Potlatch, particularly in the north where they were influenced by the Kwakiutl culture. They generally lived in cedar plank houses facing rivers or the sea. And, where in contact with the

Left: Kwakiutl war dancer with hoisting frame, photographed in 1904 by Charles H. Carpenter. Charles Nowell, who posed for this picture, was one of the last Kwakiutl dancers to be suspended by his pierced skin. The artifacts are now in the Field Museum, Chicago. Cambridge University Museum of Archaeology & Anthropology.

Below: Bella Coola Indians, brought to Germany by the Norwegian ship's captain Adrian Jacobsen, performing a dance from the winter ceremonial cycle in Berlin, c. 1885. Cambridge University Museum of Archaeology & Anthropology.

Kwakiutl, have a tradition of complex woodcarving art, which weakened to the south into simpler art forms. Two dominant subsistence and material resources among the Salish were salmon and red cedar, and they excelled in basketry and textiles. They were essentially a river and bay people in a heavy forest area with a moist, mild climate.

BELLA COOLA (NUXALK) These were a Salish people living on the north and south Bentinck Arm of the Burke Channel, British Columbia, surrounded by northern branches of the Kwakiutl and sharing with them the typical Northwest Coast cultural traits. They have continued to occupy the village of Bella Coola, and were reported to number 311 in 1902, 334 in 1949, 597 in 1970 and 1,398 in 2005. They are not to be confused with the Bella Bella, a local Kwakiutl branch.

COMOX Comox were a Salish people at the northern end of the Strait of Georgia, on both sides of Discovery Passage and centering on Cape Mudge. Culturally they were heavily influenced by the Southern Kwakiutl. Their descendants are still connected with their former villages at Klahoose, Homalco and Sliammon on the Islands and British Columbia mainland, plus the Courtenay and Campbell River bands on Vancouver Island. The tribe was reported to number 828 in 1970, and 1,957 in 2005. The Seechelt and Pentlatch were very closely related to the Comox, and they are now called collectively "Northern Coast Salish."

SEECHELT these are a Salish people on the southern arms of Jervis Inlet, British Columbia, numbering 236 in 1902 at their village. The same village was returned at 471 in 1970, 708 in 1987 and 1,159 in 2005.

PUNTLATCH or **PENTLATCH** The Puntlatch are a small group on Vancouver Island near Qualicum, sometimes classed as Comox or Cowichan. There were 42 people under the name Qualicum in 1970 and 104 in 2005.

SQUAMISH A Salish people at the northern end of Howe Sound and Burrard Inlet, mainland British Columbia, originally in many villages but restricted to six villages in 1909. In 1970, 1,143 were reported from Burrard Inlet and 1,089 from Squamish. In 2005 a total of 3,888 was registered

NANAIMO and **SNONOWAS** These are two small Salish groups who belong with the Cowichan group, with whom they are often considered as one, living on Vancouver Island near present Nanaimo. In 1907 the Nanaimo were given as 161; in 1970, 525. The Snonowas are now listed under the name Nanoose, given as 46 in 1907, 86 in 1970 and 210 in 2005.

COWICHAN or **ISLAND HALKOMELEM** The Cowichan occupied the southeastern coast of Vancouver Island between the Comox to the north and the Songish to the south, including a number of islands. The term is also sometimes extended to the mainland Stalo or Fraser River Cowichan. Their native life was disrupted in the early 19th century when Hudson's Bay traders came to the area, leading to the foundation of Victoria. There are six major Vancouver Cowichan groups — Chemainus, Cowichan, Halalt, Lyacksun, Malahat and Penelakut. Their descendants numbered 2,184 in 1970, and 15,560 in 2005, but this total no doubt includes a number of Coast Salish groups and mainland Stalo.

SONGISH or **SANETCH** or **STRAITS** A group of Salish people on the southern coast of Vancouver Island including adjacent islands are known as Songish. The founding of Victoria in the 1840s brought to an end independent native life. A number of Songish reserves still exist — Tseycum, Beecher Bay, Panquachin, Tsawout, Esquimalt, Tsartlip, Sooke and Songhees — in their old territory, and they numbered about 1,130 in 1970, and 3,176 in 2005. The Songish, Cowichan, Squamish, Semiahmoo, Lummi, Clallam and Nooksack are now sometimes collectively termed "Central Coast Salish."

STALO or **STAWLO** or **FRASER RIVER COWICHAN (MAINLAND HALKOMELEM)** The mainland Cowichan occupied the lower Fraser River valley from Yale to where the city of Vancouver now stands. In 1809 Simon Fraser passed through their country, and their subsequent history was linked to the Hudson's Bay Company. By the end of the 19th century, approximately 30 small villages became Indian reserves that still exist. The largest are Katzie, Chehalis, Cheam, Skwah, Soowahlie, Tzeachten, Seabird Island and Musqueam. In 1970 they numbered 2,650 or so, and a total of 6,031, when including their Vancouver Island relatives (Island Halkomelem). Their numbers have been counted among the Cowichan since.

SEMIAHMOO These were a small, apparently separate Salish band at the boundary between British Columbia and Washington State, where 24 were reported at a small reserve bearing their name in 1970. That number had grown to 76 by 2005. They were probably closely related to the Songish and Lummi.

Left: Cowichan/Halkomelem spirit dancer. An early representation of the Spirit Dance headdress originally of hair, sometimes later of wool, and topped with feathers. Dancers used twirling movements hinting at the identity of the spirit power, usually an encounter with an animal in human form as a guardian spirit. The complex, still active among modern Coast Salish, with initiation and dramatic ritual, is usually held in winter, and used as therapy for illness, and alcohol or drug abuse.

Top Left: Masked "Sxwayxwey" dancer, Mainland-Halkomelem (Fraser River-Cowichan), British Columbia, Canada, c.1920. These masks have characteristic eye protrusions and horns or ears, usually carved in the form of a bird or beast. They are used in one class of public performance for persons undergoing life crises or changes in status, usually during potlatches. These masks are generally made from cedar wood and are most often attributed to the Central Coast Salish groups.

Top Right: Cowichan warrior in a feather headdress—a Curtis photo published in volume 9 of The North American Indian.

Above Left: A family of Lummi Indians in native regalia, c. 1915.

Above Right: A Cowichan tule gatherer—a Curtis photo published in the supplement to volume 9 of The North American Indian.

NOOKSACK The Nooksack were a small Salish tribe on the Nooksack River, northern Washington State. After the Point Elliott Treaty of 1855, they were to move to the Lummi Reservation, but few did. They have maintained themselves around Everson, Nooksack and Deming, Whatcom County, on fragmented allotments of 3,000 acres (1,200 ha), with a population of 505 in 1970; 1,168 in 1991; and 1,537 in 2001.

LUMMI The Lummi were related to the Songish of southern Vancouver Island and lived around Lummi and Bellingham

bays, Washington. Signatories to the Point Elliott Treaty, 1855, they relinquished a large area and moved to the Lummi Reservation, where they numbered 3,889 in 2001. A small group, *Swallah*, on the San Juan Islands, were probably very closely related to or were part of the Lummi.

SAMISH A small group inhabiting various islands south of Bellingham Bay, Guemes Island area, Washington, were the Samish. A few joined the Lummi, but most maintained themselves off reservations around the Anacortes district. One modern group, known as *San Juan Indians*, are probably descendants at least in part of this tribe. They have a few hundred descendants, mostly counted among the San Juan. They are related to the various groups now called "Central Coast Salish."

UPPER and LOWER SKAGIT

This includes a group of Indians on the Skagit River in Whatcom and Skagit counties, Washington. Influenced by the Hudson's Bay traders from 1827 onward, they were included in the Point Elliott Treaty of 1855. The Lower Skagit of Whidbey Island, Puget Sound and the mouth of the Skagit River have a few descendants in the Bow and Edison area, but have largely disappeared. The Upper Skagit descendants live in numerous scattered public domain allotments in Skagit County, near Sedro Woolley and other places. They number 300 or so. Another modern group in the area, the *Sauk-Suiattle*, are also descendants of the Skagit River Indians and number about 260. A few members of this group joined the Lummi and Swinomish. The small *Kikiallus* band of Mount Vernon and the *Stillaguamish* at Arlington and on the river of the same name can be included in this group. In 1992, the Upper Skagit numbered 552. The Upper and Lower Skagit were reported at 708 in 2001.

SWINOMISH

This tribe occupied the mouth of the Skagit River and Whidbey Island, being closely related to the Skagit. They were a sea-oriented people, living on fish and other marine life. After the Point Elliott Treaty of 1855, most Swinomish people moved to the Swinomish Reservation. In 1985 the "Swinomish" numbered 624, but a number of Skagit, Samish, Snohomish, Suquamish and Duwamish have joined the Swinomish over the years. The early population of these Salish coastal tribes cannot be accurately estimated as serious epidemics reduced many in the early years of the 19th century. The Swinomish, Skagit, Stillaguamish and Snohomish are now collectively called "Northern Lushootseed."

SNOHOMISH

This tribe lived at the mouth of the Snohomish River near Marysville and southern Whidbey Island, Washington. They were among the various tribes trading at Fort Nisqually from 1833 on. After the Point Elliott Treaty of 1855, they moved to the Snohomish Reservation, now called the Tulalip Reservation, where they formed a large part of the multitribal grouping there, numbering 1,099 in 1985 under the name "Tulalip." That number — again, combining numerous tribes — increased to 4,027 in 2001.

SNOQUALMIE and SKYKOMISH

These are two closely related groups of the Snoqualmie and Tolt river basins. As signatories to the Point Elliott Treaty some were included with the Snohomish at Tulalip, but most remained off reservations in their old territory. They now number perhaps 700 descendants.

SUQUAMISH

The Suquamish occupied an area between Hood Canal and Puget Sound. Suquamish subsistence depended upon the harvest of fish, shellfish, roots and berries. The Port Madison Reservation was established for the Suquamish after the Point Elliott Treaty of 1855. Some 200 tribal members still lived on the reservation in 1985, but many more live in surrounding areas. In 1990, 780 Suquamish were reported, and 863 were counted in 2001.

DUWAMISH

The Duwamish lived on the east side of Puget Sound, near the site of the present city of Seattle. Chief Seattle was a member of this tribal group. A few members of this group moved to Port Madison, Muckleshoot and other reservations, and a number survived off-reservation. They have about 400 descendants, although many have merged with the Suquamish. The *Sammamish* were a Duwamish subtribe.

Above: Salish temporary house, c. 1870. The coast Salish people around Puget Sound built cedar plank houses of monopitch, double pitch, and hip end forms, though lacking the carved and painted façades of more northerly tribes. Temporary summer camp dwellings, as illustrated, were constructed of poles covered with cedar bark or skillfully woven cattail mats.

TWANA or SKOKOMISH

A large body of Salish on the Hood Canal, Washington are the Twana. They had wide trading ties, and a complex ceremonial and social structure, including the use of slaves. They signed the Point-No-Point Treaty of 1855 and moved to the Skokomish Reservation at the head of Hood Canal. Their population was 507 in 1984; 630 in 1990; and 750 in 2001. This also included the last of the Chimakum people and a few Clallam. In 2010, 13,241 "Puget Sound Salish" as a whole were reported.

CLALLAM

The most numerous, warlike and powerful tribe of the Coast Salish people in present Washington State were the Clallam. Their population before the epidemics of the early 19th century was between 2,000 and 3,000. As traders, they linked with their relatives on Vancouver Island and Twana, and even with Indians beyond the Cascade Mountains. Their location was present Clallam County below the Strait of Juan de Fuca, between Port Discovery Canal and the Hoh River. They were under the influence of the Hudson's Bay Company until the Point-No-Point Treaty of 1855, when a few moved to the Skokomish Reservation, but most remained in Clallam County. Three reservation

Right: Muckleshoot tumpline basket, 19th century. For collecting and storing fruit, vegetables and shellfish, women of the Coast Salish tribes used baskets — large ones being supported by a tumpline across the forehead. Baskets in the Cascades region were mainly coiled: stiff coils of cedar or spruce roots decorated by covering with strips of colored bear grass or cherry bark — a technique known as imbrication. Twined basketry was favored north and south of this region. This young Muckleshoot woman wears a rain-repellent cape and skirt of shredded cedar bark.

communities have been established over the years — Lower Elwha near Port Angeles, Jamestown and Port Gamble — with a total enrolled population of more than 2,500, but they have more descendants in the greater west coast area. They now prefer the name of S'Klallam.

MUCKLESHOOT These were a Salish tribe on the White River, a few miles inland from Puget Sound near present Kent and Auburn, where a reservation is located that bears their name. They were probably an amalgam of several minor groups combined after the Medicine Creek Treaty of 1854. The Muckleshoots numbered 194 in 1937; 425 in 1984; and 1,712 in 2001.

PUYALLUP A Salish group related to the Nisqually who lived at the mouth of the Puyallup River and the southern end of Vashon Island, near the present city of Tacoma, Washington, were the Puyallup. After the Medicine Creek Treaty, the Puyallup were located mainly on the reservation that bears their name, a few miles from Tacoma. They were reported to number 322 in 1937; 1,286 in 1984; and 2,490 in 2001, but other groups have joined them over the years, including Cowlitz, Nisqually, Squaxon and others. By no means do all live on the reservation.

NISQUALLY The Nisqually were a large body of Indians in 40 villages on the Nisqually River, Thurston County, Washington, near present Olympia. They were included in the Medicine Creek Treaty of 1854, and most located at the Nisqually Reservation. The *Steilacooms* were a band probably related to the Nisqually or Puyallup, but never moved to either Nisqually or Puyallup reservations. The population of the Nisqually Reservation was 62 in 1937; 182 in 1984; 390 in 1990 and 525 in 2001 — a vast decline from their original population. The nonreservation Steilacooms claim several hundred descendants, mostly around the Tacoma area. The Nisqually, Squaxon. Steilacoom, Puyallup, Suquamish and Snoqualmie are now collectively called "Southern Lushootseed."

SQUAXON or **SQUAXIN** Related to the Nisqually, the Squaxon and closely connected *Sahehwamish* lived on the innermost inlets of Puget Sound, between Hood Canal, Budd Inlet and Nisqually River. After the Medicine Creek Treaty, a small reservation was established on Squaxon Island. But only a portion of these groups have lived there, given at 29 in 1949 and 302 in 1984. The so-called Shaker Church, a mixture of Christian and native beliefs, had its origins among the Squaxons and still has a following. Together with their linguistic relatives in the "Lushootseed" group and Twana they form the Southern Coast group of the Salishan family.

COWLITZ This includes several Salish groups on the middle and lower course of the Cowlitz River, Lewis County, Washington. They appear to have mixed with the *Kwalhioquas* and branches of the neighboring Chehalis groups, but probably numbered in excess of 1,000 in the early 19th century. They also had contacts with the interior tribes, particularly the Klickitats. Much reduced by epidemics in the 1850s, the Cowlitz merged with the Chehalis, Chinook and Klickitats, with descendants now counted at Puyallup, Quinault and Yakima reservations, although a number have maintained themselves in their ancestral homelands. They number 400 or so, but many others claim their descent.

UPPER CHEHALIS or **KWAIAILK** A number of Salish groups on the Upper Chehalis River, Washington, around present Oakville and Tenino in Grays Harbor, Lewis and Thurston Counties are considered Upper Chehalis. A combined group of Kwaiailks, Lower Chehalis and Chinook have occupied a small reservation at Oakville since 1864, with a population given as 382 in 1984, and 485 in 1993. In 2001, the total given for Upper and Lower Chehalis (and related bands) was 866.

LOWER CHEHALIS These were an important Salish group on the lower course of the Chehalis River, Washington, at the entrance to Grays Harbor. A few combined with the Upper Chehalis on the Chehalis Reservation; others merged with the Satsops, Humptulips and others on Quinault Reservation. A few may also have incorporated with the Chinook on the Shoalwater Indian Reservation, Tokeland. They do not exist today as an independent tribe. In the same general area are other minor tribes who seem to have been either divisions of the Chehalis groups or Quinault, but have been given independent status by various writers — the *Copalis*, north of Grays Harbor; the *Humptulips* and *Whiskah*, on the north shore of Grays Harbor; the *Wynoochee*, on the Wynoochee River; and the *Satsop* on the Satsop River — though these no longer exist as separate peoples. The Chehalis groups with the Cowlitz and Quinault form the Southwestern Coast Salish.

QUEETS or **QUAITSO** These were a Salish people on the Queets River, Jefferson County, Washington. They moved to the Quinault Reservation following the Quinault River Treaty in 1855, and are no longer reported separately from the other Indians on that reservation, although they probably have some 100 descendants.

QUINAULT The largest and most important Salish people on the Pacific shore of Washington State, living mainly in the valley of the Quinault River and near Taholah, the site of their principal village, are the Quinault. They remained fairly isolated until the Quinault River Treaty of 1855 and the establishment of their reservation. They probably numbered more than 1,000 at the time of Lewis and Clark's arrival in 1805. Diminished to a reported 196 in 1907 (probably a partial count), they numbered 1,293 in 1945; 1,623 in 1984; and 2,454 in 2001, with accessions from other tribes over the years. The tribe still holds canoe races, salmon barbecues and dances at Taholah at various times each year.

TILLAMOOK The Coast Salish domain was broken by the Chinook on the lower Columbia River, but they reappear south of that great river in present northwestern Oregon. The Tillamook and closely related bands, *Nehalem* and *Nestucca*, lived around the Nehalem and Salmon rivers in present Tillamook County, Oregon, and were the largest Coast Salish group south of the Columbia. Lewis and Clark estimated the group at 2,200 in 1805, but they had declined to 200 by 1900. A few Nestuccas appear to have been reported among the Grand Ronde Indians. The census of 1970 gave 139 for the whole group.

SILETZ The Siletz were the southernmost Salish tribe on the river that bears their name in Lincoln County, Oregon. Remnants were included on the Siletz Reservation as part of the much larger "Confederated Siletz" and are no longer reported separately.

CHIMAKUM

This describes a small linguistic family formed by the grouping of three tribes: the Chimakum proper, Quileute and Hoh. The Chimakum proper may have been a Quileute subgroup who lived around the southern shores of the Strait of Juan de Fuca, Washington State. They signed the Point-No-Point Treaty of 1855, but numbered fewer than 100 at that time. They joined the Twana at the Skokomish Reservation, where only three remained separate in 1890, and a few others merged with the Clallam.

QUILEUTE or **QUILLAYUTE** This was the principal tribe of the Chimakum family, at the mouth of the Quillayute River in Washington. The Pacific Ocean was their main source of subsistence, and they were proficient seal and whale hunters. They traded with American and Russian seafarers from 1792 on. Refusing to move to the large Quinault Reservation, they were assigned their own reservation at La Push, Washington, in 1889. They numbered 383 in 1985; 784 in 1992; and 658 in 2001.

HOH This tribe may have been originally a division of the Quileute people on the Hoh River, Washington. A small reservation was established for the tribe in 1893, at the mouth of the Hoh River, where a few people have lived ever since, with a population of 91 in 1985 and 139 in 2001.

CHINOOKIAN

A small family of Indians inhabiting the lower Columbia River in Washington and Oregon as far up that river as The Dalles were the Chinooks. The Chinooks were primarily a bay and river people, dependent on fishing (salmon) as well as hunting game. They lacked the developed woodcarving art of the West Coast tribes of British Columbia and northern Washington, although are often classified in the same cultural area. They have been classified as the Upper and Lower Chinook, referring to their location on the Columbia River. They were first noticed by Lewis and Clark in 1805, and afterwards were greatly diminished in numbers by diseases brought by white traders. The majority of the individual tribes forming this family became extinct as separate identities before 1900, but a few hundred have fused with other tribes on the Warm Springs, Yakima, Chehalis, Quinault and Grand Ronde reservations in Washington and Oregon. The largest single element by 1950 were the Wasco at Warm Springs, Oregon. A few have maintained themselves off reservations.

Before their decline in population, the Chinookian tribes became the greatest traders on the Columbia River, a great

water highway stretching from the immense interior land to the area of the coastal tribes. Their geographical position at the mouth of that river up to The Dalles gave them the opportunity to become middlemen in the development of trade relationships between the coast and the interior. The development of the Chinook Jargon, an Indian trade language based originally on Chinook words but later incorporating an increasing vocabulary of European origin, bears witness to the importance of the Chinook tribes in pre-1840 trade relations. Contacts and trade took place largely on the Columbia River at Celilo or The Dalles, when material culture from the northern edge of the Plains mingled with and was exchanged for material from as far as Alaska. From there the Nez Perce were the main outlet to the northern Plains via their associations with the Crow and, to a lesser extent, the Flathead.

THE "LOWER CHINOOK" CHINOOK PROPER or **LOWER CHINOOK** This was a Chinookian tribe inhabiting the mouth of the Columbia River, giving their name to include tribes to the interior, of similar language under the name Chinookian stock. Their territory extended to Shoalwater Bay in the north, and the tribe numbered 800 in 1800. They gained considerable fame through their trading with British and American companies, and the Chinook Jargon, a trade language of the northwest originally based on the Chinook language, existed until 1900. From Lewis and Clark, Nov. 1805:

"This Chinook nation is about 400 souls, inhabit the country on the small river which runs into bay below us and on the ponds to the northwest of us, live principally on fish and roots, they are well armed with fusees and sometimes kill elk, deer, and fowl."

Above: Head reshaping, c. 1846. Several Northwest Coast tribes, from the Bella Coola in the north to the Alsea in the south, reshaped the heads of babies, by use of an additional wooden slat slanting downward from the top and bound to the head or tied to the cradle base. The Chinook of the Columbia River valley practiced the most extreme flattening of the forehead. However, the so-called Flathead of western Montana did not follow this practice, despite their popular name.

Their few remnants mixed with the Chehalis or remained in public domain, and had almost disappeared as a separate people by 1945 when 120 "Upper Chinook" remained on the Quinault Reservation, Washington. Although of mixed origin, they included descendants of the Chinook proper. A few more have been associated with Shoalwater Bay and Chehalis reservations, and some have never been on reservations. In 1970 609 "Chinook" were reported, excluding Wasco, apparently accounting for the whole family. Two smaller groups, the *Wahkiakum* and *Willapa* Indians, probably belong to this group.

CLATSOP An important coastal Chinookian tribe of the Cape Adams area, Clatsop County, Oregon, were the Clatsop. From Lewis and Clark, who estimated their population at 300, in 1806:

"The Clatsaps, Chinnooks, Killamucks etc. are very loquacious and inquisitive; they possess good memories and have repeated to us the name and capacities of the vessels etc. of the many traders and others who have visited the mouth of the river (Columbia); they are generally low in stature, proportionably small, reather lighter complected and much more illy formed than the Indians on the Missouri and those of our frontier; they were generally cheerfull but never gay. With us their conversation generally turns upon subjects of trade, smoking, eating and women.

In common with other savage nations they make their women perform every species of domestic drudgery; their women are also compelled to gather roots and assist them in taking fish which articles form much the greater part of their subsistence; notwithstanding the servile manner in which they treat their women they pay much more respect to their judgement and opinions in many respects than most Indian nations."

With the mixed remnants of the other ruined neighboring tribes, they moved to the Grand Ronde Reservation, Oregon. In 1910 they were reported as numbering 26 persons. The Clatsop are not now separately entered among the general Indian population of the Grand Ronde Agency, the population of which was about 700 in 1955, although most had lost their identity as Indians. In 1956 the reservation and Indian people of Grand Ronde were no longer recognized, and the reservation as such was terminated. However, they have recently (1983–84) been reactivated and have filed land claims against the U.S. Government.

In 2001, population from the Grand Ronde Reservation was given as 4,706, including members of the Calapooya or Kalapooya, Clackamas, Tumwater (Chinook), Clatsop, Umpqua, Rogue River and others. They are known as the "Confederated Grand Ronde," and they receive the bulk of their income (since 1996) from a casino, but still derive some revenue from lumber as well.

CATHLAMET The Cathlamet was a tribe forming a dialect division of the Chinookian stock, near the mouth of the Columbia River in Oregon and Washington, to a point up that river near the present city of Rainier, on the south bank. In 1806 Lewis and Clark estimated them at 300:

"The Killamucks, Clatsops, Chinooks, Cathlahmahs and Wac-ki-a-cums resemble each other as well as in their person and dress as in their habits and manners their complexion is not remarkable, being the usual copper brown of the most tribes in North America."

About 50 or 60 were reported in 1849. A remnant of the Cathlamet may have moved to the Grand Ronde Reservation with the Clatsop, or to the Quinault Reservation with the mixed Chinook-Chehalis, but as a distinct group they no longer exist.

THE "UPPER CHINOOK" (KIKSHT)

SKILLOOT A small Chinookian tribe at the junction of the Cowlitz River and the Columbia River in Washington State are known as Upper Chinook. Their principal subdivision was the *Cooniac*. Dialectically, they were said to be close to the Clackamas. At the time of Lewis and Clark (1806) they were living on both sides of the Columbia, opposite the mouth of the Cowlitz and perhaps numbered 1,000, although often

reported considerably higher. In 1850 they numbered about 200, and continued to diminish until they lost separate identity. A few may have accompanied relatives to reservations, but they are not returned as separate. A number of nonreservation Indian descendants claim their ancestry.

CATHLAPOTLE These were a tribe or group of Chinookian Indians on the Lewis River in Clarke County, Washington, about 150 miles (290 km) from the mouth of the Columbia River. A few may have lasted until reservation days, but they are now extinct as an independent group.

MULTNOMAH or WAPPATO A Chinookian tribe of the Sauvie Islands at the mouth of the Willamette River, Oregon, were the Multnomah. Remnants joined with related groups and lost separate identity. They were closely related to the Clackamas. Several bands can be attributed to this tribe.

Above and Below: These bowls from the Wishram/Wasco region are made from mountain sheep horn. The carving style of the Chinookian and Salishan-speaking peoples of the Columbia River area of Washington is characterized by formal surface decoration that differs from the figural imagery of the more northerly regions. These elaborately carved bowls, with their raised ends and designs of interlocking triangles, were used for ceremonial purposes. They were probably made in the late 18th to mid-19th century.

WATLALA OR CASCADE INDIANS The Watlala were a Chinookian tribe at the Cascades of the Columbia River and the Willamette River in Oregon. Remnants joined the Wishram and Wasco and lost separate identity. They were related to the Clackamas.

CLOWWEWALLA These were a Chinookian tribe of the Clackamas dialect, formerly living in Oregon on the Willamette River, a tributary of the Columbia. They have for many years been extinct as a separate people. The *Cushooks, Chahcowahs, Willamette-Tumwater* and others were divisions of this tribe. The last of this people were said to be on the old Grand Ronde Reservation.

CLACKAMAS A tribal division of the Chinook stock giving their name to a dialect group were the Clackamas. They apparently moved to the Grand Ronde Reservation, Oregon, and remained separate until recently, 89 being reported under this name in 1945. This may, however, be a combination of various Chinook remnants.

CHILLUCKITTEQUAW This was a Chinookian tribe of Hood River on the south side of the Columbia, and on the north side of the Columbia in Klickitat and Skamania Counties, Washington, along the White Salmon River. A few remained separate as late as 1895, mixed with a few Tenino (Waiam) at Celilo Falls, Warm Springs and Yakima reservations.

WISHRAM Probably the largest of the Chinookian tribes, the Wishram, lived farther up the Columbia River than any of their kinsmen. They lived principally in the present Klickitat County, Washington, and were closely related to the Wasco on the opposite (south) side of the Columbia. In 1800 they numbered about 1,000. In 1855 the remnants of the Wishram, with a few other Chinook families, were assigned to the Yakima Reservation. About 250 were incorporated with other tribes on that reservation, and the 274 "Upper Chinook" reported in 1910 may have been these Indians. They are not reported separately from the other Indians of the Yakima nation today, although a marked strain of their blood may survive.

WASCO Wasco were a Chinookian tribe of the inland branch, their closest relatives being the Wishram, living near the present The Dalles in Wasco County, Oregon, on the Columbia River. They were joined by the remnants of the Watlala and others, and removed to the Warm Springs Reservation, where a portion still remain as a separate people. In 1910 they returned a number of 242 persons; 227 in 1937; and 260 in 1945. They are the only independently reported Chinook group today; being a substantial portion of the "Warm Springs" who numbered 3,831 in 2001. The *Dalles Indians*, *Wasco* and *Wascopan* were divisions of this tribe.

COOS or **KUSAN** This was a small language family formed by two tribes in a narrow strip of the Oregon coast between the Coos and Coquille rivers. The northern division were the *Hanis* or Coos proper, who lived around the bay and river that bears their name. The southern division were the *Miluk* on the Lower Coquille, near its estuary. The combined population of the two groups has been estimated as being 2,000 in 1780. They obtained subsistence from the sea, gathered clams, and from the land obtained camas roots and berries. They also had dugout canoes. Some members of both groups were ultimately placed at the Siletz Reservation on the southern "Yachats" portion of the agency. In 1910, 93 were reported under the name Kus; in 1937, only 55; and 228 "Kusa" in 1945.

Today, two reorganized groups, descendants of several tribes but including Coos people who lost ancient lands around Coos Bay and on the old Yachats (Alsea) Reservation, Siletz agency, are petitioning the U.S. Government for financial compensation. The total number of people with Coos ancestry is about 300, considerably mixed with other tribal groups and whites. The Coos have been linked linguistically to the Siuslaw and Lower Umpqua and with the other Alseans as the Oregon branch of the Penutian stock.

YAKONAN or **ALSEAN** A group of Indians on the Oregon coast, forming a small linguistic family, are the Yakonan. From north to south these were the *Yaquina*, on the Yaquina River near present Newport, Oregon; *Alsea*, on the Alsea River; *Siuslaw*, on the Siuslaw River near Florence, Oregon; and *Kuitsh* or Lower Umpqua, on the lower Umpqua River near

Reedsport, Oregon. The Siuslaw were the most linguistically divergent. They were coastal and riverine people, wealthy in dentalium shells. They hunted seals, and held slaves.

Because of their coastal location they came into contact with white trading vessels in the late 18th century. In 1780 they perhaps numbered 5,000. The usual reductions followed, hastened by the activities of the Hudson's Bay Company, the influx of white miners and the Rogue Wars of the 1850s. Remnants were moved to the Siletz Reservation on that part known as the Southern or Alsea Reservation. In 1910, a census reported only 29 Alsea, 19 Yaquina, and seven Siuslaw and, in 1930, nine Kuitsh. They are all now part of the so-called "Confederated Siletz Indians of Oregon."

KALAPUYAN This was a group of eight tribes speaking three languages, formerly inhabiting the valley of the Willamette River, Oregon. They were probably related to the Takelma and more distantly to the Coos and Yakonan, into a stock called Oregon-Penutian.

The *Atfalati* lived around Forest Grove, northwestern Oregon, and the *Yamel*, above present McMinnville, Oregon, these forming one dialect division of the family. Continuing south were the *Luckiamute*, on the river that bears their name; the *Santiam*, around present Lebanon, Oregon; *Chepenafa* or *Mary's River*, near Corvallis, Oregon; *Chelamela*, on Long Tom Creek west of Eugene, Oregon; and *Calapooya*, near Eugene, Oregon, all of whom spoke the central Kalapuyan dialect. Finally, above Oakland, Oregon, were the *Yoncalla*, who spoke the southern dialect.

The Kalapuyans as a whole suffered greatly from the smallpox epidemics of 1782 and 1783. After coming into contact with white fur traders, they ultimately abandoned their native economy, and were unable to resist white encroachments into the Willamette valley. Following treaties in 1851 and 1855, the remnants of all the Kalapuyan tribes moved to the Grand Ronde Reservation, Oregon, where their descendants are now organized as the "Confederated Tribes of the Grand Ronde Community of Oregon." Although the reservation lost its recognition by the Bureau of Indian Affairs in 1956, it was reactivated at the request of the so-called confederated tribes, which now derive most of their income from a casino.

The census of 1910 reported 44 Atfalati, five Calapooya, eight Luckiamute, 24 Chepenafa, nine Santiam, five Yamel, and 11 Yoncalla. However, in 1930, the whole group was reported at 45 persons.

At least 24 different tribes were included in the Siletz-Grand Ronde complex, making it almost impossible for any one small group to preserve its identity. In 1955, 700 people were reported descended from the original tribes of Grand Ronde Reservation shortly before termination, when the Federal Government suspended its responsibility for any services and removed restrictions on their property. In 2001, 4,706 enrolled "Grand Ronde" were reported.

TAKELMA This is a small linguistic family comprising two separate tribes: the *Takelma*, on the east side of the Klamath and Coast Mountains in the middle Rogue River area around Grants Pass, Oregon; and the *Latgawa*, in the upper Rogue River area around Jacksonville, Oregon. Their houses were small brush shelters in summer and constructed of split sugar pine boards for winter. They decorated their costumes with

Above: Wishram fisherman, middle course of the Columbia River, c atching salmon. Photographed by Edward S. Curtis, 1911.

Above Right: Wishram woman wearing a heavily beaded buckskin dress, several necklaces, beads, shells, dentalium-shell nose ornament and a headdress of beads and hollow-centered Chinese coins. Published in the supplement to volume 8 of Curtis's The North American Indian.

Below: Three women from the Warm Springs Indian Reservation, Wasco County, Oregon, holding beaded bags.

Right: Woman's skirt, Hupa, c. 1880. From part of a woman's two-part apron of hide thongs hanging from a waistband. Each thong is strung with pinenuts and wrapped with bear grass. Royal Albert Memorial Museum, Exeter, UK.

dentalia shells, and tattooing was common. They also had cultural traits from California, and they prized obsidian stone and Shasta basket hats.

The Takelma resented intrusions on their lands and were involved in the so-called "Rogue Wars" of the 1850s, after which the U.S. Army decided to send the remaining Takelma and Latgawa to the Grand Ronde Reservation many miles to the north, where they arrived both overland and by sea. The Takelma probably numbered in excess of 1,000 in 1800, but later figures incorporate them in a mixed group known as "Upper Rogue River." Two groups of "Rogue River" were returned from Grand Ronde in 1937, numbering 58 and 46.

WEST COAST ATHABASCANS

We do not know for certain when the Athabascan tribes arrived in the area, but it was probably along the coast, perhaps 1,000 years ago. They seem to have left three small tribes in their wake: the Nicola, among the Thompson River Indians of British Columbia; the *Kwalhioqua*, in the Willapa Hills of southwestern Washington; and the *Clatskanie*, probably Kwalhioqua who crossed into Oregon before 1775 and occupied an area about 70 miles (110 km) inland from the mouth of the Columbia River. These tribes are extinct. However, the large territory held by the major communities of the Pacific coast Athabascans extended not quite continuously from the Umpqua River in Oregon to the head of the Eel River in California. The Californian tribes numbered about 7,000, and the Oregon groups about the same in aboriginal times.

COQUILLE Sometimes known as Upper Coquille, or Mishikhwutmetumme, they were an Athabascan tribe on the east fork of the Coquille River, Oregon, west of Myrtle Creek. They lived in lean-to houses of cedar planks and subsisted on acorns, deer and fish, including salmon. Some were forced onto the Siletz Reservation, where 15 "Upper Coquille" were reported in 1910. A mixed-blood faction known as the "Coquille tribe" are a few dozen people of Coos-Coquille extraction, living in their old location, who are today seeking settlement of their land claims. The "Confederated Tribes of Siletz" numbered about 900 shortly before termination of reservation status in 1956. They are now a federally recognized tribe and received self-governance in 1992. The Coquille were one of many ancestries who form the group. In 2001, 769 "Lower Coquille" were reported seperately.

UMPQUA Often known as "Upper Umpqua," these people lived mostly on the south fork of the Umpqua River, Oregon, near present Roseburg, where they were met by Astorian fur traders in the early 19th century. They numbered some 400 in the mid-19th century, eventually forced north to the Grand Ronde Reservation, they reported 84 in 1902. One band, the *Cow Creek Indians*, survived in their old homes, and a few descendants still live around Riddle, south of Myrtle Creek, Oregon, numbering 221 in 1985. These were part of a reported 700 people in southwestern Oregon in 1956, descendants of Athabascans, Coos, Siuslaw and others living in some 37 different locations, but chiefly around the Roseburg and Coos Bay areas. The same general group were reported as numbering 730 in the 1970 census. In 2001 1,162 "Cow Creek" were given, living in Oregon.

TUTUTNI This is an Athabascan tribe of the Illinois and lower Rogue rivers in southwestern Oregon, who also occupied the coast south to the Chetco River. They are commonly called "Coast Rogues." They were contacted by the British explorer George Vancouver in 1792. Although subsequent contact with other vessels and inland fur traders brought epidemics, they still numbered around 1,300 in 1850. They suffered the same fate as many other southwestern

Oregon groups, being shipped to the Siletz-Grand Ronde complex in 1857. By 1910 only 383 survived. In 1930, just 41 were reported under this name; a few others under the names "Maguenodon" and "Joshua," numbering 39 and 45, respectively in 1945, seem to be of Tututni origin. They are now part of the "Confederated Siletz." A group known as the *Naltunnhtunne* may have been very closely related to, or a subgroup of, the Tututni. In 2001, 3,660 enrolled "Confederated Siletz" were reported.

CHASTACOSTA A small Athabascan tribe on the lower course of the Illinois River, near its junction with the Rogue River were the Chastacosta. They joined the general Indian resistance to white settlement in their lands, but were moved north to the Siletz Agency, where a few remain. They were given as 153 in 1858; 30 in 1937; and 20 in 1945.

TALTUSHTUNTUDE This was a small Athabascan tribe from the upper-middle course of the Rogue River, Oregon, on Galice Creek, who were subsequently moved to the Siletz Reservation. A group called "Galice Creek" numbered 42 in 1937, and 10 in 1945.

DAKUBETEDE
This small Athabascan tribe from Applegate Creek, a tributary of the upper Rogue River, Oregon, is probably now extinct.

CHETCO An Athabascan people of the mouth of the Chetco River, near present Brookings, Oregon, were known as Chetco. They lived in wooden plank houses and were closely allied to the Tolowa to the south. They aided other "Coast Rogue" Indians in the general resistance of 1853–56, and were moved north to the Siletz Reservation, where they numbered only nine in 1910. A few descendents are reported in their old location.

TOLOWA or **SMITH RIVER** These were an Athabascan tribe who occupied the Smith River drainage and some of the nearby coast in the extreme northeastern corner of California. Linguistically they were closer to the Rogue River tribes to the north than to their relatives to the south. They resided in permanent villages along the coast in winter, and in late summer they moved inland for salmon and acorns. Their house types were low-peaked redwood plank dwellings with gable-end entrances. Tolowa society was

dominated by acquisition of wealth, usually dentalium shells, obsidian blades and woodpecker scalps.

Ceremonialism associated with the taking of the first salmon and sea lion suggests that they belonged with the northern Californian "World Renewal" complex of the Karok, Yurok and Hupa type (see p. 188).

The overland explorations of Jedediah Smith were their first contact with whites, and intensive white settlement of this region came after 1850. They probably numbered more than 1,000 in precontact times, but the census of 1910 gave only 121 Tolowa, a result of diseases and numerous attacks by whites on their settlements.

Two small reservations (called "rancherias" in California), at Crescent City and Smith River, Del Norte County, California have been home for some Tolowa descendants, reported as numbering 37 and 113 respectively in 1945. In 1990, approx. 1,000 Tolowa, Tututni and Chetco descendants were reported, and 896 "Smith River" in 2001.

Above: Hupa White Deerskin Dancer, c. 1896. The Hupa, Yurok and Karok had two major World Renewal rituals, correlating with seasonal availability of major food resources: the Jump Dance for the spring salmon run, and the Deerskin Dance for the fall acorn harvest and second salmon run. Performers held albino or other oddly colored deerskins aloft on poles, or carried obsidian blades covered with buckskin. Some, as here, wore wolfskin headbands and kilts of civet pelts.

Left: Tolowa woman, c. 1890. Classic two-piece skirt of the Klamath River area: a narrow buckskin apron panel with clam and abalone shells covers a fiber and beaded skirt, fringed with abalone "tinklers." Note the strings of shell beads, and the basket hat.

Far Left: Sam Lopez, Curtis' assistant, head-and-shoulders portrait, wearing Tolowa costume including a redheaded woodpecker scalp headress and strings of dentalium shell beads, holding a traditional painted bow and an obsidian blade, a sign of wealth. Edward S. Curtis photograph of c. 1923, published in volume 13 of The North American Indian. Library of Congress, Prints & Photographs Division LC-USZ62-118596.

Above: California/Hupa plank house, c. 1870. Tribal groups in northwest California made permanent family houses of split redwood cedar planks, supported on eaves beams and roof poles. The three-pitched roof and circular entrance were characteristic of the Hupa, Yurok and Karok. Interiors were excavated, leaving a "shelf" between exterior walls and pit, and the pit sides were revetted with horizontal planks.

HUPA or **HOOPA** Probably the largest and most important Athabascan tribe in California are the Hupa, living principally on the Trinity River, above its junction with the Klamath. Salmon and acorns provided the bulk of their diet. They were participants in the elaborate northwestern California rituals called "World Renewal" or "Big Time," involving complex ceremonial such as the White Deerskin and Jump Dances. Wealth display linked them culturally northward rather than to central California. They lived in small villages of rectangular plank houses, wore buckskin aprons and skirts and excelled in basketry.

Extensive contacts with whites came after 1850, but the establishment of the Hupa Reservation in their homeland helped maintain their numbers. They probably numbered more than 1,000 in 1851; 420 were reported in 1906, and 992 in 1962. Over the years they have settled into a rural American lifestyle, are self-supporting and economically are perhaps the most advanced among the surviving Indians of California. They still hold the White Deerskin Dance. In 2001 1,893 were reported consolidated with other groups.

CHILULA AND WHILKUT These are two small Athabascan tribes who were almost indistinguishable from each other, and from the Hupa. The Chilula lived on Redwood Creek west of the Hupa, and the Whilkut on the upper course of Redwood Creek and part of the Mad River to the southwest. The last of the Chilula moved to the Hupa Reservation and are no longer reported separately. The Whilkut suffered heavily at the hands of whites. A few "Redwood Indians" seem to have been incorporated on the Round Valley Reservation, although a few continued to live in their old homes and have mostly intermarried with whites. Consequently neither element still exists as a distinct group.

MATTOLE A small Athabascan tribe on the Bear and Mattole rivers, northwestern California, and a strip of adjacent coast about 45 miles long were the Mattole. They perhaps numbered 1,000 in precontact times. The census of 1910 reported only 34, and 30 "Bear River Indians" were living at the Rohnerville Rancheria, Humboldt County, California, in 1970, and part of 265 reported there in 2001.

NONGATL This was a minor Athabascan group on the middle Eel River, upper Mad River and Van Duzen River east of Ruth Lake. A few may have survived until reservation days at Hupa or Blue Lake.

SINKYONE An Athabascan group living mostly on the south fork of the Eel River, northwest California, to Shelter Cove on the coast were the Sinkyone. They are probably no longer separate.

LASSIK These Indians occupied the drainage of the main Eel River and headwaters of the Mad River in northwest California. They are no longer distinct as a separate group. The last joined the various groups on the Round Valley Reservation with their relatives.

WAILAKI Occupying the Eel River, south of the Lassik, to Big Bend Creek, the Wailaki were probably intermediate culturally between the central Californian Wintu and their own relatives to the north. The last of these people seem to have been located on the Round Valley Reservation and are no longer a separate group. In 1990, 1,090 "Wailaki" were reported from Round Valley, being a composite of true Wailaki, Yuki, Pit River, Pomo, Maidu and others which increased to 3,494 in 2001.

KATO or **CAHTO** The Kato were the southernmost Athabascan tribe of California in present Mendocino County, the area of the upper drainage of the south fork of the Eel River. Originally numbering some 500, they had been reduced to about 60 by 1910, residing on the Round Valley Reservation and the small rancheria at Laytonville. In 1972 they numbered 95; 81 in 2001. All traces of their former culture have apparently gone.

PRINCIPAL NATIVE VILLAGES OF THE NORTHWEST PACIFIC COAST, SOUTHERN ALASKA AND BRITISH COLUMBIA

Synonymy of Indian names for villages on map

Tribe	Village	Alternative
Tlingit	Hoonah	Huna
Tlingit	Angoon	Hutsnuwu
Tlingit	Kloqwan	Kate
Tlingit	Wrangell	Stikine
Tlingit	Klawock	Henya
Tlingit	Ketchikan	Tongas
Haida	Massett	Masset
Niska	Gitlakdamik	Gitlakdamix
Gitksan	Kitwancool	Kitwancoola
Haisla	Kitamat	Kitamatt
Heiltsuk	China Hat	Kitasoo or Haihais
Kwakiutl	Rivers Inlet	Oweekano
Kwakiutl	Smith Inlet	Quawshelah
Kwakiutl	Blunden Harbour	Nakwakto
Kwakiutl	Watson Sound	Kwawaineuk
Kwakiutl	Kingcome Inlet	Tsawataineuk
Kwakiutl	Gilford Island	Kwiksootainuk
Kwakiutl	Kight Island	Mamalillikulla
Kwakiutl	Turnour Island	Tlawttsis
Nootka	Hesquiat	Hesquiaht

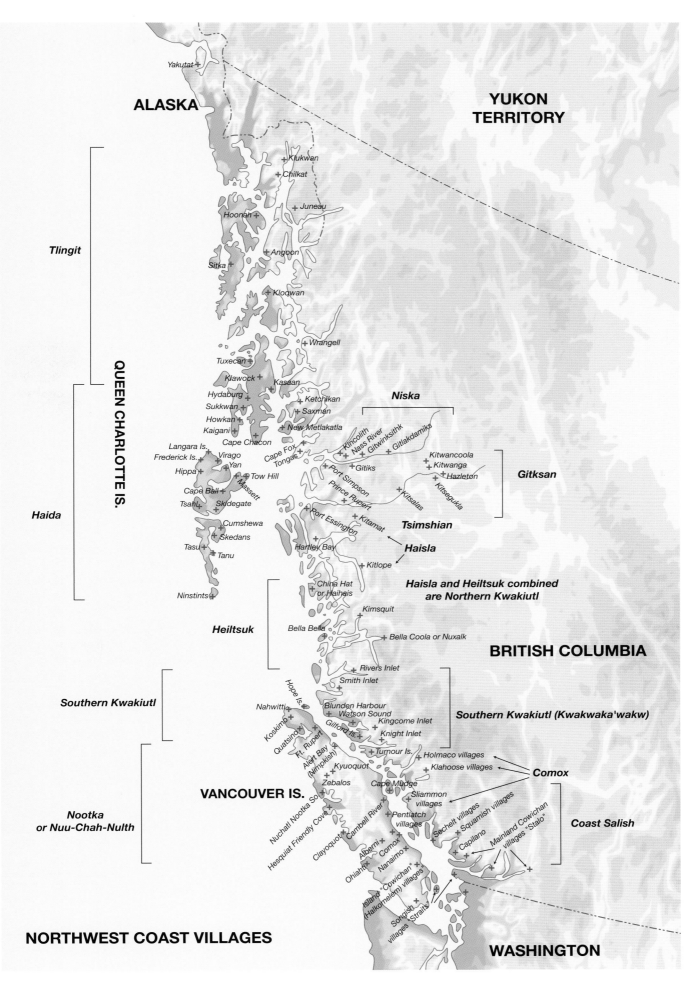

Yakutat

ALASKA

YUKON TERRITORY

Klukwan
Chilkat

Juneau

Hoonah

Angoon

Sitka

Tlingit

Kloqwan

Wrangell

Tuxecan

Klawock   Kasaan

Hydaburg
Sukkwan   Ketchikan
Howkan   Saxman
Kaigani   New Metlakatla
      Cape Chacon

Langara Is.
Frederick Is.   Virago
Hippa   Yan
          Tow Hill
Cape Ball   Massett
Tsahl   Skidegate
      Cumshewa
       Skedans
Tasu   Tanu

Ninstints

QUEEN CHARLOTTE IS.

Haida

Cape Fox
Tongas
       Gitiks

Port Simpson
Prince Rupert

Port Essington
        Kitamat
Hartley Bay

Kitlope

China Hat
or Haihais

Kimsquit

Bella Bella

Bella Coola or Nuxalk

Heiltsuk

Rivers Inlet
Smith Inlet

Niska

Kincolith
Nass River Gitwinksithk
        Gitlakdamiks

Kitwancoola
   Kitwanga
     Hazleton

Kitsalas   Kitsegukla

Gitksan

Tsimshian

Haisla ←

Haisla

**Haisla and Heiltsuk combined
are Northern Kwakiutl**

BRITISH COLUMBIA

Southern Kwakiutl

Hope Is.
Nahwitti
Koskimo
Quatsino
   Ft. Rupert
Alert Bay
(Nimpkish)
Zebalos

Blunden Harbour
Watson Sound
   Kingcome Inlet
Gilford Is.
   Knight Inlet

Turnour Is.

Holmaco villages

Klahoose villages

Cape Mudge
   Sliammon
   villages

VANCOUVER IS.

Nuchatl Nootka So.
Hesquiat Friendly Cove

*Nootka
or Nuu-Chah-Nulth*

Kyuoquot

Clayoquot
      Cambell River
Alberni   Comox
Ohiaht   Nanaimo

Island "Cowichan"
(Halkomelem) villages

Songish
villages Straits

Pentlatch
villages

Southern Kwakiutl (Kwakwaka'wakw)

Comox

Sechelt villages   Squamish villages

Capilano

Mainland Cowichan
villages "Stalo"

Coast Salish

WASHINGTON

NORTHWEST COAST VILLAGES

SUBARCTIC

Language family and tribe	Meaning/origin of tribal name, where known
Athabascan (Northern Athabascan):	
Ingalik	Eskimo name
Kolchan	–
Tanaina	"people"
Koyukon	"people of the river"
Tanana	"Tanana River people"
Ahtena	"ice people"
Han	"those who dwell along the river"
Eyak (possibly separate family)	–
Kutchin	"those who dwell on the flats"
Tutchone	"crow people"
Tagish	place name
Inland Tlingit	"people"
Tahltan	place name
Tsetsaut	"those of the interior"
Kaska	–
Sekani	"dwellers on the rocks"
Beaver	English name
Carrier	English name
Chilcotin	"people of the river"

Language family and tribe	Meaning/origin of tribal name, where known
Nicola	English name
Slavey	English name
Mountain	English name
Hare	English name
Bear Lake	English name
Dogrib	English name
Yellowknife	English name
Chipewyan	"pointed skins"
Algonkian★:	
Northern Ojibwa	
Cree	French version of own name
West Main Cree	
Western Woods Cree	
Tête de Boule (Attikamek)	French — "round heads" ("whitefish")
Montagnais–Nascapi	French — "mountaineers"
Beothuk	"human body"

★ see p. 17

The Subarctic is a cultural area of North America comprising the whole of present Quebec, Newfoundland, the northern parts of Ontario, Manitoba, Saskatchewan, Alberta, the northern interior of British Columbia, the Yukon, the drainage of the Mackenzie River about Great Slave and Great Bear lakes, and the interior of Alaska. The Indians, except for the Beothuk, are drawn exclusively from the Algonkian family in the east and the Athabascan family in the northwest. Within this vast area culture remained quite constant, though flexible, within strictly hunting and fishing parameters. The climate is harsh, with long, severely cold winters and short, warm summers. Temperatures below −40°F (−40°C) are common, but often reach 80°F (27°C) in summer, accompanied by a dense insect life that plagues man and animal alike.

Much of the area is Arctic lowlands, with abundant coniferous spruce, tamarack, willow and alder. The topography of the whole area ranges from forest to lake, swamp, prairie, tundra, mountain and sea.

Animals of economic significance to the Indians include moose, caribou, bear, fox, wolf, otter and beaver. Fish include whitefish, grayling, trout and pike. A significant number of Athabascan groups were found in the great mountain chain of the Yukon Territory and British Columbia, in the lush river valleys of spruce, fir, cedar and hemlock forests. Only at Cook Inlet, Alaska, were the Indians partly dependent upon the sea for food. Salmon was important to some Alaskan groups. Fishing became more important near the close of the fur trade era.

Religion focused on the relationship between the animal spirits and man, and the impersonal spirits of animated natural elements such as fire, wind and water. Shamans were important in helping to prevent disease and to enlist the power of animals. Communal ceremonies were few, except where sometimes influenced from other cultures such as Inuit or Northwest Coast. The Ingalik, Tanaina and other western Athabascans had a rich ceremonial life, in part derived from coastal cultures.

Northern life became influenced by the network of fur trading ports from the late 18th century on. European goods gradually transformed clothing, housing and settlement patterns, and missionary influence modified religion, which also produced a few semi-Christian nativistic cults similar to those found elsewhere in North America. Artistic traditions were also modified as floralistic beadwork on cloth largely replaced porcupine quillwork and painting in the decoration of native costume.

ATHABASCAN, ATHAPASCAN or ATHAPASKAN

One of the most widely spread linguistic families of North American Indians is the Athabascan. The family has been tentatively allied to the Haida and Tlingit into a larger generic group. They are believed to be the last Indian group, exclusive of the Inuit, to enter North America from Asia via the Bering land bridge, perhaps c. 5000 B.C.–8000 B.C., and have for the most part occupied — in scattered groups — vast areas of Subarctic Alaska and northwest Canada beyond Hudson Bay. Perhaps 1,600 years ago some Athabascans emigrated to the Pacific coast in southwestern Oregon and northern California. About a thousand years later a significant group entered the American Southwest to become the Navajo and Apache.

NORTHERN ATHABASCAN sometimes called DENE

These terms cover the northern groups of Athabascan speakers, in all about 30 languages, who occupied in relatively small bands an area embracing the Canadian and Alaskan Subarctic from the west coast of Hudson Bay to the interior of Alaska. This includes the northern parts of Manitoba, Saskatchewan, Alberta, Yukon and British Columbia, much of the drainages of the Peace, Liard, Pelly, Peel, Mackenzie, Porcupine, Yukon, Tanana and Copper rivers. In this vast area their culture was relatively uniform, being wholly without agriculture and primarily dependent on moose, caribou or deer hunting. Houses were constructed of bark or skins, modified into the log houses of fur trade influence during the late 19th century. Before trade goods became available, clothing was of dressed skins cut to fit the whole body. Vessels, toboggans and canoes utilized wood, bark, sinew and skins. The fur trade gradually modified Northern Athabascan culture. Guns, knives and steel traps were adopted in pursuit of fur-bearing animals. Despite their meager resources and harsh environment these peoples excelled in decorative porcupine quillwork and later in beadwork on clothing.

Above: Northern Athabascan dog blanket, c. 1910. These strapped-on "tapies" were part of the embellishment added for show on arrival at a settlement. Of dark cloth or velvet, backed with canvas, they had wool fringes, sleigh bells and beadwork in tight floralistic forms popularized in the Northwest during the fur trade era through Cree and Métis influence.

Below: Northern Athabascan dog team, c. 1910. The dog team and its accoutrements were added to the aboriginal flat-bottomed, hand-drawn toboggan by Europeans and Métis during the fur trade era, using European breeds stouter than the lightly built aboriginal dogs. For deep snow and narrow trails a toboggan was preferred to a runnered sledge, with a team of four to eight dogs in a tandem hitch. A fully caparisoned team had belts, tasseled and beaded blankets, and standing irons adorned with pompons. Sledges with raised runners and cariole sleighs of white manufacture were also used later in some areas.

Above: Museum model of Northern Athabascan hunter, c.1980, wearing a leather beaded jacket, mittens and pouch and holding a gun scabbard. Museum of Mankind, London, Living Arctic Exhibition, 1988. Photograph: M. G. Johnson

INGALIK the Ingalik were a group of Athabascans living in the basins of the Yukon and Kuskokwim rivers, north and east of Holy Cross, the most westerly group in Alaska. A northern division on the Innoko River, the *Holikachuk*, are sometimes now considered as a separate group. Their ceremonial life seems to have been influenced by the Inuit, from whom they borrowed heavily, and their Potlatches suggest Northwest Coast influences. The Russians established trade with the Ingalik during the early 19th century and modified their culture and religion as a consequence. A population for the group has been estimated at 1,500 at contact, reduced to about 500 during the late 19th century. In 1974, 530 were estimated at Holy Cross, Anvik and Shageluk with some Inuit and white admixture added over the years. Although not reported separately in 2001, reliable estimates suggest there are now around 1,500. The Holikachuk descendants are at Grayling and number perhaps around 100.

KOLCHAN This is a group of Athabascan bands on the upper Kuskokwim River in Alaska, sometimes considered a branch of the Ingalik, but related more closely to the Tanana, with whom they are much mixed. Their life and culture was similar to that of the Ingalik and Tanana. They have about 150 descendants at McGrath, Nikolai and Takotna.

TANAINA (DENA'INA) The Athabascan groups in the vicinity of Cook Inlet, Kenai Peninsula, and the areas north and west in Alaska are known as Tanaina — not to be confused with the Tanana. Their culture was somewhat intermediate between the coastal Tlingit and the interior Athabascans, being much more dependent in early times on salmon, but they also hunted moose and caribou. Contact with Russians in the late 18th century established their association with the fur trade and the Orthodox Church. Much reduced by severe epidemics during the 19th century, their population decreased from 4,000 to 1,500. In 1974, about 530 persons of largely Tanaina descent lived at Nondalton, Pedro Bay, Tyonek, Lime Village and Eklutna. That number is now around 1,200.

KOYUKON These were Athabascan bands in three groups occupying the middle area of the Yukon River, Alaska, plus parts of the Koyukuk and Tanana rivers. An older name for at least part of these people was Koyukokhotana. Direct contact began in 1858, when the trading post at Nulato was established by the Russian-American Company. The Koyukon viewed the supernatural world through the animal spirits, and held elaborate mortuary ceremonials and memorial Potlatches. They have been slowly modified over the years by Roman Catholic and Episcopalian missionaries.

Their clothing featured the double-V caribou hide tunics and trouser-moccasins (see p. 272). Their vast habitat was a mixture of forest, mountain and lowland flats. Their population was perhaps 2,000 in pre-white contact times. Today about that number are reported at the villages of Kaltag, Nulato, Koyukuk, Galena, Ruby, Hughes, Allakaket, Stevens and Rampart, mostly Koyukon with other Athabascan and Inuit admixture.

TANANA Tanana (not Tanaina) is a convenient name to cover several Athabascan Indian groups along the Tanana River, Alaska, in three divisions: the *Lower Tanana*, near present Fairbanks, the *Tanacross*, around the town of the same name, and the *Upper Tanana* or *Nabesna*. Contact with whites came

first to the Lower Tanana. Closest to the Yukon River trading posts in the early 19th century, they were gradually modified in culture due to the fur trade, mining activities and missionary influence .

They were dependent for food on caribou, other big game and fishing. Their material culture included toboggans, fish weirs, canoes, skin boats, and sleds, as well as caribou skin clothing, dyed porcupine quills and intricate beadwork on decorated festive costumes. The Tanana groups perhaps numbered 700 in 1880, but there had already been a reduction due to introduced diseases, which continued well into the early 20th century. Today about 600 descendants are at Minto, Nenana, Tanacross, Tetlin and Northway.

Above: Tanana dog, c. 1880. The only domesticated animal in the North in aboriginal times was the small dog, and only among the Chipewyan were they used to carry burdens. Not until larger varieties were introduced by whites did most native peoples use them as pack and sledge animals.

AHTENA (DEG HIT'AN) The Ahtena were a group of Athabascans of the Copper River basin region of Alaska, often divided into lower and upper divisions, but who were never a tribal political unit. Russians attempted to ascend the Copper River in 1796. During most of the early 19th century the tribe was hostile to foreigners, including the coastal Inuit. The Ahtena

Right: Moccasins of smoked buckskin, moose, and caribou, thread, quillwork and ribbon. Northern Saskatchewan/Alberta/Yukon area. Subarctic type, possibly Chipewyan or Mackenzie River drainage-area Métis. Silk or cotton thread embroidery on the vamp with quillwork at the junction of the vamp and bottom unit. Castellated ankle collars.

Far Right: Moccasins, probably Northern Athabascan, made of smoked buckskin, moose and caribou, thread and quillwork, 27cm long and made c. 1900. These are typical Subarctic moccasins made for sale. The vamp-instep is decorated with cotton or silk-thread floral embroidery with porcupine quills and horsehair wrapped horsehair margin.

Center Left: Caribou-skin cartridge belt, Southern Tuchone, Whitehorse, Yukon, collected 1911; also, caribou antler tool (blade missing), Tanaina, Alaska, collected before 1921, and three skinning knives.

Center Right: Guncase, probably Kutchin or Tanana, c. 1910. A smoked buckskin gun scabbard characteristically from the upper Yukon River area of Alaska and the Yukon, Canada. The double end tabs are a common feature on guncases from that area. There are three areas of beadwork decoration in floral pattern all couched on dark cloth and trimmed with wool yarn tassels with large "necklace" beads. Sinew thread has also been used in the construction. It is 130 cm long.

Below Northern Athabascan baby belt, c. 1890. Used to hold a baby or young child on a mother's back whilst working or moving. Made of dark tradecloth, buckskin, and edged with military braid and decorated with floral beadwork, probably Tanana or Kutchin (Gwich'in) from the upper Yukon and Tanana river areas of Alaska. The bottom decorated with large necklace beads and woollen tassels. The large beads may be Russian beads, and the floral beadwork and edging is sinew strung.

Opposite: Northern Athabascan woman's summer costume, Kutchin, mid 19th century. Consisting of caribou skin, hood, tunic, and mittens which provided protection against insects in summer. Decorated with quillwork and elaegnus seeds. Usually longer and fuller than men's costume, otherwise they were virtually the same.

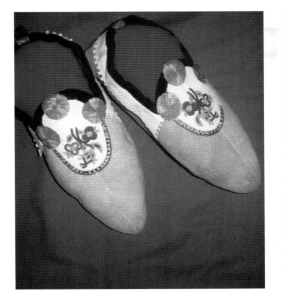

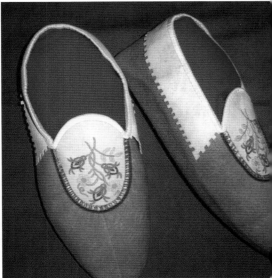

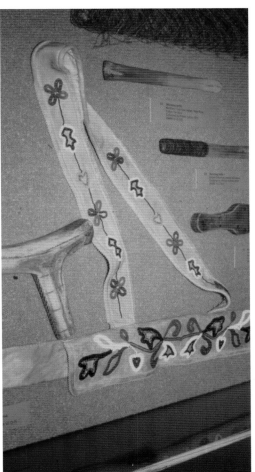

were linked to a trade network with other natives involving animal hides, native copper and, later, European trade goods. Except for the changes brought by trade goods and guns obtained from whites there were few permanent contacts with Europeans until about 1900. They still hold Potlatch ceremonies given by wealthy chiefs to honor both the living and the dead. They numbered perhaps in excess of 500 at the time of Russian contact, but were reduced to some 300 by about 1900. They seem to have recovered their numbers, but not all the 500 or so Indians in the old Ahtena area are true Ahtena. Most of their descendants are at Cantwell, Chistochina, Cakona, Gulkana, Cooper Center and Chitina in Alaska.

HAN A small Athabascan group on the Yukon River close to the present boundary between the Yukon Territory and Alaska, in a heavily forested region, are the Han. In similar fashion to other Northern Athabascans the Han wore clothing of caribou skins with leggings and moccasins made in one piece. They used bark and skin canoes, snowshoes and toboggans and depended on fish and meat for food. They were one of the last Athabascan groups to be contacted by whites, from Fort Yukon, but missionary influence followed. The Gold Rush effectively destroyed much of the traditional Han culture. Their few descendants remained at Eagle and Moosehide, later Dawson, where about 671 were reported in 2005.

Above: Ahtena woman, c. 1870, using the tumpline to carry camp equipment. This tribe of the Copper and Chitina rivers, Alaska, belonged to an ancient trade network involving other Athabscan tribes, including Inuit, Eyak, Tlingit and possibly the Siberian Chukchi. Travel was mostly on foot. In winter snowshoes and hand-drawn load-bearing toboggans were used.

Above: Ahtena chairlike birch bark cradle allowing the legs to dangle astride a central flap fastened to the chest by cross ties. The cradle was carried on the mother's back by a robe or blanket and held in position by a wide band around her shoulders or head.

EYAK A small group of Athabascans who lived on the southern coast of Alaska between Prince William Sound and the Tlingit of Yakutat Bay, close to the mouth of the Copper River, were the Eyak. A few descendants remain at Eyak (Cordova). Some studies have suggested that these people and their culture may have been a mixture of Tlingit, Athabascan, Inuit and even Asiatic origins, and suggest that they should be treated as a separate family. Five speakers were left in the 1960s in the villages of Yakutat and Cordova, the youngest a woman of 42.

KUTCHIN (QWICH'IN) The Kutchin were one of the most important branches of the Athabascan family, scattered in nine or ten groups over a wide area extending from the middle Yukon River region in Alaska, including the upper Koyukuk River tributaries, eastward along the Porcupine River, and thence into the area, which drains into the Mackenzie River basin, including the Peel River and Arctic Red River areas. Their habitat varies from the broad lowlands of the middle Yukon and Mackenzie rivers to the cordillera and

boreal forests, all characterized by long, severe winters and short, warm summers. The easternmost bands — those of the Mackenzie drainage — have usually been referred to as "Loucheux." The hunting of caribou for food, clothing and tools provided most basic raw materials, but freshwater fish and fowl were also important. Caribou hide clothing for males and females was characterized by fitted garments, hoods and combined trouser-moccasins decorated with porcupine quillwork and painting. During the late 19th century traders introduced beads and European clothing. House types were both surface and semisubterranean log and brush structures.

The earliest known encounter between the Kutchin and Europeans was with the Mackenzie party in 1789. In 1806 Fort Good Hope was established, and in 1847 Fort Yukon was founded in the territory of the western Kutchin bands. Gradually modified in culture throughout the 19th and 20th centuries, they numbered perhaps 5,000 in pre-European contact times but declined to fewer than 1,000 in 1860. In 1968, 2,150 Kutchin were reported at Arctic Village, Venetie, Fort Yukon, Circle and Chalkyitsik in Alaska and Old Crow (Yukon), Fort McPherson, Arctic Red River, Aklavikand Inuvit (Northwest Territories) in Canada. The Canadian population was 2,623 in 2005, but the Alaskan population was not reported separately.

TUTCHONE These were Athabascans of present southern Yukon Territory east of the Saint Elias Mountains, through a vast plateau dissected by the Teslin and Pelly rivers, forming the tributaries of the upper Yukon River. This area was a mixture of tundra, boreal forest and meadowlands, which supported moose, caribou and mountain sheep which, together with salmon, provided their main food and clothing sources. They seem to have been the intermediate traders between the Tlingit and the interior Upper

Right: Kutchin man, c. 1862. Northern Athabascan mens' summer dress of Western tribes was characterized by a long-sleeved pullover shirt with a distinctive pointed lower edge, combined moccasin-trousers and mittens. Usually of caribou hide, garments were decorated with dentalium shells and porcupine quillwork, the seams often highlighted with red ochre. After about 1850 Subarctic clothing began to be greatly modified in cut and materials by European influences.

Tanana and Han. During the 19th century their own efforts to secure a direct trade with the coastal tribes seem to have been blocked. The Klondike Gold Rush and the building of the Alaska Highway effectively changed native northern life. The total number of people covered by the term "Tutchone" was perhaps fewer than 1,000 in 1880, and about the same number of descendants are still reported from Ross River, Pelly Crossing, Carmacks, Whitehorse, Champagne, Aishihik and Kluane, all in Yukon Territory, but including some Tagish and others. A total of 2,825 were reported in 2001.

TAGISH The Tagish are a small but important Athabascan group near Tagish Lake at the headwaters of the Yukon River in southern Yukon Territory, Canada. Two mountain passes connected the Tagish with the Tlingit of the Northwest Coast, and the interaction between the groups led to the adoption of many coastal traits by the Tagish. The first direct contacts with whites were in the 1880s, but the Klondike Gold Rush of 1898 brought major changes. Their general culture was similar to that of other cordilleran Athabascans, perhaps with greater dependence on fishing. The coastal public display of status and wealth distribution ceremony known as "Potlatch" is still an important native function. About 600 people of Tagish descent were reported living at Carcross and Whitehorse in the Yukon in 2005. Some are probably part of the Inland Tlingit.

INLAND TLINGIT A group of Indians near Teslin village in southern Yukon and Atlin in northern British Columbia were known as the Inland Tlingit. Despite their name, some students believe them to be an Athabascan people originally called Taku, who adopted Tlingit as their language owing to extensive trade and intermarriage with the coastal Tlingit. Others claim they were Tlingit who moved into the Taku Basin from the coast. Their material culture, including their dress, was a colorful mixture of coastal and interior traits, including the varied use of west coast totemic decoration. They also held traditional style Potlatches until recently. In 1978 250 were at Teslin and 161 at Atlin. By 2005 those numbers had grown to 545 and 371, respectively.

TAHLTAN The Tahltan were Athabascan bands centered on the upper basin of the Stikine River in the northwestern interior of British Columbia, particularly around Telegraph Creek. The Tahltan, together with the Kaska, Tagish and Taku, were once referred to as Nahani. Their habitat included parklands and heavy forests, with moose and caribou providing meat and hides for clothing. They had extensive contact with the coastal Tlingit and indirectly with the white fur trade, but direct European contact became established after 1874. The Tahltan used pitched and lean-to wooden shelters and smokehouses. They probably numbered 1,000 in pre-

Kutchin, c. 1920. Older infants were sometimes carried by means of a sturdy band looped around the child's buttocks, carried over the mother's shoulders, and tied at the front. These belts were heavily beaded, and fringed with wool.

European contact times, but declined to fewer than 300 by 1900. They are still principally located on a reserve near Telegraph Creek, and numbered 702 in 1969, including a few at Kinaskan Lake. By the turn of this century their numbers had increased to near 2,000. Hunting, trapping and fishing remained basic to Tahltan subsistence until the mid-20th century.

TSETSAUT A small Athabascan group from the interior cordillera of northern British Columbia who seem to have moved to the upper Nass River and then to the Portland Canal are the Tsetsaut. In 1885 a remnant of 12 men and their families moved to the Anglican mission at Kincolith, where they merged with the Niska. They subsequently became extinct as a separate people.

KASKA (DENA) These people occupied a stretch of the Liard River, where present Yukon Territory and British Columbia adjoin at Watson Lake, and also along the Dease River tributary. They are very closely related to the Tahltan and Tagish Athabascans, and were once collectively called Nahani. They shared some cultural traits with their relatives and thence with Northwest Coastal culture, but also with more distant relatives of the Mackenzie River drainage area. Continuous contact with whites began in the 1820s, with the establishment of a Hudson's Bay post on the Liard, followed by increasing intrusion by miners and freelance traders and trappers. In 1969 there were 533 Kaska in the Liard River Band near Lower Post and Watson Lake, excluding a few who have joined other groups over the years. By 2001 they were reported at 645.

SEKANI (TSEKENE) The country of the Sekani was the valleys of the Finlay and Parsnip branches of the Peace River in north-central British Columbia. Their language suggests a close relationship with the Beaver Indians and Sarsi, and they may originally have been all one people. Their land was a vast area of high plateau, mountains, numerous rivers, lakes and streams, often covered with dense forest. As the Peace River is part of the interior Mackenzie drainage, there was little dependence on salmon, but they hunted moose, caribou, mountain sheep and, in the eastern part of their domain, bison and wapiti. White traders had an early impact on Sekani culture, and Simon Fraser established two North West Company posts in their territory in the early 19th century. In recent times they have been associated with trading posts at Fort Ware, Fort Grahame and Fort McLeod. They suffered greatly from an influx of white miners from 1861 onwards. Their population may have been 800 in early times, but only 160 were reported in 1923; 290 in 1934; 336 in 1949; 523 in 1973; and 835 by 2001. Not all were true Sekani, many being of mixed descent and a number now being considered Métis. Their present population is principally located at Finlay River (Ware) and McLeod Lake, British Columbia.

Above: Kutchin baby belt, c. 1890, constructed of leather and velvet cloth and decorated with beadwork. The floral beadwork style of the Northern Athabascan tribes such as the Kutchin, shows one of many variations inspired by European influence, which spread through much of North America during the 19th century. Formerly M. G. Johnson Collection

BEAVER (DUNNEZA) These people lived in the prairies and woods on both sides of the Peace River, northwest of Lesser Slave Lake. They were among the first Northern Athabascans to experience European contact in 1792. They were gradually pushed westward by the Cree, who were armed with guns. During the 19th century they were bound to the trading posts at Forts Dunvegan, Vermillion and St. John. Their present descendants are at the Boyer River reserves near Fort Vermillion, Horse Lake and Clear Hills, all in Alberta, but are heavily mixed with Cree at John D'or, Halfway River and West Moberly Lake. They probably numbered about 1,000 in aboriginal times, though scattered over a vast area. They are closely related to the Sekani and Sarsi. In 2001 a total of 1,855 was reported.

CARRIER (DAKELHNE) A group of Athabascan bands inhabiting the upper branches of the Fraser River in north central British Columbia, particularly in the areas around Babine, Stuart and François lakes are known as the Carrier. Their first contact with Europeans came with the Alexander Mackenzie expedition in 1793. Subsequently, following Simon Fraser's visit in 1805, trading posts were established in their territory. They lived in semisedentary villages, leaving at regular seasons for fishing and hunting.

The Carrier borrowed many customs from the coastal Tsimshians in the Hazelton area, and there has also been considerable intermarriage. The impact of fur traders, missionaries and miners had begun to erode their Potlatch-rank complex by the end of the 19th century. They were heavily dependent upon fishing, collecting roots and berries, as well as hunting beaver, goat, moose and caribou for subsistence. Their structures included wooden gabled houses of the coastal type, semisubterranean earth-covered lodges and brush shelters. They numbered about 8,000 in 1793. The Carriers who lived about Babine Lake were sometimes referred to as *Babine* by traders, from the French word meaning labret, or lip ornaments. Their present-day descendants are at Moricetown, Burns Lake, Omineca, Lake Babine, Fraser Lake, Stony Creek, Stuart-Trembleur Lake, Takla Lake, Nazko, Ulkatcho, Kluskus

and Quesnal, scattered through about 100 small reserves with a registered population exceeding 7,000 in 2001.

CHILCOTIN (TSILHQOT'IN) These are a branch of the Athabascans living on the Chilcotin River, a western branch of the Fraser system in central British Columbia. They are closely related to the Carrier tribes to the north, and together are sometimes called *Takulli*. Their material culture was fairly simple, including wooden rectangular and gabled houses, snowshoes for winter travel, spruce bark and dugout canoes, fur blankets and robes, buckskin moccasins, aprons and kilts. They hunted elk, deer, caribou, mountain goat and, more recently, moose. Fishing was also important. They had coiled basketry with imbricated designs, but few other plastic or graphic arts. In the late 18th century, indirect contacts were made with the European-stimulated fur trade, and Fort Alexandria was established in Carrier country.

By the late 19th century they were in six bands: Toosey at Riske Creek below Williams Lake; Stone and Anaham south and north of the Chilcotin River; Alexis Creek at Redstone on the upper Chilcotin; Alexandria above Williams Lake; and Nemaiah Valley at Chilko Lake. Their present descendants (2001) number more than 2,000 people — perhaps twice their ancient population. Their traditional resources are now largely depleted.

NICOLA This is a designation given a small group of Athabascan-speaking Indians in the Nicola and Similkameen valleys, British Columbia, possibly of Chilcotin origin, though culturally they belong with the Thompson Indians with whom they have now apparently merged. The language has been extinct since about 1910.

SLAVEY or **SLAVE (DENETHAH)** The Slavey are a group of Athabascans who lived along southwestern tributaries of the Mackenzie River, the Hay, Liard and Nelson systems where the present boundaries of Alberta, British Columbia and Northwest Territories adjoin. They also occupied the Mackenzie valley itself, from Great Slave Lake to Great Bear River. The Slavey people and their relatives to the north and east, lived in a region of relatively poor resources, and their subsistence was won from one of the harshest regions of North America. While the lakes and waterways were rich in fish and berries (helping to supplement a diet of moose and caribou), starvation was a constant threat.

They had snowshoes, bark canoes and conical skin- or bark-covered structures resembling the Plains tipi. A low wooden shelter of logs, chinked and covered with earth or moss, was also used. Meager and scattered resources precluded permanent settlements until early 20th-century influences reduced their seminomadic way of life. Their clothes were made from moosehide. They excelled in the ornamentation of clothes with porcupine quillwork, and later with glass beads obtained from European traders. The Slavey seem to have been pushed north by invading Crees, and their name may derive from their status as Cree captives.

Initial European contact came with the Alexander Mackenzie expedition in 1789. Subsequently, the Hudson's Bay Company founded a number of trading posts in their territory, and Slavey life and culture were gradually modified. For many generations Slavey descendants have been concentrated in a number of areas influenced by specific trading posts, and some 6,100 people are today distributed as follows: Hay River, Fort Providence (Great Slave Lake), Fort Liard, Fort Simpson, Fort Wrigley and Fort Norman, all in the Northwest Territories; Fort Nelson in British Columbia; and on several reserves in the Upper Hay River region near Lake Assumption, Alberta. The present number is twice their original population, although a proportion are Métis.

Above: Slavey or Chipewyan woman, c. 1885. Northern Athabascans of the Mackenzie drainage have a tradition of relatively tailored clothing, although this dress is also heavily influenced by European materials. The cape and cuffs are black velvet, decorated with floralistic beadwork. The moccasins are the common Subarctic form with a center seam and U-shaped instep vamp.

MOUNTAIN AND GOAT INDIANS (SAHTUOY'INE) These are terms applied to some Athabascan bands on the eastern slopes of the Mackenzie Mountains, between Forts Liard and Good Hope, sometimes reported as members of other groups such as Kaska, Dogrib or Slavey. However, on historical, environmental and linguistic grounds they are now considered independent. Their largest group seems to be those at Fort Norman, but they are not reported separately from the Slavey by the Canadian Indian Affairs Branch.

HARE These people lived in the forested areas west of Great Bear Lake, Northwest Territories, including part of the lower Mackenzie River Valley.

Although they are not a tribe in the usual sense, communal feasting, dancing and gambling have created a strong sense of identity among them. They seem to be linguistically related to the Slavey, Mountain and Bear Lake Indians. Living in one of the coldest and harshest environments, starvation was a persistent feature of their existence. Their culture was generally similar to that of the Slavey, Dogrib and Kutchin, with subsistence dependent on the supply of caribou, moose and fish. Hare skins were used for some clothing, hence their group name, but tunics and, later, jackets were usually of moose or caribou hide. They have long been associated with Fort Good Hope on the Mackenzie River, where their descendants still numbered more than 1,200 in 2001.

BEAR LAKE INDIANS Athabascan people of Great Bear Lake, previously considered as mixed Hare, Slavey or Dogrib, are now separately recognized as Bear Lake Indians, although they are essentially a mixed people. About 1,000 people, mostly at Fort Franklin on Great Bear Lake, consider themselves to be Bear Lake Indians, although they are reported as "Hare" by the Canadian Indian Affairs Branch.

DOGRIB (TLICHO YATII) The Athabascan people living between Great Slave Lake and Great Bear Lake are known as Dogrib. Their general culture echoed that of other Northern Athabascans, characterized by scarce resources, particularly in the intensely cold winters. Fish, caribou, moose and hare were subsistence food. Clothing consisted of caribou-hide coats and dresses, usually tailored, unlike the V-front garments of the Kutchin. Footwear included moccasins of the ankle-wrap type and moccasin boots.

They have been known to Europeans from the mid-18th century, and their culture was partly modified from that period by guns, knives and other goods introduced by traders. Until about 1950 they spent most of their time in the bush, with seasonal activities of a traditional pattern — in particular hunting fur-bearing animals to be exchanged at trading posts. Most modern Dogrib descendants are in the Fort Rae district (or Rae settlement) at Yellowknife, Detah and also mixed with others at Snowdrift and Fort Franklin. As

Left: Slavey, c. 1880. Among the Northern Athabascans and Métis, newborn babies were carried and nursed in cloth bags laced up the front, but lacking the back board of the Cree and Ojibwa. These "moss bags" (from their sphagnum moss internal padding) were sometimes carefully decorated in beaded or silk floralistic designs.

of 2005 they numbered about 4,800, including Métis, which exceeds their aboriginal numbers. Their name is thought to be of Cree origin, meaning "dog side."

YELLOWKNIFE (T'ATSAOT'INE) So named from copper found in their territory, this Athabascan group, who appear to be closely related to — if not strictly part of — the Chipewyan Indians, lived east of the Dogrib Indians, who were often openly hostile to them. In the early 19th century they were described as suffering periods of starvation and disease. They seem to have been absorbed by the Dogribs at Yellowknife or by the Chipewyans at Snowdrift and Fort Resolution. The Yellowknife Indians reported by the various Canadian census in recent years usually refer to the "Dogrib people at Yellowknife" in the District of Mackenzie.

CHIPEWYAN (DENE SULINE) One of the largest Northern Athabascan groups, the Chipewyan should not be confused with the Chippewa. They inhabited a vast forest-tundra area of present northern Manitoba, Saskatchewan and the Northwest Territories District of Mackenzie, south and east of Great Slave Lake. They have had the longest and most continuous contact with Europeans of Northern Athabascans, beginning in about 1682, with the establishment of York Factory by the Hudson's Bay Company. Subsequently, they became middlemen in extensive trade with more remote tribes. Their ancient domain has been modified over the years by their involvement in the Canadian fur trade, resulting in a number of bands moving south from their forest-tundra domain to true boreal forest. They were often on unfriendly terms with the Crees, who encroached on their territory, and were seriously affected by European-introduced diseases. The northern bands depended upon the Barren Ground caribou in a region affected by long, severe winters.

Their traditional beliefs were based on the concept of power given in dreams by spirit animals. This power controlled game, and could be used for curing. Their dress was originally of caribou hides, but European clothes were adopted in the 19th century. Shelters were often conical tipis of caribou skins. During the late 19th century the Chipewyans gradually affiliated into groups associated with various trading posts. In aboriginal times they are thought to have numbered more than 8,000; a number that has been more than exceeded by their current population of close to 14,000.

Right: Saulteaux woman, c. 1820. One of the earliest recorded women's dresses in the Northeast was the skin (later, trade cloth) slip, supported over the shoulders with two straps to which a separate cape or sleeves were added in cold weather. This very loose garment required a belt tied behind.

Their principal bands today are at Fort Churchill, Brochet and Northland (Manitoba); Lac La Hache (northeastern Saskatchewan); Fond Du Lac and Stony Rapids, east of Lake Athabasca, and several minor groups collectively known as Portage La Loche, English River, Peter Pond Lake (all in northern Saskatchewan). In Alberta they are at Janvier, Gregoire Lake, Fort McMurray, Fort Mackay, Fort Chipewyan, Fort Fitzgerald and Fort Smith; and in the Northwest Territories at Salt River, Resolution and Snowdrift. In all areas there has been intermarriage with the Crees. Despite their harsh environment Chipewyan women have produced very fine quillwork, beadwork and silk embroidery over the years, and their work is well represented in museum collections.

SUBARCTIC ALGONKIAN

NORTHERN OJIBWA and **SAULTEAUX** Although originally an Eastern Woodland people the Ojibwa, like their northern cousins the Crees, these people were from early contact days induced north and west by the fur trade activities of the Hudson's Bay Company. From the 1670s onward the Northern Ojibwa have occupied the interior of Ontario and the so-called Saulteaux — the areas around Lake Winnepeg, Lake Manitoba and Lake Winnipegosis in present Manitoba, and Lake of the Woods in western Ontario. They became dependent upon European trade goods, which they secured in return for furs — at first from posts on James and Hudson bays, and later from interior posts. Their material culture became a mix of native and European elements. They retained native snares, birch bark canoes, toboggans and birch bark, spruce or hide dwellings. But they also adopted guns, commercial traps, canvas tents, log cabins and lately even outboard motors. Native dress also changed to European style, though moccasins were still used until recently. Their Woodland traditions reveal themselves in the Midewiwin (Grand Medicine Society), vision quest and certain forms of decorative art. They also seem to have had a belief in Kitchi-Manitou, a paramount beneficent force, a power in all natural things and the comic culture hero they call Nanabush. Many Saulteaux communities are now Christian, often Pentecostal.

Many have moved to urban Winnipeg, and they have suffered more than most through disruptive Euro-Canadian influences. Their early population is difficult if not impossible to separate from other Ojibwa, but their descendants were reported to number about 30,000 in 1978, a number that —now approaches 100,000 in Canada which combines Eastern, Northern Ojibwa and Plains Ojibwa together. The greatest numbers of Northern Ojibwa are at Big Trout Lake, Caribou Lake, Fort Hope, Deer Lake, Osnaburgh and other places in north central Ontario, plus Garden Hill, St. Theresa Point and other locations in northeastern Manitoba. The so-called Saulteaux have 30 reserves near Lake Winnipeg, Lake of the Woods and Lac Seul. The largest groups of these are Roseau River (sometimes given as Plains Ojibwa), Berens River, Fort Alexander,

Peguis, Little Grand Rapids, Fairford and Lake St. Martin in Manitoba; and Pikangikum, Islington, Grassy Narrows, Rat Portage, Whitefish Bay, La Seul and other places in southwestern Ontario, numbering more than 30,000. In some locations Ojibwa speakers are called "Cree."

CREE The Kristineaux or Cree Indians were one of the largest and most important native tribes of the North American continent. They were an Algonkian people related to the Montagnais, Menomini, Sauk, Fox, Kickapoo and Shawnee. The term "Kristineaux," from Kenistenoag is the French version of their native name, the form "Cree" being contracted from Kristineaux during the fur trade period. The designation has no literal translation, nor does the Plains Cree term for themselves, "Nehuawak" or "Nehiyawak."

The Crees' importance was due mainly to the position they held in the Canadian fur trade, and the influence that position gave them with other tribes. During the rearrangement of the Cree bands in western Canada while engaged in the activities of the Hudson's Bay Company, the Cree were scarcely a tribe in the popular sense, but rather a collection of bands, groups — even families — scattered through an immense area. At the height of Cree power no tribe in North America ever occupied such a large area. While the Cree were scattered so widely there were only minor dialectical differences between most of the bands. However, due to long separation there were slight differences between the languages of the Plains and Woods Cree. In short, before their historic westward expansion they were a typical eastern Subarctic tribe of the Algonkian linguistic stock. They can be generally subdivided into the *West Main Cree*, *Woods Cree* and *Plains Cree*. However, there were probably Cree in the west before the advance of the fur trade, and an old group known as the Rocky Cree may have been in Saskatchewan before European contact. Missionaries organized a form of written syllabary of the Cree language which is still widely used. The total population of all groups of Cree in Canada is now approaching 160,000, a number that is considerably larger than their population in precontact days, although many of the modern Cree are intermixed; and a further 21,000 are reported as Ojibwa–Cree combined.

WEST MAIN CREE This is the modern term to cover the Cree bands formerly occupying the low-lying west coast of James Bay in northern Ontario, and formerly more commonly known as (or at least as part of) the *Swampy Cree* or *Maskegon*; more specifically, the Barren Ground, Fort Albany, Monsoni and Kesagami Cree. Beginning in the late 17th century these coastal Cree had adapted to the fur trade and missionary teachings with a gradual modification in their native culture. Contacts with Europeans go back to 1668 and 1671, when trading posts were established in reach of the Swampy Cree.

Besides being skillful hunters, they also fished. Both meat and fish were heat-dried to be preserved as winter food, often mixed with berries and grease. The Swampy Cree shared with the Northern Ojibwa and Saulteaux most religious beliefs, including the "shaking tent" rite, in which power was acquired from nonhuman helpers. Their descendants are at Moose Factory, Fort Albany, Attawapiskat, Winisk, Severn, York Factory, Fox Lake, Shamattawa and Churchill.

WESTERN WOODS CREE The Woods Cree are usually designated the western extension of the Swampy Cree in Manitoba, Saskatchewan, and Alberta, during the later decades of the 18th century and early 19th century. These Cree retained their basic boreal forest culture, though modified by their dependence upon the fur trade. They followed the European traders and explorers deep into the north country, forcing the Chipewyans north and the Beaver to the Rocky Mountains. Their material culture was largely replaced by European goods at an early period, but they retained snowshoes, toboggans, skin lodges and bark canoes, plus some elements of aboriginal dress, such as moccasins. They seem to have excelled in decorative porcupine quillwork, painting, silkwork and beadwork.

They believed in a Great Spirit and feared the Windigos (ice giants) who caused cannibalism. The Hudson's Bay Company

Above: Pouch of black-dyed buckskin decorated with horizontal bands of woven porcupine quillwork of a style once common among the northern Great Lakes Indians, but by the 19th century restricted to the Cree, Northern Ojibwa and Athabascans of Canada. This pouch is probably Cree, c. 1820. Formerly M. G. Johnson Collection

Right: Swampy Cree woman, c. 1780. A few painted garments with dot, circle and linear designs have survived in museums, attributed to Eastern and Swampy Cree of the Hudson Bay area before European styles and materials became influential. The rare side-fold dress, cape, hood, moccasins and pouch display painted, quilled and beaded ornamentation.

Left: Cree domed wigwam.

278

Above Left: Calling a moose — Cree, a photograph dated c.1927 and published in The North American Indian, volume 18. Library of Congress, Prints & Photographs Division LC-USZ62-123167.

Above Right: Banner, probably Woods Cree, c. 1875. Beadwork on dark heavy cloth edged with cord piping. The floral beaded style is of an early generation using a combination of sinew and thread to sew on the beads. Probably a wall hanging for a house or log cabin.

Left: Woods Cree watch pocket, late 19th century, decorated with imported glass beads and silk ribbon — European-manufactured replacements for the indigenous materials of dyed moose and deer hair, bird and porcupine quill.

Right: Guncase or scabbard, Northern Athabascan, c. 1920. Smoked caribou skin probably from one of the Northern Athbascan groups of northern Canada such as Slavey, Kaska, or Kutchin. There are two areas of black velvet cloth decorated with typical floral beadwork of that area. The scabbard is also trimmed with woollen tassels.

Below Left: James Cree bag. M.G. Johnson Collection.

Below Right: Man's cloth leggings with selvedged edge and panels of floral beadwork on black cloth. Probably either Athabascan-Metis or Western Woods Cree-Métis, c. 1860. M.G. Johnson Collection.

(Cross Lake, Fisher River, Gods Lake, Mathias Colomb, Nelson House, Norway House, Oxford House, The Pas and others); Woods Cree nine bands in Saskatchewan (Lac la Ronge, Montreal Lake and Peter Ballantyne being the largest); and 13 bands in Northern Alberta (Driftpile, Little Red River, Wabasca, Whitefish Lake, Sturgeon Lake, Fort Vermillion and several others). In a number of locations they are much mixed with Northern Ojibwa and Saulteaux. In 2005 a total of 159,370 Cree were reported in Canada being the total of Plains, Woods, West Main and East Cree divisions. For many years Cree and Cree Métis women have made moccasins, pouches, mittens and jackets decorated with rich floralistic patterns in beads and silk and thread for sale or trade at the trading posts. Such items have found their way into many museums in the United States, Canada and Europe.

TÊTE DE BOULE or **ATTIKAMEK** These are a branch of the Cree who still inhabit the upper St. Maurice River region in Quebec, and were perhaps contacted by Europeans as early as 1630. The general culture was similar to the Montagnais-Nascapi to the north, and the Algonkin to the south. Although heavily influenced by the French-controlled fur trade of the area, and subjected to Iroquois penetration, they continued to live independently until the introduction of Euro-Canadian industrialization in recent times.

Their native dress seems to have disappeared at an early time, but they excelled in birch bark work and made excellent canoes. They presently have more than 4,000 descendants at Obedjiwan, Weymontachie and Manouan in central Quebec. Most still speak their native language, and they are politically organized with their Montagnais neighbors.

MONTAGNAIS-NASCAPI These are the Algonkians of Quebec and Labrador, from the St. Lawrence north and west to James Bay. The Labrador and northern Quebec bands are sometimes given separate status as Nascapi (Naskapi). They belong to the Cree dialectic branch of the family, and the bands on the east coast of James Bay are now locally called *East Main Cree* or *East Cree*. They were skillful hunters, using snares, traps and bows, and when near the sea killed seals with harpoons. They fished with lines and bone hooks, and used wooden spears with bone points and light birch bark canoes. They were without agriculture, although they collected wild berries and roots, and hunted moose, caribou and deer. Clothing was made from caribou or moose hides and included coats, leggings, mittens and fur robes with hoods attached. They had toboggans, portable conical lodges and wigwams.

They ritualized their supernatural powers around good health and hunting, and a belief in the trickster-transformer figure. The Montagnais, a term used for most of the southern bands, were met by Champlain in the early 17th century. Missionary and fur trade influences followed, but until fairly recently the northern bands have been quite remote from white culture. Today, television, computers, snowmobiles, prefabricated homes and white-run schools are found in most communities.

In 1650 they perhaps numbered 5,500, gradually diminishing to 2,183 in 1906, but were numbered as 11,697 in 1971, and 12,640 in 2005. Their main southern (St. Lawrence) bands are at St. Augustin, Bersimis, Romaine, Mingan, Sept-

Above: Cree warrior/hunter from the James and Hudson Bays area, c. 1815, clothed against the harsh climate. Native in origin, the hood, coat, leggings and mittens already show European influence in the tailored cut and decorative refinements. Yet more baroque, Europeanized forms would develop as time passed. The woolen leggings, powder horn strap and bullet pouch are heavily beaded in floralistic designs, probably of European inspiration. But the painted designs on the coat and porcupine quilled belt and shoulder decoration are old native techniques. Most Eastern Cree moccasins are of moose or caribou hide, with a heavily puckered seam around the instep vamp. Western Woods Cree moccasins have a center seam from vamp to toe.

was the economic authority of the whole region until the introduction of modern Canadian influences, such as housing programs, health centers and the developing micro-urban community. Their language, however, is still widely used.

The population of the ancestors of Swampy and Woods Crees may have been 20,000 in the 18th century; they numbered 35,550 in 1978, exclusive of Métis: Swampy Cree in eight bands in Ontario (Constance Lake, Timagami with Ojibwa, Matachewan and others); and 15 bands in Manitoba,

Above: "Moss for the baby-bags," a Cree woman photographed in c. 1927 by Edward S. Curtis. Library of Congress, Prints & Photographs Division LC–USZ62–106995.

Left: Tahltan-style shoulder bag from the late 19th century, made of cotton fabric with red trade cloth facing and a backing of green coarse-weave wool cloth. The front is beaded and tasseled. The strap is made of cotton cloth and red trade cloth.

Right and Top Right: Two "octopus bag" or "four-tab" pouches (actually eight, but only four visible at the front). Top, a Cree or Cree-Métis bag collected before 1847. Toward the end of the 19th century, octopus bags were also being made and used by the Tlingit and the Salishan-speaking nations on the Northwest Coast and Plateau. The bag at right is from Northwest Canada, possibly Inland Tlingit or Athabascan. This form of bag of beaded cloth edged with silk had spread northwest across Canada with the Métis and Cree from the Western Great Lakes and Red River during the 19th century. Courtesy Mark Sykes.

Iles, Escoumains and Natashquan; their interior bands at North West River (Labrador), Lake St. John, Mistassini, Nemaska, Waswanipi and Chimo (largely transfered to Schefferville in the 1950s); and their James Bay bands are at Fort George, Eastmain, Rupert House, Paint Hills and Great Whale River — these latter groups usually being referred to as "East Main Cree." They were noted for the very fine linear and curving painted designs on their ceremonial dress, examples of which survive in museum collections in Europe and North America. Today the Montagnais-Nascapi use the term "Innu" for themselves.

BEOTHUK The Beothuk are the original inhabitants of the island of Newfoundland, perhaps met by Europeans as early as 1497, and subsequently known to explorers and fishermen. They were known for their use of red ocher, hence "Red Indians." Over the years they were in constant dispute with invading French, English and Micmac, and were often murdered on the slightest provocation. By the 18th century they were restricted to Red Indian Lake and Exploits River. They

Above: Nascapi man, c. 1880. Caribou hide clothing, perhaps partly fitted, seems to have been characteristic of circumpolar costume in aboriginal times, probably being modified by European contact into more complex tailoring. The Nascapi, Montagnais and Eastern Cree have a tradition of magnificent painted garments, paint being applied in lines scored on the skin surface. Designs (apparently once predominantly linear) were no doubt symbolic hunting aids, and often used the flattened form of double curve typical of Northeast Algonkians. Note the cap, rounded bullet pouch, mittens and moccasins without front seams but gathered around a large vamp.

Above: Mongtagnais-Nascapi woman of c. 1891, wearing the style of hat traditional around North West River, Labrador. Made in sections of alternating red and blue cloth, the hat has the upper portion folded over on itself. The hair was wound on a small piece of wood and then bound with cloth or beads.

perhaps numbered 450 in 1768; 72 in 1811; and only 14 in 1823. Shanawdithit or Nancy April, the last of her people, died in 1829. From the limited data available, the Beothuk language appears to be an isolated family, though perhaps very distantly related to Algonkian. They were a river and bay people, living in wigwams and using a very distinctively shaped bark canoe.

Below Left: Eastern Cree canoe. The Cree and Montagnais of Quebec province developed this "crooked" shape, thought to aid turning. In the far north the frame was sometimes spruce or larch, and spruce bark was occasionally used. In later years, canvas, nails, tacks and twine replaced native materials.

Bottom: Beothuk canoe. Only models have survived. Of almost V-shaped sections, they appear to have had a flared and upswept profile, and were reported to need ballast to maintain stability.

Below Right: Trade cloth pouch decorated with beadwork in applique floralistic technique and a panel of woven beadwork. East Cree/Swampy Cree, mid 19th century. Courtesy Mark Sykes.

ARCTIC

Language family and tribe	Meaning/origin of tribal name, where known
Eskimoan or Eskimaleut:	
Aleut	*"island"* (possibly)
Inuit (formerly Eskimo)	*"people,"* (*"raw meat eaters"*)

The Arctic cultural area, exclusively the home of the Inuit — formerly called Eskimo — and the Aleut, extends in a 5,000-mile (8,000 km) sweep from Siberia to Greenland, including most of the islands and coastal areas of Alaska, Canada (including Labrador) and Greenland. Their land is almost treeless, and is bounded by tundra to the south. It is a region where the climate is so cold and the coasts lashed by storms of such magnitude that it seems beyond the margins within which human beings can survive, let alone flourish.

The Inuits' ancestors seem to have been the last major influx of people from Siberia across the Bering Strait, perhaps between 5000 and 6000 B.C., with the Aleuts probably splitting from the main body fairly early on. These proto-Inuit people probably reached modern Greenland in about 2000 B.C. Archaeologists have discovered there the remains of settlements that they term the "Dorset Culture." Further west, along the coast of the Beaufort Sea, the remains of another early culture have been found, which has been termed Thule. It is believed that the Thule people or their descendants rapidly swept eastward from about A.D. 800. They settled along the ice-free shores of Greenland and absorbed the Dorset people. At about the same period, they abandoned most of the northernmost islands in the Arctic, perhaps due to climatic changes.

The Inuit for the most part relied for their subsistence on the sea, where the food chain ensured a large population of seals, whales and walrus. In summer, when the usually featureless landscape briefly became warm and sustained exuberant flora and fauna, they turned inland to hunt caribou, returning to the coast in fall and winter to fish and hunt sea mammals through blowholes in the ice or along deep fissures. They survived mostly on fat and meat — much of which was eaten raw — which

Above: Baffin Island Inuit man, c. 1577. Sketches made during Frobisher's expedition show both men and women wearing sealskin parkas with a long rear tail. This later disappeared from men's costume, perhaps in imitation of European jackets, but was retained by women.

gave them all the vitamin C required for health. Their tools, spears, harpoons, sleds, kayak frames and even bows often had to be pieced together in composite constructions from driftwood and antler, since they had only limited access to trees (although in Alaska they fashioned wooden masks that are reminscent of Northwest Coast culture, and there were other cultural exchanges with the Subarctic Athabascans).

The tribes most markedly divergent from what we think of as typically Inuit were the Chugachigmiut or Chugach, on Prince William Sound, Alaska, and the Kaniagmiut of Kodiak Island. Both mummified their noble dead, built house types of wooden slabs that resembled those of the Tlingit, and developed whale-hunting techniques strangely similar to those of the Nootka far to the south. Inuit housing varied from the iglu (igloo) of ice blocks among some Canadian Inuit to sod, wood and whalebone semisubterranean huts at winter village sites, and seal or caribou skin lodges in summer.

They were, and still are, superb sea and ice navigators, traveling by kayak or dog-drawn sleds. Their world swarmed with supernatural beings, usually interpreted by shamans. They practiced infanticide and left old people to die alone in times of great hardship, but exaggerated stories mask their unique ability to survive in their harsh, cold and dark environment. Beyond the family, social organization was largely lacking.

In this respect they were unlike the Aleuts, who had a structured society of chiefs, commoners and slaves. The Aleuts were influenced by Europeans from the mid-18th century, when Russian mariner explorers settled on their islands and began the sea-otter fur trade in which the Aleuts participated. Conversion to the Russian Orthodox Church followed. They were makers of fine waterproof clothing and, unlike the Inuit, excelled in basketry. They also used a two-man kayak, or baidarka.

The Eskimo people of Arctic Canada are

now called Inuit. The Arctic peoples of Alaska have also recently introduced terminology that more correctly represents their linguistic and cultural divergences. The northern Alaska Inuit known before as Northern, Northern Interior, Kotzebue and Bering Strait Inuit are now collectively known as Inupiat. They are linguistically related to the Canadian Inuit. The remaining Arctic peoples of Alaska (also once called Eskimo) are now collectively called Yupik. There are four Yupik languages:

1. Central Alaskan Yup'ik including two sub-groups Cup'ip and Cup'ik. They are principally located on the Yukon and Kuskokwim river deltas, Kuskokwim River and Bristol Bay and are by far the largest of the four groups.
2. Alutiip or Suqpiag also called Pacific Yupik or Chugach, living on the Alaskan Peninsula and the coastal islands of South-central Alaska including Kodiak Island.
3. Siberian Yupik, of far eastern Russia and also St. Lawrence Island of Alaska.
4. Naukan, a small group of far eastern Russia.

The Aleut or Unangan, the indigenous people of the Aleutian Islands are both culturally and linguistically independent from both Yupik and Inuit but are classed under the same general phylum.

The Siberian Inuit may be a resettlement from Alaska or the remains of the original people from whom all the Inuit originally split, or a mixture of both. The Greenland Inuit have had a long association with first the Norsemen, and later Danes, with considerable mixture among the East Greenland Inuit. European influences came later to the Canadian Inuit tribes, but by the early 20th century, twill tents, whiteman-made whale boats, guns and sewing machines were used widely — as was a form of syllabary similar to the Cree system, introduced by missionaries.

It is difficult to estimate their population before the introduction of European diseases — perhaps 60,000, reduced to half that number by 1900. But a recent estimate, including those in Greenland, would indicate a recovery to a figure well in excess of their original population.

ESKIMOAN or ESKIMOALEUT

The linguistic family of the northern edge of the New World, extending into Greenland in the east, along the Canadian and Alaskan coastline and into Siberia is referred to as Eskimoan. The family combines the Inuit, formerly termed Eskimo, and the divergent Aleut of the Aleutian Island chain. Their racial separation from the Indian is emphasized by a combination of linguistic, cultural and racial divergence, which taken together, suggest a separate people. They are distinctly Mongol, of short, stocky build — perhaps a relatively late arrival from Asia. The culture area known as "Arctic" is that of the Inuit and Aleut together.

ALEUT These are the original inhabitants of the long Aleutian Islands chain and the Alaska Peninsula, in two general divisions. The *Atka* division held several of the outer islands as far as Attu Island, and including parts of Agattu Island, Unalga Island in the Andreanof group, and Atka Island. The *Unalaska* division held the inner islands from Unalaska Island in the Fox group, Unimak Island, the Shumagin and Pribilof Islands and the western Alaskan Peninsula, almost to Pilot Point. They became known in the 1740s to the Russians, who cruelly mistreated and exploited them. Within a few decades their numbers were reduced from 16,000 to little more than 2,000.

In their rain-soaked islands they developed waterproof clothing made from translucent seal skin, often with caribou hair seam decoration of extraordinary delicacy. During the early 19th century, the remaining Aleuts were converted by the Russian Orthodox Church, generally assumed some of the culture brought by Europeans and there was considerable intermarriage. In 1867 they were — with Alaska — transferred to the control of the United States. In 1910 they were reported to number only 1,451, many of mixed descent. Today, small communities are still found, notably at Atka, on St. Pauls and St. George islands, Unalaska, Akutan, King Cove, Belkofski, Sand Point, Port Noller, and in a few other locations outside their former area. A 2001 estimate placed them at about 8,000, total.

1 Caribou Inuit kayak. About 20 feet (16 km) long and usually narrow, this decked, one-man hunting canoe was more widely employed than the umiak. The flat-bottomed or V-shaped frame of (usually driftwood) fir, pine, spruce, or willow is rigid without its (usually seal) skin covering — unlike bark canoes, which collapse on removal of the bark. The Inuit or "Caribou Eskimo" on the northwest side of Hudson Bay favored an extended prow and upraised stern, tilted cockpit, and double-bladed paddles.

2 Aleut baidarka. About 25 feet (8 km) long, these have two, occasionally three, cockpits and sharp sterns. The term also has come to be used in Alaska to designate Aleut or Inuit kayaks with forked bows. Provision was often made to hold a harpoon catch or trade goods on the deck, sometimes in a wooden frame.

3 Western Alaskan kayak. About 15 feet (4.5 m) long, these typically had sharp vertical ends, a handling hole in the bow and a flat-rimmed cockpit. They were noted for their speed. Single-bladed paddles were sometimes used.

4 Inuit umiak. These were known in various forms, up to 40 feet (12 m) long, from Kodiak Island to Greenland. This open-topped cargo boat was sometimes used for walrus hunting and whaling. Its wooden frame was covered with seal, whale or walrus hide. As many as a dozen crew could paddle, though sails (or recently, outboard motors) might be installed.

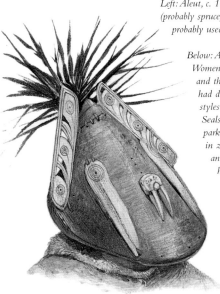

Left: Aleut, c. 1850. Long-billed wooden hat (probably spruce), with walrus ivory attachments, probably used as a sun visor when sea hunting.

Below: Alaskan Inuit woman, c. 1895. Womens' caribou parkas of northern Alaska and the Mackenzie delta region of Canada had deep side scallops and hood ruffs. Parka styles varied considerably across the Arctic. Sealskin was important in the east. Men's parkas sometimes had ears and attachments in zoomorphic reference to prey animals as an aid to hunting. Women's sometimes had circular or diagonal inserts projecting a uterine reference, symbolizing the maternal role. Hoods were often large enough to carry babies. Leggings and boots were combined. In winter, two layers of clothing were often worn, the inner layer with fur inside, the outer with fur outside.

INUIT While the Inuit constitute one complete linguistic family with the Aleut, they are usually considered independently from the native inhabitants of the rest of the continent, chiefly on physical grounds. The earliest archaeological sites in the Arctic have been dated to between 2500 and 2000 B.C., and are designated as Independence I, Pre-Dorset, Dorset and Thule cultures, the latter dated to approximately the 13th century. All are direct ancestors of the Inuit people. They seem to have spread east and south to the Gulf of St. Lawrence, around the entire northern and northeastern coast of Canada, plus some parts of Greenland; along the coast of Hudson Bay, Baffin Land and other northern islands; the coast of Alaska including Kodiak Island, and to the detached Chugach on Prince William Sound.

Despite a number of separate tribes and a range of occupation of over 3,000 miles, the Inuit languages vary sufficiently only to be classified into two major divisions: the Pacific or Alaskan (Yupik) division, and the Canadian or Northern group. The distribution of the Inuit was as follows:

Labrador Inuit — included those groups that extended from the Strait of Belle Isle along the coast of Labrador, Ungava Bay, Hudson Strait and the east side of Hudson Bay, as far south as Fort George. The most important groups were the *Tahagmiut* or *Tarramiut* of northern Quebec, *Itivimiut* of the east coast of Hudson Bay and *Kigiktagmiut* or *Qikirmiut* of Belcher Islands. Their present communities are at Rigolet, Hopedale, Nain, Makkovik, Port Burwell, Port Chimo, Tasiujaq, Aupaluk, Koartac, Wakeham, Saglonc, Ivujivik, Akulivik, Povungnituk, Port Harrison, Sanikiluaq and Poste-de-la-Baleine.

Baffin Island Inuit — includes the inhabitants of the eastern half of the Island, who include the *Nugumiut* of Frobisher Bay, *Akuliarmiut* below Amadjuak Lake, *Padlimiut* on Home Bay, *Qaumauangmiut* on the Meta Incognita Peninsula, *Akudnirmiut* of Buchan Gulf and *Sikosuilarmiut* of the Foxe Peninsula. Their present settlements are at Cape Dorset, Lake Harbor, Frobisher Bay, Broughton Island, Clyde River and Pangnirtung.

Iglulik Inuit — held the western part of Baffin Island, and the Melville Peninsula south, beyond Wager Bay, almost to Chesterfield Inlet. They include the *Tununmirmiut* of Eclipse Sound, *Tununirushirmiut* of Admiralty Inlet, *Aivillirmiut* or *Aivilingmiut* on the Ross Welcome Sound and Melville Peninsula and *Sagdlirmiut* or *Sadlermiut* on Southampton Island. Their present communities are at Arctic Bay, Pond Inlet on Baffin Island, Igloolik, Hall Beach, Repulse Bay and Coral Harbor.

Netsilik Inuit — held the area west and south of the Gulf of Boothia. They include the *Arveqtormiut* or *Arviqtuurmiut* of Somerset Island, *Netsilingmiut* on the Boothia Peninsula, *Utkuhikhalingmiut* or *Ukkusiksaligmiut* on Back River and *Iluilermiut* on Adelaide Peninsula and King William Island. Their settlements today are at Grise Fiord, Resolute, Spence Bay, Pelly Bay and Gjoa Haven.

Caribou Inuit — included a number of groups on Chesterfield Inlet, Baker Lake and Thelon River, almost to Churchill in northern Manitoba. Their present settlements are at Chesterfield Inlet, Baker Lake, Rankin Inlet, Whale Cove and Eskimo Point.

Copper Inuit — held the southern part of Banks Island, Victoria Island on both sides of Coronation Gulf, Bathurst Inlet and Queen Maud Gulf, including amongst others the *Kanghiryuarmiut* on Banks Island, *Kogloktogmiut* or *Kogluktomiut* on the lower part of the Coppermine River. Their descendants are at Sachs Harbor, Holman, Cambridge Bay, Coppermine, Bathurst Inlet and Umingmaktok.

Mackenzie Inuit — includes a number of groups around the delta of the Mackenzie River and Cape Bathurst. Their present groups are at Tuktoyaktuk, Paulatuk, Aklavik and Inuvik, the latter two settlements shared with the Athabascan Kutchin.

Greenland Inuit — encompasses a number of groups chiefly on the western coast, including a northern section above Cape York on the Hayes Peninsula known as *Polar Inuit*, and an eastern group around Angmagssalik on the east coast.

Below: Alaskan Inuit Wolf Dancer, c. 1915. He wears a wolf-head mask, and sealskin dance mittens with rattling puffin beaks.

Alaskan Inuit — can be divided as follows:

North Alaskan Inuit — extended from Point Barrow to Point Hope (Inupiat).

Northern Interior Inuit — were to the south, on the Colville River, south to the Continental Divide (Inupiat).

Kotzebue Inuit — chiefly on Kotzebue Sound and Kobuk River (Inupiat).

Bering Strait Inuit — located on Norton Sound. There were a number of Inuit groups on the southern part of Norton Sound and the mouth of the Yukon River.

Kuskwogmiut — on the Kuskokwim River (Yup'ik).

Nunivagmiut — on Nunivak Island (Yup'ik).

Togiagmiut — on Togiak Bay and River (Yup'ik).

Aglemiut — on the upper Alaska Peninsula (Alutiip).

Kaniag or *Koniag* — on Kodiak Island (Alutiip).

Chugach — on Prince William Sound (Alutiip).

Ugalakmiut — of Kayak Island (Alutiip).

Siberian Yupik — of Cape Chukotsky, Siberia and St. Lawrence Island.

The total population of the Alaskan Inuit (Alutiip, Yup'ik and Inupiat) is currently approximately 80,000 combined. This is more than 100% increase since 1970 when the Alaskan Inuit were then distributed as follows:

- North Alaskan Inuit at Barrow and Point Hope, in about six groups numbering over 3,000 (Inupiat).
- Northern Interior Inuit at Anaktuvuk Pass, numbering about 200 (Inupiat).
- About 12 communities of Kotzebue Inuit, the largest being Kotzebue, Noatak, Selawik and Noorvik, and totaling about 4,000 (Inupiat).
- Bering Strait Inuit in about 30 small settlements, the largest at Nome, Shishmaref, Wales, Teller, White Mountain, St. Michael, Mountain, Koyuk, Unalakleet and Shaktoolik, numbering in all over 5,000 (Inupiat).
- The Yukon River delta area has about 20 groups including those south to Toksook Bay, the main ones being at Kotlik, Alakanuk, Scammon Bay, Hooper Bay, Cheyak, Tanunak, Kipnuk and totaling over 4,000 (Yup'ik).
- The Kuskokwim River groups are at Kwigillingok, Eek and Kwethluk, plus Togiamiut at Togiak, Clarks Point and Dillingham, numbering together about 5,000 (Yup'ik).
- On Nunivak Island are about 300 at Nash Harbor and Mekoryuk (Yup'ik).
- On St. Lawrence Island about 1,000 people live at Gambell and Savoonga (Siberian Yup'ik).

- On the upper Alaska Peninsula are about six communities, including Chignik, Pilot Point, Egegik and others, totaling perhaps 1,000 (Alutiip).
- The Kodiak Island Inuit have about 10 groups, the largest at Kodiak, totaling about 1,500 (Alutiip).
- Prince William Sound Inuit at Port Graham and Seward, (much mixed with Athabascans,) number perhaps 300 (Alutiip).

Canadian Inuit distribution numbers from 1970 (then about 20,000 total) were given as follows:
- Labrador Inuit groups number about 4,000.
- Baffin Island Inuit, with groups at Pangnirtung, Frobisher Bay and Lake Harbor, about 2,500.
- Iglulik Inuit include about 1,000 in the Pond Inlet area, 500 in the Chesterfield area, and 200 on Southampton Island.
- The Netsilik number perhaps one thousand in the Spence Bay district. Caribou Inuit of the Chesterfield, Baker Lake and Eskimo Point areas total some 2,000.
- Copper Inuit of the Cambridge Bay and Coppermine areas, 1,500.
- Mackenzie Inuit, about 1,500 in the Aklavik district.
- The population of the Greenland Inuit was about 13,500 in 1922.

The above is by no means a complete list, but a total recent population estimate of more than 140,000, including the Siberian Inuit but excluding the Greenland Inuit, seems probably correct, and compares fairly favorably with their original numbers. (See also Native Populations.)

On April 1, 1999, Nunavut — meaning "our land" in Inuit — was separated officially from the Northwest Territories. Its capital is Iqaluit (formerly Frobisher Bay) on Baffin Island. Its inhabitants are called Nunavummiut. As of the 2001 Census the population of Nunavut was 26,745, with 22,560 people identifying themselves as Inuit, 95 as First Nations, 50 Métis and 3,945 as non–aboriginal.

The Inuit was — and in many locations still is — a hunter, and with a few exceptions (such as the Caribou Inuit), a shore-dwelling sea hunter who is wholly carnivorous. They were skilled in making the equipment necessary to win all the food they required from the sea and its margins in a climate and a terrain that seem beyond the limits at which man could survive. Their seal skin or caribou hide clothes, with the hair left on, were skillfully prepared and stitched to provide astonishing insulation against the cold. A person so dressed could sleep in the open at −22°F (−30°C). Their fitted tunic, called parka in the west or anorak in the east, was worn with trousers of polar bear or seal skin, and seal skin boots. In extreme cold, two layers of clothing were worn for added insulation. Numerous regional styles of tunic displayed variations in cut and decoration, characterized by hoods and long tails front and back, sometimes reaching down to the ankles.

The iglu was a dwelling known only to the Central Inuit groups of northern Canada, built of compacted snow blocks accurately spiraled to form a domed structure. Heat and light were generated by oil lamps, which kept the temperature inside just below freezing point. Most Inuit, however, built the *karmat* — a hut of stone, whalebone and/or sod. Modern prefabricated bungalows with electric cookers and oil-fired furnaces are now known to all parts of the north.

Two forms of water transportation were known. The kayak was common in the east, and umiak in the west. They also used a true sled, with runners drawn by dog teams on ice or frozen mud. Their principal food supply during the dark winter was seal, and caribou was eaten during the summer. Other sources of food included walrus, whale, musk-ox and wild fowl.

Two major rituals were celebrated annually: one to release the sea animals; the other to celebrate the return of the sun — the welcome herald of winter's end. In both celebrations costumed figures, often masked and simultaneously male and female, suggest the renewal of creation.

Above: Polar Inuit summer tent, c. 1915. In summer, all Inuit moved into skin tents. This tupik varied in construction and size, the simplest a seal or caribou skin cover lashed to a wooden frame, with thin-scraped hide over the doorway to admit light. More substantial interseasonal qarmaq dwellings had covers that could be raised over collapsed iglus, or supported on whale-rib arches and poles, insulated with moss and secured to the ground with boulders.

Below: Central Inuit igloo, c. 1950. Although popularly synonymous with the Inuit peoples, the iglu or igloo, was actually used only by the central tribes — the Iglulik, Netsilik and Copper Inuit. It was made in a domed shape of skillfully angled blocks of frozen snow, excavated from the floor by a cutter working inside. Daylight was admitted by a translucent piece of ice fitted above the entry tunnel. Communal and multichambered examples are reported, but the average diameter was about 12 feet (3.6 m). Still made today, they afford protection against winter weather for short periods, or as temporary hunting bases.

Shamans used symbolically decorated costumes.

Female tattooing earned the subject rewards in the afterlife for her endurance of pain for the sake of beauty. Female parkas had extended hoods to allow the carrying of babies. The tailoring and manufacture of the parka established a metaphysical identification with the animals upon which these peoples relied for their existence.

Their oral history and cosmology comprise a series of opposites — male/female, land/sea, man/animal, dark/light, winter/summer — simultaneously separate and joined. When ritualized, the engendered tensions were released.

In recent times the Inuit have negotiated a series of policies and agreements with central governments, which they historically distrust. The aims of the community and of centralized power are often at odds. But these native peoples know that they are the custodians of a land of precious resources — a prize far greater than the institutions of commercial and industrial development that threaten its, and their, future.

Above: Polar Inuit mother at Thule, Greenland, c. 1940, wearing sealskin coat with a hood large enough to accommodate infants up to two or three years old.

Below Left: Polar Inuit winter house, c. 1900. Northern Greenland winter house, similar to those of the ancestral Thule people, constructed of flat stones, whale ribs, driftwood and sod. Here the central entrance is flanked by two side doorways to storerooms; and surmounted by a window — these were sometimes covered with translucent gut skin.

Right: Kaniag Inuit, c. 1850. This Kodiak Island hunter's carved-wood seal decoy helmet may have been invested with symbolic power to attract prey, in addition to providing practical camouflage.

Above: This cloth doll, made in the 1970s by a woman in the village of Hall Beach, Nunavut, wears seal skin kamiit (boots) and carries her child in the hood of her amautik (parka).

Above Right and Right: Specialist skills are needed to live in the frozen north.

Below: Eskimo berry pickers.

MAPS DETAILING THE FIRST NATIONS OF CANADA AND NATIVE PEOPLE OF ALASKA

The maps on pages 288–293 show the distribution of the band reserves of the Canadian Indian First Nations based upon treaties with the Crown and Canadian Government. The Native People of Alaska are as recognized by the US Department of the Interior, Bureau of Indian Affairs.

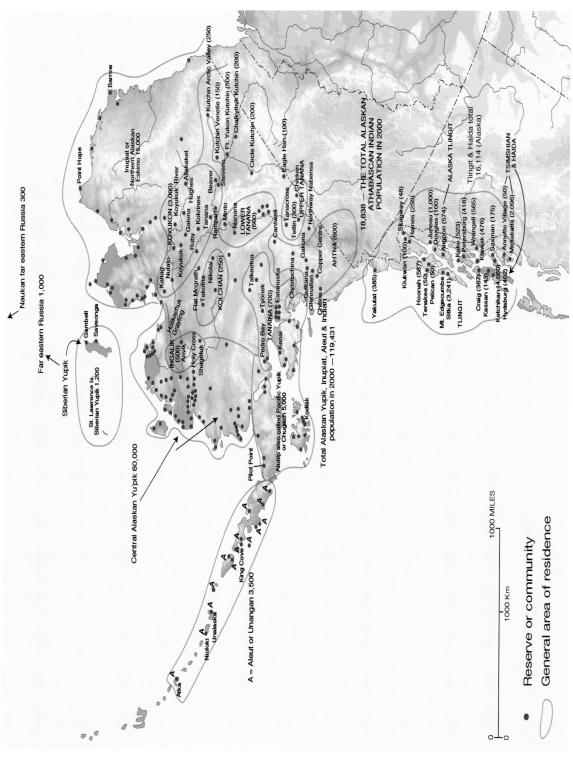

Naukan far eastern Russia 300

Far eastern Russia 1,000

Siberian Yupik

St. Lawrence Is.
Siberian Yupik 1,200

Gambell
Savoonga

Central Alaskan Yupik 60,000

A = Aleut or Unangan 3,500

Barrow

Point Hope

Inupiat or Northern Alaskan Eskimo 15,000

Kutchin Arctic Valley (250)

Kutchin Venetie (150)
Ft. Yukon Kutchin (500)
Chalkyitsik Kutchin (200)

Circle Kutchin (200)

Eagle Hain (100)

Koyukuk River
Allakaket
Hughes
Beaver
Stevens
Kokrines
Galena
Ruby
Tanana
Rampart
Minto
Nenana
LOWER TANANA (600)
KOYUKON (3,000)

Kaltag
Nulato
Koyukuk

Flat Mcgrath
Takotna
Nikolai
KOLCHAN (250)

Hoilkachuk
Grayling
Anvik
Holy Cross
Shageluk
INGALIK (500)

Talkeetna

Cantwell

Tanacross
Tetlin (300)
Chicken
UPPER TANANA
Northway Nabesna

Gakona
Copper Centre
AHTNA (600)

Christochina
Gulkana
Glennallen
Chitina

Eatamuska

Pedro Bay
Tyonek
TANAINA (700)
Kenai

Pilot Point

Aleutiip also called Pacific Yupik or Chugach 5,000

Kodiak

18,838 — THE TOTAL ALASKAN ATHABASCAN INDIAN POPULATION IN 2000

Yakutat (385)

Skagway (48)
Haines (250)

Klukwan (100)

Juneau (1,000)
Douglas (574)
Angoon (574)

Tlingit & Haida total 16,114 (Alaska)

ALASKA TLINGIT

TSIMSHIAN & HAIDA

Annette Village (50)
Metlakatla (2,096)

Hoonah (587)
Tenakee (50)
Pelican (50)
Mt. Edgecumbe
Sitka (3,241)
TLINGIT

Kake (523)
Petersburg (418)
Wrangell (565)
Klawak (476)
Saxman (175)
Craig (367)
Kassan (143)
Ketchikan (4,660)
Hydaburg (402)

Total Alaskan Yupik, Inupiat, Aleut & Indian population in 2000 — 119,431

King Cove

Niolokii
Unalaska

Atka

1000 MILES

1000 Km

● Reserve or community

General area of residence

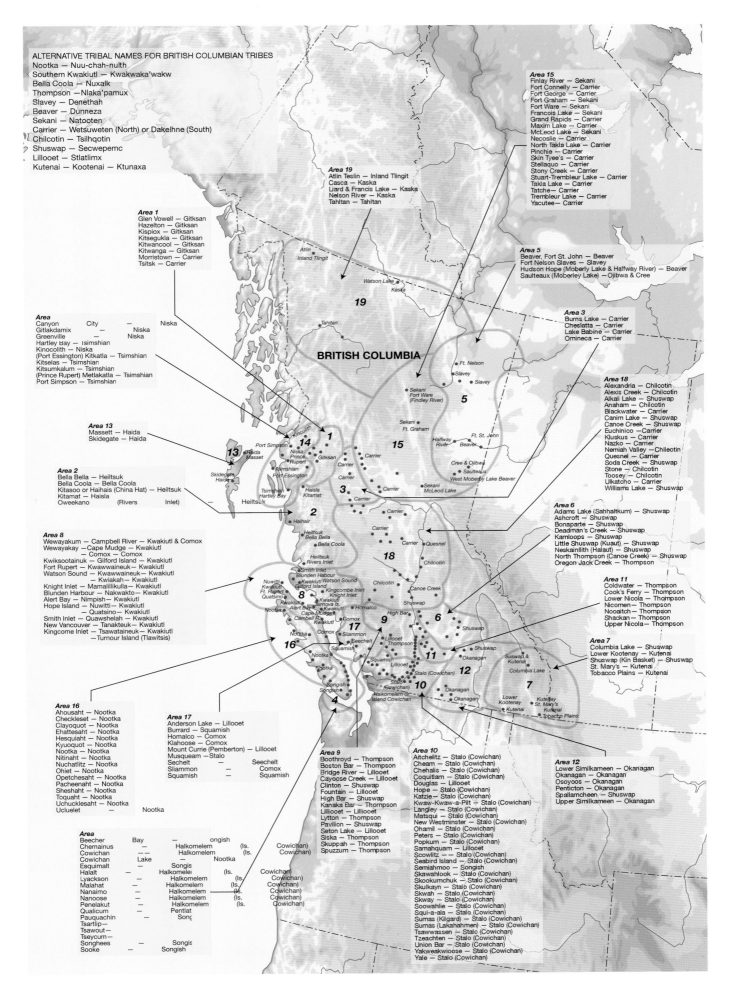

ALTERNATIVE TRIBAL NAMES FOR BRITISH COLUMBIAN TRIBES
Nootka — Nuu-chah-nulth
Southern Kwakiutl — Kwakwaka'wakw
Bella Coola — Nuxalk
Thompson —Nlaka'pamux
Slavey — Denethah
Beaver — Dunneza
Sekani — Natooten
Carrier — Wetsuweten (North) or Dakelhne (South)
Chilcotin — Tsilhqotin
Shuswap — Secwepemc
Lillooet — Stlatlimx
Kutenai — Kootenai — Ktunaxa

Area 15
Finlay River — Sekani
Fort Connelly — Carrier
Fort George — Carrier
Fort Graham — Sekani
Fort Ware — Sekani
Francois Lake — Sekani
Grand Rapids — Carrier
Maxim Lake — Carrier
McLeod Lake — Sekani
Necoslie — Carrier
North Takla Lake — Carrier
Pinchie — Carrier
Skin Tyee's — Carrier
Stellaquo — Carrier
Stony Creek — Carrier
Stuart-Trembleur Lake — Carrier
Takla Lake — Carrier
Tatche — Carrier
Trembleur Lake — Carrier
Yacutee — Carrier

Area 19
Atlin Teslin — Inland Tlingit
Casca — Kaska
Liard & Francis Lake — Kaska
Nelson River — Kaska
Tahltan — Tahltan

Area 1
Glen Vowell — Gitksan
Hazelton — Gitksan
Kispiox — Gitksan
Kitsegukla — Gitksan
Kitwancool — Gitksan
Kitwanga — Gitksan
Morristown — Carrier
Tsitsk — Carrier

Area 5
Beaver, Fort St. John — Beaver
Fort Nelson Slaves — Slavey
Hudson Hope (Moberly Lake & Halfway River) — Beaver
Saulteaux (Moberley Lake) — Ojibwa & Cree

Area
Canyon City — Niska
Gitlakdamix —
Greenville — Niska
Hartley Bay — Isimshian
Kinocolith — Niska
(Port Essington) Kitkatla — Tsimshian
Kitselas — Tsimshian
Kitsumkalum — Tsimshian
(Prince Rupert) Metlakatla — Tsimshian
Port Simpson — Tsimshian

Area 3
Burns Lake — Carrier
Cheslatta — Carrier
Lake Babine — Carrier
Omineca — Carrier

Area 18
Alexandria — Chilcotin
Alexis Creek — Chilcotin
Alkali Lake — Shuswap
Anaham — Chilcotin
Blackwater — Carrier
Canim Lake — Shuswap
Canoe Creek — Shuswap
Euchinico — Carrier
Kluskus — Carrier
Nazko — Carrier
Nemiah Valley —Chileotin
Quesnel — Carrier
Soda Creek — Shuswap
Stone — Chilcotin
Toosey — Chilcotin
Ulkatcho — Carrier
Williams Lake — Shuswap

Area 13
Massett — Haida
Skidegate — Haida

Area 2
Bella Bella — Heiltsuk
Bella Coola — Bella Coola
Kitasoo or Haihais (China Hat) — Heiltsuk
Kitamat — Haisla
Oweekano (Rivers Inlet)

Area 6
Adams Lake (Sahhaltkum) — Shuswap
Ashcroft — Shuswap
Bonaparte — Shuswap
Deadman's Creek — Shuswap
Kamloops — Shuswap
Little Shuswap (Kuaut) — Shuswap
Neskainllith (Halaut) — Shuswap
North Thompson (Canoe Creek) — Shuswap
Oregon Jack Creek — Thompson

Area 8
Wewayakum — Campbell River — Kwakiutl & Comox
Wewayakay —Cape Mudge — Kwakiutl
— Comox — Comox
Kwiksootainuk — Gilford Island — Kwakiutl
Fort Rupert — Kwawwaineuk — Kwakiutl
Watson Sound — Kwawwaineuk— Kwakiutl
— Kwiakah — Kwakiutl
Knight Inlet — Mamalilikulla — Kwakiutl
Blunden Harbour — Nakwakto — Kwakiutl
Alert Bay — Nimpish — Kwakiutl
Hope Island — Nuwitti— Kwakiutl
— Quatsino — Kwakiutl
Smith Inlet — Quawshelah — Kwakiutl
New Vancouver — Tanakteuk — Kwakiutl
Kingcome Inlet — Tsawataineuk — Kwakiutl
—Turnour Island (Tlawitsis)

Area 11
Coldwater — Thompson
Cook's Ferry — Thompson
Lower Nicola — Thompson
Nicomen — Thompson
Nooaitch — Thompson
Shackan — Thompson
Upper Nicola — Thompson

Area 7
Columbia Lake — Shuswap
Lower Kootenay — Kutenai
Shuswap (Kin Basket) — Shuswap
St. Mary's — Kutenai
Tobacco Plains — Kutenai

Area 16
Ahousaht — Nootka
Checkleset — Nootka
Clayoquot — Nootka
Ehattesaht — Nootka
Hesquiaht — Nootka
Kyuoquot — Nootka
Nootka — Nootka
Nitinaht — Nootka
Nuchatlitz — Nootka
Ohiet — Nootka
Opetchesaht — Nootka
Pacheenaht — Nootka
Sheshaht — Nootka
Toquaht — Nootka
Uchucklesaht — Nootka
Ucluelet — Nootka

Area 17
Anderson Lake — Lillooet
Burrard — Squamish
Homalco — Comox
Klahoose — Comox
Mount Currie (Pemberton) — Lillooet
Musqueam — Stalo
Sechelt — Seechelt
Sliammon — Comox
Squamish — Squamish

Area 9
Boothroyd — Thompson
Boston Bar — Thompson
Bridge River — Lillooet
Cayoose Creek — Lillooet
Clinton — Shuswap
Fountain — Lillooet
High Bar — Shuswap
Kanaka Bar — Thompson
Lillooet — Lillooet
Lytton — Thompson
Pavilion — Shuswap
Seton Lake — Lillooet
Siska — Thompson
Skuppah — Thompson
Spuzzum — Thompson

Area 10
Aitchelitz — Stalo (Cowichan)
Cheam — Stalo (Cowichan)
Chehalis — Stalo (Cowichan)
Coquitlam — Stalo (Cowichan)
Douglas — Lillooet
Hope — Stalo (Cowichan)
Katzie — Stalo (Cowichan)
Kwaw-Kwaw-a-Pilt — Stalo (Cowichan)
Langley — Stalo (Cowichan)
Matsqui — Stalo (Cowichan)
New Westminster — Stalo (Cowichan)
Ohamil — Stalo (Cowichan)
Peters — Stalo (Cowichan)
Popkum — Stalo (Cowichan)
Samahquam — Stalo (Cowichan)
Scowlitz — — Stalo (Cowichan)
Seabird Island — Stalo (Cowichan)
Semiahmoo — Songish
Skawahlook — Stalo (Cowichan)
Skookumchuck — Stalo (Cowichan)
Skulkayn — Stalo (Cowichan)
Skwah — Stalo (Cowichan)
Skway — Stalo (Cowichan)
Soowahlie — Stalo (Cowichan)
Squi-a-ala — Stalo (Cowichan)
Sumas (Kilgard) — Stalo (Cowichan)
Sumas (Lakahahmen) — Stalo (Cowichan)
Tsawwassen — Stalo (Cowichan)
Tzeachten — Stalo (Cowichan)
Union Bar — Stalo (Cowichan)
Yakweakwioose — Stalo (Cowichan)
Yale — Stalo (Cowichan)

Area 12
Lower Similkameen — Okanagan
Okanagan — Okanagan
Osoyoos — Okanagan
Penticton — Okanagan
Spallamcheen — Shuswap
Upper Similkameen — Okanagan

Area
Beecher Bay — ongish
Chemainus — Halkomelem (Is.
Cowichan — — Halkomelem (Is.
Cowichan Lake — Songis
Esquimalt — Nootka
Halalt — Halkomelem (Is.
Lyackson — Halkomelem (Is.
Malahat — Halkomelem (Is.
Nanaimo — Halkomelem (Is.
Nanoose — Halkomelem (Is.
Penelakut — Halkomelem (Is.
Qualicum — Pentlat
Pauquachin — Song
Tsartlip —
Tsawout —
Tseycum—
Songhees — Songis
Sooke — Songish

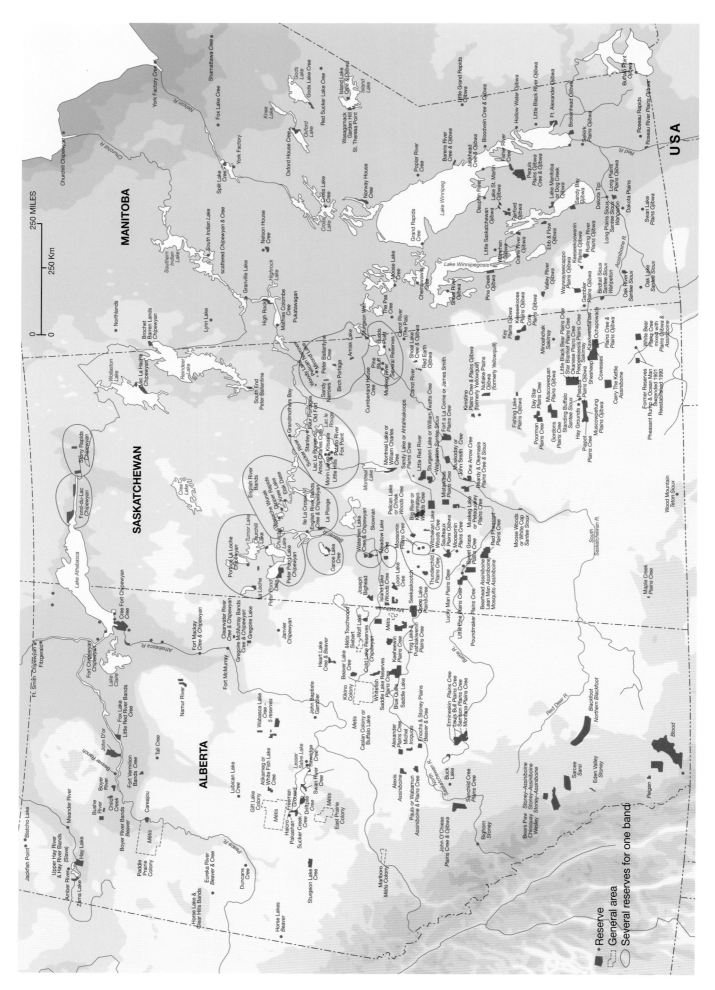

250 MILES

250 Km

MANITOBA

SASKATCHEWAN

ALBERTA

USA

• Reserve

General area

Several reserves for one band

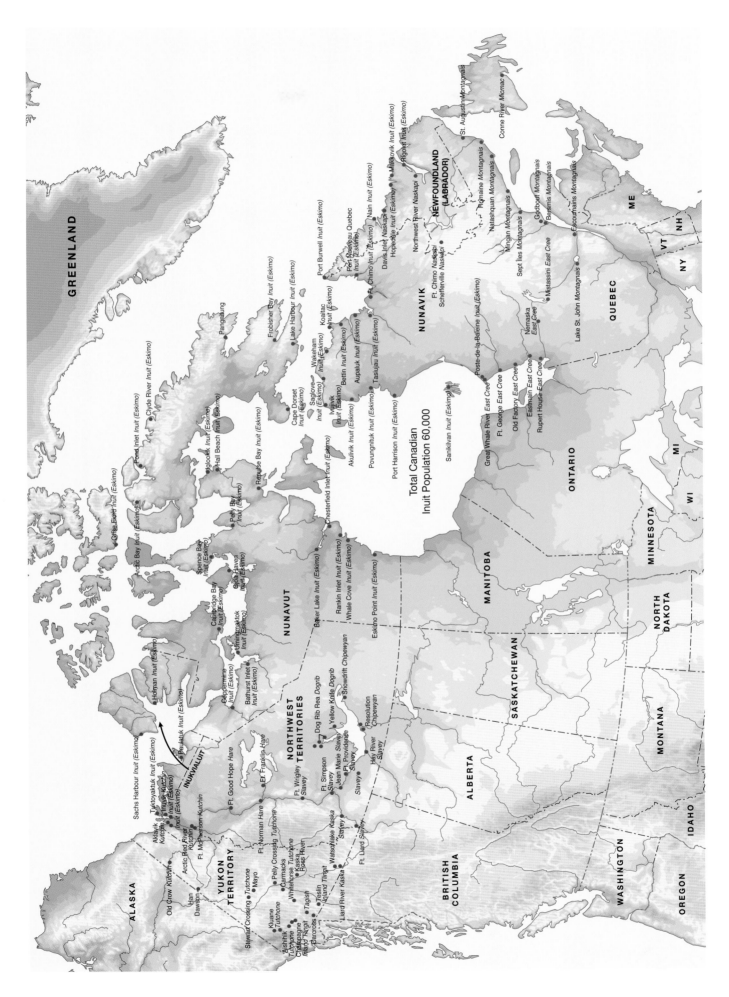

GREENLAND

Grise Fiord Inuit (Eskimo)

Clyde River Inuit (Eskimo)
Pond Inlet Inuit (Eskimo)

Pangnirtung

Igloolik Inuit (Eskimo)
Hall Beach Inuit (Eskimo)
Frobisher Bay Inuit (Eskimo)
Lake Harbour Inuit (Eskimo)

Repulse Bay Inuit (Eskimo)

Cape Dorset Inuit (Eskimo)
Saglove Inuit (Eskimo)
Wakeham Inuit (Eskimo)
Koaltac Inuit (Eskimo)
Ivujivik Inuit (Eskimo)
Bettin Inuit (Eskimo)
Aupaluk Inuit (Eskimo)
Tasiujaq Inuit (Eskimo)

Port Burwell Inuit (Eskimo)
Port Nouveau Quebec Inuit (Eskimo)
Nain Inuit (Eskimo)
Hopendle Inuit (Eskimo)
Rigolet Inuit (Eskimo)
Makkovik Inuit (Eskimo)

St. Augustin Montagnais

Conne River Micmac

NEWFOUNDLAND (LABRADOR)

Northwest River Naskapi
Ft. Chimo Naskapi
Schefferville Naskapi

Ft. Chimo Inuit (Eskimo)
Davis Inlet Naskapi

Tromaine Montagnais
Natashquan Montagnais
Mingan Montagnais
Sept Îles Montagnais
Godbout Montagnais
Bersimis Montagnais
Escoumains Montagnais

Akulivik Inuit (Eskimo)

Powungnituk Inuit (Eskimo)

Port Harrison Inuit (Eskimo)

NUNAVIK

Poste-de-la-Baleine Inuit (Eskimo)

Mistassini Montagnais
Lake St. John Montagnais

ME
NH
VT
NY

Total Canadian
Inuit Population 60,000

Sanikiluan Inuit (Eskimo)

Great Whale River East Cree
Ft. George East Cree
Old Factory East Cree
Eastmain East Cree
Rupert House East Cree
Nemaska East Cree

QUEBEC

ONTARIO

WI

MI

MINNESOTA

NORTH DAKOTA

Arctic Bay Inuit (Eskimo)

Spence Bay Inuit (Eskimo)
Pelly Bay Inuit (Eskimo)
Gjoa Haven Inuit (Eskimo)

Chesterfield Inlet Inuit (Eskimo)

Baker Lake Inuit (Eskimo)
Rankin Inlet Inuit (Eskimo)
Whale Cove Inuit (Eskimo)

Eskimo Point Inuit (Eskimo)

MANITOBA

Holman Inuit (Eskimo)

Cambridge Bay Inuit (Eskimo)
Umingmaktok Inuit (Eskimo)

Coppermine Inuit (Eskimo)
Bathurst Inlet Inuit (Eskimo)

NUNAVUT

SASKATCHEWAN

Sachs Harbour Inuit (Eskimo)
Tuktoyaktuk Inuit (Eskimo)
Paulatuk Inuit (Eskimo)

INUKVIALUT

Inuvik Inuit (Eskimo)

Dog Rib Rea Dogrib
Yellow Knife Dogrib
Snowdrift Chipewyan

Resolution Chipewyan

Aklavik Kutchin
Arctic Red River Kutchin
Ft. McPherson Kutchin

Ft. Good Hope Hare
Ft. Franklin Hare

Ft. Wrigley Slavey
Ft. Norman Hare

Ft. Simpson Slavey
Jean Marie Slavey
Ft. Providence Slavey

Hay River Slavey

NORTHWEST TERRITORIES

ALBERTA

Old Crow Kutchin

Han
Dawson

YUKON TERRITORY

Ft. Norman Hare

Pelly Crossing Tutchone
Carmacks
Mayo

Stewart Crossing Tutchone
Kluane Tutchone
Aishihik Tutchone
Champagne Tutchone
Inland Tlingit
Carcross

Whitehorse Tutchone
Kaska
Ross River

Teslin
Inland Tlingit
Tagish

Liard River Kaska

Watson Lake Kaska
Slavey
Ft. Liard Slavey

BRITISH COLUMBIA

ALASKA

WASHINGTON

OREGON

IDAHO

MONTANA

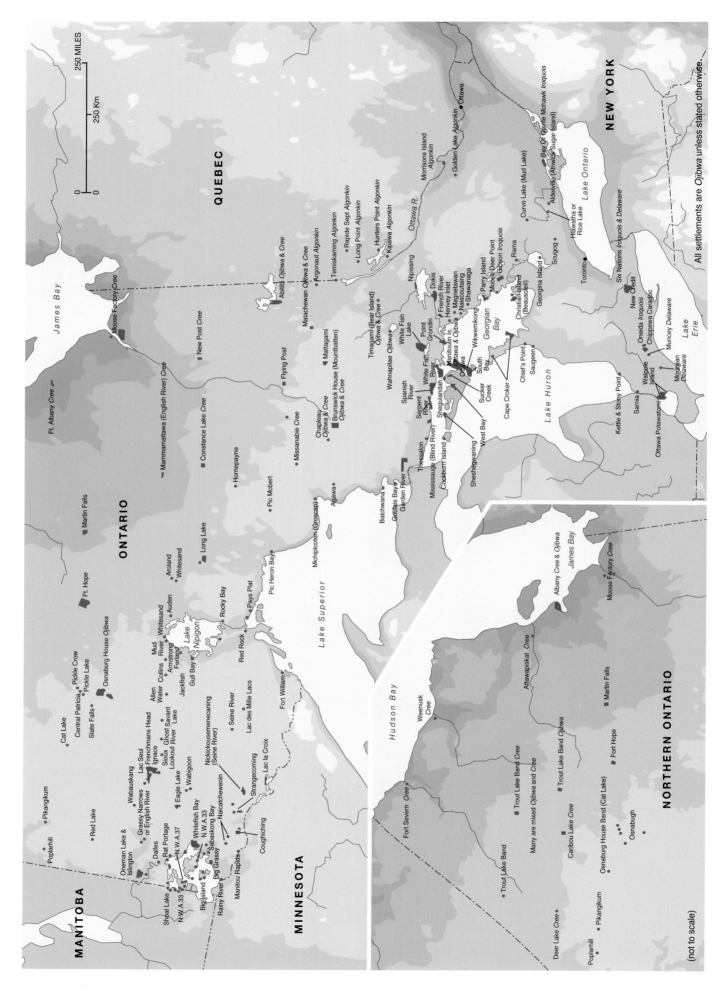

250 MILES

250 Km

QUEBEC

NEW YORK

James Bay

ONTARIO

Moose Factory *Cree*

New Post *Cree*

Ft. Albany *Cree*

Mammamattawa (English River) *Cree*

Martin Falls

Constance Lake *Cree*

Flying Post

Homepayne

Missanabie *Cree*

Chapleau *Ojibwa & Cree*

Brunswick House (Mountbatten) *Ojibwa & Cree*

Mattagami *Cree*

Matachewan *Ojibwa & Cree*

Abitibi *Ojibwa & Cree*

Argonaut *Algonkin*

Temiskaming *Algonkin*

Rapide Sept *Algonkin*

Long Point *Algonkin*

Hunters Point *Algonkin*

Kipawa *Algonkin*

Morrisons Island *Algonkin*

Golden Lake *Algonkin*

Ottawa

Ottawa R.

Nipissing

Dokis

French River

Henvey Inlet

Naisoutaing

Magnetawan

Shawanaga

Parry Island

Moose Deer Point

Gibson *Iroquois*

Georgian Island

Rama

Scugog

Curve Lake (Mud Lake)

Bay Of Quinte Mohawk *Iroquois*

Alderville (Ahwick Sugar Island)

Hiawatha or Rice Lake

Lake Ontario

Toronto

Six Nations *Iroquois & Delaware*

New Credit

Oneida *Iroquois*

Chippewa Caradoc

Muncey *Delaware*

Lake Erie

Moravian *Delaware*

Walpole Island

Sarnia

Ottawa Potawatomi

Kettle & Stony Point

Sarnia

Timagami (Bear Island) *Ojibwa & Cree*

White Fish Lake

Wahnapitae *Ojibwa*

Spanish River

Serpent River

Sheguiandah

Thessalon

Mississauge (Blind River)

Cockburn Island

Sheshegwaning

West Bay

Point Grondin

Manitoulin Is.

Ottawa & Ojibwa

Ottawa

South Bay

Sucker Creek

Wikwemikong

Cape Croker

Chief's Point

Saugeen

Georgian Bay

Christian Island (Beausoleil)

Lake Huron

Batchwana

Goulais Bay

Garden River

Agawa

Michipicoten (Groscap)

Lake Superior

Pic Mobert

Pic Heron Bay

Pays Plat

Rocky Bay

Long Lake

Aroland

Whitesand

Ft. Hope

Martin Falls

Cat Lake

Central Patricia

Pickle Crow

Pickle Lake

Slate Falls

Osnaburg House *Ojibwa*

Red Rock

Fort William

Lake Nipigon

Mud River

Whitesand

Armstrong

Ferland

Collins

Auden

Allen Water

Jackfish

Gull Bay

Sioux Lookout

Ghost River

Savant Lake

Seine River

Lac des Mille Lacs

Lac la Croix

Nickickousemenecaning (Seine River)

Strangecoming

Coughiching

Manitou Rapids

Rainy River

Big Grassy

Sabaskong Bay

Naicatchewenin

Whitefish Bay

N.W.A.33

Big Island

Shoal Lake

N.W.A.33

Rat Portage

Dalles

Oneman Lake & Islington

Grassy Narrows or English River

Eagle Lake

Wabigoon

Lac Seul

Frenchmans Head

Ignace

Wabauskang

Red Lake

Poplarhill

Pikangikum

MANITOBA

MINNESOTA

All settlements are *Ojibwa* unless stated otherwise.

Hudson Bay

James Bay

Weenusk *Cree*

Fort Severn *Cree*

Attawapiskat *Cree*

Albany *Cree & Ojibwa*

Moose Factory *Cree*

Trout Lake Band *Cree*

Trout Lake Band *Ojibwa*

Many are mixed *Ojibwa and Cree*

Trout Lake Band

Caribou Lake *Cree*

Osnaburg House Band (Cat Lake)

Osnabugh

Fort Hope

Martin Falls

Deer Lake *Cree*

Poplarhill

Pikangikum

NORTHERN ONTARIO

(not to scale)

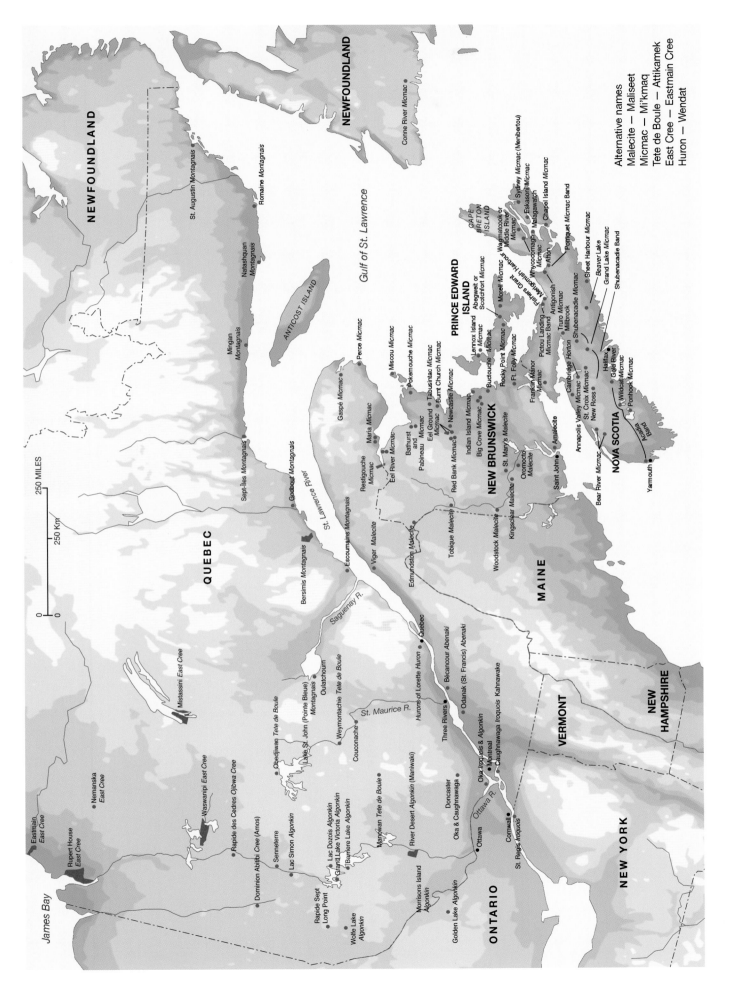

Alternative names
Malecite — Maliseet
Micmac — Mi'kmaq
Tete de Boule — Attikamek
East Cree — Eastmain Cree
Huron — Wendat

NEWFOUNDLAND

NEWFOUNDLAND

Conne River Micmac

St. Augustin Montagnais

Romaine Montagnais

Natashquan Montagnais

Mingan Montagnais

Gulf of St. Lawrence

ANTICOST ISLAND

Sept-Îles Montagnais

Godbout Montagnais

Escoumains Montagnais

St. Lawrence River

Bersimis Montagnais

Saguenay R.

QUEBEC

Péré Micmac

Misoou Micmac

Pokemouche Micmac

Gaspé Micmac

Maria Micmac

Restigouche Micmac

Eel River Micmac

Bathurst and Pabineau Micmac

Tabusintac Micmac

Burnt Church Micmac

Newcastle Micmac

Eel Ground Micmac

Big Cove Micmac

Indian Island Micmac

Red Bank Micmac

Budtouche Micmac

Rocky Point Micmac

Lennox Island Micmac

Abegweit or Scotchfort Micmac

PRINCE EDWARD ISLAND

Morell Micmac

Ft. Folly Micmac

Franklin Manor Micmac

St. Mary's Malecite

Oromocto Malecite

Saint John

Amalecite

Annapolis Valley Micmac

St. Croix Micmac

New Ross

Bear River Micmac

Yarmouth

Acadia Band

NOVA SCOTIA

Wildcat Micmac

Ponhook Micmac

Gold River

Halifax

Sheet Harbour Micmac

Beaver Lake

Grand Lake Micmac

Shubenacadie Band

Millbrook

Cambridge Horton

Shubenacadie Micmac

Truro Micmac

Antigonish

Pictou Landing Micmac Band

Fisher's Grant

New Nagonish Harbour

Whycocomagh

Afton

Malagawatch

Wagmatcook or Middle River Micmac

Sydney Micmac (Menibertou)

Eskasoni Micmac

Chapel Island Micmac

Pomquet Micmac Band

CAPE BRETON ISLAND

NEW BRUNSWICK

Kingsclear Malecite

Woodstock Malecite

Tobique Malecite

Edmundston Malecite

Viger Malecite

MAINE

NEW HAMPSHIRE

VERMONT

NEW YORK

St. Regis Iroquois

Cornwall

Ottawa

Oka-Iroquois & Algonkin

Montreal

Caughnawaga Iroquois Kahnawake

Doncaster

Oka & Caughnawaga

Ottawa R.

River Desert Algonkin (Maniwaki)

Manówan Tete de Boule

Three Rivers

Bécancour Abenaki

Odanak (St. Francis) Abenaki

Hurons of Lorette Huron

Québec

St. Maurice R.

Weymontachie Tete de Boule

Coucouache

Ouatchouan

Lake St. John (Pointe Bleue) Montagnais

Obedjiwan Tete de Boule

Senneterre

Lac Simon Algonkin

Lac Dozois Algonkin

Grand Lake Victoria Algonkin

Barriere Lake Algonkin

Rapide des Cedres Ojibwa Cree

Dominion Abitibi Cree (Amos)

Rapide Sept Long Point

Wolfe Lake Algonkin

Morrisons Island Algonkin

Golden Lake Algonkin

ONTARIO

Mistassini East Cree

Waswanipi East Cree

Nemanska East Cree

Rupert House East Cree

Eastmain East Cree

James Bay

250 MILES

250 Km

0

0

THE INDIAN TODAY

The present Native American population is found in every state and every major urban area of the United States, and is particularly significant in states in which reservations were established during the 19th century, for example Oklahoma, New Mexico and South Dakota. During the recent past many Indians have migrated to California and New York, with large concentrations in various cities. Conversely, a few states have almost no Indian population and no sizeable Indian communities or government reservations founded for native people; typical of these are Kentucky and Tennessee.

In Canada every province has a sizeable Indian population, since historically the native peoples were not pressured to move (or at least, not great distances) from their traditional homes. The reserves are more evenly distributed, if smaller, than in the United States. On the whole Canadian Indians—now called "First Nations"—seem to have fared somewhat better than many in the U.S., and traditionally have had a more positive attitude to government and the white culture. The belief that this is so, while probably not wholly true, is widely held by Indians and whites.

On the face of it the reservation system (or band reserve system in Canada) seems to have been a positive move to secure and preserve at least a fraction of Indian land in perpetuity. It should be remembered, however, that the infamous Dawes or Allotment Act of the 1880s disposed of areas of land unallocated to Indian families on many reservations — a process unchecked until the Indian Reorganization Act of 1934, by which time many reservations were simply jurisdictional areas rather than continuously Indian-owned areas of real estate. Today we find some reservations in the least accessible parts of the country, often long distances from urban centres of employment, with poor economic opportunities and a diminished land base: a classic environment for social deprivation.

Modern Ceremonial Clothing

Back row, from left:
Blackfoot dress clothes, mid-20th century. Buckskin shirts and leggings with matching beadwork strips are popular with Blackfoot men for special occasions, particularly among the Canadian branches; the costume is usually of white buckskin, heavily tailored. The bonnet is of eagle feathers tipped with white discs, the frontal cloth bindings wrapped diagonally.

Oklahoma shawl dancer, c. 1989. Pan-Indian intertribal woman's dress: a ribbon blouse and separate skirt in the Woodland tradition, worn with moccasin boots made by a Kiowa lady, and a shawl made by a member of the Comanche Parker family, items acquired by the author in Oklahoma.

Oklahoma woman's dress, c. 1960. The modern buckskin dress developed by the Kiowa, Comanche, Cheyenne and others in Oklahoma and elsewhere, was derived from older Southern Cheyenne and Kiowa dresses, and retains several old features: a deep yoke with scalloped edges at the seam with the skirt, horizontal bands of beadwork and often an associated belt and set of three beaded bags (formerly carrying women's tools). Many women wear beaded "princess crowns" and carry shawls or fans for the dance and princess contests.

Northern Plains Grass Dancer, mid-20th century. So-called Northern Grass Dance costume probably originated in its presently recognizable form among the Plains Ojibwa and Cree of Saskatchewan. The style, which became popular on the northern U.S. reservations in the 1950s, derived from the spread of the original Grass Dance northward into Canada in the 1880s, and utilized the head-roach with beaded headband with a frontal rosette or heart. The harness, rosettes, armbands, collar, tie, belt and cuffs were in geometrical or floralistic beadwork, and sometimes matched. These were worn over a shirt and leggings of dark cloth, often fringed at the shoulder, aprons, knees, and ankles with buckskin, ribbon or wool. Completely wool-fringed outfits have recently become popular with young men.

Second row from right: Oklahoma Straight Dancer, mid-late 20th century. Costume worn by Osage, Ponca, Oto and Pawnee men who dance in the older style, to the songs of the Ponca Hethuska and Osage Inlonska. The costume reinforces family, tribal and ethnic ties, and echoes an older tradition from the days when these Prairie tribes were first settled on reservations in Indian Territory; it descends from the last of their war and clan society rituals. "Straight Dance" refers to the lack of exaggerated dress or movements. The costume consists of a roach with a single feather, scalp feathers, cloth shirt, beaded belt, otter fur trailer, cloth leggings with ribbonwork, scarf, and tie slide and frontally knotted white headband. It is particularly popular at the three annual Osage powwows in northern Oklahoma.

Northern Plains woman's "jingle dress," c. 1985. Originating among the Chippewa and Santee Sioux of Minnesota, North Dakota and adjacent Canada late in the 19th century, this spread to many tribes with the development of newer forms of women's dances, and is very popular at modern celebrations. The cloth dress is decorated with rows of long tin cones, giving a loud "jingle" rhythm when dancing.

Sioux "Contemporary Traditional" dance costume, c. 1985. In the 1870s, the Sioux had distinctive men's dress for the Grass Dance: roach, belts or bustles of scavenger birds' feathers, belt braids of sweetgrass, quilled armbands, cuffs and otter fur or hairpipe breastplates, later worn over dyed trade underwear for modesty due to missionary influence. It lost popularity to the Fancy Dance and Grass Dance costumes adopted from other tribes during this century; but the early 1970s saw the development of a modern version, "Contemporary Traditional," which has become very popular; recently it is characterized by a feather visor over the eyes. This, along with the Fancy, Straight (Oklahoma) and Northern Grass Dance costumes can all be traced to the spread of the original Grass or Omaha Dance 120 years ago.

Fancy Dance or Feathers costume, mid-late 20th century. A very popular young men's pan-Indian costume from Oklahoma, apparently developed in about 1930, giving expression to the Fast War Dance at secular powwows and dances. Although specific parts of the costume can be traced to older native models, the combination of large back and arm bustles with multicolored fluffy feathers, capes, beaded harness, belt, aprons and roach or feather headdress was new, and changed from year to year. The costume was adopted in the 1940s–50s by the Sioux and many others, displacing indigenous dance clothes.

Above: Gladys and Harold Tantaquidgeon, Mohegans, Uncasville, Connecticut, May 1988. Photographed outside the small museum founded by their father, John, in 1931. The author is standing behind Gladys, who was age 95 in 1995 but was still the Mohegan tribal historian and matriarch, and who has written several scholarly works about her tribe and race. The Tantaquidgeons are descendants of the real Uncas — or one of his captains — who fought with the early English settlers in Connecticut against the Pequots in 1636–37. The tribal name "Mohican" used in popular fiction (The Last of the Mohicans) confuses two separate tribes — the Mohegan of Connecticut, Uncas's people, and the Mahican of the Hudson River Valley of New York State. Both people have several hundred descendants, the Mohegans in Connecticut and the Mahicans under the name "Stockbridge" in Wisconsin, and various other places. Photograph: Samuel Cahoon, May 1988.

In Canada and the U.S.A. alike no single generalized description can accurately portray Indian economic, cultural or social status relative to dominant white culture or to older traditional Indian values. So broad is the variation in the lifestyles of Native Americans that a number of very different descriptions could truthfully be applied to the social and economic conditions prevalent on particular reservations and in particular communities. The loss of a land base was accompanied by other pressures militating against the continuity of distinctively native culture, religion, kinship, dress and ceremony. Among these were the suppression of native speech, and the boarding school system which took youths to off-reservation establishments where they were subjected to excessively harsh discipline. Despite the generally more enlightened philosophy and improved teaching techniques of more recent times, Indian scholastic achievements are often disappointing.

There was further U.S. Government pressure during the 1950s for the termination of federal services to a number of Indian reservations where the people had made an almost complete transfer to Euro-American culture; at a stroke the Klamath (Oregon), Menomini (Wisconsin) and a number of other smaller groups were no longer federally recognized as Indians. During the 1970s federal domination of U.S. Indian Service programmes served to retard rather than enhance the progress of Native American people. Gradually the government has come to encourage tribal officials to plan and administer their own programmes for themselves; but many groups have yet to solve the difficulties posed by history, isolation, disruption, poor Bureau of Indian Affairs administration, which leave Native Americans as the poorest ethnic group in North America.

There are, however, some reasons for cautious optimism. What remains of Indian lands are today often described by native people as "sacred," and jealously guarded. Some land has been successfully reclaimed, and substantial sums of money have been obtained from federal and state sources in recompense for land loss in times past. (Some of these claims, by groups whose ethnic heritage is a mixture of Indian, African-American and Euro-American, appear to be encouraged by the possibility of such rewards.) Present Indian leaders claim that their ancestors' view of land tenure was so different from that of whites that Indians did not understand fully the implications of the treaties which they signed with government agents.

Many Indians and people of Indian descent have successfully accommodated Euro-American culture, some for many generations, and have always viewed the dominant culture as a goal. Native American people are found in all the professions, and in social, industrial and commercial concerns; they count a U.S. Vice President, a World War II general, a premiere ballerina, movie stars, two Olympic gold medal winners, the president of an oil company, historians, anthropologists and artists amongst their ranks. Many present day tribal communities boast up-to-date administrative offices complete with computer facilities, libraries and museums, and run programmes to preserve tribal histories and languages. Many of these advances have been achieved by tribes who, through various changes in their fortunes, fell heirs to mineral or oil deposits, such as the Oklahoma Osage; or by tribes with a long association of social and commercial contact with Euro-American culture. Gambling operations have brought increased wealth to some groups.

Considering their disadvantages, the Native American communities remain a vibrant section of the American and Canadian population; and since the general re-evaluation of social attitudes born of the 1960s Indians can claim, with some justification, a special place as conservationists and protectors of natural resources, with a clearer perception of man's meaningful existence and with a strong spiritual attachment to their fellow beings and their natural surroundings. Presumably because so many of the older Indian traditions reported by the earliest ethnographers in the 19th century now seem to have been lost (with the exception of those of some Southwestern groups), it would appear that some ideas have been reciprocally adopted from the general American sub-culture prevailing in the 1960s. Not all the rhetoric now employed to promote "Indian culture" seems to agree with the finer points of known cultural or historical detail; but it is sufficient to note that many Indians believe these things implicitly.

They also feel that their culture, and specifically their material culture, has been stolen by whites. It is certainly the case that deserted and archaeological sites have been desecrated by white curio-hunters, and that economically deprived native people sold their heirlooms at a fraction of their true value. Nevertheless, we should recognize that very little material culture would have been salvaged had not European and American collectors, antiquarians, explorers and latterly art dealers promoted interest and research into indigenous cultures and their arts, notwithstanding their sometimes dubious motives and methods.

But Indian culture does survive, both old and new. Amongst the older nativistic traditions (sometimes rejuvenated) are the Longhouse religion of the Iroquois, the Green Corn Ceremony of the Seminole and Creek, the Sun Dance of the Plains and Plateau, and the timeless calendrical ceremonies of the Pueblos. The newer Indian culture is termed "Pan-Indianism" by anthropologists. It is expressed outwardly in social and political contexts, but perhaps most visibly by the ubiquitous "Powwow" which merges traditions of song and dance from various Indian cultures, heavily modified and largely bereft of old religious traits. Each year many groups present their own Powwows, organized by elected officers, inviting Indians from far and wide to attend, providing feasts and cash prizes for the best dancing and costume, and promoting tribal and Indian ethnic unity and cohesion. The choreography is largely derived from the dramatic warrior society dances of the eastern Plains people, notably Omaha and Ponca adopted by the Sioux (amongst whom it was known as the Omaha dance and Omaha society), and by Oklahoma Indians who also adopted the dance to the exclusion of their own clan ceremonies. The dance, which at times took on quasi-religious overtones, has a history of diffusion for well over one hundred years. Known variously as War Dance, Omaha Dance or Grass Dance, it involves ever-changing regalia referred to as Fancy Dance, War Dance, Straight Dance or Grass Dance clothes, traditional or contemporary, dependent upon the Indian fashion of the day. Women have developed their own dances to accompany the men: Round Dances and Owl Dances of partly white origin, the Stomp Dance originally from the Southeast, and the Eagle Dance from the Southwest, all contribute to the contemporary scene. The Powwow has been adopted by tribes well outside the Plains area; the Iroquois, for example, use the Powwow dances as an adjunct to their own social dances. Powwows had arrived to most Iroquois communities by the 1970s.

Readers should also recognize that the racial separation of white and Indian was never as clear as popular history would have us believe. For many generations from the 17th century onward French trappers and traders mixed with the Crees and Ojibwas, leaving a marked strain of their blood, which resulted in the emergence of the Métis (see page 99). This people, who in the early 19th century settled around the Red River near present Winnepeg, Manitoba, have been described as a cultural bridge between whites and the Native Canadians. Following the Riel Rebellion of 1885 they also dispersed west to Alberta, and the Northwest Territories.

In the eastern United States a number of other mixed-blood groups claim Indian ancestry. Although detailed histories of these groups are often lacking, there are general similarities. They have been, until recently, isolated rural people of mixed Indian, Euro-American and African-American background. The tribal origins are often blurred, perhaps because of a multi-remnant background; in colonial times refugees of various marginal peoples banded together until the present day tri-racial groups emerged.

The largest such group in the U.S.A. are the socalled *Lumbee* (see page 91) of Robeson County, NC, numbering 27,520 in 1970. Physically they appear distinctly Indian, but they lack all knowledge of an Indian language or customs save for adopted Pan-Indian traits. So far they have been unable to persuade the U.S. Government that their genealogy is complete enough for them to be recognized as an Indian people. In this regard we should also note other post-colonial Indian mixed-blood groups or claimants to such ancestry, briefly: the *Pools* around Towanda, PA; *Keating Mountain Cherokee* of Pennsylvania; *Jackson-Whites* or *Ramapoughs* of Ramapo Valley, NJ; *Sandhill Indians* of Monmouth County, NJ; *Pineys* or *Powhatan-Renápe* of Burlington County, NJ; *Moors* of Cumberland County, NJ, and Kent County, DE; *Wesorts* and *Portobacco* of Maryland; *Guineas* of West Virginia;

Above: The Foxwoods Casino on the Mashantucket Pequot Reservation, Ledyard, Connecticut. The reservation was one of the two colonial land grants from the English in 1666, for a handful of the remaining members of the Pequot tribe destroyed in 1637 by the combined English and Mohegan. A few families had occupied the Mashantucket Reservation down to the 20th century, reported to number 25 persons in 1907 of mixed descent, and 55 in 1974. In 1983 they obtained federal recognition as a "nation" with a degree of autonomy allowing a high-stake bingo operation on the reservation, and in 1992 a gambling casino opened. Close to large urban populations the operations have been enormously successful, bringing immense wealth to the enrolled membership, which has increased to 282 (1991) and 353 (1997) if tribal ancestry can be proven. The tribe has now been able to purchase more land. September 1995 photograph.

Browns of Rockbridge County, VA; *Issues* or *Monacan* of Amherst County, Virginia; *Cubans* of Person County, North Carolina; *Haliwa* of Halifax and Warren Counties, North Carolina; *Coharie* of Sampson County, North Carolina; *Waccamaw* of Columbus County, NC; *Cheraw* of Rockingham County, NC; *Melungeons* of Magoffen County, KY; *Coe Clan* of Cumberland County, KY; *Blues* or *Peedee* of Marlboro County, SC; *Summerville Indians* (see page 000) in several counties of South Carolina; *Carmel Indians* and others in Hardin, Drake and Vinton Counties, OH; *Altamaha* of Burke County, GA; *Creoles* in Florida and Alabama; and *Cane River*, *Sabine-Red Bone* and *Apache-Choctaw* of Louisiana; some of these designations, it should be noted, are derogatory.

These groups add several thousand to the increasing number of people who are still proudly Native Americans but who present a bewilderingly complex range of ethnic, cultural and social variations drawn from many sources. What such groups have in common is that they usually subsist at the lowest economic levels; often live in inadequate, crowded and unsafe homes; endure limited employment opportunities; and are beset by various problems which once seemed endemic, but which are now moving slowly toward the hope of solution, principally through their own efforts.

The establishment of casinos and associated motels in many reservations in the past 20 years has brought considerable wealth but also corruption and factionalism. In Canada misuse of government funds by leaders of a Cree reserve in northern Ontario was given considerable attention by Canadian television. Such occurrences deflect the challenges the native people have endured from one generation to another because of disease, removal, war, and land loss following white domination.

GLOSSARY

Allotment. Legal process, c. 1880s-1930s, by which land on Indian reservations not allocated to Indian families was made available to whites.

Anthropology. The study of humans.

Anthropomorphic. An animal or god in the shape, or having the characteristics, of humans.

Appliqué. Decorative technique involving sewing down quills (usually porcupine) and seed beads onto hide or cloth, using two threads, resulting in a flat mosaic surface.

Apron. Male apparel, front and back, which replaced the breechcloth for festive costume during the 19th and 20th centuries.

Argillite. A steatite (soapstone) found on the Queen Charlotte Islands, British Columbia, used by the Haida people to fashion pipes and small totem poles.

Babiche. Leather thongs, usually for making snowshoes and hunting bags, in northern Canada.

Bandolier bag. A prestige bag with a shoulder strap, usually with heavy (often floralistic) beadwork, worn by men and sometimes women at tribal dances. Common among the Ojibwa and other Woodland tribes.

Beads. European glass beads seem to have been traded in native America from the earliest days of contact, replacing native shell, bone or stone beads. The early trade beads were mostly of the large necklace type, followed later by many types of small "seed" beads. On the Plains, the traders introduced a larger "pony" bead during the early 19th century. Most of the seed beads came from Italy, and later Bohemia, in many colors, opaque, transparent, translucent and in many sizes.

Beadwork. Glass or china beads from Europe were worked into designs by sewing to buckskin or buckskin substitute (cloth or canvas), using sinew or traded thread. Two varieties of stitching are common, overlaid or spot-stitch, or appliqué (q.v.) or lazy stitch (q.v.). The use of simple hand looms by the Great Lakes tribes for sashes and bandoliers may have been introduced by Europeans. Beadwork was traditionally largely in geometric patterns, but floral designs became hugely popular after about 1850.

Above: Fine beaded appliqué work on this Cree man's vest or waistcoat.
M.G. Johnson Collection

Below: Floral beadwork on an Ojibwa bandolier bag. M.G. Johnson Collection

Above center: The American bison was fundamental to the survival of many Native American tribes.

Above right: A selection of Plains moccasins showing beadwork on top surfaces.

Above: Assorted Micmac birch bark items decorated with quillwork. R.Green Collection.

Right: Blackfoot man's skin shirt, leggings and moccasins. The shirt is a classic mid-19th century chief's shirt, of two large deer skins, the bottom two-thirds of each forming the front and back. The remaining skins form the two sleeves. The shirt is decorated with beaded strips, large chest discs, painted stripes and hairlock fringes. It is reported to have been collected from Crowfoot, a Blackfoot chief in Alberta, by Cecil Denny of the North West Mounted Police, who passed it on to Edgar Dewdney (1835–1916). Dewdney, born in Devon, England, became Lieutenant-Governer of the Northwest Territories in Canada, and his widow gave donations of Indian items to the Royal Albert Memorial Museum, Exeter, U.K., in 1920 and 1927.

Birch bark. One of the most important resources of the American Indian was bark. White birch grows throughout the northeastern United States, from the Atlantic coast to the Rockies, and north to the Mackenzie River basin. Strong, thick, generally waterproof bark was used for canoes and various shaped wigwam coverings. It was used as well for a wide variety of containers and receptacles that were also adapted for the European souvenir trade by the addition of colored porcupine quills — such as those produced by the Micmac, and later by the Ojibwa and Ottawa (Odawa) of the Great Lakes area.

Bison or buffalo. The way of life of the nomadic High Plains peoples depended almost entirely on the bison; the parts of the animal they did not eat, were used to make robes, tipis and artifacts.

Boots. Hide boots or combined leggings and boots worn by Inuit, Athabascan and Southwestern tribes.

Buckskin. Hide leather from animals of the deer family, wapiti, moose or elk, used for clothing. Less commonly used for clothes were buffalo, mountain sheep, mountain goat and caribou.

Cacique. The chief or leader of a Native American tribe in the Southwest and other areas previously dominated by Spanish culture.

Canoes. Two main types were the birch bark-covered wooden frame used in the Northeast and Subarctic, and the dugout (hollowed) log form of the Southeast. Characteristic variations are illustrated in color illustrations to be found in this book. *See also Kayaks and Umiaks.*

Catlinite. A slate or steatite, usually red, named after the artist-explorer George Catlin, who visited the site of the mine at present-day Pipestone, Minnesota. It was made into pipes for ceremonial smoking.

Above: Photograph shows Catherine MacDonald's infant in a cradleboard hanging against a wall with examples of native crafts. Métis, Ft. Coleville in present-day Washington State, c. 1859.

Right: Plateau cradle, probably Nez Perce, c. 1890. Elliptical board covered tight with skin and beaded for the top section. The shallow bag to hold the child is on the lower, narrower section..

Below: Beautiful beadwork on this Cheyenne baby carrier. R.Green Collection.

Opposite, inset: Floral beadwork designs on these Ojibwa vest and leggings. R. Green Collection.

Opposite, Top to Bottom: A variety of beadwork designs
1 Moccasin fully beaded in stepped geometric designs typical of the Canadian Plains if the second half of the 19th century. Probably Assiniboine or Plains Cree. Courtesy Dave Sager.

2 A panel of floral beadwork with a border and roll-edge beadwork typical of the Cree-Saulteaux of Manitoba and Saskatchewan on a buckskin Cree or Saulteaux tobacco bag, c. 1880.

3 This c. 1880 tobacco bag probably from Saskatchewan or Manitoba, Canada and from an area of mixed Plains Cree and Plains Ojibwa or Northern Ojibwa and Woods Cree. Floral beaded panels on each side with an upper border of porcupine quillwork on the buckskin pouch with fringing. The edges are beaded. This pouch was formerly in the collection of James Hooper, owner of the Totems Museum, Arundel, Sussex, UK.

4 Panels of beadwork in geometric and curving designs on a buckskin tobacco bag. The style of beadwork suggests a Stoney or Plains Cree origin, and from the Canadian Plains, probably Alberta. 50cm long + fringe x 18cm wide.

Clan. Families descended from a common ancestor.

Coiling. A method of making pottery in the American Southwest, in which walls of a vessel are built up by adding successive ropelike coils of clay.

Complex. Social or religious traits and beliefs, often consisting of several elements and ideas, usually related, giving a strong sense of ethnic and emotional cohesion.

Confederacy. A group of tribes or villages bound together politically or for defense (e.g., Iroquois, Creek).

Coup. From the French, "a blow": To approach an enemy or animal close enough to touch by hand or "coup stick" was considered an honorable feat among Plains Indians.

Cradles. From the Ute north to the Blackfoot, Crow, Flathead and across the Rockies, the cradle base is a flat wood boars cut into a long ellipsoid wider at the top than bottom, curved both ends and covered with buckskin or cloth with the top half usually beaded. The bag to hold the baby is the lower narrower half. The Ute added an eye shade of basketry. The Crow replaced the bag with a series of fairly wide straps. The Arapaho used a "U" shaped skin-covered frame with the child held in place by a ladder-like band of quilled rawhide. The central Plains Sioux and Cheyenne used a cradle of beaded or quilled buckskin bag sometimes attached to a large rectangle of cloth. The baby is laid on this, then the cloth is folded around its body and legs.

The Southern Plains tribes such as the Kiowa and Comanche used a deep straight-sided skin bag, in the case of Kiowa often covered with beadwork, which was attached by buckskin lacing to a pair of wooden boards. This type of cradle was also used by the Arapaho and Cheyenne southern bands and occasionally by the Sioux.

The origin of the so-called "lattice cradle" is unknown, but it is likely not old. Surviving examples date from about 1880. The lattice cradle consisted of a cover made of buckskin or later of canvas or wool wrapped around rawhide supports at the heel and foot. This assemblage was laced to a frame of two narrow boards held apart by two shorter and narrower boards at the head and foot. The boards were pointed at the top and often decorated with brass tacks or silver buttons. The "V" shape provided an opening for the mother's head and when placed against a tree, the boards either side prevented it from falling.

The Iroquois and Great Lakes Indians used a basic cradle of a flat board with a narrow wood bow projecting forward from near the top to give the baby protection. Bark or wood sides (Cree) and a small foot board completed the basic construction. A cloth then bound the baby to the board (Iroquois and Southern Ojibwa) or a buckskin laced cloth front attached to the sides held the baby (Cree and Northern Ojibwa).

Curvilinear. Patterns made up of or bounded by curved lines.

Double-curve designs. Two opposed incurves, usually in quills or beads, attached to each other at the ends, used to decorate articles of ceremonial clothing among Northeastern tribes.

Drum or **Dream Dance**. A variation of the Plains Grass Dance adopted by the Santee Sioux, Southern Ojibwa (Chippewa) and Menomini during the 19th century. Among these groups the movement had religious features that advocated friendship, including with whites.

Ethnic. Designation of the divisions of humankind.

Ethnology. A branch of anthropology that deals with comparitive cultures, distribution of peoples, characteristics and folklore of races.

Floral designs. Truly realistic designs are thought *not* to be indigenous to North American Indian art, but were adopted by Northeastern tribes in the 17th century from French missionary influence, along with certain embroidery techniques. Floral designs, sometimes in quills but usually in beadwork, spread west either by further missionary influence or by inter-tribal contact in the late 18th century, and by other European contacts in the 19th century. Floral beadwork patterns are common in Woodland, Subarctic and Northern Plains beadwork of the 19th and early 20th centuries.

Generic. Describing the origin of a group with common characteristics, animal, human or material.

Gens. A clan united by descent through the male line from a common ancestor.

Geometric designs. These patterns are characterized by lines, angles, triangles, squares, and rectangles, or a composition of these elements, used to decorate clothing in quillwork or beadwork.

German silver. A nonferrous alloy of copper, nickel and zinc, known also as nickel silver; traded to Woodland and Plains tribes, who became expert metal workers.

Give-a-way. The Indian custom of presenting gifts as a way of honoring guests or recipients at a celebration or powwow.

Grass house Dwellings used by many tribes, particularly the Southern Caddoan tribes (see page 84).

Hairpipes. Tubular bone beads made by whites in the 19th century and traded to the Indians, often made up into vertical and horizontal rows called breastplates. Originally made from shells and, later, cattle bones.

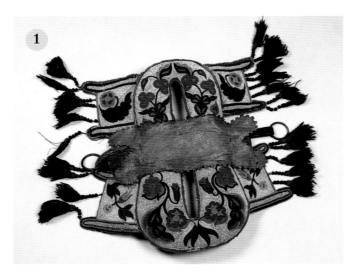

Hamatsa Society. The most important winter ceremonial of the Kwakwakawakw (Southern Kwakiutl) was that of the Hamatsa Society, during which a number of articulated masks were worn. (See page 254.)

Horse equipment. Saddles devised by North American Indians of the Plains in the 18th and 19th centuries were adapted from those seen in use by Europeans (Spanish, etc.) and other Indian tribes. Pad saddles, saddles with pommel and cantle, horse blankets, martingales, cruppers, headstalls, masks and bridles were all used and decorated with quill- or beadwork.

Housepost. Part of the structure of a Northwest Coast house to support the roof, often carved with family or ancestral emblems.

Incising. A method of scraping decorative or symbolic designs on a rawhide or bark surface.

Kachinas. Supernatural beings impersonated by costumed Pueblo Indians in religious ceremonies. Dressed Kachina dolls instruct children to recognize the different spirits.

Kayaks and Umiaks The kayak is a distinctive style of boat invented in the Arctic smaller than usual canoes, that is easily righted, developed many years ago and used by the people of the Arctic and Subarctic from the Aleutian Islands to Greenland. They were designed for use in lakes and rivers as well as in the waters of the Arctic Ocean, and Bering Sea. They were used primarily for hunting—the term "kayak" is translated as "hunter's boat." The Aleut and Inuit (Eskimo) people constructed the original kayaks using a light wood frame, over which they stretched a naturally water-resistant sealskin covering. The umiak is a larger, multiperson vessel which is more similar to the traditional idea of a canoe. An ocean-going vessel, it is open-topped and used for carrying goods.

Kiva. The structure, often subterranean, which serves as a ceremonial chamber for Pueblo Indians in the Southwest. Each village usually has several kivas.

Lazy stitch. A Plains Indian technique of sewing beads to hide or cloth, giving a final ridged or arch effect in lanes about eight or 10 beads wide. Also called "lane stitch."

Leggings. Male or female, covering ankle and leg to the knee or thigh (male), usually buckskin or cloth.

Longhouse. The religion of conservative Iroquois, whose rituals still take place in special buildings (rural grange type) also called longhouses. These buildings represent the old bark longhouse, and a microform of Iroquoia itself.

Medicine bundle. A group of various objects, sometimes animal, bird or mineral, etc., contained in a wrapping of buckskin or cloth, which gave access to considerable spiritual power when opened with the appropriate ritual. Mostly found among the eastern and Plains tribes.

Moccasins. Buckskin footwear, either hard-soled (Plains) or soft-soled (Woodland and Subarctic).

Moiety. A ceremonial division of a village or tribe.

Octopus bag So-called octopus bags or four-tab bags were usually made of red or blue trade cloth with two pairs of four tabs terminating in tassels of wool yarn. The origins of this style are likely to have been ancient painted skin pouches of the Great Lakes Indians with tabs, fringes, or animal paws hanging down. The cloth octopus bag seems to have appeared about 1840 among the Red River Métis of Manitoba, people largely of Ojibwa origin, and the Cree of northern Ontario. These bags were decorated with a variety of floralistic patterns, often bilaterally symmetrical. During the nineteenth century this form of bag spread to other Cree groups, Cree-Métis, Northern Athabascans, Tlingit, and into British Columbia, each group with its own distinct decorative beadwork style.

Pan-Indian. Describes the modern mixed intertribal dances, costumes, powwows and socializing leading to the reinforcement of ethnic and nationalist ties.

Parfleche. A rawhide envelope or box made to contain clothes or meat, often decorated with painted geometrical designs.

Opposite, from top to bottom:
1 Heavily decorated Cree or Plains Ojibwa saddle. R.Green Collection

2 Umiak.

3 Kayak hunter.

4 Kiva, Nambe Pueblo, Santa Fe County, NM

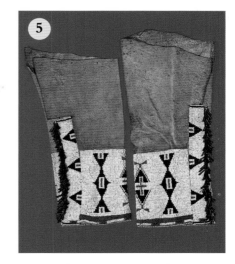

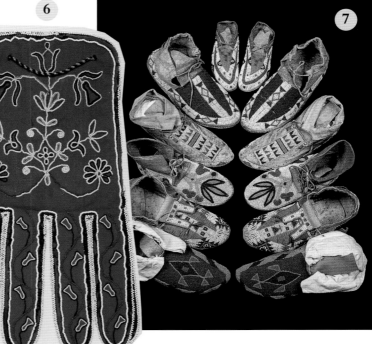

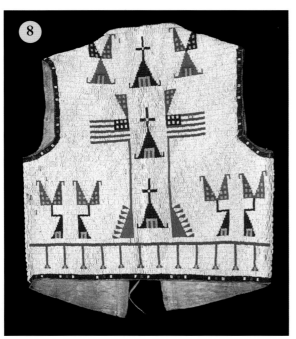

Right, from top to bottom:
5 Arapaho woman's beaded leggings. c. 1880 R. Green Collection

6 Octopus bag.

7 Assorted Plains moccasins. R. Green Collection

8 Geometric lazy-stitch beadwork on a Sioux man's waistcoat. R. Green Collection

9 Jicarilla Apache man's buckskin leggings.

Parka. Invented by the native people of the Arctic region, who — obviously — needed clothing that would protect them from windchill and wet while hunting and kayaking. Parka is of Aleut origin and anorak —today almost interchangeable — in fact is Inuit, coming from the Greenlandic Inuit word *anoraq*.

Peyote. *Lophophora williamsii*. A stimulant and mildly hallucinogenic substance obtained from the peyote button a small, spineless cactus of the Rio Grande valley. Not to be confused with mezcal.

Peyote cult. The Native American Church, a part-native and part-Christian religion originating in Mexico, but developed among the Southern Plains tribes in Oklahoma, which has spread to many native communities.

Plateau "Flat Bags" or "Panelbags"

Cornhusk bags, also called "flat bags" were made by the Yakima, Nez Perce, Umatilla and other Plateau tribes. Square and rectangular storage bags for eatable roots made of hemp fiber and originally decorated with beargrass. Later, after cultivated corn was introduced into the Plateau area, dyed cornhusk using a false embroidery technique was used for the geometric and naturalistic surface designs. Later still, wool was also used on bags of smaller size and used by women as purses and wallets.

By the late 19th century cornhusk bags had been largely replaced by beaded "flat bags" of buckskin or canvas and cloth. They were carried by womem during parades and many were given as gifts. They were made by tribes anywhere between western Montana and the Oregon coast. Some examples show animal and pictorial images of Indian women or men in native dress and many are beaded in floral designs. Many are still being made; the Yakima (Yakama) who have a preference for orange beads in their designs, the Nez Perce often use cut and small beads.

Above: Two Inuit women wearing knee-length parkas. Photograph by Edward S. Curtis, February 28, 1929, and published in volume 20 of The North American Indian. *Library of Congress. Prints & Photographs Division LC-USZ62-88326.*

Right: Aleut hooded ceremonial parka or kamleika, a waterproof overdress made of translucent seal skin. The panel at the chin is dyed gut applique with red wool embroidery, and fur and dyed gut applique trim the cuffs and hem. Human hair decorates the seams. Worn by a person of high rank or by a shaman when making contact with the spirit world. Collected before 1869.

Below left: Parfleche. R. Green Collection.

Below center: Nez Perce cornhusk bag. The Nez Perce, like neighboring peoples, had a long tradition of making small bags from twined grass or thin roots. Once confined to the reservations from the mid-19th century, people could no longer forage for the most suitable materials as before, and they began to make bags from corn husks, wool and cotton twine instead.

Below right: Elk design on a beaded Nez Perce "flat bag," early 20th century.

Porcupine quillwork. One of the principal decorative media of North America was the use of porcupine quills. The animal was found in the northeastern and much of the western United States, and throughout Canada and Alaska. Its southern limit is a matter of debate, as quillwork has been reported as far south as the lower Mississippi valley and among the Cherokee.

Quills were softened by water, teeth or nails, dyed with natural plant dyes, or — after 1850 — by traded commercial aniline dyes, or boiled-out colors from traded blankets. Quills were applied to buckskin by various techniques, such as wrapping, braiding and weaving, by Woodland, Plains and Subarctic tribes. Among the Micmac, Ojibwa and Ottawa, quills were also attached to birch bark. Beadwork largely replaced quillwork by the 1860s, but has continued to be done in a number of places.

Potlatch. A wealth distribution ceremony among Northwest Coast Indians.

Powwow. Modern celebration, often intertribal and secular, held on most reservations throughout the year.

Prehistoric. In American Indian archeology, this refers to Indian life and its remains dated before A.D. 1492.

Pueblo. An Indian village in New Mexico or Arizona. Most northern Rio Grande community dwellings are of sun-dried mud or adobe and straw bricks, forming honeycombs of rooms, sometimes terraced. The walls, thickly plastered with mud inside and out, are often whitewashed. Acoma, however, is of rubble and clay, while Zuñi pueblo are of both stone and adobe bricks. Hopi towns have walls of dressed stone laid in adobe. These are almost the only precontact towns, though many others are close to ancient sites. Most towns have plazas for public dances and subterranean kivas for secret rituals. Traditionally, each clan of a tribe occupies one section of the building. Nowadays most rooms have doors and windows, but historically, access was to upper floors only, by ladders. Taos is perhaps the most impressive of these towns, in part six stories high.

Rancherias. Small reservations in California.

Rawhide. Usually hard, dehaired hide or skin used for parfleche cases, moccasin soles, shields, drumheads and other objects.

Reservation. Government-created lands to which Indians were assigned, removed or restricted during the 19th and 20th centuries. In Canada they are called reserves.

Roach. A headdress of deer and porcupine hair, very popular for male war-dance costume, which originated among the eastern tribes and later spread among the Plains Indians along with popular Omaha or Grass Dance, the forerunner of the modern War and Straight dances.

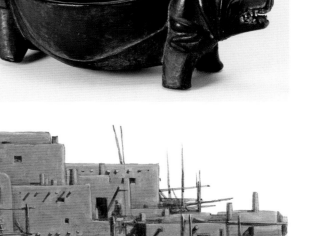

Top: Ottawa-Ojibwa quillwork boxes.

Center: Nuu-chah-nulth (Nootka) oil or grease dish carved at one end in the form of the head of a wolf, the mouth set with otter teeth. A human sits astride the neck of the wolf. At the other end is an unidentified creature. This piece would have been commissioned for the host of a Potlatch.

Above: Taos Pueblo. Note Spanish/Moorish-derived domed ovens in foreground.

Right: The Crane, probably a Winnebago warrior, possibly photographed in Sioux City, Iowa, by Gurnsey and Illingworth, c.1860s. The buckskin shirt and leggings are not native dress, but the roach and turban are typical of western Woodland groups.

Left: Making snowshoes.

Below inset: A pair of 19th-century Eastern Woodland snowshoes.

Below: Blackfoot (Blackfeet) man c.1900, undergoing self-torture in the Sun Dance ceremony, photographed inside the Medicine Lodge. The ties are attached to the center pole. Fasting and pain-induced visions satisfied vows taken beforehand to give thanks for health or tribal welfare. It was a major Plains Indian ceremony, and versions of it are still performed by the Cheyenne and Sioux.

Rosette. Disc or circular area of decoration using quills or beads, such as found on Plains men's shirts.

Silver. Sterling and coin silver used in Southwestern jewelry, originally using melted-down or hammered U.S. and Mexican coins.

Sinew. The tendon fiber from animals, used by Indians and Inuit as thread for sewing purposes.

Smoked tanning. A buckskin tanning process to maintain leather in a supple condition after rain.

Snowshoe. A wooden frame covered with babiche, worn on the feet to prevent the wearer from sinking into soft snow.

Stitches. Various stitches are used to sew beads to hide or cloth, usually called appliqué, lazy, spot or crow stitch.

Stroud. A coarse trade cloth imported from England.

Sun Dance. The annual world renewal religious ceremonial complex of the Plains Indians, whose sacred rituals took place in specially constructed "lodges" of poles and brush, the roof of rafters supported on the focal point for the dancers — the "center pole." For a fuller discussion and photographs, see the introduction to the *Plains and Prairie* section on pages 92-93.

Sweat lodge. A low, temporary, oval-shaped structure covered with skins or blankets, in which men sat in steam, produced by splashing water on heated stones as a method of ritual purification.

Syllabics. A form of European-inspired writing, consisting of syllabic characters used by the Cherokees in the 19th century and in other forms by the Crees and Inuit.

Termination. Withdrawal of U.S. government recognition of the protected status of, and services due to, an Indian reservation.

Thread. Fine flax, cotton, silk or modern fibers used to sew seams, beads or quills.

Thunderbird. A mystical bird whose wings caused thunder. *See also Totem poles.*

Tipi. The conical lodge of the true High Plains nomads, constructed of bison (buffalo) hide erected on a framework of "lodge" poles. Since the destruction of the bison herds the covers have been made of canvas. They are usually erected during powwows or for Peyote meetings. The conical tipi probably evolved from Subarctic prototypes. Early forms were relatively small, before the coming of the horse allowed transportation of larger covers and longer poles. Basic construction was fairly constant throughout the Plains: a tilted cone of straight, slim, peeled poles (usually lodge pole pine, cedar or spruce) slotted into a foundation frame of three or four poles. Three-pole foundations were used by the Cheyenne, Arapaho, Sioux, Assiniboine, Kiowa, Gros Ventre, Plains Cree, Mandan, Arikara, Pawnee, Ponca, Oto and Wichita. Four-pole foundations were used by the Crow, Blackfoot, Sarsi, Shoshone, Omaha, Comanche, Hidatsa, Kutenai, Flathead and Nez Perce.

Foundation poles were usually tied together over the spread ground cover, then hoisted, the remaining poles being slotted into the crotches they formed. In three-pole foundations, one pole faced east and formed a door pole on the south side. Four-pole foundations formed a rectangle, the rear two remaining low at the back and appearing as a "swallowtail" in the completed lodge. The tipi usually faced east towards the rising sun. Being an imperfect cone it had a back steeper than the front, which tended to brace it against the prevailing winds. Covers were usually of dressed buffalo cow hides before the destruction of the herds in the 1880s, and thereafter of traded canvas duck, usually white. Most 19th-century tipis were about 12 to 18 feet (3.7 to 5.5 m) high, requiring some 12 skins sewn together and cut to a half-circle plan. The cover was hoisted onto the frame with a single lifting pole and spread around the sides. The edges were pinned together at the front, and the bottom edge staked down. The cover included two "ear" extensions at the top of the sides, forming smoke flaps held out by external poles, adjusted to the

Above: A young Oglala girl sitting in front of a tipi, with a puppy beside her, probably on or near Pine Ridge Reservation.

Below: The tipi was adopted by Plateau tribes during the 19th century. (a) is an Umatilla extended lodge using canvas instead of cattail mats over a peaked construction. (b) Women erecting a Blackfoot tipi; and two others with typical Blackfoot designs: (c) a Rainbow Lodge with human figure, and (d) a Yellow Painted Otter Lodge. Blackfoot lodges usually have the bottom section painted black, or red with white spots, representing the puffballs seen on the Prairies; the upper edge may be flat, representing the prairie, or in semicircles or points, for hills and mountains. The central area, between earth and sky, is occupied by natural elements, usually dream animals with major organs highlighted, males on the south side, females on the north. The top section was usually black for the night sky, with white discs on the smoke flaps representing the Pleiades and Great Bear constellations with a maltese cross, a moth or a morning star connected with sleep and dreams.

Modern Crow people prefer their tipis unpainted for the annual "Crow Fair," with long poles protruding at the top (e). The Kiowa of the southern Plains also have a tradition of painted lodges; (g) is the Black Striped lodge of the holy man Beaver Cap, (f) is a Wind River Shoshone skin lodge owned by Chief Washakie, (h) shows the use by the Cheyenne of windbreaks to ward off dust during Oklahoma summers.

Opposite, below left and right: Constructing and using a sweat lodge—a Blackfoot sweat lodge in use, c. 1895 — woman attendant on right. Photograph: Walter McClintock.

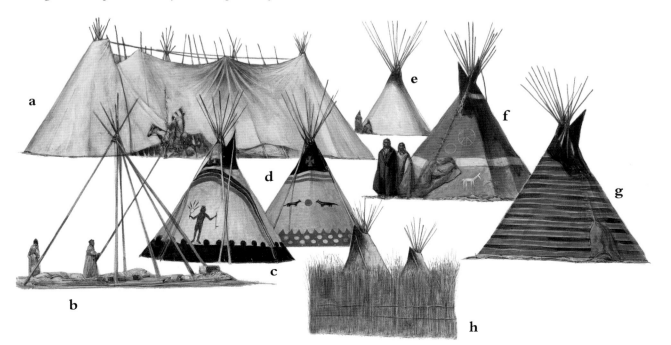

Above: Blackfoot tobacco bag and pipe. R. Green Collection.

Opposite, Left and Center: Totem pole models.

Opposite, Right: Ilchinik, a totem pole in the Royal Albert Memorial Museum, Exeter, UK.

Below: Western Sioux tobacco bag. c. 1890. R. Green Collection.

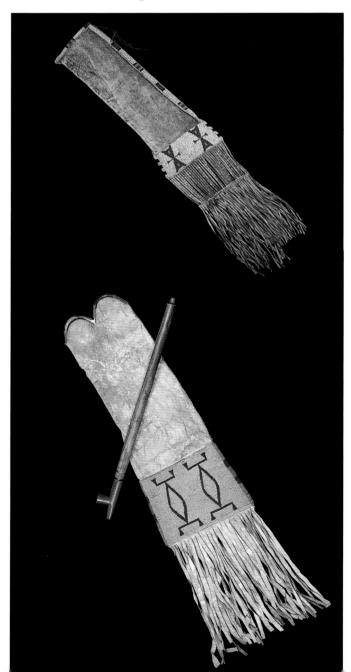

prevailing wind. These helped drag smoke through the gap left at the top. A liner 5 or 6 feet (1.5 or 1.8 m) in height ran around the inside of the poles, fastened to them and to the floor. A fireplace of stones was made centrally, somewhat toward the rear. Family beds were usually on the south side, those of guests on the north. At the rear were placed backrests of slender rods, weapons and medicine bundles. Some covers and liners were painted with naturalistic or geometrical symbolic patterns, usually peculiar to the owner and associated with the intense esoteric spiritual nature of the lodge. See page 103 for construction illustration.

Tipi bag. Bags, usually buckskin, used for storage inside tipis. See lower photograph on page 123 for example of use.

Tobacco or **pipe bag.** Bags, usually buckskin, beaded or quilled with fringing were made by most Plains Indian peoples for men to carry ceremonial tobacco and pipes.

Totem pole. A memorial post or pole set up in the front of a house, usually carved in a series of emblematic or crest symbols of family lineage, or mythical or historical events, among Northwest Coast Indians. Totem poles were of Western Red Cedar and first cut to the required length. The back was often split or cut off so that slightly more than half the column remained. The heart wood was then trimmed away leaving a cross-section shaped like the segment of a circle. The log column was carved face-up with as many as six emblematic figures on tall poles. Totem poles can be generally divided into four categories: memorial, mortuary, frontal poles and house poles, and the carved representations of animals, birds, fish, humans, mythological and supernatural beasts serve as clan or family crests. Once the salient physical details of the figures are understood the animals become quite recognizable. The art of carving large poles is not old, the greater number date from 1850 to 1910, the early poles were modestly painted with natural pigments, but later ones were painted with bright commercial paints. The availability of metal tools greatly facilitated complex carving.

The Coast Indians believed they shared the world with all living things and in a state of equality and mutual understanding and speaking a mutually understandable language. This allowed humans to share their secrets with birds and animals and vice versa. from this belief the people developed a series of myths and legends which could be illustrated in their totemic carvings. The Thunderbird is the noble and omnipotent ruler of the skies and controls the elements. He is usually represented with a carved beak and horns. He is viewed as a great helper and protector of man.

Traditionally, the Thunderbird turned the Wild Man of of the Woods into stone and was often carved below the Thunderbird with spouting lips and outstanding ears. Other mythical creatures represented on poles included various monsters, giant clam, fog woman and the double-headed monster or the Sisiutl.

Eagle — was a symbol of wisdom and is similar to the Thunderbird but does not have horns.

Bear — is a symbol of earthly power and usually has a short snout, paws with long claws, and a protruding tongue. The Grizzly Bear has ferocious canines. Grizzly bears often appear as guardian spirits on houseposts. Very similar was the Wolf with sharply pointed ears and a long tail.

Totem pole models. These were, and still are, made to satisfy the tourist market. Some models replicate full-sized poles, such as the ones opposite. The right-hand model is of an original carved in 1890 by Tlingit carver William Ukas to honor a chief named Kohlteen. It was 24 feet (8 m) tall and stood outside the Sun house at Killisnoo in the Stikine River region. This marine ivory model was made in the early years of the 20th century. It was painted in red and black pigment, now mostly worn away. The top figure represents Kicks Bay mountain glacier on the Stikine River. Then comes Frog, emblem of the Kiks'adi people. Next is Old Raven, the Creator, and Young Raven who made man. At the base of the pole is the Killisnoo Beaver, who was a chief's pet, with a small frog. The pole on the left is of the Chief Johnson or Kajuk totem pole, raised in Ketchikan, Alaska, in 1901 for the Ganaxadi Tlingit of the Raven moiety of the Tanta Kwan (Tongass) group. This model was made by Chief Johnson himself, and purchased by government agent Edgar Dewdney in 1901. A full-size replica of the original pole, carved by Israel Shotridge, was raised in 1989.

Totem pole tradition. The tradition of totem pole carving is alive and well in the Northwest as is shown by Ilchinik (*right*) — a totem pole carved by Nuu-chah-nulth (Nootka) artist and carver Tim Paul (*top*), who carved the totem pole at the Royal Albert Memorial Museum and Art Gallery, Exeter, U.K., in 1998. He was assisted by Patrick Amos, the late Francis Mark, Leslie Mickey, and apprentice carvers Tom Paul and Corey Baiden Amos. This red cedar pole is named for a successful and powerful whaler. He is seen at the base, in a state of trance, preparing himself for the hunt. He stands upon a whale, enclosed by the sides of the canoe. Also depicted are Tu-tu-ch, the elder Thunderbird; Ti-as, the New Moon; and the chief's box, Hu-pa-kwa-num. The face of the sea chief, Ha-witiisum, is on the lid of the box.

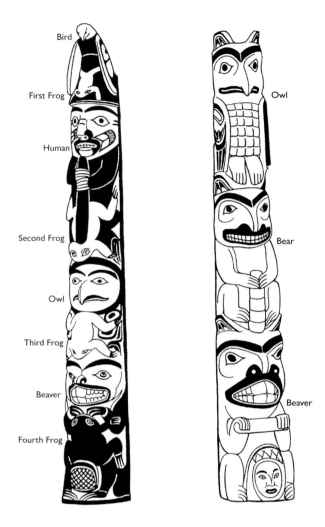

Labels on left pole (top to bottom): Bird, First Frog, Human, Second Frog, Owl, Third Frog, Beaver, Fourth Frog

Labels on right pole (top to bottom): Owl, Bear, Beaver

Above left: Haida frog totem pole.

Above right: Haida owl crest totem pole.

Below: Typical Iroquois products for the tourist trade. Alan Mitchell Collection

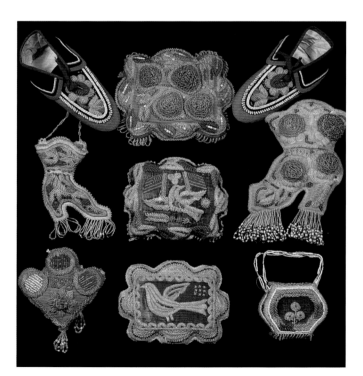

Killer whale — the much-feared lord of the seas and ruler of the underworld can be recognized by its dorsal fins. The whale was usually the villain of Indian legends.

Sea creatures — besides whales, sea lion, seal, shark, halibut and salmon were also represented on poles.

Beaver — large incisor teeth and a paddle-shaped tail turned up in front were the salient features of the Beaver.

Frog — was usually carved with a wide toothless mouth and fat little body painted green with yellow spots.

Raven — was a hero capable of changing form and appeared as man, animal or bird, and often depicted with a disc in its straight beak. Owls were often carved with a short blunt beak, turned down at the tip.

Tourist and **souvenir trade.** Native artists throughout North America often used their talents to produce beautifully decorated objects "in the native manner" for the white souvenir market. Eastern tribes were producing quill-decorated bark objects from the 18th century onward. Beadwork became very popular with white curio seekers during the 19th century. Baskets were collected from Southwestern, West Coast and Californian tribes. Such material helped the many Indian people living in poverty, although they were often sold at a fraction of their true value.

Travois. These were seen widely among the Plains peoples: a temporary load platform was tied between dragging lodge poles. Children could be confined and protected by a cage of bent willow covered with hide. The Plains Indian pony was not a beautiful animal; but it was sturdy, had great endurance and was lighter, swifter and had a longer range than the horse used by the U.S. Army. The average adult male was less than 14 hands high and weighed some 700 pounds (320 kg), exhibiting a wide range of solid and mixed colors. Its ancestry can be traced to the Barb horse introduced into Spain during the 8th century Moorish invasion; horses brought to the Americas by the Spanish early in the 16th century came from Cordoba and Andalusia, where the Barb strain survived. Although the date of large-scale diffusion into Indian hands is disputed, it is believed that the Ute, Kiowa and Kiowa-Apache were mounted by 1640, and that the Plains peoples to the north had the horse by the early 18th century. Larger horses displaced the pony during the reservation period; by the 1940s it had almost disappeared, and the only Indian-bred horse to survive to modern times is the larger, heavier Appaloosa of the Nez Perce and other Plateau tribes.

Tribe. A group of bands, sometimes (but not necessarily) linked together genetically, politically, geographically, by religion or by a common origin myth; but a common language is the main criterion. Several tribes were so scattered that they did not form a "tribe" in any popularly recognizable sense. Some "tribal" groups are only so in terms of ethnographical studies, the word being a convenient tool to describe collectively fragmented groups or collections of small groups of peoples who themselves recognized no such association.

Turquoise. Semi-precious stone in Southwestern jewelry.

Wampum. Wampum is the common name for shell beads of the North American Indian and generally refers to the white and purple cylindrical beads of the Algonkian and Iroquois Indians of the northeastern U.S. White wampum was made principally from the central column of the whelk and purple from the quahog clam. These shells found along the Atlantic coast, particularly Long Island Sound where the local Algonkians made the shell beads and traded them inland. Early white settlers gradually took over the production of shell wampum using metal implements, and for a time in early colonial America, wampum was used as a medium of exchange. Strings of wampum served to refresh or memorize ritual procedure, or as certificates of authority, but famously when woven into belts that recorded treaty negotiations by means of designs to recall the events. In these historic belts white wampum symbolized peace and purple (black) was particularly important if painted red which would symbolize war. Richard Hamell has made a careful study of historic wampum belts and has reproduced many belts from museum collections and existing old records.

War bonnet. The headdress worn by Plains Indian men, consisting of a circle of eagle feathers on a crown, which became popular among many tribal groups in the 20th century as a symbol of Indian identity. The artists George Catlin and Karl Bodmer were among the first to depict them in the 1830s.

War dance. Popular name for the secular male dances that developed in Oklahoma and other places after the spread of the Grass Dances from the eastern Plains–Prairie tribes in the 19th century, among whom it was connected with war societies. Many tribes had complex war and victory celebrations.

Weft and warp. The horizontal and vertical threads of a loom for weaving quillwork and beadwork.

Wigwam. An oval or conical lodge of the northeastern Algonkians, constructed of birch bark or rush mats fixed to a frame of saplings. The term "wigwam" applies to several Woodland forms. The four main types were domed, peaked, tipi-shaped and the bark house. The domed wigwam, of ironwood saplings driven into the ground and bent over to form arches, was covered with birch or elm bark or reed mats. The peaked-roof lodge had a series of pointed arches connected by a ridge pole, also covered with bark or mats. The tipi shape had a conical frame of poles covered with bark. The bark house was a rectangular structure of poles with bark sheet outer covering.

Most of these single-family homes had central smoke holes. Ceremonial lodges were similar to the domed type, but were longer and open-ended. Canvas was also sometimes used as a covering. Wigwams were in use in isolated areas until c. 1900. A few are still made for special occasions.

Top: Western Sioux headdress. R. Green Collection

Above: Fort Niagara Treaty Belt of 1764 reproduced by Richard D. Hamell.

Below: An improvised Cheyenne travois of c. 1870.

NATIVE POPULATIONS

The Census 2000 Figures respondents were separated into four categories and combined total. The first listed American Indians and Alaskan Native alone of one tribe; the second listed natives of two or more tribes; categories three and four were combinations with other races. However the results from these self-identification figures require to be viewed with considerable caution. It is well known that the number of full blood American Indians north of Mexico has continued to reduce as a percentage of the whole since the early days of contact with Europeans, Afro-Americans,   and latterly intermarriage with Americans. Adoption of white prisoners during the colonial wars suggests white ancestry was well established among eastern tribes (Iroquois, Delaware, Shawnee, etc.) long before the reservation period. Only in the Southwestern U.S. do full bloods predominate, eg, among the Navajo, Apache, Ute, Pueblo etc. Among the tribes east of the Mississippi only among the Choctaw and Florida Seminole do full bloods occur in numbers. The Crow tribe of Montana are one of the few present day Plains tribes where full bloods number more than tribal members of mixed descent. In some areas of the Plateau and California remnants of tribes destroyed by white invasion were absorbed by intermarriage into the greater population. The second category may contain full blood Indians as suggested, as many thousands of Oklahoma people are mixed tribally (descendants of two or more tribes) since some thirty or more tribes were forced or settled in the state (formerly Indian Territory) in close proximity to each other. 2,409,578 Indians and Eskimos (Inuit, Yupik) were reported in Category 1 in the 2000 Census, 133, 259 in Category 2, and a grand total (combining all Categories) of 4,248,873.

The Bureau of Indian Affairs, U.S. Department of the Interior (BIA) has a different method of determining who is or is not an American Indian. Most Indian Service Agencies or Indian Tribal or Reservation communities usually require a minimum of a quarter Indian ancestry of their tribe for enrollment, although some require as little as a thirty-second (Osage Oklahoma). In 2001 the total U.S. BIA figure for enrolled Native (Indian and Eskimo) people was 1,816,504. Missing from these figures are a number of predominantly eastern groups who, for various reasons, have been unable to obtain Federal recognition as Indians due partly to a lack of a documented history or proof of Indian genealogy or their social acculturation extends back beyond the establishment of the U.S. Federal system. However, some of these groups are state recognized, the largest such group being the Lumbee of North Carolina.

The discrepancy between the Census and BIA total population figures cannot easily be explained. It is possible that U.S.-based Mexican and South American people of Indian extraction and Pacific Islanders report themselves as Native American. These additions together with the considerable number of non-Federally recognized Indian elements (often triracial) in the eastern U.S., would go some way toward explaining some of the difference. All things considered, a figure of approximately two million Indians (U.S. people with an obvious degree of Indian ancestry) plus one million in Canada (including Métis) would probably be a reasonably acceptable total population figure for the Indian and Inuit (Eskimo) today— the descendants of tribes originally living north of the Rio Grande.

UNITED STATES

Table 1: North American Indian Population in the U.S., 2001. Summary.

a) BIA (Bureau of Indian Affairs) population figures enrolled in each state — not state census figures which varies because of the emigrant population in large cities.

	2001(BIA)	1990
Alabama	2,228	2,988
Alaska	119,431	95,000★
★Indian, Aleut, and Inuit (Yupik & Inupiat)		
Arizona	253,481	195,807
Arkansas	—	1,000
California	51,805	40,747
Colorado	3,387	3,639
Connecticut	2,209	585
Delaware	—	1,200
Florida	3,217	3,131
Georgia	—	200
Idaho	10,129	9,657
Illinois	—	
Indiana	379	500
Iowa	1,260	886
Kansas	9,599	2,200
Kentucky	— ⎤	
Tennessee	— ⎦—12,000	
Louisiana	2,789	8,642
Maine	7,356	3,512
Maryland	—	11,000
Massachusetts	1,001	806
Mexico	—	3,200
(North American Indians in Mexico)		
Michigan	52,446	15,734
Minnesota	52,039	23,705
Mississippi	8,823	5,438
Missouri	—	500
Montana	63,557	42,060
Nebraska	14,423	7,534
Nevada	13,664	10,887
New Hampshire	—	—
New Jersey	—	3,400
New Mexico	163,775	151,488

New York	18,505	12,280
North Carolina	12,139	44,414
North Dakota	55,167	23,751
Ohio	—	700
Oklahoma	630,586	276,691
Oregon	20,585	13,695
Pennsylvannia	—	700
Rhode Island	2,620	2,053
South Carolina	2,430	6,400
South Dakota	107,221	61,700
Texas	3,143	650
Utah	15,090	12,211
Vermont	—	—
Virginia	—	8,260
Washington	48,467	58,615
West Virginia	—	4,000
Wisconsin	52,912	26,690
Wyoming	10,537	8,038

b) North American totals

The total Indian population in 2001 based on the figures in Tables 2 and 3 (below) is as follows (All figures rounded):

	2001(BIA)	1990
Continental U.S.	1,700,000	1,125,000
Indian Alaska	40,000	35,000
(See Table 4)		
Indian Canada	640,000	530,000
Aleut & Inuit (Eskimo) Alaska	80,000	60,000
Inuit (Eskimo) Canada	60,000	55,000
Métis Canada	110,000	100,000
Total	2,630,000	1,905,000

Table 2: North American Indian population, resident and nonresident, federally and nonfederally recognized, by reservation and enclave in United States c. 2001. *See pages 316–323.*

The changes in the U.S. Indian population statistics should be viewed with caution, since the increases in recent times may *not* be due to the normal increasing birth rate. Under pressure from the Bureau of Indian Affairs, as directed by Congress during the 1950s and 1960s, the partly self-regulating (since 1934) Indian bands and reservation communities adopted changes that allowed enrollment of persons regardless of their degree of native ancestry, provided that their antecedents had at one time been tribal members. This allowed increased enrolled membership of Indian groups by persons living away from the reservation and by people of less than "one fourth degree of Indian descent," thus leaving the core band members, reservation residents, and conservatives in a minority and consequently at a disadvantage in tribal politics. This has led to factional disputes that continue. As a result, some published population figures are somewhat higher or lower than those given here.

KEY
Res. Reservation • Co.County • Cos.Counties • Par. Parish • L.I. Long Island • N.J. New Jersey • Fed. Federal • Nat. Nation

In this table, "Ref. No." keys into the reservation maps in each chapter; "Enclave" identifies location or reservation; "Tribe"
identifies the principal tribe or group name; [NFR] identifies the U.S. 2000 non-federally recognized groups' figures,
approximately 110,000 in total; "2001 (BIA)" gives the 2001 Bureau of Indian Affairs figures; and "1990" the approximate enrolled population or group membership in 1990. Note: In the text NR = not reported; 1990 figures reused.

Above: In 1987, the U.S. Supreme Court agreed that federally recognized Native American tribal entities could operate gaming facilities free of state regulation. This opened the floodgates and there are now many such casinos. Indeed, the largest casino in the United States — Foxwoods Casino in Ledyard, Connecticut — is owned by the Mashantucket Pequot Tribe.

Below: Nez Perce beaded flat bag.

REF	ENCLAVE: LOCATION OR RESERVATION	PRESENT PRINCIPAL TRIBE	[NFR]	2001 (BIA)	1990
Alabama					
1	Atmore, Escambia & Covington Cos.	Poarch Creek		2,228	1,488
2	Mobile & Baldwin Cos.	Eastern Creek, Star Clan and Machis "Creek"	[2,000]		500
3a	Citronette	Mowa "Choctaw"	[1,500]		1,000
b	Mobile Co.	(braced with 3a)			
c	Washington Co.	(braced with 3a)			
Alaska (all figures rounded)					
1	Arctic Village, Venetie Res., Fort Yukon, Circle Chalkyitsik	Kutchin		2,000	
2	Minto, Chena, Nenana, Tanacross, Tetlin, Nabesna, Northway	Tanana		2,000	
3	Eagle	Han		100	
4	Rampart, Nulato, Koyukuk, Galena, Ruby, Kaltag, Nuklukayet, Hughes, Allakaket, Stevens	Koyukon	19,000	5,000	
5	Anvik, New Shageluk, Holy Cross	Ingalik		1,250	
6	Grayling	Holikachuk		200	
7	McGrath, Big River, Nikolai, Telida, Vinasale	Kolchan		500	
8	Nondalton, Selodovia, Pedro Bay, Talkeetna, Anchorage, Lime Village	Tanaina & Ahtna		2,000	
9	Cantwell, Chistochina, Copper Center, Chitina, Glennallen	Ahtna		1,000	
10	Yakutat, Cordova	Eyak	400		50?
11	Yakutat, Klukwan, Juneau, Mount Edgecumbe, Sitka, Kake, Wrangell, Ketchikan, Klawak	Tlingit		15,000	15,000
12	Kassan, Hydaburg	Haida		2,000	2,000
13	Annette Village, Metlakahtla	Tsimshian		2,200	2,200
14	Approximately 30 locations	Aleut, Chugach, Koniag		8,000	5,000
15	Approximately 100 locations	Yupik & Inupiat Inuit		72,000	60,000
Arizona					
1	Navajo Res.	Navajo & San Juan (Paiute) (138,901) (254)		139,155	108,641
2	Hopi Res.	Hopi & Tewa		11,267	9,583
3	Ft. Apache Res.	Western Apache		12,900	13,575
4	San Carlos Res.	Western Apache		11,916	8,266
5	Ft. McDowell	Yavapai		939	887
6	Gila Bend Res.	Papago			250
7a	Gila River Res.	Pima, Maricopa		20,479	11,500
b	Maricopa Ak-Chin Res.	Papago		679	650
8	Salt River Res.	Pima, Maricopa		7,371	5,480
9	Papago & San Xavier Res. (several)	Papago (Tohono-O'dham)		25,588	18,900
10	Cocapa Res.	Cocopa		880	448
11	Yuma (California) Res.	Yuma & Cocopa		2,668	3,019
12	Colorado River Res.	Mohave, Kawia, Chemehuevi, Cocopa, Hopi & Navajo		3,526	1,716
13	Ft. Mohave Res.	Mohave, Chemehuevi		1,082	731
14a	Camp Verde Res. & nonreservation	Apache, Yavapai		1,921	800
b	Yavapai Res.	Yavapai		159	142
15	Hualapai Res, incl. Big Sandy	Walapai, Havasupai, Mohave		1,921	1,800
16	Havasupai Res.	Havasupai		674	823
17	Kaibab Res.	Southern Paiute		252	113
18	Chemehuevi (California) Res.	Chemehuevi & others		708	132
19	The Yaqui villages are at Tuscon, Tempe, Marana, Scottsdale, Eloy & Pascua	Yaqui (from Mexico)		13,231	8,206
20	Payson, Clarkdale, Middle Verde	Tonto Apache	111	145?	
Arkansas					
1	Benton, Washington, Sebastian, Garland & Pulaski Cos.	"Cherokee"	[1,600]	—	1,000
California					
	For California, e.g. Karok* and Yurok*, where no figures are shown, they are included in the totals given elsewhere.				
1a	Coast Indian Community (Resighini)	Yurok, Tolowa, Hupa.		90	85
b	Crescent City or Elk Valley	Tolowa & Hupa		100	?
c	Smith River	Tolowa		896	387
2a	Del Norte Co. Happy Camp, etc.	Karok*, Yurok*, Tolowa			5,100
b	Quartz Valley	Shasta, Karok		159	264
c	Ruffeys	Shasta			10
3a	Siskiyou Co.	Karok, Shasta, N. Wintun, Klamath, Pit River		see 5e Shasta Co.	
b	Alturas	Achumawi (Pit River), Shasta		9	10
c	Cedarville	Northern Paiute		30	25
d	Ft. Bidwell	Northern Paiute		244	177
e	Likely	Achumawi (Pit River)			60
f	Lookout 2 parcels	Pit River			50
g	XL-Ranch 4 parcels	Pit River			50
4a	Modoc County, Canby, etc.	Pit River, Northern Paiute		see 5e Shasta Co.	
b	Susanville	Maidu & Atsugewi		360	538
c	Lassen Co.	Pit River, Northern Paiute, Dixey Valley, (Atsugewi), N-E Maidu, Washo		see 5e Shasta Co.	
5a	Big Bend	Pit River (Achumawi)			12
b	Montgomery	mixed		281	10
c	Redding	Pit River			100?
d	Roaring Creek	Pit River			10
e	Shasta Co. Fall River, Burney, Hat Creek, etc.	Pit River, Apwaraki (Atsugewi)		1,667	2,329
	Pit River, Dixey Valley, Apuuraki or Apuuruge are the remnants of the Achumawi & Atsugewi tribes				
6	Trinity Co.	Northern Wintun, Chimariko			?
7a	Big Lagoon	Yurok		18	24
b	Blue Lake	Wiyot, Mattole, Nongatl, Sinkyone, Hupa, Yurok		48	33
c	Hupa Valley Res.	Hupa, Yurok, Chilula, Saiaz (Nongatl)		1,893	2,393
d	Hupa Extension, Weitchpec etc, Karok Reserve	Yurok (4,466) & Karok (3,165)		total 7,631	3,450
e	Rohnerville (Bear River)	Mattole & Wiyot		265	298
f	Table Bluff	"Miami" — Wiyot		360	239
g	Trinidad	Yurok		189	128
h	Humboldt Co.	Hupa, Yurok, Wiyot, Mattole, etc., North Wintun		—	274
8a	Coyote Valley	Northern Pomo		358	115
b	Guidiville	Northern Pomo		114	353
c	Hopland	Central Pomo		692	
d	Laytonville	Kato		81	504
e	Manchester Point Arena	Kashaya-Pomo		621	253

REF ENCLAVE: LOCATION OR RESERVATION	PRESENT PRINCIPAL TRIBE	[NFR]	2001 (BIA)	1990
8f Pinoleville	Northern Pomo		186	161
g Potter Valley & parcels	Northern Pomo		194	187
h Redwood Valley	Northern Pomo		156	129
j Round Valley Res.	Wailaki, Whilkut, Pomo, Yuki, Pit River, Lassik, Yana, Maidu		3,494	1,131
k Sherwood Valley	Northern Pomo		367	224
l Mendocino Co.	Pomo & Yuki		—	?
9a Paskenta	Nomlaki-Wintun		—	?
b Tehama Co.	Central Wintun, N-W Wintun, Yana		—	?
c Cachil Dehe	Wintun		75	?
10a Greenville & parcels	Northern Maidu, Pit River		168	317
b Taylorsville	Northern Maidu, Pit River		—	?
c Plumas Co.	Northern Maidu, Pit River		—	?
11 Sierra Co.	Washo		—	?
12a Berry Creek	Konkow-Maidu		464	304
b Chico	Konkow-Maidu & Wintun		380	45
c Enterprise	Konkow-Maidu		414	177
d Mooretown	Konkow-Maidu		1,193	808
e Butte Co.	Konkow-Maidu		157	35
13a Grindstone	Nomlaki-Wintun		75	100
b Glen Co.	Central Wintun, Patwin		136	71
14a Colusa 3 parcels	Patwin & Nomlaki		696	150
b Cortina	Patwin & Miwok		—	211
15a Big Valley	Patwin, Pomo, Miwok		—	10
b Cache Creek	Eastern Pomo & Pit River		—	10
c Lower Lake	Pomo		76	95
d Middletown	Southeastern Pomo		433	211
e Robinson	Lake Miwok & Pomo		147	147
f Scotts Valley	Southeastern Pomo		145	221
g Sulphur Bank Elem	Northern Pomo		404	188
h Upper Lake 2 parcels	Southeastern Pomo		583	?
j Lake Co.	Eastern Pomo		—	50
16a Alexander Valley	Eastern Pomo		—	273
b Cloverdale	Pomo, Miwok		—	163
c Dry Creek	Wappo		246	10
d Graton	Southern Pomo		—	183
e Lytton	Southern Pomo		—	10
f Mark West	Southern Pomo		—	243
g Stewarts Point	Kashaya-Pomo		599	?
h Sonoma Co.	Pomo, Wappo		—	?
17a Yolo Co.	Patwin		—	51
b Rumsey 2 parcels	Patwin		44	?
18a Yuba Co.	Maidu		—	?
19a Strawberry	Knokow-Maidu (Nisenan)		—	10
b Nevada City	Southern Maidu (Nisenan)		—	100
c Nevada Co.	Northern Miwok & Sthn. Maidu (Nisenan)		244	100
20a Auburn	Southern Maidu (Nisenan)		—	?
b Colfax	Southern Maidu (Nisenan)		—	?
c Placer Co.	Southern Maidu (Nisenan)		—	100

REF ENCLAVE: LOCATION OR RESERVATION	PRESENT PRINCIPAL TRIBE	[NFR]	2001 (BIA)	1990
21a Shingle Springs	Northern Miwok & Southern Maidu		310	185
21b El Dorado Co.	Northern Miwok & Southern Maidu		—	?
22 Wilton	Central Miwok		12	40
23a Buena Vista	Northern Miwok		24	10
b Jackson	Northern Miwok		30	10
c Amador Co.	Northern Miwok (Ione Band)		30	100
24a Sheep Ranch	Northern Miwok		—	15
b Cavaveras Co.	Northern Miwok		—	150
25a Chicken Ranch	Southern Miwok		21	10
b Tuolumne	Southern Miwok		350	288
c Tuolumne Co.	Southern Miwok		—	?
26a Alpine Co.	Washo		113	299
b Alpine — Washo Res. — Woodfords, see also Nevada	Washo Washo			
27 Mono Co. Bridgeport	Northern Paiute, Washo (1,582 inc Nevada)		—	500
28 Mariposa Co.	Southern Miwok		—	?
29a North Fork	Western Mono		510	280
b Pigayune	Chuckchansi-Yokuts		1,173	769
c Madera Co.	Western Mono, Yokuts		—	?
30a Big Sandy	Western Mono		331	188
b Cold Springs	Western Mono		271	265
c Table Mountain	Chukchansi-Yokuts		115	115
d Fresno Co.	Northern Hill, Kings River, Valley Yokuts & Western Mono		—	?
31a Santa Rosa	Southern Valley Yokuts "Tache"		682	356
b Kings Co.	Yokuts		100	100
32a Stratmore	Yokuts		10	10
b Tule River Res.	(Kings River, Southern Valley, Tule-Kaweah), Yokuts, Western Mono-Paiute		1,425	957
33a Big Pine (398) & Benton (136)	Owens Valley Paiute (Eastern Mono)		534	415
b Bishop (914) & Bridgeport (113)	Owens Valley Paiute (Eastern Mono)		1,027	1,350
c Independence	Owens Valley Paiute (Eastern Mono)		135	123
d Indian Ranch or Death Valley (Timbi-sha)	Owens Valley Paiute (Eastern Mono), W.Shoshone		270	?
e Lone Pine	Owens Valley Paiute Western Shoshone (Panamint)		295	296
f Inyo Co.	(E'rn Mono), Nthn. Paiute, Panamint, Tubatulabal, Palagewan		—	?
34 Kern Co.	Kawisu, Tehachipi, Kitanemuk, Tubatulabal (Tejon Tribe), Serrano & Yokuts		—	500
35 San Benito Co. Ohlone	(Mission)		—	50
36 Monterey Co.	(Mission)		—	150
37 San Luis Obispo Co.	Salinan (Mission)		—	30
38 Santa Ynez	Chumash		159	312
39a San Manuel	Serrano		151	80
b 29 Palms	Serrano, Chemehuevi		13	14
c San Bernardino Co.	Serrano, Chemehuevi		—	?
40a Agua Caliente	Serrano, Kawia (Cahuilla)		379	286
b Augustine	Kawia (Cahuilla)		8	8
c Cabazon	Kawia (Cahuilla)		30	28
d Cahuilla	Cahuilla		297	217
40e Mission Creek	Serrano, Kawia		—	20
f Morongo	Serrano, Cahuilla		1,055	1,147

REF ENCLAVE: LOCATION OR RESERVATION	PRESENT PRINCIPAL TRIBE	[NFR]	2001 (BIA)	1990
40g Pechanga	Luiseño		1,372	725
h Ramona	Cahuilla		7	3
j Santa Rosa	Cahuilla		183	135
k Soroba	Cahuilla, Luiseño		802	725
l Torres Martinez	Cahuilla (Kawia)		532	260
41a Barona	Diegueño (Ipai-Tipai)		362	420
b Campo	Diegueño (Ipai-Tipai)		294	184
c Capitan Grande	Diegueño (Ipai-Tipai)		see Viejas	36
d Cuyapaipe	Diegueño (Ipai-Tipai)		8	17
e Inaja-Cosmit	Diegueño (Ipai-Tipai)		18	17
f La Jolla	Luiseño		698	401
g La Posta	Diegueño		20	9
h Los Coyotes	Cahuilla, Diegueño		286	254
j Manzanita	Diegueño		98	81
k Mesa Grande	Luiseño, Diegueño		628	70
l Pala Mission	Luiseño		891	838
m Pauma	Luiseño		132	119
n Yuima	Luiseño			
o Rincon	Luiseño		639	432
p San Pasqual	Diegueño		529	1,698?
r Santa Ysabel	Diegueño		936	953
s Sycuan	Diegueño		67	120
t Viejas (Baron Long) Capitan Grande band	Diegueño		268	213
u Jamul	Diegueño		56	60
42 Marin Co.	Coast Miwok		—	50
43 Stanislaus Co.	Northern Yokuts		—	50

Above listing excludes c.100,000 Indians not native to California within the state, notably from the 1930s onward Cherokees (Oklahoma) and Apaches (Arizona), etc.

[NFR] Chumash [4,000] Costanoan [1,400] Esselen [100] Salinan [370] Others [530]

REF ENCLAVE: LOCATION OR RESERVATION	PRESENT PRINCIPAL TRIBE	[NFR]	2001 (BIA)	1990
Colorado				
1 Southern Ute Res.	Southern Ute		1,375	2,254
2 Ute Mountain	Wiminuche-Ute		2,012	1,325
3 Sanford	Catawba		—	60
Connecticut				
1 Ledyard (Western Pequot or Mushantuxet or Mashantucket)	Pequot		677	155
2 Stonington (Eastern Pequot or Lantern Hill)	Pequot	[100]		80
3 Norwich (Mohegan Hill)	Mohegan			250
4 Kent — Litchfield Co.	Scaticook	[250]	1,532	50
5 Bridgeport — Fairfield Co. (Golden Hill)	Paugussett	[100]		50
Delaware				
1 Kent Co. (Cheswold)	Moors	[300]	—	500
2 Sussex Co. (Millsboro)	Nanticokes	[860]	—	700
Florida				
1a Brighton Res. (Cow Creek)	1a to 3 linked together			
b Off Res. Cow Creek Seminole				

REF ENCLAVE: LOCATION OR RESERVATION	PRESENT PRINCIPAL TRIBE	[NFR]	2001 (BIA)	1990
2a Big Cypress Fed. Res. Miccosukee Fed. Res.	Miccosukee (400)			400
2b Big Cypress State Res. Miccosukee State Res. and off reservation groups Collier Co.	Seminole (2,817)	3,217	2,732	
3 Dania Res. (Hollywood) Coconut Creek, Ft Pierce, Immokalee & Tampa				
4 Apopko Dominickers & splinter groups from S. Carolina	"Choctaw"?		—	
5 Escambia Co.	"Creek"	[1,000]	—	?
6 Calhoun Co. (Blountstown)	"Creek"		—	?
Georgia				
1 Burke Co. Shell Bluff Landing	Altamaha "Cherokee" (Yamasee?)			200
2 Tama, Sac River, Echota, Chickamauga, etc.	"Creek" and "Cherokee" (Georgia, Alabama, Tennessee)	[12,000]	—	?
Idaho				
1 Ft. Hall Res.	Northern Shoshoni & Bannock		4,535	6,877
2 Lapwai Res.	Nez Perce		3,300	1,834
3 Cœur d'Alene Res.	Upper & Lower Kalispel & Cœur d'Alene		1,493	803
4 Bonners Ferry	Kutenai		121	143
Illinois				
1 Centralia	Creek?		—	?
Recent large Indian populations in Chicago area				
Indiana				
1 Miami Co., Wabash Co. (Peru)	Miami	[600]	—	500
2 Marion Co.	Shawnee?		—	?
Iowa				
1 Tama Settlement	Sac & Fox "Mesquakie"		1,260	886
Kansas				
1 Iowa Res.	Iowa		2,897	408
2 Sac & Fox Res.	Sac & Fox		433	54
3 Kickapoo Res.	Kickapoo		1,605	757
4 Potawatomi Res.	Potawatomi		4,870	781
5 Franklin Co.	Wyandot, Delaware, (Munsee), Chippewa		—	100
6 Wyandot Co.	Wyandot		—	100?
Kentucky				
1a Magoffin Co.	Melungeons (mostly removed to cities)			12,000
b Floyd Co.	Melungeons (mostly removed to cities)			
2 Pea Ridge group	Coe Clan		—	100
Louisiana				
1a Lafourche Par.	Houma			
b Terrebonne Par.	Houma	[6,800]	—	3,000
c scattered Jefferson and Orleans, Pars.	Houma			
2 Tunica Res, Marksville, Avoyelles Par.	Choctaw, Ofo, Avoyel, Biloxi, Tunica		920	176
3 Chitimacha Res, Charenton	Chitimacha		980	454

REF ENCLAVE: LOCATION OR RESERVATION	PRESENT PRINCIPAL TRIBE	[NFR]	2001 (BIA)	1990
4a Allen Co. (Kinder)	Koasati (Coushatta)		676	362
b Jefferson Davis Par. Elton	Koasati (Coushatta)		—	—
c Washington, St Landry Co., etc.	?		—	1,000
5 a b St Tammany Par., Bayou Lacombe & Pearl River Station	Choctaw (Acolapissa)		—	?
6 Calcasieu Par, Lake Charles	"Sabines" & Atakapa		—	1,000
7 Natchitoches Par.	Apache-Choctaw		—	500
8 Allen, Vernon, Beauregard Pars.	"Cane River"	[350]	—	2,000
9 a b c La Salle & Rapides Pars., Jena, Indian Creek, Clifton	Choctaw, Biloxi		213	150
10	Adai-Caddo		—	—
Maine				
1 Eastport, Washington Co. (Indian Township (1,314) and Pleasant Point (1,927) Reservations)	Passamaquoddy		3,241	1,419
2 Houlton & Aroostook Co.	Malecite (741) and Micmac (1,180)		1,921	1,042
3a Indian Island, Old Town, Penobscot Co.	Penobscot		2,194	1,051
b Lincoln & Old Lennon Islands	Penobscot		—	—
Maryland				
1 Charles and Prince George Cos.	Wesorts and Piscataway	[1,000]	—	5,000
2 Baltimore City (others northern Maryland)	Lumbee and others		—	2,000
3 Charles Co.	Portobacco Indians		—	?
4 Dorchester Co.	Nanticokes		—	700
Massachusetts				
1a Mashpee, Barnstable Co.	Wampanoag and Nauset			
b Yarmouth, Barnstable Co.	Wampanoag and Nauset	[2,300]	—	646
c Waquoit, Barnstable Co.	Wampanoag and Nauset			
2 Gay Head	Wampanoag		1,001	—
3 Fall River, Bristol Co.	?		—	?
4 Norfolk Co. (Canton, Mattapan, Mansfield)	Massachusett?		—	60
5 Worcester Co. (Grafton, Worcester, Mendon, Gardner, Freetown Forest, Webster)	Nipmuc (Hassanimisco band at Grafton)	[660]	—	100
6 Plymouth Co. (Assawompset pond)	non-existent after 1928			
Mexico				
1 Nacimiento	Kickapoo and others		—	200
2 Coahuila	Seminole		—	?
3 Sonora-Chihuahua	Pima, Papago		—	3,000
Michigan				
1a L'Anse Houghton — Keweenaw Bay Community	Chippewa		3,120	910
b Ontonagon — Keweenaw Bay Community	Chippewa			
c Lac Vieux Desert	Chippewa		442	185
2a Brimley — Bay Mills Community	Chippewa			
b Sugar Island — Bay Mills Community	Chippewa		1,462	637
c Drummond Island — Bay Mills Community	Chippewa			
3a Harris — Hannahville Community	Potawatomi		692	347
3b Wilson — Hannahville Community	Potawatomi			

REF ENCLAVE: LOCATION OR RESERVATION	PRESENT PRINCIPAL TRIBE	[NFR]	2001 (BIA)	1990
4 Isabella or Saginaw Res.	Chippewa		2,921	758
5 Athens, Calhoun Cos.	Potawatomi of Huron		428	150
6 Dowagiac, Cass Co.	Potawatomi Pokagon Band		2,730	250
7a Cross Village	Ottawa			
b Petoskey & Peshawbestown — Little Traverse band	Ottawa (3,521)			
c Fox Island, Beaver Island, Hog Island, Butt Lake	Ottawa [80]			
d Traverse City — Grand Traverse band	Ottawa (3,792)			
8a Manistee & Mason Cos. (Cent.Michigan) — Little River band	Ottawa, Chippewa (2,738)		40,651	10,134 +
b Grande Rapids — Grand River band & Match-c-be-nash-she-wish	Potawatomi, etc. (276)			2,363
9a Mikado	Ottawa			
b Oscoda	Chippewa			
c Bay City	Chippewa			
d Saginaw	Chippewa			
10 (Northern Michigan), Nahma, Isle Royale	Chippewa			
11 Sault Ste. Marie	Chippewa (30,324)			
Minnesota				
1 Red Lake Res.	Chippewa		9,610	5,126
2 Nett Lake Res. & Deer Creek	Chippewa		2,857	2,015
3 Fond du Lac Res.	Chippewa		3,905	3,265
4 Grand Portage Res.	Chippewa		1,089	349
5 Vermillion Lake	Chippewa		—	50
6 Leech Lake Res., Cass Lake, Deer Lake	Chippewa		8,294	5,803
7 Mille Lacs Res.	Chippewa		3,292	1,369
8 White Earth Res.	Chippewa		20,820	4,480
9 Lower Sioux (Morton) Res.	Santee Sioux		820	388
10 Prairie Island, Red Wing, Wabasha	Santee Sioux		622	176
11 Prior Lake	Santee Sioux		326	230
12 Upper Sioux	Santee Sioux		404	304
13 Pipestone Res.	Santee Sioux		—	150
Mississippi				
1a Leake Co. — Redwater, Standing Pine	Choctaw			
b Jones Co. — Bogue Homo	Choctaw			
c Scott Co.	Choctaw			
d Jasper Co.	Choctaw		8,823	5,438
e Winston & Neshoba Cos., Tucker, Black Jack, Bogue Chitto	Choctaw			
f Lauderdale & Newton Cos. — Conehatta	Choctaw			
g Kemper Co. — Talla Chula	Choctaw			
h Harrison and Jackson Cos.	?		—	
Missouri				
1 Jasper & Newton Cos.	? see Arkansas		—	500?
Montana				
1 Northern Cheyenne Res.	Northern Cheyenne		8,036	4,334
2 Crow Res.	Crow		10,450	6,636
3 Ft. Peck Res.	Assiniboine, Santee & Yanktonai Sioux		11,248	6,497
4 Ft. Belknap Res.	Assiniboine, Gros Ventré (Atsina)		5,426	3,652

REF	ENCLAVE: LOCATION OR RESERVATION	PRESENT PRINCIPAL TRIBE	[NFR]	2001 (BIA)	1990
5	Rocky Boys Res.	Plains Cree, Plains Chippewa		5,728	2,992
6	Flathead Res.	"Confederated Salish-Kootenai" (Flathead, Kalispel, Spokan, Upper Kalispel, Kutenai)		6,950	7,667
7	Blackfeet Res.	Piegan		15,410	7,782
8a	Scattered Great Falls, Rocky Boys	Plains Cree, Métis		309	2,500
b	Wolfpoint, Little Rockies, Hill 57, Little Shell band	Plains Chippewa (Ojibwa)	[1,000]		
Nebraska					
1	Santee Res. Niobrara	Santee Sioux		2,663	603
2	Ponca Res.	Ponca		2,095	500
3	Winnebago Res.	Winnebago		4,033	1,204
4	Omaha Res.	Omaha		5,427	5,227
Nevada					
1	Western Shoshone or Duck Valley Res.	Western Shoshone & Northern Paiute		1,888	1,278
2	Summit Lake Res.	Western Shoshone & Northern Paiute		94	13
3	Pyramid Lake Res.	Western Shoshone & Northern Paiute		2,133	1,608
4	Walker River Res.	Western Shoshone & Northern Paiute		2,219	941
5	Reno-Sparks Res.	Northern Paiute, Washo		577	850
6	Dresslerville Res.	Washo including Californian Washo		1,582	348
7	Washo Res. (Stewart)	Washo including Californian Washo			88
8	Fallon Res.	Western Shoshone & Northern Paiute		1,002	904
9	Lovelock	Western Shoshone & Northern Paiute		369	112
10	Winnemucca Res.	Western Shoshone & Northern Paiute		77	61
11	Carson	Northern Paiute, Washo			275
12	Battle Mountain Res.	Western Shoshone		575	674
13	Beowawe	Western Shoshone		—	?
14	Palisade-Carlin	Western Shoshone		—	?
15	Te-Moak (South Fork) Res.	Western Shoshone & Northern Paiute		226	239
16	Elko	Western Shoshone & Northern Paiute		1,594	150
17	Wells	Western Shoshone		202	144
18a	Ruby Valley Res.	Western Shoshone			70
b	Odgers Ranch	Western Shoshone			?
19	Ely	Western Shoshone		418	1,158
20	Duckwater Res.	Western Shoshone		337	150
21	Yomba (Reese River)	Western Shoshone		205	100
22	Moapa River Res.	Southern Paiute		295	257
23	Las Vegas	Southern Paiute & Western Shoshone		55	114
24	Ft McDermitt Res.	Northern Paiute		928	621
25	Eureka	Western Shoshone		—	100
26	Austin	Northern Paiute		—	150
27	Yerington Res.	Northern Paiute		1,150	337
28	Campbell Ranch	Northern Paiute			50
New Hampshire					
1	Manchester	Pennacook		—	?
New Jersey					
1	Ramapo Valley area	Jackson-Whites (Ramapos)	[2,000]	2,800	
2	Eatontown, Monmouth Co.	Sandhill Indians	[6]	—	100?

REF	ENCLAVE: LOCATION OR RESERVATION	PRESENT PRINCIPAL TRIBE	[NFR]	2001 (BIA)	1990
5	Burlington Co. (Rancocos)	Pineys (Powhatan-Renápe)	[1,500]	500?	?
6	Cumberland Co.	Moors		—	
New Mexico					
1	Taos	Tiwa (Tanoan)		2,443	1,816
2	Picuris	Tiwa (Tanoan)		324	236
3	Santa Clara	Tewa (Tanoan)		2,800	1,768
4	San Juan	Tewa (Tanoan)		2,723	2,240
5	Pojoaque	Tewa (Tanoan)		327	162
6	San Ildefonso	Tewa (Tanoan)		628	521
7	Nambe	Tewa (Tanoan)		643	632
8	Tesuque	Tewa (Tanoan)		404	389
9	Jemez	Jemez (Tanoan) & Pecos		3,486	3,030
10	Cochiti	Keresan		1,189	1,037
11	Santo Domingo	Keresan		4,492	3,860
12	San Felipe	Keresan		3,131	2,958
13	Zia	Keresan		773	849
14	Santa Ana-El Ranchito	Keresan		716	639
15	Laguna & villages	Keresan (Mixed)		7,825	7,201
16	Acoma, Acomita, McCartys	Keresan		6,344	6,091
17	Sandia	Tiwa (Tanoan)		485	404
18	Isleta	Tiwa (Tanoan)		4,441	3,978
19a	Zuñi Res.	Zuñi		9,780	8,725
b	Ramah Res.	Navajo		2,463	2,432
20	Mescalero Res.	Mescalero, Chiricahua, Lipan		3,979	4,289
21	Jicarilla Res.	Jicarilla		3,403	3,353
22	Alamo Res.	Navajo			
23	Navajo Res. & Puertocito	Navajo		100,976	93,608
24	Canoncita Res.	Navajo			
25	Southeast N.M. & El Paso Texas, Isleta del Sur, Senecu del Sur, Socorro del Sur *see also Texas and Mexico*	Tigua, Piro		1,270	1,284
New York					
1	Shinnecock Res., Southampton L.I.	Shinnecock	[1,200]	418	1,158
2	Poosepatuck Res., Mastic River L.I.	Poosepattuck		337	150
3	Stony Brook, Wading River L.I.	Setauket	[650]	205	100
4	Cold Springs L.I.	Matinecock		295	257
5	Montauk Point L.I.	Montauk		55	114
6	Rensselaer Co.	Van Guilders *probably no Indian ancestry*		928	621
7	Columbia Co.	Bushwhackers and Pondshiners *probably no Indian ancestry*			100
8	Orange and Rockland Cos.	Jackson-Whites (Ramapos)	[500]	*see New Jersey*	150
9	Cattaraugus Res.	Seneca and Cayuga		7,118	3,742
10	Onondaga Res.	Onondaga and Cayuga		1,034 NR	1,034
11	Allegany Res.	Seneca *incl. with Cattaraugus*			
12	Oil Springs Res.	Seneca		—	none
13	Tonawanda Res.	Seneca		689 NR	689
14	Tuscarora Res.	Tuscarora		664 NR	664
15	St. Regis Res.	Mohawk		9,020	3,631
16	Oneida Castle	Oneida		1,893	1,109
17	former Cayuga Res. and other res.	Cayuga		474	456

(continued)

#	REF ENCLAVE: LOCATION OR RESERVATION	PRESENT PRINCIPAL TRIBE	[NFR]	2001 (BIA)	1990
18	Lake George	Abenaki		—	?
19	Various upstate groups	Nams, Jukes, Slaughters, Arabs, *probably no Indian ancestry* / Honies and Clappers		—	

North Carolina

#	REF ENCLAVE: LOCATION OR RESERVATION	PRESENT PRINCIPAL TRIBE	[NFR]	2001 (BIA)	1990
1	Qualla Res.	Eastern Cherokee		12,139	10,114
2a	Robeson Co.	Lumbee or Croatan	[55,000]	—	30,000
b	Lumberton	incl. Cherokee*			
c	Bladen Co.	incl. Martins*			
d	Columbus Co.	incl. Smilings*			
e	Harnett Co.	incl. Sinkers*			
f	Cumberland Co.	incl. Brookes*			
g	Sampson Co.	incl. Cohaties* [1,200]			
h	Scotland Co.				

of Siouan, Iroquoian and Algonkian origin

#	REF ENCLAVE: LOCATION OR RESERVATION	PRESENT PRINCIPAL TRIBE	[NFR]	2001 (BIA)	1990
3	Columbus Co.	Waccamaw	[1,500]	—	1,000
4	Person Co.	Cubans (Saponi, Eno, and Tuscarora)	[350]	—	500
5	Halifax Co. & Warren Co. (splinter groups in Pennsylvania)	Haliwa (Saponi?)	[3,500]	—	1,600
6a	Dare Co.	Machapunga			few
b	Hyde Co.	Machapunga			few
7a	Rockingham Co., Stokes, Surrey Cos.	Cheraw?			?
b	Nash Co.	Lumbee			?
8	Macon Co. and Jackson Co.	Lumbee			?
9	Perquimans Co.	"Laster Tribe" *probably no Indian ancestry*			
10	Northampton Co. & Winton	"Portuguese"* & Meherrin	[600]		1,200
11	Pleasant Grove	"Occaneechi"	[100]		

* all probably descendants

North Dakota

#	REF ENCLAVE: LOCATION OR RESERVATION	PRESENT PRINCIPAL TRIBE	[NFR]	2001 (BIA)	1990
1	Turtle Mt. Res.	Plains Chippewa (Ojibwa Bungi), Métis		28,650*	9,377
2	Pembina Co. Walhalla	Plains Chippewa (Ojibwa or Bungi), Métis		1,223	1,606
3	Devils Lake Res. (Ft. Totten) or Spirit Lake	Santee, Yankton, upper Yanktonai		4,948	4,650
4	Ft Berthold Res. (3 Affiliated Tribes)	Mandan, Hidatsa, Arikara		10,789	3,776
5	Standing Rock Res.	Teton,& Yanktonai, Sioux		7,380	4,342
6	Williston & Trenton	Métis			?

* Includes several other Métis' communities in ND and Montana

Ohio

#	REF ENCLAVE: LOCATION OR RESERVATION	PRESENT PRINCIPAL TRIBE	[NFR]	2001 (BIA)	1990
1	Tampico Darke Co.	?			200
2	Hardin Co., Scioto, Carmel	Carmel Indians "Shawnee"	[100]		500
3	Vinton Co. and others	?			

Oklahoma

#	REF ENCLAVE: LOCATION OR RESERVATION	PRESENT PRINCIPAL TRIBE	[NFR]	2001 (BIA)	1990
1	former Choctaw Nation	Choctaw		148,976	44,717
2	former Cherokee Nation	Cherokee		228,307	75,940
3	former Creek Nation	Creek		52,169	76,251
4	former Chickasaw Nation	Chickasaw		46,065	13,695
5	former Seminole Nation	Seminole		13,642	6,536
6	Okfuskee Co. Creek Nation	Alabama		—	300?
7	Caddo Co. former Kiowa-Comanche Res.	Apache		488	111
8	Custer, Washita Cos. former Cheyenne-Arapaho Res.	Arapaho (*see Cheyenne*)		3,261	968
9	Caddo Co. former Caddo-Wichita Res.	Caddo-Anadarko		2,174	907
10	Caddo Co. former Caddo-Wichita Res.	Wichita-Tawakoni-Kichai		1,302	329
11	Caddo Co.	Delaware			
12	Kiowa, Comanche, Caddo Cos.	Kiowa		11,088	5,184
	Tillman, Cotton Cos.	Comanche		9,580	5,651
	former Kiowa-Comanche Res.	Kiowa Apache-Lipan		1,854	1,023
13	Roger Mills, Dewey, Custer Cos., former Cheyenne & Arapaho Res.	Southern Cheyenne (incl Arapaho)		11,459	7,543
14	Cleveland, Oklahoma, Pottawatomie Cos.	Potawatomi		23,557	2,301
	former Potawatomi Res.	Absentee Shawnee		2,926	1,180
15	Lincoln & Pottawatomie Cos. former Kickapoo Res.	Kickapoo		2,505	1,336
16	Lincoln Co., former Iowa Res.	Iowa		491	555
17	Lincoln Co. & Pottawatomie Co. former Sac & Fox Res.	Sac & Fox		3,025	1,562
18	Noble Co. former Oto-Missouri Res.	Oto-Missouri		1,505	1,412
19	Kay Co. former Tonkawa Res.	Lipan & Nez Perce		420	826
20	Kay Co. former Tonkawa Res.	Tonkawa			
21	Pawnee Co. former Oakland (Pawnee) Res.	Pawnee		2,560	2,318
22	Kay Co. former Kaw Res.	Kansa (Kaw)		2,553	604
23	Osage Co. former Osage Res.	Osage		18,415	10,594
24	Washington, Nowata, Craig and Rogers Co'., "Cherokee Nation"	Stockbridge-Munsee / Delaware		10,500	1,500
25	McIntosh (Creek Nation), Haskell Co. (Choctaw Nation)	Catawba		—	100?
26	McIntosh Cos. (Creek Nation)	Hitchiti		—	300?
27	Ottawa Cos., former Ottawa Res.	Ottawa		2,290	684
28	Ottawa Co., former Seneca Res.	Seneca-Cayuga		3,674	788
29	Ottawa Co., former Wyandot Res.	Wyandot (Huron etc)		3,860	2,203
30	Ottawa Co., former Eastern Shawnee Res.	Eastern Shawnee		2,101	429
31	Ottawa Co., former Modoc Res.	Modoc		156	218
32	Ottawa Co., former Peoria Res.	Miami (2,677/836) & Peoria (2,662/1.181) (Illinois Wea etc)		2,657	2,348
33	Ottawa Co., former Quapaw Res.	Quapaw			
34	Craig Co., former "Cherokee Nation"	Loyal Shawnee	[600]	1,100	1,100
35	Wagoner Co. "Cherokee Nation"	Natchez		100?	
36	Creek & Okmulgee Cos. "Creek Nation"	Yuchi	[300]	500?	
37	Choctaw Nation	Biloxi			
38	Noble Co. former Ponca Res.	Ponca		2,618	2,581

Alabama-Quassarte (Creek) 193; Kialagee (Creek) 277; Keetoowah (Cherokee) 7,953; and Thlopthlocco (Creek) 646; are all included in above figures.

Note: There are numerous smaller southeastern tribes or tribal remnants incorporated among the Creek, Choctaw, Chickasaw, and Cherokee. Also Black Freedmen descendants with some Indian blood at Boley; Taft and Mounds.

Oregon

#	REF ENCLAVE: LOCATION OR RESERVATION	PRESENT PRINCIPAL TRIBE	[NFR]	2001 (BIA)	1990
1	Klamath Res.	Klamath, Modoc, Northern Paiute, Shasta		3,320	2,515
2	Grand Ronde Res.	Kalapooya groups, Clackamas-Tumwater (Chinookian), Clatsop, Molala, Nestucca, Cow Creek (Umpqua), Takelna, Rogue River, (Tututni) etc, ("Confederated Grand Ronde")		4,706	3,580

REF ENCLAVE: LOCATION OR RESERVATION	PRESENT PRINCIPAL TRIBE	[NFR]	2001 (BIA)	1990
3 Siletz Res.	Yakonan, Coquille, Tututni, Chastacosta, Galice Creek, Joshua, Rogue River, Maguenodon, Klamath, Kusan, ("Confederated Siletz")		3,660	1,789
4a Coos, Lower Umpqua & Siuslaw (tog.705) + Lower Coquille (769)	Kusan, Siuslaw, Chetco, Umpqua		2,636	1,109
b Cow Creek (1,162), Roseburg scattered Oregon	Coquille, Chetco, Cow Creek			
c Empire-Coos Bay	Oregon totally in 37 locations			
5 Warm Springs Res.	Wasco, Tenino-John Day, Tyigh, N. Paiute, "Warm Springs"		3,831	2,533
6a Celilo	Yakima, Waiam etc		—	100
b The Dalles	Chinook, Klickitat etc		—	?
c Hood River, White Salmon River	Chinook, Klickitat etc		—	?
7 Umatilla Res.	Umatilla, Wallawalla, Cayuse, Northern Paiute		2,140	1,850
8 Burns Res.	Northern Paiute		295	219
Pennsylvania				
1 Cornplanter (now flooded)	Seneca		—	?
2 Keating Mountain	Cherokee?		—	200?
3 Towanda	Pools		—	500?
Rhode Island				
1 Kingston, Charlestown, Washington Co.	Narragansett		2,620	2,058
South Carolina				
1a Marlboro Co.	Lumbee & Blues			
b Dillon Co. (Latta)	Lumbee & Blues			
c Marion Co.	Lumbee & Blues	see North Carolina		
d Horry Co.	Lumbee & Blues		—	1,000
2 Chesterfield Co. & Marlboro Co. (Wallace)	Marlboro Blues		1,000	1,000
3 Catawba Res. York Co.	Catawba		2,480	400
4 Colleton Co. (Cottageville), Dorchester Co. (Four Holes, Summerville), Berkeley Co. (Moncks Corner)	Summerville, Edisto River			
5 Richland Co., Sumter Co., & Williamsburg Co.	Red Bones & Goins			
6 Bamburg Co. (groups also Hampton & Aiken Cos.)	Buckheads			5,000*
7 Sumter Co. (Dalzell)	Turks			
8 Orangeburg Co. Holly Hill	Crane Pond			
South Dakota				
1 Standing Rock Res.	Yanktonai & Teton Sioux		6,039	6,508
2 Cheyenne River Res.	Teton Sioux		13,270	9,809
3 Crow Creek Res.	Yanktonai, Yankton & Teton Sioux		3,507	2,816
4 Lower Brule	Teton Sioux		2,627	1,079
5 Pine Ridge Res.	Teton Sioux		41,226	20,806
6 Rosebud Res.	Teton Sioux		24,134	13,050
7 Yankton Res.	Yankton Sioux		7,570	4,053
8 Flandreau Res.	Santee Sioux		716	504

*The local names are derogatory terms. Summerville Indians, Crane Pond Indians, and Edisto River Indians are more appropriate terms. Some of the Edisto group at Cottageville (Creektown) are Natchez; others descend from the Peedee, Wateree, Cape Fear, Yuchi, and Winyau.

REF ENCLAVE: LOCATION OR RESERVATION	PRESENT PRINCIPAL TRIBE	[NFR]	2001 (BIA)	1990
9 Lake Traverse-Sisseton Res.	Santee Sioux		10,759	3,075
Tennessee				
1 Hancock Co., Newman's Ridge	Melungeons		see Kentucky	
Texas				
1 Alabama Koasati Res. Polk Co.	Alabama, Koasati (Coushatta)		993	890
2 Eagle Pass	Seminole		—	?
3 El Paso Co. (also see New Mexico)	Pueblo		—	200
4 Harris & Fort Bend Cos.*	?		—	?
5 Eagle Pass	Kickapoo		880	450
6 Red Oak	Creek		—	?
Utah				
1 Uintah & Ouray Res.	Uintah, White River & Uncompahgre-Ute		3,174	3,205
2 Washakie Res.	Western Shoshone		433	411
3 Skull Valley	Western Shoshone (Goshute)		118	91
4 Goshute Res.	Western Shoshone (Goshute)		433	100
5 Gandy Homestead	Western Shoshone (Goshute)		—	?
6 Kanosh Res.	Ute			
7 Koosharem Res.	Ute			
8 Indian Peak Res.	Southern Paiute		799	850
9 Cedar City	Southern Paiute, Catawba			
10 Shivwits Res.	Southern Paiute			
11 Blanding (Allen Canyon)	Ute			
12 Ouray Extension	Uncompahgre-Ute, Northern Shoshone			
13 Navajo Res.	Navajo & Southern Paiute		10,133	7,054
Vermont				
1 Swanton (Franklin Co.)	Abenaki	[2,300]	—	150?
Virginia				
1 White Oak Swamp, Charles City Co.	Chickahominy (Upper)	[1,000]	—	500
2 Near Richmond, James City Co.	Chickahominy (Lower)		—	100
3 King William Co. Pamunkey Res.	Pamunkey	[350]	—	300
4 King William Co. Mattaponi Res.	Mattaponi (Lower)		—	200
5 Adamstown	Mattaponi (Upper)	[500]	—	200
6 Several counties Indian Neck	Rappahannock		—	500
7 Stafford Co.	Potomac		—	200
8 Northumberland Co.	Wicocomoco		—	
9 Northampton Co., Drummondtown	Accohannock	[500]	—	300
10 York Co.	Wise		—	?
11 Gloucester Co., Allmondsville	Werowocomoco		—	100
12 Norfolk & Nansemond Cos.	Nansemond and Skeetertown	[150]	—	250
13 Southampton Co.	Nottaway		—	10
14 Rockbridge Co.	Browns (Tuscarora?)	?	—	1,000
15 Amherst Co.	Issues (Monacan?)	?	—	500
16 Washington, Wise, Giles, Lee, & Scott Cos.	Melungeons	[700]	—	3,000
17 Patrick Co., Halifax Co.	various groups	?	—	1,100

*There is a large emigrant Indian population in these counties, but earlier minor groups have been reported in this area.

REF ENCLAVE: LOCATION OR RESERVATION	PRESENT PRINCIPAL TRIBE	[NFR]	2001 (BIA)	1990
Washington				
1 Colville Res.	Colville, Kalispel, Okanagan, Columbia, Wenatchee, Senijextee and others now "Colville"		8,842	4,633
2 Spokan Res.	Spokan		2,305	1,230
3 Kalispel Res.	Kalispel		329	186
4 Yakima Res.	Yakima, Klickitat, Palouse, Wishram, Wasco, now "Confederated Yakima" or Yakama		8,624	13,741
5 Vancouver, The Dalles, Celillo (Oregon), Priests Rapids	Waiam & Wanapam		—	200
6 Lummi Res.	Lummi, Samish, Dumamish, Suquamish, Swinomish now "Lummi"		3,889	4,200
7 Whatcom Co.	Nooksack		1,537	740
8 Skagit & Whatcom Cos.	Sauk-Suiattle (152/273), Upper & Lower Skagit (709), Suiattle, Kikiallus		861	730
9 Swinomish Res.	Duwamish, Snohomish, Suquamish (863), Samish, Swinomish (764), Skagit-Kikiallus, Lummi, etc.		1,627	935
10 Tulalip Res. (Snohomish)	Duwamish, Snohomish,Suquamish, Samish, Lummi, Skykomish, Snoqualmie (616), Etakmur, now "Snohomish"		4,027	3,889
11 Port Gamble Res.	Clallam		984	676
12 Port Madison Res.	as Tulalip & Swinomish, etc.		—	100
13 Muckleshoot Res.	"Muckleshoot"		1,712	500?
14 Puyallup Res.	Puyallup, Nisqually, Muckleshoot, Squaxon, Steilacoom. Cowlitz		2,490	1,000
15 Squaxon Res.	Squaxon, Nisqually, Puyallup, Steilacoom, etc.		643	1,539
16 Nonreservation	several groups apparently never on reserves, incl. San Juan, Stillaquamish (182), Samish (1,154), Steilacoom, Cowlitz, Chinook		1,336	12,312
17 Nisqually Res.	as Puyallup		525	2,498
18 Skokomish Res.	Twana (Skokomish), Clallam, Chimakum		750	1,223
19 Quinault Res.	Quinault, Queets, Humptulips, Satsop, Copalis, Chehalis, Chinook		2,454	2,951
20 Shoalwater Res.	Upper & Lower Chehalis, Satsop, Chinook		237	371
21 Chehalis Res.	Upper & Lower Chehalis, Cowlitz, Chinook, Clatsop?		629	775
22 Port Angeles Res. (Lower Elwha) (984)	Clallam ⎤ s'Klallam		1,510	1,149
23 Clallam Co. & Jamestown (Jamestown 526/416)	Clallam ⎦			
24 Hoh River Res.	Hoh		139	85
25 Quilleute Res.	Quileute		658	784
26 Makah Res.	Makah & Quilleute		2,389	1,752
27 Ozette Res.	Ozette		—	?
West Virginia				
1 Taylor and Barbour Cos.	Guineas (*probably little Indian ancestry*) ?		—	4,000
Wisconsin				
1 Lac du Flambeau Res.	Chippewa		3,143	1,274
2 St Croix Res. incl. Danbury Res. (several groups)	Chippewa		982	1,409

REF ENCLAVE: LOCATION OR RESERVATION	PRESENT PRINCIPAL TRIBE	[NFR]	2001 (BIA)	1990
3 Red Cliff Res. & Apostle Islands	Chippewa		4,064	1,651
4 Bad River Res.	Chippewa		6,292	2,110
5 Lac Courte Oreilles Res.	Chippewa		5,587	4,037
6 Mole Lake Res. Sokagoan	Chippewa		1,163	512
7 Forest Co. Wabeno & Stone Lake	Potawatomi		1,186	462
8 Stockbridge Res. Shawano Co.	Stockbridge-Munsee (Mahican Delaware)		1,531	936
9 Green Bay, Brown Co.	Oneida		14,745	5,649
10 Menominee Res.	Menominee		8,074	5,422
11 Calumet Co.	Brotherton	[600]	—	150
12 Jackson Co.	Winnebago (Ho-Chunk)		6,145	2,608
13 Wood Co. Arpin	Potawatomi		—	400
14 Wanpun, & Scattered	Chippewa & Potawatomi		—	?
15 Langlade Co. Pearson	Chippewa		—	?
16 Robbins, Oneida Co.Clam Lake Res.	Chippewa		—	?
17 Tripoli-McCord	Chippewa		—	?
WYOMING				
1 Wind River Res.	Shoshoni (3,400) & Arapaho (7,137)		10,537	8,038

Most of the Indian groups of the coastal reservations of Washington now use their reservation name as a tribal designation, ie. "Lummi," "Swinomish" etc; several groups were never on reservations and many groups have existed under village names, rather than tribal. Confusing variations in spelling of names of minor groups makes the cross-checking of data from various records difficult.

CANADA

Table 3: Inuit Bands

This listing covers all Canada. The linguistic group for the list is Eskimoan and the people is Inuit. The total population is c. 60,000.

BAND	LOCATION
Rigolet	Newfoundland (Coast of Labrador)
Makkovik	Newfoundland (Coast of Labrador)
Hopedale	Newfoundland (Coast of Labrador)
Nain	Newfoundland (Coast of Labrador)
Port Burwell	Newfoundland (Coast of Labrador)
Port Nouveau	Quebec
Fort Chino	Quebec
Tasiujaq	Quebec
Aupaluk	Quebec
Payne	Quebec
Koartac	Quebec
Maricourt	Quebec
Saglouc	Quebec
Ivujivik	Quebec
Povungnituk	Quebec
Port Harrison	Quebec
Belcher Island	Quebec
Poste-de-la-Balenine	Quebec
Igloollik★	Northwest Territories
Hall Beach★	Northwest Territories
Repulse Bay★	Northwest Territories
Coral Harbour	Northwest Territories
Chesterfield Inlet★	Northwest Territories
Rankin Inlet★	Northwest Territories
Whale Cove★	Northwest Territories
Eskimo Point★	Northwest Territories
Pelly Bay★	Northwest Territories
Gjoa Haven★	Northwest Territories
Cambridge Bay★	Northwest Territories
Umingmaktok★	Northwest Territories
Bathurst Inlet★	Northwest Territories
Coppermine★	Northwest Territories
Paulatuk	Northwest Territories
Tuktoyaktuk	Northwest Territories
Aklavik (mixed with Kutchin)	Northwest Territories
Inuvik (mixed with Kutchin)	Northwest Territories
Broughton Island	Baffin Island
Pangnirtung	Baffin Island
Frobisher Bay	Baffin Island
Lake Harbour	Baffin Island
Cape Dorset	Baffin Island
Clyde River	Baffin Island
Pond Inlet	Baffin Island
Arctic Bay	Baffin Island
Resolute	District of Franklin
Grise Fiord	District of Franklin
Sachs Harbour	District of Franklin
Holman	District of Franklin

★ denotes communities in the renamed area Nunavut

Métis and Nonregistered Indians: Total population: c. 110,000

Manitoba: 99 Communities giving c. 45,000 total; the following have populations exceeding 850 people: Winnipeg, Portage, Selkirk, St. Laurent, San Clara, Camperville, Duck Bay, The Pas.

Saskatchewan: Groups total: c. 20,000

Alberta: Total c. 25,000, with six main areas — Métis Colony No. 1 Carajou, Métis Colony No. 3 Gift Lake, Métis Colony No. 4 Prairie River, Métis Colony No. 7 Whitefish, Métis Colony No. 10 Frog Lake, Métis Colony No. 9 Beaverdam.

Table 4: 2005 Canadian Indian Population Summary

The increase in the native population, as with the U.S. figures, suggests other factors than the normal increase in birth rate are involved. The change to the status of the former Non–Treaty Indians and Métis to band membership is quite probably a reason for the population to rise in many areas.

	1990	2005
Newfoundland	1,883	4,156
Prince Edward Island	—	1,100
New Brunswick	9,313	12,434
Nova Scotia	9,787	13,270
Quebec	51,754	68,735
Ontario	121,321	166,193
Manitoba	80,471	121,405
Saskatchewan	83,830	119,979
Northwest Territories	11,805	16,365
Yukon	5,854	8,073
Alberta	65,895	96,604
British Columbia	91,276	120,044
TOTAL	533,189	748,371
		excluding Inuit

Table 5: Canadian Indian Register population for all First Nations as of December 31, 2005.

Source: Indian & Northern Affairs Canada, Indian Registry System. Compiled by M.G. Johnson

RESIDENCE	TOTAL	CULTURAL GROUP
ATLANTIC PROVINCES	**30,973**	
Prince Edward Island, New Brunswick, Nova Scotia, & Newfoundland		
PRINCE EDWARD ISLAND	**1,100**	
Abegweit	310	Micmac (Mi'kmaq)
Lennox Island	790	Micmac (Mi'kmaq)
NEW BRUNSWICK	**12,434**	
Elsipogtog First Nation	2,784	Micmac (Mi'kmaq)
Buctouche	97	Micmac (Mi'kmaq)
Burnt Church	1,550	Micmac (Mi'kmaq)
Madawaska Maliseet First Nation	230	Malecite (Maliseet)
Eel Ground	860	Micmac (Mi'kmaq)
Eel River Bar First Nation	599	Micmac (Mi'kmaq)
Fort Folly	105	Micmac (Mi'kmaq)

Big Cove

RESIDENCE	TOTAL	CULTURAL GROUP
Indian Island	148	Micmac (Mi'kmaq)
Kingsclear	837	Malecite (Maliseet)
Oromocto	496	Malecite (Maliseet)
Pabineau	215	Micmac (Mi'kmaq)
Metepenagiag Mi'kmaq Nation Red Bank	529	Micmac (Mi'kmaq)
Saint Mary's	1,295	Malecite (Maliseet)
Tobique	1,888	Malecite (Maliseet)
Woodstock	801	Malecite (Maliseet)
NOVA SCOTIA	**13,270**	
Acadia	1,032	Micmac (Mi'kmaq)
Paq'tnkek First Nation Afton	491	Micmac (Mi'kmaq)
Annapolis Valley	230	Micmac (Mi'kmaq)
Bear River	276	Micmac (Mi'kmaq)
Chapel Island First Nation	584	Micmac (Mi'kmaq)
Eskasoni	3,745	Micmac (Mi'kmaq)
Pictou Landing	560	Micmac (Mi'kmaq)
Shubenacadie	2,160	Micmac (Mi'kmaq)
Membertou	1,098	Micmac (Mi'kmaq)
Millbrook	1,317	Micmac (Mi'kmaq)
Wagmatcook	645	Micmac (Mi'kmaq)
Waycobah First Nation Whycocomagh	830	Micmac (Mi'kmaq)
Glooscap First Nation	302	Micmac (Mi'kmaq)
NEWFOUNDLAND	**4,156**	
Mushuau Innu First Nation North West River	651	Nascapi
Sheshatshiu Innu First Nation	981	Nascapi
Miawpukek Conne River	2,524	Micmac (Mi'kmaq)
QUEBEC	**68,735**	
Abénakis de Wôlinak	223	Abénaki
Algonquins of Barriere Lake	629	Algonkin
Betsiamites	3,427	Montagnais
Communauté anicinape de Kitcisakik Val D'or	397	Algonkin
Conseil de la Première Nation Abitibiwinni Pikogan	836	Ojibwa & Cree
Eagle Village First Nation-Kipawa	697	Algonkin
Eastmain	633	East Cree
Innu Takuaikan Uashat Mak Mani-Utenam Sept Iles	3,456	Montagnais
Innue Essipit	412	Montagnais
Kitigan Zibi Anishinabeg	2,638	Algonkin
La Nation Crie de Chisasibi	3,655	East Cree
La Nation Crie de Mistissini	3,814	East Cree
La Nation Crie de Nemiscau	605	East Cree
La Nation Crie de Wemindji	1,321	East Cree
La Nation Innu Matimekush-Lac John Schefferville	831	Nascapi
La Nation Micmac de Gespeg	497	Micmac (Mi'kmaq)
Les Cris la Premiere Nation de Waskaganish	2,348	East Cree
Les Innus de Ekuanitshit Mingan	518	Montagnais
Listuguj Mi'gmaq Government	3,241	Micmac (Mi'kmaq)
Long Point First Nation	691	Algonkin
Micmacs of Gesgapegiag	1,206	Micmac (Mi'kmaq)
Montagnais de Natashquan	904	Montagnais

RESIDENCE	TOTAL	CULTURAL GROUP
Montagnais de Pakua Shipi	296	Montagnais
Montagnais de Unamen Shipu	1,009	Montagnais
Naskapi of Quebec	625	Nascapi
Nation Anishnabe du Lac Simon	1,532	Algonkin
Nation Huronne Wendat	3,012	Huron
Odanak	1,849	Abénaki
Première Nation de Whapmagoostui	805	East Cree
Première Nation Malecite de Viger	764	Malecite (Maliseet)
Timiskaming First Nation	1,584	Algonkin
Waswanipi	1,703	East Cree
Wolf Lake	274	Algonkin
Kahnawake	9,392	Mohawk
Mohawks of Kanesatake	2,017	Mohawk & Algonkin
Atikamekw d'Opiticiwan	2,348	Têtes de Boule or Atikamekw & Cree
Conseil des Atikamekw de Wemotaci	1,408	Têtes de Boule or Atikamekw & Cree
Les Atikamekw de Manawan	2,214	Têtes de Boule or Atikamekw & Cree
Montagnais du Lac St-Jean	4,783	Montagnais
ONTARIO	**166,193**	
Aundeck-Omni-Kaning Sucker Creek	701	Ottawa & Ojibwa
Batchewana First Nation	2,209	Ojibwa
Dokis	963	Ojibwa
Garden River First Nation	2,121	Ojibwa
Henvey Inlet First Nation	554	Ojibwa
M'Chigeeng First Nation	2,182	Ojibwa
Magnetawan	218	Ojibwa
Mississauga	1,005	Ojibwa
Nipissing First Nation	2,078	Ojibwa
Sagamok Anishnawbek Spanish River	2,290	Ojibwa
Serpent River	1,141	Ojibwa
Shawanaga First Nation	519	Ojibwa
Sheguiandah	313	Ojibwa & Ottawa
Sheshegwaning	370	Ojibwa
Temagami First Nation	650	Ojibwa & Ottawa
Thessalon	566	Ojibwa
Wahnapitae	358	Ojibwa
Whitefish Lake	866	Ojibwa & Ottawa
Whitefish River	1,068	Ojibwa
Wikwemikong	6,880	Ojibwa & Ottawa
Zhiibaahaasing First Nation Manitoulin Is. Sheshegwaning	147	Ojibwa & Ottawa
Aamjiwnaang Sarnia	1,956	Ojibwa
Alderville First Nation	973	Ojibwa
Algonquins of Pikwakanagan	1,909	Ojibwa & Algonkin
Bay of Quinte Mohawk: Six Nations	637	Mohawk
Bearfoot Onondaga: Six Nations	531	Onondaga
Beausoleil	1,702	Ojibwa
Caldwell	248	Potawatomi
Chippewas of Georgina Island	672	Ojibwa
Chippewas of Kettle and Stony Point	2,011	Ojibwa

RESIDENCE	TOTAL	CULTURAL GROUP
Chippewas of Mnjikaning First Nation — Rama	1,500	Ojibwa
Chippewas of Nawash First Nation — Cape Crocker	2,138	Ojibwa
Chippewas of the Thames First Nations	2,266	Ojibwa
Curve Lake	1,744	Ojibwa
Delaware: Six Nations	589	Delaware
Hiawatha First Nation	427	Ojibwa
Konadaha Seneca: Six Nations	437	Seneca
Lower Cayuga: Six Nations	3,105	Cayuga
Lower Mohawk: Six Nations	3,542	Mohawk
Mississauga's of Scugog Island First Nation	185	Ojibwa
Mississaugas of the Credit	1,681	Ojibwa
Mohawks of Akwesasne	10,217	Mohawk
Mohawks of the Bay of Quinte	7,533	Mohawk
Moose Deer Point	443	Ojibwa
Moravian of the Thames	1,077	Delaware
Munsee-Delaware Nation	523	Delaware
Niharondasa Seneca: Six Nations	349	Seneca
Oneida Nation of the Thames	5,127	Oneida
Oneida: Six Nations	1,734	Oneida
Onondaga Clear Sky: Six Nations	662	Onondaga
Saugen	1,559	Ojibwa
Tuscarora: Six Nations	1,926	Tuscarora
Upper Cayuga: Six Nations	3,042	Cayuga
Upper Mohawk: Six Nations	5,264	Mohawk
Wahta Mohawk	671	Mohawk
Walker Mohawk: Six Nations	431	Mohawk
Walpole Island	3,952	Ojibwa & Potawatomi
Wasauksing First Nation	1,021	Ojibwa
Albany	3,343	Cree
Animbigoo Zaagi'igan Anishinaabek Beardmore Rocky Bay	291	Ojibwa
Anishinabe of Wauzhushk Onigum Kenora	593	Ojibwa
Anishnaabeg of Naongashiing Morrow Morson	347	Ojibwa
Aroland Whitesand	577	Ojibwa
Attawapiskat	2,810	Cree
Big Grassy	619	Ojibwa
Biinjitiwaabik Zaaging Anishinaabek Macdiarmid	645	Ojibwa
Brunswick House	624	Ojibwa & Cree
Chapleau Cree First Nation	332	Cree
Chapleau Ojibway	—	Ojibwa
Constance Lake	1,429	Cree & Ojibwa
Couchiching First Nation	1,925	Ojibwa
Eabametoong First Nation Fort Hope	2,115	Ojibwa
Eagle Lake	495	Ojibwa
Flying Post	158	Ojibwa & Cree
Fort William	1,723	Ojibwa
Ginoogaming First Nation No. 77 Long Lake	770	Ojibwa
Grassy Narrows First Nation	1,235	Ojibwa
Gull Bay	1,028	Ojibwa
Iskatewizaagegan #39 Independent First Nation — Kejuk	546	Ojibwa
Lac Des Mille Lacs	506	Ojibwa
Lac La Croix	388	Ojibwa
Long Lake No. 58 First Nation	1,199	Ojibwa

RESIDENCE	TOTAL	CULTURAL GROUP
Martin Falls	577	Ojibwa
Matachewan	504	Ojibwa & Cree
Mattagami	443	Ojibwa
Michipicoten	728	Ojibwa
Missanabie Cree	358	Cree
Moose Cree First Nation	3,570	Cree
Naicatchewenin	346	Ojibwa
Naotkamegwanning Pawitik	1,022	Ojibwa
Neskantaga First Nation Lansdowne Lake	362	Ojibwa
Nibinamik First Nation Pickle Lake	384	Ojibwa
Nicickousemenecaning	256	Ojibwa
Northwest Angle No.33	423	Ojibwa
Northwest Angle No.37	333	Ojibwa
Obashkaandagaang Keewatin	270	Ojibwa
Ochichagwe'babigo'ining First Nation Kenora	322	Ojibwa
Ojibways of Onigaming First Nation	668	Ojibwa
Ojibways of the Pié River First Nation	944	Ojibwa
Pays Plat	202	Ojibwa
Pie Mobert	794	Ojibwa
Rainy River First Nations	816	Ojibwa
Red Rock	1,417	Ojibwa
Sandpoint	161	Ojibwa
Seine River First Nation	668	Ojibwa
Shoal Lake No. 40	516	Ojibwa
First Nation Fort Francis	125	Ojibwa
Taykwa Tagamou Nation Cochrane	328	Ojibwa
Wabaseemoong Independent Nations White Dog	1,665	Ojibwa
Wabauskang First Nation	251	Ojibwa
Wabigoon Lake Ojibway Nation	519	Ojibwa
Wahgoshig Matheson	259	Algonkin
Webeque	691	Ojibwa
Weenusk	512	Cree
Whitesand	1,059	Ojibwa
Bearskin Lake	806	Ojibwa & Cree
Cat Lake	588	Ojibwa
Deer Lake	1,043	Ojibwa & Cree
Fort Severn	596	Cree
Kasabonika Lake	894	Cree
Kee-Way-Win	636	Ojibwa & Cree
Kingfisher Kingfisher Lake	456	Ojibwa & Cree
Kitchenuhmaykoosib Inninuwug Big Trout Lake	1,278	Cree
Lac Seul	2,679	Ojibwa
McDowell Lake Red Lake	52	Ojibwa
Mishkeegogamang Osnaburgh	1,486	Ojibwa
Muskrat Dam Lake	358	Ojibwa & Cree
North Caribou Lake	897	Ojibwa & Cree
North Spirit Lake	430	Ojibwa & Cree
Ojibway Nation of Saugeen	192	Ojibwa
Pikangikum	2,053	Ojibwa
Poplar Hill	427	Ojibwa
Sachigo Lake	720	Ojibwa & Cree
Sandy Lake	2,364	Ojibwa

RESIDENCE		TOTAL	CULTURAL GROUP
Slate Falls Nation		216	Ojibwa
Wapekeka	Angling Lake	369	Ojibwa & Cree
Wawakapewin	Sioux Lookout	—	Ojibwa
Wunnumin		551	Ojibwa

NB: *Ojibwa — also known as Ojibway, Mississauga (southeastern Ontario), Chippewa, Saulteaux, Plains Ojibwa (western Ontario, Saskatchewan, Alberta, & British Columbia) and Anishinabe*

MANITOBA		121,405	
Barren Lands	Brochet	919	Chipewyan
Berens River		2,531	Ojibwa
Birdtail Sioux		686	Eastern Sioux
Bloodvein		1,364	Cree
Brokenhead Ojibway Nation		1,547	Ojibwa
Buffalo Point First Nation		110	Ojibwa
Bunibonibee Cree Nation	Oxford House	2,427	Cree
Canupawakpa Dakota First Nation	Pipestone	572	Eastern Sioux
Chemawawin Cree Nation		1,506	Cree
Cross Lake First Nation		6,470	Cree
Dakota Plains	Portage La Prairie	237	Eastern Sioux
Dakota Tipi		280	Eastern Sioux
Dauphin River		264	Ojibwa
Ebb and Flow	Gypsumville	2,233	Ojibwa
Fisher River		3,023	Ojibwa & Cree
Fort Alexander		6,486	Cree
Fox Lake		998	Cree
Gamblers		149	Plains Ojibwa
Garden Hill First Nations		3,748	Cree
God's Lake First Nation	Gods Lake	2,242	Cree
Grand Rapids First Nation		1,384	Cree
Hollow Water		1,479	Ojibwa
Keeseekoowenin		992	Plains Ojibwa
Kinonjeoshtegon First Nation	Hodgson	662	Ojibwa
Lake Manitoba		1,659	Ojibwa
LakeSt. Martin		2,088	Ojibwa
Little Black River		906	Ojibwa
Little Grand Rapids		1,322	Ojibwa
Little Saskatchewan		1,009	Ojibwa
Long Plain		3,362	Plains Ojibwa
Manto Sipi Cree Nation	Gods Lake	663	Cree
Marcel Colomb First Nation	Lynn Lake	314	Cree
Mathias Colomb	Pukatawagan	3,119	Cree
Mosakahiken Cree Nation	Moose Lake	1,635	Cree
Nisichawayasihk Cree Nation	Nelson House	4,882	Cree
Northlands		926	Chipewyan
Norway House Cree Nation		6,229	Cree
0-Chi-Chak-Ko-Sipi First Nation	Crane River	812	Ojibwa
0-Pipon-Na-Pawin Cree Nation		254	Cree
Opaskwayak Cree Nation	The Pas	4,815	Cree
Pauingassi First Nation	Pauingassi	557	Ojibwa
Peguis		7,846	Ojibwa & Cree
Pinaymootang First Nation	Fairford	2,586	Ojibwa

RESIDENCE		TOTAL	CULTURAL GROUP
Pine Creek		2,539	Ojibwa
Poplar River First Nation		1,320	Cree & Ojibwa
Red Sucker Lake		879	Cree
Rolling River		893	Plains Ojibwa
Roseau River Anishinabe First Nation Government		2,069	Plains Ojibwa
Sandy Bay		5,164	Ojibwa
Sapotaweyak Cree Nation	Pelican Rapids	1,875	Cree
Sayisi Dene First Nation	Tadoule Lake	686	Chipewyan
Shamattawa First Nation		1,238	Cree
Sioux Valley Dakota Nation		2,176	Eastern Sioux
Skownan First Nation		1,148	Ojibwa
St. Theresa Point		3,169	Ojibwa & Cree
Swan Lake		1,166	Plains Ojibwa
Tataskweyak Cree Nation	Split Lake	2,946	Ojibwa
Tootinaowaziibeeng Treaty Reserve	Short Lake	1,198	Ojibwa
War Lake First Nation	Ilford	234	Cree
Wasagamack First Nation		1,570	Cree
Waywayseecappo F.N. Treaty #4-1874		2,204	Plains Ojibwa
Wuskwi Sipihk First Nation	Birch River	573	Cree
York Factory First Nation		1,048	Cree

SASKATCHEWAN		119,979	
Ahtahkakoop		2,788	Plains Cree
Beardy's and Okemasis		2,799	Plains Cree
Big Island Lake Cree Nation		887	Cree
Big River	Debden	2,745	Cree
Birch Narrows First Nation	Turnor Lake	606	Cree
Black Lake	Stony Rapids	1,736	Chipewyan
Buffalo River Dene Nation	Peter Pond Lake	1,131	Chipewyan
Canoe Lake Cree First Nation		1,811	Cree
Clearwater River Dene		1,482	Chipewyan
Cumberland House Cree Nation		1,004	Cree
English River First Nation		1,291	Chipewyan
Flying Dust First Nation	Meadow Lake	1,040	Cree
Fond du Lac		1,618	Chipewyan
Hatchet Lake	Wollaston Lake, Lac La Hache	1,360	Chipewyan
Island Lake First Nation		1,153	Cree
James Smith		2,778	Cree
Kinistin Saulteaux Nation	Tisdale	827	Ojibwa
Lac La Ronge		8,030	Cree
Little Pine		1,617	Plains Cree
Lucky Man		94	Plains Cree
Makwa Sahgaiehcan First Nation	Loon Lake	1,218	Cree
Mistawasis		2,176	Plains Cree
Montreal Lake		3,218	Cree
Moosomin		1,397	Plains Cree
Mosquito, Grizzly Bear's Head, Lean Man FN		1,180	Assiniboine
Muskeg Lake		1,673	Plains Cree
Muskoday First Nation	John Smith	1,495	Cree
One Arrow		1,398	Plains Cree
Onion Lake		4,184	Cree
Pelican Lake		1,237	Cree

RESIDENCE	TOTAL	CULTURAL GROUP	
Peter Ballantyne Cree Nation	7,740	Cree	
Poundmaker	1,350	Plains Cree	
RedEarth	1,261	Cree	
Red Pheasant	1,964	Plains Cree	
Saulteaux	1,090	Plains Ojibwa	
Shoal Lake Cree Nation	779	Cree	
Sturgeon Lake First Nation	2,284	Cree	
Sweetgrass	1,611	Plains Cree	
Thunderchild First Nation	2,286	Plains Cree	
Walpeton Dakota Nation	439	Eastern Sioux	
Waterhen Lake	1,677	Cree	
Whitecap Dakota First Nation	474	Eastern Sioux	
Witchekan Lake	602	Cree	
Yellow Quill	2,455	Plains Ojibwa	
Carry The Kettle	2,237	Assiniboine	
Cote First Nation 366	2,932	Ojibwa	
Cowessess	3,359	Plains Cree	
Day Star	426	Plains Cree	
Fishing Lake First Nation	1,477	Plains Ojibwa	
Gordon	2,886	Plains Cree & Plains Ojibwa	
Kahkewistahaw	1,548	Plains Cree	
Kawacatoose	2,640	Plains Cree	Raymore Poorman
Keeseekoose	2,006	Plains Ojibwa	
Little Black Bear	439	Plains Cree	
Muscowpetung	1,119	Plains Cree & Plains Ojibwa	
Muskowekwan	1,434	Plains Ojibwa	
Nekaneet	420	Plains Cree	Maple Creek
Ocean Man	411	Assiniboine	Stoughton
Ochapowace	1,410	Plains Cree	
Okanese	560	Plains Cree & Plains Ojibwa	
Pasqua First Nation #79	1665	Plains Cree & Plains Ojibwa	
Peepeekisis	2,261	Plains Cree	
Pheasant Rump Nakota	352	Assiniboine	
Piapot	1,969	Plains Cree	
Sakimay First Nations	1,357	Plains Cree	
Standing Buffalo	1,078	Eastern Sioux	
Star Blanket	552	Plains Cree	
The Key First Nation	1,070	Cree	
White Bear	2,165	Plains Cree, Plains Ojibwa & Assiniboine	
Wood Mountain	214	Western Sioux	

ALBERTA	**98,604**		
Alexander	1,684	Plains Cree	
Alexis Nakota Sioux Nation	1,516	Stoney (Assiniboine)	
Athabasca Chipewyan First Nation	810	Chipewyan	Fort Chipewyan
Beaver First Nation	776	Beaver	High Level Boyer River
Bigstone Cree Nation	6,557	Cree	Wabasca
Blood	9,842	Blackfoot	Card
Chipewyan Prairie First Nation	661	Chipewyan	
Dene Tha'	2,449	Chipewyan	

RESIDENCE	TOTAL	CULTURAL GROUP	
Driftpile First Nation	2,179	Cree	
Duncan's First Nation	212	Cree	Brownvale
Enoch Cree Nation #440	1,967	Plains Cree	
Ermineskin Tribe	3,429	Plains Cree	
Fort McKay First Nation	601	Chipewyan & Cree	
Fort McMurray #468 First Nation	572	Cree & Chipewyan	
Horse Lake First Nation	827	Beaver	Hythe
Kapawe'no First Nation	282	Cree	Grouard
Little Red River Cree Nation	3,967	Cree	John D'or Prairie
Loon River Cree	436	Cree	Red Earth Creek
Louis Bull	1,754	Plains Cree	
Lubicon Lake	405	Cree	Peace River
Mikisew Cree First Nation	2,395	Cree & Chipewyan	Ft. Chipewyan
Montana	850	Plains Cree	
O'Chiese	832	Ojibwa & Plains Cree	Rocky Mountain House
Paul	1,667	Plains Cree & Stoney (Assiniboine)	
Piikani Nation	3,407	Blackfoot	
Samson	6,478	Plains Cree	
Sawridge	351	Cree	Slave Lake
Siksika Nation	6,021	Blackfoot	
Smith's Landing First Nation	299	Chipewyan	Fort Smith
Stoney (Bearspaw)	1,510	Stoney (Assiniboine)	
Stoney (Chiniki)	1,511	Stoney (Assiniboine)	
Stoney (Wesley)	1,331	Stoney (Assiniboine)	
Sturgeon Lake Cree Nation	2,471	Cree	
Sucker Creek	2,239	Cree	
Sunchild First Nation	1,115	Plains Cree	
Swan River First Nation	1,039	Cree	
Tallcree	1,034	Cree	
Tsuu T'lna Nation	1,544	Sarsi	
Whitefish Lake	2,020	Cree	Atikameg
Woodland Cree First Nation	934	Cree	Cadotte Lake
Beaver Lake Cree Nation	864	Plains Cree	
Cold Lake First Nations	2,244	Chipewyan & Cree	
Frog Lake	2,363	Cree	
Heart Lake	238	Beaver	
Kehewin Cree Nation	1,681	Cree	
Saddle Lake	8,404	Cree	

NB: Stoney and Assiniboine together = "Nakoda"
Peigan (Piikani), Blood, Siksika (North Blackfoot) together = "Blackfoot"

BRITISH COLUMBIA	**120,044**		
Akisq'nuk First Nation	254	Shuswap	Windermere
Adams Lake	718	Shuswap	
Ahousaht	1,781	Nootka	
Aitchelitz	—	Cowichan	
Alexandria	160	Chilcotin	
Alexis Creek	608	Chilcotin	
Ashcroft	236	Shuswap	
BeecherBay	224	Songish	
Blueberry River First Nations	395	Beaver	
Bonaparte	766	Shuswap	

RESIDENCE		CULTURAL GROUP	TOTAL
Boothroyd		Thompson	259
Boston Bar First Nation		Thompson	230
Bridge River		Lillooet	399
Burns Lake		Carrier	97
Burrard		Squamish	418
Cambell River		Southern Kwakiutl & Comox	616
Canim Lake		Shuswap	556
Canoe Creek		Shuswap	644
Cape Mudge		Southern Kwakiutl	867
Cayoose Creek		Lillooet	174
Chawathil	Hope	Cowichan	494
Cheam		Cowichan	452
Chehalis		Cowichan	945
Chemainus First Nation		Cowichan	1,095
Cheslatta Carrier Nation		Carrier	302
Coldwater		Cowichan	751
Comox		Comox	280
Cook's Ferry		Thompson	286
Cowichan	Duncan	Cowichan	3,996
Da'naxda'xw First Nation Alert Bay		Southern Kwakiutl	182
Ditidaht	Port Alberni	Nootka	689
Doig River	Rose Prairie	Beaver	245
Douglas		Lillooet	233
Ehattesaht	Zeballos	Nootka	288
Esketemc	Williams Lake	Shuswap	728
Esquimalt		Songish	233
Fort Nelson First Nation		Slave	757
Gitanmaax	Hazelton	Gitksan	2,038
Gitanyow	Kitwanga	Gitksan	706
Gitsegukla		Gitksan	874
Gitwangak		Gitksan	1,088
Gitxaala Nation	Kitkatla	Tsimshian	1,678
Glen Vowell		Gitksan	380
Gwa'Sala–Nakwaxda'xw	Port Hardy	Souther Kwakiutl	745
Gwawaenuk Tribe	Port McNeil	Southern Kwakiutl	40
Hagwilget Village	New Hazelton	Carrier	672
Halalt		Cowichan	202
Halfway River First Nation	Wonowon	Beaver	224
Hartley Bay		Tsimshian	655
Heiltsuk	Bella Bella	Northern Kwakiutl	2,130
Hesquiaht		Nootka	659
High Bar		Shuswap	66
Homalco		Comox	452
Hupacasath First Nation	Port Alberni	Nootka	256
Huu-ay-aht First Nations	Bamfield	Nootka	598
Iskut		Tahltan	621
Ka'yu'k't'h'chektles First Nations	Kyuquot	Nootka	485
Kamloops		Shuswap	1,039
Kanaka Bar		Thompson	191
Katzie		Cowichan	482
Kispiox		Gitksan	1,417
Kitamaat Haisla		Northern Kwakiutl	1,560

RESIDENCE		CULTURAL GROUP	TOTAL
Kitasoo	Klemtu, Haihais (China Hat)	Tsimshian and Northern Kwakiutl	499
Kitselas	Terrace	Tsimshian	493
Kitsumkalum	Terrace	Tsimshian	645
Klahoose First Nation		Comox	288
Kluskus		Carrier	187
Kwadacha	Prince George	Sekani	441
Kwakiutl Port Hardy		Southern Kwakiutl	654
Kwantlen First Nation	Fort Langley	Cowichan	186
Kwaw-kwaw-Apilt		Cowichan	42
Kwiakah	Cambell River	Southern Kwakiutl	—
Kwicksutaineuk-ah-kwaw-ah-mish	Simoon Sound	Southern Kwakiutl	267
Kwikwetlem First Nation	Coquitlam	Cowichan	60
Lake Babine Nation	Burns Lake	Carrier	2,181
Lake Cowichan First Nation	Victoria	Cowichan	—
Lax-kw'alaams	Port Simpson	Tsimshian	3,005
Leq' a: mel First Nation	Deroche	Cowichan	329
Lheidli T'enneh	Prince George	Carrier	314
Little Shuswap Lake		Shuswap	297
Lower Kootenay		Kootenay	206
Lower Nicolaea		Thompson	989
Lower Similkameen		Okanagan	451
Lyackson		Cowichan	184
Lytton		Thompson	1,781
Malahat First Nation		Cowichan	250
Mamalilikulla–Qwe'Qwa'Sot'Em	Campbell River	Southern Kwakiutl	372
Matsqui		Cowichan	218
McLeod Lake		Sekani	456
Metlakatla	Prince Rupert	Tsimshian	728
Moricetown		Carrier	1,776
Mount Currie		Lillooet	1,875
Mowachahr/Muchalaht	Gold River	Nootka	522
Musqueam		Cowichan	1,163
N'Quatqua	D'arcy	Lillooet	296
Nadleh Whuten	Fort Fraser	Carrier	411
Nak'azdli	Fort St. James	Carrier	1,674
Namgis First Nation	Alert Bay	Southern Kwakiutl	1,557
Nanoose First Nation		Cowichan	210
Nazko		Carrier	316
Nee-Tahi-Buhn	Burns Lake	Carrier	131
Neskonlith		Shuswap	578
New Westminster		Cowichan	—
Nicomen	Lytton	Thompson	122
Nisga'a Village of Gingolx		Niska	1,854
Nisga'a Village of Gitwinksihlkw		Niska	373
Nisga'a Village of Laxgalt'sap		Niska	1,564
Nisga'a Village of New Aiyansh		Niska	1,724
Nooaitch		Thompson	193
Nuchatlaht		Nootka	164
Nuxalk Nation		Bella Coola	1,398
Okanagan		Okanagan	1,708
Old Masset Village Council		Haida	2,581
Oregon Jack Creek		Thompson	57

RESIDENCE		TOTAL	CULTURAL GROUP
Osoyoos		435	Okanagan
Oweekeno/Wuikinuxv Nation		267	Northern Kwakiutl
Pacheedaht First Nation		258	Nootka
Pauquachin		357	Songish
Penelakut		797	Cowichan
Penticton		900	Okanagan
Peters	Hope	119	Cowichan
Popkum		—	Cowichan
Prophet River First Nation		219	Slave & Beaver
Qualicum First Nation		104	Puntlatch
Quatsino		417	Southern Kwakiutl
Red Bluff	Quesnel	138	Carrier
Saik'uz First Nation	Vanderhoof	855	Carrier
Samahquam		298	Lillooet
Saulteau First Nations		834	Ojibwa
Scowlitz		237	Cowichan
Seabird Island		763	Cowichan
Sechelt		1,159	Seechelt
Semiahmoo		76	Semiahmoo
SetonLake		605	Lillooet
Shackan		118	Thompson
Shuswap		227	Shuswap
Shxw'ow'hamel First Nation	Hope	151	Cowichan
Shxwhá:y Village	Chilliwack	300	Cowichan
Simpcw First Nation		620	Sekani
Siska	Lytton	296	Thompson
Skatin Nations	Pemberton	374	Lillooet
Skawahlook First Nation	Agassiz	72	Cowichan
Skeetchestn	Savona	474	Shuswap
Skidegate		1,373	Haida
Skin Tyee	South Bank	133	Carrier
Skowkale	Sardis	217	Cowichan
Skuppah		102	Thompson
Skwah		450	Cowichan
Sliammon		937	Comox
Snuneymuxw First Nation	Nanaimo	1,457	Cowichan
Soda Creek	Williams Lake	345	Shuswap
Songhees First Nation		461	Songish
Soowahlie		338	Cowichan
Spallumcheen		738	Shuswap
Spuzzum		204	Thompson
Squamish		3,470	Squamish
Squiala First Nation		124	Cowichan
St. Mary's		338	Kootenay
Stellat'en First Nation	Fraser Lake	405	Carrier
Stone		375	Chilcotin
Sumas First Nation		263	Cowichan
T'it'q'et		361	Lillooet
T'Sou-ke First Nation	Sooke	208	Songish
Tahltan		1,585	Tahltan
Takla Lake First Nation		632	Carrier
Tl'azt'en Nation	Fort St James	1,462	Carrier

RESIDENCE		TOTAL	CULTURAL GROUP
Tl'etinqox-t'in Government Office	Alexis Creek	1,397	Chilcotin
Tla-o-qui-aht First Nations	Tofino	881	Nootka
Tlatlasikwala	Port Hardy	52	Southern Kwakiutl
Tlowitsis Tribe	Cambell River	355	Southern Kwakiutl
Tobacco Plains		171	Kootenay
Toosey		273	Chilcotin
Toquaht		112	Nootka
Ts'kw'aylaxw First Nation	Pavilion	490	Lillooet
Tsartlip		833	Songish
Tsawataineuk	Kingcome Inlet	506	Southern Kwakiutl
Tsawout First Nation		713	Songish
Tsawwassen First Nation		265	Cowichan
Tsay Keh Dene	Prince George	362	Sekani
Tseshaht		912	Nootka
Tseycum		147	Songish
Tzeachten		368	Cowichan
Uchucklesaht		180	Nootka
Ucluelet First Nation		607	Nootka
Ulkatcho		912	Carrier
Union Bar		105	Cowichan
Upper Nicola		858	Thompson
Upper Similkameen		63	Okanagan
West Moberly First Nations		189	Beaver
Westbank First Nation		640	Okanagan
Wet'suwet'en First Nation	Burns Lake	208	Carrier
Whispering Pines/Clinton		127	Shuswap
Williams Lake	Kamloops	505	Shuswap
Xaxli'p		904	Lillooet
Xeni Gwet'in First Nations Government	Nemiah Valley	381	Chilcotin
Yakweakwioose		58	Cowichan
Yale First Nation		144	Cowichan
Yekooche		211	Carrier

NB: Cowichan = Halkomelem and Stalo together.
Northern Kwakiutl = Haisla, Heiltsuk (Bella Bella), Haihais, and Oweekano together.
Southern Kwakiutl = Kwakwaka'wakw, Nawiti, Nimpkish, Koskimo, and Kwawkewlth together.
Nootka = Nuu-chah-nulth
Songish = Straits Salish

RESIDENCE		TOTAL	CULTURAL GROUP
NORTHWEST TERRITORIES		**16,365**	
Acho Dene Koe	Fort Liard	600	Slave
Aklavik		406	Kutchin
Behdzi Ahda First Nation	Colville Lake	132	Hare
Dechi Laoti First Nations	Wekweti	157	Dog Rib
Deh Gah Gotie Dene Council	Fort Providence	1,013	Slave
Deline First Nation		896	Hare
Deninu K'ue First Nation	Fort Resolution	787	Chipewyan
DogRibRae		2,592	Dog Rib
Fort Good Hope		827	Hare
Gameti First Nation		314	Dog Rib
Gwichya Gwich'in	Rea Lakes	403	Kutchin
Inuvik Native bands	Tsiigehtchic	503	Kutchin

RESIDENCE		TOTAL	CULTURAL GROUP
Jean Marie River First Nation		123	Slave
K-atlodeeche First Nation	Hay River Reserve	550	Slave
Ka'a'gee Tu First Nation	Hay River	63	Slave
Liidlii Kue First Nation		1,190	Slave
Lutsel K'e Dene First Nation		672	Chipewyan
NahammButte		130	Slave
Pehdzeh Ki First Nation	Wrigley	327	Slave/Mountain
Salt River First Nation	Fort Smith	814	Chipewyan
Samba K'e (Trout Lake) Dene	Trout Lake Fort Simpson	109	Slave
Tetlit Gwich'in	Fort McPherson	1,311	Kutchin
Tulita Dene		585	Hare
West Point First Nation	Hay River	72	Slave
Wha Ti First Nation		568	Dog Rib
Yellowknives Dene First Nation		1,221	Dog Rib

NB: Slave at Fort Norman and Fort Franklin also called "Bear Lake Indians"

YUKON		TOTAL 8,073	
Aishihik		159	Tutchone
Carcross/Tagish First Nations		596	Tagish
Champagne	Haines Junction	581	Tutchone
Dease River		165	Kaska
First Nation of Nacho Nyak Dun	Mayo	461	Tutchone
Kluane First Nation	Burwash Landing	138	Tutchone
Kwanlin Dun First Nation	Whitehorse	959	Tutchone
Liard First Nation	Watson Lake	1,032	Kaska
Little Salmon/Carmacks First Nation		572	Tutchone
Ross River		459	Kaska
Selkirk First Nation	Pelly Crossing	500	Tutchone
Ta'an Kwach'an	Whitehorse	221	Tutchone
Taku River Tlingit	Atlin	371	Inland Tlingit
Teslin Tlingit Council	Teslin	545	Inland Tlingit
Tr'on dëk Hwëch'in	Dawson	671	Han
Vuntut Gwitchin First Nation	Old Crow	506	Kutchin
White River First Nation	Beaver Creek	136	Tanana

GRAND TOTAL 748,371

According to the 2001 Canadian Census 50 percent of band membership lived in the reserves. The 2005 total figure of 750,000 Indians for Canada compares with 630,000 for the 2001 Census and 400,000 for 1990. This increase is partly due to former Non-Treaty and Métis gaining band registration. The 2001 Census gave 480,000 with band membership with approximately 60,000 (mostly Iroquois) and 90,000 non-band members giving a total of 630,000.

Table 6: 2001 Census by Tribe for Canada

Tribe	Population
Abenaki	2,005
Algonkin	10,425
Attikamek (Tête de Boule)	4,265
Beaver	1,855
Bella Coola	1,205
Blackfoot	7,640 (+ Blood = 15,500)
Carrier	7,040
Chilcotin	2,090
Chipewyan	13,940
Tsimshian	5,140
Gitksan	5,355
Nisga	3,870
Comox	920
Cree (total)	159,330
Sioux	
Assiniboine	13,510
Stoney	
Delaware	850+ (Munsee & Six Nations-Delaware 1,960)
Dog Rib	3,795
Kutchin	2,565
Haida	2,265
Haisla	1,210
Cowichan	13,100
Han	635
Hare	1,205
Bella Bella	1,760
Huron	2,985
Iroquois	7,975 (+ 56,700)
Kaska	645
Kutenai	680
Southern Kwakiutl	4,850
Lillooet	2,115
Malecite	4,725
Micmac (Mi'kmaq)	27,240
Montagais–Nascapi	12,640
Nootka	4,920
Thompson	4,480
Ojibwa	91,685
Ojibwa-Cree	21,625
Okanagan	3,185
Pentlatch	190
Pottawatomi	290
Sarsi	875
Sechelt	775
Sekani	835
Shuswap	5,705
Slave	6,165
Squamish	245
Straits–Salish (Songish)	2,205
Tagish	750
Tahltan	1,885
Tlingit (Inland)	795
Tutchone	2,825
Tanana	180
TOTAL	479,445

+ c. 60,000 Iroquois, Blood, Delaware, not included
+ c. 90,000 non-band members
= c. 630,000 ≥

2001 CENSUS TOTAL 639,000

MUSEUMS

Since the 16th century, material culture of the native peoples of North America in contact with Europeans has been collected and dispersed around the world. These "objects of curiosity," where they survived, usually found their way into European museums, some founded in the 18th century. Unfortunately these objects usually have missing or incomplete documentation and because such material was collected during the European (British, French, Russian and later American) exploration, exploitation and colonization of North America, these collections may or may not accurately represent native cultures. Collectors in the early days were sailors (Captain Cook), soldiers (Sir John Caldwell), Hudson Bay Company Factors, missionaries and so forth.

The United States, of course, has the largest number of museums which hold vast amounts of Indian material and art objects. The Peabody Museum at Harvard University, Cambridge, Massachusetts, has for instance, over 100,000 ethnographic objects pertaining to North America, including a huge number of Northwest Coast pieces. Many collections of Indian artifacts in major American institutions were assembled by ethnologists and archaeologists who were working for, or contracted to, the various museums such as Frank Speck and Frances Densmore for the Smithsonian Institution, or George Dorsey for the Field of Natural History Museum, Chicago.

During the 20th century a number of museums have developed around the collections of a number of private individuals. The most important was that of George Heye whose museum was founded in 1916 (opened 1922) and located in New York City. It was called the Museum of the American Indian, Heye Foundation. This collection has now been incorporated into the National Museum of the American Indian, whose new building, sited on the Mall in Washington, D.C., opened on September 21, 2004. The collection includes more than 800,000 objects, as well as a photographic archive of 125,000 images.

Other notable privately owned collections subsequently purchased or presented to scholarly institutions are the Haffenreffer Museum Collection at Brown University, Rhode Island, much of Milford G. Chandler's collection, which is now at the Detroit Institute of Arts; Adolph Spohr's at the Buffalo Bill Historical Center, Cody, Wyoming; and the impressive Arthur Speyer collection at the Canadian Museum of Civilization, Hull, P.Q.

Many American and Canadian museums and institutions have been active in publishing popular and scholarly ethnographic reports including: the Glenbow-Alberta Institute, the Royal Ontario Museum, Toronto, and — most importantly — the Smithsonian Institution, Washington D.C. Most of the major American museums have organized major

exhibitions of Indian art, and their accompanying catalogues and publications, often with native input, contain important and valuable information.

In Europe, the Musée de l'Homme, Paris (now the Musée du Quai Branly), houses some of the earliest historic North American Indian material, including a wampum belt which may date from c.1611, a pair of shoes or moccasins attributed to the explorer Cartier c. 1534, and a number of painted skin robes which date from around the mid-18th century. The Linden Museum, Stuttgart, Germany, has part of the Prince Maximilian zu Wied collection, which contains the robe and costume of the Mandan chief Mato-Tope painted by Karl Bodmer in 1833. (The artist accompanied the Prince during their epic journey along the Missouri River.)

The Ashmolean Museum in Oxford, England, has a few early Northeastern Woodland pieces including the so-called "Powhatan's mantle," a cape or shirt-front decorated with shells (reported to have belonged to Powhatan, father of Pocahontas) which was in England by 1656. The Pitt Rivers Museum, University of Oxford, has a huge and varied collection of early and 19th century artifacts. There are also rare and beautiful objects at a number of British museums, such as Liverpool, Manchester, Sheffield, Aberdeen, Edinburgh, Glasgow, Exeter, Saffron Walden, Cambridge, Bristol, Norwich, and the British Museum, London. The National Museum of Ireland holds the important Jasper Grant collection of early Woodland materials.

In the recent past a number of Indian-owned and run museums have come to prominence, such as the Seneca-Iroquois National Museum, Salamanca, New York; Woodland Cultural Center, Brantford, Ontario, Canada; and the Pequot Museum, a spin-off from their successful casino operation in Connecticut. The Pequot have also sponsored a number of Indian art exhibitions. Many smaller, tribal museums are now found on a number of reservations across the U.S.

There has also been much comment, debate and honest disagreement between academics (Indian and white), museum personnel and historians about the role of museums and the validity of ownership of Indian material culture in what are, after all, white institutions. Certain Indian groups have successfully obtained from museums under legal process a repatriation of a number of funerary and religious objects, where these have been shown to be of major importance to certain ethnic groups.

There are too many museums to list them here — and the rise of the Internet and Google has made finding them much more easy than hitherto. To research the best museums to visit, go to sites such as http://www.hanksville.org/NAresources/indices/NAmuseums.html. It provides an index of Native American museums on the Internet with links.

SELECT BIBLIOGRAPHY

Andrews, Ralph W.: *Indian Primitive*; Superior Publishing Co., 1960.

Bancroft-Hunt, Norman & Norman, Werner: *The Indians of the Great Plains*; Orbis Publishing, London, 1981.

Blish, Helen H.: *A Pictographic History of the Oglala Sioux*; University of Nebraska Press, Lincoln, 1967.

Bourque, Bruce J.: *Twelve Thousand Years American Indians in Maine*; University of Nebraska, 2001.

Brasser, Ted J.: *"Bo'jou, Neejee!" : Profiles of Canadian Indian Art*; National Museum of Man, Ottawa/The National Museums of Canada, 1976.

Brasser, Ted J.: *Riding the Frontier's Crest: Mahican Indian Culture and Culture Change*. National Museum of Canada, Ottawa. 1974.

Brody, Hugh: *Maps and Dreams*; Jill Norman and Hobhouse Ltd., London, 1981.
Living Arctic; Faber & Faber Ltd., London,1987.

Coe, Ralph T.: *Sacred Circles: Two Thousand Years of North American Indian Art*; Arts Council of Great Britain, 1976.
Lost and Found Traditions: Native American Art 1965-1985; University of Washington Press in assoc. with The American Federation of Arts, 1986.

Conn, Richard: *Robes of White Shell and Sunrise: Personal Decorative Arts of the Native American*; Denver Art Museum, Denver, Colorado, 1974.
Native American Art in the Denver Art Museum; Denver Art Museum, 1979.
Circles of the World: Traditional Art of the Plains Indians; Denver Art Museum, 1982.
A Persistent Vision: Art of the Reservation Days; The L.D. & Ruth Bax Collection of the Denver Art Museum; Denver Art Museum, 1986.

Cooper, James Fenimore, *The Last of the Mohicans*. Ward, Lock & Co. Ltd, New York and Melbourne. 1826.

Corey, Peter L.; Ed.: *Faces, Voices and Dreams:* A Celebration of the Centennial of The Sheldon Jackson Museum, Sitka, Alaska, 1888-1988; The Division of Alaska State Museum & Friends of the Alaska State Museum, 1987.

Danziger, Edmund J., Jr.: *The Chippewas of Lake Superior*; University of Oklahoma Press, Norman & London, 1979.

Dixon, Dr. Joseph K.: *The Vanishing Race: The Last Great Indian Council*; Doubleday, Page & Co., Garden City, New York, 1914.

Dockstader, Frederick J.: *Indian Art In America: The Arts and Crafts of the North American Indian*; Promontory Press, New York.

Duncan, Kate C.: *Some Warmer Tone: Alaska Athabaskan Bead Embroidery*; Alaska Historical Commission Studies in History No. 131; University of Alaska Museum, Fairbanks, 1984.
Northern Athapaskan Art: A Beadwork Tradition; University of Washington Press, Seattle & London, with assistance of J.Paul Getty Trust, 1989.

Edmond, David R.: *The Shawnee Prophet*; University of Nebraska Press, Bison Books edition 1985.

Emmons, George T.,; Ed., with Frederica de Laguna & Jean Low.: *The Tlingit Indians*; University of Washington Press, Seattle & London/ American Museum of Natural History, New York, 1991.

Ewers, John C.: *Murals In the Round: Painted Tipis of the Kiowa and Kiowa-Apache Indians*; Smithsonian Institution Press, Washington D.C., for Renwick Gallery of the National Collection of Fine Arts, 1978.
Plains Indian Sculpture: A Traditional Art from America's Heartland; Smithsonian Institution Press, Washington D.C., 1986.

Ewers, John C.: *Blackfeet Crafts:* Indian Handicraft Series, Education Div., U.S. Bureau of Indian Affairs; Haskell Institute, Lawrence, Kansas, 1944.

Farr, William E.: *The Reservation Blackfeet, 1882-1945: A Photographic History of Cultural Survival*; University of Washington Press, Seattle & London, 1984.

Feder, Norman: *American Indian Art*; Harry N. Abrams, New York, 1965.

Ferg, Alan; Ed.: *Western Apache Material Culture: The Goodwin and Guenther Collections*; University of Arizona Press for Arizona State Museum, 1987.

Fleming, Paula. R. & Luskey, Judith: *The North American Indians in Early Photographs*; Dorset Press, New York,1988.

Fletcher, Alice C. & La Flesche, Francis: *The Omaha Tribe, Vols. I & II*; University of Nebraska Press, Lincoln & London, 1972.

Frazer, Patrick, The Mohicans of Stockbridge. University of Nebraska Press, Lincoln and London, 1992.

Gidley, M.: *With One Sky Above Us: Life on an Indian Reservation at the Turn of the Century*; Windward/Webb & Bower, 1979.

Gidmark, David: *The Algonquin Birchbark Canoe*; Shire Ethnography Series; Shire Publications Ltd., Aylesbury, Bucks.,UK, 1988.

Gilbert, William H.Jr.: *Surviving Indian Groups of the Eastern United States*; Smithsonian Institution, Washington. D.C., Annual Report, 1948.

Gilman, Carolyn & Schneider, Mary Jane: *The Way To Independence: Memories of a Hidatsa Indian Family 1840–1920*; Minnesota Historical Society Press. St.Paul. 1987.

Gilpin, Laura: *The Enduring Navaho*; University of Texas Press, Austin, 1968.

Gulick Bill: *Chief Joseph Country: Land of the Nez Perce*; The Caxton Printers, Ltd., Caldwell, Idaho, 1981.

Haberland, Wolfgang: *Ich, Dakota: Pine Ridge Reservation, 1909*; Dietrich Reimer Verlag, Berlin, 1986.

Hail, Barbara A. (ed): *Gifts of Pride and Love: Kiowa and Comanche Cradles;* Haffenreffer Museum of Anthropology, Brown University, 1980.

Hail, Barbara A.: *Hau, Kola!* The Plains Indian Collection of the Haffenreffer Museum of Anthropology: Vol.III, Studies in Anthropology and Material Culture, Haffenreffer Museum of Anthropology, Brown University, 1980.

Hail, Barbara A.; Essay. & Schwarz, Gregory C.,; Catalogue.: *Patterns of Life, Patterns of Art:* The Rahr Collection of Native American Art; Hood Museum of Art, Dartmouth College, with University Press of New England, Hanover & London,1987.

Hail, Barbara A. & Duncan, Kate C.: *Out of the North:* The Subarctic Collection of the Haffenreffer Museum of Anthropology; Haffenreffer Museum of Anthropology, Brown University, 1989.

Hanson, James A.: *Metal Weapons, Tools, and Ornaments of the Teton Dakota Indians*; University of Nebraska Press, Lincoln, 1975.

Harrison, Julia D.: *Métis: People between Two Worlds*; The Glenbow-Alberta Institute in assoc. with Douglas & McIntyre, Vancouver/Toronto, 1985.

Hartley, William & Ellen: *Osceola: The Unconquered Indian*; Hawthorn Books Inc., New York, 1973.

Hassrick, Royal B.: *The George Catlin Book of American Indians*; Watson-Guptill Publications, New York, 1977.

Hawthorn, Audrey: *Kwakiutl Art*; University of Washington Press, Seattle & London, 1967.

Heski. Thomas M.: *"Icastinyanka Cikala Hanzi", The Little Shadow Catcher: D.F. Barry, Celebrated Photographer of Famous Indians*; Superior Publishing Company, Seattle, 1978.

Hill, Tom and Hill, Richard W. Eds.: *Creation's Journey, Native American Identity and Belief*; Smithsonian Institution Press, 1997.

Hodge, Frederic, Ed.: *Handbook of American Indians North of Mexico*, 2 Vols., Bureau of American Ethnology Bulletin 30; Smithsonian Institution, Washington D.C., 1907-1910.

Hodge, F.W. and Orchard, W.C.: "John W. Quinney's Coat," *Indian Notes* Vol. 6, No. 4. October 1929. Museum of the American Indian, Heye Foundation, New York. 1929

Hodge, William H.: *The First Americans Then And Now*; Holt, Rinehart & Winston, 1981.

Hook, Jason: *The American Plains Indians*; Men-at-Arms Series 163; Osprey Publishing, London, 1985.
The Apaches; Men-at-Arms Series 186; Osprey Publishing, London, 1987.

Horse Capture, George P. & Pohrt, Richard A.: *Salish Indian Art from the I.R.Simplot Collection*; Buffalo Bill Historical Centre, 1986.

Howard, James H.: *The Plains-Ojibwa or Bungi:* Reprints In Anthropology Vol.7; J & L Reprint Company, Lincoln, Nebraska, 1977. *The Dakota or Sioux Indians,* Reprints In Anthropology Vol.20; U & L Reprint Company, Lincoln, Nebraska, 1980. *The Canadian Sioux*; University of Nebraska Press, Lincoln & London, 1984.

Hungry Wolf, Adolf: *The Blood People, A Division of the Blackfoot Confederacy An Illustrated Interpretation of the Old Ways*; Harper & Row, New York, Hagerstown, San Francisco, London,

1977.

Isaac, Barbara; Ed. & Brown, Ian W.: *The Hall of the North American Indian: Change and Continuity*; Peabody Museum Press, Cambridge, Massachusetts. 1990.

Jennings, Francis. Ed.: *The History and Culture of Iroquois Diplomacy*; Syracuse University Press, 1985.

Johnson, Michael G.: *American Woodland Indians*, Men-at-Arms Series 228; Osprey Publishing, London, 1990. *Tribes of the Iroquois Confederacy*; Men-at-Arms Series 395; Osprey Publishing, London, 1990. *Tribes of the Sioux Nation*; Men-at-Arms Series 344; Osprey Publishing, London, 2000. Indian *Tribes of the New England Frontier*; Osprey Publishing, London, 2006.

Jonaitis, Aldona: *From the Land of the Totem Poles:* The Northwest Coast Indian Art Collection at the American Museum of Natural History; American Museum of Natural History, New York/ British Museum Publications, London, 1988.

Josephy, Alvin M. Jr., Ed. & Brandon, William: *The American Heritage Book of Indians*; American Heritage Publishing Co.,1961.

Kaplan, Susan A. & Barsness, Kristin J.: *Raven's Journey: The World of Alaska's Native People*; University of Pennsylvania Museum, 1986.

Kelsey, Isabel Thompson: *Joseph Brant 1743–1807 Man of Two Worlds*; Syracuse University Press, 1984.

Keyworth, C.L.: *California Indians*, The First Americans Series; Facts on File, New York & Oxford, 1991.

King, J.C.H.: *Thunderbird and Lightning: Indian Life in Northeastern North America 1600-1900*; British Museum Publications Ltd., London, 1982.

Kopper, Philip: *The Smithsonian Book of North American Indians Before the Coming of the Europeans*; Smithsonian Books, Washington D.C., 1986.

Lenz, Mary Jane: *The Stuff of Dreams: Native American Dolls*; Museum of the American Indian, New York, in assoc. with National Endowment for the Humanities, 1986.

Lyford, Carrie A.: *The Crafts of the Ojibwa*; Indian Handicrafts Series, U.S.Bureau of Indian Affairs; Phoenix, Arizona, 1943.

MacDonald, George F.: *Haida Art*; Craftsman House, G+B Arta Inernational, Begium, 1996.

Macnair, Peter L., Hoover, Alan L., & Neary, Kevin: *The Legacy: Tradition and Innovation in Northwest Coast Indian Art*; Douglas & McIntyre, Vancouver/Toronto; University of Washington Press, Seattle; with The British Columbia Provincial Museum, 1984.

Mails, Thomas E.: *The Mystic Warriors of the Plains*; Doubleday & Co. Inc., Garden City, New York, 1972. *Plains Indians: Dog Soldiers, Bear Men and Buffalo Women*; Prentice-Hall Inc.,

1973. *The People Called Apache*; The Ridge Press Incd Rutledge Books Division & Prentice-Hall Inc., 1974.

Markoe, Glen E.; Ed., Demallie, Raymond J. & Hassrick, Royal B.: *Vestiges of a Proud Nation:* The Ogden B. Read Northern Plains Indian Collection; Robert Hull Fleming Museum, Burlington, Vermont, 1986.

McKenney, Thomas L., and Hall, James: *History of the Indian Tribes of North America* (three vols.); John Grant, Edinburgh, 1933.

Momaday, N. Scott; Intro.: *With Eagle Glance: American Indian Photographic Images, 1868 to 1931*; Museum of the American Indian, New York, 1982.

Mooney James: *The Aboriginal Population of America North of Mexico*; Smithsonian Misc. Coll., Vol.80, No.7, 1928.

Morgan, Lewis H. & Lloyd, H.M.; Ed.: *League of the Ho-De-No-Sau-Nee or Iroquois*, 2nd Edition, 2 Vols.; Dodd, Mead, New York, 1901.

Nabokov, Peter & Easton, Robert: *Native American Architecture*; Oxford University Press, Oxford & New York, 1989.

Pelletier, Gaby: *Micmac and Maliseet Decorative Traditions*; The New Brunswick Museum, St. John, 1977.

Penney, David W., Ed.: *Great Lakes Indian Art*; Wayne State University Press & Detroit Institute of Arts, 1989.

Powell, John Wesley: *Indian Linguistic Families of America North of Mexico: 7th Annual Report of the Bureau of American Ethnology*; Smithsonian Institution, Washington D.C., 1881.

Powell, Fr. Peter J.: *People of the Sacred Mountain, Vols. I & II*; Harper & Row. Ed. with Ann S. Merritt: *To Honor the Crow People: Crow Indian Art from the Goelet & Edith Gallatin Collection of American Indian Art*; Foundation for the Preservation of American Indian Art and Culture, Inc., Chicago, 1988.

Roberts, Kenneth G. & Shackleton, Philip: *The Canoe: A History of the Craft from Panama to the Arctic*; Macmillan of Canada, Toronto, 1983.

Roosevelt, Anna C. & Smith, James G.E., Eds.: *The Ancestors: Native Artisans of the Americas*; Museum of the American Indian, New York, 1979.

Ruby, Robert H. & Brown, John A.: *A Guide to the Indian Tribes of the Pacific Northwest*; University of Oklahoma Press, Norman, 1986.

Scherer, Joanna C. with Walker, Jean B.: *Indians: The Great Photographs That Reveal North American Indian Life, 1847-1929, From The Unique Collection of the Smithsonian Institution*; Ridge Press Inc. & Crown Publishers Inc., 1973.

Schmitt, Martin F. & Brown, Dee: *Fighting Indians of the West*; Charles Scribner's Sons, New York & London, 1948.

Scriver, Bob: *The Blackfeet: Artists of the*

Northern Plains; The Lowell Press, Inc., Kansas City, 1990.

Speck, Frank G.: *The Nanticoke Community of Delaware*; Museum of the American Indian, Heye Foundation; cont. from Vol.II, No. 4; New York, 1915. *Decorative Art of Indian Tribes of Connecticut*; Canada Dept. of Mines, Memoir 75; Government Printing Bureau, Ottawa, 1915.

Sturtevant, William C.; General Editor.: *Handbook of North American Indians*; Smithsonian Institution, Washington, D.C.:

Vol.4, History of Indian-White Relations; Ed. Wilcomb E. Washburn; 1988. *Vol.5, Arctic*; Ed. David Damas; 1984. *Vol.6, Subarctic*; Ed. June Helm; 1981. *Vol.7, Northwest Coast*; Ed. Wayne Suttles; 1990. *Vol.8, California*; Ed. Robert F. Heizer; 1978. *Vol.9, Southwest*; Ed. Alfonso Ortiz; 1979. *Vol.10, Southwest; 2nd vol.*; Ed. Alfonso Ortiz; 1983. *Vol.11, Great Basin*; Ed. Warren L. D'Azevedo; 1986. *Vol.12, Plateau*; Ed. Dewar E. Walker, Jr.; 1998. *Vol.13, Plains Vol. 1 and 2*; Ed. Raymond J. De Maillie; 2001. *Vol.14, Southeast*; Ed. Raymond D. Fogelson; 2004. *Vol. 15, Northeast*; Ed. Bruce G. Trigger; 1978.

Swanton, John R.: *Indian Tribes of the Lower Mississippi Valley and adjacent Coast of the Gulf of Mexico:* Bureau of American Ethnology, Bulletin 43; Smithsonian Institution, Washington D.C., 1911. *Early History of the Creek Indians and Their Neighbors:* Bureau of American Ethnology, Bulletin 73; Smithsonian Institution, Washington D.C., 1922. *The Indians of the Southeastern United States:* Bureau of American Ethnology, Bulletin 137; Smithsonian Institution, Washington D.C., 1946. *The Indian Tribes of North America:* Bureau of American Ethnology, Bulletin 145; Smithsonian Institution, Washington D.C., 1952.

Thomas, Davis & Ronnefeldt; Eds.: *People of the First Man: Life Among the Plains Indians in Their Final Days of Glory: The First-hand Account of Prince Maximilian's Expedition up the Missouri River, 1833-34: Watercolours by Karl Bodmer*; Promontory Press, 1982.

Thompson, Judy: *The North American Indian Collection: A Catalogue*; Historical Museum, Berne, Switzerland, 1977. *Pride of the Indian Wardrobe: Northern Athapaskan Footwear*; Published for the Bata Shoe Museum by the University of Toronto Press, 1990.

Thwaites, Reuben G.; Ed.: *Original Journals of the Lewis and Clark Expedition 1804-1806*, 8 vols.; Dodd & Mead, New York, 1904-05.

Turner, Geoffrey E.S.: *Indians of North America*; Blandford Press Ltd., Poole, Dorset, 1979.

Underhill, Ruth M.: *Red Man's America*; University of Chicago Press, Chicago, 1953.

Vidler, Virginia: *American Indian Antiques, Arts and Artifacts of the Northeast*; A.S.Barnes & Co., South Brunswick & New York/Thomas Yoseloff Ltd., London, 1976.

Viola, Herman J.: *The Indian Legacy of Charles Bird King*; Smithsonian Institution Press/Doubleday & Co., 1976.

Walters, Anna Lee: *The Spirit of Native America: Beauty and Mysticism in American Indian Art*; McQuiston & Partners/ Chronicle Books, San Francisco, 1989.

Walton, Ann T., Ewers, John C., & Hassrick, Royal B.: *After the Buffalo Were Gone:* The Louis Warren Hill, Sr., Collection of Indian Art; NW Area Foundation/Indian Arts & Crafts Board, Dept. of Interior, Washington D.C./Science Museum of Minnesota, St.Paul; 1985.

Whitehead, Ruth Holmes: *Eliteekey Micmac Material Culture from 1600 A.D. to the Present*; The Nova Scotia Museum, Halifax, 1980.

Whitehead, Ruth Holmes: *Micmac Quillwork*; The Nova Scotia Museum, Halifax, 1982.

Wildschut, William & Ewers, John C.: *Crow Indian Beadwork: A Descriptive and Historical Study*; Contributions, Vol.XVI; Museum of the American Indian Heye Foundation, New York, 1959.

Wissler, Clark: *The American Indian*; Oxford University Press, New York, 1938.

Wooley, David; Ed.: *Eye of the Angel: Selections from the Derby Collection*; White Star Press, Northampton, Maine, 1990.

Wright, Muriel H.: *A Guide to the Indian Tribes of Oklahoma*; University of Oklahoma Press, Norman, 1951.

Wyatt, Victoria: *Images from the Inside Passage: An Alaskan Portrait by Winter & Pond*; University of Washington Press, Seattle & London, in assoc. with Alaska State Library, Juneau; 1989.

No named authors:

The North American Indian Collection of the Lowe Art Museum; Lowe Art Museum, University of Miami, 1988. *The Spirit Sings: Artistic Traditions of Canada's First Peoples*; McClelland & Stewart, Toronto/Glenbow Museum, 1987. *American Indian Population and Labor Force Report 2001*; U.S. Dept. of the Interior, BIA, Office of Tribal Services, Washington D.C. Indian and Northern Affairs Canada, Indian Registry System Indian Register population for all First Nations as at Dec. 31, 2005, Ottawa, 2006. Many Trails, *Indians of the Lower Hudson Valley*. The Katonah Gallery, New York. 1974.

INDEX

Bold text indicates main entry.
Italics identify language families or major
sections thereof: see pages 10–12.